The Economics of Immigration

Örn B. Bodvarsson · Hendrik Van den Berg

The Economics of Immigration

Theory and Policy

 Springer

Professor Dr. Örn B. Bodvarsson
Department of Economics
St. Cloud State University
720 Fourth Avenue South
St. Cloud MN 56301
USA
obbodvarsson@stcloudstate.edu

Professor Dr. Hendrik Van den Berg
Department of Economics
University of Nebraska
P.O.Box 880489
Lincoln NE 68588-0489
USA
hvan-den-berg1@unlnotes.unl.edu

ISBN 978-3-540-77795-3   e-ISBN978-3-540-77796-0
DOI: 10.1007/978-3-540-77796-0
Springer Dordrecht Heidelberg London New York

Library of Congress Control Number: 2009926179

Cover design: WMXDesign GmbH, Heidelberg, Germany

Printed on acid-free paper

Springer is part of Springer Science+Business Media (www.springer.com)

Preface

The inspiration for this book came from a collaborative research project on immigration, begun in 2001, when we were colleagues at University of Nebraska-Lincoln (Bodvarsson was a Visiting Professor there in 2001–05). Our project dealt with the application of Say's Law to the supply of immigrant labor, meaning that when the supply of immigrant labor grows in an area, the new immigrants, being consumers, bolster labor demand and help to offset the lower wages they may bring about. Our test case was the seemingly obscure Dawson County, Nebraska, where the meatpacking industry experienced a relatively huge increase in Hispanic-born labor supply around 1990. We found for Dawson County this "demand effect" to be significant and our results for this test case generalizable to other, more prominent, test cases. This inspired us to study the famous Mariel Boatlift, where Miami's labor force grew suddenly by 7% due to the arrival of nearly 125,000 Cuban refugees in the spring of 1980. In that study, we showed that the *Marielitos* exerted a significant demand effect, which we argue helps to account for the stylized fact that the Mariel influx had a relatively benign effect on the Miami labor market. We had the privilege of presenting both studies at various conferences in the USA, Norway, Taiwan and Israel, and these studies have been published in *Labour Economics* and the *Research in Labor Economics* series (both studies are discussed in detail in this book).

As we delved further into the literature on the distributional effects of immigration while doing our collaborative research, we kept looking for resources where someone pulled all the literature together and provided a synthesis of past research. We found not only that that part of the immigration literature lacked a synthesis, but so did the entire field of immigration economics. Graduate and advanced undergraduate students taking migration and labor courses need a reference that ties all the academic literature on migration together and fellow researchers inside and outside of Economics need a reference to satisfy their particular interests in migration. We thus chose to fill this void by writing a book ourselves! This book project began in 2005 and we have since journeyed through the many fascinating veins of literature on the determinants of migration, the characteristics of immigrants, the distributional effects of immigration, immigration policy, and other issues. It has truly been a labor of love for both of us.

The aim of this book is twofold. First, more colleges and universities are now offering courses for graduate students and advanced undergraduate students on migration. These courses are usually populated in Economics departments, but also attract interest from students in fields such as sociology, political science and geography. We have spoken with colleagues who have taught courses on migration and they tell us that, rather than just teaching articles, they very much prefer a reference that provides an expository survey and assessment of the literature. We aim to fill this need with our book. Second, economists, sociologists, political scientists and practitioners in other fields interested in immigration need the same type of reference and we hope that this book fills their particular needs. In the book, we cut a wide swath through the literature, sometimes highlighting and detailing particularly prominent studies. We hope that by using the book, the reader gets enough detail to gain a sufficiently strong understanding of the issues without having to read further, or that the reader gets enough detail to get a solid roadmap for taking a major plunge into the literature. To use a catchy phrase from the retailing arena, we view this book as being either a "one-stop shopping" resource for those who want a quick, but detailed exposure to the field, or a reliable resource for those who wish to navigate through what is a "shopping mall" of literature. After having completed the manuscript, we have also come to see this book as a source of research topics for economists and other social scientists. As in the case of many real shopping malls here in the U.S., there is not nearly as much variety or broad coverage of our needs as the sheer size of the mall suggests. The economics literature leaves many immigration questions unanswered. The reader of this book will thus find many exciting research opportunities.

We have benefitted greatly from the advice, comments, insights and encouragement from many of our colleagues. We thank in particular our coauthor Joshua Lewer, who contributed substantially to our Mariel Boatlift reexamination study. We thank the many discussants of our papers at meetings of the Society of Labor Economists, European Association of Labor Economists, European Society of Population Economics, Western Economic Association International, Allied Social Science Association, Western Social Science Association, the Great Plains Center at University of Nebraska-Lincoln, and a special conference titled the "The Economics of Immigration and Social Diversity," held at Bar Ilan University in Tel Aviv in 2004. We also thank participants at various seminars for their very useful comments. We, of course, thank our respective academic institutions, St. Cloud State University and the University of Nebraska-Lincoln, for funding our travel to the conferences. We also thank the Institute for the Study of Labor (IZA), where we are both research fellows, for helping to promote our work. And we thank Barbara van den Berg for her enthusiastic proofreading and corrections of various drafts of the manuscript.

We reserve our most heartfelt thanks for the last, which is to our families, especially our wives Mary Bodvarsson and Barbara van den Berg, for their support, understanding, encouragement, love, and patience, as we put in the many hours preparing multiple drafts of this book. We dedicate this book to them.

April, 2009   *Örn B. Bodvarsson*
                                                                               Hendrik Van den Berg

Contents

Part II Immigration Issues and Cases

Chapter 1
Introduction to Immigration Economics

Jacques Chirac, Prime Minister of France: If there were fewer immigrants, there would be less unemployment, fewer tensions in certain towns and neighborhoods, and lower social cost.

Liberation [A Paris newspaper]: That has never been formally proven.

Chirac: It is easy to imagine, nevertheless.

–From an October 30, 1984 interview[1]

In the small Irish village of Carrigaholt, the traditional pub is named the Long Dock. The owners are from a family that has resided in Carrigaholt as long as records have been kept. The only thing that has changed in recent years is the personnel. The two bartenders are Lithuanians, and the tables are waited on by two Poles. The kitchen staff is entirely Latvian. The visiting American writer Thomas Lynch notes that on St. Patrick's day, 2006, the crowd in the Long Dock seems to be enjoying the pints of stout as usual.[2]

The scene at the Long Dock is a sign of the times. For generations, Irish had emigrated to other countries in large numbers, but in 2006 foreigners were flooding to Ireland. The booming Irish economy boasted one of the highest per capita incomes in Europe. According to the writer Thomas Lynch, whose ancestors left Carrigaholt a century ago:

Like the young of Carrigaholt and its surrounding towns, the young of Krakow and Vilnius are coming and going as they please now, citizens of the European Union and the global villages. Bartenders without borders, they travel light between cultures, common markets and currencies, picking up languages, finding in the eyes of strangers the shared lights of humanity.[3]

---

[1]Quoted in Simon (1989, p. 208).

[2]Lynch (2006).

[3]Lynch (2006).

Ö.B. Bodvarsson and H. Van den Berg, *The Economics of Immigration*, DOI: 10.1007/978-3-540-77796-0_1, © Springer-Verlag Berlin Heidelberg 2009

Carrigaholt is not the only place where the Irish pub is adjusting to immigration.

That same St. Patrick's day, in Milford, Michigan, in the United States, a crowd is gathered at O'Callaghan's, a popular local Irish style pub. O'Callahan's is a reasonable replica of an Irish pub, complete with a dart board, blarney, stew, and beer-battered fish. There is even a television screen showing curling and rugby games from Ireland. Guinness Stout is being served pint after pint by the owners and staff, all of them Palestinians. Again, the noisy crowd seems oblivious to nationality of the staff.

1.1   The Late Twentieth Century Immigration Explosion

Immigration is a prominent economic and political issue in Europe, North America, Australia, New Zealand, and many other high income countries. Today, over 200 million people, or about 3% of the world's population, live outside their country of birth. Immigration has grown rapidly in recent decades, a trend that, if continued, will result in the number of immigrants approaching 4–5% of the world's population within a generation. Immigration is one of the international economic activities that is part of the phenomenon often referred to as *globalization*. As more and more immigrants move from one country to another in search of better jobs, preferred lifestyles, and changing economic opportunities, the lives of the people already residing in the *destination* countries are often changed in unanticipated and little understood ways. For one thing, the international movement of people is subjecting people everywhere to greater labor market competition. This movement of workers affects the incomes that accrue to other factors of production. More broadly, immigration is causing more frequent conflicts between local cultures and the cultures of foreigners. President Chirac's statement that immigrants cause problems for the destination countries, as stated at the start of the chapter, refects the concerns of many people living in countries that have received foreign immigrants.

Imagine the conflict faced by the citizens of Barcelona, the capital of the autonomous region of Catalonia in Spain. The Catalonians have recently won substantial political autonomy after decades of political efforts, and there has been a revival of the Catalonian language and culture under this autonomy. However, the region of Catalonia and the country of Spain are part of the European Union, which now allows the free movement of Europeans among all the member countries. The attractive city of Barcelona and the towns along Catalonia's Mediterranean coast are attracting increasing numbers of immigrants from elsewhere in Europe. Also, growing numbers of unauthorized or, in the popular vernacular, "illegal" immigrants from Russia, Pakistan, North Africa, and Latin America are coming to work and live in Barcelona, leading a former head of the Catalonian parliament to claim that "Catalonia's collective identity was under threat by the influx of illegal immigrants."[4] Spain's national government quickly issued statements to counter

---

[4]Crawford (2001).

these widely quoted remarks, however, claiming that "Foreign labour is necessary and will become increasingly so in a country with the lowest birth rate in Europe and a rapidly aging population."[5] Often, immigration's cultural and economic effects conflict, which then pits one interest group against another in the political arena where immigration policy is discussed and formulated.

Over the latter decade of the twentieth century and the beginning of the twenty first century, the United States has received over 1 million new immigrants per year from mostly developing countries in Latin America, Eastern Europe, and Asia. In the state of Wisconsin, the so-called "Land of Bratwurst" that was the destination for immigrants from Germany and Scandinavia a century ago, the Hispanic population has tripled over the last 25 years and now numbers over 200,000. "Milwaukee feels like home," claims one immigrant from Peru.[6] A newspaper report describes how managers at the new 3Com factory in Morton Grove, Illinois, have to deal with the more than 20 different languages spoken by its 1,200 employees. It is easy to imagine the plight of the manager of one of the production lines at 3Com, a 33-year old refugee from Vietnam, Thai Chung, who is himself barely fluent in English. When he attempts to give instructions to a janitor to clean up an oil spill, Thai Chung finds the man does not speak any English. Suspecting that he is Polish, Chung calls on another assembly line worker to interpret for him. She is Serbian, however, and unable to communicate with the janitor. "I'm not even sure he's Polish," she tells Mr. Chung. "I don't know what he is." The janitor eventually cleans up the oil spill, but it is not clear how he got the message. Stella Foy, one of the few American-born workers on the line sums up the usual management style: "Around here you point a lot."[7] Tolerance is not always the chosen strategy for dealing with the social diversity caused by immigration. For example, the owner of Beauty Enterprises, a U.S. manufacturer of beauty products based in the state of Connecticut, requires that only English be spoken during working hours. Speaking foreign languages at work undermines morale, claims Beauty Enterprises' president.[8]

1.1.1 The Complexity of Immigration

Opinions on immigration vary widely because immigration is a very complex phenomenon with many different effects on many people at home and abroad. Several very distinct economic characteristics of immigration can be easily distinguished. On the one hand, immigration implies the movement of factors of production from one country to another. The movement of labor changes the relative

---

[5]Crawford (2001).

[6]Thomas (2000).

[7]Aeppel (1998).

[8]Waldmeir (2001).

quantities of factors available in economies and, therefore, the returns to all factors of production. This labor market effect causes conflicting opinions about the desirability of immigration. Workers in the destination country who compete directly with immigrant workers will often tend to view immigrants unfavorably, while people who hire immigrant workers have a more favorable opinion of immigration. Unlike machines and buildings, however, people are more than just factors of production. Immigrants are also consumers, and their arrival in a country boosts demand for all factors of production, including immigrants' own labor. Thus, the arrival of immigrants may not have the dreaded downward effect on the wages of competing workers after all. Also important is the fact that people are carriers of new ideas and knowledge; it is well known that immigration helps to spread ideas and knowledge from one country to another. This spread of ideas and knowledge is the key to economic growth and long-term improvements in living standards. On the other hand, when people with different backgrounds and traditions come together, difficult cultural clashes can occur. As President Chirac suggests at the head of the chapter, immigrants are suspected of using public services and imposing a social cost on the countries they live in. For these and many other reasons, immigration evokes even more emotion and controversy than do international trade and international investment, the other international economic activities that comprise globalization. In most countries, groups of people actively lobby their governments to impose even greater curbs on immigration than they already do. As large as the number of immigrants has become, there would be many more immigrants if countries did not intentionally restrict immigration.

1.1.2 Not Everyone Likes Immigrants

In the late 1990s, surveys by *Newsweek* and *The New York Times/CBS* reported that over 60% of Americans thought that immigration was "a bad thing" and that immigration levels "should be reduced."[9] After the terrorist attack on the World Trade Center in September, 2001, 58% of Americans stated that they favored reducing immigration. In 2004, 61% of Americans agreed that the government was "not tough enough" on immigration.[10]

There is a common belief that immigration is a threat to employment for native workers. Peter Umber of Germany's Federal Institute of Labor, an organization that actively works to neutralize German companies' increased interest in hiring foreign high-tech workers, argued that "by keeping foreigners from coming into our labor market, we intend to preserve these jobs for people who already live in Germany."[11] When, in 2002, the German government suggested that engineers

---

[9]Miller (1994).

[10]These survey results are from Blendon et al. (2005).

and computer specialists from countries such as India be permitted to work in Germany to fill the shortage of high-tech workers, one of Germany's major political parties made immigrants a major issue with the slogan "Kinder Statt Inder," which translates to "children instead of Indians." Immigrants are often perceived as a threat to a country's culture and social structure. For example, Dan Stein, the executive director of the often-cited Federation for American Immigration Reform (FAIR) stated: "Immigrants don't come all church-loving, freedom-loving, God-fearing. . .. Many of them hate America. Hate everything the United States stands for. Talk to some of these Central Americans."[12] Such fear of foreigners is so common it even has a name: *xenophobia*.

1.1.3 Economists' Perspective

Economists often view immigration favorably. Two economists, Julian Simon and Stephen Moore, conducted a small survey among leading economists in the mid-1980s, and they found that all of these economists said that immigration has either a "very favorable" or "slightly favorable" effect on economic growth.[13] None said that immigration's effect on raising living standards was "slightly" or "very unfavorable."[14] Over the past decade, as the issue of immigration has become more prominent, economists have been called on more often to weigh in on the discussion of immigration. Their conclusions seem to have become more nuanced. Some economists in the field of immigration economics now even hold much more cautious views on immigration. For example, George Borjas of Harvard argues that the massive Hispanic immigration to the U.S. in the late 1990s will not have the same benign economic consequences as did earlier immigration episodes in the U.S. Nevertheless, most economists still view immigration much more favorably than most citizens in the U.S., Europe, or other immigrant destinations. This book will make it clear why economists tend to be disposed to viewing immigration favorably, albeit with some reservations or exceptions.

This is not to say that only economists favor immigration. Despite the condemnation of immigrants recorded in the surveys sampled above, people in many countries still tend to agree that, in principle, the freedom to move from one country to another is a basic human right. And, despite all the controversy and calls for reduced immigration, no one in the U.S. has yet seriously proposed taking down the Statue of Liberty that stands in New York harbor to welcome immigrants. Recently, Canada even established a Ministry of Immigration to promote immigration and coordinate programs to help immigrants assimilate into Canadian society.

---

[11]Zachary (2000).

[12]As quoted in Carlson (1997).

[13]As quoted in Tucker Carlson (1997).

[14]Reported in Simon (1995).

This book presents what economists and other social scientists know about the complex issue of immigration. Some of what you will learn may surprise you, but you will be pleased to find that economists and social scientists actually have a fairly good handle on the economic and social effects of immigration on both the sending and destination countries. Many of the apparent contradictions can be explained. Above all, you will enjoy learning about this important economic, social, and very human phenomenon.

1.2   The Determinants of Immigration

Economic incentives to immigrate may be a function of undesirable conditions in the source country or they may be related to attractive conditions in the destination country. Immigrants are often attracted by the lure of higher income. Other attractions include better career opportunities, greater freedom to innovate, better schooling for children, less discrimination, and lower levels of taxation. Of course, there are many other reasons why people become immigrants: civil rights, political rights, religious freedom, law and order, social mobility, personal safety, climate, and peace all make a destination country attractive to potential immigrants. The many incentives that influence immigration fall into four categories: (1) negative incentives that *push* people to emigrate, (2) positive incentives that *pull* immigrants to the destination country, (3) positive incentives that induce people to *stay* at home, and (4) negative incentives that cause people to *stay away* from a foreign country. When the *stay* and *stay away* factors are strong relative to the *push* and *pull* factors, immigration is unlikely to occur on a large scale. On the other hand, when the push and pull factors are strong relative to the stay and stay away factors, immigration will grow, as has occurred worldwide over the last few decades. Figure 1.1 shows the many *push*, *pull*, *stay*, and *stay away* factors that have been discussed in the immigration literature.

1.2.1   Many Factors Discourage Immigration

Despite huge income differences across countries, there are many reasons why people decide not to emigrate. For one thing, relocating internationally can be very costly. There are the out-of-pocket costs of moving from one country to another, as well as the opportunity costs incurred during the period of transition between departure and their arrival in new homes and jobs in the destination country. For example, in 1650 ocean passage from England to one of the North American colonies cost the equivalent of half a year's wages for a farm laborer.[15] Then there are the obvious dangers of crossing oceans and passing through hostile

---

[15]*The Economist* (2001).

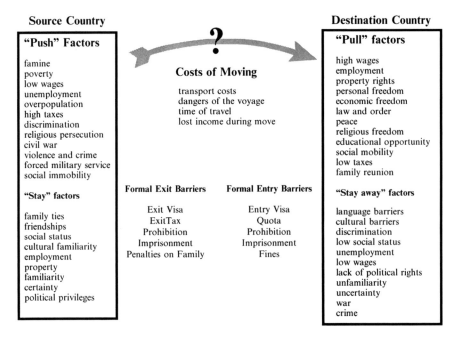

Fig 1.1 The Immigration Decision

territory. In the 1800s, European immigrants seeking to settle in Oregon, in the Northwestern United States, had to survive an ocean voyage on a sailing ship followed by a grueling 2,000-mile wagon train journey that took months and claimed many lives. For some immigrants the journey to the United States is still dangerous today: In 2000, 369 illegal immigrants died crossing the desert to reach the United States from Mexico.[16] News about African immigrants drowning in the Mediterranean trying to cross into the European Union has become all too common.

The cost of setting up a household in a new location is often large as well. Immigrants may lose social capital when they move to a new country with a new culture. They may face discrimination in the destination country that translates into lower income and more subtle costs in the form of lower life satisfaction. The psychological costs of leaving friends and family behind, adjusting to a different culture, and being treated as an "outsider" are likely to affect the immigration decision. After all, as psychology, experimental economics, and the so-called *happiness studies* have amply demonstrated, human beings are social animals

---

[16]*The Economist* (2001).

who greatly value interaction with other human beings and their status in society.[17] Lastly, psychology and experimental economics also find strong evidence that a simple fear of the unknown will tend to keep many people where they are, regardless of their present circumstances.

That immigration is a difficult decision to carry out is also clear from the widespread evidence that immigrants tend to move to where they already have family and where their countrymen moved earlier. Recent studies of immigration show that family ties have a much stronger influence on the migration decision than do employment opportunities.[18] Friends and family who have already made the move to a new location can help subsequent immigrants overcome cultural and language barriers, find work, and settle in the new community.

The difficulties that immigrants face in the destination country imply that they are often different from the native-born in terms of their skills, motivation, education, and social behavior. Because the act of moving from one country to another generally involves risk, temporary hardship, and difficult changes in culture, language, and lifestyle, immigrants tend to be especially ambitious, more willing to take risks, harder working, more open to new ideas, and energetic. Evidence suggests that this romantic view of immigrants as exceptional people may be a bit of an exaggeration, but immigrants are seldom "average" relative to the population they left behind or the ones they join.

Finally, most potential destination countries make it difficult for immigrants to enter the country. Some source countries make it hard for people to leave. The role of immigration policy has grown to where it may be the single most important determinant of worldwide immigration flows. In today's global economy, the pecuniary costs of moving from one country to another have fallen substantially. Also, improved communications and the prior movement of compatriots have increasingly lowered the social and psychological costs of immigration. The rapid increase in unauthorized immigration is a clear reflection of the growing incentives for people to emigrate and how these incentives increasingly clash with government-imposed barriers to international migration. The main determinant of immigration is the disparity in real incomes between countries. Standard economic theory predicts that immigration will arbitrage away international differences in incomes. People will tend to move from low- to high-income countries, thus increasing the supply of labor in the high-income countries and reducing the supply of labor in the low- income countries. For example, immigration to Western Europe and the United States, respectively, has exceeded one million people per year over the past decade. In contrast, we see very few people immigrating to Haiti or Ethiopia.

---

[17]See, for example, Blanchflower and Oswald (2000), Kahneman and Tversky (2000) Haidt (2006) or Camerer, Lowenstein, Prelec (2005).

[18]Madeline Zawodny (1997). See also Murayama (1991) and Kahan (1978).

1.2.2   Considering the Full Set of Push, Pull, Stay, and Stay Away Factors

The relationship between the volume of immigration and income differences is not linear. Migration from the very poorest countries of the world is actually quite small, which suggests that income levels in source countries, and not just differences in income across countries, also influence the volume of immigration. Immigration is costly and takes a long time, which simply makes immigration unaffordable for most people from very poor countries. Furthermore, people from very poor countries are less likely to have the communications and job skills necessary to be successful in higher income countries. Also, many high-income countries severely restrict the entrance of immigrants with little education, which characterizes most people in the world's poorest countries.

Some countries have prohibited their citizens from leaving; for example, before the fall of the Berlin wall, many communist states did not permit their citizens to emigrate to other countries. North Korean border guards apparently still have instructions to shoot anyone attempting to cross its border to South Korea. There are also language and cultural barriers to immigration, as well as people's psychological resistance to change.

1.2.3   Recent Shifts in the Economic Forces that Influence Immigration

Several factors have combined to increase the number of migrants over the last two centuries:

- Rapid economic growth and technological progress since 1800 have drastically lowered transport costs and eliminated the dangers of long voyages, making it much easier for people to immigrate.
- Economic growth since 1800 has varied greatly from country to country, resulting in huge discrepancies in incomes that encourage people to immigrate.
- Improved communications, also part of rapid technological progress of the past 200 years, has made people more aware of the income discrepancies across countries.
- The twentieth century surge in population growth in developing economies has greatly expanded the young, working-age population in most low-income countries, the age group most likely to immigrate.

These same factors are likely to cause further increases in immigration in future decades.

The globalization of economic activity has increased the need for people to move between countries in greater numbers. In order to produce for world markets, operate factories, market products, and take advantage of all available knowledge and technology, multinational firms increasingly view the market for labor as an international one, not a national one. Even nonprofit organizations and universities, among others, maintain operations in more than one country and routinely move managers, operatives, professors, and students across borders. All of these factors have combined to where there are few economies today that do not send substantial numbers of people to, or receive people from, other countries.

1.2.4   Immigration is a Complex Phenomenon

This discussion of the incentives for, and against, immigration still has not adequately described all the economic effects of immigration. Immigration is a complex phenomenon. The tendency for economists to view immigrants only as workers means economic analysis often fails to recognize that immigrants are also consumers and that immigrants purchase goods and services provided by others at the same time that they add to the capacity of the economy. There is also the fact that immigrants contribute to economic growth even as they add to the congestion in labor markets and public services in the short run. In the long run, immigration causes the societies of both the source and destination countries to shift to different growth paths. These many complexities explain why there are so often sharply conflicting feelings about immigrants.

The study of immigration often transcends economics. In fact, many people do not view immigration as an economic issue at all. Serious studies of immigration often ignore economic factors and concentrate on the sociological, psychological, demographic, or political aspects. Traffickers often exploit immigrants, charging high fees to carry them in overcrowded boats and trucks to other countries where they may end up working as virtual slaves in illegal factories. Many countries have waged long and hotly-debated arguments over whether growing immigrant populations will cause their societies to lose their traditional cultures. Such debates inevitably reflect various national biases against foreign cultures. Opportunistic politicians and nationalists often reduce immigration to an "us versus them" issue. Distrust of foreigners seems to be a universal human characteristic. Inaccurate beliefs about immigrants remain popular because, as Jacques Chirac says, "it is easy to imagine." Regardless of the motivations behind the immigration debates, such reactions must be understood and dealt with by policymakers.

1.3   A Brief History of Immigration

Scientists have found ample evidence suggesting that the human race originated in Eastern Africa some 150,000 or so years ago and then spread across the face of the earth. Many living species have migrated from one part of the earth to another.

Human have been especially active migrants, however. Unlike most animal species, which have tended to concentrate in certain regions and climates, humans are exceptionally adaptable. Starting about 60,000 years ago, they began to migrate throughout the world. Today, humans live on every continent and in nearly every one of the world's climates, landscapes, and altitudes.

1.3.1 Early Migrations

Early human migrations can be reconstructed using genealogical markers in DNA that permit scientists to trace the spread of humans backwards in time. When people move, they take their genes along and pass them on to their descendants in their new homes. Thus, every present-day population retains clues as to who its predecessors were. When this type of scientific analysis is combined with evidence found by anthropologists, archeologists, and paleontologists, as well as the roots of the world's languages that have been traced by linguists, a fascinating story of human migration emerges.[19] The research suggests that all humans alive today descended from earlier *homo sapiens* who lived in Africa over 60,000 years ago. These people, in turn, descended from *homo sapiens* living in what is today Ethiopia some 150,000 years ago. Homo sapiens, in turn, descended from the *homo heidelbergensis* who lived in various parts of the world nearly one million years ago. The remains of human ancestors, and what are likely to be other descendents who evolved from our human ancestors, dating back several million years have been found in Ethiopia, Java, Asia, and elsewhere in the world.[20]

People have always migrated across the face of the earth. They probably moved from one location to another for a variety of reasons, such as climate changes, glaciation, natural disasters, depletion of game, the growth of population relative to available resources, or threats from other humans or animals. Because there were no political boundaries, these movements of people are usually referred to as *migrations* rather than *immigration*. Natural barriers such as oceans, deserts, and mountain ranges slowed the spread of humans across the earth. Because there were humans living in all corners of the world by 20,000 years ago, it is obvious that there were no physical barriers that humans did not succeed in overcoming.

The very earliest migration was probably on foot over land. The first human seafaring must have taken place well over 40,000 years ago, because human remains over 40,000 years old have been found in Australia and other distant islands. The migration of people to the Western Hemisphere occurred in several waves between 10,000 and 30,000 years ago, probably across the Bering Strait from Asia. Given humans' capacity for traveling on water, migration to the Western Hemisphere did not necessarily have to coincide with the often mentioned land

---

[19]See, for example, Wells (2003), Wade (2003) or Owens and King (1999).

[20]A timeline of the likely paths of human evolution is given in Zimmer (2005).

bridge during the last ice age. People could have sailed or paddled their primitive boats across the narrow Bering Straight at any time. Europe was probably occupied by nomadic groups of humans as early as 40,000 years ago.

Growth of the human population increased when new technologies of farming, irrigation, animal husbandry, specialization, exchange, and urbanization increased humans' ability to use the earth's resources to sustain life. Beginning about 10,000 years ago, farming and urbanization created more permanent settlements, in contrast to the more mobile hunters and gatherers of earlier human societies. Permanent settlements, in turn, led to the geographic identification of societies, subject to uniform sets of institutions and surrounded by political boundaries. These boundaries, at least to some degree, restricted the movement of people even as they served to link people to political entities. Citizenship and national origin became a characteristic by which to identify people. A new term to describe the migration of people across political boundaries was invented: *immigration*. In the end, the new boundaries have not necessarily been restrictive to human migration; the economic and social development that accompanied the permanent settlements and political boundaries also served to spur technological progress that ultimately ended up improving communications and transportation, increasing commercial contacts among the different nations, and generally integrating the world into what we now often call the *global economy*.

The availability of natural resources stimulated many of the early migrations when people lived as hunters and gatherers. More recently, the driving force behind immigration is the variation in economic growth across countries. With the increasing complexity of economic organization and modern societies, economic performance has differed greatly from one country to another. People living in poor countries have been increasingly attracted to countries whose economies provide their citizens with higher standards of living.

1.3.2 Recent Immigration

The movement of people appears to have increased in modern times. The massive movement of people from Europe and Africa to the Western Hemisphere between 1500 and the present stands out as the greatest migration of modern times. It is estimated that about 75 million Europeans left their native countries and emigrated to what are now Canada, the United States, Argentina, Brazil, and many smaller countries in Latin America and the Caribbean. More than 10 million Africans were taken as slaves to the Western Hemisphere during the period from 1500 to 1900. The greatest number went to the Caribbean (4 million) and Brazil (3.6 million).

The largest single migration of people in the twentieth century took place between India and Pakistan in 1947. The partitioning of India after independence from Great Britain caused about 7 million Muslims to move from what is today India into that portion of the former British colony of India that became Pakistan, and about an equal number of Hindus were moved in the opposite direction from what is now Pakistan into India. At the close of World War II, almost 6 million Japanese moved back to Japan from China (Manchuria), Korea, and Formosa, areas occupied by Japan during the first half of the twentieth century.

Immigration increased rapidly towards the end of the twentieth century. Canada, Australia, New Zealand, and the United States, received large inflows of immigrants from Europe throughout the post-World War II period. Australia and Canada each received more than 2 million immigrants between 1946 and 1964. A number of Western European countries, which had supplied so many people to the rest of the world from 1600 through the early twentieth century, themselves began to experience large inflows of immigrants from elsewhere in Europe after World War II and, after 1960, from North Africa. Even Ireland, which sent over 4 million immigrants to the Western Hemisphere in the second half of the nineteenth century, began receiving large inflows of immigrants toward the end of the twentieth century. Because of this immigration, in 2004 Ireland's population surpassed 4 million for the first time since 1871.[21] Eight million Germans expelled from Eastern Europe after World War II settled in West Germany, and one million ethnic French moved to France during Algeria's war of independence in the late 1950s. The U.S. invasion of Iraq in 2003, and the political chaos that followed, led about 2 million Iraqis to flee to Syria, Jordan, Egypt, and other nearby countries.

The collapse of the Soviet Union and other communist governments in Eastern Europe has, since 1990, resulted in a large flow of immigrants from the Commonwealth of Independent States and Eastern Europe to the high-income Western European economies. Over 1 million immigrants legally enter European countries each year, and perhaps another 500,000 asylum seekers and unauthorized immigrants enter each year as well.[22] Immigration has greatly changed the populations of many European countries, indicated in Table 1.1 by the high percentages of foreigners living in each country. For example, Switzerland's population and labor force is about 25% foreign-born, and Luxembourg's labor force is over one-third foreign-born.

Immigrants do not only move to the developed countries of Europe and North America. An estimated 7 million Pakistanis, Filipinos, Indians, Palestinians, Egyptians, and other foreigners work in Saudi Arabia. An estimated 5 million foreigners live and work as construction workers, domestics, and day laborers in the oil-rich Gulf states on the Arabian Peninsula.[23] The newly industrialized Asian economies of Singapore, Malaysia, and Thailand also have attracted immigrants from populous countries such as Indonesia, Bangladesh, Pakistan, and India.

---

[21]Hundley (2004).

[22]*The Economist* (1998).

[23]Allen (2000).

Table 1.1 Shares of foreign-born population and labor force: 2004

New immigrant destinations			Traditional immigrant destinations		
	Population	Labor force		Population	Labor force
Austria	13.0%	15.3%	Australia	23.6%	24.9%
Belgium	11.5	11.4	Canada	18.0	17.8
Denmark	6.3	5.9	United States	12.8	15.1
France	10.0	11.3			
Germany	13.0	12.2			
Ireland	11.0	10.0			
Italy	2.5	5.9			
Luxembourg	33.1	45.0			
Netherlands	10.6	11.1			
Spain	5.3	11.2			
Sweden	12.2	13.3			
Switzerland	23.5	9.6			
Japan	1.2	1.0			

Source: OECD (2006), International Migration Outlook, Paris: OECD, Chart 1.4 and Table 1.8.

1.4   There are Many Types of Immigrants

The common image of immigrants is that they are *settlers*, people who enter another country in order to remain there permanently. Many immigrants today still fall into this category, especially those who immigrate legally to countries such as Canada, Australia, New Zealand, and the United States. But, among the millions of people who move across borders each year, many fall into other categories.

1.4.1   Not All Immigrants are Permanent Settlers

A second category of immigrants consists of *contract workers*, who are people that move to another country on a temporary basis in order to perform a specific type of work. Contract workers may work just for a tourist season or a harvest season, such as Italian hotel workers in Switzerland or Mexican agricultural workers in the United States. Or, they may remain in the country for a number of years, such as the factory workers from southern Europe and Turkey in Germany, Holland, and Belgium in the 1960s or the large numbers of Egyptian, Indian, and Pakistani workers working in the oil producing Persian Gulf states today. Another recent example of contract workers are the tens of thousands of foreign workers working for construction firms, private security firms, and the U.S. military in Iraq.

Another growing category of immigrants consists of people often referred to as *professionals*, who are immigrants who move from country to country to perform specialized technical or management jobs. Professionals often work for multinational firms and international organizations. They are also closely associated with the growing international trade in services, such as financial services, retailing, and communications. A fourth, and very different, group of immigrants consists of *asylum seekers and refugees*. These are people who left their home countries to escape political, religious, or social persecution, or other threats to their safety and well being. According to the United Nations High Commissioner for Refugees, there were over 10 million refugees in the world in 2006. Most of these people were fleeing war and ethnic strife, and most of these refugees are in Africa and the Middle East. The economic and social chaos accompanying the disintegration of Yugoslavia and the collapse of the Soviet Union led many people to seek asylum in Western Europe.

A growing number of the world's immigrants are *unauthorized immigrants*, people who cross the border in violation of the laws of the destination country and without the required approvals or documentation. Unauthorized immigrants effectively also fall into one of the above four categories, but they are given their own category because, regardless of the underlying purpose of their immigration, they find themselves in a unique legal status by not having followed mandated legal procedures to enter the destination country. The U.S. government and various research groups have estimated that there were over 10 million unauthorized immigrants in the U.S. in 2005.[24] The International Labour Organisation (ILO) estimated that in 1991 there were 2.6 million immigrants living illegally in Western Europe, and that number had doubled by the year 2000.[25] It is notoriously difficult to estimate the number of unauthorized immigrants in the U.S. and other countries because they try to avoid detection.

Some immigrants do not fall neatly into any of the categories listed above. For example, there are about 2 million students in foreign countries, nearly 500,000 in the United States alone. There are also diplomats, representatives of international organizations, employees of non-profit organizations, research organizations, employees of transportation firms, instructors and lecturers, religious workers, and many others who for one reason or another find themselves temporarily residing in foreign countries.

1.4.2 Forced Immigration

Some people are forced to move across borders against their will, a group we will call *involuntary immigrants*. People caught in the world slave trade that flourished until the nineteenth century were clearly involuntary immigrants, forced to immigrate not because of conditions in the source country, but because of coercion by conquerors or slave merchants. Some people are still forced to migrate, such as when families in one country sell their children into indentured servitude in another

---

[24]OECD (2006).
[25]*The Economist* (1998).

country. There is a fuzzy line between involuntary immigration and desperate voluntary attempts by people to better their circumstances by agreeing to near-slave working conditions in other countries. Until sound economic policies end needless starvation and destitution, we are likely to continue to be shocked by the inhumane trafficking of human beings across borders.

1.4.3   Some Immigrants are Difficult to Classify

Some immigrants fall into more than one category. It is not obvious whether the more than 1 million Cuban immigrants who arrived in the United States over the past 50 years did so to escape political persecution or to seek higher incomes. Temporary workers may become permanent residents, as in the case of the *guest workers* who went to Western Europe in the 1960s as contract workers but eventually gained permanent residency in their host countries. Unauthorized immigrants may move temporarily or permanently, and many are refugees from famine or political violence. Some unauthorized immigrants eventually gain legal status in the destination countries.

1.5   The Purpose and Organization of this Book

In writing this book, we had two goals. First, in recognition of the economic and social importance of immigration in our global economy, a growing number of universities around the world are offering courses to graduate and advanced undergraduate students on the economic analysis of immigration. We, therefore, intend for this book to serve as a comprehensive textbook for courses covering immigration issues. Second, a growing number of scholars and students are taking an interest specifically in the economics of immigration. These researchers need a central source for information about theoretical and empirical developments in the field of immigration studies. We intend for this book to effectively serve that need.

One of the challenges in writing this book was to deal with a number of large gaps in the economics literature on immigration. The field of international economics has devoted surprisingly little attention to immigration. There is only one mainstream international economics textbook that devotes more than a small portion of one chapter to immigration, and that is the one written by one of the authors of this book. Most of the economic analysis of immigration has been performed by labor economists, not international economists. Labor economists have tended to view immigrants mostly as workers, not the diverse human beings that they are. International economics has treated immigration as a relatively less important form of factor movement, and international economists have given it little more attention than it gives other special cases that require analysis that goes beyond the standard models of international trade and international investment. Hence, most of the economic analysis of immigration has failed to capture the full consequences and benefits of immigration. Fortunately, many other fields of social science have filled in many of the gaps left by economists. Sociologists have been especially active in researching immigration. This book is an attempt to take stock of the economics literature on immigration and to begin the very necessary task of building the broad field of immigration economics.

The first section of the book examines the theory and the evidence economists have developed. The economic determinants and consequences of immigration detailed in the models we survey underlie many of the political, social, and cultural disputes involving immigrants. Also, more recent models have begun to incorporate many of immigration's social and political effects discussed in other social sciences like sociology, political science, ethnic studies, and history. It will quickly become apparent that the few articles on immigration that have appeared in the mainstream economics journals only begin to analyze the complexity of the relationships between immigration and other economic and social phenomena. Especially interesting is Chap. 9, which analyzes how immigration affects a country's economic growth. It has long been suggested by historians and other social scientists that human migration is a dynamic process that has long-term dynamic consequences for societies. We will show, for example, that there are many reasons why immigration enhances economic growth.

We also hope that this book will stimulate economists and other readers to grasp the advantages of analyzing economic phenomena as processes of continual change and growth rather than one-time shocks to static systems, as so much of our traditional economic analysis does. As you will notice in the chapters that follow, most of the analysis of immigration to date has used static partial equilibrium models common to microeconomics, which not only ignores the dynamic changes that accompany immigration, but which cannot capture even static spillovers and aggregate outcomes. More specifically, we will argue that a complex phenomenon like immigration can only be understood when it is viewed from a long-run, dynamic, and interdisciplinary perspective.

The second section of the book deals with a number of special issues and cases on the economics of immigration. The section includes chapters on the determinants and consequences of unauthorized immigration, the economics of temporary immigration and forced immigration, and the interesting case of the surge in Hispanic immigration to the U.S. during the latter half of the twentieth century.

The third section of the book focuses on immigration policy. There is a chapter on the history of United States immigration policy. The U.S. makes for an interesting case study of immigration policy because not only has the U.S. received the greatest number of immigrants over the past two centuries of any country in the world, but its policies have changed quite radically over the years. There are also chapters on immigration policies in two other major immigration destinations, Canada and Western Europe. Europe is a most interesting case because it first served as a major source of immigrants for several hundred years, but it has now become a major immigrant destination.

As you will see from the chapters that follow, much work remains to be done before we achieve a full understanding of the economic and social consequences of people's increasing international mobility. Fortunately, we think that you will also find that immigration is a fascinating phenomenon to study, in large part because the act of immigration catches people in their most ambitious and vulnerable moments. The study of immigration reveals why societies often seem to struggle with the complex economic and social consequences of the movement of people between countries. The clash of cultures and the fear of strangers, which are inherent to the international movement of people, often still drive political debate and shape economic policy. Immigration is the study of both the best and the worst human behavior. We hope our exposition will do justice to both the economics and the humanity of our subject. In reference to Jacques Chirac's quote at the start of this chapter, our most basic purpose in writing this book is to enable our readers to do more than "imagine" what the causes and consequences of immigration are.

References

Aeppel, T. (1998, 30 March). A 3Com factory hires a lot of immigrants, gets mix of languages. *The Wall Street Journal.*

Allen, R. (2000, 10/11 June). A time bomb in the desert. *Financial Times.*

Blanchflower, D. G., & Oswald, A. J. (2000). Well-being over time in Britain and the USA. NBER Working Paper No. w7487, January.

Blendon, R. J., et al. (2005) Immigration and the U.S. economy. *Challenge, 48*(2), 113–132.

Camere, C., Lowenstein, G., & Prelec, D. (2005). Neuroeconomics: How neuroscience can inform economics. *Journal of Economic Literature, 43*, 9–64.

Carlson, T. (1997, 2 October). The intellectual roots of nativism. *The Wall Street Journal.*

Crawford, L. (2001, 8 March). Catalonia wrestles with its conscience over immigration. *Financial Times.*

Haidt, J. (2006). *The happiness hypothesis.* New York: Basic Books.

Hundley, T. (2004, 4 December). Booming Ireland sees population swell to 130-year high. *Chicago Tribune.*

Kahan, A. (1978). Economic opportunities and some pilgrims' progress: Jewish Immigrants from Eastern Europe in the U.S., 1890–1914. *Journal of Economic History, 38*(1), 235–251.

Kahneman, D., & Tversky, A. (2000). *Choices, values and frame.* Cambridge: Cambridge University Press.

Lynch, T. (2006, 17 March). When Latvian eyes are smiling. *The Wall Street Journal.*

Miller, J. J. (1994, 8 March). Immigrant-bashing's latest falsehood. *The Wall Street Journal.*

Murayama, Y. (1991). Information and immigrants: Interprefectual differences of Japanese emigration to the Pacific Northwest, 1880–1915. *Journal of Economic History, 51*(1), 125–147.

OECD, (2006). *International migration outlook.* Paris: OECD.

Owens, K., & King, M.-C. (1999). Genomic views of human history. *Science, 286.* 451–453.

Simon, J. L. (1989). *The economic consequences of immigration*, Washington, D.C.: Cato Institute.

Simon, J. (1995, 11 December). Immigration: The demographic and economic facts. Cato Institute: paper prepared for the National Immigration Forum.

The Economist, (1998, 4 April). Millions want to come.

The Economist, (2001, 10 May). On the move.

The Economist, (2001, 24 May). Sex, death and desert Snafus.

Thomas, P. (2000, 16 March). In the land of bratwurst, a new hispanic boom. *The Wall Street Journal*.

Wade, N. (2003, 19 February). Dating of Australian remains backs theory of early migration of humans. *New York Times*.

Waldmeir, P. (2001, 15 March). The politics of talking shop. *Financial Times*, March 15.

Wells, S. (2003). *The journey of man: A genetic odyssey*. Princeton, NJ: Princeton University Press.

Zachary, G. P. (2000, 17 January). Hire wall: as high-tech jobs go begging, Germany is loath to import talent. *The Wall Street Journal*. 2000.

Zawodny, M. (1997). Welfare and the locational choice of new immigrants. *Economic Review* (pp. 2–10). Federal Reserve Bank of Dallas, 2nd Quarter.

Zimmer, C. (2005). *Smithsonian intimate guide to human origins*. New York: HarperCollins.

Part I
Immigration Theory and Evidence

The economic theory of immigration seeks to explain why people leave one country and go and live and work in another country. Also, the economic theory of immigration seeks to highlight the economic consequences that immigration has on the welfare of others in the source and destination countries. Since people are workers, consumers, and innovators, the economic consequences of immigration on both the source country and the destination country are varied and broad. Furthermore, the analysis of the many positive and negative effects on both the demand and supply sides of the source and destination economies helps to explain why immigration is a controversial issue in so many countries.

Modeling Immigration

As discussed in the introductory chapter that precedes this first main section of the book, economic incentives to immigrate are related to a great variety of *push*, *pull*, *stay*, and *stay away* factors. Given the complexity of immigration, many different models of immigration have been developed. In preparation for this detailed examination of the many economic models of immigration, we introduce here the *labor market model of immigration* that many economists have used to explain and analyze immigration. This model is the one that appears most often in textbooks. In its simplest representation, this model assumes immigrants are only workers, and their only effect is to change the supply of labor in the source and destination countries. Clearly, this model introduced here does not do justice to the complexity of immigration. However, you are well advised to devote a few minutes to learning this model because most economic models of immigration effectively build on this popular labor market model.

I.1 The Basic Labor Market Model of Immigration

The typical demand curve for labor is known in the labor economics literature as the *value of the marginal product of labor* (VMP$_L$) curve. The VMP$_L$ curve is the product of the marginal physical product of labor, MP$_L$, and the marginal price of the output, P, or

$$VMP_L = MP_L \, P \qquad\qquad (I.1)$$

VMP$_L$ thus represents the value of the additional output produced when one more unit of labor is used in the production process. Because the marginal product of labor declines as more labor is hired, the VMP$_L$ curve is downward-sloping.

The shape of the supply curve for labor is not as obvious, however. An upward-sloping supply curve implies that the quantity supplied increases when the price rises. Certainly, the opportunity costs of leisure and nonpaying home activities rise as wages rise, and, all other things equal, a higher wage will tend to make workers *substitute* work for leisure. But higher wages also increase the income received by labor, and this positive *income effect* may very well lead people to acquire more leisure even if the opportunity costs go up. Thus, if the income effect of higher wages outweighs the substitution effect of increased opportunity costs of not working, the supply of labor curve will be backward-bending, as the curve labeled C in Fig. I.1, not upward-sloping as the more familiar-looking supply curves labeled A and B.

There is indeed evidence that the income elasticity of supply is negative. Only a century ago, in today's high income countries industrial workers routinely worked 12 h per day, 6 days per week. Today, the 40-h workweek is the norm, except where even shorter workweeks have been mandated. Recently, France legislated a 35-hr workweek.

In the simple labor market model, we draw the labor supply curves as perfectly vertical. We do this to simplify the graphs. Be reassured, however, that even if we draw the labor supply curve as upward- or backward-sloping, the conclusions reached are not qualitatively different from those that we will reach assuming a perfectly vertical supply of labor curve.

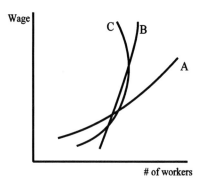

Fig. I.1 The labor supply curve

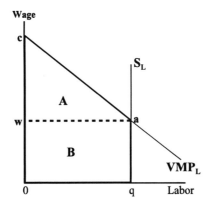

Fig. I.2 The labor market

In a competitive labor market, the wage is equal to the value of the VMP_L curve where it intersects the supply of labor curve. The area under the VMP_L curve, the demand curve for labor, represents the total value of output produced in the economy using all the factors of production, namely labor and all the other factors employed along with the labor. The area under the *marginal* curve represents the sum of all the marginal values, or the *total* value. With labor supply equal to S_L, total output is equal to the areas A plus B in Fig. I.2. The total value of output is split among labor and the other factors. At the wage w, total labor income is equal to the rectangle **B**. The remaining output, area **A**, accrues to the other factors of production such as capital and land that labor uses to produce the output.

Since we are interested in the broad consequences of immigration across both the source and destination countries, we will often examine a two-diagram graphic model such as in Fig. I.3, which shows the labor markets of two countries.

Suppose that the supply and demand curves for labor are different in two countries, say Poland and Germany, and wages are 10 euros per hour in Germany and 10 zloty in Poland. If the exchange rate between euros and Polish zloty is, say, equal to one euro = 5 zloty, we can translate the zloty wage into euros. Or, suppose Poland joins the euro area, and Polish citizens exchange 5 zloty for one euro. Then, in euro terms, wages are five times as high in Germany than they are in Poland, €10.00 as compared to €2.00.

The wage difference will tend to cause Polish workers (especially plumbers, apparently) to move to Germany. This immigration will cause the supply curve for labor to shift to the left in Poland and to the right in Germany. Figure I.4 depicts a possible outcome. Immigration is shown to have shifted the supply curve inward in Poland and outward by an equal amount in Germany, which made wages rise to €3.00 in Poland and fall to €8.00 in Germany. In the absence of any psychological or economic costs or explicit restrictions of any kind, we might have expected immigration to continue until the wages become equal in the two countries. Figure I.4, however, depicts the more realistic situation where migration tends to reduce, but not eliminate, the difference in wages between two countries. There are, no doubt, assorted stay and stay away factors, such as language differences, moving costs, and family ties, to prevent perfect wage equalization.

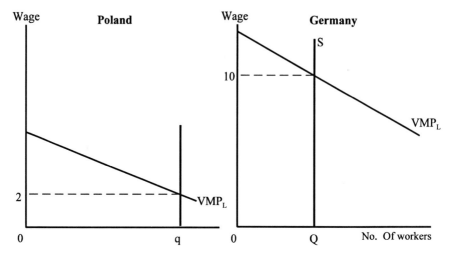

Fig. I.3 The labor markets before immigration

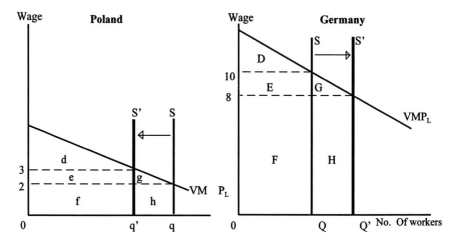

Fig. I.4 The labor market after immigration

I.2 Who Gains and who Loses with Immigration?

Figure I.4 provides useful insight into why labor migration is a controversial issue in many countries: Even though the overall worldwide gains appear to outweigh the losses, the model shows that some groups suffer welfare losses when people immigrate. Note that as a result of labor migration from Poland to Germany (represented by the shift in supply curves), migrating workers increase their welfare as they gain higher wages.

Table I.1 Gains and losses from immigration

1. Poland:	
Owners of other (non labor) factors:	loss of e + g
Remaining workers:	gain of e
Net change in real income:	loss of g
2. Germany:	
Workers originally in Germany:	loss of E
Owners of other (non labor) factors:	gain of E + G
Net change in real income:	gain of G
3. Immigrants:	
Loss of wages in Poland	loss of h
Gain of wages in Germany	gain of H
Net change in real income:	gain of H − h
World (1 + 2 + 3):	
Net change in Polish real income:	loss of g
Net change in German real income:	gain of G
Net change in immigrants' real income:	gain of H − h
Net gain:	gain of (H + G) − (h + g) > 0

More specifically, after q–q' workers depart, the supply of labor in Poland falls from S to S' and total output falls by the area g + h. The wages of the workers remaining in Poland rise from two to three euros, and their labor income increases from f to e + f. The other factors earn only d, which is smaller than their former income by the value of the areas e + g. It thus appears that labor gains real income while other factors lose income. The other factors in Poland suffer a net loss in income: The area e that other factors lose is gained by labor, but the area g is completely lost to Poland because the fall in total output, g + h, is greater than the wages that no longer need to be paid to the workers who left (area h).

Immigration causes a similar, albeit reversed, redistribution of welfare in Germany. According to Fig. I.4, native labor in Germany sees its income fall from E + F to just F, but other factors enjoy a rise in income from D to D + E + G. The income of Germany's native workers and other factors rises by the net amount of G as other factors gain more than the native workers lose. Output increases in Germany as we move down the labor demand curve in Fig. I.4; this increase is represented by the area G + H.

Figure I.4 also shows that the gain in output in Germany is greater than the loss of output in Poland. This must be the case since q–q' = Q'–Q and the average height of the areas G + H and g + h, respectively, are 9 euros and 2.5 euros. This rise in the value of total world output is the result of labor moving from a country where its marginal contribution to the real value of output is low to a country where its marginal contribution to the real value of output is higher. Table I.1 summarizes the distributional results from immigration in Fig. I.4.

I.3 Building on the Basic Labor Market Model

According to the simple labor market model developed here, the total income in the source country falls, and total income in the destination country increases. The immigrants clearly increase their welfare, which is why they were motivated to immigrate in the first place. Notice also that in the example given here, the gains of the immigrants are much larger than the net gain in the destination country. As detailed later in the book, evidence suggests that, indeed, immigrants capture the greatest part of the immediate gains from immigration. Other results of the model are that immigration causes world output to rise, wages to rise in the immigrant source country, and wages to fall in the destination country. Finally, the model effectively confirms what many people in immigrant destination countries suspect, namely that immigrants cause wages to decline.

This simple model is often used in immigration analysis. But, despite its popularity in the economics literature, the model is an extreme simplification of what actually happens in source and destination countries when people immigrate. All models are simplifications, of course, but there are some obvious extensions that can make the model more realistic. First of all, when labor moves from one country to another, there is an international transfer of not only a factor of production, but also a consumer. That implies that expenditures, and thus the demand for labor, also shift from the source to the destination countries when people immigrate. Furthermore, immigrants may introduce economies of scale effects. And, in the long run, there are dynamic growth effects associated with the movement of people because immigrants are also innovators, inventors, and entrepreneurs. These, and many more issues, are dealt with in detail in Chaps. 2–9 of this section on the economic theory of immigration.

Chapter 2
The Determinants of International Migration: Theory

Abstract The economic theory of external migration is concerned with three questions – *why* migrate, *who* migrates, and *what are the consequences* for source and destination countries? This chapter deals with the *why* question. It surveys the theoretical literature on the economic determinants of international migration. This literature is very small and relatively young, but has its roots in the much older theory of internal, or regional, migration. The standard model used implies that the immigration rate depends upon international differences in the returns to factor supply, controlling for migration costs, skill levels, income inequality, and immigration policies. We also discuss other models that focus on how the immigration decision is influenced by family considerations, the option value of waiting, and feelings of relative deprivation. There is still a big gap between theory and empirical work on the determinants of emigration, and much needs to be done on the theoretical side of this literature to bridge that gap.

> *The greatest challenge to migration theorists is the organization of all hypothetically relevant factors into one coherent theoretical framework that will specify their interaction with each other in empirically testable form and thereby serve as a guide to future research.*
>
> (United Nations, 1973)

Chapter Overview

The above quotation indicates that, as of 1973, there was no single, unified theory of why people migrate. Today, there is *still* no such convergence to a single model of immigration. Sociologists and economists have very different views about why people migrate, and politicians and policymakers seem to have yet another set of views. Economic models are based on the fundamental assumption that people's decision to relocate abroad depends on international differences in the returns to their labor, net of migration costs. This approach is useful in understanding what could be called *purely economic migration*, but not so useful in understanding refugees, family members who decide to accompany or follow immigrants, or those

Ö.B. Bodvarsson and H. Van den Berg, *The Economics of Immigration*,
DOI: 10.1007/978-3-540-77796-0_2, © Springer-Verlag Berlin Heidelberg 2009

who are forced to migrate against their will. In contrast, sociologists have tended to focus on a broader range of determinants of international migration, although important economic determinants are often given secondary emphasis in their analysis. As with any area of research that cuts across the different social sciences, often one discipline's explanation seldom matches the explanations offered by other disciplines. The economic literature has been restricted by its use of labor market models favored by the labor economists who have done most of the economic analysis of immigration.

It is certainly not obvious that the primary motive for immigration is a *factor supply* decision. Does a person relocate in order to obtain a higher price for her labor supply? Or, is migration a *consumption* decision? For example, does a person move because she expects the destination to have a more pleasant climate and attractive scenery, a preferred social culture, or better quality local public goods such as schools, parks or police protection? Or, is migration a decision to relocate *household production*? For example, does a family move because the destination has a better climate and soil for growing food or a better environment for home-schooling children? Or, do people relocate internationally to be closer to family and friends in the destination country, to seek political freedom and avoid persecution, or to safeguard one's wealth and property? A theory of the determinants of migration requires specifying what the migrant's motives are.

In this chapter, we survey the theoretical literature on the determinants of international migration. A number of things will quickly become apparent about this literature. First, it is small and young. The prevailing theory has received very little elaboration since its first presentation in Borjas (1987), who developed it primarily as a tool for understanding what determines the composition of immigrant flows. Second, the primary elements of Borjas' model come from the much older theories to explain internal migration (the flow of people within a country).

Internal migration has been studied extensively by regional, labor, and development economists. Regional economists have been interested in internal migration because of how it affects, and is affected by, local economic development. For example, a popular research question in the regional economics literature is "Do people follow jobs or do jobs follow people?" Internal migration has been of interest to labor economists because they view migration primarily as a response to geographic differences in the rates of return available to human capital. Development economists have been interested in internal migration primarily because of its distributional effects. For example, an important research question in development economics is: Does rural-to-urban migration in developing countries reduce or increase poverty?

Third, this survey of the theoretical literature on international migration will show how limited are the perspectives of the theoretical literature. Empirical researchers have often taken a much broader approach to immigration and have tested many variables representing influences not included in the available theoretical models of immigration. Much work must be done on the theoretical side to bridge the gap between theory and empirical work.

The organization of this chapter takes us first to a discussion of the very early contributions, including those made by scholars outside of economics, to understanding why people migrate internally. Second, we present an overview of the theory of internal migration since the 1960s, focusing on the human capital investment model of domestic migration developed by Sjaastad (1962). We then survey a number of other economic theories of international migration that have appeared in the mainstream literature.

2.1 The Theory of Internal Migration

Prior to the 1960s, the theory of internal migration was closely linked to the location models from regional economics and economic geography. Economic historians discussed international migration, but not from a theoretical perspective. With the development of the human capital investment model beginning in the late 1950s, internal migration began to be discussed from a more theoretical perspective. In this section, we survey the main developments in the economic theory of internal migration.

2.1.1 Pre-1960 Theory

Interestingly, an economic analysis of internal migration dates back to Smith's (1776) *An Inquiry into the Nature and Causes of the Wealth of Nations*:

> ... the wages of labour vary more from place to place than the price of provisions. The prices of bread and butcher's meat are generally the same or very nearly the same through the greater part of the united kingdom. These and most other things which are sold by retail, the way in which the labouring poor buy all things, are generally fully as cheap or cheaper in great towns than in the remoter parts of the country... But the wages of labour in a great town and its neighborhood are frequently a fourth or a fifth part, 20 or 25% higher than at a few miles distance. Eighteen pence a day may be reckoned the common price of labour in London and its neighbourhood. At a few miles distance it falls to eight pence, the usual price of common labour through the greater part of the low country of Scotland, where it varies a good deal less than in England. Such a difference of prices, which it seems is not always sufficient to transport a man from one parish to another, would necessarily occasion so great a transportation of the most bulky commodities, not only from one parish to another, but from one end of the kingdom, almost from one end of the world to the other, as would soon reduce them more nearly to a level. After all that has been said of the levity and inconstancy of human nature, it appears evidently from experience that a man is of all sorts of luggage the most difficult to be transported.[1]

---

[1] Adam Smith (1776[1976], Part I), pp. 83–84.

The above quote contains insightful observations which foreshadow research in the migration field two centuries later. Smith's observation that there is greater spatial dispersion of wages (the rural/urban wage differential is particularly large, for example) than there is of commodity prices is certainly still relevant today; international commodities seem to be more efficiently arbitraged today than labor. Smith effectively suggests that migration is potentially a response to spatial disequilibrium in labor markets. His observation of large wage differences in Britain suggest that wage differences are clearly not the only determinant of migration.

More than 150 years later, another leading economic theorist, John Hicks (1932), wrote that "... differences in net economic advantages, chiefly *differences in wages*, are the main causes of migration" (our italics). Yet, during the 150 years between Smith and Hicks, the world had seen an incredible widening of wage differences across countries and regions. Clearly, other things influenced immigration, and the rising arbitrage opportunities did not cause enough migration to prevent wage differences from growing. Indeed, Smith correctly foresaw the barriers to migration with his statement "man is of all sorts of luggage the most difficult to be transported."

Shields and Shields (1989) formalize Smith's observation in a model that hypothesizes labor moves from region i to region j if the wage is higher in j than i, and that the volume of migration is related to the wage differential in the following manner:

$$M_{ij} = \beta_{ij}(W_j - W_i), \tag{2.1}$$

where W is the wage, M is the number of migrants and β reflects barriers to migration, such as distance, imperfect information, and intentional government restrictions, that reduce the speed at which wages adjust to migration. The parameter β takes on a higher value when the barriers to migration are reduced. The theory of migration must be able to explain why wage differences do not generate enough arbitrage.

2.1.2 Ravenstein and Zipf

In between Smith (1776) and Hicks (1932), there were two scholars outside of economics who made important contributions to the study of internal migration: British geographer Ravenstein (1889) and American sociologist Zipf (1946). After extensively studying British census data on nativity of the population and place of residence along with vital statistics and immigration records, Ravenstein hypothsized seven "laws" of migration. Greenwood (1997) provides the following useful summarization of Ravenstein's 7 laws: (1) Most migrants move only a short distance and usually to large cities; (2) cities that grow rapidly tend to be populated by migrants from proximate rural areas and gaps arising in the rural population generate migration from more distant areas; (3) out-migration is inversely related to in-migration; (4) a major migration wave will generate a compensating counter-wave; (5) those migrating a long distance tend to move to large cities; (6) rural persons are more likely to migrate than urban persons; and (7) women are more likely to migrate than men.

Building upon several of Ravenstein's "laws," Zipf hypothesized that the volume of migration between two places is directly proportional to the product of the populations of the origin and destination and inversely proportional to the distance between the two. This "P(1)P(2)/D" hypothesis, where P(1) is origin population, P(2) is destination population and D is distance between origin and destination, came to be known as the *gravity model* of migration. The gravity model of migration is obviously an application of Newton's law of gravity, which predicts the level of attraction between two bodies. In applying Newton's law, Zipf treated "mass" as the population of a place, and "distance" as referring to miles between two places. Zipf's intuition is that distance is a good proxy for the costs of migration. Secondly, the gravity model effectively hypothesizes that the volume of migration is higher the greater are the populations of the origin and destination communities. The intuition behind this assumption is that at any point in time, some fraction of persons in the origin will face wage opportunities in alternative locations that exceed the wages they currently earn, net of migration costs, and those persons will migrate. Assuming that that fraction stays the same as the size of the origin population rises, the number of persons choosing to migrate will then also rise. Also, as the population of the destination community rises, the quantity and quality of employment opportunities will also be greater, inducing more migration.

It is important to note that, in terms of popularity, this gravity model of migration has received very little attention compared to another gravity model, namely the *gravity model of international trade*. The latter, which hypothesizes that the level of international trade between two countries is proportional to the product of their GDPs or populations and inversely related to the distance between the two, has been widely applied in empirical work in the field of international economics.[2]

$$M_{12} = \gamma P(1) P(2)/D$$
$$\ln M_{12} = \ln \gamma + \ln P(1) + \ln P(2) - \ln D$$

2.1.3 The Modern Theory of Internal Migration

The recent literature on internal migration can be divided into three categories, each corresponding to a particular motive for migration. Specifically, a migrant can be: (1) a supplier of her factor services or, effectively, a maximizing investor in her human capital, (2) a consumer of amenities and public goods, or (3) a producer of her own household goods and services.

---

[2]Tinbergen (1962) first applied the gravity model of trade to explain international trade patterns, and trade economists have consistently found it to explain a large proportion of the variation in trade flows, making the model attractive for testing the marginal influence of other hypothesized variables on international trade. Theoretical justifications for the gravity model of trade have been provided by Linneman (1966), Anderson (1979) and Deardorff (1998).

2.1.3.1 The Migrant as Investor in Human Capital

Most economists who study migration apply a *labor-flow* model, which posits that migration is a response to spatial differences in the returns to labor supply. At the micro level, this model implies that the migrant's goal is to maximize utility by choosing the location which offers the highest net income. Hence, users of this model implicitly assume that utility maximization is achieved through the maximization of income. These models, therefore, ignore the obvious fact that people migrate for reasons other than income maximization, e.g. family reunification, seeking refuge or political asylum, a more attractive culture, religious beliefs, etc. Those reasons are compatible with a more complex specification of utility maximization, but not with a simple assumption of income maximization.

To the extent that relocation involves up-front costs followed by an uncertain payoff in the future, migration is effectively an *investment* decision. Since labor income is a return to human capital, migration is effectively an investment in one's human capital. This view of migration draws on Becker (1962) and hypothesizes that people invest in their skills in order to maximize the net present value of future earnings.

The connection between migration and investment in human capital was first made by Sjaastad (1962). Sjaastad argued that a prospective migrant calculates the value of the opportunity available in the market at each alternative destination relative to the value of the opportunity available in the market at the point of origin, subtracts away the costs of moving (assumed to be proportional to migration distance), and chooses the destination which maximizes the present value of lifetime earnings. Nearly all recent *neoclassical* economic analyses of the internal migration decision proceed from this basic framework.[3] Within this framework, migration is usually treated as a once-and-for-all decision involving a change in the location of one's employment. This framework is, effectively, an inter-temporal version of the simple graphic labor market model we presented in the introduction to this section of the book, in which would-be migrants respond to differences in wages across labor markets in different geographic locations.

Sjaadstad uses distance as a proxy for migration costs. He justifies this by pointing out that the greater is distance traveled, the greater are the monetary costs of migration such as transportation expenses, food and lodging costs for oneself and one's family during the move, and interruptions in income while between jobs. The migration decision is also very dependent on available information about job vacancies. Such information is both informal (provided by friends and relatives, for example) and formal (advertisements in publications and employment agencies). Other pecuniary expenses include losses from selling one's home, car or appliances prior to the move, or additional expenses incurred to replace

---

[3]See expository surveys by Greenwood (1975, 1985, 1997), Molho (1986), Massey and Garcia Espana (1987), Shields and Shields (1989), Bauer and Zimmerman (1998), Ghatak, Levine, and Price (1996) and Gorter, Nijkamp and Poot (1998).

certain assets left behind at the destination. Also, a move will sometimes necessitate a loss of job seniority, employer contributions to pension plans and other types of employment benefits, which are also monetary expenses of moving. Sjaastad effectively assumes that all these types of expenses vary with distance.

Sjaastad's model does not explicitly include non-monetary gains enjoyed from moving, e.g. amenities such as better climate and recreational opportunities, a desirable social, political or religious environment, or more desirable quantities of public goods available at the destination because these are not included in the returns to human capital investment in Sjaastad's model. Instead, Sjaastad pointed out that origin-destination differences in the availability of amenities and public goods will be accounted for by differences in the cost of living. For example, a more pleasant climate in Arizona vs. North Dakota should already be reflected in higher prices for Arizona real estate. Shields and Shields (1989) point to difficulties in mixing nominal earnings differences and real costs of living. We would also argue that if one adjusts nominal income differences for differences in the costs of living, one would be mixing together the investment and consumption returns to migration, a strategy that would likely be at odds with Sjaastad's suggestions for modeling migration as human capital investment.

We can depict Sjaastad's ideas mathematically. Specifically, suppose that W_t^H represents earnings per period at home, W_t^M earnings per period if a person migrates to another market elsewhere, CL_t^H an index measuring the cost of living at home, CL_t^M an index measuring the cost of living at the destination, i the discount rate. and C the cost of migration. If a person lives T years, in discrete time, the present value of the net gain to migration Π is then

$$\pi = \sum_{t=1}^{T} \frac{(W_t^M - W_t^H)}{(1+i)^t} - \sum_{t=1}^{T} \frac{(CL_t^M - CL_t^H)}{(1+i)^t} - C(D,X), \qquad (2.2)$$

where D is distance between origin and destination and X is a vector of any other determinants of migration costs. In continuous time, the present value is

$$\pi = \int_{t=0}^{T} [W_t^M - W_t^H - CL_t^M + CL_t^H]e^{-rt}dt - C(D,X). \qquad (2.3)$$

In both the discrete and continuous time versions of the model, if $\pi > 0$, the decision-maker moves; if not, no move occurs. If there are multiple destination options, then (2.1) or (2.2) are computed for all those options and the individual chooses the option which yields the highest value of π. Nearly all theoretical and empirical studies that adopt the human capital investment approach utilize some behavioral model that is equivalent to, or is some permutation of, (2.2) or (2.3).

Sjaastad's model captures four aspects of the migration investment decision: (1) the imperfect synchronization of migration's benefits and costs in time; (2) earnings differences between origin and destination; (3) cost of living differences between origin and destination; and (4) the migrant's rate of time preference. The Sjaastad model is a single period model and, therefore, cannot explain why some people migrate on multiple occasions during their lifetimes. Also, Sjaastad's unit of analysis is the individual, which means that it cannot address the researchers who argue that the preferences and goals of persons close to the migrant such as family members must be taken into account when analyzing the migration decision. For example, if a husband and wife both work, then the husband's decision to migrate is likely to depend upon his wife's career prospects at the destination and *vice versa*. Migrants with more children tend to have a lower likelihood of migrating than those with fewer children. An explanation for this requires a model where the decision-making unit is the family, not just one person in isolation.

Another shortcoming of Sjaastad's model is its implicit assumption that migrants are perfectly informed about labor market opportunities at alternative destinations. This is a shortcoming of many investment models; uncertainty is very difficult to deal with in a model. But, in reality a prospective migrant will always face some degree of uncertainty about the size and path of his lifetime earnings stream at the destination. This uncertainty and the migrant's attitudes towards risk will influence his choice to migrate. Perhaps because Sjaastad ignored uncertainty in his model, he did not consider the role of past migration that has been shown to play such an important role in explaining both internal and international migration.

Sjaastad's model has some further shortcomings. Many international migrants remit some of their destination country earnings back home, which means that the benefits to immigration may include the benefits of remitting. Also, when remittances are part of the decision process the benefits of migrating also depend on the real exchange rate between the destination and home countries. The appreciation of the destination country's currency will boost the benefits of migration.

2.1.3.2   The Migrant as Consumer

Greenwood (1997) points out that by the early 1980s, tests of internal migration models based on the human capital investment model were consistently failing to confirm wages or earnings as determinants of migration. These empirical failures gave rise to an alternative view called the "equilibrium" perspective on migration, in contrast to the disequilibrium perspective implied by the traditional labor flow model that posits people migrate to take advantage of regional income differences.[4] The basic idea behind the equilibrium models is that people migrate as they adjust their consumption to continual changes in their incomes, prices, the supply of goods, services, and amenities, and their utility functions.

---

[4]For a sampling of important early papers using the equilibrium perspective, see Roback (1982, 1988), Graves (1979, 1983), Greenwood (1997), Green et al. (2006) and Glaeser and Shapiro (2003).

These models recognize that a person's utility function includes goods and services that are not all available in each geographic market. Desirable goods that are not universally available are called *amenities* and include such things as attractive scenery, a pleasant climate, clean air, etc. The basic idea behind this group of migration models originated with Rosen's (1974) work on hedonic prices and implicit markets.

Some of these models of migration focus on changes in the *demand for amenities*. The demand for amenities may change as a person moves from one phase of his/her life cycle to another. Or they may change as culture changes or as economic growth changes incomes and the mix of products available. For example, long term technological advances will raise peoples' real incomes and, assuming that consumption amenities are normal goods, boost the demand for those amenities. Because amenities tend to be distributed unevenly across the country, migration will occur and efficient markets will quickly re-equilibrate markets. Consequently, amenity-rich areas will experience in-migration, driving down wages and driving up land prices. In amenity-poor areas, wages will rise and rents will fall. Technological advances could have the same sorts of effects on producer demand for amenities. There will be a new set of interregional wage, rent and price differentials that emerge and they will reflect a new set of compensating differentials.

Because it focuses on demand, the equilibrium model assumes the market clears instantaneously, unlike the so-called disequilibrium approach that assumes labor flows gradually in response to earnings differences. Also, the demand-driven equilibrium model concludes that earnings differences across locations can be permanent because differences in amenities will tend to offset earnings differences in equilibrium.

The notion that people migrate internally in response to spatial differences in amenities also extends to public goods. Long before regional economists were constructing models relating spatial equilibrium to amenities, Tiebout (1956) argued that an important factor explaining why people move from one locality to another is differences in the quality of public goods such as police and fire protection, education, hospitals, courts, beaches, parks, roads and parking facilities. The idea that people "vote with their feet," picking communities which best satisfy their preference patterns for public goods, has come to be known as the *Tiebout Hypothesis*.

The consumption/equilibrium model has been used largely to explain internal migration in developed countries. The equilibrium perspective has generally not been applied to the study of internal migration in developing countries and it has not been applied at all to the study of international migration. Because of the regulated nature of international migration and the relatively higher costs of international movement, the equilibrium perspective is not very applicable to international migration. At the same time, there is no doubt that even from a disequilibrium perspective differences in amenities can drive migration.

The notion of the migrant as consumer has some relevance for the study of international migration. There are huge differences between countries, especially developing vs. developed countries, in the supply of non-tradable goods, public goods, and amenities. For example, amenities include such things as a free and democratic society, a lower perceived risk of persecution, a greater likelihood of cultural acceptance or an environment more permissive of creative expression. Furthermore, international migrants may be attracted by higher levels of public goods such as good quality health care, educational systems, and more functional judicial systems. In fact, the developed countries that have attracted most of the world's immigrants typically have a greater variety, quality and accessibility to non-tradable goods, e.g. lower cost and higher quality food, housing, home furnishings, cars, entertainment and recreation goods, that contribute overall to a higher quality of life.

As in the case of internal migration in developing countries, it is difficult to justify the assumption of immediate adjustment to a changing equilibrium in the case of international migration because that would, implicitly, assume zero migration costs. Again, this criticism does not deny the importance of amenities and the differences in the availability of nontradable goods for international migration. But the equilibrium models that incorporate the idea would not be realistic. Further relaxation of trade barriers, lower transportation costs, international regional economic and political integration, and liberalization of immigration agreements between countries could reduce international mobility costs sufficiently to enhance the equilibrium migration model's accuracy in explaining international migration.

2.1.3.3   The Migrant as Household Producer

Another set of models of internal migration assumes that a main motive for individual and family migration is the cost of household production. Shields and Shields (1989) suggested that households choose a location where they can produce the best combination of household goods and services. Their model is based on the literature of the *new household economics*, pioneered by Becker (1965), Lancaster (1966) and Willis (1973). This "migrant as household producer" view is complementary to the "migrant as consumer" view of why households move because it emphasizes the influence of amenities in the choice of migration destination.

According to the *new household economics*, all households to varying degrees produce goods and services for their own consumption. These could include meal preparation, housecleaning, growing fruits and vegetables, home repair, educational services, recreational goods and services, activities with friends and relatives, child care, etc. The household derives utility from its consumption of these goods and services, which are produced using its time, its physical capital, and various inputs purchased in the market. The household's goal is to maximize utility by choosing the optimal combination of commodities to produce and consume, subject to the household's income to purchase goods and capital and its technology of household production. Since there are significant locational differences in goods prices and amenities, there will be locational differences in the costs of household production. For example, if the household grows fruits and vegetables for its own consumption, then the cost of home grown produce will be lower in areas where climate and soil quality are more appropriate.

The implications of the household production models of migration often match those of the human capital and consumption models of migration. For example, suppose that real wages rise in an alternative location. According to the household production view, *ceteris paribus*, a household where family members allocate time to the labor market will relocate to the higher wage area because doing so will bolster income opportunities and allow for greater levels of household production. This choice of relocation matches what the human capital view would predict.

2.1.4 Further Influences on Internal Migration

Models all make assumptions that simplify the framework and permit the user to focus on a limited number of variables. For example, recall that in the original Sjaastad model, pecuniary migration costs depend only on distance traveled, that psychological and social costs are constant, and that there are zero information costs. It is, therefore, to be expected that for a complex phenomenon like immigration researchers will soon specify additional models that include variables not included in earlier models. In this subsection, we address several other strands of literature on internal migration that address other influences on people's decision to migrate.

2.1.4.1 The Role of Past Migration

Some researchers have argued that psychological and social costs, as well as information costs, are likely to fall when there is greater access to family, friends and other previous migrants in the destination. In the sociology literature on migration, the community of family and friends at the destination is often referred to as a *kinship network*, and the community of earlier migrants from a similar ethnic or regional background is referred to as a *migrant network*. Access to these networks can greatly improve the efficiency of migration. For example, as Yap (1977) has suggested: "Destination contacts have a positive effect on migration to a specific area, when contacts are measured by the presence of parents in the city, ... by potential ethnic contacts, ... by language similarity between areas or by the stock of persons in the destination who had migrated earlier from the home area." A similar point has been made by Hugo (1981), Taylor (1986) and Massey and Espana (1987). Kinship and migrant networks can lower job search costs, the costs of securing housing and child care, and reduce vulnerability to exploitation, fraud, and crime. Also, having family and members of a familiar culture at the destination can reduce the personal and cultural stresses associated with migration. To the extent that kinship and migrant networks are effective in reducing information and psychic costs, migration costs are endogenous to the volume of past migration.

One modeling approach is to enter kinship and migrant networks into the migrant's objective function under the assumption that people experience increased utility from having familiar faces and contacts in a new place. Another approach is to relate migration costs to a risk variable that varies inversely with the size of kinship and/or migrant networks. This was the approach of Taylor (1986), who argued that kinship networks serve as "migration insurance" that protects against potential income losses at the destination.

2.1.4.2 Migration as a Life Cycle Decision

Polachek and Horvath (1977) argue that migration should be modeled as an investment process undertaken at each stage of the life cycle rather than a one-investment decision. Their model generates clear, refutable predictions about when in their life cycle people are most likely to migrate and the likelihood of return migration. They argue that the Sjaastad model does generate such predictions because it says nothing about choice of locational characteristics. Polachek and Horvath's model could fit into the category of consumption demand models of migration because they assume that what matters to people are locational characteristics. They model locations as composites of various locational characteristics, including the rate of unemployment, price levels, industrial composition, occupational structure, and per capita public expenditures on education. As a person moves through the life cycle, demand for locational characteristics changes. For example, a young person in the early stage of her career may have a strong preference for locations with many other young people and high income jobs, whereas a person nearing retirement may have a strong preference for locations with good climate and healthcare. Because there are multiple stages to the life cycle, it is very likely that there will be multiple migrations during a person's life.

2.1.4.3 The Expected Income Hypothesis

A weakness of the Sjaastad model is that it assumes the probability of a migrant finding employment in the destination is 100%. If migration costs are zero and all migrants find work at the destination instantly upon arrival, a pure disequilibrium model then implies complete wage convergence between source and destination. Beginning with Todaro (1969, 1976) and Harris and Todaro (1970), many development economists have pointed out that this assumption is very unrealistic for cases involving internal rural-to-urban migration in developing countries.[5] They point out that urban unemployment rates in developing countries have historically been high and that rural migrants usually face a long wait before they find a job in the urban "modern" sector. While they search and wait, migrants are either unemployed or underemployed, occasionally performing menial tasks for low pay.

Todaro (1969) provided a model in which prospective migrants explicitly take into account the probability of obtaining work in the modern urban sector. In terms of the Sjaastad framework presented as (2.1) or (2.2) above, this involves substituting expected income at the destination for actual income:

---

[5]For a very recent and thorough review specifically of the literature on rural to urban internal migration in LDCs, see Lall, Selod, and Shalizi (2006).

$$\pi = \int_{t=0}^{T} [p(t)W_t^M - W_t^H - CL_t^M + CL_t^H]e^{-rt}dt - C(D,X), \qquad (2.4)$$

where $p(t)$ is the probability a migrant will be employed in the modern urban sector in period t. This probability is assumed by Todaro to be equal to the ratio of new modern sector employment openings to the number of "waiting" job seekers in the urban traditional sector. The number of modern sector job openings grows at the rate of industrial output growth less the growth rate of labor productivity in the modern sector. Rural-to-urban migration will continue despite high unemployment as long as the *expected* wage in the urban sector, net of migration costs, equals the average wage in the rural sector. This basic model was subsequently extended by Harris and Todaro (1970), Bhagwati and Srinivasan (1974), Corden and Findlay (1975), Fields (1979), and Calvo (1978), among many others, to take into account additional characteristics of developing countries.

2.2 The Economic Theory of Immigration

The development of theoretical models of international migration, or immigration, has gained momentum in the past several decades. One of the better-known immigration economists is Borjas (1987, 1991), who drew on the prior work on internal migration as well as work in other social sciences to develop what has become arguably the most popular model in immigration economics. It is fair to say that Borjas adds little substance to the theoretical models for internal migration presented in the previous section. His mathematical model is a close derivative of the simple graphic model presented in the introduction to this section of the book, which is, of course, a close relative of the Sjaastad migration model. Borjas does add some interesting innovations that have permitted him to address the character-istics of immigrants vs. non-immigrants. Therefore, the exposition of Borjas' model in this part of the chapter also serves as the first step towards analyzing immigrant selectivity, the topic of Chapter 4.

2.2.1 The First Borjas Model

In two papers, Borjas (1987, 1991) developed closely related versions of a human capital investment model of international migration.[6] These models assume that the incentive to migrate is driven purely by the international differences in the average

---

[6]Borjas has also presented the same models in three expository surveys of the immigration literature [see Borjas (1990, 1994, 1999)].

returns to labor and human capital in the source and destination countries. Borjas (1987) presents a model in which the distributions of human capital among workers in the source and destination countries determine immigration flows in addition to the overall differences in labor returns.

2.2.1.1 The General Intuition of the First Model

Borjas's approach reflects the observation that people in the source and destination countries are not all the same in terms of their abilities, education, age, etc. Rather, he assumes that people in both economies are characterized by entire ranges of talents, skills, education levels, and other personal characteristics. The migration decision, therefore, depends on how a would-be migrant with a specific set of skills and talents perceives his or her gains from migrating from a labor market where the labor force has a certain distribution of worker characteristics to a country where the labor force has a different distribution of talents, skills, and education levels. The migration decision thus depends not just on the average difference in wages across countries, but on where the immigrant would fit into the destination country labor market and how well the worker's abilities and other human capital can be applied there. Borjas' model is thus able to predict the flows of different types of workers between countries.

The Borjas model we discuss here is in fact the first stage of a two-stage model of international migrant selectivity. The second stage of the model will be discussed in detail in Chapter 4.

2.2.1.2 The Specification of the Model

In the simplest version of the model, Borjas assumes that migration is an irreversible "yes/no" decision and there is just one destination country. The source and destination countries have different earnings distributions, which reflect differences in earnings opportunities available to a would-be migrant. It is important to emphasize that in this model, Borjas assumes that country differences in earnings distributions are not due to differences in skill distributions (which are assumed to be the same), but to differences in markets and policies. For example, Norway has a more compressed earnings distribution than the U.S. because Norway has higher income tax rates and, through its social insurance programs, a broader system of income redistribution. As a result, a person of given skill has a greater chance of reaping a very high or a very low return to his factor supply in the U.S. than in, say, Norway.

Borjas further assumes that a person's earnings in either country are equal to the mean earnings in that country plus a random variable. Specifically, a person's earnings in his/her home country are

$$\ln(w_0) = \mu_0 + \varepsilon_0, \tag{2.5}$$

where μ_0 is the mean income home country residents would earn if they stayed at home, and ε_0 is random, uncorrelated with μ_0, with a mean of zero and a variance of σ_0^2. Some home country residents will earn less than the mean, others above the mean, and earnings differences could be due to differences in skills or random factors such as luck, unexpected health shocks, job loss, etc.

A migrant's earnings in the destination will be

$$\ln(w_1) = \mu_1 + \varepsilon_1, \tag{2.6}$$

where μ_1 is the mean income home country residents would earn if they *all* migrated to the destination country, and ε_1 is a random variable with the same assumptions as for ε_0 above. Borjas makes the assumption that μ_1 equals the mean income migrants would earn abroad if all home country residents migrated because it simplifies the model's solution without, he claims, changing the model's basic predictions.

The variance terms σ_0^2 and σ_1^2 are the parameters in the Borjas model that describe the income inequality in the source and destination countries, respectively. Holding the distribution of skills constant, the variance of earnings effectively indicates the dispersion of earnings *opportunities* in a country. If the destination country has a greater dispersion, then an immigrant with a given level of socio-economic characteristics will have a greater chance of reaping an exceptionally large return to his labor and human capital. Of course, there is also a greater risk, all other things equal, of reaping an exceptionally low income. In this version of Borjas' model, the variance of earnings in the source and destination countries is driven entirely by the variance of the error terms σ_0 and σ_1, and not by specific identifiable character and skill variables. Therefore, σ_0 and σ_1 effectively measure the returns to *unobservable* characteristics in the source and destination countries.

To incorporate skills transferability across borders, Borjas assumes that the random variables ε_0 and ε_1 have a correlation coefficient of ρ. A value of ρ that is positive and close to unity indicates that skills are easily transferrable across borders and a person who earns relatively well (poorly) in the home country is highly likely to earn relatively well (poorly) in the destination country. One would expect that the earnings correlation between home and destination countries will be positive and high if the labor markets, levels of development, industrial structures and quality of schools, for example, are similar. Canadian doctors who obtained their schooling in Canada should easily be able to transfer their skills to the U.S. and continue to earn relatively high incomes after migration. In contrast, a ρ that is positive but very small implies that skills do not transfer well across borders. It is also possible that $\rho < 0$, which is the case if a person's skills generate relatively low (high) earnings at home, but relatively high (low) earnings in the destination country. Such could be the case of a talented folk musician, who is well paid at home for performing native songs greatly appreciated by his countrymen. Were he to migrate, residents of his destination country may not know the music his countrymen are so fond of. Hence, the singer moves from being near the top of his native country's earnings distribution to singing on the street corner in the destination country for a few tips from sympathetic passers-by. Borjas suggests that ρ is positive and relatively high for pairs of developed countries, but low or even negative correlations will more often be the case for migrants from developing countries to developed economies.

In Borjas' model, if the costs of migrating are C, then a person migrates if $w_1 > w_0 + C$, or $\left[\frac{w_1}{w_0+C}\right] > 1$. Taking logs, she migrates if $I > 0$, where

$$I \equiv \ln(w_1) - \ln(w_0 + C) > 0. \tag{2.7}$$

Note that $\ln(w_1 + C)$ is approximately equal to $In(w_0) + \frac{C}{w_1}$.[7] Borjas defines $\frac{C}{w_1}$ as π, and calls this a "time equivalent" measure of the costs of migration. He assumes it to be constant across all individuals in the home country. It then follows from (2.6) that the person will migrate if

$$I = (\mu_1 - \mu_0 - \pi) + (\varepsilon_1 - \varepsilon_0) > 0 \Rightarrow (\varepsilon_1 - \varepsilon_0) > -(\mu_1 - \mu_0 - \pi). \tag{2.8}$$

According to expression (2.8), migration will occur if the destination country rewards the migrant more for her or his particular skills and if net mean earnings in the destination country are higher.

Recall that the model introduced a random element to earnings. Hence, it is the probability that $I > 0$, which we will call P, that serves as a measure of the migration rate. From (2.8), the emigration rate will be positive if $\Pr[(\varepsilon_1 - \varepsilon_0) > -(\mu_1 - \mu_0 - \pi)] > 0$. For analytical convenience, Borjas standardizes the emigration rate to a Z value by noting that P is equivalent to

$$\Pr\left(Z > \frac{-(\mu_1 - \mu_0 - \pi)}{\sigma_v}\right) = 1 - \Phi(Z), \tag{2.9}$$

where σ_v is the standard deviation of $(\varepsilon_1 - \varepsilon_0)$, $\Phi(Z)$ is the cumulative distribution function for Z, and $\sigma_v = \sqrt{\sigma_0^2 + \sigma_1^2 - 2\rho\sigma_0\sigma_1}$ under specific assumptions about the distributions. The emigration rate thus depends upon mean earnings in each country, each country's earnings variance, relative migration costs, the degree of skills transferability across borders, and the interaction of the source and destination country earnings variances (the $\sigma_0 \, \sigma_1$ term in σ_v).

---

[7]For example, suppose that home earnings are $10,000 and migration costs are $1,000. Note that Log(11,000) = 4.04 while Log (10,000) + (1,000/10,000) = 4.1, a difference of only about 1.5%.

2.2.1.3 The Predictions of the Model

Ideally, we would like to be able to integrate the density function of earnings and obtain a reduced form expression for the emigration rate. That expression would then specify an empirical model of the emigration rate. It is not possible to obtain a reduced form expression for the normal distribution, which is what Borjas necessarily assumes for his model in order to derive the relationships above. Hence, predictions about the behavior of the migration rate can only be inferred by analyzing how changes in the variables that determine the migration rate influence the distribution function.

Suppose we are interested in knowing how the emigration rate varies with some exogenous variable Ω. We can obtain the sign of $\partial P/\partial \Omega$ by deriving the expression

$$\frac{\partial P}{\partial \Omega} = -\frac{\partial \Phi}{\partial Z} \frac{\partial Z}{\partial \Omega}. \tag{2.10}$$

From a table giving areas under the standard normal curve, it can be verified that $\frac{\partial \Phi}{\partial Z}$ and $\frac{\partial^2 \Phi}{\partial Z^2} > 0$. The sign of the expression $\frac{\partial Z}{\partial \Omega}$ depends upon whether the destination is relatively rich ($\mu_1 > \mu_0 + \pi$) or relatively poor ($\mu_1 < \mu_0 + \pi$) and on the sign of $\frac{\partial \sigma_v}{\partial \Omega}$. If we assume that the destination is relatively rich and apply expression (2.9) above, we conclude that

$$\frac{\partial P}{\partial \mu_1} = \frac{\partial \Phi}{\partial Z} \left(\frac{1}{\sigma_v}\right) > 0 \tag{2.11}$$

and

$$\frac{\partial P}{\partial \mu_0} = -\frac{\partial \Phi}{\partial Z} \left(\frac{1}{\sigma_v}\right) < 0. \tag{2.12}$$

Hence, the model effectively hypothesizes that[8]:

1. *The migration rate will rise (fall) if the destination country's mean income rises (falls).*
2. *The migration rate will fall (rise) if the source country's mean income rises (falls).*

These predictions match those of the internal migration models discussed earlier, which is that when the net return to migration rises there will be a stronger incentive to migrate. However, the predictions implied by (2.11) and (2.12) also address the

---

[8]These predictions are implied by the first derivatives of the emigration rate with respect to each of its six determinants. There are also predictions implied by second derivatives (which would indicate rates of change) and cross-partial derivatives (which indicate interaction effects). Borjas did not discuss second-order effects, however.

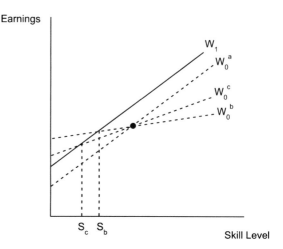

Fig. 2.1 The effects of relative income inequality when source country inequality is lower

question of why, when the mean income of an immigrant destination country is much larger, as in the case for the U.S. vs. many developing countries, we do not see a country's entire population migrating. Differences in countries' variance of earnings and the degree of skills transferability between countries means that people with different skills, talents, education, etc. will have different incentives to migrate.

To see how differences in the dispersion of earnings affects migration, consider Figs. 2.1 and 2.2. Each of the figures show a mixture of wage profiles, where each profile relates the level of earnings to the level of skills in a country. Since a higher (lower) variance of earnings opportunities increases the return to skills, a higher variance in earnings implies a steeper wage profile in the figures. In both figures, it is assumed that the destination country is relatively richer. In each figure, w_1 shows the relationship between wages and skills in the destination country and the three other profiles are for the source country. In both figures, w^a0 shows the wage profile in the source country when the variance of earnings there equals the destination country variance. When the variances are equal and skills are fully transferable, all persons in the source country have an incentive to migrate and the migration rate is 100 percent. The result that in both figures the three source country profiles intersect at a mean income level lower than the mean of w_1 reflects the assumption that the destination country is relatively richer.

According to Fig. 2.1, when the source country wage profile is less steep, as for example w_0^b, then only those persons with skill level s_b or higher will migrate. If source country inequality rises and the wage profile rotates upward to w_0^c, those persons with skill level s_c or higher will migrate, and total migration increases. As long as source country inequality is initially relatively lower, an increase in that country's inequality will result in a higher emigration rate.

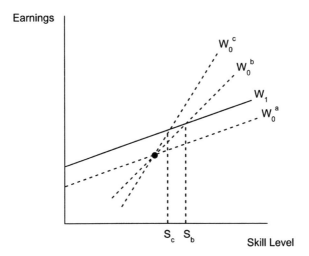

Fig. 2.2 The effects of relative income inequality when source country inequality is higher

According to Fig. 2.2, if the source country's wage profile is w_0^b, then those persons with skill level s_b or below will migrate since for those persons, the destination country offers a higher return. If income inequality in the source country rises and the wage profile rotates upwards to w_0^c, then only those persons with skill level of s_c or below will move. Hence, the emigration rate will fall. When source country inequality is greater so that the source country wage profile is steeper, an increase (decrease) in source country inequality will *lower* (raise) the emigration rate.

Borjas uses the same analysis as above to show that (1) if destination country inequality is initially relatively low, an increase in that country's inequality will raise the emigration rate, and (2) if destination country inequality is initially relatively high, the emigration rate will be positively related to that country's inequality. Furthermore, all of these predictions about the effects of income distribution are reversed if the destination country is relatively poor.

The first Borjas model also derives the following relationship

$$\frac{\partial P}{\partial \pi} = -\frac{\partial \Phi}{\partial Z}\left(\frac{1}{\sigma_v}\right) < 0, \qquad (2.13)$$

which suggests the following hypothesis:

3. *The migration rate is lower the higher are relative migration costs.*

Finally, the model generates the following relationship

$$\frac{\partial P}{\partial cov(\varepsilon_0, \varepsilon_1)} = \frac{\partial \Phi}{\partial Z}[(\mu_1 - \mu_0 - \pi)[\sigma_0^2 + \sigma_1^2 - 2cov(\varepsilon_0, \varepsilon_1)]^{\frac{3}{2}} > 0 \qquad (2.14)$$

Because the covariance measures the transferability of skills and talents, (2.14) suggests that:

4. *The migration rate rises if the degree of skills transferability rises.*

   This latter conclusion is an important result for Borjas' ultimate purpose, which is to show how differences in income distributions and skill distributions affect the characteristics of immigrants. When skills are not easily transferred, it becomes more likely that only less skilled workers will migrate, all other things equal.

2.2.2 Borjas' 1991 Model

In his 1991 study, Borjas presents a variation of the above model. Instead of assuming independently random fluctuations in earnings, Borjas (1991) assumes that the earnings of a person with socioeconomic characteristics or skill endowment X is equal to that country's average valuation of X plus a random component. This model again finds that migration is more likely to occur if the destination country values the migrant's characteristics, net of migration costs, more than the source country does. Also as before, Borjas (1991) concludes that the migration rate for persons with given characteristics X depends upon international differences in the values attached to those characteristics, each country's earnings variance, relative migration costs, and the degree of transferability of X across borders.

Borjas uses this model to show that earnings variance in a country can be driven by variations in *observable* characteristics such as schooling and experience. In this case, a person's earnings in the source and destination countries are modeled as depending on mean country earnings for a person with a set of personal characteristics other than schooling, a variable for the level of schooling, the rate of return to schooling (δ_0), and a random error. The migration rate now depends on two distributions – the distributions of unobservable characteristics in each country and the distribution of returns to schooling in each country. One of the predictions that Borjas' second model generates is:

5. *The migration rate is higher (lower) the higher (lower) is the mean level of schooling in the source country.*

   In the extreme case where mean schooling in the source country is zero, there is no "educational premium" to capture in the destination country, and hence there is no incentive to emigrate on the basis of one's education. In contrast, in a country where mean schooling is very high, the potential gains available to migrants in the destination country will be very high and there will be a strong incentive to migrate.

The important point here is that emigration rates will be higher for source countries that have more skilled labor forces.

The model also concludes that

6. *The migration rate is higher (lower) the lower (higher) is the variance of schooling in the source country.*

When the variance of the distribution of skills (measured in this case by level of educational attainment) rises, there will be a larger number of persons who fall far below the mean level of education and who have little incentive to migrate because the potential gains to education in the destination country would then also tend to be very low. There will, of course, also be more persons with exceptionally high levels of education in this case, but they would have been strong candidates for migration anyways. Hence, there is a net reduction in the overall migration rate. The implication is that in countries where there are substantial disparities in schooling across the population (such as in developing countries), smaller fractions of the population will migrate abroad.

2.2.3   Recent Extensions of the Borjas Model

Approximately 20 years have passed since Borjas first published his model of international migration in which he supplemented the role of income differences with various assumptions about the distributions of personal characteristics. Since then, others have built other determinants of international migration into Borjas' models. For example, Hatton and Williamson (2005) and Clark, Hatton, and Williamson (2007) have extended the Borjas model to account for the effects of non-pecuniary costs of migration and explicit immigration restrictions. We focus here on some novel predictions derived in Clark, Hatton, and Williamson (CHW).

2.2.3.1   The CHW Model

CHW model the decision to migrate as a function of the destination/source country wage differential, the distributions of skill levels, and several types of migration costs. The authors specify four types of migration cost:

1. *Individual-specific migration cost(z).*

According to CHW, the value of z could be a compensating differential. For example, persons who have relatives and friends in the destination country are likely to have lower levels of z. We have already discussed some reasons why relatives and friends reduce migration costs, but CHW add the important observation that persons with family members in the destination can obtain admission through family reunion or family-sponsored preference categories, as compared with other (potentially more expensive) categories. Furthermore, persons who have stronger preferences for amenities available in the destination will have lower values of z. Note that in the case of amenities, z could be negative. For example, a person's preference for the destination's warm climate could be so strong that she would migrate there even if that meant a cut in income. Refugees escaping political persecution or risk to life and limb as a result of civil war will also have a negative z.

2. *Direct cost.*

Direct migration costs are directly related to distance. Also, migration costs rise when the destination country imposes higher visa costs or imposes more difficult visa application procedures.

3. *Migration costs that result from quantitative restrictions on immigration.*

This measure uses the total cap on the number of migrants from source country y allowed to enter destination country x. The larger is the cap, the lower are the costs of waiting for permission to enter or the cost of moving to a higher-preference category.

4. *Migration costs resulting from "skill-selective" immigration policy.*

A skill-selective policy generally implies that the more-skilled face a lower cost of admission.

CHW derive a probit equation for the emigration rate using the same approach as Borjas in which they predict the effects on migration from changes in each of the four types of migration costs. CHW generate a number of novel predictions. One result is that, while the migration rate still depends on the relative variance of the destination country's income distribution, the migration rate now also depends on the level of skill-selective immigration policy and the variance of schooling in the source country. Another novel result is that different immigration policies will influence the emigration rate in different ways. For example, expanding family reunification policies lowers average person-specific migration costs μ_z, which will stimulate emigration. A reduction in an overall immigration quota will dampen emigration, as will an increase in admission standards under a skill-selective policy. However, CHW find that there is an ambiguous relationship between the parameter measuring the relative importance of skill-selective policy in the destination country. Skill-selective immigration policies may increase or decrease immigration, depending on more specific circumstances.

2.2.3.2 Migration as a Response to Relative Deprivation

Some immigration economists have applied the concept of *relative deprivation* due originally to the social psychologist Runciman (1996). The notion of relative deprivation is very fundamental: a person derives happiness not only from the goods his own income can buy, but also on how his income ranks relative to his peers. This hypothesis is solidly founded on evidence from psychology, neuroscience, and experimental economics.

Stark (1984, 1991), Katz and Stark (1986), Stark and Taylor (1989, 1991) and Stark and Yitzhaki (1988) model migration as being undertaken because it can improve a person's income relative to members of his or her "reference group," which in the immigration literature is assumed to be other income-earning persons in the source country or source community. It follows that if migration leads to higher absolute income elsewhere (assuming we have controlled for cost of living differences), the migrant experiences a higher level of welfare or satisfaction because relative deprivation is reduced.

The notion that relative deprivation motivates migration is well rooted in the psychology, happiness studies, and experimental economics literature. For example, Blanchflower and Oswald (2000), Frey and Stutzer (2002a, b), Layard (2005), and Veenhoven (1996, 1999), among others, have examined responses to life satisfaction surveys and concluded that human happiness or life satisfaction is often more influenced by their relative income than absolute income. The evidence suggests that for levels of income below $10,000, people's happiness or life satisfaction is strongly responsive to gains in absolute income, but for higher incomes, relative status overwhelms absolute income levels as the determinant of human happiness. Hence, for immigrants from high income countries, a focus on how immigration is likely to change a person's income relative to his peers in the source country is clearly called for. On the other hand, for migrants who move from poor countries to wealthy countries, improvements in both absolute income and relative income are likely to influence the migration decision.

The relative deprivation models generate potentially important testable implications of the hypothesis. First, the relative deprivations hypothesis implies that characteristics of the migrant's home income distribution will influence his decision to migrate. For example, if his absolute income stays the same, but the variance of the distribution or its degree of positive skewness rise, this will alter his utility and give him greater incentive to migrate. Since one can often obtain reasonably accurate data on the distribution of individual or household income in a community, province or country, the relative deprivation hypothesis can be tested for many cases.

There is a second and potentially very important implication of the relative deprivation hypothesis. Following Todaro (1969) and Harris and Todaro (1970), suppose people face only *expected* income. Assume, also, that the probability distribution of possible employment outcomes in the destination is such that a migrant stands only a small chance of reaping a very high reward after migrating. Assume, however, that utility is very dependent on relative income in his reference group, so were (s)he to get lucky and reap the very high reward at the destination, utility would rise substantially. Under such conditions, the expected utility from migrating could be very high even if there is no differential in expected income between the two locations. Migration could be attractive even if expected income at the origin is greater than at the destination, provided there is a higher chance of hitting the jackpot in the destination compared to the source country. In other words, the relative deprivation hypothesis is capable of contradicting the traditional hypothesis that expected income differentials between urban and rural areas must be positive in order to induce migration.

2.2.3.3 Migration as Sequential Search and the Option Value of Waiting

It is likely that someone contemplating migration will be imperfectly informed about labor market opportunities at the destination. Hence, the migration decision is generally made under some degree of uncertainty. Models like those of Todaro (1969) and Harris and Todaro (1970) explicitly recognized uncertainty and how it determined internal rural-to-urban migration. A number of theories of international migration also explain migrant decision-making when would-be migrants face probability distributions rather than full information on foreign opportunities.

Pickles and Rogerson (1984) and McCall and McCall (1987) model the decision to migrate as a sequential search process in which the migrant maximizes expected net income and faces a stationary probability distribution of wages at the destination. Every period, an observation from that distribution is revealed in the form of a wage offer, at which point the potential migrant compares the offer with the reservation wage, which is usually the wage in the source country. When a foreign wage offer exceeds the reservation wage plus migration costs, the migrant moves abroad. The model answers the question: How long does it take before a move is made? The model concludes that, all other things equal, the more favorable labor market conditions are at the origin, the longer before a sufficiently attractive wage offer arrives and migration occurs. Alternatively, the more favorable are labor market conditions in the destination country, the sooner a person decides to migrate.

These models add time as a variable in the immigration decision. They help explain the evidence showing that international migration responds only sluggishly to real income differences. For example, Burda (1995) found that following a large spike immediately after reunification of West and East Germany, migration from the East to the West was surprisingly sluggish despite very large real wage differences. This type of pattern, where migration is sluggish despite significant real income differentials between countries, has been found for most other cases of internal and external migration.

Burda (1993, 1995) provides a different explanation for the slow response of migration to the usual incentives for migration like income differences. Burda argues that uncertainty about labor market conditions in the destination country justifies delaying the decision to migrate until more information is obtained. Burda effectively models procrastination as an *option* similar to an option to purchase a stock or foreign exchange at a later date. It will pay to wait to make a decision as long as the benefits of waiting for information exceed the opportunity costs.

Consider the following example of Burda's point. Suppose a person living in Source is contemplating a move to Destination and faces a two-period decision problem in which the second period return is not certain. Specifically, suppose that by moving to Destination the migrant can increase her income by \$10,000 in the first period with a probability of 1, but in period 1 there is a 0.5 probability she will find a job with a salary \$50,000 more than in Source in period 2. But in period 1, the would-be migrant also knows that there is an equal 0.5 probability that she will not find that job and, instead, be deported and fined in period 2, in which case she will lose \$20,000 compared to her expected Source income. She also faces migration costs of \$9,500, which must be paid at the time of migration. If, for simplicity, we assume the migrant is risk neutral and has a discount rate of zero, the potential pay-offs from migrating in period 1 or waiting until period 2 when that period's outcome is known are shown in Table 2.1 below. Note the "option" value of waiting and foregoing the \$10,000 income in period 1. At the start of period 2 the migrant will know whether the \$50,000 job is available; if it is, she can cash in her "option" and migrate, but if it is not, she simply ignores the option and stays home. Had she migrated in period 1, she would have faced the risk of losing \$20,000 in period 2 and, overall, her expected gains from migrating would have been less than if she took the option of waiting.

Burda (1995) develops a formal theoretical model from which he derives an expression for the option value of waiting. He demonstrates that the value of the migration option, or the "gain from procrastination," is inversely related to the current wage gap, positively related to migration costs, has an ambiguous relationship with the discount rate, is inversely related to the wage gap when destination labor market conditions are unfavorable, and does not depend on the wage gap when destination conditions are favorable. In short, uncertainty and changing conditions at home and abroad do necessarily imply sudden large shifts in migration flows. Migrants may opt to wait and see.

2.3 The Family or Household as the Decision-Making Unit

The original economic model of migration does not distinguish between personal and family decisions. In Sjaastad (1962) the focus is on the individual, and there is no analysis of how migration by an individual may affect other persons close to him. The implicit assumption in early research on the migration decision is that if the migrant is part of a family, then the welfare of the rest of the family is unaffected by that person's decision to relocate. In other words, when the migration model is applied to individuals, it ignores the gains or losses accruing to family or household members coming along or staying behind.

Table2.1 The option value of waiting to migrate

	Period 1 income	Period 2 income	Period 2 income
Migrate	10,000 – 9,500	(50,000 – 20,000)*0.5	500 + 15,000 = 15,500
Wait	0	(50,000 – 9,500)*0.5	20,250
Option value of waiting:			4,750

For a large proportion of internal and international moves, migration is indeed a family decision, and everyone in the family is affected by it. Consequently, the migration model above needs to be extended to take account of the effects that family ties have on the migration decision, and the effects that the migration decision has on all members of the family or household. We need answers to questions such as: When family members have conflicting interests, how is the decision to migrate made? Also of interest is: Under what circumstances would only part of the family migrate, leaving the others to remain behind?

2.3.1   Conflicting Interests and the Family Migration Decision

Extensions of the standard migration model to the case of a family that migrates began with the work of Sandell (1977), Polachek and Horvath (1977) and Mincer (1978). Their models explicitly recognize that individual family members can have conflicting interests. The family's migration may enhance the well-being of some family members but reduce others' well-being. For example, while a software engineer wife may gain income when moving from India to Silicon Valley, her history professor husband might lose income or even become unemployed after the move. While the household head's income and job satisfaction may improve with relocation, other family members may suffer psychological costs that result from leaving family and friends behind, adjusting to a new language and culture, etc. Gary Becker (1974) suggests how an economist tends to view these issues when he wrote the following about a husband's migration decision: "For example, he would not move to another city if his spouse's or children's income would be decreased by more than his own income would be increased." We focus on one of the above-mentioned papers in the next section.

2.3.2   Mincer's Model

Mincer's (1978) model of the impact of the family is straightforward. Suppose, for simplicity, that the household includes two persons, a husband and a wife. Let us assume that this two-person family has two alternatives to choose from: (1) Both migrate together; or (2) Both stay at the origin. We thus rule out the possibility that one person migrates, while the other stays behind, as in the cases of "commuting couples" or broken marriages caused by career conflicts. Mincer argues that the requirement for migration to take place is not that both persons have positive gains to migration, but rather that the family's net gains, i.e. the *sum* of the family's gains be positive. If the private gains to migration for each person are positively corre-lated, then family migration is of course always the efficient action. When the private gains to migration are negatively correlated, however, Mincer's model suggests it may still be efficient for the family unit to migrate. If, for example, the husband experiences a gain from migration, the wife a loss, but the joint gains are still positive, then Mincer's model predicts the case of a *tied mover*; the wife follows her husband even though her employment outlook is better at their current residence. On the other hand, if the wife's loss from migration dominates the husband's gain, then he becomes a *tied stayer*.

2.3.3 Family Migration as a Portfolio Decision

Another strand of migration literature that focuses on the family unit emphasizes the role of immigrant remittances. This literature began with Stark and Levhari (1982), Stark (1984) and Katz and Stark (1986), who model the decision of the *household* to send a family member overseas to work. These authors model such a decision as a "family portfolio diversification decision" where the migration abroad of a family member serves to hedge against risky labor markets at home. Such hedging is especially important for low families in poor countries who have little savings to fall back on in the case of income losses.

The core feature of this collective decision making model is that the family or household, unlike the individual, can reduce risk through diversification in the same way that a portfolio manager controls the risk of investing in the financial markets. Some members of the family, for example, can be assigned to work in the local economy, while others may be sent to work in foreign labor markets where conditions are not closely correlated with local labor markets. If there is a slump in the local labor market and the household faces a liquidity shortfall, then having a family member working overseas who remits his or her income will relieve that shortfall. According to this literature, the decision to have family members migrate is a response to a lack of risk-hedging mechanisms such as unemployment insurance, welfare programs, credit institutions, crop insurance markets, futures markets, and other financial markets. This literature stands out for providing the first theoretical economic rationale for immigrant remittances, something that the immigration literature was largely silent on prior to the 1980s.

2.4 Summary and Conclusions

In this chapter, we have surveyed economic theories of why people migrate. We began with the writings of Smith (1776), who described migrants as arbitargeurs who take advantage of regional wage differences. We detailed Borjas' (1987, 1991) recent models which show that international migration is not only influenced by net earnings differences between countries, but also by factors such as international differences in income inequality and the degree of skills transferability. We also discussed Clark et al. (2007), who examine various costs of migration including explicit government policies to control immigration. We concluded with other recent models by economists that capture some of the additional complexities of immigration.

The fundamental premise of nearly all the models discussed is that migration is driven by spatial differences and distributional differences in the net returns to human labor. An important contribution was by Sjaastad (1962), who articulated a theory of internal migration as a type of human capital investment. Sjaastad argued that a person migrates to another state, province or region because, by taking advantage of higher income opportunities elsewhere, migrants in effect increase their lifetime earnings.

The shortcoming of the standard economic model of migration is that observation and research in other social sciences makes it clear that there are many motives for migration beyond the simple pursuit of higher lifetime earnings. Migration may be driven by opportunities to achieve consumption, including amenities, that more closely fits one's preferences. Some migrants may seek a more desirable capability to carry out household production. Or, migration may be motivated by a combination of social, political, or psychological factors. Some theorists have suggested that people move to assuage feelings of relative deprivation, as a solution to a household portfolio diversification problem, or to exploit migrant network effects flowing from the destination. Furthermore, migration is often a family decision as opposed to an individual one, but this obvious fact has not yet been thoroughly dealt with in the theoretical literature on immigration. The internal migration literature is at present not clear on which explanation of migration is the strongest. The international migration literature, because it is younger and less developed, is even less clear.

Much work remains to be done on the international migration model, however. Given the broad range of economic, social, political, cultural, and natural factors that enter into the migration decision, a complete model of immigration would almost certainly have to be somewhat multi-disciplinary in nature. Sociological, psychological, political, and ecological factors act alongside economic factors in pushing, pulling, rejecting, and holding back would-be migrants. An immigration model would also have to be dynamic, even evolutionary in nature. Since the labor economists who have so far dominated the development of immigration theory are still firmly wed to their neoclassical static equilibrium analysis, a dynamic unified interdisciplinary theory of migration remains a distant goal. Opportunities for progress are abundant for anyone willing to think beyond the work presented in this chapter. The upcoming chapters outlining the empirical evidence on migration provides further insight into where we still lack theories that explain the complex reality of human migration.

References

Anderson, J. (1979). A theoretical foundation for the gravity equation. *American Economic Review, 69,* 106–116.

Bauer, T., Zimmerman, K. (1998). Causes of international migration: a survey. In C Gorter, P Nijkamp, & J Poot (Eds.), *Crossing borders: regional and urban perspectives on international migration.* Brookfield: Ashgate.

Becker, G. (1962). Investment in human capital: a theoretical analysis. *Journal of Political Economy, 70*, 9–49.

Becker, G. (1965). A Theory of the allocation of time. *Economic Journal, 75*, 493–517.

Becker, G. (1974). A theory of social interaction. *Journal of Political Economy, 82*:1063–1093.

Bhagwati, J., & Srinivasan, T., (1974). On reanalyzing the Harris-Todaro model: policy rankings in the case of sector-specific sticky wages. *American Economic Review, 64*, 502–508.

Blanchflower, D., & Oswald, A. (2000). Well-being over time in Britain and the USA. NBER Working Paper No. w7487, January.

Borjas, G. (1987). Self-selection and the earnings of immigrants. *American Economic Review, 77*, 531–553.

Borjas, G. (1990). Economic theory and international migration. *International Migration Review, 23*, 457–485.

Borjas, G. (1991). Immigration and self-selection. In J Abowd, & R Freeman, (Eds.), *Immigration, trade, and the labor market*. Chicago: University of Chicago Press.

Burda, M. (1993) The determinants of East-West German migration. *European Economic Review, 37*, 452–461.

Burda, M. (1995). Migration and the option value of waiting. *The Economic and Social Review, 27*, 1–19.

Calvo, G. (1978). Urban unemployment and wage determination in LDCs: trade Unions in the Harris-Todaro Model. *International Economic Review, 19*, 65–81.

Clark, X., Hatton, T., & Williamson, J. (2007). Explaining U.S. immigration, 1971–1998. *Review of Economics and Statistics, 89*, 359–373.

Corden, W., & Findlay, R.(1975). Urban unemployment, intersectoral capital mobility and development policy. *Economica, 42*, 59–78.

Deardorff, A. (1998). Determinants of bilateral trade: does gravity work in a classical world? In J. Frankel (Ed.), *Regionalization of the world economy*. Chicago: University of Chicago Press.

Fields, G. (1979). Place-to-place migration: some new evidence. *Review of Economic Statistics, 56*, 21–32.

Frey, B., & Stutzer, A. (2002a). *Happiness and economics*. Princeton, NJ: Princeton University Press.

Frey, B., & Stutzer, A. (2002b). What can economists learn from happiness research? *Journal of Economic Literature40*, 402–435.

Ghatak, S., Levine, P., & Price, S. (1996) Migration theories and evidence: An assessment. *Journal of Economic Literature, 10*, 159–198.

Glaeser, E., & Shapiro, J. (2003). Urban growth in the 1990s: Is city living back? *Journal of Regional Science, 43*, 139–165.

Gorter, C., Nijkamp, P., & Poot, J. (1998) Regional and urban perspectives on international migration: an overview. In C Gorter, P Nijkamp, & J Poot (Eds.), *Crossing borders: regional and urban perspectives on international migration*. Brookfield, Ashgate.

Graves, P. (1979). A life-cycle empirical analysis of migration and climate, by race. *Journal of Urban Economics, 6*, 135–147.

Graves, P. (1983) Migration with a composite amenity: the role of rents. *Journal of Regional Science, 23*, 541–546.

Green, G., Deller, S., & Marcouiller, D. (2006). *Amenities and rural development theory, methods and public policy*. Northampton, MA: Elgar.

Greenwood, M. (1975). Research on internal migration in the United States: a survey. *Journal of Economic Literature, 13*, 397–433.

Greenwood, M. (1985). Human migration: theory, models and empirical studies. *Journal of Regional Science, 25*, 521–544.

Greenwood, M. (1997). Internal migration in developed countries. In M. Rosenzweig, & O. Stark (Eds.), *Handbook of population and family economics*. Amsterdam: Elsevier.

Harris, J., Todaro, M. (1970). Migration, unemployment and development: a two-sector analysis. *American Economic Review, 60*, 126–142.

Hatton, T., & Williamson, J. (2005). What fundamentals drive world migration? In G. Borjas, & J. Crisp (Eds.) *Studies in development economics and policy*. New York: Palgrave Macmillan.

Hicks, J. (1932). *The theory of wages*. London: Macmillan.

Hugo, G. (1981). Village-community ties, village norms, and ethnic and social networks: a review of evidence from the third world. In G. DeJong, & R. Gardner (Eds.), *Migration decision making: multidisciplinary approaches to microlevel studies in developed and developing countries*. New York: Pergamon Press.

Katz, E., & Stark, O. (1986). Labor migration and risk aversion in less-developed countries. *Journal of Labor Economics, 4*, 131–149.

Lall, S., Selod, H., & Shalizi, Z. (2006). Rural-urban migration in developing countries: a survey of theoretical predictions and empirical findings. World Bank Policy Research Working Paper 3915.

Lancaster, K. (1966). A new approach to consumer theory. *Journal of Political Economy, 74*, 132–157.

Layard, R. (2005). *Happiness: lessons from a new science*. New York: Penguin.

Linneman, H. (1966). *An econometric study of international trade flows*. Amsterdam: North-Holland.

Massey, R., & Garcia Espana, F. (1987). The social process of international migration. *Science, 237*, 733–738.

McCall, B., & McCall, J. (1987). A sequential study of migration and job search. *Journal of Labor Economics, 5*, 452–476.

Mincer, J. (1978). Family migration decisions. *Journal of Political Economy, 86*, 749–773.

Molho, I. (1986). Theories of migration: A review. *Scottish Journal of Political Economy, 33*, 396–401.

Pickles, A., & Rogerson, P. (1984). Wage distribution and spatial preferences in competitive job search and migration. *Regional Science, 18*, 131–142.

Polachek, S., & Horvath, F. (1977). A life cycle approach to migration: analysis of the perspicacious peregrinator. In: Ehrenberg, R (ed), *Research in labor economics*. Greenwich, CT: JAI Press.

Ravenstein, E. (1889). The laws of migration. *Journal of the Royal Statistical Society, 52*, 241–305.

Roback, J. (1982), Wages, rents, and the quality of life. *Journal of Political Economy, 90*, 1257–1278.

Roback, J. (1988). Wages, rents, and amenities: differences among workers and regions. *Economic Inquiry, 26*, 23–41.

Rosen, S. (1974). Hedonic prices and implicit markets: product differentiation in pure competition. *Journal of Political Economy, 82*, 34–55.

Runciman, W. (1996). *Relative deprivation and social justice*. London: Routledge and Kegan Paul.

Sandell, S. (1977). Women and the economics of family migration. *Review of Economics and Statistics, 59*, 406–414.

Shields, G., & Shields, M. (1989). The emergence of migration theory and a suggested new direction. *Journal of Econ Surveys, 3*, 277–304.

Sjaastad, L. (1962). The costs and returns of human migration. *Journal of Political Economy, 70*, 80–93.

Smith, A. (1776[1937]). *An inquiry into the nature and causes of the wealth of nations*. New York: Modern Library

Stark, O. (1984). Migration decision making: a review article. *Journal of Development Economics, 14*, 251–259.

Stark, O. (1991). *The migration of labor*. Oxford: Blackwell.

Stark, O., & Levhari, D.(1982). On migration and risk in LDCs. *Economic Development and Cultural Change, 31*, 191–196.

Stark, O., & Taylor, J. (1989). Relative deprivation and international migration. Demography, 26, 1–14.

Stark, O., & Taylor, J. (1991). Migration Incentives, migration types: the role of relative deprivation. *Economic Journal, 101*, 63–78.

Stark, O., & Yitzhaki, S.(1988). Labor migration as a response to relative deprivation. *Journal of Population Economics, 1*, 57–70.

Taylor, J. (1986). Differential migration, networks, information and risk. In O. Stark (Ed.), *Research in human capital and development* (vol. 4). Greenwich, CN: JAI Press.

Tiebout, C. (1956). A pure theory of local expenditures. *Journal of Political Economy, 64*, 416–425.

Tinbergen, J. (1962). *Shaping the world economy*. New York: Twentieth Century Fund.

Todaro, M. (1969). A model of labour migration and urban unemployment in less developed countries. *American Economic Review, 59*, 138–148.

Todaro, M. (1976). *Internal migration in developing countries*. Geneva: International Labour Organization.

Veenhoven, R. (1996). Happy life-expectancy: a comprehensive measure of quality-of-life in nations. *Social Indicators Research, 39*, 1–58.

Veenhoven, R. (1999). Quality-of-life in individualistic society: a comparison of forty-three nations in the early 1990s. *Social Indicators Research, 48*, 157–186.

Willis, R. (1973). A new approach to the economic theory of fertility behavior. *Journal of Political Economy, 81*, (suppl.):514–564.

Yap, L. (1977). The attraction of cities: a review of the migration literature. *Journal of Development Economics, 4*, 239–264.

Zipf, G. (1946). The [P(1)P(2)/D] hypothesis; on the intercity movement of persons. *American Sociological Review, 11*, 677–686.

Chapter 3
Why People Immigrate: The Evidence

Abstract In this chapter, we survey the empirical evidence on the determinants of international migration. The empirical literature on determinants is very small, partially due to lack of appropriate data for many countries. Existing studies focus mostly on U.S., Canadian and European immigration, and this literature provides support for the human capital investment view of immigration. However, the evidence also indicates that there are many other important social and political determinants of immigration.

Chapter Overview

In the previous chapter, we surveyed theories of why people migrate from one country to another. A major theme of the theory is that immigration is an investment in human capital, although many of the models incorporate other causal factors. In this chapter we will see how well the models discussed in the previous chapter hold up to the data.

Clark, Hatton, and Williamson (2007) accurately assess the current state of the empirical literature on immigration when they write:

> ... while the literature is long on examining the outcomes of immigration, it is surprisingly short on estimating the determinants of immigration and on testing the models of immigrant selection that underpin our understanding of those outcomes.[1]

The small size of the empirical literature is, no doubt, partly due to the lack of accurate data on international migration flows. There is little data for most source countries, and even many of the major destination countries have, at best, incomplete data on immigration. The data sets used in empirical studies of international migration are almost always incomplete because they seldom include unauthorized immigration or return immigration. Consequently, data on immigrant flows used in

---

[1]Clark, Hatton, and Williamson (2007), p. 359.

Ö.B. Bodvarsson and H. Van den Berg, *The Economics of Immigration*,
DOI: 10.1007/978-3-540-77796-0_3, © Springer-Verlag Berlin Heidelberg 2009

empirical studies usually cover only inflows of legal immigrants to a small number of OECD countries.

The data paucity does not justify the small number of empirical studies of immigration, however. There are both time-series and cross-section data available on the entry of new immigrants to most OECD countries, and these data detail the sources, ages, and many other characteristics of the immigrants. The lack of data certainly does not justify the primitive econometric methods used in much of the empirical work. Much more could have, and should have, been done. This chapter's survey of the empirical literature will, hopefully, serve as a wake-up call for economists.

Most of the empirical models detailed in this section blend elements of the modified gravity model of internal migration with elements of the standard immigration model discussed in the Introduction to this first section of the book, which hypothesizes income differences and migration costs determine migration flows. The results of the econometric analyses suggest that international migration is driven by a number of economic, social, political, and environmental determinants. In the remaining sections of the chapter, we will highlight further details of the empirical literature. You will notice that, in many ways, the empirical studies have ventured beyond the simple theoretical models presented in the previous chapter. Perhaps empirical researchers have been less enamored by their models and more driven by what they observe in the real world. In a very modest way, the brief empirical literature surveyed here can help to expand the perspective from which economists view, and model, international migration.

3.1   Regression Models of Immigration

A detailed look at the regression models used in empirical studies of immigration is a critical step in applying the scientific method. While economists like to describe their models as economic theory, those models are nothing more than hypotheses until they are verified empirically. At the same time, statistical analysis depends critically on the accuracy of the regression models used in statistical research. At this point in time, it appears that the evidence on what drives immigration is not entirely consistent across the various empirical studies that have been undertaken. Furthermore, it should also be clear that the regression models are only casually related to the theoretical models detailed in the previous chapter.

3.1.1   Empirical Models of Regional Migration

We do not intend to cover the evidence on domestic, or regional, migration in detail here. Nevertheless, it is worth briefly mentioning the general results of the empirical studies of domestic migration because, as discussed in Chap. 2 regional economics led other fields in analyzing migration. For more complete surveys of the early empirical literature on internal migration in the U.S., we recommend Greenwood (1975, 1985), Greenwood and Hunt (2003) and Shields and Shields (1989). Also, Greenwood (1997), Lucas (1997) and Lall, Selod, and Shalizi (2006) survey the empirical literature on regional migration for a range of individual developed countries.

Overall, the evidence from the literature on internal migration in the U.S. points to regional differences in earnings as the most important determinant. Among the major findings, Naskoteen and Zimmer (1980) and Kennan and Walker (2003) both estimate that a 10 percentage point increase in the wage difference between destination and source regions within the U.S. increases the probability of migration by about 7 percentage points. They also report a strong correlation between the probability that someone migrates and relative employment conditions, where the latter are proxied by unemployment rates and layoff statistics for individual states. For example, Kennan and Walker find that a 10 percentage point increase in the rate of employment growth in the sending state cuts the probability of migration to another state by about 2%. This evidence is compatible with Sjaastad's (1962) model of regional migration.

Many studies of domestic migration report a negative correlation between the likelihood of migrating internally and distance. The consensus finding is that a doubling of distance reduces the migration rate by about half. This finding supports the gravity model of migration.

There are also many case studies that provide explanations for specific episodes of internal U.S. migration. For example, Boustan (2006) documents that the great black migration of 1900–1970 was due to both the superior employment opportunities in the very strong manufacturing sector and the perception of less racial discrimination in Northern labor markets and school systems in the major cities of the Northeastern and Great Lakes regions. Another significant case of U.S. internal migration is postwar California. During much of the postwar period, many workers moved to California due to its booming economy. Following the cold war, California's defense industry underwent a significant downsizing, contributing to a loss of 750,000 jobs in the state between 1990 and 1993. Consequently, California went from being a major destination for migrants to a major source of migrants.[2]

3.1.2 The Gravity Model of International Migration

Researchers designing empirical models of the international migration rate have been influenced by two major contributions in the migration literature. First, most empirical models of the emigration rate are closely related to the *Gravity Model* of

---

[2]See, for example, "California in the Rearview Mirror," *Newsweek*, July 19, 1993, pp. 24–25.

internal migration. Second, these models usually incorporate income differences exactly as the standard model of migration in the Introduction to this Section of the book and Chap. 2 prescribes.

3.1.2.1 The Basic Gravity Model of Migration

The basic *gravity model of migration* specifies migration as a positive function of the attractive "mass" of two economies and a negative function of distance between them. The *gravity* model gets its name from physics and the familiar formula for gravity. Implicitly, in the gravity model of migration, distance is a proxy for the costs of moving from one country to another. Defining IMM_{ij} as total immigration from country i to country j, $DIST_{ij}$ as the distance between the two countries, and the gravitational "mass" as the product of the gross domestic products of countries i and j, the gravity model of immigration is

$$IMM_{ij} = f[(GDP_i \cdot GDP_j)/DIST_{ij}] \tag{3.1}$$

As a statistical regression model, (3.1) is commonly specified in natural logarithms. Representing natural logs in lower case letters, the basic gravity regression equation is thus

$$imm_{ij} = a_0 + a_1(gdp_i \cdot gdp_j) + a_2(dist_{ij}) + u_{ij}, \tag{3.2}$$

where u_{ij} is the usual random error term. The expected signs of the coefficients are $a_1 > 0$, and $a_2 < 0$.

Many researchers have specified variations of (3.2). For example, Lewer and Van den Berg (2007) specify a slightly different gravity model of migration by assuming the attractive force between immigrant source and destination countries depends on the difference between per capita incomes rather than the total GDPs of the source and destination economies. However, they recognize that the size of the populations in the source and destination countries also matter because, all other things equal, the more people there are in a source country, the more people are likely to migrate, and the larger the population in the destination country, the larger is the labor market for immigrants. Hence, Lewer and Van den Berg suggest the gravity equation

$$imm_{ij} = a_0 + a_1(pop_i \cdot pop_j) + a_2(rely_{ij}) + a_3(dist_{ij}) + u_{ij}, \tag{3.3}$$

in which pop_i and pop_j are the total populations of the source and destination countries, respectively, and $rely_{ij}$ is the ratio of destination and source country per capita incomes. The expected signs of the coefficients are $a_1 > 0$, $a_2 > 0$, and $a_3 < 0$.

When regression equations contain variables in natural logarithms, the coefficients effectively measure how the proportional growth of an explanatory variable influences the proportional growth of the dependent variable in the model. For example, in (3.3), the coefficient a_3 estimates by what percentage migration changes for a given percentage increase in the distance between the source and destination countries. Sometimes researchers enter the variables in "double log" form, or the percentage change in the rate of change, in which case the coefficient measures the elasticity of the migration rate with respect to the particular explanatory variable. For example, with the variables in double log form, a_3 measures the elasticity of the migration rate with respect to distance.

3.1.2.2 The Augmented Gravity Model

As was pointed out in Chap. 2, researchers have observed many potential determinants of international migration flows. Hence, the statistical results from estimating simple regression equations like (3.2) or (3.3) will almost certainly suffer from omitted variable bias. To mitigate such bias, researchers have introduced other variables into the basic gravity regression equation.

For example, Kahan (1978), Murayama (1991), and Rephann and Vencataawmy (2000) provide evidence supporting the hypothesis, common in the sociology literature on immigration, that immigrants tend to concentrate where earlier compatriots have settled because the cost of adapting to a new society is mitigated by the presence of compatriots familiar with both the source and destination country cultures. It is also hypothesized that immigration is larger, *ceteris paribus*, when the language and culture in the destination country is familiar. These considerations point to the augmented immigration gravity equation

$$\text{imm}_{ij} = a_0 + a_1(\text{pop}_i \cdot \text{pop}_j) + a_2(\text{rely}_{ij}) + a_3(\text{dist}_{ij}) + a_4(\text{stock}_{ij})$$
$$+ a_5\text{LANG}_{ij} + a_6\text{CONT}_{ij} + a_7\text{LINK}_{ij} + u_{ij} \tag{3.4}$$

in which stock_{ij} is the number of source country natives already living in the destination country and LANG, CONT, and LINK are dummy variables that take on a value of one when the source and destination countries share a common language, border, or colonial heritage, respectively.

Lewer and Van den Berg (2007) estimate precisely this model, and they find that all variables except contiguity are highly significant. The reason contiguity is not a statistically significant determinant of migration is, most likely, due to the many European countries in the sample and the freedom of movement within the European Union. It is just as easy (or difficult) for a Russian immigrant to move to Germany as it is for her to move one country further, the Netherlands, once the distance variable accounts for the transport costs. Lewer and Van den Berg's results also reveal high R-squares, which means the gravity model explains a very large portion of the variation in the dependent variable, immigration.

3.1.2.3 Generalizing the Gravity Model

Many variations on (3.4) are possible. Greenwood (1997) offers a general representation of the gravity model of immigration:

$$\ln(\text{IMM}_{ij}) = \ln \beta_0 + \beta 1 \ln(\text{D}_{ij}) + \beta 2 \ln(\text{Pop}_i) + \beta_3 \ln(\text{Pop}_j) + \beta_4 \ln(\text{Y}_i)$$

$$+ \beta_5 \ln(\text{Y}_j) + \sum_{n=1}^{m} \beta_{in} \ln(X_{in}) + \sum_{n=1}^{m} \beta_{jn} \ln(X_{jn}) + \varepsilon_{ij}, \qquad (3.5)$$

where:

$\text{IMM}_{ij} \equiv$ migration rate from source i to destination j
$\text{D}_{ij} \equiv$ distance (in miles) from source i to destination j
$\text{Pop}_i \equiv$ population of source i
$\text{Pop}_j \equiv$ population of destination j
$\text{Y}_i \equiv$ per capita real income or GDP in source i
$\text{Y}_j \equiv$ per capita real income or GDP in destination j
$X_i \equiv$ a vector of m characteristics of source i
$X_j \equiv$ a vector of m characteristics of destination j
$\varepsilon_{ij} \equiv$ random error term.

The variable IMM representing "migration" can take many forms. The expected signs of the coefficients, according to the intuition behind the gravity model, are $\beta_1 < 0$, $\beta_2 > 0$, $\beta_3 > 0$, $\beta_4 > 0$ and $\beta_5 > 0$. Note that the influence of total income or GDP, namely Y, is positive under the assumption that bigger economies per se increase migration flows. Greenwood's representation effectively designates per capita income or GDP to the vectors of country characteristics.

3.1.3 Some Econometric Problems Related to the Gravity Model

The vast experience with estimating gravity models by international trade economists has revealed some serious potential sources of bias in the estimation results. In the simple regression models (3.2) or (3.3), each variable is *bi-lateral* in that it applies to both countries i and j. In model (3.4), however, there is the stock$_{ij}$ variable that applies only to one of the pair of countries. The general specification (3.5) designates entire sets of variables that apply to just one or the other of the pairs of countries. Redding and Venables (2004) and Rose and van Wincoop (2001) show that such *unilateral* variables result in *standard error clustering*, which can seriously bias the estimates. Feenstra (2004) shows that in the case of a cross-section sample of countries, adding fixed effects dummies to the model eliminates this bias.

A second source of bias is related to the fact that many variables in the gravity equation model (3.5) are natural logs, which means standard regression methods require omitting observations with zero values. In larger cross-section studies of immigration, the dependent variable, migration, between pairs of countries may be zero in a substantial percentage of observations, and omitting those zero observations biases the regression results. After all, a zero outcome is just as important an observation as any other observation. All observations can be included with the *scaled ordinary least squares* (SOLS) method first applied by Wang and Winters (1992) and Eichengreen and Irwin (1995).

Finally, heterogeneity may plague a gravity model. Cheng and Wall (2005) advise including an *error ranking variable* calculated by first running regressions with the data ordered alphabetically by country and then rank ordering the average residual for each country pair.

In sum, there are unique econometric challenges associated with gravity models of migration. Few applications of the gravity model to migration have recognized these problems, even though in the international trade literature referees have for some time demanded that econometric methods deal with these issues. An example of an econometric study of immigration that does address the above-mentioned econometric problems is Lewer and Van den Berg (2007).

3.2 The Choice of Variables in Statistical Models of Immigration

Most empirical models of international migration have specified regression models based on the gravity model. Despite the same basic structure, there are nevertheless many differences in the empirical models that researchers have used to estimate the determinants of international migration. Some of these differences potentially influence the differences in the empirical results that the models generated.

Recall that the predictions of the Borjas (1987, 1991) models depend critically on the particular distribution function for the variation in population characteristics. For example, if the density of earnings is assumed to be *uniform* instead of *normal*, the equation for the cumulative distribution function is very different, and the derived interactions between determinants of migration related to the differences in source and destination country population characteristics are also different. As a result, the predictions of the theoretical model are dependent on specific assumptions about the parameters of the model. It would thus seem important that an empirical specification of a model account for the precise theoretical structure of the model it seeks to test.

Also, researchers have used different data to represent the various variables included in the theoretical models. The available data does not always match the theoretical variables very well. If different researchers use different proxies for the variables in the model, the results will vary.

3.2.1   Three Examples

In this sub-section we contrast three recent models and discuss their choice of variables to augment the gravity model of immigration. These models all include variables that fall into four broad sets of explanatory variables: (1) country differences in earnings, (2) migration costs, (3) source country levels of development and political conditions, and (4) destination country immigration restrictions. The three models are by Greenwood and McDowell (1991), who study annual immigration to the U.S. and Canada during the period 1962–1984, Clark, Hatton, and Williamson (2007), who study U.S. immigration between 1971 and 1998, and Mayda (2007), who uses data on immigration to 14 OECD countries between 1980 and 1998. Each of these models represent immigration in terms of a rate defined as $\frac{IM_{it}}{P_{it}}$ where IM_{it} is the flow of persons, and P_{it} is source country population. They differ, however, in which specific proxies they use to represent the four types of explanatory variables.

3.2.2   Representing Income Differences

Greenwood and McDowell (1991) capture the effects of cross-country differences in earnings by adding two variables to their regression model. The first is the ratio of average manufacturing earnings in the source country to the same in the destination country. The second is the ratio of the growth rate of real per capita GDP in the source country, averaged over the previous three years, to the same in the destination country.

Clark, Hatton, and Williamson (2007), who we will denote as CHW from here on, enter only the ratio of average real incomes in each source country to average real income in the U.S. They also include a variable that they claim proxies the proportion of the source country population living in poverty. However, because complete data on the incidence of poverty are not available for all source countries, CHW use the inverse of source country income squared. This is, obviously, an approximation of completely unknown quality. Mayda recognizes the possibility of a reverse relationship between income differences and migration; immigrant flows may induce changes in contemporaneous relative income opportunities because migration to country j in period t tends to depress earnings in j that period while it may raise wages in the source country i. To avoid estimation bias resulting from reverse causality, Mayda lags income per capita one period.

3.2.3   Representing Migration Costs

Greenwood and McDowell add four variables to capture the costs of migrating. First, they include geographic distance. They try to measure the costs of transferring skills to the destination country, the United States or Canada, by a dummy variable for whether or not the source country's official language is English and a variable that measures the level of educational attainment in the source country. Finally, they include a time trend to control for technological advances that may have resulted in long term declines in the costs of transportation, communications and acquiring information.

CHW include measures of various migration costs. First, they include the distance (in miles) between the source country and the U.S. They also include a dummy for whether the source country is landlocked. Like Greenwood and McDowell, they include a dummy for whether the source country is predominantly English speaking. CHW try to capture the effect of previous immigration on perceived migration costs by including the ratio of the number of persons born in the source country residing in the U.S. one period earlier to the total destination country population. The square of this ratio is also included to test whether the marginal effect of the presence of source country compatriots in the destination country diminished with the size of the immigrant population.

Mayda also follows the gravity equation by including the distance between the source and destination countries. Furthermore, she includes dummy variables set equal to one if the source and destination countries share a land border, speak the same language, or were part of the colonial empire in the past.

3.2.4 Representing Source Country Development

Greenwood and McDowell enter three variables in their model to proxy the level of development in the source country: the fraction of population that is urbanized, the fraction of the workforce employed in manufacturing, and a measure of structural similarity between the source and destination countries. The latter is calculated as the sum of squared differences between the fractions of source country employment to destination country employment in industry k. A low level of development is taken to imply limited domestic employment and earnings opportunities compared to the U.S. or Canada. On the one hand, such conditions in the source country should encourage emigration. On the other hand, a low level of development may mean that the source country's labor force has few of the skills demanded in the U.S. or Canada, in which case the effective cost of transferring the unwanted skills will be relatively high. This could discourage emigration. In short, the signs of the coefficients for the three indicators of development and political conditions could be positive or negative.

Greenwood and McDowell use the *Freedom House Index*, which is an index of economic freedom, political rights and civil liberties, to capture political conditions in the source country. CHW include the ratio of mean years of schooling in the source country relative to the U.S. to capture differences in human capital. They also add an "age" variable, namely, the share of the source country's population comprising young adults, to test whether countries with younger populations have higher emigration rates. CHW also draw on Borjas (1987, 1991) and include relative income inequality, measured by the ratio of source to destination country income inequality. Mayda measures relative income inequality as the ratio of source to destination country gini coefficients. Furthermore, she includes the share of the population in the source country that is aged 15–29 years old, the lagged migration rate to measure the influence of network effects, and the unemployment rates in the origin (destination) countries.

3.2.5 Representing Immigration Restrictions

Greenwood and McDowell use dummies to control for different immigration restrictions by source country and region, as well as changes in immigration policies. Specifically, they enter nine dummies in the Canadian regression and four in the U.S. regression.

CHW emphasize the role of immigration policy in their paper, and hence they test the statistical importance of a variety of immigration restrictions. Specifically, they include four variables that represent quotas for different kinds of visas issued by U.S. authorities divided by the populations of the source countries that qualify for them. A higher (lower) value for a specific quota variable means lower (higher) restrictions on U.S. immigration for persons choosing that channel of entry. Hence, a higher (lower) quota results in lower (higher) costs of entry and a higher (lower) emigration rate.

One of CHW's quota variables is the annual quota for non-immediate relatives. An increase in that quota should encourage more migration to the U.S., but the quota has no value to prospective migrants if they have no relatives living in the U.S. Therefore, the effect of the quota on the immigration rate depends on the number of U.S.-based relatives, which is why CHW multiply the ratio of those visas to the proportion of the source country population by the size of the source country migrant network already in the U.S. Another of CHW's quota variables is the refugee quota. Since 1980, the U.S. has adjusted this quota annually in response to changes in the source country's political and geopolitical situation. Hence, CHW multiply the actual quota by a dummy that equals unity if there was a civil war in the source country in the observation year.

CHW's remaining two policy controls reflect "special circumstance policies." These variables are designed to capture the effects of the 1986 Immigration Reform and Control Act (IRCA) and the significant increase in the backlog of unprocessed visa applications during the 1990s due to various administrative changes at the U.S. Immigration and Naturalization Service.

Mayda captures the effects of destination country immigration policy with a dummy variable that increases by one (falls by one) if in period t immigration policy is less (more) restrictive than it was in period t − 1. Mayda multiplies the policy change dummy by lagged GDP per capita in order to test for whether a lessening of restrictions accentuates the effects of pull and push factors on immigration rates. Mayda estimated alternative versions of her regression model that included an interaction between the distance variable and the immigration policy change dummy, as well as the interaction between the young population share and the immigration policy change dummy.

Comparing the three models of international migration above with (1), one can see that they are all forms of the augmented gravity model. All three models include measures of cross-country differences in income and geographic distance. They all add indicators of skills transferability, destination country immigration policy, and source country socio-political conditions. Furthermore, all three regression models are log-linear. This makes the results of the three models comparable, at least in the case of coefficients of similar variables.

There are also important differences between the models, most notably in the variables included, the number of variables included, and the samples covered. Hence, the three models will not generate identical coefficient estimates even for those variables that are identical across the three models. Omitted variable bias will differ across the models, and variations in the actual data used, sample periods, countries covered, and the statistical methods used will further cause differences in coefficient estimates.

3.3 The Empirical Evidence on the Determinants of Migration

We mentioned earlier that the empirical literature on international migration is quite small. However, there are a number of recent statistical studies of international migration in addition to the three detailed in the previous section. This section presents the results of those studies and discusses what those results tell us about the theoretical models detailed in Chap. 2.

3.3.1 Evidence on Worldwide Migration

Despite large waves of migration around the world during most of human history, empirical work has been limited by data availability. Empirical studies have, therefore, focused mostly on immigration to the U.S. and Canada, small groups of OECD countries, specific European countries, and Australia. There is one econometric study of worldwide migration by Hatton and Williamson (2005), who analyzed migration to 80 different countries using United Nations data on annual average immigration flows over five-year periods from 1970–75 to 1995–2000. Hatton and Williamson's regression model contains a small but very diverse set of explanatory variables. For example, they find a destination country's net immigration rate falls by 0.9 per 1,000 of the population, all other things equal, for every reduction of five percentage points in the share of young adults in the country's population. The "friends and family effect" is strong: for every 1,000 person rise in a destination country's immigrant community, net immigration rises by about 23 persons per year. Not surprisingly, civil war reduces annual immigration by about 2 per 1,000 of the population. Finally, Hatton and Williamson find support for the traditional model of international migration: a ten percent increase in the destination country's relative income raises immigration by 0.12 per 1,000, all other things equal. All together, these results suggest that worldwide migration is driven by a combination of economic, social, and political determinants, and no single determinant seems to dominate the process.

3.3.2   Evidence on Migration to Groups of OECD Countries

Mayda (2007) uses immigration data for a subgroup of OECD countries from the OECD's *International Migration Statistics* and its *Continuous Reporting System on Migration* (SOPEMI). Mayda finds that the elasticity of the emigration rate with respect to *destination* GDP per capita is approximately 1.9, which implies that a 10% increase in destination GDP per capita results in a 19% increase in the emigration rate, or 2.5 immigrants per 100,000 persons in the source country population. Surprisingly, earnings opportunities in the *source* country are not significantly related to immigration rates. A doubling of the distance between source and destination countries reduces the number of migrants by 41 per 100,000 persons in the source country, but common border and language do not appear to matter. The origin country's age distribution does impact emigration rates: a 10% increase in the young population share raises the emigration rate by nearly 25 migrants per 100,000 source country individuals. The coefficient on relative inequality is positive and significant and the coefficient on relative inequality squared is negative and significant, confirming Borjas' (1987, 1991) prediction that changes in relative skills and wage inequalities across countries can have both positive and negative effects on emigration rates.

   In her study, Mayda finds that the destination country's unemployment rate is negatively and significantly related to the migration rate, but the source country unemployment rate is statistically insignificant. Hence, she concludes that there is no evidence of a *poverty trap* that slows migration from very poor countries. Finally, past migration between two countries has a positive and significant effect on current migration between those same two countries. Mayda finds that distance and age distribution account for the greatest shares of the variation in migration.

3.3.3   Evidence on U.S. Immigration

Greenwood and McDowell (1991) find that U.S. immigration varies inversely with source country wages. The estimated elasticity suggests that, on average, a 10% increase in the source country wage is accompanied by a 7.5% decline in the emigration rate. They also find that distance has a strong negative effect on U.S. immigration. Furthermore, U.S. immigration is enhanced when the source country's primary language is English, its population is better educated, its population is more urban, its employment share of manufacturing is greater, and its government is more politically repressive. Greenwood and MacDowell also find that U.S. immigration restrictions were binding during the sample period.

In their 2007 paper, Clark, Hatton, and Williamson (CHW) use a data set with 2,268 panel observations (81 source countries × 28 years) covering over 80% of legal immigration to the U.S. during the period 1971–1998. CHW confirm the predictions of the Borjas (1987) model. For example, a 10% increase in a source country's income per capita reduces the emigration rate by approximately 4.5%, which confirms the "relative earnings effect." The coefficient on relative income inequality and its square are found to be positive and negative, respectively, confirming Borjas' predicted "U-shape" relationship between the migration rate and relative income inequality. Although the effect varies considerably across regions and source countries, when evaluated at the mean of all countries, a 10% increase in source country income inequality is associated with a 7.5% decline in the migration rate. The effect is on average larger for developing countries.

The coefficients on past migration and its square are positive and negative, respectively. At the mean of source country population, a 1,000-person increase in the source country's U.S.-based immigrant community will induce five more people per year to migrate there. CHW also find that a 10% increase in family-reunion immigration visas increases immigration by about 0.3%. This implies that the full effect of the family reunification provisions in U.S. immigration policy is about six new immigrants for every 1,000-person increase in the immigrant community.

3.3.4 Immigration to Other Countries

Greenwood and McDowell's (1991) results for Canadian immigration are quite similar to their results for the U.S. The impact elasticity with respect to the source country wage is remarkably close to the average elasticity for the U.S. Contrary to the U.S. case, however, political repression in the source country is not statistically significant. Canadian immigration restrictions were also found to be binding during the sample period.

Hatton (2005) uses data for the U.K. to test why, since the 1970s, Britain has shifted from a net source country to a net destination country for immigrants. Hatton incorporated income inequalities into his model. Consistent with the Borjas (1987) model, the coefficient of income inequality in the UK has a negative effect on emigration. However, the coefficient values estimated by Hatton showed that the effects on migration of the unemployment rate and income differences between countries were much stronger than the effects of income inequalities within countries.

Cobb-Clark and Connolly (1997) examine skilled immigration to Australia. Their regression model tests for the usual explanatory variables as well as for correlations with other countries' immigration. Interestingly, they find that migration flows to Australia are not independent of flows to other countries. Specifically, the number of skilled persons who apply for entry to Australia is negatively related to U.S. skilled admissions, but positively related to Canadian skilled admissions. They thus conclude that Australia's ability to induce immigration of highly skilled and educated persons depends upon the immigration policies of other nations competing for the same immigrants.

Karras and Chiswick (1999) analyze the determinants of migration to West Germany from 22 other European countries during the period 1964–1988. They found that West German immigration was strongly influenced by past West German immigration and economic growth over the entire sample period, but wage differences did not matter at all during the latter half of the period. On the other hand, Brücker, Siliverstovs, and Trübswetter (2003) study immigration to Germany from eight European countries between 1967–2000, and they find that the long run stock of immigrants in Germany is positively and strongly related to destination/source country differences in per capita income GDP levels, but only weakly related to differences in employment rates.

Rotte, Vogler, and Zimmermann (1997) analyze requests for asylum in Germany by migrants from 17 developing countries for the period 1985–1994. Interestingly, they found that the arrivals of asylum seekers are positively related to German/foreign earnings differentials, which is somewhat surprising given that one would expect asylum seekers to be influenced by more urgent factors such as wars, violence, and political oppression. It may be that requests for asylum are used as a pretext to gain entry into high income countries by people seeking to migrate for the usual economic reasons, or Rotte et al's statistical results are biased by the fact that the political and social conditions that tend to produce refugees are correlated with income and employment conditions, and the statistical procedures erroneously attribute the influence of true asylum-inducing conditions to the latter variables. Most likely, both causes contributed to Rotte et al's results.

3.3.5 Summarizing the Results

Table 3.1 summarizes the evidence from nine studies discussed above that use more or less similar augmented gravity models of immigration. Because the exact variables differ so much across the various studies, it makes little sense to compare actual coefficient values. We, therefore, report only the signs and significance levels of some of the key variables. A "+" ("–") means the coefficient on the variable was found to be positive (negative) and significant at 5% or better, a "0" means the

Table 3.1 Summary of Results of 9 Empirical Immigration Studies

Study	Receiving area(s)	Destination/ source country earnings differences	Migration costs	Destination country relative earnings inequality	Earnings correlation
H&W (2005)	Worldwide	+	−	n/i	n/i
Mayda (2007)	14 OECD countries	+	−	Inverse U-shape function	0
G&M (1991)	U.S. and Canada	+	−	n/i	+
Clark et al (2007)	U.S.	+	−	Inverse U-shape function	+
Hatton (2005)	U.K.	+	−	−	n/i
Cobb-Clark & Connolly (1997)	Australia	+	−	n/i	n/i
Karras & Chiswick (1999)	Germany	0	−	n/i	n/i
Brücker et al (2003)	Germany	+	n/i	n/i	n/i
Rotte et al (1997)	Germany (asylee inflows only)	+	−	n/i	n/i

coefficient was insignificant, and "n/i" means the study did not include this variable in the regression.

According to Table 3.1, the most consistent results across the models are that emigration is (1) positively related to earnings differences and (2) negatively related to migration costs. Only two of the nine studies confirmed an inverse U-shaped relationship between immigration and relative destination country income inequality or a positive relationship between migration and source/destination country earnings correlation, as hypothesized by Borjas (1987), but that is due to the fact that most of the nine models do not include variables to capture those influences.

It should be clear from the regression results and procedures described in this section that the differences across samples and regression models must be partially responsible for the inconsistencies in the results. Clearly, much work remains to be done before solid conclusions can be drawn about how well the data support the prevailing economic models of why people migrate. Researchers need to run many more regressions using more complete data sets, better statistical methods, and more models that include additional variables.

3.4   Summary and Concluding Remarks

Our survey of the empirical literature on why people migrate across borders and what types of people are more, or less, likely to migrate is hampered by the small size of the literature. Still, there are enough studies to venture some tentative conclusions on what the empirical evidence suggests. We draw two major conclusions from the small number of recent statistical studies: (1) People emigrate for a great variety of economic, political, social, and psychological reasons; and (2) there is so much still to do in this part of the immigration literature.

The evidence so far suggests that emigration is driven consistently by international differences in earnings and migration costs (measured by distance, past migration or destination country immigration restrictions). The regressions uncover other reasons, such as demographic factors, political shocks, poverty constraints, and international differences in income inequality, although this evidence is quite tentative given that only two of the nine studies in Table 3.1 have estimated these influences.

The empirical literature on the determinants of immigration consists of a relatively small number of studies, most of which use models closely related to the same gravity model of international migration, augmented with a variety of additional potential influences. The small size of the literature is further exemplified by the high proportion of unpublished working papers included in our survey. The data on immigration is inaccurate because they seldom include return migration or unauthorized immigration. Furthermore, most of the published studies focus on a single country, the United States. Hence, even though the studies are in some ways consistent, the small volume and the narrow focus of the literature makes it impossible to claim that these results are what statisticians would call *robust*. We need many more studies using many more regression models, data sets, time periods, countries, and replications of existing studies before economists can have very much confidence in the results of their statistical studies of immigration.

3.4.1   The Power of Statistical Models

To put the results of the small number of empirical studies into perspective, keep in mind that no one statistical study can ever provide definitive proof of any hypothesis. That is especially true for hypotheses about a phenomenon as complex as international migration. Any one study can be, and should be, critiqued for shortcomings related to the data, the specified model, and the particular statistical methods used. Also, the practical application of statistical methods inevitably requires the use of statistical models that are simplifications of the true underlying models and assumptions about the unknown distributions of the populations from which the sample data are derived. Fully justified accusations of omitted variables, simultaneity, spurious regressions, incomplete samples, biased samples, biased estimators, errors in variables, and any number of other econometric problems can be directed at any of the empirical studies we have sampled.

The very narrow range of theoretical models on which the empirical studies have been based is disturbing. Florax, de Groot, and Heijungs (2002) have shown that an unlimited number of potential models can always be found to explain any observed economic phenomenon. Hence, when researchers do not venture far from a narrow standard modeling approach, they cannot claim they have robustly *proven* a specific model's validity. We need robustness in terms of the theoretical models as well as robustness across data and econometric methods.

In reality, there is only one way to deal with the inevitable shortcomings of empirical studies, and that is to repeat the empirical process over and over until it becomes possible to claim some degree of *robustness*. Robustness is achieved when statistical results remain consistent regardless of which sample of countries is used, which time period is covered, which model is specified, or which consistent statistical methods are used. It is safe to say that robustness is not a characteristic of the empirical literature in international migration. In fact, the necessary process of serious criticism and subsequent attempts to address the criticisms has barely begun. On the positive side, think of how many opportunities economists have to engage in important research!

3.4.2   The Way Forward

Clearly, we need many more empirical studies. To get more studies and more varied studies, more economists must become interested in immigration. Given the lack of data, there is a need for more microeconomic studies and case studies that include new data on specific immigration episodes. Sociologists have taken this approach long ago; economists need to follow.

It would also be especially useful to have more micro studies on return migration and unauthorized migration, as well as studies that gather data from samples not currently included in the empirical studies of immigration. We also need better data on migration between developing countries and on migration from developed to developing countries. It would be interesting to know whether the rapidly growing so-called emerging economies attract immigrants and their human capital from the developed economies.

Finally, there should be a more detailed analysis of how immigration policy affects migration flows. There is certainly enough information available to do studies of the recent programs to promote specific types of immigrants. For example, Canada targets specific types of immigrants and discourage others. Do these programs work to promote immigration as designed? The next chapter looks at models and evidence that seek to explain what types of people tend to become immigrants and how the characteristics of the native populations in the source and destination countries help to determine the characteristics of the people who migrate between the two.

References

Borjas, G. (1987). Self-selection and the earnings of immigrants. *American Economic Review, 77,* 531–553.

Borjas, G. (1991). Immigration and self-selection. In J. Abowd & R. Freeman (Eds.), *Immigration, trade, and the labor market.* Chicago: University of Chicago Press.

Boustan, L. (2006). Competition in the promised land: Blacks, migration, and Northern labor markets, *1940–70.* Working Paper, University of California, Los Angeles.

Brücker, H., Siliverstovs, B., & Trübswetter, P. (2003). International migration to Germany: Estimation of a time-series model and inference in panel cointegration. Discussion Paper 391, German Institute for Economic Research (DIW).

Cheng, I. H., & Wall, H. J. (2005). Controlling for heterogeneity in gravity models of trade and integration. *Federal Reserve Bank of St. Louis Review, 87,* 49–63.

Clark, X., Hatton, T., & Williamson, J. (2007). Explaining U.S. immigration, 1971–98. *Review of Economics and Statistics, 89,* 359–373.

Cobb-Clark, D., & Connolly, M. (1997). The Worldwide market for skilled migrants: Can Australia compete? *International Migration Review, 31,* 670–693.

Eichengreen, B., & Irwin, D. A. (1995). Trade blocs, currency blocs and reorientation of world trade in the 1930s. *Journal of International Economics, 38,* 1–24.

Feenstra, R. C. (2004). *Advanced International trade: Theory and evidence.* Princeton, NJ: Princeton University Press.

Florax, R., de Groot, H., & Heijungs, R. (2002). The empirical growth literature: Robustness, significance and size. Discussion Paper, 2002-040/3, Tinbergen Institute.

Friedberg, R. (1992). The labor market assimilation of immigrants in the United States: The role of age at arrival. Unpublished working paper, Brown University.

Greenwood, M. (1969). An analysis of the determinants of geographic labor mobility in the United States. *Review of Economics and Statistics, 51,* 189–194.

Greenwood, M. (1975). Research on internal migration in the United States: A survey. *Journal of Economic Literature, 13,* 397–433.

Greenwood, M. (1985). Human migration: theory, models and empirical studies. *Journal of Regional Science, 25,* 521–544.

Greenwood, M. (1997). Internal migration in developed countries. In M. Rosenzweig & O. Stark (Eds.), *Handbook of population and family economics.* Amsterdam: Elsevier.

Greenwood, M., & Hunt, G. (2003). The early history of migration research. *International Regional Science Review, 26,* 3–37.

Greenwood, M., & McDowell, J. (1991). Differential economic opportunity, transferability of skills, and immigration to the United States and Canada. *Review of Economics and Statistics, 73,* 612–623.

Hatton, T. (2005). Explaining trends in UK immigration. *Journal of Population Economics, 18,* 719–740.

Hatton, T., & Williamson, J. (1994). What drove the mass migrations from Europe in the late nineteenth century. *Population and Development Review, 20,* 533–559.

Hatton, T., Williamson, J. (1998). *The age of mass migration: Causes and consequences.* New York: Oxford University Press.

Hatton, T., & Williamson, J. (2005). What fundamentals drive world migration? In G. Borjas & J. Crisp (Eds.), *Studies in development economics and policy,* New York: Macmillan.

Kahan, A. (1978). Economic opportunities and some pilgrims' progress: Jewish immigrants from Eastern Europe in the U.S., 1890–1914. *Journal of Economic History, 38*, 235–251.

Karemera, D., Iwuagwu, V., & Davis, B. (2000). A gravity model analysis of international migration to North America. *Applied Economics, 32*, 1745–1755.

Karras, G., & Chiswick, C. (1999). Macroeconomic determinants of migration: The base of Germany 1964–88. *International Migration, 37*, 657–676.

Kennan, J., & Walker, J. (2003). *The effect of expected incomes on individual migration decisions.* NBEResearch Working Paper No. 9585.

Lall, S., Selod, H., & Shalizi, Z. (2006). Rural-urban migration in developing countries: A survey of theoretical predictions and empirical findings. World Bank Policy Research Working Paper 3915.

Lewer, J., & Van den Berg, H. (2007). A gravity model of immigration. *Economics Letters, 99*, 164–167.

Lucas, R. (1997). Internal migration in developing countries. In M. Rosenzweig & O. Stark (Eds.), *Handbook of population and family economics*. Amsterdam: Elsevier.

Mayda, A. (2007). International migration: A panel data analysis of the determinants of bilateral flows. CEPR Discussion Paper No. 6289.

Murayama, Y. (1991). Information and immigrants: Interprefectual differences of Japanese emigration to the pacific northwest, 1880–1915. *Journal of Economic History, 51*, 125–147.

Naskoteen, R., & Zimmer, M. (1980). Migration and income: The question of self-selection. *Southern Economic Journal, 46*, 840–851.

Pedersen, P., Putlikova, M., & Smith, N. (2004). Selection or network effects? Migration flows into 27 OECD countries, 1990–2000. IZA Discussion Paper No. 1104.

Redding, S., & Venables, A.J. (2004). Economic geography and international inequality. *Journal of International Economics, 62*, 53–82.

Rephann, T. J., & Vencataawmy, C. P. (2000). Determinants of the spatial mobility of immigrants in Sweden. *Review of Regional Studies, 10*, 189–213.

Rose, A. K., & van Wincoop, E. (2001). National money as a barrier to international trade: The real case for currency union. *American Economic Review, 91*, 386–390.

Rotte, R., Vogler, M., & Zimmermann, K. (1997). South-North refugee migration: Lessons for development cooperation. *Review of Development Economics, 1*, 99–115.

Shields, G., & Shields, M. (1989). The emergence of migration theory and a suggested new direction. *Journal of Economic Surveys, 3*, 277–304.

Sjaastad, L. (1962). The costs and returns of human migration. *Journal of Political Economy, 70*, 80–93.

Wang, Z. K., & Winters, A. (1992). The trading potential of eastern Europe. *Journal of Economic Integration, 7*, 113–131.

Yang, P. (1995). *Post-1965 immigration to the United States: Structural determinants.* Westport, Connecticutt: Praeger Press.

Yuengert, A. (1994). Immigrant earnings, relative to what? The importance of earnings function specification and comparison points. *Journal of Applied Econometrics, 9*, 71–90.

Zavodny, M. (1997). Welfare and the locational choices of new immigrants. *Economic Review*, Federal Reserve Bank of Dallas: second quarter.

Chapter 4
Who Immigrates? Theory and Evidence

Abstract Do immigrants differ from their source country and destination country native-born peers with respect to their personal characteristics and labor market performance? This chapter surveys recent theoretical work and empirical evidence since the late 1970s that examines how immigrants self select with respect to partially-unobservable characteristics such as innate ability or fully observable characteristics such as years of schooling. Specifically, this chapter examines how immigrants self-select in response to international differences in returns to skill and education, migrants' cost constraints, and immigration policy, among other factors. This chapter also examines the literature on how immigrants assimilate in their destination societies, which indirectly has influenced discussions about the characteristics of those who immigrate. Unlike the last two chapters, which discussed the theoretical and empirical models separately, this chapter covers both the theoretical and empirical literatures.

Chapter Overview

In 1919, the U.S. Senator (and economist) Paul H. Douglas wrote a paper on U.S. immigration entitled: "Is the New Immigration More Unskilled than the Old?" Douglas's answer at that time was *no*. Today, the same question has dominated discussions on immigration policy in the major destination countries in North America and Europe. To answer Douglas' question, we need to know what kind of workers, consumers, and innovators are among the immigrants arriving in, or leaving, countries. We need to know how immigrants self-select and how they fare in the destination countries.

Chiswick (1979) points out that "U.S. immigration policy has historically been based primarily on the premise that immigrants have a favorable impact on the destination country's economic development."[1] Some have argued that for

---

[1]Chiswick (1979, p. 359).

Ö.B. Bodvarsson and H. Van den Berg, *The Economics of Immigration*,
DOI: 10.1007/978-3-540-77796-0_4, © Springer-Verlag Berlin Heidelberg 2009

immigrants to have "a favorable impact," they should have different skill sets from natives so that they are *complementary* to, and not *competitive* with, native workers. Yet, others argue that immigrants cause less social conflict if they speak the same language, have similar levels of education, and have compatible cultural backgrounds to natives in the destination country. This conflict between wanting noncompetitive workers and yet similar people to immigrate clearly reflects factors that go beyond the field of economics to sociology, psychology, and cultural anthropology. We will deal with these other factors in later chapters. In this chapter we focus on the economics of immigrant selection by surveying how some recent theorists have modeled *immigrant selectivity*, or, put more simply, sought to determine *who* immigrates.

If immigrants are different from those they left behind in the source country or the native-born that await them in the destination country, we say there is *selection bias* in immigrant flows. According to Heckman (1987, pp. 287–88):

> The problem of selection bias in economic and social statistics arises when a rule other than simple random sampling is used to sample the underlying population that is the object of interest. The distorted representation of a true population as a consequence of a sampling rule is the essence of the selection problem. Distorting selection rules may be the outcome of decisions of sample survey statisticians, self-selection decisions by the agents being studied, or both.

Figure 4.1 shows two possible forms of selectivity bias. If immigrants have skill levels below Q1, even though the overall distribution of skills follows the full curve shown, we say there is a selection bias towards low skilled immigrants. If all immigrants have skill levels above Q2, there is a selection bias towards high skilled workers.

Selection bias has been studied by labor economists in many different environments. For example, workers who decide to join a labor union tend to be, on

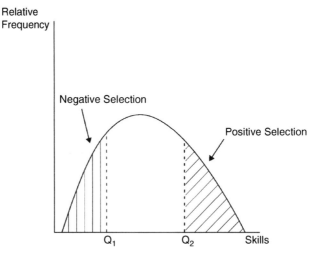

Fig. 4.1 The distribution of worker skills in the source country

average, distinctive from those who choose not to join a union. Non-joiners are likely to be younger, they may see their jobs as less permanent, they may be less interested in confronting their employer, and they are most likely less interested in actively participating in union activities. Therefore, one cannot assume that the observed wages union members earn are the same wages non-union members would earn *if they became union members*. Similarly, the observed earnings of college-educated persons will differ from the wages of current non college-educated persons *had the latter somehow been induced to enroll in college*. They would still be people with characteristics that made them choose to *not* attend college in the first place. In general, wages estimated using evidence from samples of immigrants do not provide an accurate estimate of what the wages of other members of the source country population would be if they also migrated.[2]

The concept of *self-selection* is a behavioral term closely related to the statistical concept of selection bias. Self-selection implies some deterministic process to select who does, and who doesn't, do something. The previous two chapters show that there are many factors that determine whether people decide to migrate or stay home, so self-selection is likely to result in a group of migrants whose personal characteristics are distributed differently from the way the personal characteristics of the whole source and destination country populations are distributed. Because immigrants self select, they are unlikely to be an unbiased sample of either the origin country's population or the destination country's population.

In the first part of this chapter, we survey the models that immigration economists have developed to explain the causes, and some of the consequences, of selection bias in *immigrant flows*. We follow this discussion with a survey of the empirical evidence from testing those models. Then we survey the closely related theoretical literature on *immigrant assimilation*, which links immigrants' labor performance to, among other things, immigrants' personal characteristics.

4.1 Immigrant Selection: The Chiswick Vs. Borjas Debate

One popular point of view of immigrant selection dates back to Chiswick (1978), who presented evidence that, in the United States, immigrants tended to be relatively more productive and earn more than native-born Americans. Another point of view, prominently argued by Borjas (1987, 1991), is that immigrants from developing countries tend to be less productive and earn less than natives in more developed destination countries. These discussions on immigrant labor market performance have become intertwined with discussions on whether immigration is beneficial or harmful. The argument between Chiswick and Borjas has been carried out at an intellectual level, but some of the tentative conclusions have been brought into the much less nuanced news media and political dialog. The purpose of

---

[2]For a detailed discussion of the econometric implications of self-selection behavior, see Heckman (1979).

this chapter is to describe what mainstream economists have concluded about immigrant selectivity.

4.1.1 Some Unfortunate Terminology

It is customary for labor economists studying immigration to use terms such as "positive selection bias" or "unfavorable selection bias." By positive (negative) selection bias economists mean that immigrant skills and earnings are on average above (below) the mean skill levels or earnings of the source country's population. Words such as "positive" and "negative," or "favorable" and "unfavorable," are inherently offensive, however, and they certainly will not be interpreted correctly in discussions in the public sphere. It is not even generally the case that "unfavorably-selected" or "negatively-selected" migrants, that is, relatively less educated, experienced, or skilled migrants, have "unfavorable" or "negative" consequences for either the source or destination economies.

If labor economists cannot be more sensitive and accurate, we can. In this book we will describe groups of people by using more specific terms that clearly refer to their human capital, age, education, and other explicit characteristics. For example, we will use terms such as "high-skill selection" or "youth bias" if a group includes a relatively large share of skilled or young people, and we will avoid subjective terms such as "negative" or "favorable."

4.1.2 The Chiswick View

Chiswick (1999) developed a model to show how immigrants self-select in ways that tend to make them, as a group, relatively more ambitious, harder working, and more likely to succeed in their destination country. Chiswick's model makes a number of assumptions to simplify the analysis, as all models do. For example, in order to abstract from explicit observable differences in immigrant characteristics, Chiswick assumes that wages in the origin and destination countries are invariant to the amount of labor market experience. He also assumes that age is irrelevant because workers live forever. Chiswick specifies the *rate of return to migration* as

$$r = \frac{W_D - W_S}{C_I + C_E} \qquad (4.1)$$

where W_D represents destination earnings, W_S represents earnings in the source, C_I equals the implicit opportunity costs of migration, and C_E represents explicit out-of-pocket costs. In this simple framework, migration occurs if the rate of return r from investing C_I+C_E in relocation is greater than the opportunity cost of the interest that could be earned from investing those funds. Therefore, migration occurs if $r > i$, where i is the rate of interest faced by the would-be migrant.

Suppose there are two types of worker, low-skilled and high-skilled, and skills are fully observable and known. We define r_L and r_H as the rates of return to immigration for low-skilled and high-skilled persons, respectively. If both persons have the same interest cost, the person with the higher rate of return will have a greater likelihood of migrating. Suppose, now, that source and destination country wages are k percent higher for the high-skilled. It then follows that

$$W_{D,h} = (1 + k)W_{D,l}, \tag{4.2}$$

$$W_{S,h} = (1 + k)W_{S,l}, \tag{4.3}$$

where h (l) stands for high (low) skills. Finally, Chiswick initially assumes that direct migration costs C do not vary with skill levels.

Because they earn more in their native countries, high-skilled workers have higher implicit opportunity costs, namely $C_{i,h} = (1 + k)C_{i,l}$ Therefore, the return to migration for high-skilled migrants is

$$r_h = \frac{(1 + k)[W_{D,l} - W_{S,l}]}{(1 + k)C_{I,l} + C_E} = \frac{W_{D,l} - W_{S,l}}{C_{I,l} + \frac{C_E}{(1+k)}}. \tag{4.4}$$

For example, if $k = 0.5$, $W_l = 50{,}000$ in the source country and 75,000 in the destination country, and $C_E = 10{,}000$, then, $r_l = 0.4167$, and the wage gain enjoyed by the low-skilled worker is 41.67% of the "investment" in migration. On the other hand, $r_h = 0.4412$. Equation (4.4) implies that high-skilled migrants experience higher rates of return than low-skilled migrants if (a) mean earnings in the destination are higher ($W_{D,l} > W_{0,l}$), (b) the labor market rewards higher skilled workers more ($k > 0$), and (c) there are positive out-of-pocket costs of migration ($C_E > 0$). In sum, given the three assumptions, the probability of migration is higher for the high-skilled and migrants exhibit self-selection bias.

Chiswick then examines how changes in various assumptions and variables change the model's conclusions. For example, he demonstrates that if high-skilled immigrants are more efficient in using their time than low-skilled immigrants, they will enjoy a selection advantage even if there are no out-of-pocket costs. On the other hand, even if the rate of return to migrating is higher for a low-skilled than it is for a high-skilled person, there can still be a selection bias towards high-skilled migrants if there are very high direct costs of migrating, such as high visa expenses or high transport costs due to long distance. Chiswick's model shows that under many plausible circumstances, higher migration costs are associated with a selectivity bias towards those who expect to earn the highest wages in the destination country, probably the relatively high-skilled, highly-educated, and well-connected immigrants.

4.1.3   The Borjas Model

Borjas (1987, 1990, 1991, 1999a) developed several closely-related models to counter Chiswick's conclusion that, all other things equal, self-selected immigrants tend to be relatively more skilled, talented, and educated, and, therefore, likely to be highly successful in the destination countries. He developed a model to explain immigrant selection that drew on the work of Roy (1951), Heckman (1979), and other economists who studied self-selection in labor markets. His model predicts that, all other things equal, immigrant selectivity results from international differences in the return to skills and the degree to which skills are transferable across borders. Effectively, he allows the "k" in Chiswick's model, the skill premium, to vary across countries. He finds that immigrants who self-select in response to the skill premium, the observed distributions of skills across the source and destination countries' populations, and their perceptions of their own skills, do not unambiguously end up earning high incomes in the destination economy.

In Chap. 2, equation (2.8), we showed how Borjas' (1987) model yields an expression for the emigration rate. Here we detail how that same model yields expressions for immigrant selection bias. Recall that Borjas' model assumed that a person's wage in the source country is equal to

$$\ln(w_o) = \mu_o + \varepsilon_o, \tag{4.5}$$

where μ_o is the mean income home country residents would earn if they stayed at home, and ε_o is random, uncorrelated with μ_o, with mean zero and variance σ_o^2. In the destination country the wage is similarly equal to

$$\ln(w_1) = \mu_1 + \varepsilon_1. \tag{4.6}$$

The Borjas model predicts that immigrants exhibit a self-selection bias towards people who are relatively highly-skilled or highly-educated in the source country's skill/education distribution when $E[\ln(w_o)] < \mu_o$, or when the average expected wage in the source country is below the mean. Also, migration exhibits a similar selection bias towards high-skill or highly-educated people relative to the destination country's skill/education distribution when $E[\log(w_1)] > \mu_1$.

Borjas then defines a measure of selection bias, B, so that

$$E(\log(w_0)) = \mu_0 + B_0 \tag{4.7}$$

and

$$E(\log(w_1)) = \mu_1 + B_1. \tag{4.8}$$

These two equations can also be expressed as follows:

$$E(\log(w_0)) = \mu_0 + \left(\frac{\Omega}{\sigma(\varepsilon_0 - \varepsilon_1)}\right)\sigma_1\sigma_0\left(\rho - \frac{\sigma_0}{\sigma_1}\right) = \mu_0 + B_0 \qquad (4.9)$$

and

$$E(\log(w_1)) = \mu_1 + \frac{\sigma_0\sigma_1}{\sigma(\varepsilon_1 - \varepsilon_0)}\left(\frac{\sigma_1}{\sigma_0} - \rho\right)\Omega = B_1. \qquad (4.10)$$

Since the term Ω is defined as $\frac{\phi(Z)}{P}$, where $\phi(Z)$ is the density of the standard normal distribution and P is the emigration rate, it is clear that the self-selection of immigrants who respond to source and destination country wage differences depends also on the earnings dispersion in each country and the degree to which skills are transferable from the source country to the destination country.

Borjas points out that the high-skill selection bias Chiswick (1978) hypothesized requires that (1) earnings in the source and destination countries are sufficiently positively correlated and (2) the dispersion of earnings opportunities in the destination country is greater than in the source country. Positive correlation in earnings is necessary because if a high-skill worker is to migrate, skills must be transferable. Greater wage dispersion in the destination country makes the return to highly-skilled workers higher, and the return to low-skilled workers lower, in the destination country, all other things equal. These conditions are not generally true, however, which implies that the high-skill selection bias for immigrants is not generally true either.

To highlight the influence of skills on migration, the two diagrams in Fig. 4.2 show the functional relationships between earnings and skills in two countries under the assumption that the average wage is the same in both countries. The figure shows, for example, that if the destination country's "earnings-skills line" is steeper because the return to skills is greater there and, hence, the dispersion of

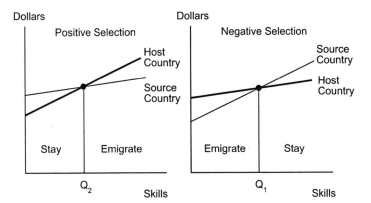

Fig. 4.2 Selection bias in immigrant flours

wages is greater there, only those with skill level Q_2 or *greater* will migrate. On the other hand, if the wage dispersion across skills is greater in the source country, all other things equal, then only the relatively less-skilled workers will migrate. In sum, Borjas' model shows that selection bias depends on the specific circumstances.

4.1.4 A More Detailed Look at the Borjas Model

By incorporating the distributions of skills, education, and other personal characteristics of people in the source and destination countries into the model, Borjas (1987) permits us to detail the role in determining who immigrates. This feature of the Borjas model is very important because, in general, migration occurs between countries with varied populations. The model shows that differences in the distribution of personal characteristics, such as age, skill, and education, across populations affect both the composition and scale of international migration.

Borjas' model distinguishes between the *composition* and *scale* effects of immigration. According to (4.10), the magnitude of migrant selectivity bias is

$$\left(\frac{\sigma_0 \sigma_1}{\sigma(\varepsilon_1 - \varepsilon_0)} \right) \left(\frac{\sigma_1}{\sigma_0} - \rho \right) \Omega = \psi \Omega, \tag{4.11}$$

where $\psi \equiv \left(\frac{\sigma_0 \sigma_1}{\sigma(\varepsilon_1 - \varepsilon_0)} \right) \left(\frac{\sigma_1}{\sigma_0} - \rho \right)$. The term ψ reflects the *income mix* or *skill mix* of a given-sized pool of migrants in the source country. The income mix can change only if there is a structural change in either of the skill or immigrant earnings distributions, that is, if the higher moments of the distribution change. The sign of ψ determines the type of bias, while its absolute value influences the magnitude of bias. Z is a constant that varies strictly with the size of the migrant pool; the bigger the migrant flow, the smaller is Ω. Hence, the size of Ω does not influence the type of selection bias, only its magnitude.

Since $B_1 = \psi \Omega$, the marginal effect of an exogenous variable κ on selection bias is

$$\frac{\partial B}{\partial \kappa} = \Omega \frac{\partial \psi}{\partial \kappa} + \psi \frac{\partial \Omega}{\partial \kappa} \tag{4.12}$$

Borjas calls the first term on the right-hand side of equation (4.12) the *composition effect*. It measures the marginal effect of a change in the exogenous variable on the income or skill mix, holding the size of the migrant pool constant. The second term is called the *scale effect*, and it measures the marginal effect of a change in the exogenous variable on the size of the migrant flow, holding the income or skill mix constant. Differentiating between the composition and scale effects permits Borjas to conjecture how specific variables influence immigrant flows and the selectivity of those flows.

Borjas obtains a number of important predictions for selection bias in the destination country.

1. *A shift in the source country's earnings distribution induces only a scale effect.*

For example, suppose there is discovery of a large reservoir of oil off the source country's coastline, which makes everyone there wealthier. The greater prosperity in the source country will reduce the emigration rate because it improves the position of the "marginal" immigrant so that he no longer has an incentive to migrate. Greater prosperity in the source country will thus cut the size of the emigrant flow and reduces average emigrant earnings. Exactly the opposite occurs if there is a drop in mean earnings in the source country.

2. *An increase (decrease) in migration costs will enhance (reduce) selectivity.*

This conclusion assumes that migration costs do not vary with skills. Higher costs have the same effect on selectivity as lower destination country mean earnings and *vice versa* for lower costs. Changes in migration costs induce only scale effects.

These first two conclusions involved only a shift in the means of the source and destination country earnings distributions, which can only induce scale effects. When there is a change in the variance or higher moments, however, then there can be both scale and composition effects. As a result:

3. *An increase (decrease) in earnings dispersion in the source country will unambiguously reduce (increase) average earnings of the emigrant pool, assuming that mean earnings in the destination country, net of migration costs, are higher.*

An increase in source country earnings dispersion reduces the income of the poorest residents, while the position of the richest residents is improved. The composition effect is unambiguously biased towards promoting migration by the poorest workers in the source country. When the earnings dispersion widens, the mix of emigrants will include more persons from the expanded lower tail area of the earnings distribution. The scale effect will also be biased towards low income workers because as income inequality in the source country rises, the worst-off persons will still want to migrate, while the relatively higher-earnings persons find their income opportunities at home have improved. Exactly the opposite happens if income inequality in the source country declines. Thus, the composition and scale effects of a change in relative earnings inequality reinforce one another.

Note that these predictions will not generally be true if mean earnings in the source country are higher than in the destination country. In that case, the composition and scale effects will be in opposite directions. For example, if mean earnings in the source country are higher and income inequality at home rises, then the average earnings of the emigrant pool can rise if the scale effect dominates.

4.1.5   Selection by Observed Characteristics

In the preceding analysis, it was assumed that immigrants self select with respect to some unobservable characteristic, such as ability, known only to the migrant. However, selection obviously also occurs according to observable characteristics. Borjas (1991) extended his model to allow for selection with respect to both observable and unobservable characteristics. Borjas uses this model to explain the conditions under which the average schooling of immigrants differs from the average schooling of the source country's population. For example, he concludes that if the destination country labor market rewards schooling more, self-selection will result in a migrant pool with relatively high levels of education.

Interestingly, Borjas points out that negative selection in an unobservable characteristic like ability could occur jointly with positive selection in an observable characteristic like education. Borjas (1991) writes: "Simply because the United States attracts highly educated persons from some countries does not imply that these highly educated persons are the most productive highly educated persons in that particular country of origin."[3] Borjas further notes that "Since the two kinds of selections are independent, *nothing* (his italics) can be said about how the average migrant performs in the destination country unless the kinds of selections that occurred in each of the two dimensions ... are known." Realistically, people migrate for a variety of reasons, the exact combination of which they themselves may not understand precisely. This makes empirical work on the determinants of immigration difficult because it is inherently problematic finding proxies for non-observable or partially-observable characteristics.

4.2   Extensions of the Borjas Model

Borjas' (1987) model has been extended by relaxing the assumption that a migrant's cost constraint is unrelated to his or her earnings, skills, or other characteristics. First, the model has been extended to allow for variation in migration costs (π from above and in Chap. 2) across members of the immigrant pool. Second, the model has been extended to include credit constraints and the ability of would-be migrants to cover the up-front costs of their investment in migration.

4.2.1   Variable Migration Costs and Migrant Selection

In his 1991 study, Borjas allowed for random variation in migration costs:

---

[3] Borjas (1991, p. 38).

$$\pi = \mu_\pi + \varepsilon_\pi, \tag{4.13}$$

where μ_π is the mean migration costs in the population and ε_π is the usual random disturbance with mean zero and variance σ_π^2. However, he also assumed that the random disturbance is correlated with the random variation in unobserved migrant characteristics ε_0 and ε_1 from (4.4) and (4.5), and that this correlation is measured by $\rho_{\pi 0}$ and $\rho_{\pi 1}$, respectively. In effect, such correlated migration costs change the source and destination earnings distributions, which we have already shown to be potential determinants of migrant selectivity.

Suppose migration costs and earnings opportunities are positively correlated. This could occur, for example, if high-ability migrants take longer to find employment. High-ability migrants are likely to be better educated and possess high-levels of special skills. While these skills may provide them with greater earnings opportunities, the kinds of jobs they seek may be more difficult to find and/or the search process may be more costly and time-consuming. A positive correlation between ability and migration costs therefore reduces the likelihood that highly-skilled and highly-educated persons will migrate. On the other hand, Chiswick's (1999) assumption that more-able persons are more efficient at securing employment would lead to the opposite effect. Since many highly-educated immigrants have job offers in hand when they arrive in the destination country, the latter case may the more realistic one in most destination countries.

Inspired by Borjas' treatment of random migration costs, Chiquiar and Hanson (2005) suggest that migration costs are likely to be inversely related to earnings for four reasons: (1) more educated persons are more likely to possess the skills necessary to satisfy the many bureaucratic and paperwork requirements to obtain legal admission to the U.S.; (2) given that the costs of using the legal services industry for the purpose of obtaining U.S. admission tend to be fixed, those costs will be relatively lower for migrants who earn more; (3) for the case of unauthorized immigration, the costs of securing transportation across the border and for obtaining counterfeit residency documents tend to be fixed, thus higher-wage persons face lower relative costs of unauthorized immigration; and (4) lower-income individuals typically face higher borrowing costs because of a higher likelihood of default, hence they will face proportionally higher migration costs. Chiquiar and Hanson add some more features to the Borjas model, which enables their model to explain the often-discussed fact that Mexican immigrants in the U.S. are at the same time more educated than the average Mexican living in Mexico but less educated than the average native-born American.

First, Chiquiar and Hanson assume that migration costs are lower for higher skilled migrants. Furthermore, they assume selection occurs with respect to just one observable characteristic, schooling, and they assume away any random components to wage determination. Residents of Mexico, therefore, face an earnings equation given by

$$\ln(w_0) = \mu_0 + \delta_0 s, \tag{4.14}$$

where w_0 is the wage available in Mexico, μ_0 is the base wage, s is the level of schooling, and δ_0 is the return to schooling in Mexico. Earnings available to Mexican immigrants in the U.S. are specified as

$$\ln(w_1) = \mu_1 + \delta_1 s, \tag{4.15}$$

where w_1 is the U.S. wage available to Mexican migrants, μ_1 is the migrant base wage, and δ_1 is the return to schooling in the U.S. Suppose the return to schooling is higher in Mexico ($\delta_0 > \delta_1$) due to scarcity of higher-level skills there.

Chiquiar and Hanson specifically assume that migration costs, π, are inversely related to the level of schooling:

$$\ln(\pi) = \mu_\pi - \delta_\pi s, \tag{4.16}$$

where μ_π are migration costs in the absence of schooling and δ_π reflects the savings in costs (measured in units of labor supply) from acquiring an additional year of schooling.

According to this model, therefore, very low-skilled Mexican migrants face relatively high migration costs, and thus the least skilled will tend to remain in Mexico. While migration costs of high-skill migrants are lower, they face very high opportunity costs of leaving Mexico because the return to education there is higher. Consequently, they will tend to remain in Mexico. Hence, Mexican migrants to the U.S. will tend to be modestly educated and modestly skilled.

4.2.2 Credit Constraints and Immigrant Selection

Orrenius and Zavodny (2005) develop a model to explain the predominance of migrants with intermediate skill levels among unauthorized immigrants to the U.S. Like Chiquiar and Hanson, they assume that the return to education is higher in Mexico than the U.S., but they also include an additional feature in the migrant's costs not found in earlier models: credit constraints. They argue that undocumented migrants typically must pay border crossing expenses in advance and, because they usually lack access to credit markets, border-crossing costs must be financed from savings. Savings, however, depend on earnings, and earnings depend on skill. Thus, savings and skill are positively related to skills and education, which implies the lowest-income and least-skilled workers will be less likely to migrate.

It should be intuitive that credit constraints, as a percentage of income, are higher for the poor. At the same time, relatively high-income Mexicans face relatively high opportunity costs in a country where skills are scarce. Therefore, it will be mostly people with intermediate levels of education and income who seek to migrate. Hence, Orrenius and Zavodny's model explains the empirical observation that, like legal Mexican immigrants, unauthorized Mexican immigrants to the U.S. tend to be more educated than the average Mexican native.

4.2.3 Family Migration and Selection Bias

As we discussed in Chap. 2, migration is often a family decision. When the decision making unit is a family, selection bias may be different than when the decision to migrate is purely an individual decision.

Borjas and Bronars (1991) addressed this issue with a model based on earlier work on family economics by Becker (1964) and Mincer (1974). Specifically, their model represents the case of a two-person family consisting of members i and j. Earnings for person k (k=i,j) in the source country are given by

$$y_{0k} = \mu_0 + v_{0k}, \tag{4.17}$$

and earnings in the destination country are

$$y_{1k} = \mu_1 + v_{1k} \tag{4.18}$$

The parameter μ_0 is mean income in the source country, μ_1 is the mean income that immigrants would earn in the destination country if all persons in the source country migrated, and v_{0k} and v_{1k} are random variables that measure person-specific deviations from mean incomes due to differences in skills or education.

Borjas and Bronars (1991) assume that skills are perfectly transferable, so that v_{0k} and v_{1k} are perfectly correlated. This allowed Borjas and Bronars to write country earnings as

$$y_{0k} = \mu_0 + \eta v_k, \tag{4.19}$$

$$y_{1k} = \mu_1 + v_k, \tag{4.20}$$

where η is the relative price of skills in the source country (the price of skills in the destination country is unity). They show that η is equivalent to the relative dispersion of earnings opportunities in the source country

$$\eta = \frac{\sigma_0}{\sigma_1}, \tag{4.21}$$

where σ_0 and σ_1 are the standard deviations of earnings in the source and destination countries, respectively. Finally, earnings across family members are assumed to be correlated, with the correlation coefficient $-1 < \rho < 1$.

Borjas and Bronars derive index functions corresponding to the migration decisions of persons i and j. Specifically, if person k (k=i,j) were not part of a family, then (s)he would migrate when

$$I_k = (1 - \eta)v_k - (\mu_0 - \mu_1) - M = (1 - \eta)v_k - \Delta\mu > 0 \qquad (4.22)$$

where M is migration costs (assumed constant across individuals) and $\Delta\mu = (\mu_0 - \mu_1) - M$. But when i and j form a family, the family migrates when the sum of members' gains is positive, or when

$$I_i + I_j + (1 - \eta)(v_i - v_j) - 2\Delta\mu > 0 \qquad (4.23)$$

Borjas and Bronars use expression (4.23) to derive the average skill of person k (k=i,j) who migrates with their family, which is the conditional expectation of v_k:

$$E(v_k) = \left[\alpha \left(\sqrt{\frac{(1 + \rho)}{2}} \right) \sigma \right] \lambda \left\{ \alpha \sqrt{\frac{2}{(1 + \rho)}} z \right\}, \qquad (4.24)$$

where $\alpha=1$ if $\eta<1$ and $\alpha=-1$ if $\eta>1$. Equation (4.24) also defines $\lambda(x) \equiv \frac{\phi(x)}{[1-\Phi(x)]}$ and $z \equiv \frac{\Delta\mu}{(1-\eta)\sigma}$, where ϕ is the standard normal density function, and Φ is the standard normal distribution function.

The average earnings of a migrant who migrates as part of a family depends upon international differences in the rewards to skills, as determined by α in equation (4.24), the correlation in earnings across family members (ρ) and the dispersion of skills in the source country's population (σ).

According to (4.24), when earnings of family members are always the same ($\rho=1$), selectivity is no different from the case of non-family migration:

$$E(v_i) = \alpha\sigma\lambda(\alpha z), \qquad (4.25)$$

which is the same condition derived in Borjas' (1987, 1991) earlier models of individual selection.

However, the average skill level of migrants under family migration differs from the case of individual migration when $-1<\rho<1$. Borjas and Bronars show that when returns to skill are greater in the destination country, there will be selection bias towards higher-skill migrants under both family and individual migration, but the degree of positive selection will be lower under family migration. This result is intuitive since families include tied movers, who are less skilled and find it less profitable to move. Tied movers effectively dilute the degree of selection bias. Similarly, if returns to skill are lower in the destination country, selection will be biased towards lower-skilled migrants under both family and non-family migration, but the degree of the bias will be less under the latter.

4.3 The Empirical Evidence on Immigrant Selectivity

The models detailed above predict that the characteristics of immigrants, such as education levels, skill levels, age, gender, and family size, depend on the distributions of those characteristics among the overall populations in both the source and destination countries. In this section we discuss the results from the empirical literature on immigrant selectivity, beginning with the original Borjas (1987) study and continuing through studies by economists who contested Borjas' findings.

4.3.1 Borjas' Empirical Results

Borjas is well-known for his hypothesis that the average skill levels of U.S. immigrants have declined since the 1965 immigration law that changed immigrant visa criteria from national quotas to family reunion. To test his hypothesis, Borjas (1987) used data from the 1970 and 1980 U.S. Censuses to estimate the wage differentials for natives and various immigrant cohorts classified according to the number of years they had been living in the U.S. Borjas restricted his analysis to men ages 25–64. His results thus depend critically on whether relative immigrant skills can be represented by *wage* differentials between immigrants and natives.

In order to gauge the reliability of Borjas' statistical results, it is important to understand the tenuous links between the variables in Borjas' theoretical model and the actual data used to proxy those variables. For example, mean level of income in the source country was measured by the logarithm of per capita GNP in 1980 (in U.S. dollars). The variance of income in the source country was measured by the ratio of household income accruing to the top 10 percent of households to the income accruing to the bottom 20 percent of households in 1970. The change in income inequality was measured by the change in the share of GNP attributable to central government spending over that period, under the assumption that a government with greater participation in the source country's economy engages in more income redistribution. Migration costs were measured by the number of air miles between the source country's capital city and the nearest U.S. gateway city. Borjas included additional variables such as the share of immigrants with good proficiency in English, the mean age of migrants, and dummy variables to capture the level of political participation, the level of democracy, political violence, and the continents from which immigrants came. If you have doubts about some of these variables, then you are in good company. When accurate data are scarce, even the most objective application of statistical models may seem more like an art form than a scientific exercise.

To test his model, Borjas regressed the estimated entry wage differential between the 1979 immigrant cohort from each source country and comparable U.S. natives on various country-specific measures. Among other things, Borjas found no significant evidence to support the hypothesis that higher income inequality in the source country lowers the education and skill levels of U.S. immigrants. Nor did he find distance to be related to the migrant quality measures. He did find source country GNP to be positively and significantly related to immigrant education and skills. Most important for Borjas' hypothesis, he finds evidence, abeit weak, that U.S. immigrants from advanced industrial countries are more likely to be highly skilled, while immigrants from poor countries are likely to be relatively less skilled compared to the native U.S. population. Borjas claims these results plus the observation that U.S. immigrants increasingly came from developing countries provide some support for his hypothesis that U.S. immigrants have become less skilled in recent decades.

Borjas (1987) admits that, overall, the above results are not entirely consistent with his model's theoretical predictions. He attributes the poor statistical results to the measurement errors in the various country-specific proxies. Furthermore, there is the likelihood of omitted variables bias because there were no controls for destination country income inequality, destination country mean income, or earnings correlation.

4.3.2   Further Tests of Borjas' Model

In a critique of Borjas (1987), Jasso and Rosenzweig (1990) argue that "interpretation of the effects of origin-country characteristics on the changes in the earnings of age-entry cohorts of the U.S. foreign-born thus is likely to require a richer model of self-selection, incorporating decisions to migrate to the United States and to remain there after migration."[4] In his 1991 study, Borjas (1991) tests the determinants of migrant characteristics by pooling three destination countries, Australia, Canada, and the United States, and estimating a regression of the immigrant/native wage differential at the time of arrival on sets of source and destination continent characteristics. In this "international" test of migrant selectivity, Borjas found strong and positive relationships between his measure of migrant education/skills and both the relative per capita GNP of the origin continent and the level of income inequality in the destination country. All other things equal, migrants from richer regions earn more *no matter the destination*, and migrants from regions with large amounts of income inequality do worse than other immigrants, all other things equal. Finally, the U.S. immigrant policy dummy was negative and significant, which Borjas interpreted as confirming that U.S. immigration policies in recent years have had the effect of reducing average skill and education levels of U.S. immigrants.

Other studies have provided mixed support for Borjas' hypothesis that the average skill levels of U.S. immigrants have fallen relative to the native population. For example, Cobb-Clark (1993) reports evidence of selection bias towards lower-skill migrants among female immigrants to the U.S. from countries with higher returns to skills. Barrett (1993) shows that U.S. immigrants arriving with a family reunification visa earn less when they originate in countries where the income distribution has a relatively high variance. Bratsberg (1995) shows that foreign

---

[4] Jasso and Rosenzweig (1990, p. 303).

students who stay in the U.S. after completing their degrees earn relatively high wages if their country of origin provides a low rate of return to skills, but earn relatively low wages if the homeland offers a high return to skills.

4.3.3   Tests Based on Counterfactual Density Functions

DiNardo, Fortin, and Lemieux (1996) argued that changes in immigrant wages over time are the combined result of a changing distribution of immigrant characteristics as well as changes in the overall wage structure in the U.S. economy. Borjas' methodology cannot separate these two potential explanations for variations in immigrant earnings, and the wages of the least educated workers in the U.S. have suffered substantial declines in wages over the past 40 years, while university graduates have enjoyed substantial wage increases, Borjas' results are likely to have been biased towards finding a decline in immigrant earnings over this period. DiNardo, Fortin, and Lemieux developed a decomposition method based on Oaxaca (1973) to estimate the separate contributions of each of the two potential determinant of immigration. Their method involves comparing the actual distribution of skills of the population with a constructed distribution that controls for the overall changes in the wage structure in the U.S. economy.

Using the DiNardo, Fortin, and Lemieux (1996) methodology, Butcher and DiNardo (2002) found that the counterfactual income/skill distribution for 1990 closely resembled the actual 1990 distribution. They thus concluded that the widening of the immigrant/native-born mean wage gap during 1970–1990 was linked to the well-documented increase in the wage premium for college-educated workers in the U.S. and does not reflect a reduction in the skill levels of immigrants. Indeed, Butcher and DiNardo also directly dispute Borjas: "The emphasis on post-1965 changes in United States immigration policy in explaining the relative wages of immigrants and natives may be misplaced."[5]

Chiquiar and Hanson (2005) applied the same DiNardo, Fortin, and Lemieux methodology to compare the earnings of immigrants from Mexico with residents of Mexico. Their analysis focused on Mexican immigrants that came to the U.S. within the previous 10 years. Their results do not support the Borjas (1987, 1991) prediction of a decline in immigrant skills. They found that for 1990, immigrant men were taken disproportionately from the middle and upper middle parts of the Mexican wage distribution, and that low- and high-wage men were the least likely to migrate to the U.S. For women in 1990 and 2000, the results also strongly indicated a bias toward the middle and upper middle parts of the Mexican wage distribution. For men in 2000, their results again indicated intermediate selection, but not as clearly. All these results are supportive of the hypothesis that there is intermediate selection of Mexican migrants in the U.S.

---

[5] Butcher and DiNardo (2002, p. 116).

Finally, Orrenius and Zavodny (2005) examine data on unauthorized Mexican immigrants to the U.S. and find strong evidence of intermediate selection similar to the legal Hispanic immigration to the U.S. Among household heads, those with the lowest probability of migrating had at least a high school education, followed by those who have completed secondary school only, then those with little or zero formal education. For the portion of the sample comprising sons, high school graduates, and those with zero schooling are found to have the lowest likelihoods of migration. Higher real agricultural income or manufacturing wages in Mexico were found to reduce the probability of migration by heads of family in all educational categories, but the greatest reductions were found in the two highest categories. These results undermine Borjas' (1987, 1991) prediction that migration from developing countries to developed countries is characterized by a decline in immigrant skills relative to destination country natives.

The Chiquiar and Hanson (2005) and Orrenius and Zavodny (2005) studies also provide valuable information about Hispanic immigration to the U.S., one of the most substantial cases of massive immigration from a low income to a high income country in the latter half of the twentieth century. Chapter 12 analyses Hispanic immigration to the U.S. in detail.

4.4   The Asymmetric Information Model

The process of selection, whether by the migrants themselves, by policymakers, or those who employ or sponsor immigrants in the destination country, depends on how the actors view the relative differences in income, skills, and the distributions of those incomes and skills. In short, there is an important informational component to the migration decision. This begs the obvious question: How is immigration affected when information is missing?

Kwok and Leland (1982) develop an interesting model of migrant selection bias that is the result of asymmetric information in the international labor market. They apply the well-known concepts from the labor economics literature, specifically the work of Akerlof (1970) and Leland (1979, 1980) on the market for lemons (as in used automobiles) when sellers know more about product quality than buyers, Spence (1973) and Riley (1975) on job market signaling, and Stiglitz (1975) on employer screening of workers' job qualifications.

4.4.1   Kwok and Leland's Model

Kwok and Leland (1982) set up a simple case in which employers in one country are better informed about an individual migrant's productivity than are employers in the other country. However, there are no informational differences between employers and workers in the same country and workers are fully informed about their own productivities. Note that Kwok and Leland (1982) specifically model the case of skilled persons that have been studying abroad who must choose to stay or return. This case contrasts with the more traditional case of positive selectivity in *out*-migration, e.g. the case when the high-skilled professionals leave a developing economy in search of more lucrative opportunities in the U.S.

To illustrate, suppose that Indian graduate students studying in the United States have to decide whether to remain in the U.S. to work or to seek work back in India. Kwok and Leland begin by assuming that there is some fraction $k < 1$ such that an Indian student is indifferent between working in the USA for a wage W, and returning to India for a wage kW. If there was perfect information and a fully integrated global labor market, each new graduate would be offered the same wage in India as he would in the USA, and all Indian graduate students would return home. However, suppose there are two types of Indian students/workers trained in the USA: Type A workers have productivity 10 and type B workers productivity 5. Suppose, moreover, that equal numbers of each type of student graduate from U.S. universities. Finally, suppose Indian graduates require a wage in India of at least 80% of the U.S. wage in order to return home, i.e. $k = 0.8$.

In the face of uncertainty about returnee productivity, Kwok and Leland assume that Indian employers set their pay offers equal to expected productivity for all students abroad. Since there are equal fractions of type A and type B graduates, Indian pay offers will be $(0.5)(5) + (0.5)(10) = 7.5$. Suppose that Indian employers are not completely uninformed, and that they know how productive type A and type B graduates are and the fraction of each type out of the Indian graduate student pool in the U.S. But, they can't match each individual graduate with his or her personal productivity.

The problem Indian employers face is that the average productivity of returning graduates is 7.5, the average productivity of the entire graduate pool, but type A graduates are offered a wage in the U.S. of 10 by U.S. employers who are able to discern between type A and type B students. Those type A students need a wage offer from India equaling $(0.8)(10) = 8$ to return. Thus, all type A graduates remain in the USA. The Type B graduates, who require a wage in India of $(0.8)(5) = 4$, do return. There is thus a *separating equilibrium* where the lower productivity workers return and the high productivity workers stay.

Indian employers, unable to distinguish between Type A and Type B returnees, at first pay all returnees a wage equaling the average productivity of all Indian graduates of U.S. universities. Type Bs are thus overpaid in India relative to their true value by 2.5, as well as relative to their reservation wage for returning by 3.5. The Type As understand this too, and they are deterred from returning because they expect to be underpaid relative to their true productivity by 2.5 and 0.5 relative to their reservation wage. Eventually, Indian employers realize that type B employees only produce a value of 5, and eventually the market settles close to that wage. In this case, type B students still return to India, however, because their reservation wage for returning is 4. The Indian migrants have effectively been selected into a group consisting entirely of type B students.

An important implication of the Kwok and Leland model is that the Indian/USA wage differential is not the *cause*, but the *result*, of negative selectivity in return migration. This conclusion is important because a casual observer might attribute the negative selectivity of returnee migrants to lower wages in India. It is also worth emphasizing that Kwok and Leland's results are sensitive to the values assumed for the parameters in their model. For example, suppose that $k = 0.7$. In this case, all Indian graduates would return home if Indian employers offer the average productivity wage of 7.5. Also, suppose that type A workers have a productivity of 7. In that case, the wage offered in India to all returnees would be 6. Type B students would return because they would make 2 more than their reservation wage, and type A students would also return because their reservation wage in India is 5.6. Finally, all graduate students would return as well if a very large fraction of workers were type B, say, 80% of the pool.

Kwok and Leland (1982) consider a variety of other cases, such as when the informational advantage is with Indian employers rather than U.S. employers. In each case, immigrant selection is different. In general, the nature of migrant selectivity depends upon the location of the ignorant employers, the distribution of workers according to skill type, worker preferences for remaining at home, and the difference in wage structures between the destination and source countries.

4.4.2   Restoring Symmetric Information

There are measures that can be taken to mitigate the selection bias in immigration caused by employer ignorance and information asymmetries. Katz and Stark (1987) show that immigrants can invest in a signaling device such as an examination or professional qualifications such as a university degree or professional certification. Suppose the signaling device allows a worker's skill level to be completely identified, but it requires a fixed cost investment by the worker and it does not vary with skill level. The worker thus faces a dual decision: Do I invest in the signal *and* do I migrate? Katz and Stark demonstrate that the high-skilled individuals will be the ones most likely to invest in the signal since the most skilled workers have the most to lose when they are paid a wage equaling the expected productivity of the entire group. In contrast, the relatively low-skilled workers will usually not wish to invest in a device that reveals their below-average productivity. Hence, the investment in signals is biased by a self-selection process, but note that it is biased in a way that offsets the bias caused by asymmetric information in the labor market.

4.5   The Theory of Immigrant Assimilation

The word "assimilation" has its roots in physiology and biology, where it is defined as the transformation of food into living tissue. In the social sciences, assimilation is generally defined as the process by which a group of persons, new to an area, adapt to the destination area's culture, values, and traditions. To economists studying immigration, assimilation is often applied in a much more mechanical way, specifically used to describe the process whereby immigrants' incomes catch up to native incomes in the destination country. Income assimilation is hypothesized to be strongly influenced by immigrant selectivity, hence the reason for discussion of assimilation in this chapter. For example, Chiswick (1978, pp. 919–920) writes:

> That the foreign born eventually have higher earnings than the native born suggests that they may have more innate ability, are more highly motivated toward labor market success, or self-finance larger investments in post-school training. The higher earnings may therefore be a consequence of a self-selection in migration in favor of high ability, highly motivated workers, and workers with low discount rates for human capital investments.

If Chiswick is correct, earnings assimilation will be stronger and faster the more biased is the selectivity of immigrants towards immigrants with "innate ability" and "motivation."

There is actually very little theoretical work that we can draw on. Even those researchers who have articulated a theory of immigrant earnings assimilation have usually done so as a small piece in a much larger empirical study. We examine Chiswick's (1978) often-referenced empirical study here.

4.5.1 The Chiswick Study of Assimilation

In a pioneering study, Chiswick (1978) elaborated on an important point made by Ben-Porath (1967), namely that younger workers will have stronger incentives to invest in human capital than older workers. If immigrants tend to be relatively young, they will have especially strong incentives to invest in human capital, particularly right after arrival. Both Chiswick (1978) and DeFreitas (1980) argued that time spent in the destination country, particularly during the first years, yields information to the immigrant about job opportunities and the value of his/her own skills. This "informational capital" that immigrants produce for themselves permits them to sort themselves into jobs in which earnings are greatest.

Chiswick, therefore, hypothesized that immigrant earnings will be lower than native earnings at the time of arrival due to the absence of country-specific human capital. However, after arrival the immigrant begins to acquire country-specific human capital, and if immigrants acquire this capital more rapidly than similar native workers, immigrant wages will *converge* to native wages.

To test his hypothesis, Chiswick (1978) examined earnings differences between native U.S. workers and foreign-born male immigrants in the U.S. Chiswick used data from the 1970 U.S. Census, which provided detailed earnings of immigrants, broken down by the number of years the immigrants had been in the U.S. Chiswick estimated a regression model with the general structure

$$\ln W_i = \lambda X_i + \beta t_i + \varepsilon_i, \tag{4.26}$$

where W_i is the labor income, or "wage," of immigrant i, X_i is a vector of socioeconomic characteristics of the worker, t_i measures years since migration, and ε_i is the usual random error term. The coefficient β effectively measures whether there is wage convergence, or income assimilation. Chiswick's regression equation included a large number of other influences on earnings, such as education, years of work experience, and location in the U.S. so that the coefficient β would not suffer from omitted variable bias.

The estimated value of Chiswick's β implied that immigrants earned about 17% less than comparable natives at the time of arrival, but the gap narrowed by over 1% per year. The earnings of the foreign-born in the U.S. in 1970 were just 9.5% lower than natives if they had been in the country for 5 years, they were equal, on average, if they had been in the U.S. for 13 years, and they were 6.4% *greater* for immigrants in the country for 20 years. Chiswick thus concluded that immigrants' earnings overtake the earnings of natives after about 10–15 years, depending upon the country of origin.

Subsequent cross-section analyses by Carliner (1980), DeFreitas (1980), Long (1980), Borjas (1985), and Borjas and Tienda (1985) analyzed both male and female immigrants, used alternative data sets such as the 1976 *Survey of Income and Education*, and focused on specific immigrant populations, e.g. Hispanics or Asians. These studies produced similar results. Immigrants enjoyed more rapid earnings growth than native-born Americans.

4.5.2   Potential Bias in Chiswick's Results

In an immigrant country like the United States, these results were well-received. They reinforced the common myth that immigrants were harder working, more ambitious, and more able than either those that chose to remain in their native countries or the natives in the destination country. But, were Chiswick's regression model and its results accurate?

Borjas (1985) argued that Chiswick's finding of earnings convergence is only a statistical illusion. He pointed out that there is a fundamental weakness in Chiswick's approach of using census data from 1 year to calculate a rate of assimilation. Chiswick used cross-section data to estimate a dynamic process. Figures 4.2 and 4.3 illustrate this weakness.

Figure 4.3 shows the age earnings profiles for immigrants and natives, and the specific shapes of the two curves reflect the results reported by Chiswick (1978). When newly-arrived young immigrant workers enter the U.S. labor force, all other things equal, their earnings are 17% less than similar native workers. However, after 15 years, they "catch up" to the natives, after which they earn higher incomes than natives. The immigrant's age-earnings profile is steeper, supposedly the result of a self-selection process that results in immigrants having the ability and motivation to accumulate human capital more rapidly than natives.

Now, suppose that the study's data covered a period of time over which the self-selection process changed so that immigrants who arrived in different years have

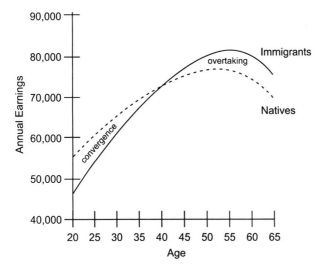

Fig. 4.3 Immigrant and native age-earnings profiles

different personal characteristics. For example, suppose Borjas is correct and immigrants who arrived in more recent years have fewer of those special traits that Chiswick hinted at. In this case, each group has a different age-earnings profile.

Figure 4.4 shows three age-earnings profiles, one each for immigrants who arrived in 1987, 1997, and 2007. Someone doing a study like Chiswick's using a cross section sample from 2007 would notice that immigrants who had been in the country for 20 years were earning more than natives, those who had come in 1997 and had been in the labor force for 10 years had income about equal to natives, and those who just arrived in 2007 were earning less than natives.

But there is no way to tell from the 2007 cross-section data whether the income differences among immigrants were due to their ability to raise their wages quickly or because the three groups of immigrants were on different age-earnings profiles, each of which is no steeper than the native age-earnings profile. The latter case is the one Borjas suggests. He would conclude that the immigrant cohort will never catch up to native workers and later immigrants to the U.S. will forever remain poorer than native Americans. Figure 4.4 illustrates this latter case; for example, notice that the 2007 cohort's age-earnings profile lies below the profile of natives no matter how many years each has been in the workforce. If that age-earnings profile represents Hispanic immigrants, then Borjas' hypothesis is correct.

4.5.3 Borjas' Empirical Results

To test his hypothesis, Borjas (1985) used 1970 and 1980 census data to estimate the degree of bias due to *cohort effects*, or differences in the cohorts. His analysis

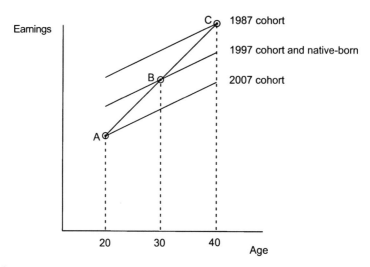

Fig. 4.4

was restricted to males ages 18–54 in 1970 and 28–64 in 1980, but he conducted the analysis separately for six major immigrant groups – Mexican, Cuban, other Hispanic, Asian, white, and black. He explicitly separated cohort effects from human capital accumulation effects, and found that within-cohort earnings growth was found to be much slower than what would be predicted by a simple cross-section study. Specifically, the cross section approach overestimated the growth rate of country-specific human capital by as much as 20%. To further support his conclusion that the cross section approach overestimates earnings convergence substantially, Borjas (1985) provided detailed data showing that the relative earnings of many immigrant cohorts experienced little change and sometimes even a slight decline between 1970 and 1980.

Borjas (1985) suggested another source of bias in estimating the slope of the path of country-specific human capital accumulation even if the omitted variable problem is addressed: *return migration*. Because the least successful immigrants are more likely to return to their native countries, the sample of remaining immigrants overstates the success of immigrants in general.

4.6   Addressing Borjas' Critique

Following Borjas' (1985) critique, the empirical literature on immigrant assimilation recognized the need to separate the cohort effects from the accumulation of country-specific human capital. It is, of course, impossible to eliminate all omitted variable bias because there are never enough data and degrees of freedom to capture all potential influences in a regression model.

Chiswick (1986) used detailed data from the U.S. Immigration and Naturalization Service, the 1970 and 1980 censuses, and the 1976 *Survey of Income and Education* to examine how immigrant skills have changed over time. He reasoned that difficult-to-quantify immigrant characteristics such as skill, work experience, and talent could be detected by comparing earnings profiles of immigrants with natives of the same racial and ethnic origin, or by comparing the profiles of immigrants relative to other immigrants. Chiswick found that unexplained earnings differences varied by country of origin, with UK and Canadian immigrants to the U.S. earning the most and those from parts of Asia, Latin America, the Caribbean region and Africa earning the least. Chiswick concluded that, overall, the data suggested little change in the unmeasured components of skill for white non-Hispanic immigrants, but he did detect a slight decline for U.S. immigrants from Mexico.

Borjas (1999b) and others estimated the regression

$$\ln W_{\ell\tau} = \beta_\tau X_{\ell\tau} + \delta_\tau I_{\ell\tau} + \varepsilon_{\ell\tau} \tag{4.27}$$

in which $W_{\ell\tau}$ is the wage of individual ℓ in the census observed in year τ ($\tau = 1960$, 1970, 1980, 1990, 2000, for example), X is a set of socioeconomic characteristics, and $\varepsilon_{\ell\tau}$ is a random error term. The variable $I_{\ell\tau}$ is a dummy set equal to one if individual ℓ is an immigrant and zero otherwise. What has typically been found from estimating (4.27) using U.S. data is that δ_τ has declined, typically going from positive in the earlier censuses (1950 and 1960, for example) to increasingly negative with more recent ones. This is taken as a confirmation that unobservable immigrant skills and human capital are lower for more recent immigrant cohorts.

The second strategy is to identify within-cohort (aging) effects. What researchers have done is to estimate (4.27) on a pooled sample that tracks cohorts over different years. The problem is, however, that the likelihood of the same person being interviewed across time periods is quite low. As Borjas (1985) pointed out, there is selective return migration and census sampling procedures have changed over time. Furthermore, there could be differences in labor supply, likelihoods of being self-employed, and rates of mortality, which will create additional cohort differences over time.

Borjas (1995) extended his 1985 study by adding the 1990 census to his analysis. He observed that the relative decline in wages across successive immigrant cohorts in the U.S. from the 1960s to the 1970s continued into the 1980s. After adjusting for changes in the wage structure between 1970 and 1990, Borjas (1995) estimated that the entry wage of immigrant cohorts arriving in the 1970s was 9 percentage points lower than in the 1960s and the entry wage of cohorts arriving in the 1980s was 6 percentage points lower than in the 1970s. He found no tendency for the earnings of immigrant cohorts from the 1980s to overtake the earnings of native-born workers. In fact, Borjas predicted that the relative wages of post-1970 immigrants would remain roughly 15–20% below those of natives over their entire working lives. Third, he predicted that Mexican and Asian immigrants who arrived in the 1980s would fail to even attain wage parity with ethnically similar natives.

Borjas and Friedberg (2007) show that over the 30 year 1960–1990 period there was a continuous decline in the relative earnings of new immigrants. More important, they found that the rate of wage convergence declined for more recent immigrant cohorts, as did the rate at which cohorts overtook even the earnings of their native counterparts from earlier migrations. Butcher and DiNardo (2002) earlier found that the decline in the mean relative wage of successive immigrant cohorts over the two decades between 1970 and 1990 was due to the increasing likelihood that new arrivals land in the very bottom of the native wage distribution. Other studies of U. S. immigration who also find that the strength of income convergence has weakened for more recent immigrants include Duleep and Regets (1997), Funkhouser and Trejo (1995), LaLonde and Topel (1992), and National Research Council (1997, Chap. 5).

Finally, Lalonde and Topel (1997) provide a more general model of immigrant assimilation and income convergence. They construct a model that addresses many of the alleged weaknesses of the Chiswick (1978) and Borjas (1987) models. Lalonde and Topel's model explicitly recognizes that the current wage earned by an immigrant from a particular arrival cohort depends upon his observable human capital characteristics, the rate of return available in the destination country for supplying those characteristics, the average level of unobservable characteristics for his cohort, current conditions in his occupation or industry, the amount of time members of his cohort have spent in the destination country, and the reward the destination country's labor market offers for supplying country-specific human capital. Lalonde and Topel emphasize, however, that assimilation can be difficult to confirm empirically because there are likely to be a multitude of other influences on relative immigrant earnings growth and existing data sets often preclude the researcher from being able to adequately control for those influences.

4.7 Conclusions

In this chapter we have surveyed the theoretical work over the last 30 years on how immigrants will differ from native-born workers. The literature can be conveniently divided into two parts – studies on *immigrant selection bias* and studies on *assimilation*. The fundamental point made in the literature on selection bias is that immigration is by nature an act of self selection. The fundamental points made in the literature on assimilation is that (i) assimilation is in part a form of human capital investment, and (ii) how well immigrants fare in the labor market *relative to natives* depends on how well they are able to invest in human capital. Empirically, the evidence suggests that immigrant selection does influence both *why* people migrate and *who* decides to migrate. However, the evidence is very tentative and of questionable accuracy.

We have already discussed the difficulties of finding data to perform statistical tests of hypotheses related to immigration. When we consider the issues brought up in this chapter, which require detailed data on the distributions of human characteristics among immigrant groups and the populations of source and destination countries, the potential for data shortcomings to bias statistical analysis becomes even more serious a problem. Perhaps we can best conclude, as we did at the end of the previous chapter, by calling for much more theoretical and empirical work. The few statistical studies we have do not use enough sources of data, enough different samples, enough different statistical models, or the most modern statistical methods for anyone to claim any degree of "robustness" in the available statistical results. Worse yet, there is not much consistency across the results from the small number of empirical studies that we do have. At best we have "suggestions." It is up to future researchers to do the empirical work to upgrade these "suggestions" to serious hypotheses.

References

Akerlof, G. (1970). The market for lemons: Quality uncertainty and the market mechanism. *Quarterly Journal of Economics, 84*, 488–500.

Barrett, A. (1993). Three essays on the labor market characteristics of immigrants. *Unpublished doctoral dissertation*. Michigan State University.

Becker, G. (1964). *Human capital: A theoretical and empirical analysis, with special reference to education*. Chicago: University of Chicago Press.

Ben-Porath, Y. (1967). The production of human capital and the life-cycle of earnings. *Journal of Political Economy, 75*(4), 352–365.

Borjas, G. (1985). Assimilation, changes in cohort quality, and the earnings of immigrants. *Journal of Labor Economics, 3*, 463–489.

Borjas, G. (1987). Self-selection and the earnings of immigrants. *American Economic Review, 77*, 531–553.

Borjas, G. (1990). Economic theory and international migration. *International Migration Review, 23*, 457–485.

Borjas, G. (1991). Immigration and self-selection. In J. Abowd, & R. Freeman, (Eds.), *Immigration, trade, and the labor market*. Chicago: University of Chicago Press.

Borjas, G. (1995). Assimilation and changes in cohort quality revisited: what happened to immigrant earnings in the 1980s. *Journal of Labor Economics, 13*, 201–245.

Borjas, G. (1999a). Immigration and welfare magnets. *Journal of Labor Economics, 17*, 607–637.

Borjas, G. (1999b). The economic analysis of immigration. In O. Ashenfelter, & D. Card, (Eds.), *Handbook of labor economics* (vol. 3A). New York: Elsevier.

Borjas, G., & Bronars, S. (1991). Immigration and the family. *Journal of Labor Economics, 9*, 123–148.

Borjas, G., & Tienda, M. (1985). *Hispanics in the U.S. economy*. New York: Academic Press.

Bratsberg, B. (1995). The incidence of non-return among foreign students in the United States. *Economics of Education Review, 14*, 373–384.

Butcher, K., & DiNardo, J. (2002). The immigrant and native-born wage distributions: evidence from United States censuses. *Industrial and Labor Relations Review, 56*, 97–121.

Carliner, G. (1980). Wages, earnings and hours of first, second, and third generation males. *Economic Inquiry, 18*, 87–101.

Chiquiar, D., & Hanson, G. (2005). International migration, self-selection, and the distribution of wages: evidence from Mexico and the United States. *Journal of Political Economy, 113*, 239–281.

Chiswick, B. (1978). The effects of Americanization on the earnings of foreign-born men. *Journal of Political Economy, 86*, 897–921.

Chiswick, B. (1979).The economic progress of immigrants: some apparently universal patterns. In F .William, (Ed.), *Contemporary economic problems*. Washington, DC: American Enterprise Institute.

Chiswick, B. (1986). Is the new immigration less skilled than the old. *Journal of Labor Economics, 4*, 168–192.

Chiswick, B. (1999). Are immigrants favorably selected? *American Economic Review, 89*, 181–185.

Cobb-Clark, D. (1993). Immigrant selectivity and wages: The evidence for women. *American Economic Review, 83*(4), 986–993.

DeFreitas, G. (1980). The earnings of immigrants in the American labor market. *Unpublished doctoral dissertation.* Columbia University, New York.

DiNardo, J., Fortin, N., & Lemieux, T. (1996). Labor market institutions and the distribution of wages, 1973–1992. *A semiparametric approach. Econometrica, 64*, 1001–1044.

Duleep, H., Regets, M. (1997). Are lower immigrant earnings at entry associated with faster growth? A review. Unpublished Paper, The Urban Institute.

Funkhouser, E., Trejo, S. (1995) The decline in immigrant labor skills: did it continue in the 1980s? *Industrial and Labor Relations Review 48*:792–811.

Heckman, J. (1979). Sample selection bias as a specification error. *Econometrica 47*:153–161.

Heckman, J. (1987). Selection bias and self-selection. In *The new Palgrave dictionary of economics, Vol. 4.* New York: Macmillan Press Ltd.

Jasso, G., Rosenzweig, M. (1990). Self-selection and the earnings of immigrants: comment. *American Economic Review 80*:305–308.

Katz, E., & Stark, S. (1987). International migration under asymmetric information. *The Economic Journal, 97*, 718–726.

Kwok, V., & Leland, H. (1982). An economic model of the brain drain. *American Economic Review, 72*, 91–100.

Lalonde, R., & Topel, R. (1997). Economic impact of international migration and the economic performance of migrants. In M .Rosenzweig, & O. Stark, (Eds.), *Handbook of population and family economics.* Amsterdam: Elsevier.

Leland, H. (1979). Quacks, lemons, and licensing: a theory of minimum quality standards. *Journal of Political Economy, 87*, 1328–1346.

Leland, H. (1980). Minimum quality standards and licensing in markets with asymmetric information. In S .Rottenberg, (Ed.), *Occupational licensure and regulation.* Washington, DC: American Enterprise Institute.

Long, J. (1980). The effect of Americanization on earnings: some evidence for women. *Journal of Political Economy, 88*, 620–629.

Mincer, J. (1974), *Schooling, experience and earnings.* Columbia University Press: New York.

Oaxaca, R. (1973). Male-female wage differentials in urban labor markets. *International Economic Review, 14*, 693–709.

Orrenius, P., & Zavodny, M. (2005). Self-selection among undocumented immigrants from Mexico. *Journal of Development Economics, 78*, 215–240.

Riley, J. (1975). Competitive signaling. *Journal of Economic Theory, 10*, 174–186.

Roy, A. (1951). Some thoughts on the distribution of earnings. *Oxford Economic Papers, 3*, 135–146.

Smith, J. P., & Edmonston, E., & National Research Council (1997). *The new Americans: Economic, demographic, and fiscal effects of immigration.* Washington, DC: National Academy Press.

Spence, A. (1973). Job market signaling. *Quarterly Journal of Economics, 87*, 355–374.

Stiglitz, J. (1975). The theory of screening, education and the distribution of income. *American Economic Review, 65*, 283–300.

Chapter 5
The Effects of Immigration on the Destination Economy: The Theory

Abstract When immigrants enter a country, they affect the destination country's economy in a variety of ways. This chapter surveys theoretical research since the 1960s on the macroeconomic and microeconomic effects of immigration on the destination country. Macro effects are measured by an "immigration surplus" that is usually positive but very small. The "micro" studies have focused on the distributional effects, and these have been substantial in magnitude. Estimates of how immigration affects natives depends on the assumptions of the model used to frame the analysis, such as the production function, number of goods produced, local immigrant consumption, native migration, and the time frame. We appraise the traditional labor market model's predictions, and then we move to more detailed models that present a more nuanced story. Finally, this chapter examines how economists have begun to model immigration from a longer-run perspective, which requires the explicit recognition of "feedback mechanisms" that supplement the initial labor market effects covered in the traditional models.

Chapter Overview

There have been few issues in economics that stir up as much controversy among politicians, business owners, and consumers as the debate on the impact of immigration on the destination country. Economists have tried to answer some of the questions that seem to concern so many people, such as:

1. Does immigration raise or lower average destination country income?
2. Which native-born people in the destination country enjoy income gains, which suffer losses, and how much are the gains and losses?
3. How does immigration affect product markets in the destination economy?
4. How do answers to the above differ for the short run vs. the long run?

The first question concerns the aggregate, or macro, effects of immigration. The second is *distributional*, or *micro*, in nature. The second question has received

Ö.B. Bodvarsson and H. Van den Berg, *The Economics of Immigration*,
DOI: 10.1007/978-3-540-77796-0_5, © Springer-Verlag Berlin Heidelberg 2009

the most attention and is at the heart of most political debates. The third question has both macro and micro implications in that immigration affects aggregate demand as well as the demand in specific market segments in the destination economy. The *demand* effect of immigration has been discussed in the business press, but it has been left largely unaddressed by the mainstream economics literature. This is a major failure of this field of economics, especially because the shifts in demand, and thus production, change people's lives and their culture. There is little doubt that much of the emotion surrounding immigration is directly related to these changes in economic and social structures that immigration is perceived to cause. Finally, the fourth question concerns the *dynamic* effects of immigration that determine the full consequences of immigration in the long run.

This chapter surveys the theoretical literature on the first three questions. The very important dynamic effects will be discussed in Chap. 9. As we compare and contrast models developed since the 1980s, it will be clear that there are still many unanswered questions. To some degree, the controversy that has engulfed political discussion also characterizes discussion among economists. This chapter will hopefully contribute to moving the debate within our profession towards accurate and useful conclusions that will, ultimately, also serve to enlighten the public debate.

5.1   The Macro Effects of Immigration

Traditional economic analysis of immigration shows that when immigrants enter the country, some native-born groups gain while others lose. Traditional economic analysis has focused on trying to determine whether the sum of the gains and losses is a positive or a negative number. To arrive at such a number, economists must set the time frame of their discussion, model the supply of native labor and other factors, and specify the economy's production function.

There will be several important themes to the discussion below. Most models conclude that some natives of the destination country *must* lose welfare for others to gain welfare. Second, macro effects depend critically on the shape of the economy's production function. We develop five specific cases to illustrate this literature.

5.1.1   Homogeneous Labor with Fixed Capital

We first use the standard model presented in the Introduction to this section of the book, in which capital is fixed and native-owned, a given quantity of immigrants moves from a source country to the destination country, and immigrant and native-born workers are perfect substitutes. Specifically, we define a production function $Q = f(L,K)$, in which Q is the quantity of output, L is the quantity of labor input, and K is the quantity of capital input. L is the sum of native-owned labor, N, and immigrant-owned labor, M. Furthermore, we assume that labor and capital are complementary, labor supply is perfectly inelastic, markets are competitive, and there are constant returns to scale in production.

If the economy's production function $Q = f(L,K)$ exhibits constant returns to scale and there is perfect competition in all markets, then (a) output changes in exact proportion to a simultaneous change in all inputs, and (b) the economy's total product is fully distributed to the owners of the factors used in production, in this case the labor force and owners of capital. That is,

$$Q = MP_L(L) + MP_K(K) \tag{5.1}$$

where MP_L and MP_K are the marginal products of labor and capital, respectively. This latter relationship, which depends critically on the assumptions of perfect competition and constant returns to scale, is known in the economics literature as *Euler's Theorem*. In terms of the price of output, the total value of the economy's output is

$$P \cdot Q = (P \cdot MP_L)L + (P \cdot MP_K)K \tag{5.2}$$

Furthermore, the assumption of profit maximization by producers implies that $w = P \cdot MP_L$ and $r = P \cdot MP_K$, and thus

$$PQ = wL + rK \tag{5.3}$$

This relationship implies that firms earn zero economic profit.

We can analyze how immigration affects national income by a simple graph of the labor market. At point B on Fig. 5.1, employment consists of N natives, each earning a wage of W_0. National income equals the area under the value of marginal

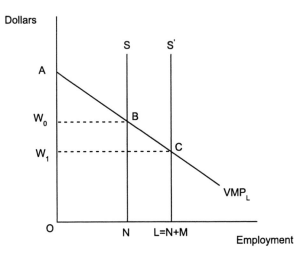

Fig. 5.1 Labor market equilibrium with immigration

product of labor (VMP$_L$) curve for N workers. While not shown, the rate of return to capital is r_0 and K_0 units of capital are used. Thus, national income = $w_0N + r_0K_0$, or area OABN.

Suppose there is an *exogenous* increase in labor supply of M immigrants ("supply-push" immigration). This assumption is in contrast to *endogenous* ("demand-pull") immigration, where an increase in destination country labor demand raises the wage, thus inducing an increase in the quantity of immigrants. The exogenous supply curve shift to the right to S' leads to a total of N + M workers being employed. Greater competition causes the wage to fall to w_1 and because the labor force is larger, more output is made and there is more consumption. National income rises to OACL. Assuming there is no output lost from absorbing immigrants, such as training immigrants or legal costs, the country's economic pie expands.

Figure 5.2 illustrates how natives are affected by immigration. Specifically, the increase in national income attributable to immigration is the sum of triangle BCD and rectangle NDCL (equivalent to $w_1 \bullet M$). The area NDCL, which is claimed by immigrants, usually accounts for most of the destination country's income gains. Natives claim area BCD, which is called the *immigration surplus*. As long as the demand curve slopes downward, there is an immigration surplus and native factor owners *as a whole* gain from immigration.

According to the traditional labor demand model of immigration, not all natives share in the immigration surplus. From Fig. 5.2, native workers do not gain welfare because they now are paid a lower wage of w_1 and their employment is assumed to remain unchanged. Native workers lose national income equaling the area of rectangle w_0w_1BD. Native *capital* owners, on the other hand, capture the area w_0w_1BD formerly earned by native workers. And native capital owners gain the surplus BCD. Therefore immigration causes native workers to lose welfare and native capital owners to gain welfare, and the gains to capitalists are greater than the

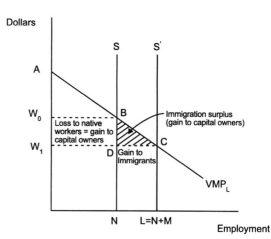

Fig. 5.2 Measuring the immigration surplus

losses suffered by workers. Immigration redistributes income from the destination country's native labor force to its capital owners.

There are three important implications of the immigration surplus. First, a surplus requires redistribution of income; some native groups lose income in order for the nation as a whole to gain. Second, natives lose if they substitute for immigrants, but not if they are owners of the complementary factor, capital. Gains from immigration and the adverse effects on substitute natives are directly related. Third, the immigration surplus results from a downward sloping demand curve. The flatter is the curve the greater is the fraction of national income gains enjoyed by immigrants. If the demand curve is perfectly elastic, there is no surplus, and all gains go to immigrants.

The surplus depends upon a number of factors. As a fraction of national income (Q), the immigration surplus can be shown to be equal to

$$\frac{Surplus}{Q} = -1/2(s \cdot e \cdot m^2) \tag{5.4}$$

where s is labor's share of national income, e is the *factor price elasticity*, and m is the share of the labor force comprising immigrants. The factor price elasticity is the percentage change in the wage relative to the percentage change in labor supply. If immigration induces a very large (small) wage decline, the elasticity is very high (low). With two inputs, the elasticity equals $(1 - s)^2\eta$, where η is the price elasticity of labor demand. If the labor demand curve is steep (flat), the factor price elasticity will be high (low) and immigration will induce a relatively large (small) loss in national income to native workers.

Hamermesh (1993) reports that e is about -0.3 in the U.S., which means that a 10 percent increase in the size of the labor force reduces the wage about 3%. A low factor price elasticity results from a high degree of substitutability between labor and capital, whereas a large elasticity results from labor-capital complementarity. If we then suppose that s is equal to 0.7 and m is equal to 0.1, the surplus is national income multiplied by 0.00105, or about 1/10th of 1% of national income. In 2006, nominal U.S. GDP was $13.195 trillion, which makes the U.S. immigration surplus $14.65 billion, or about $45 per capita. A result such as this may lead you to ask why the net welfare gains are so small. One reason is that the factor price elasticity is very small. If the wage is insensitive to changes in labor supply, then immigration won't have much effect on the wage, and capital owners stand to gain little. Another reason is that immigrants make up only a small fraction of the labor force. The biggest influence on the relative size of the immigration surplus is the factor price elasticity. If e = -0.3, then the surplus as a fraction of national income will tend to be very small.

The small immigration surplus masks huge changes in how the destination country's economic pie is distributed by immigration, however. In general, the labor income that is transferred from workers to capitalists, the area W_1W_0BD, is much larger than the surplus area BDC. For example, Borjas (1999) shows that, expressed as fractions of national income, the loss to native workers and gains to capital owners are roughly equal to

$$\frac{W_1 W_0 BD}{Q} = s \cdot e \cdot m(1 - m) \tag{5.5}$$

and

$$\frac{W_1 W_0 BD + BDC}{Q} = -s \cdot e \cdot m\left(1 - \frac{m}{2}\right) \tag{5.6}$$

Applying these formulas to 2006 U.S. data, the loss to native workers is about 1.9 percent of GDP, or \$263.66 billion, whereas the gain to capitalists is roughly 2.0% of GDP, or \$278.30 billion. The immigration surplus is the difference between these two numbers, \$14.64 billion. While the net surplus is very small, the distributional effects are substantial. This may help to explain why many labor groups object to immigration while business owners often welcome it.

5.1.2 Homogeneous Labor with Variable Capital

In the previous case, an immigration surplus arises because immigration lowers wages. That result assumed a constant supply of capital and other factors. What happens if capital supply is variable? We begin by examining the polar opposite situation of perfectly elastic supply of capital.

Suppose that capital is available both domestically and internationally and that we are looking at a very small country so that capital prices are entirely determined by the world market and the supply of capital to the small country is perfectly elastic. Assume that the production function is of the convenient Cobb-Douglas form:[1]

$$Q = AK^\alpha L^{1-\alpha} \tag{5.7}$$

When markets are competitive, the value of the marginal product (VMP) in equilibrium is the factor price and

$$w = (1 - \alpha)AK^\alpha L^{-\alpha} = (1 - \alpha)A\left(\frac{K}{L}\right)^\alpha \tag{5.8}$$

and

$$r = \alpha AK^{\alpha-1} L^{1-\alpha} = \alpha A\left(\frac{K}{L}\right)^{\alpha-1}. \tag{5.9}$$

---

[1]The Cobb-Douglas function is "convenient" because is exhibits constant returns to scale, diminishing returns to each individual factor of production, and the exponents represent the factors' shares in national output.

Note that the partial derivatives of wages and capital returns with respect to labor supply L are, respectively, $\partial w/\partial L < 0$ and $\partial r/\partial L > 0$. Therefore, by increasing L, immigration pushes down the wage w and raises the return to capital r. Under the small country assumption and the free flow of capital, the fact that immigration tends to raise r above the world level in the small country means that capital flows to the destination country. Because labor and capital are complementary, more capital boosts overall labor demand. The wage thus rises, which attenuates the initial adverse effect of immigration on native workers.

The capital stock rises until there is zero profit, i.e. the return to capital has fallen back to the world level. According to (5.9), K rises by enough to reduce r and to restore the capital/labor ratio to its pre-immigration level. According to (5.8), however, if (K/L) returns to its pre-immigration level, so must the wage. This leads to a very different implication for the effects of immigration on native workers and capitalists: When the supply of capital is perfectly elastic, immigration will not alter factor prices in the long run and the immigration surplus is zero.

Figure 5.3 illustrates the above story. Initially, supply-push immigration of M workers lowers the wage to w_1, but this stimulates the inflow of capital and leads to greater labor demand. The labor demand curve shifts from VMP_L to $VMP_L^{'}$ and the wage returns to its pre-immigration level (w_0). This example suggests that in a small country in the global economy, (a) the immigration surplus is at best only temporary, and (b) the more easily capital flows between countries, the greater are the gains to immigrants. These results depend, critically, on the "small country" assumption, however. If the immigration flows are very large and the destination country is a major player in the global capital market, the world return to capital is unlikely to remain unchanged in the face of growing capital demand from the destination country.

This example also implies that immigration has complex macroeconomic effects. For example, the inflow of 1.3 million immigrants to the U.S. in 2006, as

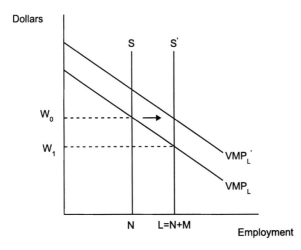

Fig. 5.3 Capital adjustments to immigration

reported by the OECD, is likely to have stimulated the inflow of foreign capital to the U.S. Economists have provided many explanations for the huge inflow of foreign capital to the U.S. over the past two decades, and the equally huge trade deficits that balance those capital inflows. Immigration has not been brought into the discussion very often. Perhaps it should be.

5.1.3   Heterogeneous Labor

The cases discussed above both assumed that natives and immigrants are identical in production. Suppose, instead, that there are just two inputs to the production function, namely two different labor inputs: skilled labor (L_S) and unskilled labor (L_U). Assume, for the time being, that skilled (unskilled) natives are perfect substitutes for skilled (unskilled) immigrants. Suppose, furthermore, that labor supply is perfectly inelastic, and that there are constant returns to scale. The production function is

$$Q = f(L_S, L_U) = f\{[bN + \beta M], [(1 - b)N + (1 - \beta)M]\}, \qquad (5.10)$$

where b and β are the shares of skilled workers among natives and immigrants, respectively.

If immigrants and natives are equally skilled, so that $\beta = b$, immigration has *no* effect on wages. However, if skill levels differ, immigration moves wages in *opposite* directions. For example, if immigrants are more skilled, immigration makes skilled labor relatively more abundant and unskilled labor less so. These changes in relative labor supply, along with complementarities in production between skilled and unskilled labor, cause the skilled wage to fall and the unskilled wage to rise. Skilled workers suffer a loss in income, but unskilled workers gain.

Borjas (1995) shows that the immigration surplus depends on the disparity in skill distributions. If this case is correct and the goal of immigration policy is to maximize the immigration surplus, then immigration should be restricted to those workers who *differ most* from natives. Since, for example, Canada's workforce is relatively skilled, Borjas' model prescribes that, all other things equal, Canadian immigration policy should restrict the admission of skilled workers. The fact that Canadian immigration policy seeks to accomplish exactly the opposite with its near open invitation to highly educated immigrants makes this model suspect. What is it missing?

5.1.4   Heterogeneous Labor with Constant Capital

Suppose next that the supply of capital is perfectly inelastic. In this case, there is a surplus even when natives and immigrants have identical skills. Borjas (1995b) shows that, in this case, the surplus depends on the fraction of the destination economy's workforce that is unskilled and the share of national income accruing to unskilled labor, provided the capital stock is brought into the analysis. The arrival of immigrants increases the labor supply, and if labor and capital are complementary, capital owners gain regardless of the skill level of immigrants. But the outcome for labor depends on the relative skill levels of immigrants and natives. For example, suppose the native workforce is primarily skilled and the immigrant labor pool is primarily unskilled. Then, immigration causes the unskilled wage to fall and the skilled wage to rise. Thus, native owners of capital and native skilled workers benefit from immigration, while native unskilled workers lose.

5.1.5 Heterogeneous Labor and Perfectly Elastic Capital Supply

We now extend the previous case to allow for capital adjustments. Assume, again, that we are analyzing a "small country," and capital's price is set exogenously on the world market. Immigration will trigger capital inflows, and the elastic supply of capital keeps wages invariant to changes in the relative supply of immigrant labor. In the case where the native workforce is primarily skilled, the surplus is largest if all admitted immigrants are unskilled. In general, immigrant skills *must* be different from native skills, on average, in order for the destination country to benefit from the admission of immigrants.

5.1.6 How Big is the U.S. Immigrant Surplus?

Most measures of the immigrant surplus have assumed theoretical models, which were then used largely for "back of the envelope" calculations. A more detailed study of immigration by the National Research Council (NCR) of the National Academy of Sciences estimated that the net benefits to the United States from immigration in the 1980 were between $1 and $10 billion per year, a miniscule fraction of total U.S. GDP.[2] A study by the RAND Corporation reaches similar conclusions: "While the effects on the least educated workers may be substantial, the economy-wide effects are small."[3]

Freeman (2006) estimates that a 10 percent increase in immigration will generate an increase in GDP of only about 0.2%. According to Freeman, native owners of capital and workers in professions that complement immigrants gain 4.2% in national income, while workers who compete directly with immigrants lose 4%.

---

[2]National Research Council Panel on the Demographic and Economic Impacts of Immigration (1997).

[3]Robert F. Schoeni (1997).

These small effects of immigration on the U.S. economy mirror the results of the many studies that have estimated the costs of immigration.[4]

Some researchers have estimated the size of the surplus through more complex computer simulations, among others Borjas (1995a), Borjas, Freeman, and Katz (1997), and Johnson (1997). While the simulations are quite sensitive to assumed parameter values, they indicate that regardless of skill distributions, the measured impact of immigration is always very small.

To summarize, native-born residents in the destination country will in aggregate benefit from immigration depending upon how responsive factor prices are to immigration, native/immigrant skill disparities, and the adjustability of capital. In practice, estimated immigration surpluses tend to be very small relative to GDP. The small immigration surplus may explain why the national debate on immigration tends to focus much more on how certain native-born groups' shares of the destination country's economic pie change as a result of immigration. These "distributional" effects have been much larger than the net effect of immigration.

5.2   Detailing the Distributional Effects of Immigration

The macro effects of immigration have really been a "sideshow" in the theory of how immigration affects the destination economy. The spotlight has been on how the gains and losses from immigration are distributed across different factor groups, with particular interest paid to how native-born workers are affected by immigration.

The traditional models have made many strong assumptions that may have biased the conclusions. A number of studies have extended the traditional model of immigration to account for other potential determinants of how immigrants cause the economic pie in the destination to be split among the various categories of native factors and immigrants.

5.2.1   The Johnson Model (1980)

Johnson (1980) extended the basic models above to the case where the immigrant and native skill distributions differ. Johnson was interested in policy implications, particularly those relating to the control of unauthorized immigration. His model focuses on the distributional effects of unauthorized immigration of low-skilled workers to a market comprising both high- and low-skill native workers. Johnson's model explains the impact each additional immigrant has on the wage and employment of native low-skill and high-skill workers, the returns accruing to native capital owners, and the level and distribution of national income.

---

[4] See the survey of this evidence by Friedberg and Hunt (1995).

Johnson's model suggests that different native-born groups in the destination country will be affected differently by immigration. High-skill workers and owners of capital are likely to be complementary to low-skill immigration, and they are, therefore, likely to gain from immigration. However, low-skilled immigration may have certain fiscal effects that could harm high-skill workers and owners of capital. Specifically, if immigration results in unemployment of low-skill native workers, greater unemployment compensation must be paid. When the tax system is progressive, high-skill workers and capitalists (who typically have higher incomes) may bear the tax burden imposed by higher unemployment compensation.

Interestingly, Johnson speculates that a higher wage gap between low- and high-skill workers and the relative increase in the returns to high-skill occupations may encourage a larger share of the population to invest in higher levels of education and training. Johnson suggests that the skill distribution may be *endogenous* to immigration, not unlike the capital inflows to immigrant-intensive industries discussed earlier.

5.2.2   The Altonji and Card Model (1991)

Altonji and Card (1991) extended Johnson's analysis to include two additional features of the labor market: (1) skill diversity within the immigrant pool; and (2) the endogeneity of local demand to immigration. In contrast to Johnson's model, which is of a national economy, Altonji and Card's model is of a city economy. Immigrants can be skilled or unskilled in their model, but natives and immigrants are perfect substitutes within each skill category.

By making product demand endogenous to immigration, Altonji and Card allow for immigrants to buy at least part of their own output, which attenuates any adverse wage and employment effects of immigration. They point out that this feedback effect of immigration on wages through local demand is important because many goods produced locally are non-tradeable, that is, because transport costs and trade barriers prevent perfect product arbitrage between countries, the location of workers affects the location of product demand. "The observation that the demand for labor with a local economy arises in part from the demand for location-specific goods and services implies that a partial equilibrium model of the labor market is potentially misleading"[5] This recognition of the product market effects of immigration foreshadows more recent work, discussed below.

The Altonji and Card model hypothesizes that the effects of immigration on the outcomes of unskilled natives depend upon the skill distributions of the local population and pool of new immigrants, the production function, the output demand and labor supply functions, and the fraction of the locally produced good that is consumed locally. In addition, the model includes skill diversity within the

---

[5] Altonji and Card (1991, p. 203).

immigrant pool and characteristics of product demand as other influences. Immigration shifts the labor supply and consumer demand curves, creating wage and employment changes for both skill groups. As in Johnson (1980), the wage and employment effects of immigration depend upon labor demand and supply elasticities and skill shares.

The Altonji and Card model yields three important insights. First, immigration need not always have adverse effects on natives. For example, if skill distributions are identical and all local output is consumed locally, then immigration leaves wages of unskilled natives unchanged. For immigration to affect wages, skill distributions must differ and at least some of the locally consumed products must be imported and locally produced goods must be exported. In general, the adverse wage and employment effects experienced by natives are reduced the larger is the fraction of locally produced goods that are consumed locally.

There are three limitations to the Altonji and Card model. First, it does not allow for internal migration as a response by natives. While the model allows for a reduction in per capita labor supply when the wage falls, it assumes the total native population remains unchanged. It is likely, however, that when the unskilled wage falls, unskilled natives will leave. Such out-migration tends to reduce the adverse wage effect of immigration. Finally, the local labor market is assumed to always clear. However, in the market for unskilled labor there could be obstacles to market clearing, e.g. minimum wages, fixed welfare benefits, or unionization. These constraints are likely to dampen wage effects and accentuate employment effects.

5.2.3   The Ottaviano and Peri Model

Ottaviano and Peri (2005, 2006, 2008) demonstrate that the specific form of the production function can greatly influence the predicted distributional effects. First, they argue that immigrants and natives will not be perfect substitutes. Even within the same occupation or at the same levels of education or experience, the human capital endowment of a native differs from an immigrant's because of source/destination country differences in education, language, culture, and family environment. They write: "... Chinese and American cooks do not produce similar meals, nor do Italian and American tailors provide identical types of clothes."[6] Ottaviano and Peri's model treats natives and immigrants as distinct inputs both across and within skill levels. Second, Ottaviano and Peri point out that when a country experiences immigration, labor supplies in many different occupations will increase. It is thus important to recognize interrelationships in production across different skill levels.

Ottaviano and Peri follow an approach used earlier by Borjas (2003), which defines a labor market as a national market for workers comprising a *skill cell*.

---

[6]Ottaviano and Peri (2005, p. 13).

A skill cell is defined to include workers with k years of education and j years of experience. Within a cell, natives (immigrants) are perfect substitutes for other natives (immigrants), but natives are imperfectly substitutable for immigrants. Across cells, workers will be complements if they have different levels of education, but substitutes if they have the same level of education. In Ottaviano and Peri's study, there are precisely 32 different skill cells –4 educational categories ×8 experience categories. The four educational categories include (1) incomplete secondary education, (2) secondary school graduates, (3) some post-secondary education, and (4) university graduates. Workers within each education category are grouped into eight different experience intervals of 5 years between 0 and 40. Within each cell, there are two inputs – natives and immigrants – making for a total of 64 different labor inputs.

Previous literature mostly assumes a fixed capital stock and treats immigration as an unexpected and instantaneous shock. In reality, immigration is an ongoing and anticipated process and capital adjusts continually to actual and anticipated flows of new immigrants. Ramsey (1928) and Solow (1956) show that when there is international capital mobility and/or domestic capital accumulation, a flexible market economy will operate on its *balanced growth path* in the long run. When an economy is on its balanced growth path, the capital-labor ratio rises at a constant rate equaling the growth rate in technology. We saw earlier that when the supply of capital is perfectly elastic, factor prices in the long run are invariant to immigration. This is because the economy is operating on its balanced growth path. Ottaviano and Peri's model permits immigration shocks to cause the capital-labor ratio to fall below its long run trend and for the average wage to fall. This stimulates growth in the capital stock, boosts labor productivity, and, in the long run, restores the pre-immigration wage.

Ottaviano and Peri point out that most of the immigration literature tends to focus only on the short run effects within one labor market or, in their terms, skill cell. The literature has assumed that workers in other cells are not impacted, i.e. there are no interrelationships in production across cells. Furthermore, previous studies have customarily assumed that natives and immigrants within a skill category are perfect substitutes. If workers across cells are interrelated in production and if there are capital adjustments, then there are additional effects on wages. These effects include:

1. *Temporary effects on the capital-labor ratio*

Initially, the capital-labor ratio falls, which reduces labor productivity and the wage. As the ratio returns to its balanced growth path, however, productivity and the wage return to their pre-immigration levels.

2. *Positive feedback effects on workers in different education cells.*

It is presumed that workers with different levels of education are complementary to the workers comprising the cell experiencing immigration. Immigration to one cell boosts the productivities of workers in the other cells, which in turn boosts the productivity of workers in the first cell. This effect is bigger the less substitutable workers are across different educational categories.

3. *Negative feedback effects on workers that have the same education, but different experience.*

While workers within a cell are substitutes for one another, workers in other cells are substitutes as well, but the substitutability is lower. Immigration thus lowers the productivities of workers in the other cells, which then feeds back negatively on the productivities of native-born workers in the first cell.

Ottaviani and Peri also point out that when a country experiences immigration, over time the new immigrants begin flowing into many different skill cells. The strength of this effect depends upon how substitutable workers are across educational categories, as well as the pre-immigration size of the labor force. Also important are the effects generated by short- and long-term changes in the capital-labor ratio that occur in response to an increase in the labor force.

5.3   Long-Run Adjustment Processes

Exogenous immigration shocks lead to both short- and long-term distributional effects on the destination economy. The long-term effects differ from the short-term effects because economies adjust to immigration shocks in many ways. Wage and employment changes trigger many other changes throughout the economy, some right away, others in later periods. Above, Johnson (1980) and Ottaviano and Peri (2005, 2006, 2008) discussed the adjustment of capital stocks, and Altonji and Card (1991) discussed local consumer demand. There are other adjustment processes that may occur. One of the most-often noted adjustments is that native workers react to the wage and employment changes induced by the arrival of immigrants and migrate out of the region where the immigrants settle.

5.3.1   Internal Migration Responses

Borjas (2006) presents a model of the regional wage structure that explicitly includes native migration responses to immigration. Borjas' model shows how internal migration spreads the wage impact of immigration from the local labor markets to the national labor markets.

Borjas assumes that even in the absence of immigration there could be excess supply or demand of native workers in each region during any period, and there will generally be migration responses of native workers to imbalances across regional labor markets. He then introduces a permanent exogenous influx of immigrants each period, where each region receives the same number of immigrants. Immigrants are assumed not to migrate internally. As a result, natives continue to make relocation decisions, but now they have two reasons for relocation: (1) relocation occurs in response to regional wage differences that would occur in the absence of immigration; and (2) relocation results from immigration-induced wage disparities. Borjas' model assumes that relocation induced by immigration occurs with a one-period lag. Wages respond immediately, but there is a lagged labor supply response because internal migration is a longer run response to immigration. Not surprisingly given Borjas' assumption of rational forward-looking native workers, the national wage prevails after all internal migration responses have occurred. The model concludes that over time, internal migration neutralizes the effects of the immigration shock on the regional wage structure.

5.3.2   Multiple Goods

Card (2005), Dustmann, Fabbri, and Preston (2005), Dustmann and Glitz (2005), and Gaston and Nelson (2000) argue that if an immigration shock alters the skill distribution, a one-good economy can only react to the shock through a change in its wage structure. When there are multiple goods, however, the economy will also adjust the mix of products it produces.

For example, consider a *small* (price-taking) open economy with two labor markets – skilled and unskilled – and two goods whose prices are set at world levels. Holding the goods ratio fixed, immigration of unskilled workers will in the short run drive down (up) the relative unskilled (skilled) wage. Since unskilled-intensive sector profits are higher, that sector will expand, pushing up the demand for unskilled labor and its wage. If immigration is not too large, wages will return to their old levels, and immigration affects only the *output mix*. The economy reacts to the increase in the supply of labor from immigration by expanding the sector that uses immigrants more intensively. This effect is known as the Rybzcynski Theorem in international trade theory, and this theorem is derived from the standard Heckscher-Ohlin model of international trade.

The Rybczynski theorem states that, in a neoclassical world of perfect competition, free international trade, two products, and two factors, the increase in one factor of production in a small country, all other things equal, causes that country to increase production of the good that uses that factor relatively intensively and decrease production of the other product. The result that for a small country the factor prices remain unchanged after the open economy adjusts its product mix is stated by Leamer and Levinsohn (1995) as the *hypothesis of factor price insensitivity*.

A formal derivation of this result is provided by Dustmann, Fabbri, and Preston (2005). Their model is a blend of a traditional labor market model and the Heckscher-Ohlin trade model. Accordingly, they assume two factors in the form of two types of labor – skilled and unskilled. Also, like the simple Heckscher-Ohlin model of trade, they assume two traded goods. Furthermore, natives and foreigners are perfect substitutes in each skill class, there is no joint production, production in each sector operates under a different production function that exhibits constant returns to scale, and markets are fully competitive. Under their small country assumption, the return to capital r is determined in the world market. Dustmann, Fabbri, and Preston show that the effects of immigration on native-born outcomes differ dramatically depending on whether we use a traditional labor market model of distributional effects with a single-sector with two inputs, or we follow international trade economists and specify a model with multiple sectors and inputs. In effect, for a small country, immigration induces shifts in production that have the same effect as the inflow of capital; only this time the wage effects of immigration are muted by a shift to producing immigrant labor-intensive products.

5.3.3 Choice of Technology

There is another possible long-term response by firms. Acemoglu (1998) argues that even in the absence of relative wage changes, firms may adopt technologies that emphasize more the factor whose relative supply has increased. Suppose there is unskilled immigration. Then, firms may substitute technologies that require more intensive use of unskilled labor, which are likely to be less advanced. Lewis (2004) argued for example, that the 1980 "Mariel Boatlift" of some 125,000 relatively low-skilled Cubans to Miami induced local employers to adopt more unskilled-intensive technologies. Lewis (2005) also argued that during 1988–1993, manufacturers in cities where low-skill labor supply grew faster adopted automation technologies at slower rates. He observed cases where employers actually abandoned more capital-intensive technologies. If technology is endogenous to factor endowments, immigration is likely to trigger changes in choice of technology.

5.3.4 The Demand Effect of Immigration

The labor market model is not a good model of the overall effects of immigration because it makes the convenient "all other things equal" assumption in order to focus attention on the direct effects on wages or employment of the sudden arrival of immigrants. All other things *do not* remain the same when immigrants arrive in the destination economy, as suggested in the previous section where immigration-induced shifts in native workers, capital investment, and production were analyzed. The next section details another effect of immigration not captured by the traditional labor market model of immigration: When immigrants arrive, they become consumers as well as workers. That is, immigration shifts product demand in the destination country.

5.4 The Demand Effect of Immigration

Most models suppress the goods market by assuming either a "small" open economy where prices are set at world levels, or a closed economy with fixed prices. Prices are fixed either because immigration is very small or because product prices are simply not the focus of analysis. In general, however, immigration will trigger shifts in both the demand and supply curves for output. Immigrants are not only workers, they are consumers too. If immigrants spend at least part of their earnings locally, their consumption activities will stimulate the derived demand for labor. This link between goods supply and immigration is virtually untouched in the literature.

Also, if immigration boosts product supply, native consumers may benefit. Furthermore, if immigration cuts labor costs, product supply will rise and prices will fall. Thus, accurate measurement of distributional effects requires an analysis of product market reactions. The next sub-section details recent studies on the potentially substantial demand effects of immigration.

5.4.1 Say's Law of Immigration

New immigrants spend their income on housing, food, and many other goods and services produced in the economy. New immigrants buy food, transportation, lodging, and other goods and services before they find a job. Thus, the demand for labor may rise even *before* the supply of labor does![7]

Immigrants thus cause the value of the marginal product (VMP) of labor curve to shift up when they take up residence in a country.[8] This rise in income will cause the demand curve for labor, the VMP curve in Fig. 5.4, to rise. In Fig. 5.4, the wage does not fall from A to B, as the static model of labor suggests. Rather, it is likely to fall to a lesser degree, say to C because immigrants cause the demand for labor to increase along with the supply of labor.

Technically, the demand effect of immigration requires that international trade is not complete in the sense that goods and services can be traded across borders without any cost or impediments of any sort. If trade is complete, then immigrants would already have been spending a portion of their income in the destination country prior to their arrival, and they would continue to spend the same portion of their total income in the destination country. Immigrants' higher income after migrating to the higher wage country would lead to an increase in demand world-wide, only a small fraction of which would show up in the destination country. The world is not anywhere close to complete trade, of course. The fact that immigrants respond to large wage differences across countries suggests that products do not move freely enough to equate prices of factors, as true free trade under competitive

---

[7]This point is made by Simon (1989).

[8]This diagram was first presented in Van den Berg (2004).

Fig. 5.4 Immigration and
Demand for Labor

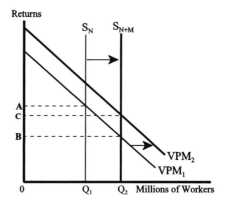

conditions would do, and, therefore, the assumption that not all goods are tradeable is appropriate. In reality, there are transport costs, marketing expenses, trade barriers, distributional rigidities, and many other factors that cause a home bias in consumption. When not everything can be transported across borders, then it matters where consumers are located. Thus, the movement of people shifts demand from one economy to another. Therefore, immigrants will spend a substantial portion of their income in the destination country, and this raises the derived demand for the labor services they supply. This suggests an extension of *Say's Law*: Immigrant labor supply creates its own demand.

5.4.2 Regional Migration and Local Demand

The effect of immigration on demand has attracted the attention of several regional economists. In three expository surveys of the regional economics literature, Greenwood and Hunt (1984), Greenwood and McDowell (1986), and Greenwood (1994) all discuss demand responses to migration. Greenwood and McDowell (1995) argue that demand is one of five channels through which migration can affect the employment and wages of native residents in the destination region or country. They note that greater immigrant labor supply can increase or decrease local aggregate labor income depending upon whether immigrants and natives are substitutes or complements and the specific factor price elasticities of demand. Furthermore, Greenwood and Hunt suggest that the extent to which immigration stimulates local demand depends upon the per capita wealth, non-labor income, and capital holdings of immigrants. They sketch a general equilibrium model in which immigration influences demand, but the model is not used to generate predictions about how the demand-augmenting effects of immigration influence native labor market outcomes.

5.4.3   A Few Models of Immigrant Demand Effects

Mishan and Needleman (1966, 1968) first suggested a link between demand and immigration. They argued that immigration can create excess aggregate demand and will influence the balance of payments. However, they did not consider how immigrant consumption can influence the labor market. It was Harrison (1983) who explicitly sketched a labor market model where immigrant consumption influences native wages and unemployment.[9] He argued that (1) immigrant employment will lag consumption and initially contribute to consumption independently of employment, and (2) the effects of immigration on native labor market outcomes will depend on immigrants' relative propensities to consume and find work. According to Harrison's model, for immigration to cut native unemployment, immigrant propensity to consume and the native job-getting success rate must both be large.

Harrison concludes that there will be conflicting effects on native unemployment. On the one hand, native unemployment tends to increase because immigrants displace natives and native consumption falls. On the other hand, native unemployment will tend to fall because immigrants spend locally. Immigrants cause native unemployment to increase if, overall, natives have a higher propensity to consume and are less efficient at finding work. On the other hand, native unemployment falls if immigrants spend more of their income than natives do.

Hercowitz and Yashiv (2002) build on Harrison's (1983) point that immigrant labor market participation lags consumption, calling it "differential entry" into the labor and goods markets. Their model also includes product supply effects of immigration. Hercowitz and Yashiv's model was inspired by the mass migration of Jewish Russian immigrants to Israel after the collapse of the Soviet Union, mostly during the early 1990s. The model features an open one-good economy produced with three inputs – labor L, imported capital M, and an unadjustable input M_0 – using constant returns to scale technology.

The key feature of Hercowitz and Yashiv's model is their incorporation of the goods market, and they are the first to derive a closed form, general equilibrium, solution for output price that links exogenous immigration to product prices. Product supply is a function of native population, immigrant labor and the relative price of domestic goods to imports. The higher immigrant labor supply increases the price of domestic goods because immigrants stimulate demand. At the same time, immigrants are substitutes for native workers, which lower production costs and domestic prices. Hence, the full effect of an immigrant shock on price is the result of two opposing price effects. Which effect dominates depends upon wage and price elasticities, labor and capital output shares, and the extent to which immigrants participate in the goods market relative to the labor market. For example, if immigrants delay getting jobs but participate strongly in the goods market right after arrival, the first effect will dominate and the relative price of

---

[9]Harrison's model was analyzed later in Simon (1989, pp. 226–28).

domestic goods will rise, which reduces the negative effect of immigration on native wages.

5.4.4 Bodvarsson and Van den Berg's Lexington Model

Bodvarsson and Van den Berg (2006) and Bodvarsson, Van den Berg, and Lewer (2008) explicitly model the local demand effects of immigration. They point out that immigration's demand effect is determined by several factors, such as the relationship between natives and immigrants in production, immigrant remittance rates, wage elasticities, and whether there is demand-pull or supply-push immigration. Bodvarsson and Van den Berg (2006) consider the case where immigrants work exclusively in an export industry, but spend some portion of their earnings on locally-produced goods and services. This is a special case based on the experience of a small rural city, Lexington, Nebraska, in the U.S. It is, however, a realistic case, one that has been repeated in many high-income countries where immigrants have come to dominate the labor forces of manufacturing plants recently moved from major urban areas to small rural cities. These plants often appear to "revive" the economies of these cities, which often struggle to maintain their populations with the mechanization of agriculture and the increasing concentration of populations in larger urban regions.

In their model, Bodvarsson and Van den Berg assume there are two labor markets – export and retail. The export labor market employs both natives and immigrants, who are perfect substitutes. The export good's price is set on the world market, out-migration is allowed to occur, and immigrants remit some earnings back to their native countries. In the retail market, only natives are employed, out-migration can occur, and price is endogenous. Retail workers spend all their earnings on the retail good. The analysis focuses on how immigration affects the retail labor market.

An important feature of Bodvarsson and Van den Berg's model is that retail consumer demand depends largely on labor earnings in the export sector. The model is used to derive two general equilibrium expressions, one for the retail product price, the other for the general equilibrium retail wage. Bodvarsson and Van den Berg use both expressions above to analyze the demand effects of immigration.

The model predicts that, if immigration is the result of an increase in demand for the export industry's products in the world market, there will be demand-pull immigration and retail wages and employment will definitely rise. The reason is that since immigration would be driven by higher export industry wages, immigration will always increase local retail demand and all workers in both sectors experience wage increases. On the other hand, if immigration is of the supply-push type, driven by conditions overseas and, therefore, exogenous to the local community, immigration depresses the export wage and results in some out-migration. Hence, the number of consumers could rise, fall or stay the same. Also, because export wages fall with the increase in labor supply, each consumer has less to spend.

The effect on the local retail sector, therefore, is ambiguous. Bodvarsson and Van den Berg find that, according to their model, retail wages and employment rise only if export labor demand is sufficiently wage elastic, the export wage elasticity of supply is relatively low, and the immigrant inflow is relatively large.

5.4.5   The More General Case

While Bodvarsson and Van den Berg (2006) examine a realistic case to prove there are demand effects of immigration, the case is not general. Therefore, Bodvarsson, Van den Berg, and Lewer (2008), henceforth referred to as BVL, develop a model for the more general case where immigrants and natives are imperfectly substitutable and work in the same market where they consume.

BVL find that exogenous immigration will induce four effects on local prices, which they take as the indicator of changes in local demand. The first three – out-migration, a drop in native earnings, and a drop in immigrant's earnings – always cause the product price to fall. The fourth effect – more consumers – always boosts price. The net effect of immigration on product prices will be positive if the stimulus to consumer demand from more consumers dominates the depressing effects on demand due to out-migration and the drop in earnings.

Through the influence on product prices, BVL's model predicts that, in general, immigration also has an ambiguous effect on wages. Specifically, BVL's model can be solved to derive two separate effects on the wage: (i) an *input substitution effect* and (ii) a *consumer demand effect*. The former effect results in a lower native wage because immigrants are substituted for natives. The latter effect could raise or lower the native wage depending upon whether immigration raises or lowers total local consumer demand. The marginal effect of immigration on the native wage is the *sum* of the input substitution and consumer demand effects. If a positive consumer demand effect dominates, the wage can rise. However, for the demand effect to dominate, there must be a relatively large immigration shock, little out-migration, and certain assumptions about the various elasticities must be satisfied. For example, if a city experiences an extraordinary inflow of immigrants who send few earnings home, labor supply elasticities are low, and demand elasticities are high, then the inflow of immigrants is likely to result in higher product prices and wages. BVL's model suggests that, in any case, immigrants have a substantial demand effect, and this demand effect helps to explain the mild effect immigration is so often found to have on wages in the destination country.

5.4.6   Further Models of Immigrant Demand Effects

Lach (2007) argues that exogenous immigration affects the composition of demand. He studies mass migration of Russian Jews to Israel during the 1990s after the fall of the Soviet Union. Lach models immigration as inducing a *size effect* and a *composition effect* on consumer demand and prices. According to the size effect, as immigrants flow into an area, assuming there is little or no out-migration, prices rise because there are more consumers. With the composition effect, if immigrants' socioeconomic characteristics (tastes, incomes, job search effort, etc.) differ from those of natives, then the price elasticity of demand can change. If immigration flattens the demand curve, prices will fall, whereas a steepening of the curve raises prices. Thus, the composition effect could either reinforce or offset the size effect.

Several researchers have considered the effects of immigration on the housing market. This research is important for several reasons. First, all immigrants need housing, and housing typically comprises a very substantial share of a household's consumption expenditures. Consequently, immigration is expected to exert significant effects on the area's housing market. Second, immigration-induced changes in area housing prices are expected to influence area labor market outcomes. Since real wages depend a lot on housing costs, immigration could lower real wages. Higher housing prices lower employment if labor supply falls due to out-migration responses. Third, if low housing costs and high housing quality are an amenity that is highly valued, immigration could induce out-migration (or deter future immigration) if it reduces the value of that amenity. Finally, the housing industry often employs immigrants, who would be expected to also consume the good they help produce. Thus, immigration to the industry will influence demand and supply in both the retail housing and housing labor markets.

Saiz (2003) analyzed the effects of unskilled immigration to a city on local rental prices and wages. The setting is the rental market in Miami following the Mariel Boatlift. Saiz assumes that a continuum of housing quality is available to all workers. Skilled workers earn more and they are willing to pay more than unskilled workers for a dwelling of the same quality. The unskilled wage varies inversely with the number of unskilled workers, but the skilled wage is fixed. Saiz shows that with skilled/unskilled differences in rental demand, the rental market will be segmented in the pre-immigration spatial equilibrium, with skilled workers residing in the relatively higher quality housing. Segmentation creates a "cutoff quality level" that separates skilled renters from unskilled ones. At this level, the unskilled bid the same as the skilled, but below the cutoff quality level skilled workers' bids are below unskilled workers' bids and above the cutoff quality level, skilled workers bids are higher than the unkilled workers' bids.

Suppose there is unskilled immigration, and unskilled immigrant demand is the same as unskilled native demand. Then, the relative demand for lower-quality housing rises. Saiz argues that there will be three effects. First, in the short run, the unskilled experience greater rent hikes than the skilled. This is because, if the range of qualities occupied by unskilled renters is small, prices must rise significantly to induce an increase in supply. Second, unskilled renters displace skilled renters from dwellings popular with the unskilled, but at the lower end for the skilled. In other words, the immigration shock raises the "quality cutoff level" of housing. Since large price increases are needed to induce an increase in the supply of lower quality housing, those same increases would be expected to induce skilled renters to search for more upscale housing. Third, if an immigration shock spikes prices of low quality housing in the short run, the resulting drop in the real unskilled wage induces out-migration of unskilled natives and, all other things equal, increases the nominal unskilled wage. If moving costs are negligible, the nominal wage should return to pre-immigration levels, as out-migration will continue until the marginal unskilled person is indifferent between any two locations. Consequently, the nominal and real unskilled wages should be invariant to immigration in the long run and most of the short-run impact of immigration on unskilled persons is felt through higher housing prices.

Saiz (2003) does not formally derive his third effect from his model, however, a shortcoming he corrects in Saiz (2007). In the latter paper, Saiz formally derives the rental price and uses it to analyze the effect of unexpected immigration on price in both the short and long runs. His model shows that the long run response of the market includes supply adjustments and out-migration, which cause the impact of the immigration shock on rental prices to be less than in the short run.

5.5 Concluding Remarks

Theoretical models of the distributional effects of immigration in the destination country have moved beyond the traditional labor market model, but many areas have not yet been investigated. One reason for the gap in economists' research on immigration's effects on destination countries is the long-standing split between labor economists and international trade economists on how to model distributional effects. Trade economists traditionally build multi-sector models of an open economy, focusing their analyses on longer term effects. In contrast, labor economists traditionally build single-sector models of a closed economy and focus their analyses on short term effects. Labor economists tend to focus on how the production, labor demand, and labor supply functions influence short run distributional effects. In contrast, trade economists focus on the long run features of post-immigration equilibrium.

Because of these distinct approaches, there are two big missing pieces to the theoretical puzzle. The first missing piece is a general equilibrium model that differentiates between short and long run adjustments to immigration and takes account of the product market effects of immigration for open versus closed economies, as well as for economies with single versus multiple goods sectors. For example, there is no model that examines the long run effects of immigration when the destination economy experiences a complete set of secondary adjustments – capital responses, internal migration, changes in output mix, and technological and product market responses. We will return to the long-run consequences of immigration in Chap. 9, where we specifically address the effect of immigration on long-run economic growth.

The reason that it is so important for theoretical work in this area to continue is because, as we will see in the next two chapters, there remain large discrepancies between what theoretical models predict and what the data tell us regarding the wage and employment responses of native-born workers to immigration shocks. While it is tempting to dismiss these discrepancies as being due to data and econometric problems, theory also has a very important role to play in their resolution. If theory does not distinguish reasonable hypotheses, empirical work cannot ask the right questions or be confident in the answers.

We conclude this chapter by noting that economic theory has probably not induced enough reasonable hypotheses yet. Why has it taken so long to inspire models that look at the product demand effects of immigration when the field of macroeconomics has for decades linked employment to product demand? Seemingly trapped within the culture of labor economics, the economic theory of immigration has focused predominantly on the labor market effects, specifically, how immigration affects the wages of native-born workers. Policymakers, most likely, are more directly interested in what immigration means for tax revenue, government expenditures, school-age populations, and crime rates. Native workers want to know whether immigrants will actually take their jobs, and homeowners want to know how immigration will change housing values. Native residents also seem to be very concerned about how immigrants will change their culture and their communities. These latter issues go well beyond economics, of course, but economics can still say a lot about how economic forces will shape social change. The economics of immigration needs to address these issues.

In the next two chapters, we detail the empirical evidence on immigration's economic effects on the destination economy. Some of this empirical evidence was inspired by the models in this chapter. Some of the evidence was motivated by policymakers and social scientists seeking answers to broader questions about immigration.

References

Acemoglu, D. (1998). Why do new technologies complement skills? Directed technical change and wage inequality. *Quarterly Journal of Economics, 114*, 1055–1089.

Altonji, J., & Card, D. (1991). The effects of immigration on the labor market outcomes of less-skilled natives. In J. Abowd, & R. Freeman (Eds.), *Immigration, trade and the labor market*. Chicago: University of Chicago Press.

Bodvarsson, Ö., & Van den Berg, H. (2006). Does immigration affect labor demand? Model and test. In S. Polachek, C. Chiswick, & H. Rapoport (Eds.), *Research in labor economics* (vol. 24). New York: Elsevier.

Bodvarsson, Ö., Van den Berg, H., & Lewer, J. (2008). Measuring immigration's effects on labor demand: A reexamination of the Mariel Boatlift. *Labour Economics, 15*(4), 560–574.

Borjas, G. (1995a). Assimilation and changes in cohort quality revisited: What happened to immigrant earnings in the 1980s. *Journal of Labor Economics, 13*, 201–245.

Borjas, G. (1995b). The economic benefits from immigration. *Journal of Economic Perspectives, 9*, 3–22.

Borjas, G. (1999). The economic analysis of immigration. In O. Ashenfelter, & D. Card (Eds.), *Handbook of labor economics* (vol. 3A). Amsterdam: Elsevier.

Borjas, G. (2003). The labor demand curve is downward sloping: Reexamining the impact of immigration on the labor market. *Quarterly Journal of Economics*, *118*, 1335–1374.

Borjas, G. (2006). Native internal migration and the labor market impact of immigration. *Journal of Human Resources*, *41*, 221–258.

Borjas, G., Freeman, R., & Katz, L. (1997). How much do immgration and trade affect labor market outcomes? *Brookings Papers on Economic Activity*, *1*, 1–67.

Card, D. (2005). Is the new immigration really so bad. *Economic Journal*, *114*, F300–F323.

Dustmann, C., Fabbri, F., & Preston, I. (2005). The impact of immigration on the British labour market. *Economic Journal*, *115*, F324–F341.

Dustmann, C., & Glitz, A. (2005). Immigration, jobs and wages: theory, evidence and opinion. London: Centre for Research and Analysis of Migration.

Freeman, R. (2006). People flows in globalization. *Journal of Economic Perspectives*, *20*, 145–170.

Gaston, N., & Nelson, D. (2000). Immigration and labour-market outcomes in the United States: A political economy puzzle. *Oxford Review of Economic Policy*, *16*, 104–114.

Greenwood, M. (1994). Potential channels of immigrant influence on the economy of the receiving country. *Papers in Regional Science*, *73*, 211–240.

Greenwood, M., & Hunt, G. (1984). Migration and interregional employment redistribution in the United States. *American Economic Review*, *74*, 957–969.

Greenwood, M., & McDowell, J. (1986). The factor market consequences of U.S. *immigration. Journal of Economic Literature*, *24*, 1738–1772.

Greenwood, M., & McDowell, J. (1995). Economic effects of immigrants on native and foreign-born workers: Complementarity, substitutability, and other channels of influence. *Southern Economic Journal*, *61*, 1076–1097.

Hamermesh, D. (1993). *Labor demand*. Princeton, NJ: Princeton University Press.

Harrison, D. (1983). *The impact of recent immigration on the South Australian labor market.* Unpublished report to Committee for the Economic Development of Australia.

Hercowitz, Z., & Yashiv, E. (2002). A macroeconomic experiment in mass immigration. IZA Discussion Paper No. 475.

Johnson, G. (1980). The labor market effects of immigration. *Industrial and Labor Relations Review*, *33*, 331–341.

Johnson, G. (1997). Estimation of the impact of immigration on the distribution of income among minorities and others. Unpublished paper, University of Michigan.

Lach, S. (2007). Immigration and prices. *Journal of Political Economy*, *115*, 548–587.

Leamer, E., & Levinsohn, J. (1995) International trade theory: The evidence. In G. Grossman, & K.Rogoff (Eds.), *Handbook of international economics* (vol. III). New York: Elsevier.

Lewis, E. (2004). How did the Miami labor market absorb the Mariel immigrants? Federal Reserve Bank of Philadelphia Working Paper No. 04–3.

Lewis, E. (2005). Immigration, skill mix, and the choice of technique. Federal Reserve Bank of Philadelphia Working Paper 05–8.

Mishan, E., & Needleman, L. (1966). Immigration, excess aggregate demand and the balance of payments. *Economica*, *33*, 129–147.

Mishan, E. & Needleman, L. (1968). Immigration: some long term consequences. *Economica Internazionale*, *21*, 281–300

National Research Council Panel on the Demographic and Economic Impacts of Immigration (1997). Report, In J. P. Smith, & B. Edmonston (Eds.), *The New Americans: Economic, Demographic, and Fiscal Effects of Immigration*. Washington, D.C.: National Academy Press.

Ottaviano, G., & Peri, G. (2005). Rethinking the gains from immigration: Theory and evidence from the U.S. NBER Working Paper No. 11672.

Ottaviano, G., & Peri, G. (2006). *Rethinking the effects of immigration on wages*. NBER Working Paper No. 12497.

Ottaviano, G., & Peri, G. (2008). *Immigration and national wages: Clarifying the theory and the empirics*. NBER Working Paper No. 14188.

Ramsey, F. (1928). A mathematical theory of saving. *Economic Jounral*, *38*, 543–559.

Saiz, A. (2003). Room in the kitchen for the melting pot: Immigration and rental prices. *Review of Economics and Statistics, 85*, 502–521.

Saiz, A. (2007). Immigration and housing rents in American cities. *Journal of Urban Economics, 61*, 345–371.

Schoeni, R. (1997). *The effects of immigration on the employment and wages of native workers: Evidence from the 1970s and 1980s.* RAND Corporation Report DRU/1408/IF, March.

Simon, J. (1989). *The economic consequences of immigration.* Oxford: Basil Blackwell.

Solow, R. (1956). A contribution to the theory of economic growth. *Quarterly Journal of Economics, 70*, 65–94.

Van den Berg, H. (2004). *International economics.* New York: McGraw-Hill.

Chapter 6
How Immigration Impacts the Destination Economy: The Evidence

Abstract This chapter supplements the previous chapter by examining the available evidence on how immigration impacts the destination country's labor markets. In this chapter, we discuss studies that use one of the three popular statistical modeling approaches to estimating the labor market effects of immigration: *the spatial correlation method, the production function method*, and *the skill cell method*. The spatial correlation method exploits geographic variation in immigrant concentrations and yields estimates from regressions of labor market outcomes on those concentrations. The production function method produces estimates of immigration's impact through the estimation of factor price elasticities. The skill cell method partitions the national labor market into measured skill categories and estimates the impact of exogenous immigration to those categories. Studies applying the production function and spatial correlation methods show that immigration has little or no impact on native-born wages or employment, while the skill-cell method suggests more substantial impacts, at least in the short run.

Introduction

Since the late 1970s, many researchers have estimated the effects of immigration on destination country labor markets. In their recent meta-analytic assessment of the empirical literature, Longhi, Nijkamp, and Poot (2005) note more than 350 estimates of the elasticity of the native wage with respect to the relative supply of immigrant labor. The empirical literature on immigration's impact on the labor market is much larger than the empirical literature on the determinants and composition of immigrant flows. Perhaps wages and employment are what most people and policymakers are most interested in, and economists have simply responded to the demand for analysis by providing estimates of immigrants' effect on destination country labor markets. People and policymakers in destination countries are probably concerned about other issues related to immigration, like government expenditures, tax receipts, law enforcement, education, and other social changes, but, given

Ö.B. Bodvarsson and H. Van den Berg, *The Economics of Immigration*,
DOI: 10.1007/978-3-540-77796-0_6, © Springer-Verlag Berlin Heidelberg 2009

that it has been the field of labor economics that has most enthusiastically embraced the issue of immigration, economists have produced predominantly studies that estimate the impact of immigration on destination country wages.

Recall the popular elementary textbook model discussed early in the previous chapter where native- and foreign-born workers are substitutes. That simple model predicts that the wages of native workers in the destination economy fall when immigrants arrive. The consensus from the many statistical studies is actually quite unsupportive of this model: Immigration appears to have little or no effect on native-born labor market outcomes. In a survey of the literature, Friedberg and Hunt (1995, p. 42) conclude: "Despite the popular belief that immigrants have a large adverse impact on the wages and employment opportunities of the native-born population, the literature on this question does not provide much support for this conclusion." More recently, after many more studies, Borjas (2003, p. 1335) observes that "The measured impact of immigration on the wage of native workers fluctuates widely from study to study (and sometimes even within the same study), but seems to cluster around zero."

This chapter explains why the evidence is so unsupportive of the elementary textbook model. We first discuss the methods used as well as the results generated from their application. We then sort through past and current debates over why the evidence is so unsupportive of the basic labor market model. We break the empirical literature into three parts according to the methods used. The two parts discussed in this chapter correspond to two popular methods for estimating immigration's impact on destination country labor markets – the *spatial correlation* and the *production function* methods.

The spatial correlation approach has been the most widely-used, but most researchers now agree that it is biased towards underestimating immigration's true impact. Many researchers suggest that *the skill cell method* may be the most accurate of the three approaches.

6.1   The Spatial Correlation Method

The *spatial correlation*, or geographic correlation, method has been the most commonly used method to estimate the wage and employment effects of immigration in the destination country. To grasp the logic behind the spatial correlation method, suppose the world consists of two regions in the same country, say region A and region B, that have identical labor markets. Suppose that workers in A are perfect substitutes for workers in B and that labor supply is perfectly inelastic in both locations. Suppose that region A receives a group of immigrants, who are perfect substitutes for workers already residing there, but region B receives no immigrants. This model, therefore, predicts that wages fall in A after immigration, but wages remain the same in region B.

Suppose, however, that at the time the immigrants arrive in region A, both regions are negatively impacted by a recession that lowers demand throughout the national economy. In this case, the researcher running a regression in which immigration is the explanatory variable is likely to attribute the decline in wages entirely to immigration and nothing to the fact that a recession is at least partially responsible for the wage decline in region A. The spatial correlation method prescribes that the researcher include not only data on region A in the regression, but also data for a *control* region that does not receive immigrants and whose wage level is, therefore, exclusively the result of national economic conditions. The researcher then can test to see whether immigration explains the difference in the wage changes. Such tests are used to see if differences between regions or years explain the differences in labor market outcomes. This is why this type of analysis is often referred to as "difference in differences" analysis in the econometric literature.

The difference-in-differences test has been applied to the case of immigration in two different ways. The first is called the *cross section* approach, which involves using a large number of observations on different regions in a regression equation with controls for other explanatory variables that are hypothesized to also affect wages or employment. One or a few of the regions experience immigration inflows, while most of the others experience little immigration. The second approach is to take advantage of unexpected sudden surges in immigration, which we call the *unexpected extraordinary supply shock* (UESS) study. This approach uses time-series data that consists of many "normal" years and one exceptional year when there is a sudden, huge inflow of immigrants. Regression analysis is then used to look at the differences between the regions or years with little immigration and the region and year with a large amount of immigration to distinguish the effect of immigration on wages, employment, and other labor market outcomes. We detail both methods below.

6.1.1 Cross Section Applications

The cross section approach involves estimating a regression equation where the dependent variable is some labor market outcome like wages, and the most often-used explanatory variable is the proportion of immigrants in the population, or what labor economists refer to as *immigrant density*. The observations may be for a set of different geographic regions, or they may be for a set of different occupations. In the case of a set of geographic observations, a cross-section regression model takes on the form

$$\ln(Y_{jt}) = \beta(\ln M_{jt}) + \alpha(\ln X_{jt}) + \varepsilon_{jt}, \tag{6.1}$$

where Y_{jt} is a labor market outcome experienced by natives who live in region j during period t, M_{jt} is the fraction of immigrants comprising region j's labor force during t, X_{jt} is a vector of other variables hypothesized to influence immigration in region j during period t (the so-called "control variables"), and ε_{jt} is a random error term. If native-born and immigrant workers are substitutes in the sense that they compete in the same labor market, this standard model of immigration hypothesizes that $\beta < 0$, that is, the higher is the concentration of immigrants in the local labor market, the lower is the wage, all other things equal. Unbiased estimation of (6.1) requires that the allocation of immigrants across regions is random. That is quite unlikely, however. For example, U.S. immigrants tend to cluster in a small number of states (California, New York, Texas, Florida, Illinois and New Jersey) and cities (Los Angeles, New York, Chicago and Miami). There are two likely reasons for this clustering. First, immigrants have a strong tendency to settle where labor markets are strong, hence immigration is also endogenous to local economic conditions. This endogeneity creates the problem of *simultaneity bias* in estimates of β. If immigrants choose areas where pay is higher (ε_{jt} is high), then the correlation between pay and immigration is the result of the simultaneous influences of each variable on the other. High pay influences immigration, and immigration influences the wage. The resulting positive correlation between Y_{jt} and M_{jt} will bias the estimate of β. The solution is to modify the immigration variable so as to cut the line of causality from the wage to the immigrant density variable.

Another source of bias in the regression (6.1) is that immigrants tend to settle in areas where there are high concentrations of immigrants from their home countries who arrived in earlier periods. If those areas may coincidentially experience persistently soft or strong labor markets, then the estimate of β will be biased by the *spurious correlation* between immigration and wages that has nothing to do with the direct influence of immigration on wages. If immigrants choose to settle where there are large concentrations of immigrants and those areas also have relatively low wages, β will be biased downwards and thus overestimates immigration's true impact. The downward bias is due, first, to the fact that the regression fails to account for the influence of historical immigrant settlement patterns on M_{jt}. Second, the regression omits a control for characteristics that are unique to the location, or what econometricians call the *fixed effect* of location. The solution is to remove the influence of the fixed effect(s) and to control for the source of the correlation between wages and immigrant density.

6.1.2   Dealing with Simultaneity and Spurious Correlation

Fortunately, there are several econometric solutions to treating both problems above. The first is to exploit variation in immigrant density and labor market outcomes *within* each spatial unit across two consecutive periods. In the regression model (6.1), the variables in *levels* are, therefore, replaced with variables in *differences*. In applying the first difference model, *changes* in labor market outcomes are regressed on *changes* in immigrant density and other control variables. A generic version of such a model is

$$\Delta Y_{js}(t, t') = \beta_t \Delta M_{js}(t, t') + X_{js}(t) + \varepsilon_{js}(t, t'), \qquad (6.2)$$

where $\Delta Y_{js}(t,t')$ is the change in a labor market outcome experienced by residents of region j who belong to skill group s between years t and t', $\Delta M_{js}(t,t')$ is the size of the immigrant supply shock to region j for that skill group over the (t,t') time interval, X is a vector of control variables, and $\varepsilon_{js}(t,t')$ is a random error term. The β_t coefficient measures the impact of immigration on the change in labor market outcomes. Note that when there is no immigrant population in t, the variable measuring immigration is the same as in the non-differenced specification and β_t has exactly the same interpretation as in the non-differenced model.

Testing for changes over time requires time-series data. If time-series data are not available, the difference in differences method can also use cross-section data to test differences across different markets at the same point in time. For example, suppose that there is substantial variation in the amount of immigration and wages across occupations. Then, the researcher can estimate the effect of immigration in each profession by testing those differences across different occupations.

Goldin (1994) applied a differencing model to city-level data for 1890–1923 from the U.S. Census to estimate the effect of changes in immigrant density in cities on changes in native wages in different occupations and industries. She found that a 1 percentage point rise in the city's fraction of immigrant residents reduced native wages by 1.0–1.6%.[1] LaLonde and Topel (1991) performed first difference regressions using 1970 and 1980 U.S. census data for individual males in cities. An advantage of working with individual data is that it is possible to control for many of the variables and personal characteristics that induce people to move to areas with strong demand for labor, which reduces the likelihood of encountering spurious correlation. LaLonde and Topel focus on the effects that different immigrant cohorts have on each other's wages. Overall, LaLonde and Topel's results indicate no significant effects of immigration on wages in U.S. cities. However, they did find that for the sub-group of recent male immigrants, an increase in the fraction of immigrants comprising the city's male labor force by 10% reduces the wage of the average worker in that group by 0.3%. Immigration was not found to affect the wages of young native blacks and Hispanics.

First differencing prevents spurious correlation, but does not prevent simultaneous equations bias if immigration depends upon *anticipated* changes in the wage. The solution is still to first difference, but to convert the immigrant density into an exogenous variable through instrumental variables (IV) estimation. What would be a sensible instrument? Recall our earlier discussion about how immigrants prefer to settle in areas with already high concentrations of immigrants. Pre-existing immigrant concentrations are unlikely to be correlated with current economic conditions if these concentrations are measured with an adequate time lag.

---

[1]Friedberg and Hunt (1995) point out that Goldin's results may be affected by a "composition" problem, which results from the use of aggregate data. In Goldin's study, city-level wages are a composite of immigrant and native wages. If immigrants on average earn less, then cities with higher immigrant densities will have lower mean wages, even absent an adverse effect of immigration. This problem can be avoided by the researcher distinguishing between native and immigrant earnings in the data, something Goldin could not do.

Altonji and Card (1991) sought to explain changes in wages and unemployment rates of low-skill workers across U.S. cities from 1970 to 1980, controlling for changes in educational attainment and mean age in each city. The low-skilled include white males who did not finish high school and black and white females and black males with a high school degree or less.[2] The reason for their focus on the low-skilled is that they are most likely to be adversely affected by immigration. Like Lalonde and Topel, Altonji and Card's results indicate that immigration generally exerts only very modest effects on the labor market outcomes of low-skilled native-born workers. Employment effects are ambiguous and very small, while there is some evidence of negative, but still small, effects on wages (wages are measured as log earnings per week). Altonji and Card estimate that for their full sample, if the immigrant population share increases by 1%, the wage will fall by 1.2%. However, the magnitude of this effect is not large because it measures a percentage point change in the immigrant share. For example, suppose that immigration increases from 5 to 6% (a 20% increase) and the wage is predicted to fall by 1.2%. Then a 10% increase in immigrant share implies only a 0.6% drop in weekly earnings.

Altonji and Card also found that for black male high school graduates, immigration exerts a slightly positive effect on the employment rate and a very modest negative effect on earnings (a 10 percentage point increase in the city's foreign-born share is predicted to reduce earnings by 1.9%). For comparable black females, there is no effect on immigration on the employment rate and only a very mild negative effect on earnings (a 10 percentage point increase in the city's foreign-born share reduces earnings by 1.37%). For white males without a high school degree, there are no effects on employment and very mild adverse effects on the wage (a 10% increase in foreign-born share reduces earnings by just 1.1%). There are no wage and employment effects of immigration on white female high school graduates.

Applications of the spatial correlation approach continued through the 1990s. Important studies during this period include Butcher and Card (1991), Borjas, Freeman, and Katz (1997), Schoeni (1997), DeNew and Zimmerman (1994) and Pischke and Velling (1997), to name just a few. These studies all found little effect of immigration on native-born labor market outcomes. Some of the more recent spatial correlation studies used both time-series and cross-section data, or what is often referred to as panel data. Butcher and Card (1991) tracked relative growth rates of wages for low- and high-paid workers in 24 U.S. cities using *Current Population Survey* data from 1979 to 1989. They found no evidence of a negative wage effect of immigration, either across cities or within cities over time. Growth in wage inequality was positively correlated with growth rates in immigration, but higher inequality came in the form of more rapid increases in the 90th percentile of wages, but not with a relative decline in the 10th percentile.

---

[2] The choice of members of this group may be a result of the researchers recognizing discrimination in the labor markets, where blacks and females with high school degrees are treated similarly to white males who did not finish high school.

Borjas et al. (1997) estimated a version of (6.2) for the years 1960, 1970, 1980, and 1990 across U.S. states and occupations, and they found that the β coefficient changed significantly across decades. For example, they found a negative coefficient for the 1960s, but a positive one (and larger in absolute value) for the 1970s, followed by a negative coefficient during the 1980s. Schoeni (1997) observed a similar pattern. He found that a three-point increase in the foreign-born share of the population, e.g. from 6 to 9%, cut the earnings of male high school graduates by 1% in the 1970s, but would have increased the same group's wages by 0.8% during the 1980s.

6.1.3 Recent Applications of the Spatial Correlation Method

As the number of applications of the spatial correlation method grew, so did concern over the failure of these studies to confirm the predictions of basic labor market models. For example, Borjas (1994, p. 1700) wrote: "A fair appraisal of the literature thus suggests that we still do not fully understand how immigrants affect the employment opportunities of natives in local labor markets; nor do we understand the dynamic processes through which natives respond to these supply shocks and reestablish labor market equilibrium." Borjas (1999) suggested that the reversal of sign on the estimated effect of immigration on native wages may be due to long term changes in the wage structure that are not fully understood and accounted for in the regressions.

Recall, also, the Leamer-Levinsohn (1995) hypothesis discussed in the last chapter. Local effects of large immigrant flows to some areas will be diffused elsewhere by internal migration responses, capital adjustments, product market responses and other secondary adjustment processes. The degree to which an uneven distribution of immigrants across areas results in persistent and observable differences in native labor market outcomes depends on how flexible markets are in the destination economy. If changes in wages or unemployment induce quick and large shifts in workers between regional labor markets, then factor prices are likely to equalize across areas.

In one of the most thorough applications of the spatial correlation approach, Card (2001) considered the possibility of internal migration responses. Earlier studies, such as Altonji and Card (1991) and LaLonde and Topel (1991), had modeled demand responses to immigration, but they did not include empirical controls for demand in the empirical models. In contrast, Card (2001) estimates regression equations derived directly from his theoretical model.

Like most previous applications of the spatial correlation approach, Card uses the city as his spatial unit, but he further stratifies the sample along *occupational* lines. Card argues that there is ample evidence that the population of U.S. immigrants consists of a great variety of people with very different backgrounds, cultures, work experiences, and lifestyles: "Given this heterogeneity, the overall fraction of immigrants in a city is simply too crude an index of immigrant competition for any particular subgroup of natives"[3] It would make little sense to conduct a study where, for example, native-born high school teachers are assumed to compete for jobs with foreign-born dental hygienists (and for immigrant high school teachers to compete with native-born dental hygienists). Card effectively argues that it is more sensible to distinguish between public school teaching and dental hygiene as separate labor markets and then have natives and immigrants competing within each market. He thus uses local *occupational* density, the fraction of local population comprising an occupation, rather than overall immigrant density in the local market, as most previous studies have done.

Card's data set is a cross-section drawn from the 1990 U.S. Census, and includes labor market outcomes of men and women aged 16–68 in 1989 who had at least 1 year of potential labor market experience. He used 100% of all foreign-born persons in what is described as a 5% public use micro sample from the full Census sample (approximately 840,000 observations) and a 25% random sample of all native-born persons (approximately 1,900,000 persons) in the 5% public use sample. The dependent variable is hourly earnings, computed from total annual earnings (including self-employment and wage and salary earnings), information about weeks worked, and hours per week over the year. The data set includes the 175 largest U.S. cities.

Card corrects for some potential sources of bias. For example, there is a problem with stratifying by occupation, which is that occupational choice is often endogenous. People are likely to switch out of an occupation if there is excess supply (due to the arrival of immigrants, for example) in a particular occupation. Second, there is the problem of selection bias in the measurement of occupation-specific labor supply. Census data only include information about occupation for those that are employed, however the proper way to measure labor supply to occupation A is the population of individuals who could *potentially* work in A.

Card's most important finding here is that inflows of new immigrants put more supply pressure on less-educated natives than on other native groups. In general, Card's results suggest that immigration exerts only modest effects on local employment rates. The estimated coefficients on the occupational density ranged from -0.1 to -0.2. There are several ways to interpret these coefficients. First, a one percentage point increase in the occupation's population share will, all other things equal, lower the employment rate by 0.1–0.2 percentage points. For example, if the share of the lowest occupation group were to rise from 10 to 14%, the employment-population rate is predicted to fall by 0.02–0.04.

With regard to the question of whether immigrant inflows induce offsetting outflows of natives and previous immigrants, Card estimates a separate outflow rate equation

$$P_{ijc} = X_{ijc}b_j + Z_{jc}\beta + \gamma R_{jc} + d_j + \theta_c \qquad (6.3)$$

---

[3]Borjas (1994, p. 1700).

in which P_{ijc} is the out-migration probability for person i in occupation group j who lived in city c, X is a vector of characteristics for the individual, Z_{jc} is a vector of group-level characteristics, R_{jc} is the inflow rate of new immigrants, and θ_c is a dummy variable to capture city fixed effects. Card found that city outflow rates of natives and older immigrants were generally not influenced by inflow rates of new immigrants. Card's results, therefore, suggest that researchers may not need to worry about internal migration when estimating the impact of immigration.

Card's estimates from the wage regressions confirm the general finding of earlier studies that immigration appears to induce very mildly adverse to zero effects on native-born wages. Corrected for selectivity bias, the estimated coefficients on the immigrant density for the full sample are −0.15 for native-born men, 0.063 for native-born women, zero for pre-1985 immigrant men and −0.251 for pre-1985 immigrant women. The first two coefficients predict that an immigrant inflow rate of 10% reduces native male wages by just 1.5% and raises native female wages by 0.63%. The coefficient estimates across various demographic, occupation and city groups range from −0.15 to zero. All these results generally match the kinds of results found in earlier studies.

Dustmann, Fabbri, and Preston (2005) performed a cross section spatial correlation analysis on British data to test for the effects of immigrant population shares on both wages and employment rates of native-born persons. Their regression specification incorporates two important implications of their theoretical model: (1) wages depend not only on relative immigrant supply, but also on the diversity of skills in the native population; and (2) the native skill mix and the immigrant labor force share should be separate variables in a regression. The data set is the British Labour Force Survey, an annual household survey providing a wide range of data on labor market variables.

Dustmann, Fabbri, and Preston estimated their regressions equations using OLS, first differences, and instrumental variables. Coefficient estimates vary widely across estimation procedures. The OLS results show a negative and significant relationship between the native unemployment rate and the regional immigrant share, but there is no significant relationship generated by the instrumental variables estimates, however. For native wages, OLS shows a strong positive relationship, no relationship in the first differences equation, and a positive relationship (only significant at 10%) in the instrumental variables equation. Overall, these results indicate no strong evidence of immigration's impact on native unemployment rates and very mixed results for wages

6.1.4 Applications of the Unexpected Exogenous Supply Shock Method

The *unexpected exogenous supply shock* (UESS) approach is similar to the two-region example given at the beginning of this section. Only now there is one exceptional year in terms of immigration rather than one exceptional region or city. There have been many surges in immigration that were framed by earlier and later years of very small inflows of immigrants. Choice of the counterfactual is extremely simple in that example because region II is identical to region I save the immigration episode. In reality, the choice of the counterfactual is more complicated because no spatial units are ever alike. Choice of the proper counterfactual is clearly crucial when using the UESS application.

Two prominent applications of the UESS include the classic study by Card (1990) of the 1980 "Mariel Boatlift" of Cuban refugees to Miami and Friedberg's (2001) often-cited study of mass migration of Russian Jews from the former USSR to Israel during the early 1990s. Other important studies include Carrington and De Lima's (1996) analysis of the repatriation of roughly 600,000 Portugese from Angola and Mozambique following independence of those two former colonies in the mid 1970s, Hunt's (1992) study of the impact of the arrival in France of approximately 900,000 people of mostly French origin from Algeria in 1962 after that country gained its independence from France, and Angrist and Kugler's (2003) analysis of the effects of the Balkan Wars on migration to European countries. What all these studies have in common are (1) an unexpected case of extraordinary immigration triggered by a political shock in the sending country, and (2) an application of the difference-in-differences test to assessing the effects of the shock on native-born labor market outcomes in the destination country.

The UESS studies generally find very little impact of immigrants on native labor market outcomes. In Hunt's (1992) study, the repatriation to France of skilled Algerians resulted in the French labor force rising by 1.6%. Hunt found that a 1% increase in the immigrant share of the labor force induced a drop in the regional wage by at most 0.8% and raised the unemployment rate of natives by 0.2%.

Carrington and De Lima's (1996) study of the massive repatriation of overseas Portuguese after the independence of Mozambique and Angola, which suddenly increased Portugal's labor force by nearly 10%, first used Spain and France as the counterfactuals. Secondly, they used a series specification to apply the UESS method. Overall, they found that the Portugese repatriation did induce some short run unemployment among natives, but the primary reason for rising unemployment in Portugal was that unemployment rates rose all across Europe during the period of oil price shocks during the 1970s. In the long run, once other outside influences were controlled for, immigration seems to have had little effect on wages or employment.

6.1.5   The Mariel Boatlift

The *Mariel Boatlift* in 1980 provides an interesting case study on the impact of immigration on a specific labor market. Between May and September of 1980 about 125,000 Cuban immigrants arrived in the United States after the Cuban dictator Fidel Castro suddenly reversed his policy of prohibiting Cubans from leaving.

Castro required immigrants to leave through the small port of Mariel, which is why the mass migration came to be known as the *Mariel Boatlift*. A flotilla of chartered boats paid for mostly by Cuban-Americans carried the immigrants from Mariel to the United States. About half of the 125,000 immigrants settled in Miami, suddenly and unexpectedly expanding the labor force by about 7%. "There is no way this community can absorb so many people without serious socioeconomic problems," lamented a local school board member.[4]

Card (1990), in what has become a classic study of the consequences of immigration on a destination country, reaches a surprising conclusion about the Mariel Boatlift: the sudden large inflow of Cuban immigrants had almost no effect on wages in Miami. This clearly is not what the traditional labor supply model of immigration predicts. Card's analysis shows that there was no effect of the immigration surge on average wages in Miami for the population as a whole or among specific groups such as low-wage workers, Cuban-Americans, or other minorities, but there was some shift in migration patterns into and out of Miami. Specifically, the Mariel Boatlift seems to have reduced in-migration and encouraged competing workers, most notably the lower-skilled from minorities other than Cuban-Americans, to move elsewhere in Florida.

Card used individual micro-data for 1979–1985 from the Merged Outgoing Rotation Group (MORG) samples of the Current Population Survey (CPS) to test for the effects of the Mariel influx on the wages and unemployment rates for five different groups of workers – white, black, non-Cuban Hispanic, earlier Cuban immigrant and all low-skilled workers for the first 5 years following the influx. Card's counterfactual group included four cities – Tampa, Atlanta, Houston and Los Angeles. Card selected these cities because they experienced patterns of economic growth similar to Miami during the period.

Card observed that during 1979–1981, only the Cuban wage fell in Miami, whereas the wage for whites, blacks and Hispanics in the comparison cities all fell. The white unemployment rate even fell from 5.1 to 3.9% in Miami while it fell only slightly in the comparison cities from 4.4 to 4.3%. While the black unemployment rate rose from 8.3 to 9.6% in Miami, it rose even more in the counterfactual group from 10.3 to 12.6%. This is unusual because blacks are likely to be the non-Cuban group most substitutable for the Mariel immigrants. Card's difference-in-differences calculation on black unemployment rates reveals that the unemployment rate fell in Miami by 1% relative to the rate in the counterfactual group during 1979–1981.

For the most part, the Miami labor market seems to have absorbed the new workers relatively easily by expanding employment opportunities. Card (1990, p. 23) suggests that "in many respects Miami was better prepared to receive [the immigrants] than any other city." Miami's industrial structure was already skewed toward low-skill jobs and its large Hispanic population made it easier for Spanish-speaking immigrants to find employment. The relatively flexible labor markets

---

[4]*Business Week* (1980), "The New Wave of Cubans is Swamping Miami," August 25, 1980.

throughout the United States also helped to dissipate the effects throughout the region, as suggested by the out-migration of competing workers. Miami had already proven it could absorb earlier waves of Latin American immigrants from Cuba, Central America, and the Caribbean.

Perhaps the most important question posed by Card's study is: Did the Boatlift reduce the relative earnings of less-skilled natives in Miami? If the Boatlift reduced the wage of less-skilled natives, then one would see a decline in the wage of workers occupying the lowest skill quartile relative to workers occupying the upper quartiles. By calculating predicted wages using the coefficients obtained from the counterfactual regressions, Card adjusted Miami wages for economic conditions in the comparison cities. He found no evidence that those in the lowest quartile were made worse off relative to the other quartiles, even during 1979–1981. Card concluded that there is no evidence to support the hypothesis that the Boatlift had an adverse impact on native-born workers in the Miami labor market.

Card suggested that the primary reason for the benign effects of the immigration shock was that it triggered offsetting out-migration from Miami and deterred prospective migration to Miami. The expansion of employment in response to the massive Cuban immigration in 1980 also suggests, however, that the expansion of the number of workers increased demand for labor. The new workers spent some of their incomes to demand local goods and services. That is, immigrants may be employed providing some of the goods and services they themselves demand, or others demand, as a result of the multiplier effect of the immigrants' local expenditures. The traditional models of immigration generally ignore these direct and indirect effects that immigrants have on the demand for their own labor services.

6.1.6 Russian Immigrants in Israel

Friedberg (2001) studied the nearly one million Russian immigrants who arrived in Israel during the 1990s. When the Soviet Union lifted emigration restrictions in 1989, many Jewish Russians chose to leave, and most went to Israel because that was their only immediate alternative. Unlike most other potential destination countries, Israel had no entry restrictions and no waiting period for immigrants who were Jewish. This is not to suggest Israel was or is open to all immigrants; in fact, Israel routinely expels Palestinians and other non-Jewish people residing in territory that Israel claims. Friedberg reports that during 1990 alone, the influx of Jewish Russians increased population growth in Israel by 4% during each of the years 1989–1995. These annual levels of migration were proportionally much larger than anything experienced by the U.S. or Western Europe.

There are several important features of this particular natural experiment. First, it is a clear-cut case of exogenous immigration driven by a change in policy in the source country. Second, Israel is a very small country, and there were really no geographic areas unaffected by the Russian immigration. Recall that if an immigration shock penetrates only part of a country, then flexible markets will diffuse the effects of the shock to unaffected areas, thus hampering the researcher from estimating the true effects of immigration. Third, the Jewish Russians who immigrated to Israel were highly educated and experienced. Friedberg points out that while in the short run, labor market outcomes in the destination country may not depend on the immigrant skill distribution because language difficulties force many immigrants to compete with less-skilled natives for blue-collar jobs, in the long term the country's reaction to immigration may be different if the migrants are high-skilled.

Friedberg stratifies the labor market along occupational lines to make it possible to use the spatial correlation method. Equalization across occupations is unlikely because large investments in retraining are required and workers may have a strong preference for remaining in their original occupations of choice. This is especially likely for high-skill persons who have incurred years of expensive training. Friedberg effectively assumes that any disequilibrium caused by immigration will persist much longer than for the case of immigration to a region. Second, the likelihood of endogenous immigration to an occupation is also assumed to be less likely.

Friedberg's data set was drawn from several sources. Information about the Russian immigrants came from the Israeli Immigrant Employment Survey (IES), which interviewed a random sample of 3,300 new immigrants who came to Israel in 1990. She specifically used information coming from a survey of a cohort of Russian immigrants who arrived in Israel or received immigrant status between October and December of 1990. This cohort was interviewed annually during 1992–1994. The data set includes information on an immigrant's education and job experience prior to immigration.

Friedberg found large differences between the estimated wage effects of immigration across various specifications of regression models. For example, the estimate of her OLS regression for groups of people in each profession yielded a coefficient on r_j, the immigrant density for employment group j, equaling -1.54, i.e. a 10% gain in employment due to immigration induced a 15.4% drop in average wages, whereas the first differenced version yielded a coefficient of -0.616. However, the 2SLS first differenced version yielded a statistically insignificant coefficient. These results suggest that the OLS regressions reflect simultaneity bias. Since the 2SLS method explicitly tries to account for this bias, its results are probably the more reliable in this case. Thus, it appears that the Russian immigrant influx did not adversely affect native Israeli labor market outcomes. Friedberg achieved wider ranging estimates from her regressions for samples of individuals rather than groups of individuals, but she still failed to find consistent evidence showing immigration reduced the welfare of natives.

In assessing her results, Friedberg speculates that there may be complementarity between the Jewish Russian immigrants and the native Israelis. For example, many Russian doctors took lower-paying, less desirable positions in Israeli hospitals, which may have allowed native Israeli doctors to move to more desirable and more lucrative positions. Second, there was rapid growth of the high tech industry in Israel, which is likely to have stimulated labor demand across many occupations, including those with higher Russian immigrant concentrations.

6.1.7 Assessing the Spatial Correlation Method

A drawback of the spatial correlation method is that estimates of immigration's effects on destination country labor markets will tend to be biased towards zero because of endogenous movement between regions and particular labor market segments. That is, the adverse effects on wages caused by immigration will induce natives to move elsewhere or pursue other careers. It is not clear to what extent this potential bias affected the studies reviewed above, which strongly suggest that immigration has little or no effect on local native labor market outcomes.

Interestingly, Borjas, Freeman, and Katz (1996) applied the method to 1980 and 1990 U.S. Census data for 236 U.S. cities, splitting their sample by decade and gender, and measuring immigrant density as the ratio of immigrants to natives in each city. Then they repeated the regressions after aggregating their data from individual cities to states, and then finally to regions. They showed that the larger the region, the more negative the coefficient on immigrant density. That is, the overall state effects of immigration were more adverse than the individual city effects, and the regional effects were more adverse for native workers than the state effects. They concluded that this confirmed that estimates of immigration's impact were biased in spatial correlation studies because they ignored the offsetting internal migration responses. Borjas, Freeman, and Katz (1996, p. 249) wrote: "If native migration responses are sufficiently large over the relevant period, comparisons of small areas will mask the true effect of immigrants on native wages"

Friedberg (2001) agrees, suggesting that factor price equalization is much less likely across borders than within because of restrictive immigration policies, international differences in tax rates on capital, investment risks, and trade restrictions. Accordingly, the effects of immigration shocks on the *national* labor market should be easier to detect than effects on local labor markets. This serious shortcoming of the spatial correlation method served as the inspiration for the next two empirical strategies, which we begin to discuss below.

6.2   The Production Function Method

In contrast to the spatial correlation method, in which wages or employment rates are directly regressed on measures of immigrant labor supply, the strategy behind the production function method is to first estimate the degree of substitutability between native and immigrant workers. The method requires the researcher to specify a production function where immigrants and natives are distinct inputs, estimate it using national, regional or local data, and use coefficient estimates to calculate the factor price elasticity of native-born labor with respect to foreign-born labor.

6.2.1 Grossman's Pioneering Production Study

The production function method was pioneered by Grossman (1982). She assumes that the destination economy is a city with four inputs – the quantity of native labor with native parents (N), the quantity of native labor with immigrant parents (SG), the quantity of immigrant labor (FN) and the capital stock (K). She began with a translog production function, from which she derived factor shares denoted as S_j, where j = N, SG, FN, and K. Grossman estimated factor share equations, from which she computed a measure of factor complementarity, C_{ij}, which measures the percentage change in the relative wage of factor i in response to a one percentage point change in the employment of factor j, holding price and other inputs constant. Two inputs are substitutes (complements) if $C_{ij} < (>) 0$. The factor price elasticities (η_{ij}) were then computed as follows:

$$\eta_{ij} = S_j C_{ij}. \tag{6.4}$$

The factor price elasticity measures the percentage change in the market price of factor i due to a one percentage point change in the supply of factor j. A large and negative elasticity of the native wage with respect to immigrant supply, for example, indicates a high degree of substitutability between natives and immigrants and that immigration will generate strongly adverse effects on natives. A positive elasticity indicates that natives and immigrants are complements and that immigration boosts native wages.

Grossman focused on estimating the elasticities of first and second generation natives with respect to the supply of immigrant labor. She found that the elasticity of the first generation native wage with respect to the supply of immigrant labor was -0.02, meaning that the wage of first generation natives falls only 0.02% when the supply of immigrants increases by 1%. The elasticity of the second generation native wage was just -0.03. Therefore, immigration's effects on native wages overall appear to be very mildly negative. However, the immigrant group's own factor price elasticity was estimated to be more negative (-0.23), indicating that immigrants' primary competitors in the labor market are other immigrants.

Grossman's results point to two likely causes of immigration's mild labor market effects on natives. First, immigrants' labor market share was less than 10% for the U.S. at the time of Grossman's study, and as (6.4) indicates, if immigrants comprise only a minor portion of the labor force, then even a very strong degree of substitutability still yields an elasticity close to zero. Second, estimates show that immigrants are least substitutable for first generation natives ($C_{n,f} = -0.32$), more substitutable for second generation natives ($C_{s,f} = -0.61$) and most substitutable for immigrants

($C_{f,f} = -4.65$). Thus, immigrants compete much more with immigrants than with natives.

In Grossman's study, the labor force is divided into only three very broad groups. Borjas (1987) later argued that Grossman's failure to control for within-group variation biased her estimates of elasticities of complementarity and factor price elasticities. To control for within-group heterogeneity, Borjas broke the labor force down into nine categories – white, black, Hispanic and Asian native males, white, black, Hispanic and Asian immigrant males, and females. The dependent variable is 1979 annual earnings and the nine earnings functions were estimated simultaneously. Controls were included for years of schooling, years of labor market experience and experience squared.

After making these adjustments, Borjas (1987) found that immigrants generally are substitutes for the white native-born population, but increases in immigrant labor supply exert only modest adverse effects on the earnings of white natives. Factor price elasticities of white natives with respect to immigrant labor supply range from just -0.002 for black immigrants (a 10% increase in black immigrants reduces the white native wage by 0.2%) to -0.025 for white immigrants. There is evidence of both substitutability and complementarity between immigrants and other native groups, though. Black natives are complements to white immigrants (elasticity = 0.02), but neither substitutes nor complements with respect to the other three immigrant groups. Hispanic natives are substitutes for white and black immigrants (elasticities are -0.015 and -0.021, respectively), but complements for Hispanic immigrants and Asian immigrants (elasticities are 0.01 and 0.014, respectively). There was no evidence of any relationship between the wages of Asian-Americans natives and immigrants.

6.2.2   Gang and Rivera-Batiz

The production function approach was also applied to a study of the U.S. and Europe by Gang and Rivera-Batiz (1994). They questioned the appropriateness of treating natives and immigrants as distinct inputs. Gang and Rivera-Batiz asked (p. 159): "... in what sense is the labor of immigrants and native-born workers of the same sex with identical human capital characteristics (education, experience, etc.) different?" They suggested that rather than regarding nativity or ethnicity as having distinct roles in production, one should follow human capital theory and concentrate on worker differences in human capital endowments, specifically differences in education, experience and other skill indicators.

Gang and Rivera-Batiz first estimated a traditional individual earnings equation, and then they estimated rates of return to the human capital in the earnings equation. Factor price elasticities were obtained by estimating an assumed translog production function, and the elasticities were then used to calculate the *income elasticity of natives with respect to immigrant supply*. The income elasticities measure the percentage change in the wage of native group t due to a one percentage point change in the supply of immigrant group i. The factor price and income elasticities indicate complementarity or substitutability between education, experience and unskilled labor. If the elasticities are negative, this indicates that immigration exerts downward pressure on a native's earnings, all other things equal. However, the technical relationships between education, experience and unskilled labor aren't the only determinants of how immigration impacts natives. What matters also is how important each of these characteristics is in production and what impact they have on native/immigrant differences in skill distributions.

A principal finding from Gang and Rivera-Batiz' estimation is that education contributes roughly the same to income in both the U.S. and Europe (44% for the U.S. and 43% for Europe). In the second stage, estimating the human capital factor price elasticities, Gang and Rivera-Batiz found that in both the U.S. and Europe, unskilled labor, education, and experience are all complementary. They also found that the elasticities are quite small in absolute value for both the U.S. and Europe, with the relatively larger elasticities observed for those pairs of groups with the biggest differences in skill endowments. This confirms Borjas' (1995, 1999) points that the distributional effects of immigration are most important when there are big differences in skills between immigrants and natives.

The more detailed U.S. data allowed Gang and Rivera-Batiz to disaggregate their sample into 11 native groups and 13 immigrant groups classified by ethnicity or national backgrounds. Overall, the factor price elasticities were found to be close to zero, with positive and negative elasticities scattered widely across all the native/immigrant pairs of groups. Elasticities with respect to the European-born group were found to vary from -0.037 for Mexican Americans to 0.0293 for Americans of East Indian ethnicity. Elasticities with respect to the Mexican-born group varied from -0.158 for Mexican Americans to 0.142 for Indian Americans. Assessing their results for Europe and the U.S., Gang and Rivera-Batiz conclude that "... it appears that employed United States and European workers have very little to fear from immigration."[5]

6.2.3 Assessing the Production Function Method

We should also mention a study by Suen (2000), who applied the production function approach to simulating the effects of the continual immigration from mainland China to Hong Kong over the past several decades on the wages of persons born in Hong Kong. He found the effects of mainland immigrants to be extremely modest. Suen's simulations show that a 40% increase in the stock of new Chinese immigrants lowers wages by only 1% or less.

Comparing the studies that estimated production functions and the elasticities of labor substitutability, there appears to be a very consistent pattern: Immigration appears to exert relatively modest effects on native labor market outcomes. While

---

[5]Gang and Rivera-Batiz (1994, p. 159).

all the factor price elasticities in Grossman's study are negative, only about 60% in Borjas' study are negative, and less than half in Gang and Rivera-Batiz's study are negative. There is even some weak evidence that immigration *raises* natives' wages. The very mild effects of immigration appear to be due to low degrees of substitutability stemming from large differences in skills. The generally small immigrant labor shares also serve to keep estimates of substitutability low.

6.3 The Skill Cell Approach

Researchers often suspected that estimates of immigration's effects on local wages were biased because their regression models failed to account for shifts in native worker migration in response to the arrival of immigrants in a particular city or region. Some researchers addressed this concern by adopting an estimation approach that looked at wages in specific skill groups across larger geographic areas. This method became known as the *skill cell method*. If there is little mobility between skill cells, and there are observations for workers in skill cells across an entire country, then the estimates of immigrants entering that particular skill cell should not be biased by geographic migration.

6.3.1 Borjas' Use of National Data versus Regional Data

Borjas (2003) defined the "labor market" as a nationwide group of workers comprising a skill cell. A skill cell is a group of workers with the same level of measured skills. For example, skill cells are often defined according to workers' education and work experience. In such a case, skill cells might be defined so that cell A includes persons with 16 years of education and 0–5 years of employment experience, cell B includes those with 16 years of education and 5–10 years of experience, etc. If there is little or no mobility between skill cells, this approach allows for an unbiased test of immigration's impact because immigrant inflows to a cell will not be expected to trigger out-migration the way inflows to geographic regions do. Hence, the researcher avoids the biased estimates of immigration's impact when immigration causes outflows of native workers.

Borjas (2003) used data from the four decennial Censuses from 1960 through 2000 for men aged 18–64 who were civilian labor force participants. Borjas classified the male workers into four distinct schooling groups: workers who did not graduate from high school, high school graduates only, those with some college, and those with at least one university degree. He further distinguished eight work experience groups, which gave him 32 education/experience skill cells for five decades, that is, a pooled data set with 160 observations.

In contrast to much of the evidence discussed in the two sections above, Borjas found statistically significant adverse effects on native workers' earnings. When the dependent variable was weekly earnings, the elasticity with respect to immigration was estimated to be -0.40, which implies that a 10% rise in immigrants reduces weekly earnings by 4%. The elasticity for annual earnings was -0.64, and the elasticity for time worked was -0.37.

Borjas then compared these results with those that would have been obtained if skill cells were defined by state of residence. While in this case estimates of factor price elasticities were still consistently negative, Borjas found that defining labor cells geographically (by state) diminished the impact of immigration by approximately two-thirds. He cited this as strong evidence that the effects of immigration to a state are diffused to other states through internal migration, capital reallocation, and other adjustment processes. This indicates the importance of looking at immigration's effects beyond the labor market of one region or city.

Borjas' estimates were not without their potential sources of bias. One potential shortcoming of his results, which he openly recognized, is that they don't account for an important source of measurement error in the experience variable. According to the findings of Chiswick (1978), U.S. employers attach less value per year of pre-migration experience than they do to post-migration experience due to the imperfect transferability of human capital. Thus, failure to correct for lower valuation of pre-migration experience of immigrants relative to the valuation of native workers' experience can result in biased estimates. To correct for this measurement error, Borjas converted the data on experience into destination country equivalents, calling the corrected variable "effective experience." Borjas then re-estimated his regressions with effective experience substituted for reported experience. His new estimates differ little from his earlier results.

Borjas also recognizes that his results may be biased by his assumption that each cell comprises an isolated labor market. To test for this possibility, he again adjusts his model, this time incorporating a specific production function that explicitly accounts for interrelationships in production across inputs. After making a number of assumptions and generating cross-cell elasticities, Borjas found that immigrant inflows adversely affected the pay of most natives, especially those at the ends of the education distribution. For example, Borjas found that workers who did not finish high school experienced a relative wage decline of 8.9%, and university graduates experienced a 4.9% drop. Workers with only a high school degree experienced the smallest drop in relative wage, 2.6%, while the pay of workers with some post-secondary education hardly changed. These results are compatible with the observation that the educational attainment of immigrants to the U.S. is, relative to the native U.S. population, strongly skewed towards the extremes of very little education or very high levels of education. Overall, the wage elasticity of the average native worker with respect to immigration is -0.32, which implies that a 10% increase in immigrant labor supply reduces the wage by 3.2%.

In sum, Borjas' use of national data rather than regional or city data avoids the estimation bias of models that do not explicitly account for changes in regional migration by native workers in the face of immigrant arrivals. His national sample of workers classified by skill cells avoids the bias, and Borjas' (2003) results more closely mirror the effects predicted by the traditional labor market model of immigration.

6.3.2   Ottaviano and Peri's Extension of Borjas' Skill Cell Model

Ottaviano and Peri (2005, 2006, 2008) extended Borjas' (2003) model to include endogenous adjustments of the capital stock to immigration shocks and imperfect substitutability between native- and foreign-born workers within a skill cell. In their 2005 study, Ottaviano and Peri analyzed the same period as Borjas (2003), 1960–2000, using the same data sources. They also used the same 32 skill cells. Elasticities were calculated from simulations, where the values for some parameters were taken from other studies while others were calculated using their own data. It is important to recognize that estimates such as these are highly dependent on the particular models used, the data used, and the assumptions made.

Ottoviano and Peri found that during the decade 1990–2000 in the U.S., the elasticity of mean wages to immigration was 0.275, that is, the 8% increase in foreign-born workers that occurred during that decade *increased* the average wage by 2.2%. More specifically, the top three schooling groups all gained from immigration, but the lowest schooling group experienced a 2.4% decline. Immigration thus appears to benefit all labor groups except the least educated.

In their 2006 study, Ottaviano and Peri focused on estimating the effect of immigration during the 1990–2004 period. Using the same procedures as in their 2005 study, they estimated that the within-cell elasticity of substitution averaged 5.88, again confirming imperfect substitutability. University graduates' real wages are estimated to have risen by 0.7% and high school graduates' wages by 3.5%. The real wage of workers who did not complete secondary school is estimated to have fallen by only 1.1% during 1990 and 2005 because of immigration. Note that the impact of immigration on the extremes of the educational distribution is similar, but not identical, to what Borjas (2003) found.

Ottiaviano and Peri noted that their results change substantially when they assume perfect substitutability between natives and immigrants rather than the partial substitutability their model suggests. Also, when they use Borjas' (2003) model and assume a fixed capital stock, their results change quite substantially. Therefore, it appears that assuming imperfect substitutability between natives and immigrants and including endogenous capital investment in the model substantially changes estimates of immigration's impact; Ottaviano and Peri's results are, on the whole, more similar to the results derived by the models in the first two sections of this chapter.

Borjas, Grogger, and Hanson (2008) argued that the Ottaviano and Peri results are fragile and are very sensitive to the way the sample of working persons is constructed. Borjas, Grogger, and Hanson find that Ottaviano and Peri's finding of imperfect substitution disappears once the analysis adjusts for the heterogeneity of labor market classifications. For example, the finding of immigrant-native complementarity disappears entirely if high school students are removed from the data; Ottaviano and Peri had classified currently enrolled high school juniors and seniors as workers without a high school degree. More generally, when other standard methods of classification of workers are introduced, it is no longer possible to reject the hypothesis that comparably skilled immigrant and native workers are substitutes.

Ottaviano and Peri (2008) respond to Borjas, Grogger, and Hanson by retesting the theoretical model used in their earlier studies on a larger data set (1990–2006) and improving their estimates of elasticities of low-skill native wages with respect to low-skill immigrant labor supplies. They emphasize that to obtain these factor price elasticities, it is imperative to obtain accurate estimates of the elasticity of substitution between workers who have not graduated from high school and workers with at most a high school degree, something previous studies had not been as successful in doing. They found small negative effects in the short run on natives without a high school degree (factor price elasticity is −0.7%) and on the average native wage (−0.4%), but small *positive* effects in the long run (which takes into account capital adjustments) on natives without a high school degree (0.3%) and on the average native wage (0.6%). As with the 2005 and 2006 studies, these estimates indicate that immigration has a less adverse effect than earlier literature suggests.

We should point out that at the time of the writing of this book, neither the Ottaviano and Peri studies or the latest Borjas, Grogger, and Hanson paper had yet been published in a peer-reviewed journal. Nevertheless, the points made in the papers are valid ones. Clearly, when native and immigrants workers are not perfect substitutes, statistical results based on a model that assumes perfect substitutability will tend to overstate immigration's adverse effects (or, perhaps we should say understate immigration's benefits). There are likely to be complementarities in production generated by immigration, and there is also the long run adjustment in the capital stock triggered by immigration shocks. However, it is important to emphasize that their studies suppress other responses to immigration that could be important, e.g. labor demand responses, changes in industry mix, choice of production technologies, as well as native labor supply responses (in all three studies, native labor supply is perfectly inelastic, for example). Once these other responses are accounted for, estimates of the wage impact of immigration could vary, perhaps significantly. Fortunately, there are sure to be more papers by authors on both sides of the argument about the impact of immigration on native wages, so, perhaps, a consensus will eventually develop.

In a recent working paper, Cohen-Goldner and Paserman (2007) extend the skill cell model by analyzing how distributional effects generated by the arrival of a new group of immigrants will be felt in the long-run. They estimate to what extent immigrants with different amounts of time in the destination country exert different effects on natives in the labor market. Cohen-Goldner and Paserman run regressions with and without cell fixed effects, and with and without Borjas' "effective experience" variable. They find that coefficient estimates are very sensitive to the omission of cell fixed effects and the use of the effective experience variable.

For male workers, Cohen-Goldner and Paserman find that when skill cell fixed effects are excluded, immigrants have a statistically significant negative initial effect and a positive long run effect on native wages. This suggests that male natives and immigrants are substitutes in the short run, but adjustments in other inputs over the longer term will drive wages back towards pre-migration levels. However, when they included skill cell fixed effects in their regression, the short and long run effects were no longer statistically significant. For female workers, Cohen-Goldner and Paserman found a similar pattern as they found for males; when skill cell fixed effects were included in the regression, the short-run and long-run effects were much weaker. They also ran regressions with employment as the dependent variable, but immigration had no significant effect in any case.

Cohen-Goldner and Paserman's results thus suggest that immigration does not have a negative impact on native wages, contrary to Borjas' (2003) estimates. Furthermore, Cohen-Goldner and Paserman's results suggest the importance of taking into account assimilation when measuring immigration's impact.

6.3.3   Other Types of Labor Market Cells

The creation of schooling-experience cells, as in the case of the studies in the previous section, is obviously not the only way of segmenting the national labor market in a non-geographic way. Card (2001), Friedberg (2001), and Orrenius and Zavodny (2007), for example, segment by occupation under the assumption that occupational barriers to entry such as training and certification costs keep people from quickly moving between occupations.

Orrenius and Zavodny focused on three groups of occupations – professional workers, service-related workers and manual laborers. Their results show considerable variation in the impact of immigration across occupation groups and type of immigration. For example, in the case of a subgroup of immigrants to the U.S. who adjusted their status from illegal to legal after the 1986 legislation giving amnesty to long-term unauthorized immigrants living in the U.S., there appears to be no impact of immigration on natives in both the professional and service groups. For manual laborers, a 1% increase in the supply of new immigrants lowers the average native wage by just 0.04%. For the subgroup of new arrivals, the results are considerably different. Immigration to the professional group has positive effects on natives (a 1% increase in immigration induces a 0.094% increase in the wage), but no effect on native wages in the other two groups.

In sum, when Borjas (2003) applied the skill cell method to estimate immigration's effect on U.S. wages, he found that immigration lowered native wages. On the other hand, other economists who applied the skill cell method in order to trace immigration's effects found immigration to have a more benign effect on wages. The discrepancies between the studies are largely due to the way substitutability between the skill cells and between immigrants and natives is estimated. The discrepancy between the traditional labor market model of immigration and the empirical evidence thus remains to be explained.

6.4   Concluding Remarks

In this chapter we surveyed and assessed three empirical methods used to estimate the impact of immigration on the destination country's labor market – the *spatial correlation* method, the *production function* method, and the *skill-cell* method.

The spatial correlation method has received the most attention, and it continues to be used despite the likely bias in of its estimates. There was a brief flurry of interest in the production function method in the 1980s, but the method has lost favor among researchers. Recently, empirical work on the destination country labor market responses to immigration has increasingly applied something akin to the skill cell method in order to examine the effects of immigration across larger geographic areas. It is widely believed that immigration causes shifts in regional migration by native workers, and this migration effect biases the results of studies that use data for small regions.

A comparison of the evidence from all the studies surveyed in this chapter makes it clear that, with very few exceptions, there is no strong statistical support for the view held by many members of the public, namely that immigration has an adverse effect on native-born workers in the destination country. In fact, there is even evidence from some studies surveyed in this chapter that native-born wages and employment rates increase in response to immigration. But, it should also be clear from this brief survey of the empirical literature that the statistical evidence is not definitive.

The popular statistical modeling strategies described in this chapter have missed many potentially important economic effects of immigration. The arrival of immigrants triggers many reactions, and not only in the labor markets. Changes in the quantity and price of different categories of labor will, all other things equal, cause changes in the demand for products in the destination economy, the mix of products produced, the technologies with which the products are produced, the amount of education acquired by native workers, and the amount of capital provided to workers, among other things. Some of these changes occur quickly and are often picked up in the data used to estimate the effects of immigration, but others are long-run adjustments that only gradually show up in the data. The likelihood that immigration triggers a variety of dynamic responses throughout the economy suggests that the empirical methods described in this chapter do not come close to accurately capturing the full long-run effects of immigration.

In the next chapter, we focus on estimating additional hypothesized effects of immigration that the methods described in this chapter were not designed to pick up, such as adjustments in the capital stock that are likely to accompany the growth of the immigrant labor force and the increase in the demand for labor and other factors triggered by immigrants' consumption in the destination economy. Then, in Chap. 9 we will examine the long-run growth effects of immigration, which are likely to completely overwhelm the short-run wage effects estimated in the studies covered in this chapter.

References

Acemoglu, D. (1998). Why do new technologies complement skills? Directed technical change and wage inequality. *Quarterly Journal of Economics, 114*, 1055–1089.

Altonji, J., & Card, D. (1991). The effects of immigration on the labor market outcomes of less-skilled natives. In J. Abowd, & R. Freeman (Eds.), *Immigration, trade and the labor market*. Chicago: University of Chicago Press.

Angrist, J., & Kugler, A. (2003). Protective or counter-productive? Labour market institutions and the effect of immigration on EU natives. *Economic Journal, 113*, F302–F331.

Bartel, A. (1989). Where do the new U.S. immigrants live? *Journal of Labor Economics, 7*, 371–391.

Borjas, G. (1986a). The demographic determinants of the demand for black labor. In R. Freeman, & H. Holzer (Eds.), *The black youth employment crisis*. Chicago: The University of Chicago Press.

Borjas, G. (1986b). The sensitivity of labor demand functions to choice of dependent variable. *Review of Economics and Statistics, 68*, 58–66.

Borjas, G. (1987). Immigrants, minorities, and labor market competition. *Industrial and Labor Relations Review, 40*, 382–392.

Borjas, G. (1994). The economics of immigration. *Journal of Economic Literature, 32*, 1667–1717.

Borjas, G. (1995). The economic benefits from immigration. *Journal of Economic Perspectives, 9*, 3–22.

Borjas, G. (1999). The economic analysis of immigration. In O. Ashenfelter, & D. Card (Eds.), *Handbook of labor economics* (vol. 3A). New York: Elsevier.

Borjas, G. (2003). The labor demand curve is downward sloping: Reexamining the impact of immigration on the labor market. *Quarterly Journal of Economics, 118*, 1335–1374.

Borjas, G. (2006). Native internal migration and the labor market impact of immigration. *Journal of Human Resources, 41*, 221–258.

Borjas, G., Freeman, R., & Katz, L. (1992). On the labor market effects of immigration and trade. In G. Borjas, & R. Freeman (Eds.), *Immigration and the work force: Economic consequences for the United States and source areas*. Chicago: University of Chicago Press.

Borjas, G., Freeman, R., & Katz, L. (1996). Searching for the effect of Immigration on the Labor Market. *American Economic Review, 86*, 246–251.

Borjas, G., Freeman, R., & Katz, L. (1997). How much do immigration and trade affect labor market outcomes. *Brookings Papers on Economic Activity, 1*, 1–67.

Borjas, G., Grogger, J., & Hanson, G. (2008). Imperfect substitution between immigrants and natives: A reappraisal. NBER working paper 13887.

Business Week, (1980, 25 August). The new wave of Cubans is Swamping Miami.

Butcher, K., & Card, D. (1991). Immigration and wages: Evidence from the 1980s. *American Economic Review, 81*, 292–296.

Card, D. (1990). The impact of the Mariel Boatlift on the Miami labor market. *Industrial and Labor Relations Review, 43*, 245–257.

Card, D. (2001). Immigrant inflows, native outflows, and the local labor market impacts of higher immigration. *Journal of Labor Economics, 19*, 22–64.

Card, D. (2005). Is the new immigration really so bad. *Economic Journal, 115*, F300–F323.

Card, D., & DiNardo, J. (2000). Do immigrant inflows lead to native outflows? *American Economic Review, 90*, 360–367.

Card, D., & Lemieux, T. (2001). Can falling supply explain the rising return to college for younger men? A cohort-based analysis. *Quarterly Journal of Economics, 66*, 705–746.

Carrington, W., & De Lima, P. (1996). The impact of 1970s repatriates from Africa on the Portugese labor market. *Industrial and Labor Relations Review, 49*, 330–347.

Chiswick, B. (1978). The effects of Americanization on the earnings of foreign-born men. *Journal of Political Economy, 86*, 897–921.

Cohen-Goldner, S., & Paserman, M. (2007). The dynamic impact of immigration on natives' labor market outcomes: Evidence from Israel. IZA Discussion Paper 1315 (www.iza.org).

De New, J., & Zimmerman, K. (1994). Native wage impacts of foreign labor: a random effects panel analysis. *Journal of Population Economics, 7*, 177–192.

Dustmann, C., Fabbri, F., & Preston, I. (2005). The impact of immigration on the British labour market. *The Economic Journal, 115*, F324–F341.

Freeman, R. (1977). Manpower requirement and substitution analysis of labor skills: A synthesis. *Research in Labor Economics, 1*, 151–183.

Friedberg, R. (2001). The impact of mass migration on the Israeli labor market. *Quarterly Journal of Economics, 116*, 1373–1408.

Friedberg, R., & Hunt, J. (1995). The impact of immigrants on destination country wages, employment and growth. *Journal of Economic Perspectives, 9*, 23–44.

Gang, I., & Rivera-Batiz, F. (1994). Labor market effects of immigration in the United States and Europe. *Journal of Population Economics, 7*, 157–175.

Goldin, C. (1994). The political economy of immigration restrictions in the United States, 1890 to 1921. In C .Goldin, & G. Libecap (Eds.), *The regulated economy: A historical approach to political economy*. Chicago: University of Chicago Press.

Grossman, J. (1982). The Substitutability of natives and immigrants in production. *Review of Economics and Statistics 64*:596–603.

Hunt, J. (1992). The impact of the 1962 repatriates from Algeria on the French labor market. *Industrial and Labor Relations Review, 45*, 556–572.

Jaeger, D. (1996) Skill differences and the effect of immigrants on the wages of natives. Unpublished paper, U.S. Bureau of Labor Statistics.

Johnson, G. (1980). The labor market effects of immigration. *Industrial and Labor Relations Review, 33*, 331–341.

LaLonde, R., & Topel, R. (1991). Labor market adjustments to increased immigration. In J. Abowd, & R. Freeman (Eds.), *Immigration, trade, and the labor market*. Chicago: University of Chicago Press.

Leamer, E. (2000). What's the use of factor contents? *Journal of International Economics, 50*, 17–49.

Leamer, E., & Levinsohn, L. (1995). International trade theory: The evidence. In G. Grossman, & K. Rogoff (Eds.), *Handbook of international economics* (vol. 3). Amsterdam: Elsevier.

Longhi, S., Nijkamp, P., & Poot, J. (2005). A meta-analytic assessment of the effect of immigration on wages. *Journal of Economic Surveys, 19*, 451–477.

Orrenius, P., & Zavodny, M. (2007). Does immigration affect wages? A look at occupation-level evidence. *Labour Economics, 17*, 757–774.

Ottaviano, I., & Peri, G. (2005). Rethinking the gains from immigration: Theory and evidence from the U.S. NBER Working Paper 11672 (http://www.nber.org/papers/w11672).

Ottaviano, I., & Peri, G. (2006). Rethinking the effects of immigration on wages. NBER Working Paper 12497 (http://www.nber.org/papers/w12497).

Ottaviano, I., & Peri, G. (2008). Immigration and national wages: Clarifying the theory and the empirics. NBER Working Paper 14188 (http://www.nber.org/papers/w14188).

Pischke, J., & Velling, J. (1997). Employment and effects of immigration to Germany: An analysis based on local labor markets. *Review of Economics and Statistics, 79*, 594–604.

Schoeni, R. (1997). The effect of immigrants on the employment and wages of native workers: Evidence from the 1970s and 1980s. Unpublished paper, Rand Corporation.

Suen, W. (2000). Estimating the effects of immigration in one city. *Journal of Population Economics, 13*, 99–112.

Welch, F. (1969). Linear synthesis of skill distribution. *Journal of Human Resources, 4*, 311–327.

Welch, F. (1979). Effects of cohort size on earnings: the baby boom babies' financial bust. *Journal of Political Economy, 87*, S65–S97.

Chapter 7
Estimating Immigration's Impact: Accounting for all Adjustments

Abstract This chapter surveys the evidence of the long-run effects of immigration on the destination economy. We specifically discuss the most recent literature on how immigration affects domestic migration by native workers, the demand for domestic production and, hence, domestic labor, the industrial mix, and producers' choice of technology. Studies on how immigration affects product demand conclude that the broader long-term reactions to immigration imply that immigration is likely to have positive welfare effects and certainly no strong negative effects. However, evidence on other potential long-run adjustment responses is more complex.

Chapter Introduction

In Chap. 5 we surveyed the economic models of immigration, most of which concluded that the effects of immigration on the destination country cause modest changes in destination country wages or overall employment levels. The previous chapter discussed the empirical estimates of the effects highlighted by the traditional models of immigration. Generally, the empirical results confirm what the theory suggests, namely that immigration causes only small changes in overall welfare, but the net change obscures some rather large redistributional effects.

The empirical results may have been biased by the failure of the underlying regression models to capture the full effects of immigration on the destination country economy. As discussed in the latter part of Chap. 5, the traditional labor market models of immigration fail to take account of the fact that the inflow of immigrants normally induces a series of reactions by native workers, native investors, foreign investors, entrepreneurs, policymakers, and other immigrants, among others. Specific reactions include the out-migration of native workers located in the communities where immigrants arrive, shifts by native workers to other professions, increases in demand as immigrants spend their earnings in the destination country,

Ö.B. Bodvarsson and H. Van den Berg, *The Economics of Immigration*,
DOI: 10.1007/978-3-540-77796-0_7, © Springer-Verlag Berlin Heidelberg 2009

and new investment in capital that complements the new immigrant workers. Many of these reactions by other actors in the economy occur later in time, and regression analysis using contemporaneous data generally misses these effects.

One of the proposed solutions to this bias in the estimates of immigrants' impact is to test directly for additional reactions to immigration. By including all the short-run and long-run reactions in the analysis, the final estimate of the effects of immigration on the destination economy should be more accurate. But, it is not easy to test for the long-run reactions and adjustments to immigration. Such estimates require more dynamic models that relate current immigration flows to future adjustments. Most important, economists must abandon the traditional labor market models that have restricted the analysis to the immediate labor market effects. Immigrants are consumers, innovators, home owners, students, and community members as well as workers. Below, we describe the early attempts of economists to test and quantify the broader long-term consequences of immigration.

7.1　Does Immigration Trigger Internal Migration?

In the previous chapter we reviewed evidence from Card's (2001) study, in which he concluded that increases in the supply of labor to an occupation in a city appears to induce little or no out-migration of natives. Recall that Card tested whether immigration's benign effect on wages was due to a rise in out-migration by native workers. Card found that city outflow rates of natives and older immigrants were generally not sensitive to inflow rates of new immigrants. Card's results, therefore, suggest that researchers may not need to worry about internal migration when estimating the impact of immigration. However, Card's (1989) earlier study on the Mariel Boatlift had suggested that out-migration by native workers was likely to have played an important role in preventing a decline in wages in Miami after the arrival of 125,000 Cuban immigrants in one summer.

7.1.1　Evidence That Immigrants Drive out Natives

More thorough evidence on how native out-migration mitigates immigration's downward pressure on local wages in a labor market receiving large numbers of immigrants was provided by Filer (1992). He used data from the 1980 U.S. Census to examine mobility patterns by natives during 1975–1980 for 272 U.S. cities. Recognizing that native migration responses are likely to occur with a lag, he identified the number of immigrants living in an area in 1975 who were admitted between 1970 and 1974, and these immigrants were used to explain native out-migration during 1975–1980. Filer looked at net native migration, which he defined as the net sum of native workers in the city's labor market in 1980 who resided elsewhere in 1975 minus the number who lived in the city in 1975 but resided elsewhere in 1980, divided by the size of the city's workforce in 1975. He limited his sample of native workers to adult males. Across cities, the average percentage of adult males who arrived as immigrants was about 1% of the male labor force, and the mean increase in the adult male labor force from native in-migration was just under 1%. Filer found that mobility patterns of natives and rates of immigrant inflows across cities varied substantially.

Filer regressed native mobility rates on immigrant arrival rates while controlling for a wide range of characteristics of the city, its labor force, and the region. As controls, he included variables such as the growth in adult women and younger workers in the labor force, housing, pollution, commuting and demographic characteristics, various amenities and regional controls. The OLS regressions provide reasonably strong evidence that higher immigrant arrival rates deter inflows of natives, but there is little evidence suggesting that out-migration is encouraged. Filer found that a 1% increase in immigrants reduces native net migration by 0.12% and reduces native in-migration by 0.83%. There was no significant statistical evidence of out-migration.

Filer recognized that location decisions can be endogenous to city and region characteristics, which would bias his OLS estimates. To test for this possibility, he specified a simultaneous equations model that explicitly accounted for endogenous reactions. The estimated coefficients from this model suggest a much larger migration effect among natives than he estimated in his OLS model. The 3SLS model estimated that a 1% increase in immigration reduces native net in-migration by 3.34%. Because the 3SLS coefficients were so much more negative, the OLS coefficients likely suffer from simultaneity bias, as a result of both immigrants and natives being pulled in at greater rates to those cities with stronger labor markets.

Both OLS and 3SLS estimation indicated negative correlation between native net migration and the immigrant arrival rate, thus providing robust evidence that native migratory responses *more* than offset immigrant arrivals. Both the 3SLS and OLS results show that mobility responses were stronger among low-skilled natives. One possible explanation for this "native flight" is that natives leave because they perceive that their labor market opportunities have weakened. Filer actually draws a different conclusion, however. He found that mobility responses were stronger among whites. Filer reasoned that since evidence shows that white wages are impacted less by low-skilled immigration than black wages, there is something other than direct labor market effects influencing native migration. Obviously, prejudice against immigrants and the foreign culture they introduce into the community may drive a substantial portion of native migration. Also, while all native groups may have incentives to leave when immigrants arrive, wealthier whites may be better able to respond due to their having greater access to capital markets, can more easily find jobs in other cities, and, because native white culture dominates in all parts of the country, they will find it easier to move elsewhere compared to minority groups.

Strong evidence of native migratory responses was also found by Frey (1995) and Frey and Liaw (1996). Frey (1995) studied out-migration by natives from California, and Frey and Liaw (1996) studied multiple U.S. regions. Both studies reported a positive correlation between immigrant inflows and native outflows, a phenomenon Frey called "demographic balkanization" of U.S. cities.

Borjas, Freeman, and Katz (1997) compared native interstate migration during 1970–1990 to immigration during 1960–1970 by estimating *first difference* and *double difference* regression models. They pointed out that one disadvantage of a first difference specification is that it implicitly assumes each state would have had the same growth rate in native population absent immigration. However, many states probably would have had different growth paths during 1970–1990 compared to 1960–1970 even if there had been no immigration. The double-difference model controls for that possibility.

The double difference model used by Borjas et al. is the following:

$$\Delta n_j(70, 90) - \Delta n_j(60, 70) = \alpha + \beta[\Delta m_j(70, 90) - \Delta m_j(60, 70)] + v_j \qquad (7.1)$$

In this equation, $\Delta n_j(t, t') = \frac{\frac{N_{jt'} - N_{jt}}{L_{jt}}}{(t' - t)}$ is the growth rate of natives in state j between time period t and t' relative to the state's population in t (L_{jt}), N_j is the number of natives residing in state j, $\Delta m_j(t, t') = \frac{\frac{M_{jt'} - M_{jt}}{L_{jt}}}{(t' - t)}$ is the growth rate of immigrants in state j between periods t and t' relative to the state's population in t, M_j is the number of immigrants in the state, β measures the impact of a gain in immigrants on the size of the native population relative to pre-immigration conditions in the state, and v_j is a random error term. Note that Borjas, Freeman, and Katz' first difference model estimates the impact of an additional immigrant arriving in the state between 1970 and 1990 on the change in the native population during that period. In contrast, their double difference model estimates whether a change in the growth rate of immigrants entering the labor market between the two periods induced a change in the growth rate of natives entering the same labor market.

Using the first difference model, Borjas, Freeman, and Katz found a positive association between immigration in each state and the growth rate of the state's native population. The double difference model, on the other hand, showed a negative relationship. Therefore, immigration does not decrease the native population, but it does decrease the native labor force. Apparently, immigration causes natives to commute to neighboring labor markets.

Hatton and Tani (2005) analyzed geographic migration between 11 UK regions using annual data for the years 1981–2000. Hatton and Tani found relatively strong evidence of a negative native mobility response to immigration, particularly for the UK's 6 Southern regions. For all 11 regions, a 1% increase in net foreign immigration to region i relative to region j is estimated to have reduced net in-migration to region i by 0.064%. When estimation was restricted to the six Southern regions, however, the mobility response coefficient was 0.162%. Hatton and Tani noted that gross flows of international migration historically have tended to be larger for the Southern regions, particularly London, hence the importance of doing a separate estimate for that group of regions. Overall, their results strongly confirm that immigration induces native-born residents to relocate to other cities, either because of a softening in the labor market or because of other factors about the locality that they perceive as becoming less attractive with the arrival of immigrants.

7.1.2 Evidence that Immigration has Little Effect on Native Migration

Contradicting the empirical results reviewed above, Wright, Ellis, and Reibel (1997) found no correlation between native migration and immigrant arrivals after controlling for area size, a factor they argued could have biased other studies. They also tested for whether native out-migration varied across five different educational categories. Wright, Ellis, and Reibel found that variation in out-migration by unskilled natives across cities was due more to variation in the population size of cities than variation in immigrant arrival rates. They confirmed their results through robustness checks, using different samples of cities, and excluding outliers such as the highest immigration cities.

Card and DiNardo (2000) used 1970–1990 census data to test whether immigrant inflows during the 1980s altered the distribution of native-born skills across 119 U.S. cities. Card and DiNardo's study is the first to focus on the relocation decisions of specific native skill groups. They estimated the effect of immigrant inflows on the relative proportion of native-born workers in three equally sized occupational groups defined by average weekly wages in each occupation. They estimated the following equation, which relates the relative growth rate of natives in skill group j in a city to the growth rate of immigrants in that same skill group:

$$\left(\frac{\Delta N_{jc}}{P_{jc}} - \frac{\Delta N_c}{P_c}\right) = a + b\left(\frac{(\Delta M_{jc})}{P_{jc}} - \frac{(\Delta M_c)}{P_c}\right) + v_{jc} \tag{7.2}$$

where ΔN_{jc} (ΔM_{jc}) is the change in natives (immigrants) in skill group j in city c, ΔN_c (ΔM_c) is the change in natives (immigrants) in city c, P_{jc} is the population of skill group j in city c, P_c is the population of city c, and v_{jc} is a skill-group- and city-specific random error term. A value of $b = -1$ means the arrival of a new immigrant to skill group j results in one native from that skill group relocating. If $b = 0$, the mobility of natives in a skill group is independent of immigration to that group. In general, a zero value for b, however, does not mean that native location decisions are immune to immigration, only that changes in native population are not affected by changes in the arrival rate of immigrants to the same skill group.

Card and DiNardo estimated (7.2) using first weighted OLS and then instrumental variables to mitigate the potential bias due to immigrant and native population growth being endogenous to city- and skill-group-specific labor market conditions. The OLS estimates do not show any evidence that, within the lowest skill group, immigrants displace natives out of an SMSA. In fact, these estimates indicate a positive association between native in-migration and foreign-born in-migration.

After controlling for relative growth of the native population, city population growth, the fraction of immigrants in the skill group in 1980, and other city effects, weakly significant estimates showed that a 1% increase in immigrants to the lowest-skill group in a city induces a 0.24% increase in native in-migration to the same skill group in that city. The instrumental variables estimate was considerably larger, although also barely statistically significant. Even though these estimates are not strong, they do directly contradict the findings of Filer and others who found that immigrants displaced natives.

7.2 Migration Biases Estimates of Immigration's Wage Effect

Borjas (2006) asked how much of the difference between the estimated wage effects of immigration obtained from national studies and those obtained from local studies can be explained by the diffusing effects of internal migration. Recall from Chap. 5 that Borjas' theoretical model predicts that the longer after an immigration shock when the wage is measured, the closer the wage will be to what it would be in the absence of immigration. Borjas (2006) provides a framework that connects the parameters measuring the wage effect of immigration at a national level, the parameters that measure the effect at a local level, and the geographic mobility of native labor.

Borjas' approach was to estimate the wage effect of immigration in the national labor market, the labor markets defined by the boundaries of the nine U.S. Census regions, state labor markets, and individual city labor markets. Specifically, he estimated the following wage regression

$$\log w_{ijt} = \theta_w P_{ijt} + s_i + r_j + \pi_t + s_i \pi_t + r_j \pi_t + s_i r_j + \phi_{ijt} \qquad (7.3)$$

where w_{ijt} measures the wage paid to a worker in skill group i in spatial unit j at time t, P_{ijt} is the foreign-born share of the labor market for workers in skill group i, s_i is a vector of fixed effects which controls for the group's skill level, r_j is a vector of fixed effects controlling for place of residence, π_t is a vector of fixed effects controlling for the time period, and ϕ_{ijt} is a random error term. He applies data for 1960–2000. He then analyzes how the coefficient θ_w, which is intended to capture the wage effect of immigration, varies with the size of the geographic area.

When the labor market is national and the sample includes both men and women, Borjas estimated the coefficient at -0.532, which implies a 10% increase in the immigrant share reduces weekly earnings by 5.32%. The coefficient was -0.35 when the spatial unit is the Census division, -0.27 for the state-level regression, and between zero and -0.06 for the city regression. The estimated wage effect thus nearly evaporates when the labor market is disaggregated down to the local level.

Borjas also directly estimated the impact of the immigrant share on the native workforce and migration rate. He found that the impact of immigration on the native workforce diminished with the size of the area. At the city level, for every ten immigrants that arrive, slightly over 5 natives leave. At the state level, around 2 natives will leave the workforce for every ten immigrants that enter. At the Census division level, the estimated effect was found to be unstable, varying between nil and approximately 2 natives.

The final step in Borjas' strategy was to examine whether the large differences in the wage effects of immigration across geographic definitions of the labor market could be accounted for by native labor mobility. He assumed that the national labor market approximates a closed economy, so that the estimated wage effects of immigration at the national level reflect the true elasticity of the native-born wage with respect to immigration. Borjas concluded that: (1) native mobility responses account for about 40% of the gap between state-level wage effects and national-level effects; and (2) mobility responses account for as much as 60% of the difference between city wage effects and national effects. Overall, these results all suggest that internal migration is a very important secondary adjustment process.

Federman, Harrington, and Krynski (2006) tested for natives' response to the arrival of immigrants within an occupation. That is, they tested whether natives "migrated" out of a profession when immigrants entered. Their test case is the manicurist profession in California. The proportion of Vietnamese-born immigrants in the profession of manicurist in California jumped from 10% in 1987 to nearly 60% in 2002. At the same time, the population density of manicurists in the state grew from 1 to approximately 1.5 per 1,000 residents, an increase three times the 12% growth of real per capita income. While the growth of per capita income suggests there was an increase in the demand for manicuring services, the very high increase in the number of manicurists also implies an increase in supply driven primarily by an influx of mostly Vietnamese-born women who had the appropriate skills. The question is whether this large influx of immigrants into the profession induced native-born manicurists to abandon the profession and whether it deterred prospective native manicurists to enter the profession.

Federman, Harrington, and Krynski ran regressions using weighted least squares (the weights are population of each city) and instrumental variables. Coefficient estimates from both types of estimation confirmed a negative displacement rate. The weighted least squares regression estimates predict that for every ten Vietnamese manicurists that entered the local market, approximately five non-Vietnamese manicurists were displaced. The instrumental variable estimates predict that about four non-Vietnamese manicurists were displaced. Inflows, as well as exit rates, of non-Vietnamese manicurists were regressed on the Vietnamese manicurist density and other controls to ascertain the underlying reason for the observed displacement effect. The authors concluded from this analysis that the displacement effect was primarily due to the entry of Vietnamese manicurists deterring the entry of native manicurists, rather than the exit of natives.

In summary, the evidence on internal migration responses to immigration is very mixed, with some studies showing strong evidence of offsetting native mobility responses, others showing little or no evidence, and still others indicating a positive association. An appropriate description of the state of the evidence is given by

Freeman (2006, p. 157): "Analysts have reached no consensus about the extent to which internal migration explains the absence of any relation between immigration and wages among local labor markets."

7.3   Does Immigration Change Industry Structure?

International trade theory suggests that the inflow of immigrants will, all other things equal, change the industrial structure of the destination economy. As described in Chap. 5, traditional trade theory suggests that the inflow of a certain category of workers will increase the share of production of those industries that require relatively high amounts of that category of labor in their production process. This is known as the *Rybczynsky theorem* of the Heckscher-Ohlin model of trade. Very little empirical work has been done to test the hypothesis that immigration triggers changes in industry structure, however.

Lewis (2003) studied how U.S. cities absorbed inflows of workers in four different education groups during the 1980s. Applying U.S. Census data to a first difference specification, Lewis tested for a positive association between a city's share of immigrants in education group j and the employment share of industries that employ large amounts of group j workers, that is, industries that are *relatively j-intensive*. Lewis found that the relative sizes of the j-intensive industries were weakly related to immigration in that education group. In contrast, he found a strong positive association between inflows of workers in education group j and the share of an industry's workers from that group. Lewis concluded, therefore, that immigration does not increase immigrant-intensive industries, but only increases employment shares of immigrants across all industries.

Card and Lewis (2005) used 2000 U.S. Census data on employment shares in 3-digit classified industries for 150 larger cities to determine whether local reactions to immigration shocks are changes in industry shares or changes in skill-group employment shares within industries. They used the decomposition method introduced by Lewis (2003) to distinguish how immigration affected labor market shares in industries. They focused on high school dropouts. Card and Lewis' analysis effectively rejected the standard international trade model. They found that when U.S. cities experience an increase in the supply of workers with less than a high school education, local industries respond by adjusting their labor forces in favor of poorly educated workers, not by growing those industries that normally employ large numbers of poorly educated workers.

Card and Lewis' (2005) results supports the models of endogenous technological change by Acemoglu (1998) and Beaudry and Green (2003). These models predict that production technology is driven by the relative scarcities (prices) of factors of production. Also supporting the endogenous technology explanation is Lewis (2004), who used data on the number of advanced production techniques adopted by U.S. manufacturers in the late 1980s and early 1990s and found that the adoption of advanced techniques slowed significantly following inflows of unskilled workers to local labor markets. Similar evidence was obtained for Israel by Gandal, Hanson, and Slaughter (2004), who examined how production techniques of Israeli industries adjusted to the massive inflows of Jewish Russians in the early 1990s. A large proportion of adult Russian immigrants to Israel were highly educated and had held high-skilled professions in Russia. About the time of the immigrants' arrival, Israel's high-tech industry began a period of rapid growth. It is not clear that the adoption of high skilled-intensive technologies in Israel was endogenous to the Russian immigrant inflows, however; there were many other fundamental reasons why Israel's high tech industry grew rapidly, such as foreign investment, the high level of education of Israel's native population, and shifts in government policies to promote economic growth.

7.4 Measuring the Demand Effects of Immigration

As pointed out in Sect. 5.3 of Chap. 5, immigrants are not only workers, they are also consumers. This suggests there is likely to be a "Say's law of immigration" in the sense that immigrants at least partially demand their own labor. Specifically, if immigrants spend at least part of their destination economy earnings on goods and services produced locally, then immigration will trigger changes in the derived demand for their own labor. They will also affect the demand for other categories of labor, and thus they will affect native-born wages and employment rates. Changes in immigrant remittance rates and changes in public spending on goods and services for immigrants could further shift derived demand. Finally, if new immigrants compete with native-born workers for jobs, then the resulting lower labor costs will shift the product supply curve and generate lower costs for consumers. Thus, immigration is likely to change product prices directly through consumer demand or indirectly through product supply channels.

This demand effect of immigration has not been widely analyzed, as evidenced by the small number of studies cited in Chap. 5. There have even fewer attempts to actually quantify the demand effect of immigration.

7.4.1 Hercowitz and Yashiv's Estimates

The theoretical model developed by Hercowitz and Yashiv (2002) predicts that an exogenous immigration shock will trigger offsetting effects on product price, among other things. Hercowitz and Yashiv develop a dynamic model that captures the timing of the various effects of immigration. The model predicts that immigrants will delay entry to the destination economy's labor market but will enter the goods market immediately. As seems to have happened in a number of recent cases of mass immigration, the adverse labor market effects of immigration will be delayed.

Specifically, Hercowitz and Yashiv tested these predictions using the following empirical specification:

$$\ln p_{m,t} = a + bX_t + \sum_{q=1}^{Q} c_q \frac{\Delta P_{I,t-q}}{P_{N,t}} + \varepsilon_t, \tag{7.4}$$

where $p_{m,t}$ = the real price of output in period t, X is a vector of controls, $P_{I,t-q}$ is an exogenous immigrant inflow that occurred q periods earlier, P_N is native population, and ε_t is a random error term.

Of particular importance in (7.4) is the sum of right-hand terms, namely the product of c_q and the past immigrant inflows. The variable c_q is a vector of immigrant "participation factors" that describes how labor market participation varies with the length of time since immigration. In (7.4), these terms generate what statisticians call *impulse responses*, which in this case are the effects of immigration on prices after various lengths of time immigrants have been in the destination country. The impulse responses are assumed to be linearly related to immigrant participation in the labor and product markets according to the following specification

$$c_q = -\omega_1 (\theta_y)_{-q} + \omega_2 (\theta_1)_{-q} \tag{7.5}$$

The vector $\theta_y = \{(\theta_y)_{-1}, (\theta_y)_{-2}, \ldots\ldots\}$ consists of immigrant "participation factors" that describe how differences in time since migration influence the extent of labor market participation. The coefficients ω_1 are functions of the elasticities of native labor supply and other labor market characteristics. The vector $\theta_1 = \{(\theta_1)_{-1}, (\theta_1)_{-2}, \ldots\}$ consists of immigrant participation factors in the product market, determined by the price elasticities of demand and the time since migration, among other things.

Note the negative sign on ω_1 and the positive sign on ω_2 in (7.5). The opposite signs reflect the conflicting effects that immigration has on the product market. As consumers, immigrants push up product demand and price. But, as workers, they cause prices to fall by lowering wages, all other things equal. Furthermore, shifts in immigrant participation factors over time determine whether, overall, immigration raises or lowers prices. New immigrants are likely to immediately enter the product market as consumers, but they may not enter the labor market until after they have had some time to settle in the destination country. Hence, the impulse response term will exert a positive effect on price for low values of q, but since cohorts that have been in the destination country longer will be participating in both markets, those older cohorts will exert an ambiguous effect on prices.

Hercowitz and Yashiv estimate their regression model based on (7.5) using quarterly data on the arrival and assimilation of Jewish Russian immigrants to Israel over the years 1990–1999. The chosen number of lags, Q, was 9 quarters, and the coefficients on immigration lags were restricted to lie on a polynomial distributed lag for the technical reason that this distribution allows for more convenient estimates of the impulse responses.

Hercowitz and Yashiv found that the impulse response of immigration on product prices was positive at the first lag, negative from lag 2 onwards, but only statistically significant at lags 4 and 5. Those significant estimates were negative; the only positive coefficient occurred for the first lag, but that was statistically insignificant. These results very weakly confirm a decline in *relative* participation by immigrants in the goods market with length of stay. Hercowitz and Yashiv also found that significant negative effects of immigration on native employment occur after a year following an immigration shock. They interpret this result to also reflect the net stimulus effect of immigration on the product market during the first year.

Hercowitz and Yashiv's study has two important implications for future research on the product market effects of immigration. Unlike other adjustment processes, the consumer demand response to immigration starts up very quickly. Therefore, in the short term native-born workers can enjoy net benefits from immigration. However, while the consumer demand response continues for the long term, it will lose its ability to counteract the adverse labor market effects of immigration on native-born workers and that loss occurs faster than many would probably expect.

7.4.2 Bodvarsson and Van den Berg's Lexington, Nebraska, Study

Bodvarsson and Van den Berg (2006) estimated a model of an immigration shock to a local export-driven industry, inspired by the case of Lexington, Nebraska, a small rural city that received several thousand Hispanic immigrants in the early 1990s. Lexington provides a special case that facilitates the estimation of immigrants' demand effect because immigrants work almost exclusively in the "export" market, namely new large food processing plants producing for the national market. Yet, the immigrants consumed in the local market. Hence, after controlling for other changes that affected the local market, including native migration, immigration can be entered into the regression equation to estimate its effect on local demand without having to worry about immigration's effect on the labor market for local production.

Lexington, Nebraska, is located in the west-central part of the Great Plains corn and cattle region. Lexington experienced an extraordinary episode of endogenous immigration in 1990 when a multinational meat processing firm retrofitted an abandoned agricultural equipment manufacturing plant in the county to a state-of-the-art meatpacking facility. Virtually overnight, Dawson County saw an influx of approximately 2,500 workers, almost all of whom were foreign-born Hispanics. Following the initial immigration shock, there were subsequent waves of Hispanic migrants during the 1990s, many desiring closer proximity to family and friends, and soon other meatpacking and assorted manufacturing plants settled in Lexington. By 2000, about half of the city's residents were Hispanic immigrants, compared to just 3% before 1990.

To estimate the demand effect of immigration, Bodvarsson and Van den Berg first estimated the effect on retail wages using the regression equation

$$W_R = \delta_0 + \delta_1 I_0 + \delta_2 IM + \delta_3 N_0 + \delta_4 OM + \delta_5 P_X + \delta_6 V_N + \delta_7 V_1 + \alpha' X'$$
$$+ \emptyset' Z' + \varepsilon \tag{7.6}$$

in which W_R is the real county retail wage, I_0 is the initial stock of immigrants, IM is the volume of net in-migration during the period, N_0 is the initial stock of native-born persons, OM is net out-migration in the county during the year, P_X is the price of the export good, V_N is the real reservation wage of native-born workers, V_I is the real reservation wage of foreign-born workers, X' is a vector of county fixed effect controls, Z' is a vector of other control variables, and ε is an error term. The coefficients of the most interest are δ_2, which measures the effect of the immigration shock on the wage, and δ_4, which measures the native mobility response to the immigration shock.

Bodvarsson and Van den Berg included eight other counties in Nebraska, Kansas, South Dakota and Iowa in their sample. These other counties were chosen because they most closely resembled Dawson County, in which Lexington was located, but, unlike Dawson County, they experienced little or no immigration during the sample period. These other eight counties serve as the *counterfactual* in the sample. The sample period begins in 1980 and ends in 1999.

Bodvarsson and Van den Berg found that, all other things equal, the addition of one new immigrant raised the annual retail wage by $0.17, implying that the arrival of nearly 6,000 immigrants raised annual real wage income in the local economy by about $1,000. Furthermore, using data on real median housing prices in the 9 counties, Bodvarsson and Van den Berg tested for the Hispanic influx's effects on the local housing market. Estimating an equation like (7.6), but using the real median housing price as the dependent variable, they found that the addition of one immigrant to Dawson County raised the housing price by over $2, all other things equal. Bodvarsson and van den Berg thus conclude that there indeed were positive demand effects linked to immigration.

7.5.3 Estimating the Demand Effect of the Mariel Boatlift

Bodvarsson, Van den Berg, and Lewer (2008) reexamined the Mariel Boatlift to determine to what extent Card's (1990) finding that the Boatlift had a benign effect on Miami's labor market can be attributed to a boost in local consumption spending by immigrants. Recall from Chap. 5 that Card conjectured that the small effect of the Boatlift on Miami wages and unemployment rates was due to offsetting out-migration of native workers. Lewis (2004) argued that the Boatlift encouraged Miami's industries to adopt more unskilled-intensive production technologies. Bodvarsson, Van den Berg, and Lewer argue that while these adjustment processes may have been at work, Saiz's (2003) finding of strong positive effects of the

Boatlift on housing prices suggests that immigration also caused an increase in local product, and thus labor, demand. But how important was this demand effect for keeping wages and unemployment rates largely unchanged despite the arrival of nearly 100,000 immigrants?

To estimate the demand effect of immigration, Bodvarsson, Van den Berg, and Lewer set up a regression model in which an exogenous immigration shock is the net sum of (1) the substitution of immigrants for natives and (2) the stimulation of labor demand due to the consumer demand effect. In general, when labor demand is stimulated, native wages can rise, fall or stay the same, depending upon the shock's intensity and the various labor elasticities.

The authors applied an econometric methodology developed by Wacziarg (1998, 2001), which allows for the estimation of a simultaneous equations regression model in which an independent variable affects the dependent variable through different *channels* of influence. Specifically, the Wacziarg model includes a set of *channel equations*, each describing one of the processes by which the fundamental causal variable influences the channel variable, and an *aggregate equation* that explains the dependent variable and includes, among other determinants, each of the channel variables as explanatory variables. The overall effect of the fundamental causal variable on the dependent variable is the sum of the effects of the causal variable on each channel variable, each multiplied by the channel variable's influence on the final dependent variable. In this case, the native wage as the final dependent variable, and the two channel variables represent, respectively, the input substitution effect and the consumer demand effect.

Specifically, the following model was used to estimate the net effects of immigration on Miami wages:

$$W_N = a_0 + a_1(W_I) + a_2(P) + a_3(Z) + \delta, \tag{7.7}$$

$$W_I = b_0 + b_1(\theta_1) + b_2(R) + \varepsilon, \tag{7.7}$$

$$P = c_0 + c_1(\theta_1) + c_2(S) + \omega, \tag{7.8}$$

where W_N and W_I are the wages of natives and immigrants, respectively, P is product price, Z, R and S are vectors of other variables hypothesized to influence native wages, immigrant wages, and product prices, respectively. The variable θ_1 is the proportion of immigrants in the local labor market, and δ, ε, and ω are random error terms. The effect of immigration on wages through the immigrant wage channel is $(b_1 \cdot a_1)$, and the effect of immigration through the product price channel is $(c_1 \cdot a_2)$. The total effect of immigration on the native wage is $(a_2 \cdot c_1) + (a_1 \cdot b_1)$, of which the consumer demand effect accounts for the proportion $(a_2 \cdot c_1)/[(a_2 \cdot c_1) + (a_1 \cdot b_1)]$.

Bodvarsson, Van den Berg, and Lewer used the same data set and the same 4 comparison cities as Card's (1990) study. Like Card, they also broke the sample down into four categories of workers (whites, blacks, Cubans and Hispanics) and three categories for the other cities (whites, blacks and Hispanics). Estimation of

(7.7) and (7.8) confirmed that the Boatlift induced a negative input substitution effect. However, estimation of (7.9) confirmed a strong, positive consumer demand effect. Specifically, a 1% increase in the Cuban share of the Miami population induced an increase in retail sales per capita in excess of $23, all other things equal. More important, the positive contribution of the post-Boatlift consumption stimulus to the native-born wage exceeded the negative contribution that resulted from the substitution of immigrants for natives in the retail labor market. In fact, the consumer demand effect was nearly *twice* as strong as the input substitution effect, implying that the Mariel Boatlift net boosted the native-born wage. Similar results were found when the sample was split into three unique ethnic groups. The positive consumer demand effect for whites, blacks, and Hispanics suggests that the new Cuban immigrants patronized shops and businesses of all ethnic backgrounds. However, while native white wages were positively affected by a larger Cuban immigrant share, native black and Hispanic wages were on balance not affected by the Mariel influx. These findings led Bodvarsson, Van den Berg, and Lewer (2008, p. 35) to conclude that "... there is a 'Say's Law of Immigration': Immigrants do indeed spend a substantial portion of their incomes in their new home communities and thus demand at least some of the labor they supply."

7.5.4 Additional Estimates of the Demand Effects of Immigration

Lach (2007) explicitly analyzed the price effects of Russian Jewish immigrants to Israel. By estimating the price effects, Lach effectively estimates the effect of immigration on local demand. Lach looks at demand in more detail than Bodvarsson and Van den Berg (2006) and Bodvarsson, Van den Berg, and Lewer (2008), and he analyzes both the shift and change in the shape of the demand curve.

First, Lach used the 1990 Russian Jewish immigrant supply shock in Israel to test the immigrant price elasticity of demand. Lach's sample includes store-level price data for over 900 products sold in about 1,800 retail stores located in 52 cities during 1990. There is considerable cross-city variation in the Russian immigrant density, and Lach took advantage of this variation to identify the effect of immigration on prices. Overall, Lach found a negative effect of immigration on consumer prices: a one percentage point increase in the ratio of immigrants to natives in a city will *decrease* prices by 0.5 percentage points. He attributed this result to the change in the composition of demand. He found that immigrants were more price sensitive and more likely to substitute cheaper goods for more expensive goods. Hence, it is not certain that the price decline in any way implies that immigrants have a negative demand effect. To the contrary, since Lach builds supply growth into his analysis, his results probably show only that immigrants are more careful shoppers than natives and, therefore, do not increase demand as much as a similar increase in the number of natives would. Nevertheless, his results do suggest that immigrant remittances are not the only thing that reduces the demand effect of immigrant workers below that of increases in native workers.

A number of studies have estimated the effects of immigration on housing prices and house rents. Housing price data is often readily available, and all immigrants must acquire housing. Saiz (2003) hypothesized that immigration causes unskilled individuals to experience greater escalation in rental prices than skilled individuals and unskilled renters to displace skilled ones from dwellings at the lower end of the rental market. He used observations from rental units in the 1974–1983 national and SMSA Annual Housing Survey (AHS) to perform a difference-in-differences test on Miami-area prices following the Mariel Boatlift. Saiz compared the evolution of rental prices in Miami with that of 10 metropolitan areas with the closest median growth rate to Miami. The identifying assumption in his sample is that there is no factor other than the Mariel shock specific to Miami that accounts for any deviation in the trend of rental prices.

According to Saiz, the Boatlift contributed to a significant spike in all rental prices. The differential rent increase varies from just over 7% to approximately 10%, depending upon the comparison group used. Through 1981, the differential rent hike was even larger, varying between approximately 8.5 and 12%. Saiz also observed that units in the bottom three quartiles were the ones significantly affected by the Boatlift, whereas prices in the top quartile were generally unaffected. Thus, the Boatlift had a disproportionate impact on the rental prices of dwellings used by persons with lower incomes. Furthermore, the impact of the Boatlift appears to have been strongest in low-income Hispanic neighborhoods, where the Mariel immigrants were most likely to have settled.

Although it was not a focal point of their study, Ottaviano and Peri (2005) estimated regressions of housing values on increases in local employment due to immigration using data for individuals in 86 U.S. cities (1970–2000) and 117 cities (1970–1990). They found that the impact of immigration on housing values of native-born local residents was substantially positive. Specifically, Ottaviano and Peri estimated that an increase of foreign-born workers equal to 1% of total city employment generates a 1.1–1.6% increase in native-born housing values.[1]

7.6   The Costs of Government Services for Immigrants

Discussions of the economic effects of immigration in destination countries often focus on immigrants' use of public services and their receipts of government

---

[1]Cortes (2008) addresses another more specific question, which is: How does immigration affect the product supply curve? She uses U.S. data for 1980–2000 to measure local immigrant densities and low-skilled labor shares, as well as store-level price data to construct estimates of local price indices for non-tradeable low-skilled services. Cortes finds that an increase of 10 percent in the share of low-skilled labor in a city decreases the price of these services by approximately 2.5%. However, her estimate does not take into account any effects of immigration on service demand.

transfers. In most developed economies, which are the principal destination countries for immigrants, such services and transfers are a large portion of GDP. This means that even small changes in the amount of taxes paid by immigrants or services used by immigrants are much greater than the small estimated overall net economic effects of immigration on the destination country. It is not entirely surprising, therefore, that policymakers and taxpayers in the destination countries are concerned about how government costs are affected by the arrival of immigrants.

7.6.1 Recent Studies for the United States

The evidence does not support the popular belief that immigrants are a fiscal burden in the United States, however. First of all, except for refugees and elderly immigrants, the remaining immigrants to the United States actually use government services to a lesser degree than natives. If we include refugees, who are high users of government services and recipients of government transfers, immigrants as a group still use government services only slightly more often and receive only slightly more welfare payments than natives. For example, according to the 1990 census, 9% of immigrant families received welfare payments, a percentage that was only slightly more than the 7.4% of U.S.-born families that received welfare payments. Pre-1982 legal immigrants to the United States living in the six states with the largest immigrant populations were found to pay more in total taxes than they received in government-provided benefits.[2] Another study shows that, counter to some popular myths, immigrants do not seem to make settlement decisions based on the availability of welfare and social services; they settle where there are jobs and where they have close family. That is, immigrants use state and local government services, but they do not seem to immigrate just to take advantage of those services.[3]

A 1992 study for the United States Department of Health and Human Services determined that the fiscal burden of immigrants fell mostly on state and local governments. The federal government actually enjoyed net gains from increased income tax and Social Security tax revenues.[4] According to the historical data, the average immigrant in 1990 was less educated and had a larger family compared to natives, and immigrants were, therefore, more likely to use state and local government services, especially education. But, because immigrants were also younger than natives, they were large contributors to Social Security, a federal program.

With time, however, the situation changes at the local government level. The children of immigrants pay more taxes and receive fewer transfers, and their

---

[2]Kirchner and Baldwin (1992).

[3]See Zawodny (1997), referenced earlier, and Vedder, Gallaway, and Moore (2000).

[4]Kirchner and Baldwin (1994).

increased incomes make them even greater net contributors to the Social Security fund. According to a recent Federal Reserve Bank study: "When it's all added up ... most long-run calculations show that immigrants make a net positive contribution to public coffers."[5]

A study of immigration in Europe suggests that the tax-transfers ratio is not as burdensome as is often feared because governments adjust both taxes and transfer programs in order to improve the balance for native workers. A study by Razin, Sadka, and Swagel (2002) found that for 11 European countries, both taxes on workers and transfers to the poor were reduced as immigrants came to represent a higher percentage of the population. The recent welfare reforms in the United States, which reduced benefits to non-citizens, are further evidence that the political process adjusts immigrants' access to welfare benefits as immigration rises.

7.6.2 *Are U.S. Immigrants More Costly Today than in the Past?*

The image of the many immigrants that arrived in the United States at the end of the 1800s and the early 1900s is that they "came to this country not with their hands out for welfare checks," but "for freedom and the opportunity to work."[6] Since so many Americans are descendants of those turn-of-the- century immigrants, the myth of the self-reliant immigrants is enthusiastically kept alive, even as polls reveal that many Americans believe that today's immigrants are coming to the U.S. for the welfare benefits and free schools.

One hundred years ago, in 1909, about half of all public welfare recipients in the U.S. were members of immigrant families, even though immigrants made up about 15% of the total population. At about the same time, two-thirds of people receiving public assistance in Chicago were foreign-born.[7] According to the 1990 census, 9% of immigrant families received welfare payments, a percentage that was only slightly more than the 7.4% of U.S.-born families that received welfare payments. In the early 1900s, nearly three-quarters of all students in New York City's public schools were children of immigrants; over half of all students in public schools of the 30 largest U.S. cities were children of immigrant families. The so-called fiscal burden of immigrants, if there is one at all, is clearly not a recent phenomenon.

---

[5]Zeretsky (1997, p. 5).

[6]The words of Rep. Bill Archer of Texas, chairman of the House Ways and Means Committee, in describing earlier immigrants and justifying his committee's 1995 bill to deny welfare payments to most legal immigrants.

[7]Rose (1995).

7.7   Immigration's External Effects

Immigration may generate externalities that cause gains or losses that exceed those represented in the static model of immigration. For example, the arrival of immigrants can increase productivity throughout the economy by increasing the size of the market and thereby raising the level of competition. Or, immigrants may raise the level of technology by introducing new products and production methods, which raises the productivity of all factors in the economy. Also, by increasing the total size of the economy, immigrants permit greater exploitation of economies of scale.

7.7.1   Economies of Scale

Economies of scale refer to the case where output increases faster than inputs, a common attribute of large-scale production. The effect of population on economies of scale has been emphasized by Julian Simon (1992, p. 397):

> In addition to the acceleration of progress in knowledge-creation and technology, . . . , a larger population also achieves economies of scale. A larger population implies a larger total demand for goods; with larger demand and higher production come division of labor and specialization, larger plants, larger industries, more learning-by-doing, and other related economies of scale. Congestion is a temporary cost of this greater efficiency, but it does not seem to present an ongoing difficulty in the context of production.

Simon's point is essentially the same as Adam Smith's well-known discussion in *The Wealth of Nations* on how the *extent of the market* determines the size of the gains from specialization. The larger is the population, the more opportunities there are for people to specialize in particular tasks and professions, and, therefore, raise per worker productivity.

Nathan Rosenberg, an economic historian noted for studying the growth of technology over the ages, attributes the rapid economic growth of the United States in the 1800s to "rapid growth in demand and circumstances conducive to a high degree of product standardization." (Rosenberg 1994, p. 113) That is, the United States was able to exploit economies of scale because its market grew rapidly and, because of the country's large middle class, the market was very uniform. What caused this growth of the market? According to Rosenberg (p. 113): "Probably the most pervasive force of all was the extremely rapid rate of population growth . . . with immigration assuming a role of some significance in the 1840s." This discussion of scale effects and U.S. economic growth in the nineteenth century deals with an important issue; despite having a very protectionist trade policy in the 1800s, the U.S. was able to grow rapidly without taking advantage of international trade because immigration increased its population and thus mitigated the constraints of national borders on the division of labor. Effectively, the United States used immigration rather than international trade to achieve economies of scale.[8] Immigration enabled U.S. industry to exploit increasing returns to scale despite the strong protectionist bias of U.S. trade policy throughout the nineteenth century.

Suppose for a moment that the static labor market model of immigration correctly describes the effects of immigration, and we can ignore for the moment the demand-side effects of immigration discussed earlier in this section. The *externalities* from immigration cause output to rise, and the demand for labor to increase, and thus the VPM_L curve shifts up. The combined effects of immigration, (1) the increase in the supply of labor and (2) the rise in the VPM_L curve, are illustrated in Fig. 7.1. The positive externalities, perhaps in the form of increasing returns to scale, prevent the wage from falling from w_1 to w_2. Instead, if the externalities are large enough, the wage could even rise, say to w_3. If the wage does rise, there are gains to everyone in the destination economy, even the labor that competes directly with the new immigrants. Native labor gains the checkered area between w_1 and w_3, which is equal to the shaded area **a**, immigrants gain additional income equal to **b**, and other factors gain area **c**. Researchers have produced little formal evidence measuring such externalities to immigration, and certainly no one has come up with a credible estimate of the magnitude of areas such as **a** and **c**.[9] Obviously the fortuitous outcome shown in Fig. 7.1, where everyone gains from immigration, is only one possible outcome; the wage could fall rather than rise even with positive externalities. The positive externalities have to be added to the demand-side effects of immigration, which also shifts the VMP_L curve.

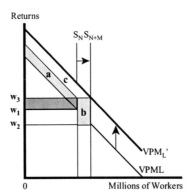

Fig. 7.1 Immigration: Positive Externalities in the Destination Country

---

[8]Other economic historians who reach similar conclusions about nineteenth century U.S. immigration and economic growth are Irwin (2000), Hill (1971), and Crafts and Venables (2001).

[9]For example, Borjas (1995) presents exactly the model we present in Figs.3–5, but offers no clues as to the likelihood or magnitude of areas a and c.

7.7.2   Are There Negative Externalities Associated with Immigration?

Immigrants may cause negative externalities. The arrival of immigrants can cause increased congestion in public services such as schools, roads, sewers, electric power systems, and parks. Many people in fact criticize immigration because they feel their community is getting "too crowded," and some people attribute increased crime, pollution, and the destruction of traditional culture to the arrival of immigrants in their country. The increase in the number of people holding more than one passport, a situation openly promoted by many source countries as a way to increase immigrant remittances, has caused concern to some nationalists. Mark Krikorian, director of the Center for Immigration Studies, a lobby organization sponsored by special-interest groups opposed to immigration, suggests that dual citizenship will loosen the traditional notion of "us" and "them." He asks: "If people can become dual citizens, why not have allegiances to three, four or even eight countries?"[10] Well, why not?

Immigration's negative externalities, all other things equal, cause a downward shift of the demand for labor curve that partially offsets the positive effects of higher demand and increased investment. Figure 7.2 illustrates the case where the negative consequences of congestion lower real output and, hence, the VMP curve. Note that in this case immigration causes the wage to fall not to w_2, but to w_3. So long as w_3 is high relative to the source country wage, immigrants will still tend to come to the destination country, but the destination country no longer gains welfare from immigrants' arrival. In this case, if there are no positive demand-side effects, total welfare for natives will fall if the negative externalities cause a large enough downward shift in the VPM_L curve so that $f > g$. Recall from earlier diagrams that

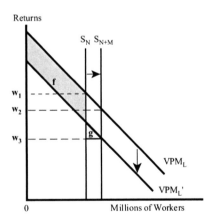

Returns

S_N S_{N+M}

w_1

w_2

w_3

f

g

VPM_L

VPM_L'

0   Millions of Workers

Fig. 7.2 Immigration: Negative Externalities in the Destination Country

[10]As quoted in Pascal (1998).

the area **g** is immigration's net gain in welfare for the destination country. There is little evidence that immigration generates negative externalities large enough to generate the result shown in Fig. 7.2. Recall that studies of immigrants' use of government services and transfers do not confirm that immigrants are a large fiscal burden on destination countries.

7.8 Concluding Remarks

This chapter has surveyed recent research on the longer-term effects of immigration in the destination country. This literature includes studies on internal migration responses, capital adjustments, product market responses, and adjustments in industrial composition and technological choice, to immigration. The majority of the research has focused on internal migration responses, and this effect has been found to be ambiguous. Nor is it clear how important internal migration is as a long term adjustment process. Little is known empirically about how the capital stock adjusts to immigration. The small number of studies done on industrial structure responses to immigration suggests that capital adjustments may not be substantial.

The strongest long-term adjustments to immigration involve the so-called demand effects. The evidence in that particular literature is clear: Immigration boosts the prices of local goods and services, especially housing, through increases in consumer demand. Furthermore, there is preliminary evidence that immigration, by lowering labor costs, can lower product prices too.

Clearly, one of the promising areas for future research on the effects of immigration is the development, and empirical testing, of models that account for both the short term and long term effects of immigration shocks in destination countries. It would certainly be interesting to blend elements of the models by Ottaviano and Peri (2005, 2006), Hercowitz and Yashiv (2002), Borjas (2006) and Card and Lewis (2005) to specify a "unified" general equilibrium theory of the distributional effects of immigration in the destination country, and to estimate such a model while controlling for the various adjustment processes. However, it is even more important that the adjustment processes themselves be modeled and tested more rigorously. Internal migration responses, capital stock adjustments, and demand effects are, by themselves, at least as important as the small estimated net effect of immigration in the specific destination community. The labor literature has been constrained by the simple labor-market model to analyzing only the labor market outcomes of immigration. It has, therefore, missed much of the action that accompanies and follows immigration flows.

Finally, the finding that there are substantial long-run adjustments to immigration flows suggests that economists need to take a dynamic approach to immigration. Static analysis simply cannot accurately capture the many slow adjustments that the arrival of immigrants causes in an economy. In particular, conspicuously absent from the immigration literature in economics is the analysis of immigration's long-run effects on economic growth. This is surprising because some of the countries that received the greatest number of immigrants have also been the economies that have grown to be among the world's wealthiest economies. The net static gains captured by the traditional labor market model of immigration cannot begin to explain immigration's full, and varied, long-run effects on, say, Australia, Canada, New Zealand, or the United States. Chapter 9 will take up the role of immigration on economic growth and suggest how researchers can proceed to bring growth into their analysis.

References

Acemoglu, D. (1998). Why do new technologies complement skills? Directed technical change and wage inequality. *Quarterly Journal of Economics, 114*, 1055–1089.

Altonji, J., & Card, D. (1991). The effects of immigration on the labor market outcomes of less-skilled natives. In J. Abowd, & R. Freeman (Eds.), *Immigration, trade and the labor market.* Chicago: University of Chicago Press.

Beaudry, P., & Green, D. (2003). Wages and employment in the United States and Germany: What explains the differences? *American Economic Review, 93*, 573–603.

Bodvarsson, Ö., & Van den Berg, H. (2006). Does immigration affect labor demand? Model and test. In C. Chiswick, S. Polachek, & H. Rapoport (Eds.), *Research in Labor Economics* (vol. 24). New York: Elsevier.

Bodvarsson, O., Van den Berg, H., & Lewer, J. (2008). Measuring immigration's effects on labor demand: A reexamination of the Mariel Boatlift. *Labour Economics 15*, 560–574.

Borjas, G. (1995). Assimilation and changes in cohort quality revisited: What happened to immigrant earnings in the 1980s? *Journal of Labor Economics, 13*, 201–245.

Borjas, G. (2003). The labor demand curve is downward sloping: Reexamining the impact of immigration on the labor market. *Quarterly Journal of Economics, 118*, 1335–1374.

Borjas, G. (2006). Native internal migration and the labor market impact of immigration. *Journal of Human Resources, 56*, 221–258.

Borjas, G., Freeman, R., & Katz, L. (1997). How much do immigration and trade affect labor market outcomes. *Brookings Papers on Economic Activity, 1*, 1–67.

Butcher, K., & Card, D. (1991). Immigration and wages: Evidence from the 1980s. *American Economic Review, 81*, 292–296.

Camarota, S. (1997). The effects of immigrants on the earnings of low-skilled native workers: Evidence from the June 1991 Current Population Survey. *Social Science Quarterly, 78*, 417–431.

Card, D. (1990). The impact of the Mariel Boatlift on the Miami labor market. *Industrial and Labor Relations Review, 43*, 245–257.

Card, D. (2001). Immigrant inflows, native outflows, and the local labor market impacts of higher immigration. *Journal of Labor Economics, 19*, 22–64.

Card, D. (2005). Is the new immigration really so bad. *Economic Journal, 115*, F300–F323.

Card, D., & DiNardo, J. (2000). Do immigrant inflows lead to native outflows. *American Economic Review, 90*, 360–367.

Card, D., & Lewis, E. (2005). The diffusion of Mexican immigrants during the 1990s: Explanations and impacts. NBER Working Paper 11552.

Card, D., & Lemieux, T. (2001). Can falling supply explain the rising return to college for younger men? A cohort-based analysis. *Quarterly Journal of Economics, 66*, 705–746.

Chiswick, B. (1978). The effect of Americanization on the earnings of foreign-born men. *Journal of Political Economy, 86*, 897–921.

Cohen-Goldner, S., & Paserman, M. (2007). The dynamic impact of immigration on natives' labor market outcomes: Evidence from Israel. IZA Discussion Paper 1315.

Cortes, P. (2008). The effect of low-skilled immigration on U.S. prices: Evidence from CPI data. *Journal of Political Economy, 116*, 381–422.

Crafts, N., & Venables, A. (2003). Globalization in history: A geographical perspective. In M. Bordo, A .Taylor, & J. Williamson (Eds.), *Globalization in historical perspective* (pp. 323–364). University of Chicago Press: Chicago.

Federman, M., Harrington, D., & Krynski, K. (2006). Vietnamese manicurists: Are immigrants displacing natives or finding new nails to polish. *Industrial and Labor Relations Review, 59*, 302–318.

Filer, R. (1992). The effect of immigrant arrivals on migratory patterns of native workers. In G. Borjas, & R. Freeman (Eds.), *Immigration and the work force: Economic consequences for the United States and source Areas*. University of Chicago Press: Chicago.

Freeman, R. (2006). People flows in globalization. *Journal of Economic Perspectives, 20*, 145–170.

Frey, W. (1995). Immigration and internal migration 'flight' from U.S. metropolitan areas: Towards a new demographic balkanization. *Urban Studies, 32*, 733–757.

Frey, W., & Liaw, K. (1996). The impact of immigration on population redistribution within the United States. Unpublished paper, Population Studies Research Center, University of Michigan.

Friedberg, R. (2001). The impact of mass migration on the Israeli labor market. *Quarterly Journal of Economics, 116*, 1373–1408.

Gandal, N., Hanson, G., & Slaughter, M. (2004). Technology, trade, and adjustment to immigration in Israel. *European Economic Review, 48*, 403–428.

Hatton, T., & Tani, M. (2005). Immigration and Inter-Regional Mobility in the UK, 1982–2000. *Economic Journal, 115*(507), F342–F358.

Hercowitz, Z., & Yashiv, E. (2002). A macroeconomic experiment in mass immigration. CEPR Discussion Paper 2983.

Hill, P. (1971). The economic impact of immigration into the United States. *Journal of Economic History, 31*(1), 260–263.

Johnson, G. (1980). The labor market effects of immigration. *Industrial and Labor Relations Review, 33*, 331–341.

Katz, L., & Murphy, K. (1992). Changes in the wage structure, 1963–1987: supply and demand factors. *Quarterly Journal of Economics, 57*, 35–78.

Kirchner, J., & Baldwin, S. E. (1992). *The fiscal impact of eligible legalized aliens*. A study performed under a contract between the KRA Corporation and the U.S. Department of Health and Human Services.

Lach, S. (2007). Immigration and prices. *Journal of Political Economy, 115*, 548–587.

Lewis, E. (2003). Local open economies within the U.S.: How do industries respond to immigration? Federal Reserve Bank of Philadelphia Working Paper No. 04–1.

Lewis, E. (2004). How did the Miami labor market absorb the Mariel immigrants? Federal Reserve Bank of Philadelphia Working Paper No. 04–3.

Lewis, E. (2005). Immigration, skill mix, and the choice of technique. Federal Reserve Bank of Philadelphia Working Paper No. 05–8.

Orrenius, P., & Zavodny, M. (2007). Does immigration affect wages? A look at occupation-level evidence. *Labour Economics, 17*, 757–774.

Ottaviano, G., & Peri, G. (2005). Rethinking the gains from immigration: Theory and evidence from the U.S. NBER Working Paper No. 11672.

Ottaviano, G., & Peri, G. (2006). Rethinking the effects of immigration on wages. NBER Working Paper No. 12497.

Pascal, G. Z. (1998, 25 March). Dual citizenship is double-edged sword. *The Wall Street Journal*.

Razin, A., Sadka, E., & Swagel, P. (2002). Tax burden and migration: A political economy theory and evidence. *Journal Of Public Economics, 85*(2), 167–190.

Rose, F. (1995, 26 April). Muddled masses, the growing backlash against immigrants includes many myths. *Wall Street Journal*.

Rosenberg, N. (1994). *Exploring the black box, technology, economics, and history*. Cambridge: Cambridge University Press.

Saiz, A. (2003). Room in the kitchen for the melting pot: Immigration and rental prices. *Review of Economics and Statistics*, *85*, 502–521.

Saiz, A. (2007). Immigration and housing rents in American cities. *Journal of Urban Economics*, *61*, 345–371.

Vedder, R., Gallaway, L., & Moore, S. (2000). The immigration problem, then and now. *The Independent Review*, *4*(3), 347–364.

Wacziarg, R. (1998). Measuring the dynamic gains from trade. Stanford University Working Paper, May.

Wacziarg, R. (2001). Measuring the dynamic gains from trade. *World Bank Economic Review*, *15*, 393–429.

Wright, R., Ellis, M., & Reibel, R. (1997). The linkage between immigration and internal migration in large metropolitan areas in the United States. *Economic Geography*, *73*, 234–254.

Zawodny, M. (1997). Welfare and the locational choice of new immigrants, Economic review, Federal Reserve Bank of Dallas 2nd Quarter: 2–10.

Zeretsky, A. M. (1997). A burden to the economy? Immigration and the economy, *Regional economist*, Federal Reserve Bank of St. Louis, October.

Chapter 8
Immigration and the Source Country

Abstract This chapter examines the effect of migration on the source country. The standard labor supply and demand model shows that immigration causes the destination country to gain welfare while the source country loses welfare. There are more complex outcomes, however. This chapter first focuses on income *remittances*. The second half of this chapter covers the *brain drain*. The policy debate has been complicated by the lack of consensus on the actual costs and benefits of the brain drain for the source country. Offsetting the obvious negative consequences, the brain drain may also increase remittances back to the source country, and overseas opportunities provide incentives for all people in the source country to acquire more education.

The simple labor supply model of immigration, presented in the introduction to this section of the book, suggests that the source country suffers a decline in total production but enjoys a rise in per capita income after immigrants depart, all other things equal. These are the net results of an increase in income of workers that remain behind and a decrease in welfare of the owners of the economy's other productive factors whose marginal products decline with the departure of the immigrants. Just as is the case for an immigrant destination country, the full effects of immigration on the source country are much more complex than the simple labor supply model of immigration suggests. This chapter discusses the many potential economic changes that immigration causes in the source country beyond the obvious reduction of the labor force.

Among the issues discussed in this chapter are the source country demand effects of workers leaving the country to both earn and spend labor income in another country, the positive and negative externalities associated with the decline in population, the effects of remittances back to the source country by overseas workers, and the dynamic effects of the loss of innovative resources when people leave the country. The latter phenomenon has been referred to as the *brain drain*.

Ö.B. Bodvarsson and H. Van den Berg, *The Economics of Immigration*,
DOI: 10.1007/978-3-540-77796-0_8, © Springer-Verlag Berlin Heidelberg 2009

8.1   Remittances and Demand Effects in the Source Country

Most early articles on the effect of immigration on the source economy found unambiguous negative effects. For example, Grubel and Scott (1966), Bhagwati and Hamada (1974), and Kwok and Leland (1982) conclude that the source economy suffers a loss in income when natives immigrate to other countries. However, the more recent literature is more ambiguous in its conclusions. By linking immigration itself to human capital formation, introducing real world complications such as return migration and network effects, and technology flows between countries, source countries need not suffer economic declines from the departure of people. This chapter discusses the contributions of both the early and more recent literature. To begin the discussion, however, we go back to the familiar static labor supply and demand model.

8.1.1   Demand Effects

Recall from the basic labor supply model of immigration in the Introduction to Section I that when some source country workers leave to go to their destinations, the supply of labor is reduced in the source economy. Figure 8.1 illustrates that the leftward shift in labor supply causes wages in the source country to rise from A to B for the remaining workers. As a result, immigration increases total wages accruing to the remaining workers from the area f to f + e in the source country. On the other hand, the income accruing to the economy's other factors declines from d + e + g to just d. The size of the source country economy shrinks by the areas g + h that lie between the original and post-immigration labor supply curves S and S' and under the fixed value of the marginal product of labor, or labor demand, curve. The effect of immigration on the source country is a mixed result, with per capita total income rising, the size of the economy shrinking, and some groups gaining at the expense of others.

The simple labor supply model of immigration is incomplete, however. First of all, the departure of a substantial number of workers implies that there are fewer consumers living in the source country, and the total income of that reduced number of consumers is also lower by the areas g + h. All other things equal, immigration reduces labor demand in the source country.

Figure 8.2 illustrates how the demand effect of out-migration alters the conclusion of the simple labor supply model in the source country. When the immigrants depart from the country, total output and income fall, the demand for labor declines from VMP_1 to VMP_2, where VMP stands for the "value of the marginal product" of labor. The wage thus rises only to C, not all the way to B as in Fig. 8.1.

Recall from Chap. 7 that immigration has a *demand effect* when there is some barrier to the completely free flow of goods and services across borders. If there are no transport costs, trade restrictions, or any other constraints that favor local products over foreign products, then demand will be optimally spread across

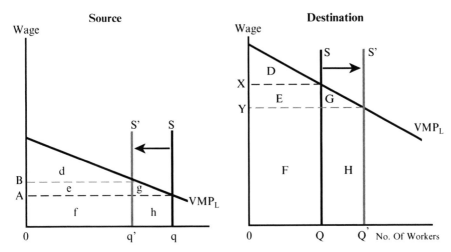

Fig. 8.1 Immigration's effect on labour markets

all products produced throughout the world. Immigrants would already be spending a portion of their income in the destination country prior to their arrival, and they would continue to spend the same portions of their total income in the source, destination, and remaining countries of the world after they immigrate. More precisely, immigrants' higher income after migrating to the higher wage country would, in the case of completely costless and unrestricted trade, increase total worldwide demand, and some fraction of that increase in overall demand shows up as an increase in labor demand in the source country. In the real world, however, trade is not costless. There are transport costs, customs procedures, tariffs, marketing costs, distribution costs, and myriad other costs associated with exporting and importing. Many goods and services are still what economists call "nontradables." Thus, the movement of people from one country to another also shifts some demand from one economy to another. The conclusions from the basic labor supply model of immigration, therefore, must be modified as suggested in Fig. 8.2.

8.1.2 Immigrants and Remittances

Many immigrants send a portion of the income they earn in the destination country back to the source country to support family left behind or to store wealth for their own future return to their native country. Such transfers of income are commonly referred to as immigrant *remittances* in the economics literature. Immigrant remittances shift income, and thus labor demand, from the destination country to the source country. In fact, if immigrants remit a substantial enough portion of their higher destination country incomes to the source country, then total demand for labor in the source country could actually increase even though people leave the country.

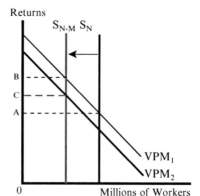

Fig. 8.2 Immigration and demand for labor in the source country

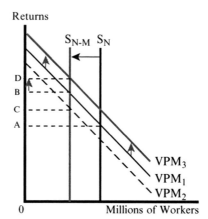

Fig. 8.3 Immigration and demand for labor in the source country with remittances

If remittances exceed the loss in income due to the shrinking of the economy after the departure of the immigrants, the demand curve for labor could on balance shift upward rather than downward. Figure 8.3 shows two different scenarios in the source country for labor demand following emigration. In the absence of remittances (scenario 1), labor demand falls from VMP_1 to VMP_2, causing the wage to fall from B to C. With remittances (scenario 2), labor demand rises from VMP_1 to VMP_3, causing the wage to rise to D. Note, however, that the fraction of income remitted back to the source country must be sufficiently high for the wage to rise.

8.1.3 A Two-Country View of Remittances

The increase in the demand for source-country labor comes at the expense of demand for labor in the destination country. Demand for labor decreases in the destination country when purchasing power residing in the destination country is remitted to consumers in the source country. In fact, critics of immigration in destination countries often claim that their country does not gain from immigration precisely because immigrants send their earnings back to the source countries. Evidence suggests that immigrant remittances are not large enough to substantially reduce the demand for labor in high-income destination countries. Rather, immigrant remittances make possible the interesting case where immigration generates total income gains in both the destination and source countries.

The labor supply model of immigration in Fig. 8.4 shows that in the absence of remittances, the total income of the workers and owners of other factors remaining in Source following emigration decreases by the area g. This implies that if remittances exceed g, income will rise in Source. This requirement is not difficult to meet. Since immigrants usually move from low-income countries to countries where the marginal return to labor is many times greater, they need only remit a small portion of their high Destination wages for Source to enjoy an increase in total income. In Fig. 8.4, the pre-immigration wage is assumed to be €2 in Source and the post-immigration wage in Destination is €8. Such a four-fold difference in incomes between source and destination countries may actually be a conservative assumption; when a Mexican worker immigrates to the United States, his or her wage is likely to increase nearly ten-fold. In Fig. 8.4, the area g is only about one-sixteenth the size of the area H, the total earnings of immigrants in Destination, and the area h is one-fourth of the area H. If immigrants send home to Source more than €2.50 for every €8 they earn, the source country's total income increases. There will then tend to be an increase in labor demand in Source, shown as a shift from VMP_1 to VMP_2 in Fig. 8.4. The destination country still experiences a net gain in total income following immigration so long as the area G plus the gains in real output caused by the demand effect discussed above, the areas J + K, are greater than the g + h remitted. In sum, remittances by immigrants open up the possibility

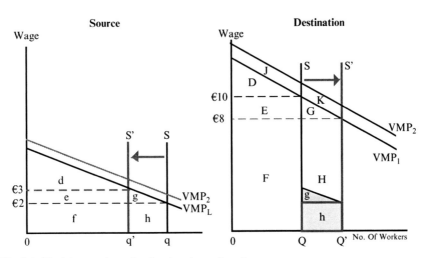

Fig. 8.4 The labor markets after immigration and remittances

that the economies of both the source and destination countries increase their gross national incomes. The income of the workers and other factor owners remaining in Source thus rises with immigration so long as remittances exceed the area g in Fig. 8.4. The requirement that remittances equal one-eighth of immigrant earnings overseas is an even less restrictive criterion. The gross domestic product (GDP) of Source still shrinks with the departure of the immigrants, although the total income of Source natives, migrants and those remaining, definitely increases.

8.2   What We Know About Immigrant Remittances

Immigrant remittances have become an important component of the balance of payments for many countries. Immigrant remittances are recorded as unilateral transfers in the current account of a country's balance of payments. Because most immigrant remittances are from high income immigrant destination countries to lower income immigrant source countries, unilateral transfers have become large net negatives in the accounts of the former countries and large positives in the accounts of the latter. Balance of payments data have been supplemented by other data and case studies to provide a more complete picture of immigrant remittances.

8.2.1   The Growth of Immigrant Remittances

The growth of immigration over the past 50 years has been accompanied by an even more rapid growth of remittances. Not surprisingly, immigrants in the United States send the most money back to relatives in their native countries. A 2004 survey of immigrants living in the U.S. revealed that more than 60% of Latin American immigrants in the U.S. send some money to relatives in their native countries, and total U.S. immigrant remittances to Latin America alone were estimated by the Inter-American Development Bank to exceed $30 billion in 2004.[2] More recent data shown in Table 8.1 below suggests the number was greater than that. According to several reports, Mexican immigrants in the United States sent $6 billion to family and relatives in Mexico in 1999, they sent $6.8 billion in 2000, in 2003 they remitted $14.5 billion, and in 2005 they reportedly remitted over $20 billion.[3] According to a Federal Reserve Bank of Dallas report, Mexicans living in the United States sent over $23 billion back to Mexico in 2006.[4] Research suggests that temporary Mexican workers in the United States send about half of their income home, while permanent Mexican immigrants to the United States still send about

---

[2]Inter-American Development Bank (2004).

[3]The 1999 number was reported in *The Economist* (2000) October 29, the 2000 figure is reported by Fidler (2001), the 2003 figure is from Thompson (2003), and the 2005 estimate is from Laper (2006).

[4]Cañas, Coronado, and Orrenius (2007).

Table 8.1 Immigrant remittance payments received by developing countries, by region, 2000–2006 (Billions of U.S. Dollars)

	2000	2001	2002	2003	2004	2005	2006[a]
Total	85	96	117	143	165	193	206
East Asia and Pacific	17	29	29	35	39	43	47
Europe and Central Asia	13	13	14	179	23	31	32
Latin America & Caribbean	20	24	28	35	41	48	53
Middle East and North Africa	13	15	16	20	23	24	25
South Asia	17	19	24	31	31	36	41
Sub-Saharan Africa	5	5	5	6	8	9	9

[a]Estimated
Source: World Bank (2007), *Global Development Finance 2007*, Washington, D.C.: The World Bank; Box 2.2, p. 54. Numbers are the sum of the categories Workers' Remittances, Compensation of Employees, and Migrant Transfers from the *Balance of Payments Statistics Yearbook 2007*, Washington D.C.: International Monetary Fund.

15% of their U.S. income to family in Mexico.[5] Immigrant remittances account for more than 1% of GDP in many developing economies, and more than 5% in some.

8.2.2 Remittances as a Percentage of Source Country GDP

India has received immigrant remittances in excess of 1% of its gross domestic product for many years. For example, as far back as 1982, remittances by Indians working overseas were estimated to be equal to 1.6% of Indian GDP. Total remittances by overseas Indians were reported to have reached $8 billion by 2000, about 2% of Indian GDP.[6] By 2006, they were double that amount, although because of India's rapid economic growth over the past half decade, the share of remittances in Indian GDP grew only slightly.

El Salvador reportedly received $1.2 billion in remittances from overseas relatives in 1998, about 15% of national product. Egypt had so many of its citizens working in other countries that its balance of payments recorded remittances equal to over 10% of its GDP throughout the 1990s. Filipinos reportedly sent home some $6 billion annually by the late 1990s, nearly 10% of GDP.[7] Some Caribbean nations receive over half of their national income from remittances by former citizens living overseas.[8] Cuba receives over $1 billion from Cuban-Americans annually,

---

[5]Handlin, Krontoft, and Testa (2002).

[6]From NationsBanc Montgomery Securities, Tokyo-Mitsubishi International, as reported in *The Wall Street Journal* (1998).

[7]*Wall Street Journal* (1998).

[8]Siegel (1993), p. 150.

which enables it to partially overcome the U.S.-led trade embargo and earn dollars to pay for needed imports.[9]

8.2.3 The Reliability of Remittance Data

The most recent estimates suggest that total worldwide remittances by overseas immigrants exceeded $200 billion in 2006. Such estimates of immigrant remittances must be used with caution, however. Money is often carried back home in the form of cash, and is, therefore, not recorded in the balance of payments accounts. Furthermore, because foreign exchange transactions are often regulated and restricted in many developing countries, remittances often are carried out in parallel markets where exchange rates are more favorable compared to official exchange rates, and such transactions are also unlikely to be accurately recorded in the balance of payments accounts from which estimates of remittances are often derived. For a variety of reasons, the estimates have probably gotten more accurate in recent years. First, fewer countries restrict foreign exchange transactions, so there are no longer such large differences between official and "black" exchange rates; this has, no doubt, brought remittance payments back to official channels where they can be recorded. Also, private banks have reduced their fees and captured a larger role in intermediating remittance payments through official channels, where they can be recorded. Finally, estimates of remittances have increasingly found alternative sources of information to amend the numbers that show up in the official balance of payments accounts. Cañas, Coronado, and Orrenius (2007) attribute a large part of the estimated increase in immigrant remittances to improved data gathering rather than an increase in actual remittances. Past estimates were much larger than earlier estimates suggested. Today's more accurate estimates are welcome, of course, but they may have given the wrong impression about the growth of immigrant remittances. Table 8.1 reflects data that have, to some unknown degree, corrected for past failures in the data.

8.2.4 The Recent Data on the Growth of Immigrant Remittances

Beyond the simple data problems, the fact remains that immigrant remittances have indeed grown substantially over the past several decades. That remittances have grown so large is a direct consequence of the growth of immigration. The acceleration of immigration in recent years, both legal and illegal, further contributes to the sharp rise in immigrant remittances because recent immigrants tend to send more money back to source countries than immigrants who have been in the destination

---

[9]Barrionuevo and Cordoba (2004).

country longer. Also, many immigrants from poor countries left their native countries with the specific intent to remit foreign income. For example, according to a recent poll of Ecuadorian families who have members working overseas, "the majority of Ecuadorian emigrants were motivated for reasons other than personal economic problems. Instead, their decision to emigrate is the product of a family consensus, in which the younger, healthier and best-equipped family members were chosen to make the journey."[10] The poll also found that the cost of emigration was usually financed by the family remaining behind. Thus, remittances by recent Latin American immigrants to the U.S. are large because remittances were the principal reason for immigrating.

8.2.5 *Policies to Encourage Remittances*

The growth of remittances and the potentially positive impact of remittances on the source country's overall welfare is well understood by source country policy makers. Governments in some labor abundant countries have even adopted policies that effectively encourage people to immigrate to countries where incomes are much higher. The Philippines, for example, has a state-sponsored program to send workers abroad. When the Prime Minister of India made an official visit to the United States in 2002, he formally asked the United States to streamline the process for Indians to get visas to work in the United States.

Of course, the source country's eventual gains from the out-migration of its citizens depend on future remittances, so governments have also taken measures to ensure that remittances continue long after immigrants have taken up foreign residence or even foreign citizenship. Evidence shows that immigrant remittances decline the longer immigrants reside in their destination countries. Over time, family ties weaken, young relatives become adults who can take care of themselves, and older relatives pass away. To prevent a decline in remittances, some source countries have recently changed their national laws to encourage permanent immigrants to keep their native country citizenship. In the past, nearly all countries cut off citizenship when citizens immigrated and acquired citizenship in another country. In recent years, however, Colombia, Ecuador, Brazil, Mexico, and the Dominican Republic, among others, have changed their laws to permit dual citizenship. Mexico now even allows former citizens to reclaim Mexican citizenship after they had lost it by becoming citizens in the United States. In 2004, President Fox asked the Mexican Congress to approve letting millions of Mexican citizens living in the United States vote in the 2006 Mexican presidential election.[11] The Mexican state of Zacatecas passed a law in 2003 to let the 800,000 Zacatecans who now live in the United States come back to run for local political office.[12] The motive for these

---

[10]Reported by Quesada (2003).

[11]Weiner (2004).

[12]Authers (2004).

legal changes was clearly to maintain ties with the people who left the country and to encourage their continued remittances to relatives at home. The increase in the number of people holding more than one passport has caused concern among some nationalists in the destination countries.[13] While it is unlikely that formal allegiances will multiply as much as some people fear, dual citizenship has become a common occurrence in the twenty first century world.

To facilitate remittances, many source country governments have pressured banks and other financial institutions to lower the costs of making remittance payments. The banks and other financial services companies have long enjoyed hefty profits from remittance payments. For example, one study found that for some Latin American countries, the cost of remittances in amounts under $500 exceeds 20% of the amount remitted![14] McKinsey & Company, the management consulting firm, estimated in 2004 that banks and other firms earned $12 billion worldwide from immigrant remittances.[15] Most Latin American immigrants use relatively expensive wire transfer companies to move money to their relatives abroad because they do not have bank accounts. Only about half of all Latin American immigrants have bank accounts, and among illegal immigrants, an even smaller percentage have bank accounts. A recent program approved by the U.S. government and several governments of immigrant source countries permits foreign consulates in the United States to issue identification cards that can legally be accepted by U.S. banks as identification for opening a bank account, and this has substantially increased the use of banks by foreign immigrants.[16] The recent growth of international banking, which has led to large multinational banks operating in both developed and developing economies, is likely to reduce remittance costs because immigrants and the recipients of remittances will be able to deal with the same bank in both the sending and receiving countries. For example, in 2004, the Citigroup Inc. banking subsidiary California Commerce Bank began offering a binational account that permitted immigrants in the U.S. to deposit funds that relatives could access with credit cards overseas. In the case of Mexican immigrants, for example, the California bank offers the U.S. account and simultaneously authorizes Banamex, Citibank's Mexican subsidiary, to issue family members a card on that U.S. account.[17]

---

[13]As quoted in Pascal (1998).

[14]See, for example, Suro, Bendixen, Lowell, and Benavides (2002).

[15]McKinsey & Company (2004).

[16]Federal Reserve Bank of Dallas, El Paso Branch (2004).

[17]Associated Press (2004).

8.2.6   How Remittances are used in the Source Countries

The welfare effects experienced by the source country from remittances depend critically on how remittances are used. If remittances are used for high-return investments, then the long-run welfare effects will be greater than if they are used for short-run consumption needs. This is not to say that consumption is bad for human welfare; to the contrary, remittances can greatly alleviate poverty in source countries by providing people with the means to raise their consumption levels above mere subsistence. However, when remittances are used to acquire consumer durables, to improve housing, and, perhaps most important, to increase education, they can raise long-run welfare by much more than their current consumption value.

Statistical tests of how remittances affect source countries face several econometric problems. First of all, the data on remittances are notoriously inaccurate, largely because many private transfers pass through informal financial channels. Secondly, because remittances are, at least in part, more like insurance payments than steady income flows, remittances are likely to rise when economic conditions worsen in the source country. That is, recent immigrants send home more money to family in the source country when their family needs the money most. Hence, remittances will appear to be correlated with declining economic conditions. Finally, omitted variables influence remittance flows, which makes any estimated relationship between remittances and source country economic conditions suspect. There are, fortunately, econometric methods to take account of these difficulties, and several recent studies provide suggestive results.

Yang and Martínez (2006) study remittances to the Philippines from overseas Filipinos. They use *instrumental variables* to address the econometric problems described in the previous paragraph, and they find a clear positive relationship between remittances and reductions in poverty in the Philippines. They find that remittances raise incomes, all other things equal, of the families who directly receive them, and overall poverty is also reduced in the communities where remittances are received. Yang and Martínez suggest that these spillovers to other households in the community may be due to a multiplier effect from the recipient families' increased expenditures or from direct transfers within the communities.

A detailed World Bank study of Guatemala by Adams (2006) reveals that remittances substantially reduce the severity of poverty. In Guatemala, remittances from relatives working overseas, mostly in the United States, account for over half the household income of the very poorest households and raise their levels of consumption. Another study by Cox Edwards and Ureta (2003) finds that in El Salvador remittances have a very strong influence on whether children remain in school. Their empirical analysis confirms that schooling is positively correlated with income in general, but in El Salvador's urban areas increases in income from remittances have ten times more impact on school attendance than general increases in income. This evidence suggests that one of the reasons why family members emigrate and remit their foreign earnings is specifically to finance the schooling of children and siblings.

Not all studies find that remittances have positive effects on source country economic welfare. An econometric study of remittances for a large sample of countries over the period 1970–1998 by Chami, Fullenkamp, and Jahjah (2003) of the International Monetary Fund is not as optimistic about the long-run benefits of immigrant remittances. Their study specifically examines the moral hazard associated with remittances. They ask whether recipients of remittances behave more carelessly once they have remittance income than they would normally behave with money they themselves earned. An example of such a moral hazard problem is from a 2002 *New York Times* story on a young Bangladeshi wife in an arranged marriage to an older disabled military man. She went to Penang, Malaysia to work for five years, sent back as much of her income as she could, and when she returned, not only had all the money been spent, but her husband had actually increased the family's debt.[18] In their empirical study of the issue, Chami, Fullenkamp, and Jahjah (2003) conclude:

> The dependency on these transfers induces recipients to use remittances as a substitute for labor income, and to lower their work effort ... The aggregate impact of moral hazard can be quite significant, and our empirical results suggest that this particular moral hazard problem does affect economic activity in many economies.[19]

Moral hazard extends beyond the immediate recipients of remittances, however:

> Governments, too, may succumb to a moral hazard problem created by the receipt of remittances...the government may be able to ignore imbalances in the domestic economy and avoid taking politically costly steps to address them. At worst, governments could intentionally pursue politically beneficial but economically unwise policies, in the expectation that remittance flows will continue to insulate the domestic economy from any negative consequences. Such policies would likely exacerbate the conditions that led to large-scale migration and remittance transfer, leading to heavier dependence on immigrant remittances and decreased effort on the part of domestic workers, firms, and entrepreneurs.

Unlike most other studies of remittances, Chami, Fullenkamp, and Jahjah conclude that, all other things equal, remittances have a negative effect on economic growth. Some source countries have tried to mitigate immigrants' fears of moral hazard. For example, the state government of Zacatecas, Mexico, offers three dollars in government funds toward specific infrastructure projects in migrants' native towns and villages for every dollar migrants contribute to the investment funds. Immigrants must still have confidence in the source country government's ability to spur economic growth for this scheme to stimulate remittances, however. Ratha (2003) finds that worker remittances are a contributor to developing country economic growth only in countries "with sound economic policies."[20]

---

[18]Somini Sengupta (2002).

[19]Chami, Fullenkamp, and Jahjah (2003).

[20]Ratha (2003).

8.2.7   Remittances: Tentative Conclusions

We know that immigrant remittances are large, that they are much larger than official overseas development assistance (foreign aid), and that they account for huge percentages of some countries' national products. Remittances are clearly an important result of immigration, and they can substantially alter the costs and benefits of immigration experienced by the destination and source countries. In general, it is not clear whether remittances turn immigration into a positive factor for source countries.

There is clearly a need for much more research. First, we do not yet have accurate data on remittances. We do not yet know exactly how large remittances are, and we know even less about exactly who remits, who receives the remittances, and what people do with the remittances. We also need to examine the long-run dynamic growth effects of remittance payments in source countries.

Complicating matters is the fact that remittances are just one component of the overall phenomenon of immigration, which in turn is just one component of the overall phenomenon of globalization. As the world integrates, goods, services, investment, and people increasingly move, and all types of payments between countries expand. As important as remittances have become, a final judgment of how immigration affects the source country depends on much more than remittances. In the remainder of this chapter, we examine several other important consequences of immigration in the source country that are not easily captured in the standard immigration models.

8.3   Negative Externalities from Agglomeration

The departure of migrants to another country can have both negative and positive externalities in the source economy. Immigration serves as a "safety valve" when employment opportunities are lacking in the source country, as Bhagwati and Rodriguez (1975) suggested. If immigrants were unemployed in the source country and they find work overseas, then the departure of the immigrants will almost definitely raise the average income of those remaining behind. Also, the departure of unemployed or under-employed natives reduces the need for housing and other infrastructure investments, the crime rate may fall, and lines at the movie theater will be shorter. On the other hand, economies of scale may be lost when the population shrinks, which may raise costs and reduce per capita real income. In the latter case, negative externalites would shift the labor demand curve to the left, lowering wages, all other things equal, for those workers remaining behind. Welfare could also decline in more subtle ways as well; there may no longer be a market for certain products, product variety could decline, and available infrastructure may simply fall into disuse and no longer be maintained.

Externalities from economies of scale are potentially troublesome for source countries for more complex reasons. The next section looks at how immigration driven by worldwide economies affects the countries who supply the immigrants to the global economy's centers of agglomeration.

8.3.1 Economies of Scale, Agglomeration, and Source Countries

High income economies produce a very different mix of goods and services than poor economies do. High income countries also tend to use very different production methods. Economic growth, therefore, changes the concentrations of economic activity. By itself, such changes in specialization do not imply the movement of productive resources, like people, from one economy to another. Changes in specialization can be achieved by simply moving an economy's existing resources from one set of tasks to another set of tasks. However, the newer economic activities, such as industrial activity and innovative activity tend to be subject to economies of scale. Krugman (1991) attributes the agglomeration of industrial activity to increasing returns to scale. Glaeser, Kallal, Scheinkman, and Schleifer (1991) link agglomeration more closely to innovation rather than industrial concentration. Innovation is even more likely to agglomerate: "After all, intellectual breakthroughs must cross hallways and streets more easily than oceans and continents."[21] Florida (2005) shows how research and development activities and creative activities that generate patents and copyrights are even more concentrated than industrial activity.

Economic growth has gradually increased industrial and innovative activity relative to the more traditional dominance of agricultural activity. Over the past 200 years, human migration has been motivated by the tendency for economic activity to concentrate geographically, or, as economists say, to *agglomerate*. One of the characteristics of economic growth is the movement of people toward cities, regions, and even other countries where the economic activities that are subject to economies of scale, industrial and innovative activity, have agglomerated. The year 2006 reached a major population landmark: Over half of the world's 6.5 billion people now live in urban areas.

The agglomeration of economic activity and the population necessarily led to migration within countries and, naturally, across borders because natural population growth is still highest in rural areas and the poorest agricultural countries. The growth of immigration is, therefore, a very natural outcome of the changing structures of economies as they grow. Agglomeration is likely to continue for the foreseeable future, and immigrants will continue to be attracted by the higher wages and better job opportunities in the regions where production and innovation concentrates.

---

[21]Glaeser, Kallal, Scheinkman, and Schleifer (1991).

8.3.2 Agglomeration Causes the Source Countries to Shrink

Agglomeration may be the reason why incomes are higher in some countries than others, as described in the labor market model of immigration. The departure of immigrants from the source country may reduce the size of the source country's economy and even per capita income if there are economies of scale. The opposite may happen in the destination country. Hence, with economies of scale and agglomeration, the returns to all factors of production, including labor, may rise in the destination country and fall in the source country. Economies of scale, therefore, exaggerate income differences that may already exist for other reasons, thus further stimulating immigration. In one sense, the various conclusions from the labor supply and demand model of immigration concerning the gains and losses to the various groups in the source country are even more relevant. However, since the economies of scale and agglomeration of economic activity are also related to innovative activity, there are dynamic effects that are not captured by the labor supply and demand model of immigration.

Immigration may serve to both promote and hinder the spread of technology and, hence, the spread of the benefits of innovative activity in the centers of agglomeration. First of all, immigration will tend, all other things equal, to reduce resources in the source country, and this may delay the adoption of new technologies necessary for growth. On the other hand, immigration increases innovative activity in the center countries where activity clusters, which generates more new technology that, potentially, becomes available throughout the world. Furthermore, to the extent that immigrants build networks through which new ideas and technologies pass, immigration driven by innovative agglomeration can both increase innovation and speed the spread of innovative new ideas and technologies. Both the destination and source countries may, therefore, raise their rates of economic growth.

Most obviously, the innovation that occurs in countries that are centers of innovative activity causes changes throughout the world. Technological change alters production everywhere, depending, in part, on how fast technology moves from one economy to another. Technological change also alters the prices of resources throughout the world, and the resulting price changes can have a variety of beneficial and detrimental effects on the source economy.

History shows how varied the effects can be. For example, the technological progress and the growth of industrial activity that agglomerated in the economies of Europe and North America during the nineteenth century increased the demand for many raw materials produced in Latin America, Asia, and Africa, which led Robertson (1938) to famously describe the resulting growth of international trade in primary products as an "engine of growth." In other words, technological progress can raise the value of what people in the source countries produce. On the other hand, technological progress may also reduce demand for source country output. For example, demand for primary products in general has not kept pace with overall economic activity in the world. Economic growth and the growth of incomes have resulted in more demand for services that do not require primary products as inputs, and industrial technologies have also greatly increased the efficiency of resource use. In short, the income gains from agglomeration have an ambiguous effect on incomes in the source countries that tend to shrink relative to the centers where innovative activity clusters.

Technological progress, or the way in which economies transform resources into welfare enhancing output, is the fundamental source of economic growth. The benefits for the source country from emigration to the innovative centers therefore depend on how quickly technology is applied in the source country. Evidence suggests that technology moves slowly across countries because the adoption and application of new technologies requires resources. It may not take as many resources to adopt and apply existing technology than it does to create new technology from scratch, but it does still require some costly resources. Abramovitz (1986, p. 405) concluded that "differences among countries in the productivity levels create a strong potentiality for subsequent convergence of levels, provided that countries have a 'social capability' adequate to absorb more advanced technologies ... the institutional and human capital components of social capability develop only slowly as education and organization respond to the requirements of technological opportunity and to experience in exploiting it." All other things equal, therefore, technological progress and economic growth will be faster in those locations where there are more resources that facilitate the absorption of new technologies.

The fortuitous outcome described above, in which agglomeration and immigration accelerates technological progress and, through the spread of technology, increases incomes everywhere, may not occur under most real world circumstances. If immigration leads to the departure of a large portion of the source country's most skilled workers, who are critical to applying new technologies, source country economic growth may slow even if, worldwide, technological progress accelerates.

8.4   Immigration and Technology Transfers, Investment, and Trade

The conventional wisdom that talented, entrepreneurial, and educated people are needed to adopt and apply foreign technologies is supported by the evidence. However, that does not imply that the departure of exceptionally talented people necessarily leaves a source country less able to gain from foreign technological progress. The transfer of knowledge, ideas, and technology from technologically more advanced countries to less advanced countries requires people on both ends of the transfer. Immigration helps build networks and channels that facilitate the flow of technology. In fact, it is very well possible that a compatriot who recently immigrated to an advanced technology country is better able to communicate information back to the source country. Agrawal, Cockburn, and McHale (2003) find that social capital, the subtle relationships among people that have been shown to facilitate the sharing of knowledge and technology, endures even after immigration separates people. That is, even after immigrants move overseas, they maintain close ties with former colleagues and associates in the source country. Analysis of patent citations reveals that former colleagues and associates that subsequently separated by emigration continue to influence each others' research. This effect is especially important for countries such as India, China, Taiwan, and others that have many university graduates living overseas.

Obviously, other factors also influence the flow of technology. For example, Kuhn and McAusland (2006) show that technology flows benefit the source country the most the stronger is intellectual property rights protection in the destination country and the weaker is such protection in the source country.

8.4.1 Immigration and International Investment

Devan and Tewari (2001) report that expatriates working in Silicon Valley in the U.S. accounted for the majority of new investments in the rapidly growing technology industries of Bangalore and Hyderabad in India. Ex-patriots have played a similar role in Taiwan, with current and former Silicon Valley residents responsible for a substantial share of investments in new technology industries.[22] Light (1985) and Saxenian (2002) suggest that entrepreneurial immigrant communities stimulate significant flows of international investment. Gould (1994) and Head and Ries (1998) suggest that immigration stimulates international investment by reducing the transaction costs associated with language, business practices, and culture.

The relationship between immigration and investment flows is complex. Traditional trade theory suggests that capital should move to labor-abundant countries, which includes most of the major immigrant source countries. Lucas (1990), however, noted that capital does not always move to labor abundant countries. Lucas attributes this lack of capital mobility to institutional failures. Immigrants have been observed to form ethnic and cultural networks that can mitigate the institutional failures that prevent capital from moving across borders. Light (1985) and Saxenian (2002) provide evidence that entrepreneurial immigrant communities stimulate significant flows of international investment back to their native countries. Saxenian's study of foreigners in Silicon Valley during the 1990s concluded that immigrants build "social networks that span national boundaries and facilitate flows of capital, skill and technology. In so doing, they are creating transnational communities…that allow local producers to participate in an increasing global community."[23] Gould (1994) and Head and Ries (1998) argue that immigration still stimulates international investment by reducing the transaction costs associated with language, business practices, and culture. Lewer and Van den

---

[22]World Bank (2003).

[23]Saxenian (2002), p. 28.

Berg (2009) find that, on average, a 10% rise in immigration is associated with a 5% increase in FDI from immigrants' new home countries back to their native countries.

8.4.2 Immigration and International Trade

Van den Berg and Lewer's (2009) empirical study finds that immigrants cause international trade between immigrant source and destination countries to expand for several reasons: (1) immigrants create trade networks, (2) they stimulate the presence of multinational firms from richer destination countries in poorer source countries, and (3) they induce governments in both the source and destination countries to reduce trade barriers. Gould (1994), Head and Ries (1998), Rauch and Trindade (2002), and Greif (1989) have convincingly argued that dispersed immigrant communities linked by common cultures often build trade networks that encourage international trade when other institutions are weak. This role of immigrant diasporas may, therefore, be especially important for developing economies that still lack the sophisticated institutions required for long-distance trade.

Culture-based trade networks are by no means a recent phenomenon. Greif (1989) details how the Maghribi traders in the Mediterranean spread across distant cities and facilitated trade when other institutions to support trade were absent after the fall of the Roman Empire. Ensminger (1997) describes Islamic trade networks in the Mediterranean Region and Africa more than 1,000 years ago.

The Indian software industry views the work permits for Indian programmers as necessary for expanding its global business.[24] In 2000, during a visit to the United States, the Prime Minister of India surprised many commentators when he openly lobbied U.S. policymakers for a change in U.S. immigration law in order to permit more Indian engineers and computer programmers to gain U.S. work visas. In addition to the overseas experience that Indian programmers and engineers gain overseas, they are also the people who can sell Indian software services in the U.S. Exporting services often requires the physical presence of people in the export market. The United States accounted for about 60% of India's $4 billion in software exports.

8.4.3 Immigration and Services Trade

Immigration may be especially important for international trade in services, which has become an important source of export earnings for India. After the terrorist attacks in the United States in 2001, it became more difficult for Indian firms supplying information technology services to enter the United States and other

---

[24]Madhavan (2000).

high income countries to obtain temporary work permits for its employees. According to an Indian IT industry representative:

> An IT service contract is as much of a perishable commodity as fruit or vegetables.
> Delaying a visa application on an outsourcing contract is no different from Indian customs
> holding up a shipment of American fruit for three months to check for pesticide.[25]

If services must be personally delivered, then the temporary migration of people
and trade are one and the same thing. In the case of India's growing service
industry, the movement of highly talented people is clearly not a brain drain in
the traditional sense. This immigration reflects the spread of multinational service
firms, which provide what is arguably a very efficient and direct channel for
spreading technology across countries.

8.5   The Brain Drain

When people immigrate, they carry both their own labor and their accumulated
human capital with them. Development economists have occasionally extended
their analyses beyond the overall numbers of immigrants to evaluate the implications of the simultaneous movement of humans and human capital. That this
distinction matters is evidenced by the fact that destination countries often favor
highly educated and talented immigrants over less educated immigrants. There is a
widespread belief that human capital is beneficial to economic growth. On the flip
side, the departure of highly educated and talented immigrants has been singled out
as a serious cost of immigration for source countries.

8.5.1   Human Capital of Immigrants

Evidence shows that immigrants from less developed countries are usually much
more educated than the average residents of their source countries. These findings
may surprise Europeans or Americans, who observe the arrival of many foreigners
who are less educated than they are. However, while it is true that the average
Mexican immigrant arriving in the U.S. is less educated than the average American,
those immigrants have more education than the average Mexican.[26] More worri-
some to development economists is the finding that it is often the most educated
people who leave a poor country and immigrate to high income countries. This
phenomenon has even been given its own ominous name: The immigration of
university graduates, doctors, and other professionals from developing countries

---

[25]Quoted in Madhavan (2000), op. cit.
[26]Boucher, Stark, and Taylor (2005).

to high income countries in Europe, North America, and the Pacific region is usually referred to as the *brain drain.*

Immigration policies in the high income countries have stimulated the brain drain by making it easier for highly educated people to enter the country while making it more difficult for poorly educated people to acquire work visas. Australia, Canada, and New Zealand have instituted *point systems* for selecting immigrants in place of traditional *country of origin* criteria. Points are awarded for many personal characteristics, but education and professional experience count heavily in the scores used to qualify potential immigrants for entry visas. Even the United States, whose immigration qualifications are predominantly based on the principle of "family reunion," increasingly award resident visas on the basis of job skills and education. A number of European countries, such as France, Ireland, the United Kingdom, and Germany, have introduced immigration promotion programs to explicitly target highly educated and technical workers.

8.5.2   The Brain Drain as a Development Issue

The brain drain has been seen as a problem for less developed countries. Bhagwati and Hamada (1974) and Bhagwati and Rodriguez (1975) argued that educated and skilled immigrants take with them the education and training that was, at least in part, paid for by people remaining in the source country. In effect, capital-scarce developing countries were investing in human capital that was subsequently carried out of the country when educated people immigrated to high income countries. More recently, the brain drain has been linked to the "Schumpeterian" growth models, in which highly educated people are viewed as critical resources for the creation of new technologies and the adaptation of existing technologies from other countries. For example, Miyagiwa (1991) and Wong and Yip (1999) focused on the role of education in the growth process and analyzed how the departure of educated workers affects the source country's rate of economic growth. Growth models that focus on technological progress suggest that the long-run economic growth rate of immigrant source countries will fall when people move away to other countries. In short, the economic development literature has come to view the brain drain as a serious problem for developing economies. Subsequent analysis and research, however, suggest that the consequences of the brain drain for the source countries are not always so detrimental to growth.

The profession of nursing provides an interesting example that is often used to illustrate the negative effects of the brain drain on source countries. There is a shortage of nurses in most high-income developed economies, in large part because demographic shifts in those countries are causing their populations to age rapidly. Older people require more nursing services than young people. The market for nurses is increasingly global because qualified nurses from poor countries can raise their incomes many-fold by immigrating to high income countries. Nurses are one of the largest categories of brain drain we observe in the world. Hospitals and nursing homes in the United States, Britain, and other developed economies routinely travel to Africa and Asia to entice nurses to immigrate. One doctor from Ghana suggests that efforts to meet his country's needs for nurses would be futile; increase nursing school enrollments means that "we may end up educating more, only to have more leave."[27] That these strong "pull factors" in developed countries could damage living standards in poor countries has been recognized by government officials in the destination countries. For example, the British government's guidelines for the National Health Service include a prohibition on recruiting nurses from countries where there are severe shortages of nurses. However, these guidelines are open to interpretation and, therefore, not easily enforceable.[28]

8.5.3   How Big is the Brain Drain?

During the past three decades, over 70% of newly trained physicians in Pakistan left the country. Over 60% of Ghana's doctors emigrated to more developed countries. There are more Haitian physicians practicing medicine in the United States than in Haiti. Siegel (1993) reports that in 1987 an estimated 30% of Sub-Saharan Africa's educated population had immigrated to other parts of the world. This is not a recent phenomenon, as U.S. immigration data show that during the 1970s, of the 500,000 technical and professional workers admitted into the country, nearly three-fourths were from developing economies such as India, Pakistan, and South Korea. Worldwide, the most important source country of professional and highly educated immigrants is India, with Pakistan, Ghana, Sri Lanka, Argentina, and Chile following India in importance. One news report estimated that during the late 1990s over half of India's yearly total of 100,000 engineering graduates moved to other countries after graduation.[29]

Many economists have related these departures of professionals from developing countries as a function of the poor economic performance in developing countries. However, the brain drain persists even for economies like Chile, India, and China, whose economies have performed spectacularly in recent years. Of course, the relative differences in wages between these countries and developed countries like the United States and those of the European Union remain very large. In the meantime, the demise of the Soviet Union and the decline of living standards in most former soviet republics and eastern European satellites have created new brain drains. The pool of talented labor in the former Soviet Union and other Eastern European countries is large. Education in engineering and the physical sciences was stressed by the communist governments, and these technical skills are in high demand in Western Europe and North America.

---

[27]Zachary (2001).

[28]World Bank (2003).

[29]Sender (2000).

Carrington and Detragiache (1998) used data from the 1990 United States Census, the OECD, and United Nations sources to estimate the extent of the brain drain. Their study covers migration from 61 developing economies to 25 developed economies. This data set permits the authors of the study to calculate the education levels of immigrants from developing to developed countries. They classify the immigrants according to whether they completed primary, secondary, or higher education, and this information is then combined with other data on the overall educational attainment of the populations of each of the 61 developing economies in order to arrive at the fraction of each educational category (primary, secondary, or higher-educated people) that migrates to developed economies.

Carrington and Detragiache admit that, for the lack of data, they do not include the many unauthorized immigrants in their analysis. Nor do they account for immigrants who have returned to their countries of origin. Despite these short-comings, however, their estimates of the brain drain are stunningly large for a majority of developing countries. The study results, reported in Table 8.2, also show that the great majority of legal immigrants from developing countries have secondary or higher educations. Immigrants tend to be much better educated than the rest of the population of their country of origin. Also, the percentage of highly educated people who immigrate to the more developed countries exceeds 30% for some Central American, Caribbean, and African countries. There is little doubt that the brain drain is a substantial phenomenon.

Docquier and Marfouk (2006) build on the Carrington and Detragiache study detailed above by addressing several methodological shortcomings of the latter and calculating alternative estimates of the proportions of skilled workers among source countries' general populations and among each source country's immigrants. Despite the substantial changes in methodology, Docquier and Marfouk reach conclusions that are similar to those of Carrington and Detragiache

Tables 8.3 and 8.4 summarize Docquier and Marfouk's results for 2000. Table 8.3 provides estimates for various groups of countries. The first two columns of percentages give the rates of emigration for source countries' populations in general and their skilled populations in particular. The right-most two columns present estimates of the share of skilled workers in the source countries' general population and the source countries' migrants.

Table 8.4 provides some summary information based on Docquier and Marfouk's estimates for individual countries. Note that the largest stocks of skilled immigrants living outside their native countries are not predominantly from developing economies. The developed countries Australia, Canada, France, Germany, the United Kingdom, and the United States, together, were the destination of 85% of the world's skilled immigrants. The inclusion of Canada and the United States among the largest *sources* of skilled labor is interesting because these nations are also the two largest *destinations* for skilled immigrants, with the latter receiving about half of all skilled immigrants in the world. So one can not really speak of a brain drain for these net recipients of skilled workers from overseas. The highly skilled workers from these countries often work overseas as businesspeople, teachers, technicians, consultants, and any variety of professional positions.

Table 8.2 Estimated immigration rates to OECD countries by educational levels for 61 LDCs, 1990[a]

	Schooling level		
	Primary or less	Secondary	Tertiary
Asia			
China	–	0.2–0.2	3.0–3.1
India	–	0.3–0.3	2.6–2.7
Indonesia	–	0.1–0.1	1.5–1.6
Iran	–	2.0–2.1	25.6–34.4
Korea	0.5	3.3–3.4	14.9–17.6
Malaysia	–	1.2–1.2	22.7–29.4
Pakistan	–	0.5–0.5	6.9–7.4
Philippines	0.1	6.0–6.4	9.0–9.9
Sri Lanka	–	0.5–0.5	23.6–31
Syria	0.1	2.3–2.3	3.0–3.1
Taiwan	0.1	0.8–0.8	8.4–9.0
Thailand	–	1.7–1.8	1.5–1.6
Africa			
Cameroon	–	0.1–0.1	3.2–3.4
C.A.R.	–	0.1–0.1	1.7–1.8
Congo	–	–	0.5–0.6
Egypt	–	0.8–0.8	5.0–5.3
Gambia	–	0.6–0.6	61.4–100.0
Ghana	–	0.7–0.7	25.7–34.6
Kenya	–	0.3–0.3	10.0–11.1
Lesotho	–	–	2.9–3.0
Malawi	–	0.1–0.1	2.0–2.0
Mali	–	0.1–0.1	0.9–0.9
Mauritius	–	0.1–0.1	7.2–7.7
Mozambique	–	0.5–0.5	8.6–9.4
Rwanda	–	–	2.2–2.3
Sierra Leone	–	1.2–1.3	24.3–32.1
South Africa	–	0.4–0.4	7.9–8.5
Sudan	–	0.1–0.1	1.8–1.8
Togo	–	0.1	1.3–1.4
Uganda	–	0.6–0.6	15.5–18.4
Zambia	–	0.1–0.1	5.0–5.3
Zimbabwe	–	0.3–0.3	4.7–4.9
Central America & *Caribbean*			
Costa Rica	0.1–0.1	10.1–11.2	7.1–7.7
Dom. Rep.	0.6–0.6	30.5–43.8	14.7–17.2
El Salvador	1.6–1.6	66.6–100.0	26.1–35.4
Guatemala	0.4–0.4	29.1–41.1	13.5–15.6
Honduras	0.2–0.2	15.7–18.7	15.7–18.6
Jamaica	0.7–0.7	33.3–50.0	77.4–100.0
Mexico	1.6–1.7	20.9–26.4	10.3–11.5

(*continued*)

Table 8.2 (Continued)

	Schooling level		
	Primary or less	Secondary	Tertiary
Nicaragua	0.3–0.3	33.3–50.0	18.8–23.2
Panama	0.1–0.1	9.4–10.4	19.6–24.4
Trinidad	0.3–0.3	16.0–18.9	57.8–100.0
South America			
Argentina	–	1.0–1.0	2.7–2.8
Bolivia	–	2.2–2.2	4.2–4.4
Brazil	–	1.6–1.6	1.4–1.4
Chile	–	1.9–1.9	6.0–6.4
Colombia	–	3.8–3.9	5.8–6.1
Ecuador	0.1–0.1	11.4–12.9	3.8–4.0
Guyana	0.9–0.9	23.7–31.1	77.5–100.0
Paraguay	–	0.7–0.8	2.0–2.0
Peru	–	2.7–2.7	3.4–3.9
Uruguay	–	2.3–2.4	3.8–3.9
Venezuela	–	0.8–0.8	2.1–2.2

Source: Table 3 from William J. Carrington and Enrica Detragiache (1998)[a] All figures are percentages of the full population grouped according to educational attainment.

The brain drain was clearly most substantial for small countries like Guyana, Grenada, Jamaica, and other small island countries. Docquier and Marfouk find five countries for which in the year 2000 over 80% of their skilled populations left the country. One of those five is not a small country: Haiti has a population of over 5 million. In general, however, the larger countries have lower emigration rates for their skilled populations. The two right-most columns of Table 8.4 give the countries with, respectively, the highest and lowest skilled to unskilled emigration ratios. These ratios are surprisingly high for many developing economies, whose populations are predominantly unskilled. In short, in countries where most of the population has little education and few of the skills needed in a modern economy, those that immigrate to high income countries are from among the relatively small group of skilled and educated workers. Even the middle-income source countries that send mostly unskilled workers to high-income countries, such as Mexico, Morocco, or Turkey, still see many of their most educated and skilled workers leaving for higher wage countries. Mexico's stock of skilled emigrants numbers nearly one million people. And, as pointed out earlier, even the so-called "un-skilled" workers are relatively skilled compared to the source country population.

In sum, the Carrington and Detragiache (1998) and Docquier and Marfouk (2006) studies show that, compared to countries with large populations, small countries see larger proportions of their populations immigrating to other countries. Small island economies in Oceania and the Caribbean are most likely to see their skilled workers migrate to other countries. They also find that workers with above-average education levels are almost three times as likely to immigrate as all workers in developing economies. There is also a non-linear immigration reaction to income differences

Table 8.3 Immigration of skilled workers in 2000

	Rate of emigration		Share of skilled workers	
	Total population (%)	Skilled (%)	Residents (%)	Migrants (%)
By country size:				
Large - Pop > 25 million	1.3	4.1	11.3	36.4
Upper- middle - 25 < Pop < 10	3.1	8.8	11.0	33.2
Lower-middle - 10 < Pop < 2.5	5.8	13.5	13.0	33.1
Small - Pop < 2.5 million	10.3	27.5	10.5	34.7
By income group:				
High-income	2.8	3.5	30.7	38.3
Upper-middle income	4.2	7.9	13.0	25.2
Lower-middle income	3.2	7.6	14.2	35.4
Low-income	0.5	6.1	3.5	45.1
Selected groups:				
Middle East and North Africa	2.8	8.9	9.4	32.0
Eastern Europe, Former U.S.S.R.	2.7	4.8	17.1	30.3
European Union	4.8	8.1	18.6	32.5
America:				
North America	0.8	0.9	51.3	57.9
Caribbean	15.3	42.8	9.3	38.6
Central America	11.9	16.9	11.1	16.6
South America	1.6	5.1	11.1	16.6
Africa				
Total	1.5	10.4	4.0	30.9
Sub-Saharan Africa	0.9	12.9	2.8	42.6
Asia:				
Eastern Asia	0.5	3.9	6.3	55.5
South-Central Asia	0.5	5.3	5.0	52.5
South-Eastern Asia	1.6	9.8	7.9	51.4
Western Asia	1.6	6.9	11.4	22.9
Oceania				
Australia and New Zealand	3.7	5.4	32.7	49.2
Melanesia	4.5	44.0	2.7	45.0
Micronesia	7.2	32.3	7.1	43.6
Polynesia	48.7	75.2	7.1	22.7

Source: Frédéric Docquier and Abdeslam Marfoukin (2006, pp. 170–171), Table 5.3, pp. 170–171.

because a substantially greater proportion of people in middle-income developing countries immigrate to higher income countries than do people in very low-income countries. Finally, the brain drain is greatest from the poorest countries; the lower

Table 8.4 Immigration of skilled workers in 2000

Emigration stocks		Rate of emigration				Skilled migrants/Total migrants			
		All countries		*Population> 5 milllion*		*Highest*		*Lowest*	
United Kingdom	1,441,307	Guyana	89.0%			Taiwan	78.0%	Suriname	18.4%
Philippines	1,126,260	Grenada	85.1%			Qatar	69.6%	Moçambique	17.7%
India	1,037,626	Jamaica	85.1%			Kuwait	67.8%	Italy	17.3%
Mexico	922,964	St. Vincent	84.5%			UAE	67.3%	Bosnia & Herz.	17.0%
Germany	848,414	Haiti	83.6%			Philippines	67.1%	Angola	16.9%
China	816,824	Trinidad & Tob.	79.3%			Nigeria	65.0%	Senegal	16.7%
South Korea	652,894					Saudi Arabia	64.6%	Bulgaria	16.4%
Canada	516,471					Japan	63.8%	San Marino	16.0%
Vietnam	506,449			Haiti	83.6%	Oman	62.7%	Cape Verde	15.2%
Poland	449,059			Ghana	46.9%	South Africa	62.6%	Tunisia	14.9%
United States	431,330			Moçambique	45.1%	Hong Kong	61.9%	Mexico	14.4%
Italy	408,287			Kenya	38.4%	Mongolia	61.1%	Guinea-Bissau	14.2%
Cuba	332,673			Lao PDR	37.4%	India	60.5%	Algeria	14.1%
France	312,494			Uganda	35.6%	Canada	60.1%	Tuvalu	13.8%
Iran	308,754			Angola	33.0%	Venezuela	60.1%	Comoros	13.4%
Jamaica	291,166			Somalia	32.7%	Uzbekistan	59.5%	Morocco	12.9%
Hong Kong	290,482			El Salvador	31.0%	Brunei	59.3%	Equatorial Guin.	12.4%
Russia	289,090			Sri Lanka	29.7%	Malaysia	59.2%	Portugal	12.0%
Taiwan	275,251			Nicaragua	29.6%	Egypt	58.9%	Mali	10.9%
Japan	268,925			Hong Kong	28.8%	Iran	58.5%	Turkey	8.8%

Source: Frédéric Docquier and Abdeslam Marfoukin (2006, pp. 175–176), Table 5.4.

the per capita income in the source country, the more likely that the immigrants that leave for high income economies are educated and skilled. It is clear that the brain drain is a very real phenomenon, but not all developing countries experience large brain drains. There are clearly additional characteristics that determine the size of a country's brain drain.

8.5.4 Why Human Capital Flees Capital-Scarce Countries

If it is indeed true that highly educated and talented people are an important productive and innovative resource in source countries, it is fair to ask: Why are they so poorly compensated at home and paid so much more after they immigrate? It appears that the fundamental cause of the brain drain is that professional and technical skills are not fully exploited in immigrant source countries. The lack of demand for educated labor in developing economies may be the result of poor economic policies that repress the demand for the things that highly educated people can provide, such as technical know-how for modern production, entrepreneurship, innovation, the adaptation of foreign technology, the education of others in society, and informed public policies. Immigrants leave their native countries in part because they have better opportunities elsewhere. However, they also leave because they see *no* opportunities at home.

Labor markets may not function properly. Restrictions on wages paid, taxation of high wages and incomes, and even confiscation and theft of the gains from innovation and successful enterprises may explain why people with high amounts of human capital migrate to countries where human capital is already relatively abundant. Or, perhaps technology is so much less developed in developing economies that the returns to all factors, even the scarcest factors, are lower. Finally, for human capital to earn high returns it must have other inputs to work with. For example, physicians may be very scarce in Malawi, and if they have no hospitals to work in or medicines to dispense, they cannot be very productive. Those same doctors, in well-equipped and well-staffed hospitals, provide much greater health services in developed countries.

On the other hand, even though the marginal physical product of healthcare workers is higher, the full monetary rewards for providing health services in rich and poor countries do not accurately compare the true relative values of those services. The price for health services is higher in wealthy countries for the simple reason that incomes are much higher there. This higher price of health care, and higher pay for healthcare workers, does not imply that human life is worth more in rich countries. The same conclusion holds for the many other jobs performed by immigrants in high income countries: Many locally provided services reflect local demand factors as well as differences in productivity. To the extent that it is local income levels that drive the higher wages, the gain in measured monetary output overstates the gains from shifting scarce resources to high-income countries.

8.5.5   Brain Drain and Brain Waste

Another "drain" associated with the immigration of highly educated persons from poor countries is the inefficient matching of immigrants' skills to the jobs they perform. There are many anecdotal accounts of trained engineers from poor countries driving taxis or immigrant scientists tending bar in high-income countries. Özden (2006) in fact finds that highly skilled immigrants do not always use their skills after they immigrate. He refers to this as *brain waste* rather than *brain drain*. Özden also relates the performance and earnings of skilled immigrants to their countries of origin, and he finds "striking" differences in the earnings of skilled immigrants from different source countries. Özden's analysis distinguishes a number of factors that cause such variations in earnings of skilled workers in the destination countries.

Özden finds that when the same language is spoken in the source and destination countries, immigrants are more likely to fully exploit their talents and skills in the destination country. Cultural similarities between source and destination countries also improve skilled immigrants' earnings. These results reflect the importance of social capital for a person's economic success. They may also reflect ethnic discrimination in destination labor markets. Immigration policies in the destination country also matter, and destination countries that more finely base visa requirements on specific skills are more likely to match immigrant skills to their economies' needs. Özden specifically mentions the United States' emphasis on *family reunion* as a criterion for awarding visas as a detrimental factor for immigrant earnings and the likelihood of brain waste because it does not directly match immigrant job skills and job opportunities in the U.S. Finally, Özden finds that the quality of education in the source country determines the earnings of skilled immigrants in destination countries. Skilled immigrants from source countries with better education systems earn considerably more in their destination countries than immigrants from countries with poor education systems.

In sum, skilled immigrants are not all the same. Therefore, generalizations based on the estimates of the brain drain in Tables 8.1 through 8.4 should be used with caution.

8.6   A Reassessment of the Brain Drain

The recent literature on the brain drain has challenged the conclusions of the early literature. This literature has distinguished several reasons why the brain drain may not be a net drain on the source economy. For example, Bhagwati and Rodriguez (1975) suggested that the brain drain serves as a "safety valve" in a poor economy suffering from high rates of unemployment or underemployment of educated workers. If the talents of educated workers are not employed in their native countries, these workers may benefit the source country more by becoming productively employed overseas.

8.6.1 Remittances Again

We documented earlier in this chapter that when workers move overseas they often send money back to the source country. Highly skilled and educated migrants are likely to remit more income back to the source economies for the simple reason that they are likely to earn much more income abroad than less skilled workers would. An obvious example is the large number of talented baseball players from the Dominican Republic who play in the United States. They have no opportunity to earn high salaries playing baseball in their own country because there is no major professional league in the Dominican Republic. But those Dominicans who have reached the major leagues in the United States, and there have been quite a few, earned salaries that exceeded what they could have earned in the Dominican Republic by a huge multiple. Most of these players eventually returned to their native country with their accumulated incomes. Even those who have not returned sent more money back to family and relatives than they would have earned had they stayed in the Dominican Republic.

8.6.2 The Brain Drain as an Incentive to Seek Education

Education levels have improved substantially in most developing countries of the world over the past two decades, the period when the brain drain also became a more prominent phenomenon.[30] This coincidence of the brain drain with increased education has led several economists to build models linking the two phenomena. For example, Stark, Helmenstein, and Preskawetz (1998), Vidal (1998), and Beine, Docquier, and Rapoport (2001) developed models suggesting that overseas opportunities provide incentives for all people in the source country to acquire more education, even if only some people actually find overseas jobs. This induced rise in education can actually end up contributing to source country growth despite the departure of some of the educated natives. The option of immigrating to a high-income country, where education is rewarded more highly than in a poor country, adds to the incentives for people to acquire more education.

   In the absence of other mechanisms through which immigrants raise income in the source countries, the incentive for more people to become more educated will be a benefit for the source country only if a substantial percentage of those who acquire more education with an eye on immigrating actually end up remaining in

---

[30]See, for example, World Bank (2006) or UNDP (2006).

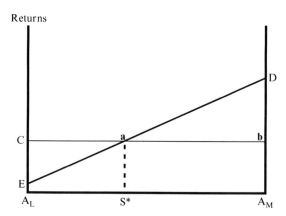

Fig. 8.5 The returns to
education with immigration

the country. To the extent that education requires an up-front investment by the
source economy, immigration clearly has a "drain" effect for the source country. If
education has positive externalities, the drain is even greater. However, if the
possibility of immigrating to higher-income countries causes people remaining in
the country to also acquire more education suggests that there may be a net "brain
gain," not a brain drain. These possibilities are depicted graphically in Fig. 8.5
through 8.9, which apply a model from Commander, Kangasniemi, and Winters
(2002).

8.6.2.1 Simple Case

Suppose that basic human ability and talent are distributed unequally among the
source country population. Such inherent ability and talent determines people's
ability to enhance their productivity by acquiring education. Workers are listed
from the least able to the most able along the horizontal axis from A_L to A_M, and the
vertical axis shows the returns to education. The marginal product of workers is
shown as an upward-sloping line ED under the assumption that the returns to
education increase with ability.

Whether people invest in education depends on whether the marginal gains are
greater than the marginal costs of education. To simplify the analysis, we assume
that the private returns to education are identical to the social returns and that
people earn wages equal to the marginal returns of their education-reinforced labor.
Hence, in the case of a constant cost of education at C, people who reside to the
right of S* along the continuum of abilities will find it in their interest to acquire
an education. Hence, the number of people who decide to acquire an education is
the difference between S*, the individual for whom the return from education
just equals the marginal cost of education, and the most able person at A_M. The
proportion of people seeking education is thus $(A_M - S^*)/(A_M - A_L)$. In general, not
all people acquire education. Only when the private cost of education is very low or
the returns to education are very high will everyone acquire education. The total

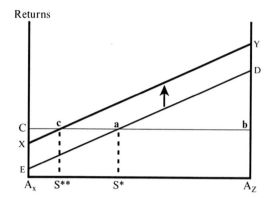

Fig. 8.6 The social returns to
education

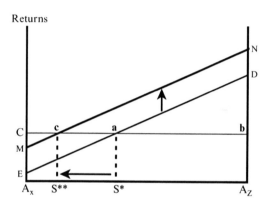

Fig. 8.7 The foreign returns
to education

gains from education are equal to the net area under the upward-sloping returns to
education curve to the right of S*. The net gains to the economy are the area under
the line ED and above the cost line C, or the triangle abD in Fig. 8.5.

If there are positive externalities to education, then society's marginal returns to
education exceed the private returns. Psacharopoulos (1994) and Schutz (1988)
present evidence suggesting this is indeed the case for most countries. In this case,
the social returns to education lie above the line ED in Fig. 8.5. For example,
society's marginal product of educated workers line may be the line XY in Fig. 8.6.
If private individuals pay for their own education and make the choice about
whether to acquire education, society will end up with too few educated workers.
$A_Z - S^{**}$ workers should acquire an education, but only $A_Z - S^*$ do.

This under-investment in education can be corrected for by means of a subsidy
or the provision of public education funded by taxation. Alternatively, workers
could be induced to acquire education by offering them the opportunity to use their
education in other countries where the earnings of educated workers are higher.
A simple version of this latter case is illustrated in Fig. 8.7. The line MN represents
the returns to education when people can immigrate to another country. In this case,
$A_Z - S^{**}$ people will indeed get an education, but they will then also immigrate and

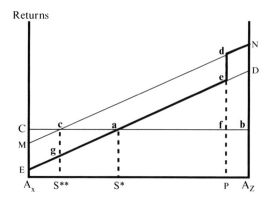

Fig. 8.8 The returns to education and immigration

use their education abroad. Note, however, that the gains from education are entirely captured by the immigrants and others abroad.

This case in which all educated people in the source country immigrate is approximated in some less developed island countries according to Carrington and Detragiache's estimates in Table 8.2. The source country gains nothing from the education, and subsequent departure, of its educated workforce. If the cost of education is paid by taxpayers or parents, who remain in the source country, then this case represents the worst-case scenario in which the brain drain causes a net loss to the source country. The source economy incurs costs of education equal to $cS^{**}A_Zb$, and the immigrants overseas earn $cS^{**}A_ZN$.

The recent literature that links potential gains from the brain drain to the increase in education among the overall population in the source country assumes that only a fraction of the educated workers leave the country. Suppose also that the line MN in Fig. 8.7 exactly coincides with the domestic social returns to education line XY in Fig. 8.6. However, assume now that, instead of everyone immigrating, only a fraction of the workers who seek to immigrate to a high-income country are awarded residence visas in those countries. This is a realistic case, since many high-income countries currently ration work visas even for educated workers. More specifically, suppose that of the $(A_Z - S^{**})$ people from a source country who acquire education, high-income countries only award immigrant visas to the proportion of applicants they judge as most productive. Suppose the fraction admitted into the high-income countries is $\rho < 1$.

This latest case is illustrated in Fig. 8.8. Only the top portion $\rho(A_Z - S^{**}) = (A_Z - P)$ of educated source country workers get to enjoy the expected higher foreign returns to their education equal to **dfbN**. The educated workers remaining in the source country increase source country output by $cS^{**}Pd$, but the source country incurred educational expenses equal to $cS^{**}A_Zb$. The net gain for the country is thus $cS^{**}Pd - cS^{**}A_Zb = \mathbf{cfd} - \mathbf{fPA_Zb}$, where the right hand side of the equality consists of the net social gain **cfd** from educating the source country workers who remained to work in the country minus the the cost $\mathbf{fPA_Zb}$ the source country incurred for the education of those who left the country. If $\mathbf{cfd} - \mathbf{fPA_Zb} > 0$, the opportunity for some source country workers to use their education abroad still ends up increasing the average income of the workers who remain in the source country.

8.6.2.2   More Realistic Case

It may not be realistic to assume that all $A_Z - S^{**}$ source country workers will invest in education if the probability of getting a higher paying overseas job is less than one. Surely, many workers will rationally conclude that they may not be awarded a work visa in a high-income country. With some positive probability of failure to obtain a foreign work permit, the returns to education curve becomes the *expected* returns to education curve. This curve lies somewhere between the curves ED and MN = XY in Figs. 8.6 and 8.7. If the line representing expected private returns to education lies below the social returns to education line, private individuals would not make the optimal investment in education. It also becomes less likely that the partial brain drain increases domestic income enough to offset the lost cost of educating the immigrants.

Suppose, however, that foreign wages are much higher than source country wages. For example, suppose the MN line is as shown in Fig. 8.9. Note that MN lies far enough above the source country's social returns to education line XY to cause the expected returns to education line to again coincide with XY, then we are very likely to satisfy **cfd** > **fPA$_Z$b** so that private individuals do invest in the socially optimal amount of education. This is actually a fairly realistic case, since most educated migrants from low-income countries are able to increase their incomes by sizeable multiples when they immigrate to the U.S., Canada, Western Europe, and other high-income countries. Of course, it is not difficult to imagine that in the case of a very poor country people could over-invest in education, and many people will

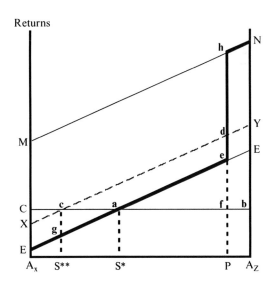

Fig. 8.9 The returns to education and immigration

end up unemployed and unable to use their education while only a small number of compatriots succeed in immigrating to high-income countries.

8.7   Conclusions

The standard labor supply and demand model shows the effects of immigration in both the source and destination countries. Overall, if immigrants are counted as residents of the destination country, then the destination country appears to gain welfare while the source country loses welfare. The immigrants definitely gain from their move. As we have already shown in earlier chapters, there are more possibilities than the simple labor supply model of immigration lets on.

In this chapter, we focused first on income transfers, or what the immigration literature calls *remittances*. Remittances enable the source country to share in the gains from immigration that accrue to immigrants. Remittances have grown more than proportionately to immigration, in part because incomes of immigrants have risen and in part because more immigrants are going abroad specifically to earn income that can be remitted back to relatives in the source country.

Secondly, this chapter focused on the brain drain. There are no clear solutions to the brain drain. Walls and taxes are unlikely to be successful in keeping human capital in the source country. A number of policies to deal with the brain drain have been suggested, although few have actually been implemented. Policies to restrict the departure of people inevitably clash with the civil right to leave the country. Measures to prevent people from leaving often solicit comparisons with East Germany and its infamous wall. More humanitarian schemes have been devised to prevent the brain drain, including requirements that highly educated people stay in the source country for a minimum number of years or pay an exit tax to "compensate" the source country for their education and experience. Many developing country governments have argued that they effectively subsidize developed country growth and that, therefore, they deserve foreign aid and other transfers from developed economies.

The policy debate has been complicated by the lack of consensus on the actual costs and benefits of the brain drain for the source and destination countries. For example, there is a debate on how much of the income that immigrants earn overseas is due to the immigrants' own particular character, ambition, inventiveness, and intelligence, and how much is due to the education funded by the taxpayers of the home country. Estimates vary widely. Source country economic growth may suffer when highly educated people leave because educated people are necessary for a country to adapt and apply foreign technologies. The departure of entrepreneurs could be equally damaging to source country economic growth. On the other hand, remittances serve to mitigate the negative effects of the brain drain just as they serve to reduce the costs to the source country of immigration in general. In fact, educated immigrants earn much more overseas than poorly educated immigrants. The brain drain may, therefore, increase remittances back to the source countries.

In any case, when we consider how easily people can now move between countries, how many immigrants already live in the destination countries of North America, Europe, and Asia/Oceania, and how modern communications makes the huge income differences and job opportunities across countries ever more obvious, the issue for source countries is not so much whether the brain drain is good or bad for a poor country, but rather how to make the best of the inevitable. The efforts by Mexico, Philippines, India, and other source countries to strengthen ties between immigrants living abroad and their native countries represent perhaps the best approach to the brain drain. Also, the evidence suggests that source countries should improve their economic policies in order to ensure that remittances are well invested. Of course, making the institutional and policy changes that improve the returns to investment at home would probably also help to eliminate the fundamental cause of the brain drain in the first place.

References

Abramovitz, M. (1986). Catching up, forging ahead, and falling behind. *Journal of Economic History, 46*(2), 385–406.

Adams, R. H. (2006). Remittances, poverty, and investment in guatemala. In C. Özden, & M. Schiff (Eds.), *International migration, remittances, and the brain drain* (pp. 53–80). Washington, DC: World Bank.

Agrawal, A., Cockburn, I., & McHale, J. (2003). Gone but not forgotten: Labor flows, knowledge spillovers, and enduring social capital. NBER Working Paper No. w9950.

Associated Press, (2004, 16 June). Citigroup to introduce binational credit-card.

Authers, J. (2004, 1 July). Tomato King looks to make mark for Mexican Migrants. *Financial Times*.

Barrionuevo, A., & de Cordoba, J. (2004, 2 February). For aging Castro, Chavez emerges as a vital crutch. *Wall Street Journal*.

Beine, M., Docquier, F., & Rapoport, H. (2001). Brain drain and economic growth: theory and evidence. *Journal of Development Economics, 64*, 275–289.

Bhagwati, J., & Hamada, K. (1974). The brain drain, international integration of markets for professionals and unemployment: a theoretical analysis. *Journal of Development Economics, 2*, 19–24.

Bhagwati, J., & Rodriguez, C. (1975). Welfare-theoretical analysis of the brain drain. *Journal of Development Economics, 2*, 195–221.

Branch, E. L. (2004). Workers' remittances to Mexico. *Business Frontier*, Issue 1.

Boucher, S., Stark, O., & Taylor, J. E. (2005). A gain with a drain? Evidence from rural Mexico on the new economics of the brain drain. Working Paper, August, 2005.

Cañas, J., Coronado, R., & Orrenius, P. (2007). Explaining the increase in remittances to Mexico. *Southwest Economy* July/August, Federal Reserve Bank of Dallas.

Carrington, W. J., & Detragiache, E. (1998). How big is the brain drain? IMF Working Paper WP/98/102, July, 1998.

Chami, R., Fullenkamp, C., & Jahjah, S. (2003). Are immigrant remittance flows a source of capital for development? IMF Working Paper WP/03/189, September.

Commander, S., Kangasniemi, M., & Winters, L. A. (2002). The brain drain: Curse or boon? A survey of the literature. Paper presented at the CEPR/NBER/SNS seminar on International Trade, Stockholm, May 24–25.

Cox Edwards, A., & Ureta, M. (2003). International migration, remittances, and schooling: Evidence from El Salvador. NBER Working Paper No. w9766, June.

Devan, J., Tewari, P. S. (2001). Brains abroad. *The McKinsey Quarterly, 4* December, 2001.

Docquier, F., & Marfoukin, A. (2006). International migration by education attainment, 1990–2000. In Ç. Özden, M. Schiff (Eds.), *International migration, remittances, and the brain drain.* Washington, DC: World Bank.

Ensminger, J. (1997). Transaction costs and Islam: explaining conversion in Africa. *Journal of Institutional and Theoretical Economics, 153*(1), 4–29.

Federal Reserve Bank of Dallas, El Paso Branch (2004). Workers' remittances to Mexico. *Business Frontier,* Issue 1, 2004.

Fidler, S. (2001, 17 May). New migrants spur growth in remittances. *Financial Times.*

Florida, R. (2005). The world is spiky. *Atlantic Monthly,* October.

Glaeser, E., Kallal, H. D., Scheinkman, J., & Schleifer, A. (1991). Growth in cities. NBER Working Paper 3787, July.

Gould, D. (1994). Immigrant links to the home country: empirical implications for U.S. bilateral trade flows. *The Review of Economics and Statistics, 76*(2), 302–316.

Greif, A. (1989). Reputation and coalitions in medieval trade: evidence on the Maghribi traders. *Journal of Economic History, 49*(4), 857–882.

Grubel, H. G., & Scott, A. (1966). The international flow of human capital. *American Economic Review, 56*(1), 268–274.

Handlin, E., Krontoft, M., & Testa, W. (2002). Remittances and the unbanked,' *Chicago Fed Letter* 175a, March.

Head, K., & Ries, J. (1998). Immigration and trade creation: econometric evidence from Canada. *Canadian Journal of Economics, 31*(1), 47–62.

Inter-American Development Bank (2004). Latin American immigrants in the United States send 30 billion to homelands in 2004. News release from May 17, 2004.

Krugman, P. (1991). *Geography and trade.* Cambridge, MA: MIT.

Kuhn, P. J., & McAusland, C. (2006). The international migration of knowledge workers: When is brain drain beneficial? NBER Working Paper 12761, December.

Kwok, V., & Leland, H. (1982). An economic model of the brain drain. *American Economic Review, 72*(1), 91–100.

Laper, R. (2006, 21 June). Inflow of dollars helps build good roads to empty future. *Financial Times.*

Lewer, J., & Van den Berg, H. (2009). Does immigration stimulate international trade? Measuring the potential channels of influence. *Journal of International Trade, 23,* 187–230.

Light, I. (1985). Ethnicity and business enterprise. In M. M. Stolarik, & M. Friedman (Eds.), *Making it in America.* Lewisburg, PA: Bucknell University.

Lucas, R. E. (1990). Why doesn't capital flow from rich to poor countries?. *American Economic Review, 80*(2), 92–96.

Madhavan, N. (2000, 21 August). India seeks more U.S. visas, less control for tech. *Reuters News Service,* August 21.

McKinsey & Company, (2004), Sending money back home. *McKinsey Quarterly.* Number 4, 2002.

Miyagiwa, K. (1991). Scale economies in education and the brain drain problem. *International Economic Review, 32*(3), 743–759.

Özden, Ç. (2006). Educated migrants: is there a brain waste? In Ç. Özden, M. Schiff (Eds.), *International migration, remittances, and the brain drain* (pp. 227–244). Washington, DC: World Bank.

Pascal, G. Z. (1998, 25 March) Dual citizenship is double-edged sword. *The Wall Street Journal.*

Psacharopoulos, G. (1994). Returns to investment in education: a global update. *World Development*, 22, 1325–1343.

Ratha, D. (2003). Workers' remittances: an important and stable source of external development finance. *Chapter 7 in World Bank, Global development finance*. Washington, DC: World Bank.

Rauch, J. E., & Trindade, V. (2002). Ethnic Chinese networks in international trade. *Review of Economics and Statistics, 84*(1), 116–130.

Robertson, D. H. (1938). The future of international trade. *The Economic Journal, 48*(189):1–14.

Saxenian, A. (2002). Silicon valley's new immigrant high-growth entrepreneurs. *Economic Development Quarterly, 16*(1), 20–31.

Schutz, T. P. (1988). Education investments and returns. In H. Chenery, T. N. Srinivasan (Eds.), *Handbook of development economics*. Amsterdam: North Holland.

Sender, H. (2000, 21 August). Soaring Indian tech salaries reflect country's brain drain. *Wall Street Journal*.

Sengupta, S. (2002, 24 June). Money from kin abroad helps bangladeshis get by. *New York Times*.

Siegel, A. (1993). *An atlas of international migration*. London: Hans Zell Publishers.

Stark, O., Helmenstein, C., & Preskawetz, A. (1998). Human capital depletion, human capital formation, and migration: a blessing or a curse? *Economics Letters, 60*, 363–367

Suro, R., Bendixen, S., Lowell, B. L., & Benavides, D. (2002). Billions in motion: Latino immigrants, remittances and banking. A report produced in cooperation between the Pew Hispanic Center and the Multilateral Commission.

The Economist, (2000). Home and away, migration is a complex phenomenon.

Thompson, G. (2003). A surge in money sent home by Mexicans. *New York Times*.

UNDP, (2006). *Human development report 2006*. New York: United Nations Development Program.

Vidal, J.-P. (1998). The effect of emigration on human capital formation. *Journal of Population Economics, 11*, 589–600.

Weiner, T. (2004, 16 June). Fox seeks to allow Mexicans living abroad to vote in 2006. *Wall Street Journal*.

Wong, K.-Y., & Yip, C. K. (1999). Education, economic growth, and brain drain. *Journal of Economic Dynamics and Control 23*(5–6), 699–726.

World Bank, (2003). *Global economic prospects 2004* (p. 159). Washington DC: World Bank.

World Bank, (2006). *World development indicators 2006*. Washington, DC: World Bank.

World Bank, (2007). *Global Development Finance 2007*. Washington, D.C.: The World Bank.;

Quesada, C. (2003, 28 October). Why Emigrate? *IDB América*, Inter-American Development Bank.

Yang, D., & Martínez, C. (2006). Remittances and poverty in migrants' home areas: Evidence from the Philippines. In Ç. Özden, M. Schiff (Eds.), *International migration, remittances, and the brain drain*. Washington, DC: World Bank: 81–122.

Chapter 9
Economic Growth and Immigration

Abstract The Solow model clearly shows that growth through factor accumulation cannot cause permanent improvements in living standards. Continuous improvements in per capita income can only occur if there is technological progress. The Schumpeterian model of innovation shows that immigration is likely to stimulate technological progress in destination countries, which means immigration contributes to the destination country's rate of economic growth, all other things equal. There are four channels through which immigration may influence technological progress: Immigrants can (1) facilitate the transfer of technology, (2) contribute to innovation as entrepreneurs and workers in innovative activities, (3) change the size of economies, and (4) increase innovative competition by reducing the ability of vested interests to take protectionist measures to slow the process of creative destruction. The effects of emigration on the source country are more ambiguous, however.

> A more liberal immigration policy is one of the most obvious reasons why the U.S. economy continues to grow faster than the European.
>
> −Quentin Peel, 2005[1]

The economic analysis of immigration has been conducted almost entirely with the use of comparative statics. There is considerable evidence, however, that the movement of people across borders is not a reaction to current economic conditions alone, as the standard labor market model of immigration assumes. Immigrants are humans who seek to improve their lives, and the lives of their children. That is, they react not only to the current relative incomes across countries, but the long-run economic and social prospects at home and abroad. Hence, immigration reacts to countries' long-run prospects for economic growth and development.

At the same time that immigrants react to long-run economic growth rather than only short term changes in economic conditions, the economic impact of immigrants is not a one-time static change either. Generally, the departure or arrival of immigrants sets off a series of changes that affect countries' long-run economic growth.

---

[1]Peel (2005).

Ö.B. Bodvarsson and H. Van den Berg, *The Economics of Immigration*,
DOI: 10.1007/978-3-540-77796-0_9, © Springer-Verlag Berlin Heidelberg 2009

In this sense, the static labor market model of immigration does not accurately describe the long-run consequences of immigration. The long-run effects of immigration on an economy, therefore, depend on how immigrants affect the economy's rate of economic growth.

Growth theory shows that long-run economic growth is driven by technological progress; mere factor accumulation cannot sustain permanent growth in a country's per capita income.[2] Therefore, when assessing the full long-run impact of immigration we must explicitly examine how immigrants contribute to innovation and the technological progress that underlies long-run economic growth. The question we seek to answer in this chapter is: Does the inflow of immigrants increase the destination country's rate of economic growth? Equally important is the question: Does the outflow of immigrants reduce the source country's rate of growth?

This chapter reviews the principal models of economic growth and systematically introduces immigration into those models. In effect, our analysis moves beyond the simple labor market model of immigration, which treated immigrants as workers, or factors of production. We extended this model to recognize the fact that immigrants are also consumers. In this chapter, however, we examine the third dimension of immigration, namely that immigrants contribute to the innovative process. In the case of a destination country, this approach explicitly examines immigrants as (1) *workers* that increase the labor force, (2) *consumers* that increase the demand for national output, and (3) *innovators* that induce technological progress. The results of this modeling exercise will reveal that the standard static labor market model of immigration is inadequate for determining the long-run economic effects of immigration on source and destination countries. The changes in innovation and technological progress that immigrants cause soon overwhelm their effect on the labor force and consumer demand because the power of compounding quickly translates even small adjustments in a country's rate of growth into very large long-run welfare changes.

9.1 The Early Models of Economic Growth

Economists have studied economic growth for a long time, and recent models build on ideas and theories developed over the previous two centuries. Fortunately, recent advances in the field of economic growth have pushed the analysis of economic growth in a direction that proves to be especially useful in understanding the long-run effects of immigration. To understand these recent advances, however, a review of contributions over the past two centuries is necessary.

In this section, we begin with Adam Smith, and we then move on to the classical economists, such as Thomas Malthus and David Ricardo, who in the early nineteenth century provided a somewhat pessimistic view of economic growth by

---

[2]See, for example, Barro and Sala-i-Martin (2004), Jones (2002), or Van den Berg (2001).

focusing on diminishing returns to factors of production. We conclude with the Harrod–Domar model.

9.1.1 Adam Smith's Broad View of Growth

Adam Smith is best known for his 1776 work, *An Inquiry into the Nature and Causes of the Wealth of Nations*. Writing at the start of the industrial revolution, Smith was clearly fascinated by the economic changes that he was witnessing, and he provided insights that to this day remain useful for understanding economic growth. Adam Smith's observations from travels around Europe and his vast knowledge of history led him to conclude that one of the key characteristics of the growing economies is the increasing specialization of individual economic activity:

> The greatest improvements in the productive powers of labour, and the greater part of the skill, dexterity, and judgment with which it is any where directed, or applied, seem to have been the effects of the division of labour.[3]

In today's language, Smith saw economic growth as fundamentally a process of increasing *specialization and exchange*. In his analysis of the Industrial Revolution that was beginning to take form around him, Smith also uncovered another important phenomenon that we now call *economies of scale*. He observed large differences in productivity between the traditional cottage system of production and the *factory system* that characterized the Industrial Revolution, and he explained that those differences in productivity could not be generated by simply multiplying the number of cottage industries. In effect, he preceded Robert Solow in pointing out that increased productivity and economic growth require improvements in technology.

Smith also recognized that increased specialization not only improves efficiency, but it also serves to increase the efficiency of technological innovation:

> Men are much more likely to discover easier and readier methods of attaining any object, when the whole attention of their minds is directed towards the single object, than when it is dissipated among a great variety of things ... .[4]

This insight is closely related to the modern concept of *learning-by-doing*.

Some modern growth theorists have depicted the learning-by-doing process as an unintended by-product to production undertaken for other reasons. The recent endogenous models of growth are credited with dispelling such notions. However, over two centuries ago, Smith already recognized that technological improvements were created as a result of intentional efforts to innovate:

> All the improvements in machinery, however, have by no means been the invention of those who had occasion to use the machines. Many improvements have been made by the ingenuity of the makers of machines, when to make them became the business of a peculiar

---

[3] Adam Smith (1776 [1976], p. 7).
[4] Adam Smith (1776 [1976,] p. 13).

trade; and some by that of those who are called philosophers or men of speculation, whose trade is not to do any thing, but to observe every thing; and who, upon that account, are often capable of combining together the powers of the most distant and dissimilar objects. In the progress of society, philosophy or speculation becomes, like every other employment, the principal or sole trade and occupation of a particular class of citizens... Each citizen becomes more expert in his own peculiar branch, more work is done upon the whole, and the quantity of science is considerably increased by it.[5]

That is, innovation became a "business." The "philosophers and speculators" Smith mentions are now usually referred to as *entrepreneurs*.

9.1.2 The Classicals and Diminishing Returns

The view of population growth as a positive factor for economic growth was not shared by all early economists. Thomas Malthus and many other early nineteenth century economists, known as the *Classical School*, are well known for a model of economic growth in which population growth and economic growth interact to doom the world to stagnation and, most likely, eternal poverty.

The *Classicals* hypothesized that output is a function of labor and land, where the amount of land is fixed in quantity but labor can grow or contract depending on birth and death rates. Output is determined by how much labor is combined with the fixed stock of arable land. Because labor is combined with a fixed stock of land, production is subject to *diminishing returns*. The classical production function is shown in Fig. 9.1; the more labor is added to society's fixed stock of land and natural resources, the smaller are the marginal increments in output.

The Classicals introduced a second hypothesis, namely that population growth is a function of real per capita income. Effectively, this hypothesis reflects the seemingly reasonable assumption that when people are well off, they eat better, they are healthier, they live longer, and they have more surviving children. Decreases in real per capita income, on the other hand, inevitably increase the death rate due to increases in starvation and disease, making labor more scarce and effectively raising marginal productivity and incomes.

Combined with diminishing returns, this second hypothesis leads to the conclusion that whenever any improvement in per capita output occurs, say because of some fortuitous increase in technology or an expansion of trade, population growth will accelerate, the supply of labor will expand, diminishing returns will set in, and per capita income will again decline. Therefore, there can be no permanent economic growth, and people are effectively doomed to eternal poverty!

Malthus and the Classicals have been unfairly criticized for their pessimistic predications of eternal stagnation of incomes. Their predictions were not unreasonable given the evidence available to them at the start of the nineteenth century. Table 9.1 presents Angus Maddison's (2006) estimates of economic growth over the past two millennia. The automatic reversion to subsistence and poverty appears

---

[5]Adam Smith (1776[1976]), pp. 13–14.

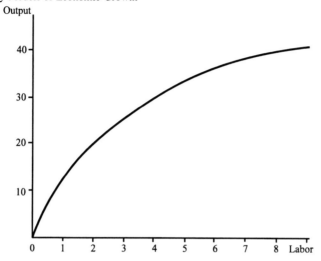

Fig. 9.1 Production with diminishing returns to labor

Table 9.1 World population, real GDP, and per Capita GDP: 1500–2003

Year	Population (millions)	GDP (1990 $)	GDP Per Capita (billions 1990 $)	Period	Population	GDP	GDP/Capita (Annual % growth rates)
0	231	103	445				
1000	267	117	436	0–1000	0.01	0.01	0.00
500	425	240	565	1000–1500	0.10	0.15	0.05
1820	1,068	695	651	1500–1820	0.29	0.33	0.04
1870	1,260	1,128	895	1820–1870	0.33	0.97	0.64
1913	1,772	2,726	1,539	1870–1913	0.79	2.05	1.64
1929	2,047	3,696	1,806	1913–1929	0.90	1.90	1.00
1950	2,512	5,372	1,138	1929–1950	0.97	1.78	0.80
1973	3,896	16,064	4,123	1950–1973	1.91	4.76	2.86
2003	6,314	27,995	6,432	1973–1992	1.60	2.92	1.44

Source: Angus Maddison (2006). Growth Rates are from Angus Maddison (2003), Table 8b.

to be a reasonably accurate description of what had occurred in the real world up to Malthus' time. Population growth accelerated over time, apparently keeping per capita real income from growing hardly at all. Also, it should be pointed out that the Classicals' were very correct in predicting that, after 1800, economic growth would cause population to increase. Unlike Adam Smith, though, the Classicals failed to grasp the potential for a surge in technological progress that would characterize the nineteenth and twentieth centuries.

9.1.3   The Role of Immigration in the Classical Model

Given the classical view that population growth will inevitably prevent long-run economic growth, in a destination country immigration will only accelerate the economy back toward income stagnation whenever there is a short-run increase in income. The static model of immigration suggests that people will leave countries where incomes are falling and move to countries where incomes are rising. Therefore, immigration causes population to grow faster than the population would grow naturally in countries where incomes rise above the subsistence level, and it causes a faster population decline in countries where incomes fall below subsistence.

In this light, the rapid growth of per capita incomes in countries that received large numbers of immigrants in the nineteenth century represents a strong refutation of the Classical model. During the late 1800s, fast-growing economies like Argentina, the United States, Canada, and Australia experienced huge inflows of immigrants equal to over one percent of their total populations each year. Something enabled economies to grow and raise living standards, despite the acceleration of both natural population growth and the increased movement of people across borders in response to those increases in living standards. The coincidence of population growth and economic growth suggests that population growth may stimulate technological progress.

9.1.4   The Simplistic Harrod–Domar Growth Model

In the latter half of the nineteenth century, when much of the world economy was firmly embarked on an unprecedented path of persistent growth and change, economists seemed to lose interest in economic growth. In the latter half of the nineteenth century, economists focused more on resource allocation and how individual markets functioned, topics that today make up the field of microeconomics. The Great Depression of the 1930s shifted economists' priorities away from the study of the economy's component parts and back to how the overall system performed. The shortcomings of economists' focus on individual production and consumption decisions became apparent in the 1930s, when aggregate output fell, economic growth turned negative, and unemployment surged in many countries.

It was during the 1930s that the British economist, John Maynard Keynes, developed a macroeconomic model of an economy that explicitly showed how the major components of the economy interacted. Keynes' *macroeconomic* model served to help policymakers deal with the obvious failure of most of the world's major economies to reach efficient general equilibria in which product and labor markets cleared. But, because Keynes assumed fixed prices and unlimited supplies of resources in his model, reasonable assumptions in light of the conditions of the Great Depression, the *Keynesian* model is inappropriate for analyzing long-run economic growth. Despite the inherent short-run nature of the Keynesian model, however, Roy Harrod and Evsey Domar simultaneously used the model to derive what quickly became a very a popular twentieth century growth model.[6]

Like the Keynesian macroeconomic model, Harrod and Domar assumed an unlimited amount of unemployed labor that would permit investment to increase output without diminishing returns. With capital not subject to diminishing returns, the Harrod–Domar model specifies that output is a constant function of the stock of capital. Specifically, the model assumes that the *capital-output ratio*, which is the amount of capital needed to produce a unit of real output over some period of time (usually a year), is a constant. A constant capital output ratio implies that the rate of output *growth* is directly and linearly related to the rate of saving and new *investment* in capital. Capital-output ratios are not constant or similar across countries and time periods, and the model has proved to be a very poor predictor of economic growth and a worse prescription for growth policy. The model's most noted accomplishment may be that it stimulated Robert Solow to develop a new model that has provided very valuable insight into the growth process.

9.2 The Solow Growth Model

Robert Solow won the Nobel Prize in economics for developing a simple model that qualifies the Harrod–Domar model's suggestion that a country's rate of economic growth is directly proportional to the economy's rate of investment.[7] Solow's model incorporated the marginalist thinking of the nineteenth century Classical School by assuming that capital investment is subject to diminishing returns, just as the Classicals assumed that population growth suffered from diminishing returns (plural). Solow showed that capital accumulation moves the economy along the production function, which can only cause, at best, temporary growth. Continued growth can only occur if the entire production function is shifted upward, which requires technological progress.

9.2.1 A Graphic Representation of the Solow Model

Suppose that output is a function of two factors, labor and capital,

$$Y = f(K, L) \tag{9.1}$$

In the function (9.1), Y is defined as total output, K is the economy's stock of capital, and L is the number of workers. The partial derivatives of output with

---

[6]Domar (1946), and Harrod (1939).
[7]Solow (1956, 1957).

respect to capital and labor are assumed to be positive; to model diminishing returns, the second derivatives are assumed to be negative.

Solow also assumed that capital depreciates, and that the rate of depreciation, defined as the proportion of the stock of capital that wears out each year, is a constant fraction δ of the stock of capital, K. The larger the capital stock, the greater the amount of capital that needs to be replaced each year. Thus, the change in the stock of capital over the course of the year, denoted as ΔK, is equal to the difference between total new investment, I, and the amount of existing capital that depreciates:

$$\Delta K = I - \delta K \tag{9.2}$$

Solow also assumed that people save a constant fraction, σ, of income Y, or

$$S = \sigma Y. \tag{9.3}$$

If we assume that the stock of labor remains unchanged, we can write the production function simply as $Y = f(K)$. Then, if we also assume that all savings are productively invested, (9.2) becomes:

$$\Delta K = I - \delta K = \sigma Y - \delta K = \sigma f(K) - \delta K. \tag{9.4}$$

Notice that when $\sigma f(K)$ is greater than δK, and total investment is greater than what is needed to replace that portion of the capital stock that wears out, the total stock of capital and output $Y = f(K)$ increase. On the other hand, when $\sigma f(K) < \delta K$ total investment in new capital is not large enough to replace the capital that depreciates, and the total stock of K and output $Y = f(K)$ decrease.

Because depreciation, investment, and output are all functions of the capital stock K, the three functions can all be included in a single diagram in which capital is shown on the horizontal axis and Y, I, and depreciation are measured along the vertical axis. With diminishing returns to capital investment, the production function slopes upward at a decreasing rate as in Fig. 9.2. The constant savings rate, σ, implies that the savings/investment function is a constant proportion of income equal to $S = I = \sigma f(K)$, which is just a diminished version of the production function $f(K)$ that also slopes upward at a decreasing rate. Solow's assumption of a constant rate of depreciation implies that depreciation is represented by a straight line function of capital, δK. Figure 9.2 combines all three functions in one diagram.

The diagram confirms what we already noticed in equation (9.4): The economy's capital stock automatically adjusts toward a stable equilibrium level K*. When investment is greater than depreciation, or $\sigma f(K) > \delta K$, the stock of capital grows. In Fig. 9.2 this occurs to the left of K* where the investment curve $\sigma f(K)$ lies above the depreciation line δK. Because of diminishing returns the slope of $\sigma f(K)$ declines, and eventually investment only adds just enough income and saving to cover the depreciation of the ever-increasing stock of capital. At that point there is no further growth of K. To the right of K*, the situation is reversed; investment is less than depreciation and K declines back toward K*.

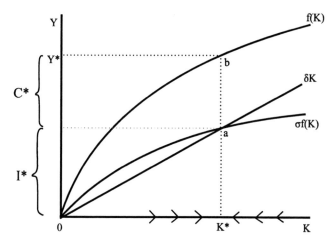

Fig. 9.2 The Solow equilibrium

Output is a function of K, and therefore output also tends toward a stable equilibrium level of $Y^* = f(K^*)$. At Y^* consumption and investment are C^* and $I^* = \sigma Y^*$, respectively. Solow defined these stable equilibrium levels of the capital stock and output as the economy's *steady state equilibrium*. Note that the Solow model generates a stunning rebuke to the Harrod–Domar model: Growth by means of factor accumulation is, by itself, not sustainable.

9.2.2 Immigration Similarly has no Long-Run Effects

In order to better understand the growth effect of immigration in the Solow model, it is convenient to put the model in per capita terms. In addition to diminishing returns to any single input, Solow also assumed that the production function exhibits *constant returns to scale*. If equation (9.1) is a constant returns to scale production function, then for any positive constant c the following must also hold:

$$cY = F(cK, cL) \tag{9.5}$$

Then, letting $c = 1/L$, the production function can be written as

$$Y/L = y = F(K/L, 1) = f(k) \tag{9.6}$$

where Y/L and K/L are defined as y and k, respectively, and we let the function F(k) represent f(k,1). Equation (9.6) describes output per worker as a function of capital per worker, which is quite appropriate given that economic growth is normally defined as the change in *per capita* output.

The basic dynamic equation of the Solow model can also be written in per capita terms. Denoting per capita investment I/L as i, per capita investment increases the per capita total stock of capital only if it exceeds the amount of per capita capital that depreciates. In per worker terms,

$$\Delta k = i - \delta k = \sigma y - \delta k = \sigma f(k) - \delta k. \qquad (9.7)$$

Now, if $\sigma F(k)$ is greater than δk, the capital-labor ratio k will increase. On the other hand, if depreciation is so large and diminishing returns have so reduced the marginal gains in output from investment in new capital that $\sigma f(k) < \delta k$, then Δk will be negative and k will decline.

Immigration changes the size of the population. To analyze the effect of population change in the Solow model, we have to drop our assumption of a constant labor stock. Suppose, therefore, that the labor force can grow at some rate $n = \Delta L/L$. For $k = K/L$ to remain constant when the labor force grows, K must grow at the same rate as L. Thus, for k to remain constant, investment must cover not only the amount of capital that depreciates, but it must also equip new entrants to the labor force. Therefore, the direction of change in k depends on whether the amount of investment per worker, $i = \sigma f(k)$, is greater than or less than capital depreciation per worker plus the amount of capital needed to equip each new worker with the same per capita amount of capital that existing people already have to work with. The change in the capital-labor ratio k will thus be

$$\Delta k = i - \delta k - nk = \sigma f(k) - (\delta + n)k \qquad (9.8)$$

Figure 9.3 illustrates population growth's effect on the steady state level of k, and hence output f(k). If $n > 0$, the intersection of $(\delta + n)k$ and $\sigma f(k)$ occurs at a lower level of k than the intersection of dk and $\sigma f(k)$. All other things equal, the higher the rate of population growth, the lower is the steady state of k: compare k_1^*, which represents the steady state for $n = 0$, and k_2^*, which represents the steady state for $n > 0$, in Fig. 9.3. And, the lower the steady state level of k, the lower the steady state level of per worker output and income. The Solow model therefore predicts that, all other things equal, countries with higher rates of population growth have lower *levels* of per capita output. Thus, continuous immigration lowers per capita income in a destination country but raises it in a source country.

The conclusion that countries receiving immigrants suffer a reduction in per capita income is similar to what the static labor market model of immigration tells us. This conclusion seems to be at odds with the observation that countries such as the United States, Canada, Australia, and New Zealand, which all have traditionally received large inflows of immigrants and continue to receive immigrants, have among the highest per capita incomes in the world. We could, perhaps, rationalize the Solow model by concluding that these countries achieved very high steady state levels of per capita income *in spite of* immigration. The Solow model suggests

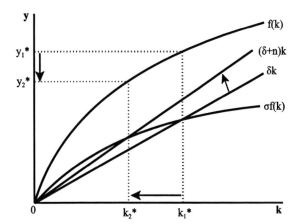

Fig. 9.3 The effect of population growth on the steady state

another, more plausible, explanation for the high per capita incomes in the major immigrant destination countries, however.

9.2.3 How an Economy Achieves Permanent Growth

The Solow model shows that the ten-fold increase in real per capita income for the world as a whole since 1800 could not have been the result of increased saving and investment. Rather, the Solow model makes it clear that the spectacular growth of the past two centuries must have been caused by technological progress.

Technological progress is defined as an improvement in the efficiency with which an economy uses its factors of production to produce welfare-enhancing output. Thus, technological progress effectively causes an upward shift in the economy's aggregate production function, as from $f_1(k)$ to $f_2(k)$ to $f_3(k)$ in Fig. 9.4. The repeated shifts in the production function change the economy's steady states from points a to b and then to c, which represent the steady state combinations of k^* and y^*, k^{**} and y^{**}, and k^{***} and y^{***}, respectively. Technological progress in effect shifts the economy's production points along the dashed line in Fig. 9.4, not along a single production function with diminishing returns, as in Fig. 9.3.

According to the Solow model, the rising standards of living that people in most countries have experienced over most of the past 200 years could not have been just the result of *more* tools and machines, it was the result of *more and better* tools and machines, technologies, and production methods. Any assessment of immigration's growth effects must, therefore, examine whether and how immigration affects the economy's rate of technological progress. If immigration causes the whole production

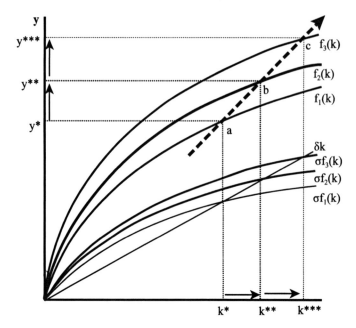

Fig. 9.4 Technological progress

function to shift upward, then immigration will, in the long run, increase per capita income, not diminish it.

9.3   Immigration and Technological Progress

Models of technological progress tend to view immigration in a very different light than the Classical, Harrod–Domar, and Solow growth models. Rather than viewing immigrants as mere factors of production that, in the destination country, reduce the returns to labor by adding more labor resources to a given set of other productive resources, models of technological progress tend to see people as the resource that thinks of new ideas, develops new technologies, and applies new methods and procedures. The arrival of immigrants, therefore, adds creative and innovative people.

This role of people as innovators and creators is not new. The early social scientist William Petty wrote in 1682 that "... it is more likely that one ingenious curious man may rather be found among 4 million than among 400 persons."[8] Simon Kuznets, the noted economist and Nobel laureate, queried more than 25 years ago: "Why, if it is man who was the architect of economic and social growth in the past and responsible for the vast contributions to knowledge and technological

---

[8]Quoted in Simon (1996).

and social power, a larger number of human beings need result in a lower rate of increase in per capita product.?"[9] Ester Boserup and Julian Simon went further and argued that it is the very congestion created by population growth that provides the incentives for technological progress.[10] Boserup and Simon effectively restate the old claim that "necessity is the mother of invention." Immigration both creates the necessity and provides the potential inventors.

9.3.1 Immigration and Technological Progress

There are many reasons why the movement of people from one country to another affects the rate of technological progress in the source and destination countries. Perhaps most obvious, immigrants are carriers of ideas and knowledge, and therefore immigration increases the transfer of technology between countries. Second, immigrants often have talents and personalities that are especially appropriate for innovation, which implies that they are an especially important factor input into the process of technological progress. This potential characteristic of immigrants implies that their migration would cause innovation and technological progress to slow in their source country and accelerate in the destination country. Third, by changing the levels of population and gross domestic product in the source and destination countries, immigrants change the size of economies. There is some evidence that technological progress is related to the size of economies. Finally, by adding new people to the population, immigration may actually reduce the ability of vested interests to take protectionist measures that slow the process of economic growth. We can examine these four possibilities in detail within the framework provided by a model derived from the ideas of the early twentieth century economist Joseph Schumpeter.

9.3.2 Joseph Schumpeter's Theory of Creative Destruction

The most popular model of technological progress is based on the ideas of Joseph Schumpeter, who early in the twentieth century criticized his contemporary neo-classical economists for being overly concerned with resource allocation and ignoring how an economy's productive capacity grows. According to Schumpeter, "the important issue is not how capitalism administers existing structures, ... the relevant problem is how it creates and destroys them."[11] Schumpeter described the capitalist economy as a "perennial gale of *creative destruction*." Every time an

---

[9]Kuznets (1973).

[10]See Boserup (1965, 1981) and Simon 1992).

[11]Schumpeter (1934, p. 84).

innovator *creates* a new business opportunity, it *destroys* the market power and profits that its competitors had gained as a result of their earlier innovations. This continual creation and destruction prevents monopolies from permanently reaping profits. More important, argued Schumpeter, the process gives society continual technological progress.

Schumpeter' view of *competition* was different from the price competition emphasized by mainstream economic theory. He saw ferocious competition among imperfectly competitive firms, but it was competition to develop new products and production processes and earn monopoly profits, not traditional price competition. In economists' favorite case of perfect competition, the market price just covers the cost of the resources used in *production*, leaving nothing to cover the up-front cost of *innovation*. Schumpeter effectively clashed with mainstream economics. Where standard microeconomic theory suggests that monopoly profit is a form of "market failure" that is costly to society, Schumpeter saw temporary profits as a necessary incentive for innovation.

Schumpeter's concept of *creative destruction* also captures another important characteristic of economic growth, which is that the creation of something new usually requires that something old be eliminated. New activities require resources, which, in the absence of unemployment or excess capacity, must be transferred from existing activities. Growing economies are therefore characterized by *structural change*. Finally, Schumpeter recognized the importance of the economic and social climate for innovation within which innovators, or *entrepreneurs*, operated. Fundamentally, an economy's rate of technological progress depends on the incentives and barriers that entrepreneurs face.

Romer (1990), Grossman and Helpman (1991), Rivera-Batiz and Romer (1991), and Aghion and Howitt (1992) have built models of endogenous technological progress around the "Schumpeterian" assumption that technological progress is the result of costly innovative activities carried out by profit-seeking entrepreneurs. There are subtle differences between the many models that have been developed, but all of them incorporate the following five fundamental ideas:

1. Innovations are generated by intentionally employing costly (scarce) resources to create new products, ideas, methods, etc.
2. Profit-seeking innovators must compete with producers to employ the economy's scarce, and thus costly, resources.
3. Innovation creates new products or techniques that are better, cheaper, more attractive, or in some other way better than existing products, which gives the new activities and products an advantage over existing producers and products.
4. Just as their innovations "destroyed" earlier innovators' profits, innovators also know that further innovations by competing innovators will eventually eliminate the profits of their innovations.
5. Innovators rationally weigh the costs of innovation and the discounted expected future profits of innovation.

This section introduces a graphic version of a typical Schumpeterian model of technological progress.

9.3.3 A Graphic Schumpeterian Model

In the traditional microeconomic model of a firm, an imperfectly competitive producer faces a downward-sloping demand curve. To simplify the analysis without losing generality, suppose that the marginal cost of production is constant at the wage level w. This assumption means the marginal cost (MC) curve is a horizontal line at price w. As shown in Fig. 9.5, the profit-maximizing producer increases production up to the point where marginal revenue equals marginal cost. The traditional static microeconomic model therefore prescribes a profit-maximizing output level of q sold at price p. Profits are equal to the markup $\mu = p - w$, multiplied by the quantity of products sold, q (the shaded box in Fig. 9.5). This model, therefore, depicts the case where successful innovators gain some market power and face downward-sloping demand curves, which permits them to set a price above the marginal cost of production so that they can recover some or all of the cost of innovation.

In the dynamic model of creative destruction, profits from innovation depend not only on the size of the shaded profit box in Fig. 9.5, but also on how long a producer can reap the profit. Innovators expect that, on average, the future stream of profits following an innovation will be large enough and continues long enough to exceed the costs of innovation. The duration of the profit stream of course depends on how quickly other innovators *destroy* the latest creation.

Models of endogenous technological progress generally assume that innovators engage in innovative activity up to the point where their expected marginal gains from innovation equal the marginal costs of innovation. Many of these models treat technological progress as the stream of products $x_1, x_2, \ldots, x_n$, where each new product replaces the product preceding it because it is in some way superior to its predecessor. Suppose that the world consumes one product, denoted as x_t, at time t, and that the innovator who created x_t reaps a profit because the innovation made x_t preferable to x_{t-1}. This implicitly assumes that all consumers are identical and that the markup is marginally less than the increase in value provided by the latest

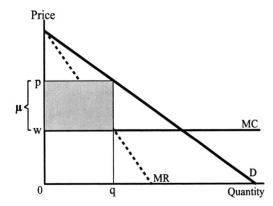

Fig. 9.5 Monopoly profit

innovation (so that consumers no longer demand any more x_{t-1} after the creation of x_t).

Profit from innovation depends on (1) markup μ, (2) the quantity of the product x_t produced during one period of time, denoted as X, and (3) the number of periods τ that the innovator produces x_t before her market is *destroyed* by a subsequent innovation. Thus, profit π is equal to

$$\pi = \mu X \tau \tag{9.9}$$

The level of production, X, depends on how many of society's available resources are devoted to production rather than research and development (R&D) activities. The total resources, R, devoted to innovative activity during the period are equal to

$$N = nR \tag{9.10}$$

Suppose for simplicity, but no loss of generality, that one unit of resources R produces one unit of output x_t. Total production during the period is therefore

$$X = (1 - n)R \tag{9.11}$$

Thus, X is directly related to the economy's total amount of productive factors and resources, R, and inversely related to the fraction of those resources devoted to innovation, n.

9.3.4 The Opportunity Costs of Innovation

The rate of innovation can be found by solving a maximization problem that takes into consideration the costs of innovation and the expected gains from innovation. Innovating firms seeking to create a new product x_{t+1} must purchase labor and other productive resources in competition with producers who demand resources to produce the most recently-developed product, x_t. The opportunity cost of innovation is the reduction in the production of products x_t caused by shifting scarce resources to innovative activities.

The cost of resources R will be lower, all other things equal, the more factors and resources are available in the economy. The cost of resources will be higher the greater is innovation. The price of resources, w, is therefore some function of N and R as follows:

$$w = g\left(\overset{+}{N}, \overset{-}{R} \right) \tag{9.12}$$

Signs over the equation reflect the partial derivatives of resource cost w with respect to N and R.

In reality, the process of innovation is highly uncertain. Devoting resources to innovative activity does not guarantee that something useful will actually be created, nor does the innovator know exactly how long it will take to successfully create that better product. It is difficult to incorporate uncertainty into the maximization problem that we are trying to model, however. To bring across the main ideas behind the Schumpeterian model, we make some simplifying assumptions. Suppose, therefore, that new products are developed according to an R&D process that has a known average outcome around which actual outcomes vary randomly. Suppose, furthermore, that the average time it takes to come up with a new product or technology is a direct function of the amount of resources devoted to innovative activities. Since we are interested in modeling the long-run growth process, we can solve for the average outcome. If innovators have *rational expectations*, then *on average* they correctly predict the future and we can substitute *expected values* for future values.

Suppose that the production function of innovations is linear with respect to the amount of productive resources, R, employed in innovative activity, and that it takes, on average, β units of resources to produce an innovation.[12] The average cost of innovation, CoI, that entrepreneurs expect to incur in generating an innovation is therefore

$$CoI = w\beta \tag{9.13}$$

Increasing innovation increases total demand for productive resources, and the prices of R rise. Therefore, the cost of innovation, denoted as CoI, is an upward-sloping function of innovative activity. Figure 9.6 shows a typical upward-sloping CoI curve relating marginal costs of innovation to the amount of factors and resources used in innovation, N. All other things equal, the CoI curve shifts up if β, the average amount of resources needed to generate an innovation, increases, and it will shift down if R, the total supply of resources, increases. In general notation, the cost of innovation is

$$CoI = h\left(\overset{+}{N}, \overset{-}{R}, \overset{+}{\beta}\right) \tag{9.14}$$

---

[12]Obvious, the R&D function need not be linear. The R&D function may be subject to diminishing returns, or it could reflect increasing returns to innovation. The latter would be the case if knowledge follows a combinatoric process in which the more researchers probe new ideas and communicate their findings, the easier it is for everyone to make progress toward finding new ideas, products, methods, etc. Since it is reasonably certain that the R&D function is an increasing function of the resources entrepreneurs devote to innovation, we appeal to simplicity and assume that the positive function is linear. This does not in any way reduce the generality of the qualitative results derived from the model.

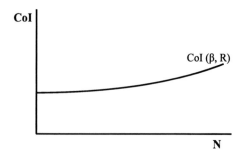

Fig. 9.6 The cost of
innovation

9.3.5 The Gains from Innovation

Equation (9.9) showed that the expected profit from an innovation, $\pi = \mu X \tau$, is a positive function of the average markup μ, the amount of output produced X, and the length of time τ that an innovator expects to enjoy the monopoly profit. The length of time τ depends on how fast new innovations are created. Since we have assumed that it takes β units of resources to generate an innovation, the expected number of innovations, **q**, during one period is

$$q = (1/\beta)N \qquad (9.15)$$

Figure 9.7 provides a graphic illustration of the relationship between the amount of resources devoted to innovation, N, and the average quantity of innovations **q** generated per period. It follows from (9.9) that the number of days that an innovator expects to enjoy his/her profit is equal to

$$E(\tau) = 1/q = \beta/N \qquad (9.16)$$

For example, if it takes one-half period before a new innovation "destroys" the current product's market position, q = 2.

According to (9.16), expected future profit is a direct function of β, a result that, at first glance, may seem counterintuitive. How could an increase in the cost of innovation *increase* the profit from innovation? Keep in mind, however, that we are specifying the *gains* from innovation; the cost function has already been specified above in (9.14), and there the costs of innovation clearly rise as β increases. But, precisely because the costs of innovation rise with β, an increase in β increases the length of time before a new innovation trumps a previous innovation, and the longer an innovator is likely to enjoy the profits of the innovation. Hence, the more difficult it is to innovate, the greater the gains from innovation.

The length of time an innovator can reap the profits from an innovation also depends on how many resources are devoted to innovation. Furthermore, the more resources are used for innovation, the fewer are available for producing profitable products derived from the innovations. Hence, there are two reasons why the present value of an innovation is inversely related to N: (1) a higher N leads to a

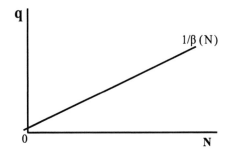

Fig. 9.7 The innovation function

faster destruction of prior creations and (2) a higher N reduces the amount of resources available to produce profit-generating output. Hence, the gains from innovation are inversely related to N, the amount of resources devoted to innovation.

An increase in total resources, R, permits more future production X, which implies that expected profits are positively related to R. And, finally, because innovations require *current* expenditures on research and development (R&D) that must be paid for from *future* profits, expected future profits must be discounted. Hence, the higher the discount (interest) rate, the less is the present value of an expected innovation. In general, therefore, the present value of future profit from innovation, or PVI, takes on the following general form:

$$PVI = f(\overset{+}{\mu}, \overset{+}{R}, \overset{-}{N}, \overset{+}{\beta}, \overset{-}{r}) \tag{9.17}$$

A more specific relationship can be derived by defining the right-hand variables in (9.17) more precisely. According to (9.9), (9.11), and (9.15), the expected profit, $E(\pi)$, accruing to an innovation is

$$E(\pi) = \mu X/q = \mu(R - N)(\beta/N) \tag{9.18}$$

The exact rate at which the future profit is discounted to the present of course depends on exactly when and how long the profit occurs. The present value of innovation thus consists of a series of future profits, each one discounted to the present. Hence:

$$PVI = \sum_{j=1}^{(\beta/N)} 1/(1 + r)^j \mu(R - N)(\beta/N) \tag{9.19}$$

PVI declines as N increases and more resources are applied to innovative activity because profit is destroyed more quickly the greater is N, all other things equal. This negatively-sloped function is drawn in Fig. 9.8. As suggested by the signs shown over the variables in (9.17), increases in the profit markup μ, the stock of productive

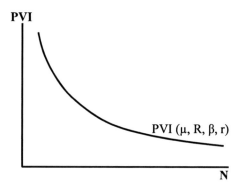

Fig. 9.8 The PVI curve

resources R, and the resources needed to generate an innovation β cause the PVI curve to shift up. An increase in the interest rate r lowers the curve.

9.3.6 The Equilibrium Level of R&D Activity

A useful simplifying assumption is that innovators are perfect competitors in the market for resources and in the innovative process. Each individual innovator, therefore, views the economy's average cost and profit functions as their marginal functions. Suppose, also, that innovators are risk-neutral so that they do not require a premium to induce them to undertake the inherently risky innovative activities. Profit maximizing entrepreneurs therefore employ resources to the point where their marginal expected cost of innovation is equal to the expected future profits from innovation. We can then show the profit maximization problem graphically as in Fig. 9.9. The top portion of Fig. 9.9 combines Figs. 9.6 and 9.8. The intersection of the CoI and PVI curves determines the equilibrium N, the amount of resources that competitive entrepreneurs devote to innovative activity. The bottom half of Fig. 9.9 is simply Fig. 9.7 turned upside down and conveniently attached along the horizontal axis that it shares with Figs. 9.6 and 9.8. The 1/β curve translates N into the number of innovations per period. Given the values of the parameters that determine the CoI and PVI curves in the upper half of Fig. 9.9 and the productivity of the innovative process as given by β, the economy produces **q** innovations per period of time.

The graphic model in Fig. 9.9 can be used to predict the changes in the innovation resulting from changes in the parameters that lie behind the PVI and CoI curves. Specifically in the case of immigration, the model can be used to predict a new equilibrium level of innovation as a result of a flow of immigrants into, or out of, a country. Equations (9.14), (9.15), and (9.17) highlight the directions of the shifts.

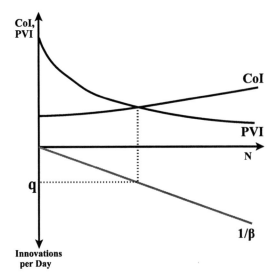

Fig. 9.9 Equilibrium innovation

9.4 Immigration in the Schumpeterian Model

Recall from our discussion above that there are at least four channels through which immigration may influence technological progress: Immigrants can (1) facilitate the transfer of technology, (2) contribute to innovation as entrepreneurs and workers in innovative activities, (3) change the size of economies, and (4) increase innovative competition by reducing the ability of vested interests to take protectionist measures to slow the process of creative destruction. This section examines the first three of these channels through which immigration has been hypothesized to influence economic growth.

9.4.1 Immigrants as an Innovative Resource

The most obvious change introduced by immigration is a change in a country's productive resources. The Schumpeterian model very clearly depicts the potential dual roles of immigrants as both workers and innovators, discussed above, by splitting resources R into productive resources, X, and innovative resources, N. Fig. 9.10 illustrates the effect on innovation of an increase in R, which would be the case when a country receives immigrants. An increase in R lowers w, which, according to (9.14), shifts the CoI curve down to CoI_1, causes the equilibrium value of N to increase, and thus increases the number of innovations to q_1.

An increase of R also shifts up the PVI curve, as specified in Equation (9.17), because an increase in productive resources implies more production of new products and, therefore, more profits, all other things equal. This effect further

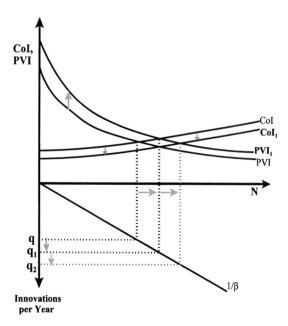

Fig. 9.10 The effects on innovation of an increase in R

increases the amount of resources allocated to innovation by profit-seeking innovators, and thus the number of innovations rises further to q_2.

Schumpeter emphasized the role of entrepreneurs in the process of creative destruction. The literature on immigration has for a long time suggested that immigrants may represent human resources that are especially appropriate for innovation and entrepreneurship. For example, Chiswick (2000) has found that the self-selection of immigrants in terms of personal characteristics favorable to economic growth is more pronounced "the greater the out of pocket (direct) costs of migration and return migration, the greater the effect of ability on lowering the costs of migration, and the smaller are the wage differences by skill in the lower income origin than in the higher income destination."[13] The fact that international migration is difficult and risky implies that immigrants are likely to be less risk averse and more adventuresome than the average person in their countries of origin. Economic research confirms that people tend to be risk averse when it comes to personal choices. The fact that so many people endure low incomes and accept limitations to their personal freedom is further evidence that familiar, if inferior, conditions are often preferable to unfamiliar, though probably better, conditions elsewhere. International migration, therefore, provides a natural selection process that distinguishes exceptionally adventuresome and enterprising people. Immigrants are, all other things equal, likely to be less risk averse and more ambitious than the majority of people in their native country and, often, the majority of people in the destination country.

---

[13]Chiswick (2000).

Whether immigrants are self-selected to favor entrepreneurship is an important question for the analysis of the economic effects of immigration on the source and destination countries. If immigrants are really more entrepreneurial, more willing to sacrifice now for future gains, better educated, and more ambitious than the average population of the country they leave behind, then the source country is likely to suffer both immediate and long-term losses. On the other hand, to the extent that new immigrants are more ambitious, educated, entrepreneurial, and forward-looking, the destination country will gain more from their arrival.

9.4.2 *Immigrants Increase the Returns to Innovation*

Nathan Rosenberg, an economic historian noted for studying the growth of technology over the ages, attributes the rapid economic growth of the United States in the 1800s to "rapid growth in demand and circumstances conducive to a high degree of product standardization."[14] That is, the United States was able to exploit economies of scale because its market grew rapidly and, because of the country's large middle class, the market was very uniform. What caused this growth of the market? "Probably the most pervasive force of all was the extremely rapid rate of population growth . . . with immigration assuming a role of some significance in the 1840s."[15] Also relevant is the observation that despite protectionist U.S. trade policy, the country was able to grow rapidly in the 1800s without taking advantage of international trade because immigration made the domestic economy sufficiently large so that its national border did not constrain the division of labor. By 1870 the United States overtook England as the world's biggest economy, and by 1900 its residents enjoyed the highest per capita incomes in the world. In a sense, the United States used immigration rather than international trade to achieve economies of scale.[16] Immigration enabled U.S. industry to exploit increasing returns to scale despite the strong protectionist bias of U.S. trade policy throughout the nineteenth century. Figure 9.11 shows how an increase in market size expanded profit and, therefore, the rate of innovation.

9.4.3 *Immigrants and Technology Transfers*

The movement of people may also cause a change in β, the resource cost of generating innovations. Immigrants inevitably carry ideas with them, and the

---

[14]Rosenberg (1994, p. 113).

[15]Rosenberg (1994, p.113).

[16]Other economic historians who reach similar conclusions about nineteenth century U.S. immigration and economic growth are Irwin (2000), Hill (1971), and Crafts and Venables (2001).

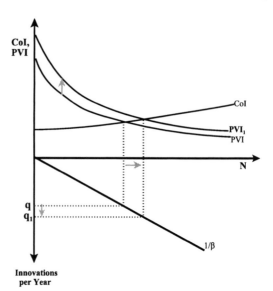

Fig. 9.11 The effects on innovation of an increase in π

arrival of ideas from abroad through immigration is likely to be much less costly than arriving at those ideas from scratch through original research. For example, the economic historian Carlo Cipolla (1978) describes the clock and watch industry from several 100 years ago, in which immigration greatly affected technological development and subsequent economic growth. The clock and watch industry played a particularly important leadership role in developing the technology of precision engineering. Many early clock makers were French, but a large percentage of the early French clock makers, who were highly literate and often interested in various aspects of science, were also active in the Reformation movement. When France expelled the Huguenots, as the French Protestants were called, a number of French clock makers went to Geneva, Switzerland, at the invitation of John Calvin, the Calvinist leader of that Swiss city. According to Cipolla, at its infancy in 1500, "to destroy or to build up the [clock] industry it was enough to dismiss or attract a few dozen craftsmen."[17] The future Swiss watch industry was founded by "the inflow of a handful of refugees-to the injection of a small but precious amount of human skills."[18] A change in β affects *all* the curves in Fig. 9.9. Suppose, for example, that β declines, which implies an increase in the efficiency with which the economy generates and applies new ideas. First of all, a decrease in β shifts the $1/\beta$ line, which relates N to q, clockwise, as shown in Fig. 9.12. Second, Fig. 9.12 also shows the CoI curve shifting down, as suggested by (9.14). Finally, (9.17) suggests that a decline in β shifts the PVI curve down as well. All other things equal, if it becomes less costly to innovate, then creative destruction occurs more frequently

---

[17]Carlo M. Cipolla (1978, p. 64).
[18]Carlo M. Cipolla (1978, p. 64).

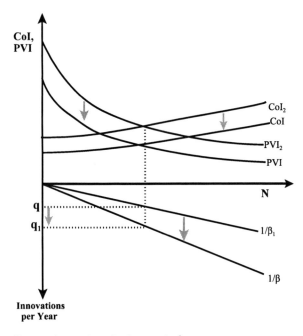

Fig. 9.12 The effects on innovation of a decrease in β

and any given innovation enjoys profits for a shorter period of time. The net result of these shifts appears to be ambiguous because a fall in β not only reduces the marginal cost of innovation, but it also reduces expected profits because the lower costs of innovation imply that the destruction side of the creative destruction process occurs more quickly. The *net* effect on innovation of the three effects of a decline in β is likely to be positive, however. The specification of the PVI and CoI curves suggest they exactly offset each other, leaving the shift of the 1/β line as the net contributor to the change in innovation.

Specifically, the PVI and CoI curves specified by (9.13) and (9.19) define the equilibrium where CoI and PVI curves intersect as

$$PVI = CoI = \sum_{j=1}^{(\beta/N)} 1/(1+r)^j \mu (R-N)(\beta/N) = w\beta \qquad (9.20)$$

Since β enters into both the CoI and PVI equations as a simple multiplicative factor, the partial derivatives of CoI and PVI with respect to β are equal:

$$\partial PVI/\partial\beta = \sum_{j=1}^{(\beta/N)} 1/(1+r)^j \mu (R-N)(1/N) = \partial CoI/\partial\beta = w \qquad (9.21)$$

Thus, at the equilibrium level of N, a decrease in β causes equal downward shifts in the CoI curve and the PVI curve, keeping N unchanged after a decline in β. Therefore, the remaining shift in the $q = (1/\beta)$ curve in the bottom portion of the diagram determines the net effect of a decline in β on innovation. We conclude that, under the plausible conditions that determined (9.13) and (9.19), an improvement in the efficiency of innovation raises the amount of innovation.

In summary, the Schumpeterian R&D model of endogenous technological progress developed here suggests that, all other things equal, the number of innovations in an economy is greater (1) the larger is the profit markup at which the successful innovator can sell her innovative new product, (2) the greater is the supply of resources available to innovators and producers, (3) the more highly innovators value future gains relative to current costs, and (4) the more efficient are innovators in employing the economy's scarce resources toward generating new innovations. These conclusions are conveniently summarized as

$$q = f\left(\overset{+}{\mu}, \overset{+}{R}, \overset{-}{r}, \overset{-}{\beta}\right) \tag{9.22}$$

Immigration is likely to increase profits, expand the amount of productive and innovative resources, and reduce the costs of innovation. The Appendix to this chapter reinforces this section's results by showing the first three channels through which immigration influences the rate of innovation in an alternative mathematical version of the Schumpeterian model.

9.5 Protectionism, Creative Destruction, and Immigration

A fourth channel through which immigration may influence economic growth has been suggested: Immigration increases innovative competition by reducing the ability of vested interests to take protectionist measures to slow the process of creative destruction. The logic of the Schumpeterian model illustrates how immigration could increase innovative competition and, therefore, the rate of economic growth.

9.5.1 Creation Requires Destruction

For the process of *creative destruction* to work, there must be *destruction* as well as *creation*. If an initial creation is not followed by a second creation that *destroys* the first creation's advantage, then there can be no continued technological progress and economic growth. Lee and McKenzie (1993) pointed out that in many societies the political environment permits previous innovators to slow the creative destruction process. More recently, Raghuram and Zingales (2003) described this situation very well:

> Instead of viewing destruction as the inevitable counterpart of creation, it is far easier for the politician to give in to the capitalist, who ostensibly champions the distressed by demanding that competition be shackled and markets suppressed.[19]

The negative relationship between protecting vested interests and technological progress was also discussed by Mokyr (1990) in his historical study of innovation and technological progress:

> The enemies of technological progress were not the lack of useful new ideas, but social forces that for one reason or another tried to preserve the status quo.[20]

Mokyr distinguished the growth of international competition in an increasingly globalized economy as a particularly favorable development for continued technological progress:

> As long as some segment of the world economy is creative, the human race will not sink into the technological stasis that could eventually put an end to economic growth.[21]

Holmes and Schmitz (1995, 1998) provide an especially insightful variation of Schumpeter's model to show how international competition limits vested interests' ability to block innovation.

9.5.2 The Holmes and Schmitz Model

In the Schumpeterian tradition, Holmes and Schmitz (1995) hypothesize that a certain country has two imperfectly competitive manufacturers who engage in Schumpeterian competition, each trying to establish technological superiority. Technological leadership enables a firm to earn a monopoly profit from production after effectively *destroying* its competition with its *creativity*. The *technological follower*, unable to profitably produce its inferior product, devotes all available resources to research and development in order to capture technological leadership. The leading firm, on the other hand, must decide how many resources to allocate to the production that generates the profit with which to recoup its past investment in creating new technology and how much to allocate to research to create further innovations that will generate new profits after its current innovation is creatively destroyed.

Holmes and Schmitz add an important wrinkle to the standard Schumpeterian model, however: they permit the technological leader to allocate resources to a *third* activity of *obstructing* the efforts of the technological followers to gain leadership. The decision to produce, research, or obstruct depends on the potential payoffs from

---

[19]Raghuram and Zingales (2003, p. 2).

[20]Mokyr (1990, p. 301).

[21]Mokyr (1990, p. 304).

each form of activity. The more resources that are devoted to R&D, the faster is the rate of technological progress. If resources are used to obstruct the follower, then technological progress slows. The question for economic growth is, therefore: What conditions are relatively more favorable to innovation than obstruction?

Holmes and Schmitz show that there will be less obstruction under free trade than under restricted trade. The intuition for this conclusion is straightforward. In a protected domestic economy, the technological leader enjoys greater returns to innovation when it only has to compete with other domestic firms for consumer dollars, and, hence, the payoff to obstructing other domestic manufacturers' research efforts is higher. In an open economy, when the manufacturer also has to compete with foreign firms, obstructing domestic competition has little effect on future profits. Worldwide competition would have to be obstructed, and that is much more difficult and costly. Hence, expending resources to obstruct domestic innovators becomes less profitable, and the domestic economy gains a more rapid rate of technological progress under free trade. Immigration can have a similar effect on innovative competition.

Joseph Schumpeter of course emphasized the role of entrepreneurs in the process of creative destruction. Schumpeter saw the entrepreneur as something of a social deviant:

> ... The reaction of the social environment against one who wishes to do something new...
> manifests itself first of all in the existence of legal and political impediments. But neglect-
> ing this, any deviating conduct by a member of a social group is condemned, though in
> greatly varying degrees according as the social group is used to such conduct or not.[22]

Schumpeter pointed out that entrepreneurs were often recent immigrants because they are less attached to the traditions of society and, therefore, less reluctant to innovate. Their lack of social capital, local connections, and personal relationships makes it more difficult for them to collude, or others to collude with them, in order to stymie creative destruction.

9.6 Growth Effects of Immigration in the Source Country

The models in the previous sections explain how immigration affects economic growth in the destination country. In this section, we briefly examine the growth effects of immigration in the source country.

9.6.1 The Overall Growth Effect of Out-Migration

The R&D model suggests that countries losing migrants grow less rapidly because its stock of innovative people declines, immigrants take knowledge and ideas with them, the size of the economy is reduced and thus there are diseconomies of scale,

---

[22]Schumpeter (1934, p. 155).

and the departure of "social deviants" make obstruction of creative destruction more likely. Recent models by Miyagiwa (1991), Haque and Kim (1995), and Wong and Yip (1999) conclude that *source* countries of immigration suffer a decline in the rate of economic growth.

Growth declines can be avoided, however, if (1) immigrants eventually return to their homelands and (2) immigrant remittances enable greater levels of investment than otherwise would occur in source countries. For example, Mountford (1997), Stark, Helmenstein, and Prskawetz (1998), Vidal (1998), and Beine, Docquier, and Rapoport (2003), among others, have suggested that the prospects for high overseas earnings may actually increase source country human capital formation. Their reasoning is straightforward: the possibility of immigrating to a high income country raises the return to education in the source country, which increases the demand for education.

A slowdown in economic growth in the source country can also be avoided if immigration opens channels for technology transfers from countries that are technological leaders. The conventional wisdom that talented, entrepreneurial, and educated people are needed to adapt and apply foreign technologies is strongly supported by the evidence, which means that a country's capacity to absorb foreign technology will diminish if talented and entrepreneurial people immigrate elsewhere. Dustmann and Kirchkamp (2002) and Mesnard and Ravallion (2002) show that immigrants often maintain ties with their native countries, and these ties can serve to create channels through which technology can be transferred. Agrawal, Cockburn, and McHale (2003) find that social capital, the subtle relationships among people that have been shown to facilitate the sharing of knowledge and technology, endures even after out-migration. Specifically, their analysis of patent citations shows that former colleagues and associates separated by immigration continue to influence each others' research disproportionately. This effect is especially important for countries such as India, China, Taiwan, and others that have many university graduates living overseas.

Lundborg and Segerstrom (2002) use a typical Schumpeterian growth model and computer simulations to find how welfare changes for immigrants, natives in the destination country, and natives in the source country. Under a variety of reasonable parameter values, they find that the spread of technological progress definitely improves the welfare of natives in the source country, but not necessarily in the destination country. They conclude that the expansion of the European Union to include Eastern European economies will likely expand economic growth more in the new members than in the original 15 EU member countries, largely because of the expected large flows of immigrants from the new members to the old members.

9.6.2 How Remittances are used in Source Countries

As discussed in the previous chapter, the analysis of remittances in the static model suggests that, all other things equal, remittances improve welfare in the immigrant source country. From the growth perspective of this chapter, a more important question is how remittances affect the long-run growth rate of the source economy. The evidence on the growth effects of remittances is not very clear, however.

Most studies of the use of remittances find that remittances are used mostly for consumption, not investment. But, remittance studies do not capture the multiplier effects. Taylor's (1999) summary of village studies in Kenya, West Java, Senegal, and Mexico concludes that multiplier effects are often small in local communities, with the countries' urban areas receiving the greatest secondary boosts. However, such secondary effects can still have a very positive effect on the country's economic growth, even if that growth does not occur in the local communities where the recipients of the remittances reside.

A comparison of Mexican families that receive, or do not receive, remittances by Germán Zárate-Hoyos (2001) shows that, all other things equal, "households receiving remittances devote a higher proportion of current expenditures to investment and savings than those households that do not receive remittances." Combined with the finding that conspicuous consumption is usually higher in villages that receive large remittances from relatives abroad, this finding suggests that it is the lack of local investment opportunities rather than the direct effect of remittances that causes the high propensity to consume remittance income. Economic growth depends on the many variables that influence capital investment, innovation, entrepreneurship, and the willingness to do things differently. Therefore, remittances by themselves are not likely to play the decisive role in a nation's economic development.

9.7 The Brain Drain Again

Now that we have introduced growth models and how immigration fits into these models, it is useful to return to the long-run consequences of the brain drain. We noted in the previous chapter that there is little that can be done about the brain drain short of increasing wages and improving working conditions in poor countries. The brain drain itself has growth effects, which suggests that the brain drain may involve both vicious cycles and virtuous cycles.

In the long run, the brain drain could raise or lower growth rates in the source country. The growth effects on the source country of the emigration of educated people can be summarized using a diagram such as Fig. 9.13. Source country per capita income is shown on the vertical axis, and time is on the horizontal axis. Suppose that at time t* the brain drain begins. Whether the brain drain has a beneficial effect on the source country depends on whether per capita income grows faster after the brain drain than it would in the absence of the brain drain. Suppose that the growth path of the economy without a brain drain is given by the curve $G_{no\ im}$. Figure 9.13 then shows two hypothetical alternative growth paths with a brain drain, labeled G_1 and G_2.

The path G_1 represents the case often suggested by traditional development economists who fear that the brain drain will cause output and income to fall in the source country in the short run, and the rate of growth will fall in the long run.

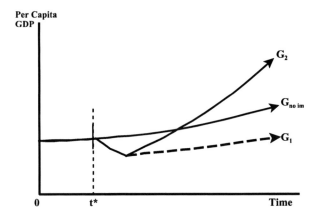

Fig. 9.13 Alternative long-run growth paths with a brain drain

Clearly, in this case, the source country would have been better off if its educated natives had not left the country. On the other hand, the growth path G_2 suggests that, despite the initial depressing effect on per capita income when the brain drain began, eventually there are increased technology flows back to the source country and growth actually rises above the rate at which the country would have grown in the absence of sending its most educated natives overseas. This increased growth could be the result of communications channels or business networks built by the immigrants between their destination and source countries. Perhaps, the knowledge and experience returning emigrants bring back with them ends up being less costly and more useful than the knowledge and technology these same people could have developed within the source country if they had stayed. Or, there may be more trade and investment flows encouraged by immigrant networks. Finally, remittances of a substantial portion of the high incomes educated migrants earn overseas can help to finance new businesses and raise the education of remaining family members, which increases economic growth beyond what could have been accomplished in the absence of the remittances.

Which of these two scenarios, G_1 or G_2, is more realistic is not clear. There are many other possible growth paths depending on exactly who migrates, how many educated people migrate, how long the migrants remain overseas, and what level of contact they maintain with the source country. Of course, the source country's other economic and social policies also play a major role in determining the answers to each of these questions. While the popular press has written frequently about remittances and the brain drain, much more serious research is needed.

9.8   Summary and Conclusions

The Solow model clearly shows that growth through factor accumulation cannot cause permanent improvements in living standards. Continuous improvements in per capita income requires continuous technological progress. The Schumpeterian model of innovation shows that immigration is indeed likely to stimulate technological progress in destination countries. Immigration is likely to enhance the destination country's rate of economic growth, all other things equal.

Because they come from other societies and cultures, immigrants usually bring new ideas to their new countries of residence. Furthermore, by increasing the number of people in the destination economy, the total supply of productive and innovative resources grows. And because immigration is costly and risky, immigrants are self-selected into a group that is likely to be more entrepreneurial and risk-taking than the average members of their original societies. Immigration also increases the size of the destination country's economy, stimulating more specialization and exchange, economies of scale, and profit from innovation. Finally, immigrants may help to prevent the status quo from obstructing the process of creative destruction. Thus, in the destination country, immigrants are likely to shift the variables in the Schumpeterian model in ways that increase innovation.

Immigrations's effect on economic growth in the source country has been studied even less than immigration's growth effects in destination countries. Theoretically, the effects of immigration on the source country are not as clear as they are in the destination country. There are obvious negative effects; all one needs to do is reverse the conclusions about how immigration influences growth by shifting labor and entrepreneurial talent. However, when it comes to the movement in knowledge and ideas, immigration can lead to bi-directional flows. A source country's former residents living abroad can send back new information and knowledge, thus expanding economic growth in the native countries they no longer reside in. Also, immigrants can remit money back home, which can also increase growth in the source country. Finally, immigrants often return home with a greater amount of human capital than they left with. Hence, the negative growth effects in the source country may not be as great as feared. In some cases, immigration may produce growth in both the source and destination countries. However, much research remains to be done before these hypotheses can be judged with any degree of confidence.

Just like any assessment of the economic effects of globalization, the overall effects of immigration on individual countries and the world as a whole depend critically on the long-run growth effects. The power of compounding implies that any change in the rate of growth will eventually overwhelm the static effects that we usually focus on, no matter how large the static effects may be. The relationship between technological progress, economic growth, and the international movement of people requires much more research. If immigration indeed has positive growth effects, then restrictive immigration policies can greatly damage long-run human welfare.

Appendix: An Alternative Mathematical Schumpeterian Model

Growth models are normally presented in mathematical form, not the graphic form embraced in this chapter. Here we present a simple mathematical growth model that follows logic similar to that of the graphic model of the previous section, albeit with one important difference. Rather than making the assumption that each successive innovation (new product) replaces earlier innovations (products), the model in this section assumes that innovation consists of new products that are added to the existing stock of products. In the growth literature, these two types of models are referred to as "quality ladder" models and "expanding variety" models, respectively. For example, in their advanced graduate level textbook on economic growth, Robert Barro and Xavier Sala-i-Martin (2004) devote separate chapters to these two groups of models of endogenous technological progress. The dichotomy between the two types of models is not as great as it seems, however. As shown below, the conclusions of the two versions of Schumpeterian models are nearly identical.

A.1 Innovation and Profit

Suppose that each act of innovation consists of creating a new firm that produces a new product. We start with n firms in the economy, each producing one of n different products. Suppose also that one unit of labor is required to produce a product; this implies that the marginal (and average) cost of producing each good is equal to the wage rate, w. Because each product is different, each producer enjoys some degree of market power so that each firm faces a downward-sloping demand curve. For simplicity, suppose that each profit maximizing firm faces an identical demand curve and, therefore, sets the same price equal to

$$p = w(1/\gamma) \tag{9A.1}$$

where $0 < \gamma < 1$ and the price markup $p - w = \mu = [(1-\gamma)/\gamma]w$. Since $w = p\gamma$, profit per unit is $p(1-\gamma)$. Because entrepreneurs face downward-sloping demand curves, they can set a price above the marginal cost of production w and, potentially, recover the cost of innovation.

The total value of output is GDP, and therefore total profits in the economy are equal to

$$\Pi = GDP(1 - \gamma) \tag{9A.2}$$

The profit of any one of the n identical firms is

$$\pi = [GDP(1 - \gamma)]/n \tag{9A.3}$$

The present value of the earnings of a successful innovation is equal to the discounted stream of future profits, or

$$PV = \sum_{i=0}^{\infty} \rho^i \pi_{t=I} \tag{9A.4}$$

where ρ is the discount factor $1/(1 + r)$, r is the interest rate, and the $\pi_{t=i}$ are the profits in each future time period i. The present value of all future profits can be thought of as the equity value of the firm.

A.2 The Equilibrium Level of Entrepreneurial Activity

Entrepreneurs will innovate and enter the market so long as the present value of future profits, PV, exceeds the current cost of product development. Suppose that β is equal to the units of labor required to develop each new product. The cost of developing a new product is thus $w\beta$. Assuming that there is a fixed number of workers in the economy, the more workers are hired by firms to develop new products, the higher will be w, the opportunity cost of those workers' marginal product in producing goods. Innovation will stop expanding when the discounted future earnings from producing the nth good are exactly equal to the cost of creating the nth good. Putting together the costs and profits from innovation, the *innovation profit*, defined as θ, is

$$\theta = PV - w\beta \tag{9A.5}$$

If there is competitive innovation, meaning that all prospective entrepreneurs can demand resources for innovation and, if successful, market their new products, then $\theta = 0$ and

$$PV = \beta w \tag{9A.6}$$

Equation (9A.6) represents the equilibrium condition for innovation profits. This equilibrium condition is similar to the intersection of the CoI and PVI curves in Fig. 9.9

A.3 The Equilibrium Rate of Technological Progress

We assume that firms live forever, even though their profits are gradually eroded by the entry of new firms with new products. In the case of an endless flow of future profits, the discounted value of future profits can be approximated by π/r, where π is the average future profit and r is the interest rate. If the growth of products is zero, or $g = 0$, the total stock market valuation of a firm is

$$(PV) = [GDP(1 - \gamma)]/nr \tag{9A.7}$$

where r is the rate of interest and n is the total number of firms and products. The total capitalization of the economy's stock market is thus

$$n(PV) = [GDP(1 - \gamma)]/r \qquad (9A.8)$$

If innovation is profitable, the number of products increases, however. For simplicity, suppose that (1) total output, or GDP, stays the same when new firms develop new products and (2) each new firm has to share a fixed amount of labor in the economy. Thus, the profit of any single firm $[GDP(1-\mu)]/n$ will decrease if the number of firms increases. Specifically, profit will continually decline by the growth rate of new products/firms $g = \Delta n/n$. If $g > 0$, then the market valuation of *existing* firms is

$$n(PV) = [GDP(1 - \gamma)]/(r + g) \qquad (9A.9)$$

The equilibrium rate of innovation, g, can be found manipulating the above results. First, combining (9A.1) and (9A.6) gives us

$$p = w/\gamma = PV/\gamma\beta \qquad (9A.10)$$

With the above result, equation (9A.10) can be rewritten as

$$p = PV/\gamma\beta = [GDP(1 - \gamma)]/\gamma\beta n(r + g) \qquad (9A.11)$$

Since it takes one unit of labor to produce each unit of output of old and new products, the total amount of labor devoted to production is exactly equal to the total quantity of output of products, which is equal to GDP/p. The amount of labor devoted to research and development is equal to the number of new products, ng, times the amount of labor required to create a new product, or βng. If the quantity of labor available in the economy is R, then the growth rate of new products must be compatible with

$$\beta ng + GDP/p = R \qquad (9A.12)$$

Using equation (9A.11) to substitute for p in equation (9A.12) yields

$$\beta ng + [\gamma\beta n(r + g)/(1 - \gamma)] = R \qquad (9A.13)$$

Multiplying all terms in (9A.13) by $(1-\gamma)$ and dividing everything by βn:

$$g(1 - \gamma) + \gamma r + \gamma g = R(1 - \gamma)/\beta n \qquad (9A.14)$$

Equation (9A.14) can be further simplified to:

$$g + \gamma r = R(1 - \gamma)/\beta n \qquad (9A.15)$$

Isolating g, the growth of new products, on the right-hand side of the equation gives us a result that is very similar to the graphic Schumpeterian model of this chapter.

$$g = [R(1 - \gamma)/\beta n] - \gamma r \qquad (9A.16)$$

That is, the growth rate of new products, which is really intended as a proxy for the creation of new ideas and technology, depends directly on R and inversely on γ, β, n, and r.

The partial derivatives of g with respect to R, γ, β, n, and r are: $\partial g/\partial R = (1-\gamma)/\beta$ n > 0, $\partial g/\partial \gamma = -R/\beta n - r < 0$, $\partial g/\partial r = -\gamma < 0$, $\partial g/\partial \beta = -[R(1-\gamma)]/(\beta)^2 n < 0$, and $\partial g/\partial n = -[R(1-\gamma)\beta]/(\beta n)^2 < 0$. The signs of the derivatives suggest that the rate of technological progress depends directly on the amount of productive resources R and inversely on γ, β, n, and r. Note that γ is inversely related to $\mu = [(1-\gamma)/\gamma]w$, or $\partial \mu/\partial \gamma = [-w(1-\gamma)/\gamma^{-2} - w/\gamma] < 0$. Given the result above that $\partial g/\partial \gamma < 0$ and the chain rule $\partial g/\partial \gamma = (\partial g/\partial \mu) \cdot (\partial \mu/\partial \gamma)$, it follows that $\partial g/\partial \mu > 0$. Hence, the results here are compatible with the simple graphic Schumpeterian model in this chapter, which effectively concluded that $\partial g/\partial \mu > 0$. Overall, the results are thus identical to those given in equation (9.22).

To find the relationship between immigration and economic growth according to the mathematical model of this section, we need to specify how immigration affects the variables in the model, such as R, β, r, and μ. For it to be true that $\partial \gamma/\partial im < 0$, then $(\partial g/\partial \gamma) \cdot (\partial \gamma/\partial im) > 0$. Similarly, if the evidence suggests that $\partial R/\partial im > 0$, then $\partial g/\partial im = (\partial g/\partial R) \cdot (\partial R/\partial im) > 0$ because $\partial g/\partial R > 0$. Finally, immigration increases growth by improving the efficiency of innovation, that is, by reducing β, provided $(\partial g/\partial \beta) \cdot (\partial \beta/\partial im) > 0$. This will be the case if $(\partial \beta/\partial im) < 0$. It remains to be proven empirically what the signs of the relevant partial derivatives are, although our reasoning suggests the relationship are as we hypothesize here. Much empirical research remains to be done.

References

Agrawal, A., Cockburn, I., & McHale, J. (2003). Gone but not forgotten: Labor flows, knowledge spillovers, and enduring social capital. NBER Working Paper No. w9950.

Aghion, P., & Howitt, P. (1992). A model of growth through creative destruction. *Econometrica*, 60, 323–351.

Barro, R. J., & Sala-i-Martin, X. (2004). *Economic growth* (2nd ed.) Cambridge, MA: MIT.

Beine, M., Docquier, F., & Rapoport, F. (2003). Brain drain and growth in LDCs: Winners and losers. IZA Discussion Paper, IZA, Bonn, Germany.

Boserup, E. (1965). *The conditions of agricultural growth*. London: Allen and Unwin.

Boserup, E. (1981). *Population and technological change*. Chicago: University of Chicago Press.

Chiswick, B. R. (2000) Are immigrants favorably self-selected? An economic analysis. IZA Discussion Paper No. 131, March, 2000.

Cipolla, C. M. (1978). *Clocks and culture*. New York: W.W. Norton.

Crafts, N., & Venables, A. (2001). Globalization and geography: An historical perspective. Working Paper, April 12.

Domar, E. D. (1946). Capital expansion, rate of growth, and employment. *Econometrica, 14*, 137–147.

Dustmann, C., & Kirchkamp, O. (2002). The optimal migration duration and activity choice after remigration. *Journal of Development Economics, 67*(2), 351–372.

Grossman, G., & Helpman, E. (1991). *Innovation and growth in the global economy.* Cambridge, MA: MIT.

Haque, N.U., & Kim, S-J. (1995). Human capital flight: Impact of migration on income and growth. *IMF Staff Papers, 42*(3), 577–607.

Harrod, R. F. (1939). An essay in dynamic theory. *The Economic Journal, 49,* 14–33.

Hill, P. J. (1971). The economic impact of immigration into the United States. *Journal of Economic History, 31*(1), 260–263.

Holmes, T., & Schmitz, J. (1995). Resistance to new technology and trade between areas. *Federal Reserve Bank of Minneapolis Quarterly Review, 19*(1), 2–17.

Holmes, T., & Schmitz, J. (1998). A gain from trade: More research, less obstruction. Federal Reserve Bank of Minneapolis Staff Report No. 245.

Irwin, D. (2000). *Tariffs and growth in late nineteenth century America.* NBER Working Paper 7639.

Jones, C. (2002). *Introduction to economic growth* (2nd ed.). New York: W.W. Norton.

Kuznets, S. (1973). *Population, capital and growth.* New York: W.W. Norton.

Lee, D., & McKenzie, R. (1993). *Failure and progress, the bright side of the dismal science.* Washington, DC: The Cato Institute.

Lundberg, P., & Segerstrom, P. (2002). The growth and welfare effects of international mass migration. *Journal of International Economics, 56,* 177–204.

Maddison, A. (2003). *The World economy: Historical statistics.* Paris: OECD.

Maddison, A. (2006). *Historical statistics for the world economy: 1–2003AD,* Statistical Appendix; this document was downloaded in August 19, 2006 from the Web site (http://ggdc.net/maddison/) maintained by the Groningen Growth & Development Centre at the University of Groningen, Netherlands.

Mesnard, A., & Ravallion, M. (2002). *Wealth distribution and self-employment in a developing country.* CEPR Discussion Paper DP3026.

Miyagiwa, K. (1991). Scale economies in education and the brain drain problem. *International Economic Review, 32*(3), 743–759.

Mokyr, J. (1990). *The lever of riches.* New York: Oxford University Press.

Mountford, A. (1997). Can a brain drain be good for growth in the source economy? *Journal of Development Economics, 58*(2), 287–303.

Peel, Q. (2005, 3 March). A dynamic Europe needs immigrants. *Financial Times.*

Raghuram, R., & Zingales, L. (2003). *Saving capitalism from the capitalists.* New York: Crown Publishing.

Rivera-Batiz, Luis A., & Paul M. Romer (1991). Economic integration and endogenous growth. *Quarterly Journal of Economics, 56,* 531–555.

Romer, P. (1990). Endogenous technological change. *Journal of Political Economy, 95,* S71–S102.

Rosenberg, N. (1994). *Exploring the black box, technology, economics, and history.* Cambridge: Cambridge University Press.

Schumpeter, J. (1934). *The theory of economic development.* Cambridge, MA: Harvard University Press.

Simon, J. (1992). *Population and development in poor countries.* Princeton, NJ: Princeton University Press.

Simon, J. L. (1996). *The Ultimate resource 2.* Princeton, NJ: Princeton University Press.

Smith A. (1776 [1976]). *An inquiry into the nature and causes of the wealth of nations.* Chicago: University of Chicago Press.

Solow, R. (1956). A contribution to the theory of economic growth. *Quarterly Journal of Economics, 70*(1), 65–94.

Solow, R. (1957). Technical change and the aggregate production function. *Review of Economics and Statistics, 39,* 312–320.

Stark, O., Helmenstein, C., & Prskawetz, A. (1998). Human capital depletion, human capital formation, and migration: A blessing or a curse?. *Economics Letters, 60*(3), 363–367.

Taylor, J. (1999). The new economics of labor migration and the role of remittances in the migration process. *Migration and Development, 37*(1).

Van den Berg, H. (2001). *Economic growth and development.* New York: McGraw-Hill.

Vidal, J.-P. (1998). The effect of emigration on human capital formation. *Journal of Population Economics, 11*(4), 589–600.

Wong, K. Y., & Yip, C. K. (1999). Education, economic growth, and the brain drain. *Journal of Economic Dynamics and Control, 23*(5–6), 699–726.

Zárate-Hoyos, G. (2001). The case for a remittance policy in Mexico. Paper presented at the Pacific Coast Council on Latin American Studies Conference, April 5–7, 2001, Tijuana, Baja California, Mexico.

Part II
Immigration Issues and Cases

Immigration affects human welfare in many ways, as the many different models and supporting evidence from Chaps. 2–9 have shown. The models and empirical studies have pointed out the likely costs for natives in destination countries, the people remaining in the source countries, and the immigrants themselves. We added complexity to our analysis by examining the long-run growth effects, externalities, and demand effects. We are not yet done, however. There is much more to learn about immigration.

In this section of the book, we apply the basic theory to some interesting issues and cases that have concerned economists, policymakers, and the public at large. In the process, we accumulate more evidence of the causes and consequences of immigration. Many policymakers have, in fact, focused more on these special issues than they have on the wage and employment effects described in many economic models. This focus on narrow issues and cases creates a problem for political leaders and social scientists interested in the overall welfare of humanity. For example, restricting one category of immigrants or favoring immigrants employed in one specific industry at the behest of specific lobby groups is unlikely to maximize national welfare. The focus on specific and isolated cases and issues inevitably misses many of the widespread effects of immigration. Each particular issue and case evolved within the complex interplay of the many natural and social forces that shape the human environment.

It is the purpose of this section of the book not only to examine some of the specific issues of immigration that seem to be of special interest, but to examine them within the broader framework built with the theory and evidence presented in the previous section. As before, we will present models where they are helpful, and we will describe the evidence that social scientists have pieced together to support or refute specific hypotheses.

The first chapter of this section covers the case of temporary immigration. Chapter 10 dispels the myth that most immigrants are permanent settlers. The fact is that immigrants often view their stay in the destination country as temporary. Even when the intent is to move permanently, people often reconsider and reverse their decision to immigrate. There have always been large return flows of people who immigrate, even during the nineteenth century immigration flows to the United States, Canada, Australia, New Zealand, and Argentina that we now hold up as "traditional" immigration experiences.

The second part of Chap. 10 also examines involuntary immigration. In the past, the slave trade forced 10 million Africans to migrate to the Western Hemisphere. It is a sober fact that even today not all immigration is entirely voluntary. There is ample evidence that many immigrants are bought and sold worldwide each year as indentured workers, bonded laborers, mail-order brides, or as sex workers. There is evidence that the international trafficking in people may be as important a source of revenue for international organized crime groups as drugs and guns. A detailed description of slavery and other forms of involuntary immigration must be part of any full story of immigration.

Chapter 11 discusses the widespread phenomenon of unauthorized immigration. The incentives for people to migrate from low-income countries to high-income countries have only grown over the past 200 years as incomes across countries diverged. At the same time, high income countries imposed a wide range of restrictions on immigration. Would-be immigrants are, therefore, left with limited options, and many have opted to immigrate without formal permission to live and work in the destination country. Chap. 11 explains that the determinants and consequences of unauthorized immigration are not identical to those of legal and fully documented immigrants.

Finally, Chap. 12 looks at the special, and very interesting, case of Hispanic immigration to the United States. The sheer size of Hispanic immigration to the U.S. makes it an important case to examine. There are some unique problems when so may people from a single foreign culture enter a single destination country. This case, therefore, is of interest to policymakers facing potential surges in immigration from a single source.

Chapter 10
Temporary Immigration, Involuntary Immigration, and Other Variations on the Standard Model

Abstract This chapter relaxes the implicit assumptions made in most immigration models, namely that people immigrate permanently and according to their own free will. Many immigrants end up returning to their native countries, either because they had explicitly decided earlier to be abroad only temporarily, or because changing circumstances led them to reverse an earlier decision to be abroad permanently. The second major issue covered in this chapter is forced, involuntary immigration. Finally, this chapter analyzes refugees, who are people seeking to escape especially threatening conditions in their native countries.

Chapter Overview

The models of immigration that we have detailed in earlier chapters almost all assume, implicitly if not explicitly, that immigration is a decision that, once taken, is irreversible and permanent. Another fundamental assumption underlying our models of immigration is that people make a conscious choice about moving from one country to another. These assumptions are not appropriate in all cases, however. Many immigrants end up returning to their native countries, either because they had explicitly decided earlier to remain abroad only temporarily, or because changing circumstances led them to reverse an earlier decision to remain abroad permanently. Also, many people leave their native countries not by choice, but because special circumstances force them to emigrate. Many immigrants are refugees from persecution and violence, *pushed* out of their countries by unbearable conditions rather than *pulled* abroad by superior conditions elsewhere. Finally, throughout history, people have been transported against their will to other countries.

Temporary immigration is often referred to as *return immigration*, although the two are slightly different. Strictly speaking, temporary immigration refers to those immigrants who never intended to remain in another country permanently, but rather view their move overseas as a temporary move in order to take advantage of foreign opportunities. The return is, therefore, part of the overall decision to immigrate temporarily. Return immigration, on the other hand, refers to the choice to return to one's native country after immigrating to a foreign country. The latter treats the decision to return as separate from the decision to immigrate in the first place. Many countries have explicit policies that permit temporary immigration, even when they tightly restrict permanent immigration. Policymakers in many countries are currently proposing measures that permit larger amounts of temporary immigration. Interestingly, many source country governments have in recent years taken measures to encourage immigrants to return after spending years abroad.

The second major issue covered in this chapter is forced or involuntary immigration. Not all immigrants actively decide to leave their native countries to seek better lives elsewhere. Some people are forced to migrate *against* their own choice. An example of such involuntary immigration is the enslavement and forced transport to the Western Hemisphere of over 10 million Africans during the 400 years of the Atlantic slave trade. While slavery is prohibited everywhere today, it effectively still exists in various forms in many countries. Coerced migration is often referred to today as *human trafficking*. Standard economic analysis cannot explain refugees or coerced migration very well. Clearly, we need alternative models to address these still prevalent forms of immigration.

This chapter presents what we know about temporary immigration and involuntary immigration. It compares these types of immigration to the more traditional one-time movement of people from one country to another as described in the models presented in earlier chapters.

10.1   Return Immigration

The models of immigration that we have detailed in earlier chapters assume that the decision to migrate is irreversible and permanent. This is not always the case, however. Immigrants often prefer to remain in the destination country only temporarily. Also, destination countries may prefer to keep immigrant workers from putting down permanent roots.

Despite the focus of our models on permanent immigration, the fact is that throughout history immigrants have often returned to their native lands after spending some number of years in their destination countries. Figure 10.1 shows that in the U.S. between 1870 and 1950, a period of immigration that is today glamorized as one when Europeans arrived to begin permanent new lives in the U.S., many of those European immigrants in fact later again returned to their native lands. In some years, there were actually large net *outflows* of immigrants from the U.S.

Note that immediately after World War I and during the Great Depression, more people returned to their native countries than arrived in the U.S. The former period

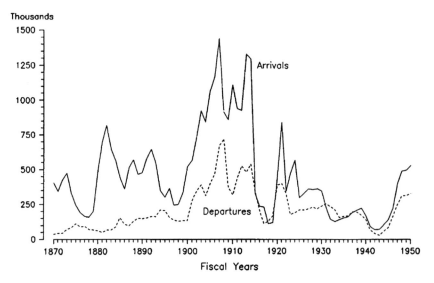

Fig. 10.1 Alien passenger Arrivals and Departures

no doubt reflects a surge of people who had for several years wanted to return to their native countries but had been prevented from doing so by the hostilities of the war. Some of the returning immigrants were refugees who sought to escape the violence of the war but had never intended to stay in the U.S. permanently. The net outflows during the Depression were a direct result of high unemployment in the U.S. Many European economies from which the immigrants came did not suffer nearly as acute a decline in output and employment as the U.S. did during the 1930s. The Great Depression in the U.S. during the 1930s radically changed the pull factors that had attracted immigrants to the U.S. during the "roaring 20s" and earlier periods of rapid economic growth. Also, unemployed immigrants had to return to their native countries in order to draw on family assistance.

10.1.1 Return Immigration as a Response to Changing Circumstances

There are many reasons why immigrants reconsider their decisions to immigrate to another country and return to the countries that they left earlier. The push and pull factors that led people to immigrate often change. For example, if people left their native countries because of war, famine, or political persecution, they might decide to return after there is a change in government or once animosities settle down in their native country. On the other hand, conditions in the destination country may change, as in the example of the Great Depression above. The fact is, unlike the picture presented by our standard immigration model, immigrants do often reconsider their initial decision to immigrate when circumstances change.

10.1.2   Correcting Mistakes in Judgement

Immigrants may return to their native countries not because circumstances change, but because they realize they misjudged conditions in the destination country relative to those of their native country. Sometimes enthusiastic immigrants find that, contrary to their inaccurate expectations, the streets are not paved with gold in the destination country. Immigrants may also encounter difficulties in the destination country that they did not anticipate. Jobs may not pay as much as expected. Life may not be as nice as expected. Homesickness may set in when immigrants re-evaluate their native cultures relative to their adopted destination country cultures; immigrants often underestimate the difficulty in building new social relationships in the destination country. Sometimes they encounter open discrimination, injustice, and harassment in the destination country.

10.1.3   Source Country Policies to Encourage Immigrants to Return

Another factor in making immigration a temporary rather than a permanent phenomenon are the growing efforts of source countries to "pull" ex-patriots back home. Recall from Chap. 8 that one of the proposed solutions to the brain drain is to induce migrants to return after they accumulate wealth and work experience overseas. The World Bank (2003) describes a variety of ways in which source country governments have encouraged skilled people to return after having worked and lived in high-income countries.[1]

South Korea has intentionally upgraded research institutions, such as the Korea Institute of Science and Technology, in order to attract returnees. Taiwan has indirectly encouraged ex-patriots to return and become entrepreneurs in Taiwan by providing incentives for investment in new upstart firms. Taiwan also offers airfare and assistance in finding employment in Taiwan for returning professionals. China has launched a program to develop 100 universities into world-class institutions that provide employment for researchers as well as teachers; the expectation is that many positions at these institutions will be taken by Chinese currently working overseas. Even the governments and groups in developed countries have taken measures to attract native scholars and researchers back. Switzerland promotes networking across borders for overseas Swiss with its Swiss-List.com

---

[1]See especially World Bank (2003, p. 159).

online network, which helps ex-patriots stay connected to events and job opportunities in Switzerland. In 2003, the World Bank (2003) reported that it found 41 such ex-patriot knowledge networks.

10.2   Temporary Immigration

Many immigrants never intended to remain permanently in the destination country. These *temporary immigrants* interpret the push, pull, stay, and stay away factors as suggesting they would be best off taking advantage of higher wages or better opportunities in the destination country only for some specified length of time. They, more than other immigrants, tend to maintain ties to the source country in order to facilitate the planned return to their native societies. In many cases, it is useful to view temporary immigration as the outcome of a rational maximization problem that weighs the economic and social benefits of immigrating against the explicit economic and social costs of leaving one's native society. The decision to immigrate temporarily may be seen as the effective *customization* of the immigration experience in which people choose to maintain their social relationships in the source country while taking advantage of the short-term economic opportunities in the destination country.

10.2.1   The Multinational Corporation and Temporary Immigration

The growth of multinational corporations over the past decade has caused a sharp increase in temporary immigration. As business organizations spread across borders, the need to move personnel throughout the organization necessarily creates the need to move people across borders. Multinational firms continually move management and technical staff between units. For example, the building of a new plant in a foreign country inevitably requires the movement of engineers and project managers. The advancement of employees' careers, especially at the higher levels of management, usually requires them to shift from one unit to another. A foreign assignment has become a normal step in a career within many multinational firms.

Countries usually treat management and technical staff of multinational firms differently from other immigrants. Special visas for personnel of multinational firms are often available without quantitative limits in most countries. For example, the United States reserves about 20% of permanent immigrant visas for immigrants with desirable skills and their family members. These are the so-called "employment-based," or EB-1 through EB-5, visas. The first of these, EB-1, cover foreigners who are managers for multinational firms. The EB-2 visa covers workers with advanced degrees or exceptional ability, and often includes employees of foreign firms with operations in the U.S. The EB-5 "Employment Creation" visa covers

foreigners who will live in the United States for the purpose of establishing a new
business and who will employ U.S. workers. Employees of multinational firms
often fall into this latter category. The U.S. also offers an unlimited number of L1
visas for "intracompany transfers." In 2001 328,500 L1 Visas were issued, about
double the number from 5 years earlier. In 2002, new U.S. legislation reduced the
former requirement that recipients of L1 visas be employed by the multinational
company for a full year to just six months.

The large rise in L1 visas has stimulated some debate, with some critics of the
program suggesting that both U.S. multinational firms and foreign multinational firms
operating in the U.S. are abusing the category in order to bring less expensive workers
from foreign operations to take jobs in the U.S. That may, indeed, be partly the case.
But the extraordinary growth in foreign direct investment in the U.S. over the past ten
years suggests that the increase in the number of L1 visa requests is also a result of the
normal cross-border shuffling of employees and expertise by multinational firms.

10.2.2 Temporary Immigration as a Destination Country Policy

Temporary immigration is also the result of specific immigration policies in destination countries. Many high-income countries make it easier to acquire temporary
residence or work visas than permanent residence visas. Such policies may reflect
destination country governments' desire to satisfy the labor needs of specific
industries. The native population of a destination country may be willing to let
employers hire temporary foreign workers who will leave before they establish long-
term social relationships or acquire long-term public benefits such as health insurance or pensions. Just as individual immigrants may prefer to maintain their cultural
links to their native countries, destination countries may want to minimize the
influence of foreigners on their cultures.

Many countries permit foreigners to live and work for some specified period of
time. For example, in response to wartime shortages of labor, the United States
instituted the so-called *Bracero Program*, which gave temporary work visas to
Mexicans when Americans were drafted into military service during World War II.
The program involved mostly farm labor. When the war ended, most returning
soldiers went to work in the growing industrial and service sectors of the U.S.
economy, and farm labor remained in short supply, at least at the wages the farmers
wanted to pay. Therefore, the Bracero program remained in effect. The program
ended only in the early 1960s, when U.S. labor organizations were finally able to
pressure the U.S. Congress to discontinue the program.

Other examples of temporary immigration programs include the various programs in Western Europe during the 1960s to bring *guest workers* from Southern
Europe, North Africa, and the Eastern Mediterranean to work in countries with
labor shortages such as West Germany, the Netherlands, Switzerland, and France.
These guest workers often ended up bringing family and staying permanently in the
destination countries. Today, Germany, Holland, Belgium, Switzerland, and many

other Western European countries have substantial numbers of foreign-born citizens and large second generation foreign ethnic groups. When only temporary work visas are offered, even foreigners interested in immigrating permanently will use them to enter the destination country. The liberal political regimes in Western Europe and their emphasis on human rights had in place legal channels that enabled temporary immigrants to stretch their stays and, eventually, to convert their temporary resident status to permanent residence status. Once permanently established, the former guest workers were often able to bring spouses and other family members to the destination countries as well.

More recently, the rapidly-growing Persian Gulf states, including Dubai, Qatar, and Kuwait, have permitted large numbers of temporary workers from labor abundant countries like Pakistan, India, Bangladesh, and Indonesia to work in construction, domestic service, and other services. The Persian Gulf states have controlled and monitored their temporary foreign workers more carefully to prevent foreigners from putting down permanent roots.

10.2.3   The Diversity of Temporary Immigration

Data on temporary migration is incomplete and inaccurate, which makes analysis of temporary migration difficult. Every country has different immigration categories, and over time visas are often issued inconsistently by category. Temporary unskilled workers often enter countries unauthorized, or by using tourist or student visas, which makes their detection difficult. Also, temporary workers related to the international trade in services, such as consultants, bankers, entertainers, teachers, athletes, etc., often use tourist and other visas rather than specific work visas when they enter other countries to provide their services in another country on a temporary basis. The best data are for highly skilled temporary workers because most countries issue temporary visas for highly skilled workers working for multinational firms with few restrictions.

The OECD provides estimates of temporary immigration. Table 10.1 presents available data for the period 1992–2000 for a number of OECD countries. It appears that the number of temporary workers increased during the 1990s, except in Switzerland, a country that has long awarded temporary visas for foreign workers in its seasonal tourist industry. Also, Germany's admittance of temporary workers seems to have fluctuated over the decade, more in line with political developments in neighboring eastern European countries rather than German immigration policy or economic trends. Australia, South Korea, the United Kingdom, and the United States admitted steadily increasing numbers of temporary immigrants during the 1990s. Australia established a number of temporary entrance programs for highly skilled workers during the 1990s, and the United States increased the number of temporary H-1B visas for highly skilled workers during that decade.

There are some shortcomings in the OECD data, and temporary immigration is defined differently across countries. Because of the large changes in the flows of

Table 10.1 Entries of temporary workers 1992–2000 (millions of workers)

	1992	1997	2000	2002	2004
Australia	40.5	81.7	115.7	128.5	136.1[a]
Canada	70.4	75.4	93.7	79.5	74.8
France	18.1	12.9	15.4	23.4	25.7
Germany	332.6	267.7	331.6	348.4	358.2
Japan	–	143.5	183.9	203.6	225.6
Korea	8.3	105.0	122.5	137.7	–
Switzerland	127.8	47.4	50.3	–[b]	–[b]
United Kingdom	57.6	89.7	134.1	62.3	106.4
United States	143.0	342.7[c]	505.1	280.3	321.0

[a]2003
[b]Status of seasonal worker abolished in 2002
[c]1998
Source: OECD (2002), Table 1.1, p. 24; OECD (2007), Table I.5, p. 40.

temporary immigrants, the variations across countries make it difficult to reach clear conclusions.

10.3   Analyzing Temporary Migration

The temporary movement of highly skilled workers cannot be analyzed with the traditional model of immigration in which wage differences are the main driving force of immigration. Such models suggest that immigration is a one-way process based on a one-time decision that depends on observed income differences. The traditional model of immigration cannot explain why immigrants would immigrate only temporarily. Only in the case of return immigration driven by changes in relative incomes across countries does the traditional immigration model make sense. Obviously, income differences play an important role, especially in the case of unskilled workers. However, for highly skilled temporary immigrants, more complex career and lifestyle issues are likely to also matter. And, for both skilled and unskilled labor, there are social issues, cultural differences, and political factors as well.

10.3.1   A Simple Model: Culture Clash versus Higher Income

Dustmann (2001) builds a simple model of temporary immigration by explicitly including a second variable to the model to supplement the role of the wage differential in the traditional model. Specifically, Dustmann assumes not only that wages are higher overseas, as the conventional model of immigration does, but he also assumes that the immigrant has a preference for consumption at home. The latter assumption can be interpreted as a preference for one's native culture, an unwillingness to adapt to a foreign culture, or the discomfort from overt antagonism toward immigrants in the destination country.

In Dustmann's model, the migrant is offered the option to immigrate at time $t = 0$, and the remainder of the potential migrant's life is a continuum from $t = 0$ to $t = 1$, the time at which (s)he expects to die. Wages in the source and destination countries are w_s and w_d, respectively. Following standard immigration models, we assume $w_s < w_d$. The flows of consumption goods in the source and destination countries are c_s and c_d. Consumption is determined jointly with the decision on how much time to spend in the source and destination countries, $t_s = 1 - t_d$ and t_d, respectively according to the migrant's lifetime utility function

$$J = t_d v(\zeta_d, c_d) + (1 - t_d) v(\zeta_s, c_s) \qquad (10.1)$$

in which $v(\zeta_d, c_d)$ and $v(\zeta_s, c_s)$ are the utility functions when the immigrant is in the destination and source country, respectively, and ζ_d and ζ_s are preference parameters whose partial derivatives are positive. The assumption $\zeta_d < \zeta_s$ means that immigrants prefer life in the source country to life in the destination country. We could call this the *homesickness assumption*. This assumption is supported by the earlier findings of Hill (1987), Djajic and Milbourne (1988), and Raffelhüschen (1992), who incorporated geographic preferences into their models.

The immigrant is assumed to effectively maximize (10.1) with respect to c_s, c_d, and t_d, subject to the budget constraint

$$t_d w_d + (1 - t_d) w_s - t_d c_d (1 - t_d) p c_s = 0 \qquad (10.2)$$

The parameter p denotes the relative price of consumption goods in the source country versus the destination country. In general, $p < 1$, which implies destination country earnings provide higher real income back in the source country than they do in the destination country. This is not an unrealistic assumption when comparing low income and high-income countries. Dustmann has shown elsewhere (Dustmann, 1995, 1997) that this price differential can have a positive effect on temporary immigration. For simplicity, Dustmann assumes a time discount rate of one which, given the purpose of the model, causes no loss of generality.

Dustmann then differentiates the associated Lagrange equation with respect to the optimal time of return t_d. Then, after combining terms, he arrives at

$$\Gamma = \lambda[(w_d - w_s) - (c_d - pc_s)] - [v(\zeta_s, c_s - v(\zeta)_d, c_d)] = 0 \qquad (10.3)$$

The first term in (10.3) represents the marginal benefit of staying in the destination country, and the second term represents the cost of staying overseas. The two bracketed terms are both positive if we assume normal preferences and that either $p < 1$ and/or $\zeta_d < \zeta_s$. Suppose, also, that the first bracketed term decreases with t_d and the second increases with t_d. Hence, the difference between benefits and costs decreases over time, or $d\,\gamma(t_d)/d\,t_d < 0$. Equations (10.2) and (10.3) determine λ, the marginal utility of wealth, and the optimal time to return t_d. If the difference between benefits and costs is always positive, then immigration will be permanent. If the difference is always negative, there is no migration. The interior solutions are more interesting because they show how the length of the immigrant's overseas stay varies with changes in source country and destination country wages. Changes in wages turn out to have both income and substitution effects, and that the net result depends on the specific form and parameters of the model.

Dustmann's model leads to the conclusion that an increase in the source country wage leads to a shorter migration duration because the wage differential decreases and the income effect provides a greater welfare gain when consumption occurs in the source country. Hence, Dustmann's simple model suggests that immigrants from very poor countries will remain in the destination country longer than immigrants from middle-income countries. On the other hand, a rise in the destination country's wage increases the wage differential, which would increase immigration and the length of stay abroad, all other things equal. However, the model predicts a U-shaped relationship between destination country wages and migration duration because there is also an income effect that favors consumption in the source country and makes a return to the source country more attractive.

The theoretical ambiguity means that the matter has to be examined empirically. To test the model, Dustmann compiled actual data on migration duration in Germany and immigrant survey responses giving the intended migration duration. He found that the actual duration data confirmed a U-shaped relationship between German wages and how long immigrants remained in the destination country. However, an increase in German wages was found to always be associated with a decrease in the intended migration duration, which is in accordance with the opinions expressed on surveys. Therefore, Dustmann's model and empirical results suggest that the standard model of immigration, which links the amount of immigration directly to wage differentials, is misleading as an indicator of the total stock of immigrants because the differential also affects the *duration* of immigration.

10.3.2   Other Determinants of Temporary Immigration

Dustmann's conclusion is suggestive, at best. He does not have data to test the relationship between duration and source country wages; he only tests the differential under the assumption that changes in the differential are the result of destination country wages alone. This distinction could be important, especially since a number of major sources of immigration, notably China and India, are growing much faster than the destination countries favored by Chinese and Indian migrants. A much more daunting problem for Dustmann's model is that it is probably still much too simplistic to accurately capture the decisions on whether to immigrate and how long to remain in the destination country. Also, there are, no doubt, many specific events and sudden changes in circumstances that drive people's decisions to first immigrate and then return. The model does not directly include discrete variables such as the loss of a job, the gain of a better job, changes in immigration policies, shifts in destination country attitudes towards immigrants, and family events such as marriage, divorce, the birth of children, or the death of a spouse. Recall Fig. 10.1 and the sharp rise in return immigration from the U.S. during the Great Depression. This sudden rise was not driven by cultural preferences and long-run trends in relative earnings; the dominant cause of the return migration was the loss of jobs and the poor economic prospects for the immediate future.

Card and Lewis (2007) find that Mexican immigration to the U.S. is driven mostly by population growth, falling real wages, and persistently weak economic conditions in Mexico. Richter, Taylor, and Yunes-Naude 2006 find that network effects dominate other determinants of Mexican immigration to the U.S. Hence, even though a large percentage of Mexican immigrants fit Dustmann's model in that they do not necessarily intend to remain in the U.S. indefinitely, relative incomes and price levels are not the most important determinants.

10.3.3 The Role of International Trade

There are other reasons why immigration may be temporary. Immigration's close relationship with other international economic activities, such as international trade and investment, explains some temporary immigration. For example, international trade in services almost certainly implies some international migration of people. Services are not shipped in a box like goods are. The export of services may require the physical presence of company employees in the export market. For example, Indian software firms have sought to make it easier for Indian computer programmers to acquire work permits overseas.[2] According to an Indian IT industry representative:

> An IT service contract is as much of a perishable commodity as fruit or vegetables. Delaying a visa application on an outsourcing contract is no different from Indian customs holding up a shipment of American fruit for three months to check for pesticide. It kills our advantage stone dead.[3]

As international trade in services expands, immigration and international trade become more closely linked; if services must be personally delivered, then the temporary migration of people and trade are one and the same thing.

The Internet may reduce the need for people to physically move to another country to deliver services, however. We already witness many customer service functions being carried out on-line and by telephone. But, at the same time, the liberalization of services trade has caused an increase in temporary migration of labor. And, since services trade is still the most restricted category of international

---

[2]Madhavan (2000).
[3]Quoted in Madhavan (2000).

trade, further efforts to reduce services trade barriers are likely to cause substantial increases in temporary immigration in the future.

The proximity of this future scenario depends on the course of international trade negotiations. Current negotiations under the GATS (General Agreement on Trade in Services) have stalled during the World Trade Organization's Doha Round in the early 2000s. Overall, immigration related directly to the supply of services overseas is still small because personally delivered services account for only 1.4% of all services traded. Most services are effectively supplied overseas through established commercial channels operated by nationals of the importing country, transferred abroad through the Internet, telephone, or other means of communication. Or, they are consumed overseas, as in the case of tourist services, transport services, and educational services.[4]

The growth of trade in goods also stimulates temporary immigration. Exports and imports require marketing activities, distribution systems, management, legal procedures, contractual arrangements, etc., all of which require people to work in other countries temporarily or for extended, but not permanent, periods of time. Most important, international trade is increasingly linked to foreign direct investment, with multinational firms operating overseas plants to produce the products, components, and other inputs into their worldwide manufacturing operations. These networks of factories, distribution systems, and marketing organizations staffed by technical and management personnel are multinational and often move throughout their firms' multinational corporate organizations. Such cross-border personnel movements constitute a major share of the temporary immigration flows we observe in the world.

10.3.4   Further Issues Related to Temporary Immigration

Future research on temporary immigration will need to address a number of other issues. Among these are the roles of remittances, technology transfers, the economic and social status of temporary guest workers, the brain drain, and the potential for labor market segmentation.

The role of remittances was discussed in detail in Chapter 8. Here we note that temporary immigrants are likely to send a higher proportion of their overseas income back to the source countries. In general, recent immigrants send more remittances than longer-term immigrants. Temporary immigrants are, on average, more recent than immigrants in general. Galor and Stark (1991) in fact found that immigrant remittances are greater for temporary immigrants than for permanent immigrants. They also found that remittances are greatest for temporary workers with a fixed date of return. This finding may reflect a natural selection process rather than a direct determinant of remittances. That is, when immigrant visas have a

---

[4]See World Bank (2003, p. 168).

specific time constraint or immigrants go overseas under a specific employment contract or job assignment within a multinational firm, they obviously view the migration as a temporary career choice undertaken for financial reasons. Permanent immigration is more likely to involve more complex motivations, many of which are not linked to the source country or family in the source country. The relationship between temporary immigration and remittances suggests another potential binary independent variable to add to Dustmann's model in the previous section.

Another issue related to temporary immigration is the role of immigration policies in shaping the length of stay in destination countries. For example, in response to both the critics of immigration and some industries that rely on immigrant workers, President George W. Bush has repeatedly proposed providing temporary work permits for foreigners in a program reminiscent of the *Bracero Program* after World War II, which permitted Mexican agricultural workers to come to the U.S. on a seasonal basis. This led some opponents of immigration to argue that a temporary worker program would merely result in more unauthorized immigrants because foreign workers entering the U.S. legally would be tempted to outstay their temporary working permit. This has indeed been a problem in other countries that have offered temporary work permits. For example, many of the temporary workers from Southern Europe and Turkey that went to work in Northern European countries in the 1960s are still there, as are now their descendants. Supporters of a temporary worker program offer solutions to this problem. They point to Taiwan, where the companies who recruit foreign workers retain part of the workers' earnings, which are then only paid out when the workers return to their native countries after their temporary employment officially ends. Under the old Bracero Program, U.S. employers were required to withhold 10% of Mexican workers' earnings and deposit them in a Mexican fund payable to workers on their return to Mexico.

Schiff (2004) proposes that any new guest worker program in the U.S. should apply three mechanisms for guaranteeing that foreign workers do not outstay their legal employment period: (1) make employers post a bond that is forfeited if the workers remain in the host country, (2) have the government withhold part of the workers' income to be paid out when workers return to their native countries, and (3) have the source country government cooperate in helping to ensure that only workers with work permits emigrate.

10.3.5 Growth Implications of Temporary Immigration

The discussion of the brain drain in Chap. 8 pointed out how the negative growth effects of the brain drain can be mitigated if skilled workers eventually return to their native countries. It was pointed out that returning workers have accumulated wealth and human capital that can be applied in the source country when they return. Since returning skilled workers are, by definition, temporary immigrants, the analysis from Chap. 8 on the relationship between immigration and economic growth applies to our discussion of temporary immigrants here. Temporary immigration's long-run growth consequences for the source country must include the accumulation of work experience overseas.

The discussion in Chap. 8 noted that there is little that can be done in the short run about the brain drain; only measures to increase wages and improve working conditions in poor countries will reverse the brain drain. We also pointed out, however, that the brain drain can raise growth rates in the source country. Many development economists fear that the brain drain will cause output and income to fall in the source country because the departure of human capital permanently reduces innovation and the capacity for a country to adopt new technologies. But, when immigration is temporary the returning immigrants bring with them a familiarity with foreign technologies, and they may increase technology flows back to the source country. Source country growth may, therefore, actually rise above the rate at which the country would have grown if it had not temporarily sent some of its most educated people overseas. The knowledge and experience returning emigrants bring back with them would have been difficult or impossible to develop in the source country.

10.3.6 Temporary Immigration and the Ageing Problem

Immigration changes the population profile of the destination country, and if immigrants are, on average, younger and of working age, then indeed immigration can reduce the burden that rapidly ageing societies face. Temporary immigrants tend to be predominantly young and of working age. A major reason for the young age of immigrants is the fact that in developing countries population growth accelerated some decades ago and the working age population accounts for an increasing share of the population. In China, for example, about one quarter of the population is under the age of 15, and only 7% of the population is over 65. In India, the population between the ages of 15 and 59 will account for three-fourths of the total population, which implies a very high worker-retiree ratio. Over the next two decades these countries have to provide employment for rapidly increasing working age populations, and they are thus in a position to provide labor to high-income countries in the rest of the world where marginal returns to labor are higher. Maximizing the income of their populations is important for these countries, of course, because in the latter half of the century, these countries will also go through the same demographic transition that today's high-income countries are going through.

Most analyses conclude that immigration cannot solve the high-income countries' ageing problem entirely. For example, the United Nations' *2004 World Economic and Social Survey* concludes that "incoming migration would have to expand at virtually impossible rates to offset declining support ratios, that is, workers per retirees."[5] According to one estimate, the European Union countries

---

[5]Quoted in Williams (2004).

as a group will have to accept between 50 and 75 million immigrants from outside the region over the next 50 years if the future burden on working people is to remain manageable.[6] Such levels of immigration equal about 20% of Europe's total population. According to the United Nations report, Japan's very low birth and death rates imply that it would have to receive 600,000 immigrants per year for the next half century just to keep its total working age population from shrinking. Such a high volume of immigrants implies that by 2050, one-third of the Japanese population will consist of immigrants and their children.

Calculating the precise effect of immigration on a country's ability to handle population ageing is not easy. There are a number of offsetting factors to consider. First of all, while immigrants increase the size of the labor force, they have a variety of influences on income in the country, as the previously discussed models of immigration made clear. Secondly, immigrants increase their human capital after they arrive in the country, which will increase their productivity and marginal effect on national income. Thirdly, immigrants, like natives, are eligible for a variety of government transfers, and how those transfer programs evolve over time influences the calculations. Finally, immigrants themselves eventually age and require pension payments and other assistance. After looking at many of these potential changes, Fehr, Jokisch, and Kotlikoff (2004) conclude that "high-skilled immigrants deliver a larger bang for the buck when it comes to paying net taxes," but it is less obvious exactly what is the full effect of immigrants on a country's ability to deal with population ageing. Fehr, Jokisch, and Kotlikoff conclude that even a large expansion of immigration, "whether across all skill groups or among particular skill groups, will do remarkably little to alter the major capital shortage, tax hikes, and reductions in real wages that can be expected along the demographic transition."

Temporary immigration may provide a better outcome for destination countries. By letting foreigners work in the country but requiring them to leave before they become old will reduce the eventual ageing of the immigrant population. Temporary immigration, assuming the temporary status can be enforced, also implies that fewer dependents are likely to accompany temporary immigrants, thus also reducing the growth of the very young dependent population in the destination country. In short, policies that concentrate immigrants tightly in the age groups where people have very high labor force participation rates ensure that immigration will decrease the destination country's dependency ratio.

Many writers have, probably correctly, observed that it is difficult to imagine Europe, Japan, and other developed countries willingly opening their borders to the very large immigrant inflows necessary to prevent an increase in the dependent-worker ratios, even if these workers are advertised as temporary guest workers. On the other hand, Weil (2002) observed that the immigrant arrivals required to keep the support ratios constant as calculated by the United Nations imply annual immigrant inflows for Europe and Japan that are less than 0.5% of their total populations, just half of what annual per capita immigrant inflows to the United States were in the

---

[6]Crawford (2001).

first decade of the twentieth century. After analyzing the incentives to move and the increasing ease with which people can travel from one country to another, the international economist, Cooper writes:

> ... the prospective decline of natural population growth likely to be observed in the coming decades suggests a prediction: Immigration into all rich countries will occur on a much greater scale than is currently envisioned in official population projections, illegally if not legally; on balance such immigration will be more welcome than it seems to be at present. Indeed, it will even be encouraged.[7]

It remains to be seen whether rich country governments will respond to the demographic transition by liberalizing immigration as Cooper predicts.

The *Financial Times* columnist Martin Wolf gives a somewhat more realistic view of how countries with ageing populations are likely to react: "Immigration could solve the West's ageing population problem but the numbers required would be unacceptable. Free migration is economically logical but politically impossible."[8] We should not forget that, while current U.S. immigration rates are lower than at the start of the twentieth century, it is also true that the high rates back then inspired the U.S. to enact a very restrictive immigration regime in the 1920s. And, as recently as 2007, the U.S. Congress attempted to pass legislation calling for balanced immigration policy that would both tighten controls to reduce unauthorized immigration and expand legal immigration. The measure failed because, while there was ample support for reducing unauthorized immigration, there was not enough support for the second part of the bill, the expansion of legal immigration programs. One of the specific measures in the failed bill was a provision for a guest worker program, but both sides of the immigration issue objected to it. Pro-immigrant groups objected because they felt temporary workers would be treated as second-class citizens who could be easily exploited. Opponents of immigration doubted that guest workers would actually return to their native countries when their temporary visas expired.

In short, the demographic transitions in the high-income countries will expand the incentives for people to immigrate. However, history tells us that there will, nevertheless, be opposition to immigration, and that an increase in temporary immigration is not a foregone outcome.

10.4 Asylum Seekers and Refugees

A group of international migrants that do not fit the standard model of immigration very well are *asylum seekers and refugees*. These are people who have left their home countries to escape actual or feared political, religious or social persecution, or other threats to their safety and well-being. They are not so much responding to

---

[7]From the conclusion of Cooper (2002).
[8]Wolf (2001).

the economic pull of higher incomes overseas as they are being pushed or driven out of their native countries by war or intolerable political and social conditions. Most countries have special legal procedures to deal with people seeking entry to escape persecution and other threats. There is also a United Nations organization, the office of the United Nations High Commissioner for Refugees, that provides assistance and temporary shelter for refugees from war, persecution, and other threats.

10.4.1 Refugees

The 1951 United Nations Convention Relating to the Status of Refugees defines a *refugee* as a person who "owing to a well-founded fear of being persecuted for reasons of race, religion, nationality, membership of a particular social group, or political opinion, is outside the country of their nationality, and is unable to or, owing to such fear, is unwilling to avail him/herself of the protection of that country." (UNCHR, 2000) The concept of a refugee was expanded by a 1967 United Nations Protocol and later Conventions to include persons who flee war and other violence in their home countries. In this book on immigration we describe only the *refugees* who leave their native country and flee to another country. The majority of refugees actually remain in their own countries in camps, relatives' homes, and other temporary shelters after they are driven from their permanent homes by war, violence, persecution, and other threats.

Today, most refugees are people fleeing civil wars and ethnic strife. Many of these refugees are in Africa and the Middle East. Wars and ethnic cleansing in the Balkans created a huge refugee problem in Europe in the 1990s. Table 10.2 presents UNCHR data showing that the estimated number of refugees in the world dropped from 10.6 million at the end of 2002 to about 8.6 million at the end of 2005, only to rise again to 9.8 million by the end of 2006. One reason the number of refugees declined from 2002 through 2005 is that several of the civil wars in Africa that had caused many people to flee their homes were brought to tentative settlements. Also, the situation in the former Yugoslavia seems to have stabilized and many people were able to return home. Some refugees also managed to permanently move

Table 10.2 Number and origin of international refugees

	End 2002	End 2005	End 2006
Africa (Except North Africa)	3,088,500	2,571,500	2,421,300
Central/South Asia, N. Africa, Middle East	3,363,500	2,716,500	3,811,800
Europe	2,593,700	1,975,300	1,733,700
Western Hemisphere	656,000	564,300	1,035,900
East Asia/Oceania	902,900	825,600	875,100
Total	0,604,600	8,653,200	9,877,800

Source: UNHCR (2007), United Nations High Commissioner for Refugees, Division of Operational Services, Field Information and Coordination Support Section, July 16; United Nations High Commissioner for Refugees (2004).

elsewhere, which reduced the number of people with refugee status. On the other hand, the conflict in Afghanistan and the U.S. invasion of Iraq has inflamed civil war and ethnic strife, causing a sharp rise in refugees to neighboring countries in 2006. Pakistan, Iran, Syria, and Jordan are now four of the top six recipients of foreign refugees. Preliminary evidence suggests the flow of refugees from Afghanistan and Iraq continued after 2007, further swelling the refugee populations in these four countries.

10.4.2   The UNHCR

The United Nations High Commissioner for Refugees (UNHCR) was formally established in 1951 to oversee the world's refugee problems. When the UNHCR was first established, the focus of the agency's activities was on resettling refugees in Europe, Palestine, and Korea. Today, its activities include operating refugee camps in many parts of the world. Wars and ethnic conflicts in Africa, Asia, and Europe have swelled the number of refugees over the past two decades.

At the end of 2006, the UNCHR oversaw nearly 10 million refugees who were living in temporary quarters, often camps set up specifically for the refugees, outside their native countries, usually in countries bordering those the refugees fled from. The UNHCR also monitored another 5 million refugees living in restricted areas within their own countries or in the process of returning home under international supervision, usually the UNHCR. In 2003, for example, the UNHCR assisted the resettlement of 26,000 refugees from, among other countries, Sudan, Afghanistan, Somalia, Ethiopia, Iran, and Iraq. Just over half (54%) of these were accepted by the United States, 17% by Canada, 15 by Australia, and 5 and 4%, respectively, by Sweden and Norway. The reluctance of countries to accept refugees for permanent settlement implies that millions of people remain in temporary camps waiting for a permanent resolution of their status. The UNHCR's greatest success has been in returning refugees to their original homes. The number of refugees actually declined between 2002 and 2005, only to rise again in 2006. The return of refugees to their homes depends on the elimination of the wars, persecution, or political strife that caused the refugees to flee their homes in the first place. Therefore, future numbers of refugees are as hard to predict as the events that trigger people's flight for safety across borders.

10.4.3   Asylum Seekers

Asylum seekers are refugees waiting to be granted permission to reside permanently in a country other than their country of citizenship. Most countries have laws that permit the government to grant asylum to people who can show they are in danger or under severe persecution in their home country. The UNHCR estimated that there were nearly 750,000 people actively seeking asylum in foreign countries at the end of 2007.

10.5   Involuntary Immigration

The above section on refugees showed that not all people move from one country to another country by their own choice. The previous section showed that refugees are more or less forced to migrate, driven from their home countries by especially dismal or dangerous conditions. However, refugees can still be modeled as improving their personal situation when they cross the border, and the standard model of immigration still applies in that people move to improve their well being. However, there is another type of *involuntary immigration* that does not fit the standard immigration model: the enslaved migrant. There are many examples of slavery that do not result in people crossing borders and, therefore, do not result in forced immigration. But there has always been a strong international component to slavery because societies are more likely to enslave foreigners than people from within their own society. Slavery is an ancient institution, but the systematic enslavement of foreigners who were subsequently transported to other societies and nations reached unprecedented proportions just 200 years ago. The consequences of this slavery still affect many destination countries. Unfortunately, the practice of enslavement has not yet been eliminated entirely.

Slavery has been an element of human societies for as long as we have records of human activity. For example, in 2000 B.C., the Hammurabi code explicitly recognized slaves as the lowest category of people. At the time of ancient Greece, Aristotle described slaves as being distinct from other people in various other states of servitude. At the height of the Roman Empire, about half the population was enslaved or in a state of long-term servitude.

Beginning about 500 years ago, slavery became an integral part of an increasingly global economy. Between 1500 and the late nineteenth century, over 10 million enslaved Africans were brought against their will to the Western Hemisphere by Dutch, English, French, Portuguese, Spanish and other European slave traders. Table 10.3 provides more detailed data on the Atlantic slave trade between 1500

Table 10.3 Estimates of the African slave arrivals in the Western Hemisphere

Period	Spanish America	Brazil	Caribbean	USA	Total	Annual Arrivals
1525–1600	75,000	50,000	0	0	125,000	1,667
1600–1700	292,500	560,000	463,500	0	1,316,000	13,160
1700–1800	512,700	1,700,000	3,131,000	391,200	5,734,000	57,340
1800–1850	628,600	1,713,700	213,300	168,300	2,723,900	54,478
1851–1870	153,600	6,400	18,400	300	178,700	200

Source: Taken from Table A.2 in Herbert S. Klein (1999, pp. 210–211), which presented data from Philip Curtin (1969) and David Eltis (1989).

and the end of the nineteenth century. The death rate for slaves during the two-month voyage in horrible conditions was nearly 10%, so actually well over 11 million Africans were actually enslaved and forced aboard ships bound for the Western Hemisphere. The largest destination for African slaves was Brazil, a Portuguese colony organized around large plantations for sugar, tobacco, cotton, cacao, and during the eighteenth century, mining.

10.5.1 A Model of International Slavery

Suppose that there are two countries with similar labor markets, as in the traditional labor market model of immigration. As shown in the familiar labor market model of immigration in Fig. 10.2, the consequences of moving people from a country named Source to a country named Destination results in the usual shift of the labor supply curve. Ironically, this basic model of immigration may be most relevant to the analysis of slavery because the international trafficking in slaves has as its fundamental purpose the movement of labor resources from one country to another. The fundamental cruelty of slavery is that the welfare of the enslaved migrant is not accounted for. Assuming that enslaved labor competes with native-born workers, the forced migration causes the wage to rise in Source and fall in Destination. The owners of other factors lose income in Source equal to the areas e + g, while the owners of other factors gain income equal to the areas E + G in Destination. Slaves do not own their own labor and they do not immigrate in order to gain higher wages. Therefore, the motivation for the international slave trade is not the same as for voluntary immigration.

The returns to the labor of slaves accrue to the slave owners. Slave owners incur costs related to acquiring ownership of the slaves; they must transport them from the source to the destination country, and they must feed, clothe, and shelter them

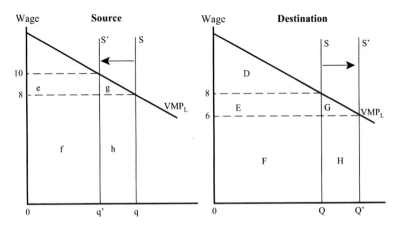

Fig. 10.2 The Labor Markets And Forced Immigration

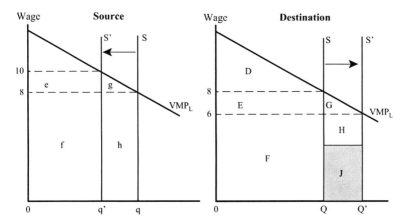

Fig. 10.3 The Economic Consequnces of Forced Immigration

lest their investment perish. Therefore, if it is possible to ignore the social consequences of slavery, international trafficking can be economically viable as long as the gains exceed the costs.

Figure 10.3 illustrates one possible case of forced migration. Suppose that the shaded area J represents the portion of slave labor's earnings that must be devoted to feeding, clothing, sheltering, and otherwise caring for the slaves so that they remain able and willing to work. In this case, forced immigration will occur if the discounted value of future surplus earnings of the slave owners, equal to the area H, is greater than the cost of acquiring and transporting the slaves to the destination country. If the sale of the slaves provides earnings for residents in Source, then the overall loss from the enslavement and export of natives from Source will be reduced. The net loss to natives remaining in Source is g; therefore, if the slaves are sold for more than the discounted value of future area g, then Source gains from the inhuman transaction. In the case of the Atlantic slave trade, the traffickers from third countries like Holland, Portugal, and England captured some of the gains over and beyond the transport costs they provided.

The model suggests that international slavery is more likely to occur if, all other things equal, (1) people can be inexpensively enslaved, (2) international transport of slaves is not very costly, (3) slaves employed in their destination country generate a large surplus over and above their maintenance costs, (4) alternative forms of labor are more expensive than slave labor, and, of course, there is no enforcement of anti-slavery laws. The model suggests that the Atlantic slave trade flourished because slaves could be inexpensively acquired in Africa, traffickers cramped large numbers of slaves into their small ships in rather uncomfortable conditions, and the employment of slaves on plantations and in mines reaped their owners large surpluses. It cost much more to entice workers from Europe to immigrate and work in the jobs slaves were forced to perform. This is not to say that employers in the Western Hemisphere did not seek other workers. Indentured workers from India and China were brought to many British colonies in the Caribbean, for example, although this occurred mostly after Britain prohibited slavery. In short, the slave trade was motivated by profit, and it endured because it continued to be profitable. The surplus accruing to the slave owner, H, was more than large enough to pay for the slaves, their transportation, and their maintenance.

Political economy factors also influence the likelihood of slavery and forced immigration. For example, the owners of other factors of production in the source country may lobby their government to prohibit or prevent the enslavement of members of their population because the forced departure of labor from Source reduces their welfare. On the other hand, workers in Source may welcome the capture and forced departure of workers who compete with them in the local labor market, especially if the enslaved workers are in other ways deemed socially undesirable. Such an outcome becomes politically more likely if there are ethnic or racial divisions within the source country, hence it becomes easy to imagine why authorities in source countries effectively cooperated in the slave trade. For example, in Africa it was often rival tribes that delivered slaves to the European slave traders.

10.5.2   Other Oppressive Forms of Immigration

Slavery is no longer officially sanctioned anywhere in the world. But, this certainly does not mean all migration is now entirely voluntary and free. There is disturbing evidence that some of the immigration occurring in the world today is at least partially involuntary. For example, there are estimates that as many as 1 million women and children are bought and sold worldwide each year as bonded laborers, mail-order brides, or as sex workers.[9] The international trafficking in people may be as important a source of revenue for international organized crime groups as drugs and guns.

One source of revenue for international traffickers of people is supplying bonded labor to sweatshops located within developed countries. Where import barriers prevent foreign products from entering an economy, as in the case of clothing in most developed economies, traffickers have huge incentives to move low-wage labor inside the protected markets. A recent report claims that there are at least 100,000 illegal immigrants working in "contract slavery," or bonded labor, in Europe, often in small clothing industries.[10] Organized traffickers recruit workers from the poorest parts of China, India, Bangladesh, and other developing countries, offer to transport them to jobs in Europe in exchange for future payments that effectively force them to work for nearly nothing during their first few years abroad. For example, one Indian trafficker living in Britain, Jogindir Singh Kaile, smuggled thousands of fellow countrymen from India to Britain. He charged $10,000 per person for the journey, and then forced the workers to repay him by working in

---

[9]Williamson (2000).

[10]*Business Week* (2000).

sweatshops that made clothing under contract to subcontractors who in turn contracted with the large clothing firms that supplied leading retailers. Until he was arrested in 2000, Kaile reportedly earned a profit of several thousand dollars per immigrant, more than enough to make him a millionaire.[11]

The system of *sponsorship* used to grant immigrant visas in the oil-rich Persian Gulf states may lead to de facto enslavement of immigrants. In some Persian Gulf states, immigrants must be sponsored by a national citizen, who then gains exclusive rights to the labor of those immigrants as long as they remain in the country. Large employers such as construction companies routinely sponsor large numbers of workers supplied by recruitment firms operating in low-wage countries such as Pakistan, India, and Bangladesh. The International Labour Organisation (ILO) contends that local labor laws are often ignored when it comes to these foreign workers. According to a *Financial Times* article: "Low pay, late pay, and 18 h days are often the norm. A labourer will earn an average of $110 a month, be expected to repay the labour supply company for his visa ($1,400) and send money back to his family. Protest means instant deportation."[12] Some of the worst abuses are by individuals who sponsor foreign workers to become housemaids and nannies. "They are often unpaid, work 18 h a day, and have no days off. They are unable to complain because they are prisoners to the villas and apartments they keep clean."[13]

The Gulf states defend the practice of sponsorship. According to one academic in the United Arab Emirates: "They want to be here. They earn good money, $15 billion [in total] a year. In their own countries they would be out of work and living in sewers."[14] It may be true that immigrants voluntarily enter into these onerous arrangements. Dire economic circumstances can lead workers to indenture themselves and induce parents to entrust their children to traffickers. There is not much difference between choosing to indenture oneself under conditions of destitution and being forced into slavery. Until sound economic policies end needless starvation and destitution, we will, no doubt, continue to be shocked by trafficking in willing humans desperate to improve their dismal circumstances.

10.6 Summary and Conclusions

In earlier chapters we have modeled immigration as a one-directional, one-time decision motivated by the welfare gains captured by the immigrants themselves. In this chapter, we looked at some variations on that theme. First, many immigrants actually move to another country for some limited amount of time and then return

---

[11]*Business Week* (2000).
[12]Allen (2000).
[13]Allen (2000).
[14]As quoted in Allen (2000).

to their native countries. In general, a complete study of immigration needs to recognize that there is also *return migration*, and often such return migration is part of a more complex decision to *temporarily* immigrate overseas. Second, some immigrants are refugees escaping especially onerous economic, social, or political conditions, and their decision to immigrate has little to do with the usual assumed comparisons of destination country incomes versus source country incomes. And thirdly, some immigrants are forced to move to another country against their will. Slavery has been outlawed everywhere today, but some forms of immigration today still border on forced migration. People with few options for dealing with their dismal social and economic conditions are sometimes willing to subject themselves to various forms of servitude that should trigger international action and concern.

Despite some of the differences between the one-way immigration we have described in earlier chapters and the return, temporary, and forced immigration described in this chapter, we were still able to make use of the basic labor market model of immigration. Nevertheless, there is clearly a need for economists to develop more detailed models of immigration to more accurately analyze the various different categories of immigrants. As the global economy increasingly integrates labor markets across countries we will, no doubt, see workers making more frequent and more varied locational decisions. People will more often immigrate several times, they will frequently return to their home labor markets, and they will be motivated by many more factors than pure wage and income differentials.

The Dustmann (2001) model, which makes the decision to immigrate, the length of stay overseas, and the date for returning all part of a single migration decision is promising. It would also be useful to incorporate people's changing economic and social circumstances more throughly into immigration models in order to reflect how immigration responds to family needs, opportunities to study abroad, career choices, and, finally, retirement choices. Some locations are better for raising children, others are home to specialized universities and institutes, multinational firms employ people in multiple locations, and retirement may be more pleasant in a warm climate. We are already seeing a steady increase in the number of people who live in several countries as children, students, workers, and retirees. These choices all imply different motivations and the weighing of different factors. A richer model incorporating changing economic and social circumstances could, in theory, generate several migrations over a person's lifetime. Then, if we can also add the effects of discrete changes in personal circumstances, such as meeting a spouse, discovering special business opportunities, and other economic, social, and political factors, perhaps we will then be able to come closer to accurately modeling the complex immigration patterns we observe in the world.

References

Allen, R. (2000, 10/11 June). A time bomb in the desert. *Financial Times*.
Business Week, (2000, 27 November). Workers in Bondage.

Card, D., & Lewis, E. (2007). The diffusion of Mexican immigrants during the 1990s: Explanations and Impacts;. In G. Borjas (Ed.), *Mexican immigration*. Chicago :University of Chicago Press.

Crawford, L. (2001, 27 June). Migrant workers obeying the cold laws of Economics. *Financial Times*, Special section on "Europe Reinvented".

Cooper, R. (2002). The economic impact of demographic change: A case for more immigration. In J. Sneddon Little, & R. Triest (Eds.), *Seismic shifts: The economic impact of demographic change*. Boston :Federal Reserve Bank of Boston.

Curtin, P. (1969). *The Atlantic slave trade: A census*. Madison, WI :University of Wisconsin Press.

Djajic, S., &Milbourne, R. (1988). A general equilibrium model of guest-worker migration: A source-country perspective. *Journal of International Economics, 25*, 335–351.

Dustmann, C. (1995). Savings behavior of migrant workers: A life-cycle analysis. *Zeitschrift für Wirtschafts- und Sozialwissenshften, 115*, 511–533.

Dustmann, C. (1997). Return migration, uncertainty and precautionary savings. *Journal of Development Economics, 52*, 295–316.

Dustmann, C. (2001). Return migration, wage differentials, and the optimum migration duration. IZA Discussion Paper No. 264, February.

Eltis, D. (1989). *Economic growth and the ending of the transatlantic slave trade*. New York : Oxford University Press.

Fehr, H., Jokisch, S., & Kotlikoff, L. (2004). The role of immigration in dealing with the developed world's demographic transition. NBER Working Paper w10512, May.

Galor, O., & Stark, O. (1991). The probability of return migration, migrants' work effect, and migrants' performance. *Journal of Development Economics, 35*, 399–405.

Hill, J. K. (1987). Immigrant decisions concerning duration of stay and migration frequency. *Journal of Development Economics, 25*, 221–234.

Klein, H. (1999). *The Atlantic slave trade*. Cambridge :Cambridge University Press.

Madhavan, N. (2000, 21 August). India seeks more U.S. Visas, less control for tech. *Reuters News Service*.

OECD, (2002). *Trends in international migration 2002*, Paris: OECD.

OECD, (2007). *International migration outlook, SOPEMI 2006*, Paris: OECD.

Raffelhüschen, B. (1992). Labor migration in Europe: Experiences from Germany after unification. *European Economic Review, 36*, 1453–1473.

Richter, S., Taylor, J. E., & Yunez-Naude, A. (2006). Impacts of policy reforms on labor migration from rural Mexico to the United States. In G. Borjas, ed., *Mexican Immigration*. Cambridge: National Bureau of Economic Research and Chicago: University of Chicago Press.

United Nations High Commissioner for Refugees (2004). *2003 Global refugee trends*, Geneva: UNHCR, June 15.

United Nations High Commissioner for Refugees (2007). *2006 Global trends*. Geneva: UNHCR, July 16.

Weil, D. (2002). Demographic shocks: The view from history. In J. Sneddon Little, & R. Triest (Eds.), *Seismic shifts: The economic impact of demographic change*. Boston :Federal Reserve Bank of Boston.

Williams, F. (2004, 30 November). Migrants cannot fix pension crisis. *Financial Times*.

Williamson, H. (2000, 2 April). Asia nations act to halt trafficking in humans. *Financial Times*.

Wolf, M. (2001, 28 November). Fighting for economic equality. *Financial Times*.

World Bank (2003). *Global economic Prospects 2004*, Washington DC: World Bank.

Chapter 11
Unauthorized Immigration

Abstract One of the results of the clash between immigration policies and economic incentives is *unauthorized immigration*. There is no accurate data on unauthorized immigration, but estimates permit some empirical work. The motives for
immigrants to enter the destination country without formal authorization are the
same as those that lead immigrants to seek legal entry, and the static labor market
model of immigration can be used to explain the flows of unauthorized immigrants.
There are additional factors to consider, however. Unauthorized immigrants do not
normally enjoy the same civil rights as legal immigrants, so the potential rewards
from immigrating are unlikely to be the same for legal and unauthorized immigrants. There are other interesting questions, such as why so many destination
countries implicitly accept substantial numbers of unauthorized immigrants, even
though their formal laws and regulations call for their strict punishment and
expulsion. Unfortunately, we have few answers.

> If the migrants run into some new...wall, they will simply go around it. Or over it. Or under
> it. Mexicans will show as much ingenuity in getting into the United States as Americans
> would in breaking into British Columbia if the Canadian minimum wage were $70 an hour.[1]

Introduction

The strong incentives for people to immigrate from low- to high-income countries
clash with the restrictive immigration policies of high-income destination countries.
One common result of this clash between policies and economic incentives is
unauthorized immigration. We obviously do not have very accurate data on unauthorized immigration; unauthorized immigrants seldom reveal their status for fear
of being detected and deported back to their native countries. Estimates do exist,

---

[1]Cooper (2006, p. 132).

Ö.B. Bodvarsson and H. Van den Berg, *The Economics of Immigration*,
DOI: 10.1007/978-3-540-77796-0_11, © Springer-Verlag Berlin Heidelberg 2009

though. For example, the ILO estimated that in 1991 there were 2.6 million immigrants living illegally in Western Europe. That number was estimated to have doubled by the end of the decade.[2] The United States Immigration and Naturalization Service estimated that there were about 5 million unauthorized workers in the United States in 1996, and that the number had risen to 6 million by 2000.[3] However, census data for 2000 suggest the number was closer to 9 million.[4] The Pew Foundation estimated that in 2005 there were between 10.5 and 11.7 million unauthorized immigrants in the U.S. Unauthorized immigrants may account for as much as one-third of all immigrants in the U.S., as official estimates by the Census Bureau showed slightly more than 36 million foreign-born residents in the U.S. in 2005.

Unauthorized immigration occurs not only in developed economies. There are several million unauthorized immigrants in South Africa, which itself is not a wealthy country and is the source of unauthorized immigrants to high income countries. But South Africa offers much higher wages than most of its neighbors. Even though wages are even higher in developed countries in Europe, another destination for African immigrants, it is usually much easier to get to South Africa. "There are no oceans to cross. From anywhere below the Sahara, anyone with a few rand for the truck-driver can hitch a ride south. South Africa's land border is roughly 4,000 km long and extremely porous."[5] Foreign workers in South Africa are important to neighboring countries; miners' remittances account for about 10% of Lesotho's GDP.

The motives for immigrants to enter the destination country illegally are the same as those that lead immigrants to seek legal entry, and the static labor market model of immigration can be used to explain the flows of unauthorized immigrants. Nevertheless, unauthorized immigrants do not normally enjoy the same civil rights as legal immigrants, so the potential rewards from immigrating are unlikely to be the same for legal and unauthorized immigrants. Also, employers may face possible punishment for hiring unauthorized immigrants, which may lead employers to discount the perceived marginal productivity of unauthorized immigrant workers by the likelihood of their being punished or having production disrupted by sudden arrests of workers. There are other interesting questions, such as why so many destination countries implicitly accept substantial numbers of unauthorized immigrants, even though their formal laws and regulations call for their strict punishment and expulsion. Unfortunately, we have few answers. The quote at the start of the chapter indicates the reason for lack of understanding in the literature of the motivations for and the costs and benefits of unauthorized immigration: There has simply been very little analysis. Unauthorized immigrants are not easily identified and counted, thus there is a huge void in the data.

---

[2]*The Economist* (1998).

[3]Data from the Immigration and Naturalization Service, Office of Policy and Planning, INS website, www.ins.gov, January 21, 2001.

[4]Parks and Tricks (2000), Ehrlich (2001) and Magnisson (2001).

[5]*The Economist* (2000).

11.1 Estimating Unauthorized Immigration

Unauthorized immigrants are not easily counted, in large part because they try to avoid detection and deportation. In a country like the United States or France, where the number of unauthorized immigrants is large, population censuses seriously undercount the true populations because they miss many unauthorized immigrants. Thus, Census data are generally not very useful for studying patterns in unauthorized immigration.

11.1.1 The Residual Method

Hanson (2006) describes the most common method for estimating unauthorized immigration. He begins with the following formula:

$$U_t = F_t - L_t = F_t - \sum_{j=0}^{\infty} L_j(1 - d_j - im_j) \qquad (11.1)$$

The variable U_t represents the stock of unauthorized immigrants in year t, F_t is total foreign-born population in the country in year t, L_j is the official count of legal documented immigration in each year from $j = 0$ up to the year t, d_j is the mortality rate for the group of immigrants entering each year j, and im_j is the emigration rate for each immigrant group documented as entering in each year j.

A complicating factor is the continual adjustment of an immigrant's status from unauthorized to legal, and vice versa, in many countries with complex immigration regulations. Immigrants with temporary work permits may overstay their allotted time, and unauthorized immigrants may change their status by marrying a legal resident, paying a fine, or gaining a legal visa through separate legal channels. The 1986 Immigration Reform and Control Act (IRCA) in the United States provided for an amnesty that eventually gave several million unauthorized immigrants legal resident status. Now, in the first decade of the 2000s, there is pressure for another general amnesty for at least some of the estimated 10–12 million unauthorized immigrants residing in the U.S. Ideally, we need to incorporate these flows of persons changing from legal to unauthorized, or unauthorized to legal, status to the above equation. Equation (11.1) can be amended as follows:

$$U_t = F_t - \sum_{j=0}^{t} L_j(1 - d_j - im_j - v_j + u_j) = F_t - L_t \qquad (11.2)$$

where all variables are the same as in (11.1) with the addition of v_j to represent unauthorized immigrants who gain legal residence visas in year j and u_j to represent formerly legal immigrants who lose their legal status in year j.

Estimates of unauthorized immigration are inherently inaccurate because it is simply impossible to come up with accurate estimates for all, if any, of the right hand side variables in (11.2). The estimate of the total unauthorized immigrant population U_t is the residual value after inserting values for all the other variables in the equation. First of all, researchers have to make assumptions about the inaccurate data available to them. For example, the estimate U_t in (11.2) depends critically on the accuracy of the values for F_t and L_j that are inserted into the equation. Most researchers assume that both F_t and L_j are undercounted in national censuses and other population surveys, with F_t undercounted more than L_j. In the United States, for example, there is substantial evidence suggesting minority groups are under-counted, and the Census Bureau has evidence that over 2% of Hispanics, to which the largest U.S. immigrant group belongs, are not counted in the official Census. Assumptions about the extent of undercounting must, therefore, be made. Specifi-cally, the estimate of the total foreign-born population is

$$F_t = F_t(1 - \lambda_t) + \varepsilon_t \qquad (11.3)$$

where λ_t is the fraction of the true total foreign population, F_t, that is not counted, and ε_t represents an unbiased random error. Hence, the best estimate of the true total foreign population would be

$$F_t = F_t/(1 - \lambda_t) \qquad (11.4)$$

provided the fraction of undercounting λ_t is correct. Similarly, the legal immigrant population is counted as

$$L_t = L_t(1 - \zeta_t) + \varepsilon_t \qquad (11.5)$$

where ζ_t is the fraction of the true total legal immigrant population, L_t, that is missed by the survey or count.

If the difference between the total and legal immigrant populations is relatively small, which will be the case in countries where unauthorized immigrants make up a small percentage of all immigrants, then different assumptions about the sizes of λ_t and ζ_t result in very large differences in estimates of the total unauthorized immigrant population. Table 11.3 below presents estimates using the residual method under alternative undercount assumptions.

The most popular estimates of the U.S. unauthorized immigrant population, at least in terms of the frequency with which they are quoted in the press and by political leaders, are those published by the Pew Hispanic Center (Passel 2006). To get their estimate of the number of foreign-born American residents, Pew research-ers start with the Census Bureau's annual Current Population Survey, which is based on 80,000 interviews in which households are asked where each member of their household was born.[6] After adjusting the Hispanic numbers by 10% for

---

[6]The Pew method is detailed in most Pew Hispanic Center reports; this and other methodologies are also discussed in Bialk (2006).

suspected Census Bureau underestimates, these results are then extrapolated to the estimated whole U.S. population. In 2005, this procedure yielded an estimate of 36 million foreign-born people in the U.S. Next, the Pew researchers sum the annual numbers of permanent residence visas issued, numbers that sum back for decades. Next, they assume that immigrants die at the average rates for each age group of the entire population, and they use estimates for return migration from several studies. Pew researchers admit the return migration numbers are the least reliable component in the estimation procedure. Finally, the estimated number of legal immigrants is subtracted from the estimated total foreign-born population to arrive at the residual estimate of unauthorized immigrants.

11.1.2   Other Methods for Estimating Unauthorized Immigration

Researchers have devised some other ways to estimate unauthorized immigration. These estimates of unauthorized immigration can be augmented with other data from assorted case studies, local government records of services provided to immigrants, and data from countries that supply most of the unauthorized immigrants. For example, the reduction in population in Mexican communities not compensated by increases in population in other Mexican communities most likely implies that the missing persons immigrated to the U.S. and are part of the unauthorized workforce there.

Another, potentially more accurate, estimation method was used by Snel, de Boom, Engbersen, and Weltevrede (2005), who estimated the unauthorized immigrant population in the Netherlands using the two-step capture/recapture method from the field of animal ecology. This method has been used to estimate animal stocks. Specifically, an estimate of the number of fish in a pond can be found by, first, capturing a certain number of fish, tagging them, and releasing them back into the pond. Second, after enough time has passed for the fish to randomly disperse throughout the pond, another group of fish are captured in the pond. Some of the fish in the second capture will be recaptures, as evidenced by their tags. By noting the proportion ρ of recaptures among the 100 fish captured in the second round, the total number of fish in the pond can then be approximated as the number of fish captured in the first round divided by ρ. For example, if 100 fish are captured and tagged in the first round, another 100 fish are captured in a second round, and five of the fish captured in the second round are tagged from the first catch, then the total fish population in the pond is estimated to be 100/0.05 = 2,000. Snel et al. (2005) estimate the number of unauthorized immigrants in the Netherlands by examining police records of random identity checks in two successive periods of time.

A study by the Swiss research group GFS (2005) used a very different method, called the Delphi method, to arrive at a consensus estimate of unauthorized immigrants residing in Switzerland. This method consists of a series of meetings, discussions, and revisions of estimates by independent researchers and panels of experts. The independent researchers must justify their estimates to the experts, who render judgments. Then, the researchers revise their estimates, followed by new judgments by the experts, new revisions by the researchers, etc., until there is a convergence of opinion. The accuracy of the Delphi approach depends critically on the quality of the initial estimates, the knowledge of the experts, and the personalities of the researchers and experts.

The U.S. government has generated measures of unauthorized immigrants from data on the number of detainees apprehended by the U.S. Border Patrol. These studies assume that a specific percentage of unauthorized border crossings are stopped by the Border Patrol, and thus as the actual number of detainees varies, total unauthorized crossings are assumed to vary proportionately. Of course, these numbers are then used to construct a total stock of unauthorized immigrants in the country after making further adjustments for return migration and age-specific death rates. Needless to say, these numbers are probably highly inaccurate.

Researchers in Spain, Italy, Portugal, and Greece have used the records of recent legalizations of unauthorized immigrants in those countries. When unauthorized immigrants step forward and reveal themselves during the legalization process, researchers can estimate what the unauthorized immigrant population was prior to disclosure of legal status. Of course, the method has to make assumptions about the proportion of unauthorized immigrants that volunteer to legalize their status. This proportion varies depending on the criteria that must be satisfied for legalization and the trust that immigrants have in the legalization process. For example, if there is widespread fear that the process is a pretext for their capture and deportation, few unauthorized immigrants are likely to participate.

It should be clear from this discussion that reported data on unauthorized immigration are unreliable. However, researchers have to proceed with the data they have available to them and make the best of it. It does mean that we have to treat the results of empirical studies of unauthorized immigration with some skepticism. In a practical sense, it means that unless a statistical result "stands out like a sore thumb," we should probably refrain from making strong claims about having discovered some truth about unauthorized immigration.

11.2 How Many Unauthorized Immigrants are There?

Despite the difficulties of estimating unauthorized immigration, estimates are available. Given the difficulty of counting unauthorized immigrants and the inherent inaccuracy of indirect methods, estimates of unauthorized immigrants vary widely. Across the various estimates of unauthorized immigration, it is clear that the number of unauthorized immigrants has grown rapidly over the past several decades, and for most destination countries, unauthorized immigrants constitute a substantial portion of the overall population.

Table 11.1 presents estimates of the unauthorized immigrant populations in a number of developed economies. These estimates were derived using one or more of the methods described above, all of which have shortcomings. These are all

Table 11.1 Estimates of the unauthorized immigrant population: selected OECD countries, 2005[a]

Country	Number	% of Population	Year
Australia	50,000	0.2	2005
Japan	210,000	0.2	2005
United States	10,300,000	3.6	2004
Netherlands	125,000–230,000	0.8–1.4	2004
Switzerland	80,000–100,000	1.1–1.5	2005
Spain	690,000	1.6	2005
Italy	700,000	1.2	2002
Portugal	185,000	1.8	2001
Greece	370,000	3.4	2001

[a]The original studies from the Netherlands and Switzerland provide only ranges rather than point estimates.
Source: Table 1.6 from OECD (2006).

estimates with wide margins of error. Nevertheless, several things stand out from the estimates in Table 11.1. First, unauthorized immigration in isolated island countries like Australia and Japan is much smaller as a proportion of total population than in the United States or Western European countries. It is also clear that unauthorized immigration is more than a marginal phenomenon. With unauthorized immigrants comprising as much as three or more percent of some countries' populations, this phenomenon must have substantial economic consequences.

The unauthorized immigrant population of the United States was estimated by the Pew Hispanic Center to be between 11.5 and 12 million persons in 2005.[7] Out of the total estimated foreign-born population in the U.S. in 2005, about 30% of all U.S. immigrants are in the country illegally. The Pew Center further estimates that 56% of the unauthorized immigrants, or 6.2 million, are from Mexico, 22% are from elsewhere in Latin America, and 13% are from Asia. The rest are from Canada, Europe, the Caribbean, and Africa. Compared to legal immigrants, unauthorized immigrants are much more likely to be from a neighboring country like Mexico. This conclusion reflects what Table 11.1 shows, namely, that distant island countries like Australia and Japan have relatively fewer unauthorized immigrants.

With a common 3,000 km border, it is difficult for the United States to stop Mexican immigrants who can increase their incomes ten-fold by crossing from one side to the other of the border. Most other unauthorized immigrants to the U.S. arrived through normal border crossings with tourist, student, or other temporary visas, although border apprehensions suggest that some unauthorized immigrants from other countries also cross the border from Mexico. The highest concentrations of unauthorized immigrants in the U.S. are in the border states of California and Texas. Table 11.2 presents estimates by the Pew Hispanic Center for the individual states of the United States.

---

[7]See Passel (2006).

Table 11.2 Pew foundation estimates of the unauthorized migrant population in the U.S: 2005

California	2,500,000–2,750,000	Indiana	55,000–85,000
Texas	1,400,000–1,600,000	Iowa	55,000–85,000
Florida	800,000–950,000	Oklahoma	50,000–75,000
New York	550,000–650,000	New Mexico	50,000–75,000
Arizona	400,000–450,000	Kansas	40,000–70,000
Illinois	375,000–425,000	S. Carolina	35,000–75,000
Georgia	350,000–450,000	Missouri	35,000–65,000
New Jersey	350,000–425,000	Nebraska	35,000–55,000
North Carolina	300,000–400,000	Kentucky	30,000–60,000
		Alabama	30,000–50,000
Virginia	250,000–300,000	Mississippi	30,000–50,000
Maryland	225,000–275,000	Arkansas	30,000–50,000
Colorado	225,000–275,000		
Washington	200,000–250,000	Louisiana	25,000–45,000
Massachusetts	150,000–250,000	Idaho	25,000–45,000
Nevada	150,000–200,000	Rhode Island	20,000–40,000
		Hawaii	20,000–35,000
Pennsylvania	125,000–175,000	Delaware	15,000–35,000
Oregon	125,000–175,000	District of Columbia	15,000–30,000
Tennessee	100,000–150,000	N. Hampshire	10,000–30,000
Michigan	100,000–150,000		
		Alaska	<10,000
Ohio	75,000–150,000	Wyoming	<10,000
Wisconsin	75,000–115,000	South Dakota	<10,000
Minnesota	75,000–100,000	Maine	<10,000
Utah	75,000–100,000	Vermont	<10,000
Connecticut	75,000–100,000	North Dakota	<10,000
		Montana	<10,000
		West Virginia	<10,000

Based on March 2005 Current Population Survey and published by Pew Hispanic Center, A Pew research Center Project, Washington D.C.20036–5610, www.pewhispanic.org.

Table 11.3 presents several alternative estimates of the unauthorized immigrant population in the U.S. The U.S. Immigration and Naturalization Service's (INS) estimates are based on border apprehensions, as stated earlier. The remaining estimates are based on finding the residual between legal immigrants estimated from immigration statistics and estimates of the total foreign-born population from the decennial Census and intermediate Census Bureau surveys. The variations in the estimates are due to alternative assumptions about the undercounts in Census Bureau surveys and counts. For example, in Table 11.3, Bean, Corona, Tuirán, Woodrow-Lafield, and Van Hook (2001) obtained estimates of the unauthorized immigrant population assuming the Census Bureau undercounts unauthorized immigrants by 15–25%; these assumptions are justified by the results from Bean and Van Hook (1998).

Table 11.3 Alternative estimates of unauthorized immigrants in the U.S. (thousands)

	INS	Census bureau study			Bean et al. (2001)			Pew 2006
Undercount rate:	–	10%	15%	20%	15%	20%	25%	–
1990	3,500	3,766	4,430	4,707	–	–	–	–
1995	5,146	–	–	–	–	–	–	–
2000	7,000	8,705	10,242	10,882	–	–	–	–
2001	–	–	–	–	5,918	7,751	9,864	
2005	–	–	–	–	–	–	–	11,100

Source: Hanson (2006), Table 1, p. 875. The studies shown are: INS (2001); Costanzo, Davis, Irazi, Goodking, and Ramirez (2001), Bean, Corona, Tuirán, Woodrow-Lafield, and Van Hook (2001) and Passel (2006).

11.3 Some Characteristics of Unauthorized Immigrants

It is difficult to describe the characteristics of unauthorized populations residing in the principal destination countries because they are not a homogeneous group. However, the Pew Hispanic Center has taken all available data from the Census Bureau and other government agencies to compile several studies that, for the first time, shed some light on who exactly are the unauthorized immigrants in the United States (Passel 2006).

Out of the 11 million or more unauthorized immigrants in the U.S. in 2005, the Pew Center estimates that two-thirds arrived in the U.S. after 1995, 40% after 2000. This implies that between 2000 and 2005, close to 1 million immigrants entered the country illegally each year. The study estimates that during the 1980s about 200,000 immigrants entered the U.S. illegally, between 1990 and 1995 about 400,000 entered each year, and close to 600,000 entered each year in the latter half of the 1990s. The study finds that slightly over half of all unauthorized immigrants in the U.S. in 2005 were natives of Mexico, and another 20% are from elsewhere in Latin America. Asia was the source of 13% of the unauthorized U.S. population, Europe, and Canada contributed 6%, and Africa 3%. Overall, out of the total U.S. foreign-born population of 36 million, unauthorized immigrants accounted for 11 million, or 30% of the total. Also, the Pew Center's (2006) research suggests that about 60% of unauthorized immigrants entered the U.S. by crossing the border clandestinely; the other 40% entered through normal entry points and then overstayed visas, student visas, or other temporary entry permits.

In 2005, unauthorized immigrants consisted of 5.4 million adult males (49%), 3.9 million adult females (35%), and 1.8 million minors (16%). Immigrant families were not neatly divided between fully documented and unauthorized immigrants. Nearly 15 million people lived in 6.6 million families that had members who were unauthorized immigrants. Therefore, there were about 4 million legal immigrants, U.S. citizens, and native-born Americans who were part of families that included unauthorized immigrants. About 3.3 million were children born in the U.S. who were U.S. citizens. This finding complicates the policy debate over what to do about unauthorized immigrants already living in the U.S.

Another important finding by the Pew Hispanic Center's research on unauthorized immigrants is that just short of 5% of the U.S. civilian labor force consists of unauthorized immigrant workers. While 83% of all adult males in the U.S. are in the active labor force, 94% of unauthorized adult male immigrants in the U.S. were working in 2005. Finally, unauthorized immigrant workers are highly concentrated in certain U.S. industries, most notably in relatively low-wage jobs in the agriculture, construction, food processing, and service industries.

11.4   The Economic Analysis of Unauthorized Immigration

Very little of the early research on unauthorized immigration was done by economists. Sociologists led the way in analyzing why immigrants crossed borders illegally, where they came from, and how they survived in their destination countries.[8] Perhaps empirically-minded economists were discouraged from analyzing unauthorized immigration due to the lack of reliable data on unauthorized immigration. Whatever the reasons, economists' focus on legal immigration flows has limited their analysis of immigration in several critical ways. First of all, since nearly one-third of all immigrants in the U.S. are in the country illegally, any analysis focusing only on legal immigration inevitably gives an incomplete picture of immigration. Second, statistical analysis using only an arbitrary two-thirds of a total sample will almost certainly result in biased conclusions, especially because the status of being unauthorized uniquely alters an immigrant's opportunities and economic outcomes. Illegality imposes costs and reduces the potential gains from immigration. Unauthorized immigrants do not enjoy the same legal protections and privileges as legal immigrants do, and they tend to have fewer employment and living options available to them. They often face various forms of discrimination and exploitation in the labor market, housing, education, and social conditions. Third, the inflows and outflows of unauthorized immigrants do not react to shifts in legal barriers to immigration in the same way as legal immigrants. In most destination countries, legal barriers to immigration cause a backlog of people seeking to immigrate.

Hence, actual annual flows of legal immigrants do not reflect current economic and social conditions as strongly as unauthorized immigration, which does seem to respond quickly to changes in current economic conditions in the source and destination countries. Given the fairly unchanging quotas on legal immigration in many immigrant destination countries, flows of unauthorized immigrants may seem to over-react to changes in conditions because unauthorized immigration is effectively a "spillover" from the constrained flow of legal immigration. For all these reasons, the study of unauthorized immigration can provide information that studies of legal immigration may not readily reveal in standard statistical studies.

---

[8]See, for example, the review of the sociology literature by Espenshade (1995).

11.4.1 The Supply and Demand for Unauthorized Workers

The standard labor supply and demand model of immigration can guide our discussion of the determinants of unauthorized immigration. First, there are costs to unauthorized immigration, which may be higher or lower than legal immigration. These costs are related to time, distance, and the costs of penetrating the barriers a destination country has erected to prevent the entry of unauthorized immigrants. The bureaucratic procedures for acquiring work or residence visas in destination countries can take a long time, sometimes years. Hence, immediate illegal entry can be an attractive alternative for many immigrants who do not qualify for visa categories for which visas are quickly available, such as highly educated workers or business executives.

Legal immigration usually involves other direct costs, such as transportation and legal fees. The United States charges some immigrants up to $5,000 for certain work visas. Unauthorized immigrants evade such legal charges, but illegal entry introduces other costs that legal immigrants do not encounter. For example, immigrants seeking illegal entry may contract the services of a trafficker, a people-smuggler, or a "coyote," as the smugglers operating on the Mexico-U.S. border are called. Cornelius (2005) reports that coyotes charge between $1,200 and $1,700 (in year 2000 US$'s) for their services, more if the immigrant's final destination is further inland from the border. In the United Kingdom, people-smugglers who bring Chinese workers from China charge £15,000 to £20,000 (US$ 27,500 to US $35,000), which is ten times the cost of a standard airline ticket between China and Europe.[9] The role of gangs in the trafficking of unauthorized workers results from immigration restrictions. There is no legal way for the Chinese workers to even get to Europe. Airlines will not let passengers board without valid entry visas, and the embassies and European Consulates in China only give tourist or student visas to Chinese who can prove they have the high incomes to be tourists or overseas students. Hence, poor fortune seekers must rely on traffickers.

The supply of unauthorized immigrants is influenced by source country conditions and the particular characteristics of the immigrants. Orrenius and Zavodny (2005) find that unauthorized Mexican immigrants to the United States are neither uneducated nor highly educated; they have above-average education for Mexico but below-average education from a U.S. perspective. Unauthorized Mexican immigrants in the U.S. also tend to be related to other unauthorized immigrants already in the country, which suggests that unauthorized immigrants follow family networks, not unlike many legal immigrants. In fact, the difficulties encountered by unauthorized immigrants may make family, ethnic, and language networks even more important for them.

Both the supply and demand sides of the labor market for unauthorized immigrants are affected by overall economic conditions. Supply is driven by both source country and destination country economic conditions, and demand is driven mostly

---

[9]Champion and Kaminski (2000).

by destination country economic conditions. Hanson and Spilimburgo (1999) examine the causes of unauthorized immigration to the U.S. using data on apprehensions at the border under the assumption that unauthorized immigration is directly related to the number of apprehensions by the U.S. Border Patrol. They find that decreases in Mexican wages sharply increase border apprehensions, and, by assumption, unauthorized immigration to the U.S. within months. They also find that U.S. wages have less influence on the flows of unauthorized immigrants from Mexico to the U.S. This result does not accord with the more traditional literature on immigration, which gives destination country wages a large influence. On the other hand, we use annual county data derived from census studies and updates and find that Hispanic immigration to the U.S. is more responsive to U.S. economic conditions than source country conditions. The differences in findings can easily be explained by the differences in data sources. Their weekly data gave Hanson and Spilimburgo the significant advantage of being able to measure short-term responses to changes in economic conditions, something annual census data cannot do. Espenshade (1995) points out the difficulties with using border apprehensions to proxy unauthorized immigration, although he admits that there are no alternatives to using border apprehension data to quantify weekly or monthly changes in unauthorized immigration.

Following his survey and analysis of the motivations for unauthorized immigrants from Mexico to the U.S., Hanson (2006) reaches the more general conclusion that it is income differences between source and destination countries that are directly correlated with immigrant flows. He also concludes that:

> "The perspective that emerges from the data that are available is that Mexico-to-U.S. illegal migration increased in the 1970s and 1980s and averaged around 200,000 to 300,000 net unauthorized entries per year in the 1990s and early 2000s. The population of illegal immigrants from Mexico in the United States includes a substantial fraction of women, is predominantly employed in nonagricultural jobs, and has schooling levels that are comparable to or higher than nonmigrating individuals in Mexico. Though many migrants maintain ties with family members in their origin communities, a majority appear to have settled in the United States on a medium or long-term basis" (pp. 886–87).

These conclusions suggest that unauthorized immigrants in the U.S. are unlikely to leave the country soon. This presents a difficult situation for those who have suggested the U.S. needs to find and deport all unauthorized immigrants.

Hanson (2006) also concludes that there must be large unobserved costs to unauthorized immigration from Mexico to the United States because, given the income differences, there should be much more immigration. Perhaps the standard model of immigration does not capture all the relevant push, pull, stay, and stay away factors. For example, poor living conditions and working conditions for unauthorized immigrants may partially offset the higher wages they earn in the destination countries. The nature of an illegal existence has been documented in the press and books, especially in the sociology literature, but it has not always been properly incorporated in the economics literature.

11.4.2   Unauthorized Immigration as a Form of Labor Market Discrimination

The economic costs and benefits of unauthorized immigration can be illustrated using the standard labor supply and demand model first presented in the Introduction to Section One of the book. We use this model in its most restricted form, which models immigrants exclusively as suppliers of labor. As Fig. 11.1 shows, immigration shifts the labor supply curves to the left in Source, and to the right in Destination. Wages rise in Source and fall in Destination, and the remaining workers increase their share of GDP by the area **e** in Source, but native workers lose a share of GDP equal to the area E in destination. The immigrants gain the difference between the areas H and h. This model, therefore, suggests that workers in Destination will seek restrictions on immigration.

This representation of immigration may not be accurate for unauthorized immigration, however, because the model effectively assumes immigrants and domestic workers are perfect substitutes. In general, unauthorized immigrants are not treated exactly the same as otherwise identical legal immigrants and natives. Unauthorized workers often end up working for lower wages and benefits, and in poorer working conditions, than native workers. Also, unauthorized workers cannot find employment in all sectors of the economy. Differences in labor union vigilance, selective government regulation, or just tradition often lead to sharp concentrations of unauthorized immigrant workers in certain industries and occupations, while virtually no unauthorized workers are found in many other industries and occupations. Table 11.4 presents some evidence of the occupational concentration of unauthorized immigrants in the United States.

Returning to the labor market model of immigration, suppose that the illegal status of immigrants results in the segmentation of the labor market into legal and

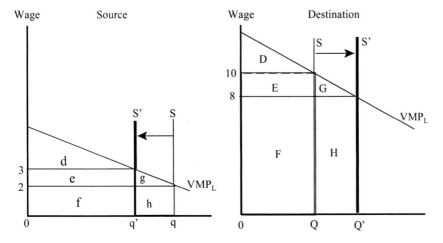

Fig. 11.1 The gains and losses from immigration without discrimination

Table 11.4 Unauthorized immigrants in U.S. occupations with 20% or greater share: 2005

Occupation	Total workers	Undocumented workers	
		Number	Share
Total U.S. Civilian Workforce	148,615,000	7,255,000	4.9%
Insulation workers	56,000	20,000	36%
Agricultural workers	839,000	247,000	29%
Roofers	325,000	93,000	29%
Drywall installers	285,000	79,000	28%
Construction helpers	145,000	40,000	27%
Meat, poultry, fish processing workers	322,000	87,000	27%
Textile, garment workers	83,000	21,000	26%
Grounds maintenance workers	1,204,000	299,000	25%
Construction laborers	1,614,000	400,000	25%
Masons	198,000	49,000	25%
Dishwashers	367,000	85,000	23%
Production worker helpers	64,000	15,000	23%
Maids, housekeepers	1,531,000	342,000	22%
Graders and sorters in agriculture	74,000	16,000	22%
Painters in construction industry	768,000	167,000	22%
Cement masons and finishers	141,000	29,000	21%
Computer hardware engineers	54,000	11,000	20%
Packaging and filling machine operators	367,000	75,000	20%
Packers and packagers	548,000	111,000	20%
Cleaners of vehicles and equipment	427,000	85,000	20%
Carpet and floor installers and finishers	330,000	66,000	20%
Cooks	2,218,000	436,000	20%

Source: Jeffrey S. Passel (2006), Table 1, p. 12; downloaded from www.pewhispanic.org.

illegal segments, and employers pay different wages in each segment. Figure 11.2 illustrates how such a discriminatory scheme distributes economic welfare. In the case where immigrants are restricted to certain jobs that would not be performed at all in the absence of immigration (say butchering hogs or cows in unpleasant meat packing plants or picking oranges in hot fields), jobs listed along the labor demand curve from **a** to **b**, the wage for immigrant workers would fall to $8. Total immigrant wages would be equal to area H in Fig. 11.1. If authorized workers refuse to work for less than $10 or if there is a minimum wage of $10 that is only enforced for authorized workers, then total wage income for the 0Q native workers will remain equal to the gray shaded area E + F. The reservation wage (or minimum wage) of $10 implies that native workers will not be employed in any of the lower-paying jobs between **a** and **b**, and the labor market will be perfectly segmented into two separate markets with wages of $10 and $8, respectively.

Notice also that owners of other factors such as capital will still gain from the immigration. They will not capture area E, which remains with native workers, but the owners of other factors do gain area G by employing immigrant workers at the lower wage of $8. Thus, schemes whereby immigrants are allowed to work only in

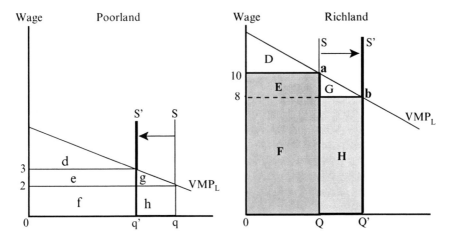

Fig. 11.2 The gains and losses from immigration with discrimination

sectors of the economy where native workers earning pre-immigration wages would not be employed will prove beneficial to immigrants and employers without lowering the welfare of native workers.

The model in Fig. 11.2 can be used to explain the political economy model of Hillman and Weiss (1999), in which an equilibrium is reached where unauthorized immigration is concentrated in sectors of the economy where domestic labor interests are not strong while the majority of voters continues to support curbs on legal immigration because they do not want immigrants to compete in the labor markets where they work.

Hillman and Weiss point out that in most European countries that attract unauthorized immigrants, undocumented foreign workers usually occupy jobs that native workers are not very interested in performing. Vigilance against unauthorized immigrants is higher in the higher wage segments of the labor market for the simple reason that domestic workers demand that unauthorized immigrants be barred from applying for those jobs. Thus, undocumented workers end up in certain low-paying segments of the labor market where they do not compete directly with native workers and employers actually gain surplus from employing unauthorized workers. Restrictions on unauthorized immigrants' use of public services, such as those passed by the federal and many state governments in the U.S. during the 1990s, also serve to keep the inflow of unauthorized foreign workers from having a negative impact on the welfare of native workers.

11.4.3   Oppression of Unauthorized Workers

The illegal status of unauthorized immigrants gives employers in the destination country added labor market power. Unauthorized workers are in constant danger of being deported and, possibly, punished for their having entered the country illegally. Employers can dismiss the unauthorized workers by simply reporting them to the authorities, who will then escort the workers out of the country and out of the normal range of responsibilities that employers have toward legal workers. The unauthorized workers know this, and they accordingly tend to avoid conflict with their employers. They also tend to accept lower wages, poorer working conditions and hours, and more abuse in the workplace.

The casual evidence suggests that many employers treat unauthorized immigrants on par with legal immigrants. Employers fearful of government punishment have an incentive to act as though they are not aware of unauthorized immigrants' illegal status. Many employers of unauthorized workers even contribute their share of social security payments and forward deducted taxes to the government from the immigrants' paychecks.[10] On the other hand, the press has reported numerous cases of mistreatment and underpayment. A 2003 *Financial Times* story describes the plight of unauthorized Burmese workers in the border city of Mae Sot in Thailand:

> Most Burmese workers receive just a fraction of Thailand's minimum wage, and risk prompt deportation by local authorities–often acting in league with enterprise owners–if they demand better conditions. Police routinely arrest, beat and threaten to deport Burmese migrants who fail to pay bribes. Deadly violence is also a growing danger. In January 2002, 17 migrants, their hands bound and throats slit, were discovered in a stream near Mea Sot. Thai police, who dubbed the murders as the "normal killing" of Burmese workers, advised villagers to float the bodies downstream, though a public outcry forced an investigation.... In June, police in Mae Sot deported 34 Burmese workers after a labor court ordered their employer to pay them back wages.[11]

Some of the worst labor conditions for unauthorized immigrants have been found in Western Europe and the United States. For example, the *Associated Press* reported many cases of unauthorized immigrants not receiving full, or in some cases, any, payments for weeks of work for contractors hired to clean up after Hurricane Katrina damaged towns and cities along the U.S. Gulf Coast in 2005.[12] And *Business Week* reported that in 2000[13], as many as 100,000 unauthorized immigrants were working in Europe in closed sweatshops and denied any contact with the outside world. In contrast, not all studies show that unauthorized immigrants are at a serous disadvantage to legal immigrants. For example, Massey (1987) found that undocumented immigrants in the U.S. earned lower wages because of their characteristics, not because they were undocumented per se. Massey explains immigrants' lower wages by their skill levels, the types of jobs that they hold, and length of tenure in their jobs. The types of jobs immigrants hold and their job

---

[10]Potter (2006), Jordan (2007).

[11]Kazmin (2003).

[12]Pritchard (2005).

[13]*Business Week* (1000), "Workers in Bondage," November 27.

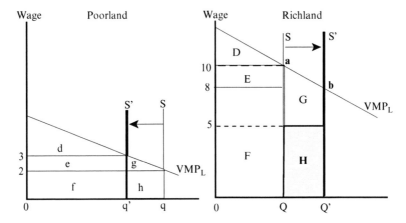

Fig. 11.3 The gains and losses from immigration with discrimination

tenure are influenced by their legal status, so it is still likely that the status of being an illegal worker causes wages to be lower compared to legal workers.

The models in Figs. 11.1 and 11.2 suggested that employers gain the area G from the presence of unauthorized workers willing to work at $8. Suppose, however, that there are many foreign workers ready to work at wages below $8, say for any wage higher than they can earn in their native countries. If employers can collude, exploit unauthorized immigrants' inability to shop around for jobs because of language barriers, threaten the workers with arrest, or if they can simply exploit the workers' lack of knowledge about the labor market in the destination country, then employers could lower the wage for unauthorized, illegal workers to say $5, as shown in Fig. 11.3. Now the area G is much larger. The immigrants still accept the work because the wage is well above the source country wage.

11.4.4 Discussion of the Labor Segmentation Hypothesis

To summarize the above discussion, employers gain from being able to employ less expensive unauthorized workers, and workers and employers in other segments of the economy are not too troubled by the presence in the country of unauthorized immigrants who work mostly in a few specific industries where they would not themselves care to work. Representative of this view are the comments by Rosie Olivares, a labor organizer in Fremont, Nebraska, who reacted to the presence of unauthorized workers in Nebraska's growing meat-packing industry as follows: "They're not taking jobs from anybody."[14] "There are only so many people who want to do that at the given pay scale," claimed a manager of the Nebraska Turkey

---

[14]Quoted in Orenstein (1995).

Growers Cooperative.[15] Economists will be somewhat leery of accepting this market segmentation argument, and the suggestion that the work performed by unauthorized Mexican workers at Nebraska meat packing plants would not be performed at all if unauthorized workers were all deported has been contested by many anti-immigrant groups and labor organizations. Workers are not so easily segmented into exclusive markets. And, the increased total supply of labor would, in the absence of strong positive externalities and demand-side effects, be likely to cause wages to fall elsewhere in the economy. But, in the case of unauthorized immigrants, there seem to be some implicit barriers to unauthorized immigrants competing in other labor markets, most likely by labor unions and, perhaps, by firms interested in avoiding labor conflicts. Governments may vary enforcement of immigration laws on an industry-by-industry basis in response to the different interests of firms, organized labor groups, and consumers in each industry.

There are obvious political implications of the market segmentation hypothesis discussed above. Potential employers who stand to gain G will lobby hard for legislators to close their eyes to the entry of unauthorized immigrants, and labor groups opposing the legalization of unauthorized immigrants would be willing to overlook unauthorized workers in segments of the market that would probably not exist without cheap exploited labor.

11.4.5 Close Variations on Illegality

Various immigration policies have been devised that directly attempt to legally achieve exactly the outcome shown in Fig. 11.2. Such schemes effectively require employers to discriminate between native and immigrant workers. For example, many countries permit foreign workers to enter the country temporarily to work at specific jobs where they do not compete directly with domestic workers, and often these jobs pay substantially less than other domestic jobs. Sometimes, temporary contract workers do not have to be paid the same benefits, and certain employment taxes are waived. Seasonal jobs in agriculture and tourism often pay wages and offer work conditions that reflect effective discrimination against foreign workers.

In the 1960s, a number of Western European countries instituted temporary worker programs that brought large numbers of foreign workers from Southern European and Mediterranean countries to specific jobs in certain industries, e.g. construction. Interestingly, the strong social welfare policies and the high levels of civil and human rights in these Western European countries soon undermined the discriminatory immigration system that was intended to only temporarily bring foreign workers to perform certain jobs for which nationals were not available. Family members of the immigrants began to arrive, families formed and grew, and the temporary work permits soon began to be converted to permanent residence

---

[15]Quoted in Orenstein (1995).

visas. Formerly homogeneous European societies have become much more diverse, and foreign-born residents have come to account for high proportions of the populations of most Western European countries.

The United States authorized the *Bracero* Program during World War II, which permitted Mexican workers to do seasonal work in the United States. This program was instituted because native U.S. workers were being drafted into the armed forces for the war, and fruits and vegetables were rotting in the fields of California and Texas. Clearly, the program covered jobs that would not otherwise have been done. The program also permitted employers to pay lower wages and avoid paying other benefits. The program continued after the war, but by the early 1960s strong opposition to it had developed. Unions sought to organize native agricultural workers, and the availability of temporary workers willing to work for low wages under the special provisions of the Bracero Program undermined organized labor's ability to press for higher wages and better working conditions in the fields of California. In the early 1960s, with labor-friendly politicians leading the U.S. Congress, the Bracero Program was ended. In 2006 and 2007, the inclusion of a temporary worker program in a comprehensive immigration bill before the U.S. Congress undermined support and, ultimately, led to the bill's rejection. A number of industries had pressed for the temporary worker program as part of a grand bargain that also included stronger measures to curb unauthorized immigration, but organized labor groups strongly opposed the discriminatory temporary worker provision, and the bargain unraveled.

This discussion suggests that unauthorized immigration is the logical result of the destination country's political process, not an unintended or unexpected outcome. Indeed, a number of political scientists have described immigration policy from this perspective, e.g. Andreas (2000), Massey, Durand, and Malone (2002), and Cornelius, Truda, Martin, and Hollifield (2004). This literature recognizes that authorities have some freedom to vary the enforcement of immigration laws and regulations. Decisions on how to patrol the borders, whether to pursue employers or the immigrants themselves after they have crossed the border, and whether to punish unauthorized immigrants, their employers, or their other accomplices within the country, are all open to considerable variation. The choices made by the authorities are, therefore, political decisions that reflect the various interest groups within the destination country and how those groups are able to translate their interests into political outcomes. Employers of unauthorized immigrants seem to have been able to reduce the enforcement of immigration laws in many countries. Many articles and studies show that U.S. immigration authorities have for many years simply not pursued unauthorized immigrants at their places of employment, although it seems to be one of the obvious places to look for unauthorized immigrants. Incidentally, there is nothing in U.S. law that prevents U.S. immigration authorities from visiting firms and inspecting identification and other types of required documents.[16]

---

[16]See, for example, the discussion in Hanson (2006, pp. 909–910).

11.4.6   Unauthorized Immigration can be Deadly

In June of 2000, the world was stunned by the death by suffocation of 58 Chinese migrants locked in an airtight cargo truck during a ferry crossing of the English Channel from France to the United Kingdom. Only two of the passengers survived to tell the story of their ill-fated trip from China. The 60 passengers had spent 4 months traveling from China's Fujian province via Moscow and Eastern Europe. They had paid traffickers to carry them to London, where they had been promised jobs that would pay wages well above what they could earn in their native China. European leaders replied to the tragedy by reiterating their determination to stop the trafficking of humans. But, as two reporters for the *Wall Street Journal* wrote just after the tragic event, "Despite the predictable promises of action from EU leaders, no easy solutions are on offer."[17] This tragedy reflects the strong incentives for immigration created by the large differences in wages between countries.

In Japan, companies who need low-wage workers have gotten around very firm barriers against immigration by taking advantage of a 1993 program that lets Japanese firms bring in foreign trainees for up to 3 years. Many of these trainees are in fact underpaid workers performing menial, repetitive jobs. More likely, as Fig. 11.2 suggests, the program was set up with the specific intention of segmenting the Japanese labor market to let foreigners perform certain jobs without impacting native workers' wages. A member of the Japanese parliament was recently caught accepting a large bribe from an organization that actively recruits overseas "trainees" for Japanese companies; the parliamentarian had pushed legislation to extend the training period from 2 to 3 years. Life for these trainees is difficult and many run away and take unauthorized work in Japan's underground economy.[18]

Increased spending on border patrols has made it more difficult for Mexicans and Central Americans to cross the Mexico-U.S. border at the most convenient, and safe, places. Therefore, traffickers are more frequently crossing the 2,000 mile-long border in remote areas. In 2000, 369 people died of hunger or thirst trying to cross into the United States by walking across remote desserts or riding in the backs of airtight, sealed trucks. In 2005 an estimated 472 would-be immigrants died trying to cross into the U.S.[19] In an ironic twist, the Mexican government has launched a program to equip unauthorized immigrants with survival kits containing water, medicines, bandages, and anti-dehydration powder.[20] This is a case of the government of the source country spending money to help immigrants overcome barriers paid for by the taxpayers in the destination country. In the meantime, unauthorized Mexican immigrants continue to enter the United States.

---

[17]Champion and Kaminski (2000).

[18]Nakamoto (2001).

[19]*The Economist* (2007).

[20]*The Economist* (2001).

11.5 The Fiscal Costs and Benefits of Unauthorized Immigration

Unauthorized immigrants are expected to generate various externalities, and the most often discussed externalities are the fiscal costs to local, state, and national governments. Evidence for the U.S. does not support the popular belief that immigrants are a fiscal burden, however. Except for refugees and elderly immigrants, the remaining immigrants, including unauthorized ones, use government services to a lesser degree than natives. Even when we include refugees, who are high users of government services and recipients of government transfers, immigrants as a group still use government services only slightly more often and receive only slightly more welfare payments than natives. For example, according to the 1990 census, 9% of immigrant families received welfare payments, a percentage that was only slightly more than the 7.4% of U.S.-born families that received welfare payments. A 1992 study for the United States Department of Health and Human Services by Kirchner and Baldwin (1992) found that pre-1982 legal immigrants to the United States living in the six states with the largest immigrant populations were found to pay more in total taxes than they received in government-provided benefits.

Not all levels of government are affected the same way by immigrants, however. The 1992 study determined that the fiscal burden of immigrants fell mostly on state and local governments. The federal government actually enjoyed net gains from increased income tax and social security tax revenues. Apparently the average immigrant is less educated and has a larger family compared to natives, so immigrants were more likely to use state and local government services. But, because immigrants are also younger than natives, they are large contributors to Social Security, a federal program.

A study of immigration in European countries suggests that the tax-transfers ratio is not as burdensome as is often feared because governments adjust both taxes and transfer programs in order to improve the balance for native workers. Razin, Sadka, and Swagel (1998) show that for 11 European countries, taxes on workers and transfers to the poor were reduced as the percentage of immigrants in the population increased. The recent welfare reforms in the United States, which reduced benefits to non-citizens, are further evidence that the political process adjusts immigrants' access to welfare benefits as immigration rises. Hence, the fiscal burden of immigrants appears to be an endogenous variable, and politics is unlikely to let the fiscal burden become more burdensome for voting native workers.

While the evidence on the fiscal effects of immigrants is sparse, there is almost no evidence on the fiscal effects of unauthorized immigrants. Unauthorized immigrants do not readily reveal themselves to the government authorities. Also, in many destination countries, especially those with strict civil rights laws and traditions, government service providers such as health clinics and schools do not ask immigrants to reveal their legal status.

Table 11.5 Major government-sponsored programs and their availability to undocumented immigrants

Unavailable	Available
Medicare	K-12 Education, Higher Ed. In some states
Medicaid	Emergency Medicaid Care
Children's Health Insurance (CHIP)	Substance Abuse Services
Food stamps	Mental Health Services
Supplemental Security Income (SSI)	Immunizations
Public housing assistance	Women and Children's Health Services
Job opp. for low income individuals	Public health
Child care and development	EMS

Source: United States Department of Health and Human Services; published as Exhibit 1 in Special Report (2006).

Table 11.6 Costs, revenues and economic impact of undocumented immigrants in Texas, 2005 (In millions of $'s)

Costs		Revenues	
Education	$967.8	State Revenue	$999.0
Healthcare	$58.0	School Property Tax	$582.1
Incarceration	$130.6		
Total	$1,156.4	Total	$1,581.1
Surplus/Deficit:	+ $425 million		

Source: Exhibit 18 in Special Report (2006).

There is a Special Report (2006) by the Texas Comptroller of Public Accounts that estimates the financial impacts of unauthorized immigrants on the Texas state budget and economy. During 2004–05, there were an estimated 1.4 million unauthorized immigrants in Texas. Table 11.5 shows which of Texas' major government-sponsored social and educational programs that unauthorized immigrants are denied access to and which ones for which they can qualify. Note that in Texas, unauthorized children can attend college at in-state tuition rates if they graduate from a Texas High School.

In its estimates, the authors of the Special Report included law enforcement and criminal justice costs generated by these immigrants. Total state expenditures for unauthorized immigrants were estimated to be $1,156 billion. Total revenue paid by unauthorized immigrants was calculated using a method that arrived at total state revenue under the assumption that immigrants suddenly disappeared. This exercise led to the conclusion that the unauthorized immigrants' presence increased the gross state product by $17.7 billion, which, in turn, increased property taxes, sales taxes, fees for services, etc., by $1.581 billion. Therefore, the state government enjoyed a net gain of $425 million from the presence of 1.4 million unauthorized immigrants in Texas. Table 11.6 summarizes the study's results.

The conclusion from the Special Report is that unauthorized immigrants are not a drain on state government coffers, as so many critics of illegal immigration suggest. To the contrary, because unauthorized immigrants do not have access to as many government services and programs as legal immigrants do and they actually pay many state and local taxes, for example sales taxes, property taxes, automobile registrations, and income tax deductions from paychecks, unauthorized immigrants were net contributors to Texas' fiscal budget.

11.6 Unauthorized Immigration: Policy Options

Immigration policy has generated controversy in most of the destination countries in Europe, North America, and the Pacific region. Given the huge differences in wages across countries, the restrictions on legal immigration that most countries have instituted almost inevitably result in people crossing borders without permission. The static labor supply and demand model suggests that there will be groups who find unauthorized immigration to work in their economic favor, so there is liable to be implicit support for unauthorized immigrants in the form of jobs. The demand effects of immigration also imply that there will be landlords willing to rent housing and retailers willing to provide goods and services to the immigrants. The opposing interests within the destination country thus place policymakers in the position of having to make difficult choices.

Among the measures that have been suggested to stop unauthorized immigration are: (1) placing barriers on the border, (2) preventing unauthorized immigrants from taking the jobs that they seek once they are in the country; or (3) creating better jobs in the would-be immigrants' own country. The latter is not a short-term option, since that would require investment flows and encouragement of international trade, among other things. The first two options are the ones commonly targeted by policymakers.

11.6.1 Border Controls

Border controls are easier for immigrant destination countries far away from source countries. For example, Australia receives relatively few unauthorized immigrants because it is an island that is thousands of miles from the most common sources of immigrants. The United States, however, shares 2,000 miles of border with Mexico, the source of over half of its immigrants over the past two decades. Western Europe receives unauthorized immigrants from Eastern Europe, and it increasingly receives unauthorized immigrants from Africa, most of whom cross the Mediterranean Sea to Spain or Italy. Some African migrants climb the fence into Ceuta, the Spanish enclave in Northern Africa. Like the desert along the Mexican-U.S. border, the Meditarranean has caused numerous deaths when overloaded boats sank or high waves overwhelmed small boats inappropriate for sea crossings.

Europe and the United States also receive unauthorized immigrants from further away. Increasingly, Western Europe and the United States receive unauthorized immigrants from China. The U.S. and Spain are destinations for Latin American immigrants from Central and South America. Some of these Latin American immigrants travel through numerous countries before crossing the Mexico-U.S. border, making Mexico now also one of the main transit countries for unauthorized immigrants. Immigrant trafficking has become a large business for Mexican "coyotes."

Many unauthorized immigrants do not actually sneak across the borders of the destination countries. Evidence suggests that half of all unauthorized immigrants enter destination countries legally with tourist visas, student visas, or other temporary entry visas. Sometimes such visas are obtained under false information; often, tourists and students decide to remain in the destination country.

11.6.2 Employer Sanctions

Sanctioning employers is often viewed as a more effective way to stop unauthorized immigration. This will be the case only if unauthorized immigrants come for work, of course, but that does seem to be the most common reason for unauthorized immigration. One reason employer sanctions are not used more frequently is that they directly confront an important domestic political constituency in the destination country. Furthermore, civil rights issues arise. To avoid charges of discrimination, the legality of all workers, including natives and legal immigrants, would have to be checked with equal seriousness. Hence, another important domestic political constituency is inconvenienced. If mistakes are made, natives and legal immigrants will be swept up in raids on employers. For example, if immigration authorities only check workers on a selective basis, say according to whether they fit some profile or are employed in jobs where unauthorized immigrants are most likely found, then natives and legal immigrants are likely to face occasional harassment, incarceration, and even deportation.

Ethier (1986) famously showed that successful border enforcement hurts the would-be immigrants but helps competing native and legal immigrant workers. Employer enforcement, on the other hand, is likely to hurt both unauthorized immigrants and legal immigrants when employers have trouble distinguishing between legal and illegal immigrants. If the employer sanctions are very costly, employers may refrain from hiring any immigrants for fear that they might be discovered to be unauthorized.

Some countries have used employer sanctions successfully, however. Japan has apparently been able to keep unauthorized immigrant numbers quite low (See Table 11.1) by using employer sanctions and frequent document checks in the workplace. Opponents to immigration in the United States increasingly call for the U.S. government to carry out more employee checks and, where unauthorized immigrants are found, more employer sanctions. After 2007, authorities increasingly targeted industries in the U.S. known for hiring undocumented workers.

11.7   Conclusions

The issue of unauthorized immigration is perhaps best summarized by the 2004 bill brought before the California legislature that would have allowed the estimated 2.5 million illegal immigrants residing in California to apply for a California driver's license. After proponents of the bill ran television commercials showing a fictional nanny riding the bus telling how she is welcomed into her employers' home and trusted to care for their children, but not allowed to drive their car, the bill was promptly dubbed the "let my illegal nanny drive my SUV" bill.[21] Note that California is the U.S. state with the highest proportion of foreign born and the largest number of unauthorized immigrants.

To the outside observer, the question of whether to issue an official driver's license to a person not legally in the country may seem absurd. However, the United States is a country designed around the automobile, and it is simply difficult for anyone to hold a job, shop, attend to family matters, and effectively live a normal life without being able to drive a car. In fact, in 2004, 10 U.S. states already permitted people who could not prove legal residence to acquire driver's licenses.[22] Critics charged that a driver's license effectively gives the holder a picture identification document that is used for many other things, such as getting on an airplane or train, cashing a check, or registering a car. A driver's license practically gives a person legal status. State driver's license agencies thus become de facto issuers of immigrant visas! In the case of the California bill to permit driver's licenses for undocumented immigrants, Governor Arnold Schwarzenegger, who is himself an immigrant, vetoed the measure.

Our models of immigration show that the benefits and costs of immigration are complex and spread in an uneven fashion across the economy and over time. Unauthorized immigration is, therefore, tolerated by some and strongly opposed by others. This chapter shows that there are some important differences between legal immigration and unauthorized immigration, which further complicates the question of who tolerates and who opposes unauthorized immigration. How the destination country should treat unauthorized immigrants when they are effectively tolerated, as is the case in many destination countries, is a difficult and uncomfortable issue. In later chapters on immigration policy, the issue will be discussed again. Recent political battles about whether to legalize the status of unauthorized immigrants with some form of amnesty and legalization of their status is similar to California's debate about driver's licenses for unauthorized immigrants. In 1986, the United States approved a broad amnesty. In 2007, the U.S. Congress refused to consider an amnesty for even some of the 11 million unauthorized immigrants. It is not clear how 2007 was different from 1986, but the decisions on how to deal with unauthorized immigrants were noticeably different.

---

[21]Alden (2005).
[22]Edds (2004).

References

Andreas, P. (2000). *Border games: Policing the U.S.-Mexico divide*. Ithica, NY: Cornell University Press.

Alden, E. (2005, March 8). Illegal immigrants divide US as backers seek their right to drive. *Financial Times*.

Bean, F., & Van Hook, J. (1998). Estimating unauthorized migration to the United States: Issues and results. In Mexican Ministry of Foreign Affairs and U.S. Commission of Immigration Reform (eds.), *Migration between Mexico and the United States, binational study* (vol. 2, pp. 211–550). Austin, TX: Morgan Printing.

Bean, F. D., Corona, R., Tuirán, R., Woodrow-Lafield, K. A., & Van Hook, J. (2001). Circular, invisible, and ambiguous migrants: components of difference n estimates of the number of unauthorized Mexican migrants in the United States. *Demography, 38*(3), 411–422

Bialk, C. (2006, 5 April). Fuzzy math on illegal immigration. *The Wall Street Journal*.

Champion, M., & Kaminski, M. (2000, 21 June). Availability of work in London lures Chinese migrants. *The Wall Street Journal*.

Cooper, M. (2006, May). Exodus, the ominous push and pull of the U.S.–Mexico border. *The Atlantic Monthly, 132*.

Cornelius, W. (2005). Controlling 'unwanted' immigration: Lessons from the United States, 1993–2004. *Journal of Ethnic and Migration Studies, 31*(4), 775–794.

Cornelius, W., Tsuda, T., Martin, P., & Hollifield, J. (Eds.) (2004). *Controlling immigration: A global perspective* (2nd Ed.). Stanford: Stanford University Press.

Edds, K. (2004, 24 September). No driver's licenses for California illegal immigrants. *Washington Post*.

Ehrlich, E. (2001, 7 March). The mystery of the missing millions. *Financial Times*.

Espenshade, T. J. (1995). Unauthorized immigration to the United States. *Annual Review of Sociology, 21*, 195–216.

Ethier, W. (1986). Illegal immigration: The host-country problem. *American Economic Review, 76*(1):56–71.

GFS (2005). Nombre de sans-papiers en Suisse. GFS Research Institute, Bern.

Hanson, G. H. (2006). Illegal immigration from Mexico to the United States. *Journal of Economic Literature, 44*(4), 869–924.

Hanson, G. H., & Spilimburgo, A. (1999). Illegal immigration, border enforcement, and relative wages: Evidence from apprehensions at the U.S.-Mexico border. *American Economic Review, 89*(5), 1337–1357.

Hillman, A. L., & Weiss, A. (1999). A theory of permissible illegal immigration. *European Journal of Political Economy, 15*(4):585–604.

Jordan, M. (2007). Even workers in U.S. illegally pay tax man. *The Economist*, April 4.

Kazmin, A. (2003), "Burmese workers Find Life Brutal in Thailand," *Financial Times*.

Kirchner, J., & Baldwin, S. E. (1992). *The fiscal impact of eligible legalized aliens*. A study performed under a contract between the KRA Corporation and the U.S. Department of Health and Human Services.

Magnisson, P. (2001, 9 April). The border is more porous than you think. *Business Week*, April 9.

Massey, D. (1987). Do undocumented migrants earn lower wages than legal immigrants? New evidence from Mexico. *International Migration Review, 21*(2), 236–274.

Massey, D. S., Durand, J., & Malone, N. (2002). Beyond smoke and mirrors: Mexican immigration in an era of economic integration. New York: Russel Sage Foundation.

Nakamoto, M. (2001, January 19). Spotlight falls on Japan's illegal workers. *Financial Times*.

OECD (2006). *International migration outlook 2006*. Paris: Organisation for Economic Co-Operation and Development.

Orenstein, D. (1995, March 12). Raids won't deter illegal work force. *Lincoln Journal Star*.

Orrenius, P. M., & Zavodny, M. (2005). Self-selection among undocumented immigrants from Mexico. *Journal of Development Economics*, *78*(1), 215–240.

Parks, C., & Tricks, H. (2000, 23 Feberuary). Illicit angels of America's economic miracle. *Financial Times*.

Passel, J. S. (2006). *The size and characteristics of the unauthorized migrant population in the U.S.*, estimates based on the March 2005 Current Population Survey. Research Report, Pew Hispanic Center, March 7.

Pew Hispanic Center (2006). *Fact sheet, estimates based on the March 2005 Current Population Survey*, April 26.

Potter, E., (2006, June 19). Here illegally, working hard and paying taxes. *New York Times*.

Pritchard, P. (2005, November 5) Immigrants often unpaid for Katrina work. *Associate Press Wire Report*.

Ramirez, R. (2001). Evaluating components of International migration. The residual Foreign born population. U.S. Bureau of the Census Working Paper No. 6

Razin, A., Sadka, E., & Swagel, P. (1998). Tax burden and migration: A political economy theory and evidence. *Journal of Public Economics*, *85*(2):167–190.

Snel, E., de Boom, J., Engbersen, G., & Weltevrede, A. (2005). *SOPEMI Report for the Netherlands*. Paris: Organisation for Economic Co-Operation and Development.

Special Report (2006). *Undocumented immigrants in Texas: A financial analysis of the impact to the state budget and economy*. Austin, TX: Texas Comptroller of Public Accounts, December.

The Economist, (1998, 4 April). Millions want to come.

The Economist, (2000, 2 September). South Africa's migrant workers, a ticket to prosperity.

The Economist, (2001, 24 May). Sex, death and desert snafus.

The Economist, (2007, 24 August). Death in the desert.

Chapter 12
Hispanic Immigration to the United States

Abstract This chapter presents some of the exceptional characteristics of recent Hispanic immigration to the United States. In 2005, there were nearly 40 million Hispanic immigrants and descendants of Hispanic immigrants living in the U.S. The assimilation experience of this large cultural group does not seem to be following the path past immigrants to the U.S. followed. Most third generation Hispanics in the U.S. still find themselves with income and education levels below the U.S. averages. Most forecasts predict that about 60 million Hispanics and Hispanic-Americans will be living in the U.S. by 2030.

> *The persistent inflow of Hispanic immigrants threatens to divide the United States into two peoples, two cultures, and two languages.*
>
> (Samuel Huntington, 2006)[1]

Americans living in smaller U.S. cities like Little Rock, Arkansas, Raleigh, North Carolina, and Omaha, Nebraska, are often surprised to learn that there is a Mexican Consulate in their city. In fact, aside from the obvious locations of consulates, such as New York City, Chicago, and Los Angeles, in 2007 there were 47 Mexican Consulates in cities throughout the U.S. This proliferation of Mexican diplomatic offices across the U.S. reflects the extraordinary increase in Mexican immigrants living in the U.S. There are about 11 million Mexican immigrants in the United States, and another ten million U.S. born Mexican Americans. Mexicans make up nearly two-thirds of the overall group of Hispanic immigrants in the United States, and Hispanics, in turn, account for nearly one-half of all foreign-born residents in the United States.

The rapid growth of immigration to the U.S. from Latin America has increased the overall Hispanic population of the U.S. The social group commonly referred to as Hispanics includes all immigrants from Latin American countries and their offspring. So large has been recent Hispanic immigration to the U.S. that, in 2002, Hispanics passed African Americans as the largest minority ethnic group in

---

Ö.B. Bodvarsson and H. Van den Berg, *The Economics of Immigration*,
DOI: 10.1007/978-3-540-77796-0_12, © Springer-Verlag Berlin Heidelberg 2009

Table 12.1 Estimates of Hispanic population in the United States: 2000 and 2005

	Census 2000[a]	%	2005 Community survey[b]	%
Total Hispanic	35,305,818	100.0	41,926,302	100.0
Mexican	20,640,711	58.5	26,784,268	63.9
Puerto Rican	3,406,178	9.6	3,794,776	9.1
Cuban	1,241,685	3.5	1,462,593	3.5
Dominican	764,945	2.2	1,135,756	2.7
Central American	1,686,937	4.8	3,114,877	7.4
Costa Rican	68,588	0.2	111,978	0.3
Guatemalan	372,487	1.1	780,191	1.9
Honduran	217,569	0.6	466,843	1.1
Nicaraguan	177,684	0.5	275,126	0.7
Panamanian	91,723	0.3	141,286	0.3
Salvadoran	655,165	1.9	1,240,031	3.0
South American	1,353,562	3.8	2,237,960	5.3
Argentinean	100,864	0.3	189,303	0.5
Bolivian	42,068	0.1	68,649	0.2
Chilean	68,849	0.2	105,141	0.3
Colombian	470,684	1.3	723,596	1.7
Ecuadorian	260,559	0.7	432,068	1.0
Peruvian	233,926	0.7	415,352	1.0
Uruguayan	18,804	0.1	51,646	0.1
Venezuelan	91,507	0.3	162,762	0.4
Other	57,532	0.2	89,443	0.2
All Other[c]	6,211,800	17.6	3,396,072	8.1

[a]Table 3 from Suro (2002).
[b]Pew Hispanic Center tabulations of the Census Bureau's 2005 American Community Survey, reported in "A Statistical Portrait of Hispanics at Mid-Decade," downloaded from http://pewhispanic.org/docs/December 1, 2007
[c]This category includes Hispanics from other Caribbean countries and people who define themselves as Hispanics or Latinos without specifying any Hispanic country. Such general classifications are more common on voluntary Census returns than in the Community Survey interviews.

the U.S. In that year, the U.S. Census Bureau estimated that there were about 37 million Hispanics in the U.S., compared to 36.1 million African Americans.[2] Table 12.1 details the 2000 U.S. Census data on the Hispanic population.

A controversial book by Samuel Huntington (2004) entitled *Who Are We? The Challenges to America's Identity* reflects the sentiments of some Americans with regard to the large inflow of Spanish speaking immigrants. As the sample quote by Huntington shown at the head of this chapter suggests, Huntington does not view the massive Hispanic immigration to the U.S. favorably. He argues that Hispanic immigrants are less likely than previous immigrants to the U.S. to assimilate, learn

English, and reach income parity with native-born Americans. Huntington is not alone in his views. Hispanic immigration seems to be the focus of the increasingly active opposition to immigration in the U.S., not unlike the anti-immigrant movement in Germany that focuses on the rapid growth of Turkish immigration to Germany or the French opposition to further immigration from North Africa. Sudden large inflows of immigrants from a single foreign culture have always led to resistance in the destination country.

There is little doubt that the current wave of Hispanic immigration to the United States will bring major economic and social changes to both the source and destination countries. It will be a challenge for the U.S. to devise a set of policies to effectively deal with this disruptive but potentially beneficial immigration episode. The difficulties the U.S. Congress faced when it tried to enact practical legislation to modify the country's poorly designed immigration system in 2006 and 2007 underscores the complexity of the issue and the many conflicting interests and views that must be dealt with. From a social scientist's perspective, we can learn a lot from the U.S. experience with Hispanic immigration. Other countries face similar movements of people and clashes of cultures, as evidenced by the conflicts surrounding the growth of the non-Christian population in many European countries. This chapter summarizes what we know about Hispanic immigration to the United States, and it points to where we need further research and analysis.

12.1   The Characteristics of Hispanic Immigration

Immigration to the United States has gone through many different phases. The latest phase, which covers the years since the 1960s, is characterized by a sharp shift in immigration source countries from Europe to Latin America and Asia. Hispanics make up the largest share of new arrivals. Nearly half of all foreign-born persons currently living in the U.S. came from Mexico, Central America, South America, or the Spanish-speaking Caribbean countries. Table 12.2 provides detailed figures for 2005.

Over 30% of foreign-born Americans are natives of Mexico. This is a very high share for one single country. The concentration of the sources of immigration has fueled fears that Hispanics will establish a permanent parallel culture in the United States rather than assimilate into the dominant culture. Recall, again, Huntington's words at the start of the chapter. Many of those who expect Mexican and other Hispanic immigrants to eventually assimilate like all other immigrant groups have done in the past nevertheless still fear that the massive inflow of people from one single foreign country will substantially change American culture.

It is interesting to ask why reactions to Hispanic immigration are so much less favorable than reactions to recent immigration from Asia. Asian immigration to the U.S. does not seem to generate the same emotional response among the native U.S. population that Hispanic immigration does. This is surprising because Asian immigration to the U.S. has grown just as fast as immigration from Hispanic

Table 12.2 Country of birth of foreign-born living in the United States the 20 largest sending countries: 2005

Country	Number	Percent of all Foreign-born	Country	Number	Percent of all Foreign-born
Mexico	10,993,851	30.7	Guatemala	644,669	1.8
Philippines	1,594,805	4.5	Germany	626,504	1.8
India	1,410,731	3.9	Jamaica	579,241	1.6
China	1,202,923	3.4	Colombia	554,821	1.6
Vietnam	1,072,881	3.0	Haiti	483,748	1.4
Korea	993,883	2.8	Poland	449,158	1.3
El Salvador	988,014	2.8	Honduras	387,002	1.1
Cuba	902,448	2.5	Italy	385,973	1.1
Canada	830,300	2.3	Russia	381,169	1.1
Dominican Republic	708,455	2.0	Peru	371,980	1.0
Region/ethnicity					
Total Hispanic	16,840,774	47.1			
South and East Asia	8,385,165	23.4			
Middle East	1,220,776	3.4			
All Other	9,322,888	26.1			
Total foreign born	35,769,603	100.0			

Source: Pew Hispanic Center (2006), "Tabulations using data from the 2005 American Community Survey," October 2006.

countries. Perhaps Asian immigration seems less threatening because its sources are spread evenly among several distinctive cultures. For example, the Philippines, India, China, Vietnam, and South Korea each account for between 3 and 4.5% of foreign-born Americans. Another possible factor is that a greater percentage of Asian immigrants are highly educated professionals while the great majority of Hispanic immigrants are laborers with less than high school education.

Another reason that Hispanic immigration may generate more openly expressed concerns is that it has been highly concentrated in a few states such as California, New York, Florida, and Texas. This geographic concentration effectively amplifies the cultural influence of immigrants in those areas. This is not to say that all Hispanic immigration to these states is from the same countries; Mexican immigrants favor California and Texas, while immigrants from Caribbean countries such as Cuba and the Dominican Republic most often settled in Florida and New York, respectively. Central Americans have favored California. Also, in recent years Hispanic immigrants have increasingly settled in Southern and Midwestern states, where food processing and other manufacturing are concentrated. It is not clear yet whether this wider dispersion of Hispanic immigrants merely makes new regions of the U.S. more aware of immigration or whether it reduces the fear that Hispanic immigration will establish a permanent parallel culture in the U.S.

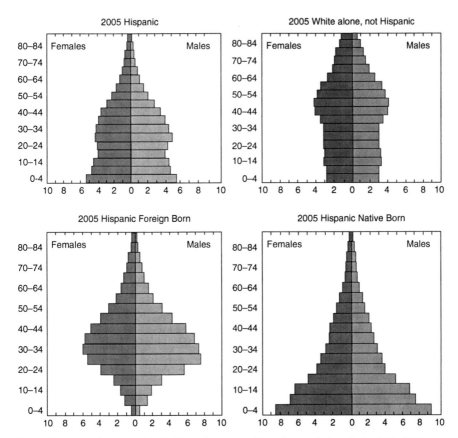

Fig. 12.1 Population pyramids for hispanic and non-hispanic populations in the U.S.: 2005

Hispanic immigrants are disproportionately young and working aged. Figure 12.1 shows the population profiles for foreign-born Hispanics in the lower left-hand diagram and non-Hispanic Americans in the upper right-hand diagram. Compared to the overall U.S. population, very few foreign-born Hispanics are either very young or very old. The great majority of foreign-born Hispanics are of working age. This implies that, all other things equal, Hispanic immigrants are likely to be self-supporting and productive. On the other hand, the lower right-hand diagram in Fig. 12.1 makes it obvious that Hispanic families have more children than Americans, on average. Hence, the U.S.-born Hispanic population is relatively young. With the youth of the native-born Hispanic population, the population profile of the combined foreign-born and native-born Hispanic population in the U.S. is, on average, younger than the overall U.S. population. In a sense, Hispanic immigration has mitigated, at least in part, the problems associated with the ageing of the U.S. population. Compared to most other high income countries, population ageing is not nearly as serious a problem in the U.S.

12.2 Assimilation

Historical evidence suggests that immigrants to the U.S. have almost always assimilated within one or two generations. Even at the previous height of immigration at the start of the twentieth century, when the foreign-born population surpassed 15% of the total population, immigrants quickly moved up to the average income and education levels of the native U.S. population. Blau's (1980) often-referenced study used detailed data for the late nineteenth and early twentieth centuries to determine that immigrants quickly caught up to native-born Americans in income. Equally well-known is Chiswick's (1978) study, which used 1970 Census data to show that immigrants' earnings caught up to, and then exceeded, native-born Americans' average incomes after just 10 or 15 years. These average outcomes do not describe all immigrants a century ago, of course. There were high rates of return immigration after World War I and during the Great Depression, and many immigrants and their descendants remained poor. However, today even the average indicators for immigrant assimilation suggest that the traditional myth of immigrants as anxious to assimilate and become "American" as quickly as possible may be inaccurate.

Perlmann and Waldinger's (1997) statistical analysis shows that in the 1990s the children of immigrants still lagged substantially behind the rest of the U.S. population in education, income, and in terms of other socioeconomic indicators. Perlmann and Waldinger's data on recent immigrants in the U.S. suggest that U.S. immigration from Latin America, and from Mexico in particular, is the main cause of the change in assimilation rates. When they eliminate Mexican immigrants from their sample, they find that the socioeconomic disadvantage among children of immigrants vanishes. Hence, they conclude that Mexican immigrants are somehow different from earlier immigrants to the U.S.

12.2.1 Hispanics' Slow Assimilation

Table 12.3 provides further insight into how Hispanic immigration differs from immigration overall and to other specific groups of immigrants. Notice that, compared to the native population or native households, immigrants and immigrant households from Mexico, Central America, the Caribbean, and South America all have higher concentrations in the lower income categories. Note also that Asian immigrants and immigrant households have higher median incomes and greater concentrations in higher-income brackets compared to the native-born American population and households. Hence, the data indeed suggest that Hispanic immigrants, on average, do not raise their economic status very quickly. Of course, assimilation is never a matter of a few years; it normally takes at least a generation. Hence, the data in Table 12.3 may not be a good indication of assimilation for the large numbers of Hispanic immigrants to the U.S. Also, there are many other

Table 12.3 Personal earnings by region of birth: total population and households, 2005

	Median earnings ($)	Percentages			
		<$20,000	$20,000–$49,999	<$50,000	Total
Total population:					
Native born	28,000	36.3	39.6	24.1	100.0
Foreign born	23,000	42,3	38.4	19.3	100.0
Mexico	17,000	56.7	37.3	5.9	100.0
Asia	30,000	31.3	37.0	31.7	100.0
Caribbean	24,000	39.6	43.7	16.7	100.0
Central America	19,000	52.2	40.0	7.9	100.0
South America	24,000	40.0	43.5	16.5	100.0
Middle East	30,000	33.5	33.3	33.2	100.0
All Other	30,000	31.2	37.4	31.4	100.0

	Median earnings ($)	Percentages				
		<$18,999	$19,000–$35,999	$36,000–$56,499	$56,000–$89,599	<$89,600
Households:						
Native born	46,000	19.6	19.9	20.0	20.3	20.2
Foreign born	42,000	21.1	22.3	20.0	18.0	18.6
Mexico	32,000	24.7	30.7	23.0	14.8	6.9
Asia	59,000	16.5	14.7	17.3	21.1	30.4
Caribbean	36,000	26.7	22.6	19.5	17.2	14.0
Central America	37,000	20.1	27.8	23.6	18.0	10.5
South America	45,000	16.9	22.5	22.7	20.3	17.6
Middle East	49,000	21.0	16.9	17.5	17.4	27.2
All Other	48,000	20.5	18.7	17.9	18.7	24.3

Source: Pew Hispanic Center (2006), "Tabulations using data from the 2005 American Community Survey," October 2006, Tables 24, 25, 28, and 29.

indicators that could be used to show how quickly immigrants assimilate, such as language fluency, mixed marriages, housing, education, and university graduation rates, and we will examine these alternative indicators below.

Research on the assimilation of Mexican Americans in the U.S. shows that new immigrants from Mexico and other Hispanic countries earn substantially less than U.S. natives. But, more ominously, studies such as Livingston and Kahn (2002) find that second generation Mexican Americans only partially catch up to the U.S. average, and third generation Mexican Americans show no further progress at all in catching up. Borjas (1985, 1994) uses evidence of the stalled economic progress after the second generation to argue that "the huge skill differentials observed among today's foreign-born groups become tomorrow's differences among American-born ethnic groups."[3] In short, there is evidence that a permanent gap between Hispanics and other Americans may be in the making.

Trejo (1997, 2003) looks at the causes of the lack of income growth for Mexican immigrants, and he concludes that the differences in income between Mexican Americans and other U.S. residents are largely explained by differences in human capital. In his studies, Trejo provides evidence showing that Mexican Americans do not continue catching up between the second and third generations because they do not continue to increase their relative levels of human capital after the second generation.

Duncan and Trejo (2006) survey the various studies of assimilation by Mexican Americans, and they report that between the first and second generations, average schooling rises by almost four years, and incomes rise by 30%. But then advancement stops, and third generation Mexican Americans still have 1.3 fewer years of education than the average American, and incomes are still about 25% lower. Suro and Passel (2003) examine income and education attainment and find the same pattern of rapid advancement from the first to the second generations of Hispanic immigrants, followed by little change from the second to the third generations. Table 12.4 summarizes the data from a special survey by the U.S. Census Bureau.

When it comes to English language skills, however, Suro and Passel (2003) find a continued improvement in English proficiency from the second to the third generations. While fewer than half of all second generation Hispanic immigrants live in households where English is the dominant language, nearly 80% of third generation Hispanics do. Table 12.5 details the English proficiency of Hispanics. Also, Suro and Passel show that Hispanics do assimilate socially after the second generation. Only 8% of first-generation Hispanics marry someone outside their ethnic group, nearly one-third of second-generation immigrants do, and 57% of third-generation Hispanic immigrants do. Therefore, in terms of this indicator, assimilation is clearly occurring.

Blau and Kahn (2005) use the U.S. Census Bureau's Current Population Survey data for 1994–2003 to distinguish the assimilation of male and female Mexican Americans in order to determine whether gender differences can explain the slow

---

[3]George J. Borjas (1994, p. 1713).

Table 12.4 Educational attainment by region of birth: 2005

	0–9th	9th–12th	H.S. grad.	Some college	College grad	Adv. Degree	Total
				Grades			
Native born	5,858,965	14,461,648	49,204,124	46,578,187	27,906,173	15,670,073	159,679,170
Foreign born	5,931,156	3,528,959	6,702,969	5,286,845	4,577,449	3,224,008	29,251,396
Mexico	3,466,811	1,630,793	1,943,943	854,833	280,827	122,158	8,299,365
Asia	652,306	478,827	1,223,479	1,320,985	2,039,894	1,455,359	7,170,850
Caribbean	404,628	369,608	795,732	640,336	326,979	183,661	2,720,944
Central America	646,885	343,244	490,353	334,400	143,590	52,628	2,011,100
South America	177,529	180,631	574,458	487,564	363,522	204,154	1,987,858
Middle East	86,164	64,236	210,685	202,084	258,214	208,729	1,030,112
All other	496,843	461,620	1,464,319	1,446,643	1,164,423	997,319	6,030,167
Percentages							
Native born	3.7	9.1	30.8	29.2	17.5	9.8	100.0
Foreign born	20.3	12.1	22.9	18.1	15.6	11.0	100.0
Mexico	41.8	19.6	23.4	10.3	3.4	1.5	100.0
Asia	9.1	6.7	17.1	18.4	28.4	20.3	100.0
Caribbean	14.9	13.6	29.2	23.5	12.0	6.7	100.0
Central America	32.2	17.1	24.4	16.6	7.1	2.6	100.0
South America	8.9	9.1	28.9	24.5	18.3	10.3	100.0
Middle East	8.4	6.2	20.5	19.6	25.1	20.3	100.0
All other	8.2	7.7	24.3	24.0	19.3	16.5	100.0

Source: Pew Hispanic Center (2006), "Tabulations using data from the 2005 American Community Survey," October 2006.

Table 12.5 English ability by age and region at birth: 2005

	Under 18			18 and Over		
	English only	Good English	Poor English	English only	Good English	Poor English
Native born	41,842,908	6,339,110	1,843,144	168,615,187	11,150,979	2,868,618
Foreign born	432,483	1,386,672	990,687	5,188,381	9,930,344	17,497,743
Mexico	20,623	522,429	544,398	333,451	1,883,592	7,570,231
Asia	117,491	263,650	154,254	787,944	3,192,561	3,782,550
Caribbean	50,884	83,931	51,842	1,004,435	716,043	1,228,361
Central America	16,578	72,820	70,230	136,374	608,609	1,581,855
South America	33,643	133,570	53,641	357,368	712,111	1,129,759
Middle East	10,805	54,386	20,409	139,904	551,051	430,431
All Other	182,459	255,886	95,913	2,428,905	2,266,376	1,774,556
Percentages						
Native born	83.6	12.7	3.7	92.3	6.1	1.6
Foreign born	15.4	49.4	35.3	15.9	30.4	53.6
Mexico	1.9	48.0	50.1	3.4	19.2	77.3
Asia	21.9	49.2	28.8	10.1	41.1	48.7
Caribbean	27.3	45.0	27.8	34.1	24.3	41.7
Central America	10.4	45.6	44.0	5.9	26.2	68.0
South America	15.2	60.5	24.3	16.2	32.4	51.4
Middle East	12.6	63.5	23.8	12.5	49.1	38.4
All Other	34.2	47.9	18.0	37.5	35.0	27.4

Source: Pew Hispanic Center (2006), "Tabulations using data from the 2005 American Community Survey," October 2006.

assimilation in terms of income. They find that immediately after immigrating to the U.S., Mexican male and female immigrants both work fewer hours per week than their average U.S. counterparts. But, in terms of hours worked they catch up within 20 years. Wages received remain far below the national average for Mexican immigrants, however, and this differential shrinks only with the second generation Mexican Americans for both men and women, largely because of increased levels of education. However, as other studies have found, there is little further improvement in education, labor supply, or wages beyond the second generation.

Mexican immigrants are more likely to be married than Americans overall, and fertility levels also exceed U.S. averages for women. Marriage rates remain above the U.S. average through the third generation, and while female fertility declines by the third generation, it remains above the U.S. average. Blau and Kahn (2005) conclude that Mexican American families continue to exhibit a family structure more similar to Mexican families than American families. Again, it appears as though Mexican Americans do not assimilate as fast as previous immigrant groups have done. Table 12.6 presents data from the Census Bureau's 2005 community Survey that support the conclusions by Blau and Kahn.

12.2.2 Further Reasons Why Hispanic Assimilation is Slow

Hispanic immigrants appear to be less entrepreneurial than other immigrant groups or Americans in general. Combined with the lower levels of education of Hispanic immigrants, the below average levels of entrepreneurial activity further reduce Hispanics' access to the traditional routes that past immigrants have used to quickly reach average U.S. income levels. Fairlie and Woodruff (2006) find that only 6% of Mexican immigrants to the United States are self-employed. This outcome contrasts sharply with other immigrant groups to the U.S., which all exhibit self-employment rates more similar to native country self-employment rates. Interestingly, Mexican immigrants' low rate of self-employment also contrasts sharply with the very high rate of self-employment in Mexico. Mexico has the highest self-employment rate of 28 OECD countries, and it is ranked fourth among a larger sample of 41 countries by the Global Entrepreneurship Monitor (2003).[4] Yuengert (1995) reports that across all immigrant groups, self-employment rates are usually positively correlated with native country rates. This relationship does not hold for Hispanic immigrants to the United States, however.

The drastic fall in self-employment when Mexicans and other Hispanics cross the U.S. border begs for an explanation. At the very least, the phenomenon suggests that Mexican American immigrants and their children face barriers to entrepreneurship. Perhaps the lack of self-employment is due to the high percentage of unauthorized immigrants among Hispanic immigrants; unauthorized immigrants do not have

---

[4]Reported in Fairlie and Woodruff (2006).

Table 12.6 Family structure of U.S. immigrants by region of birth: 2005

	Family household			Non-family household	Total
	Married couple	Female head only	Male head only		
Native born	158,063,089	40,142,786	12,818,558	41,604,783	252,629,216
Foreign born	23,367,506	4,463,987	3,165,419	4,772,691	35,769,603
Mexico	7,179,023	1,471,870	1,399,503	943,455	10,993,851
Asia	6,110,777	744,171	507,797	1,022,420	8,385,165
Caribbean	1,675,811	732,483	252,695	489,803	3,150,792
Central America	1,385,611	435,377	371,817	316,521	2,509,326
South America	1,489,419	357,092	235,919	353,848	2,436,278
Middle East	853,719	92,373	97,132	177,552	1,220,776
All Other	4,673,146	630,621	300,556	1,469,092	7,073,415
Percentages of population					
Native born	62.6	15.9	5.1	16.5	100.0
Foreign born	65.3	12.5	8.8	13.3	100.0
Mexico	65.3	13.4	12.7	8.6	100.0
Asia	72.9	8.9	6.1	12.2	100.0
Caribbean	53.2	23.2	8.0	15.5	100.0
Central America	55.2	17.4	14.8	12.6	100.0
South America	61.1	14.7	9.7	14.5	100.0
Middle East	69.9	7.6	8.0	14.5	100.0
All Other	66.1	8.9	4.2	20.8	100.0
Percentages of households					
Native born	49.2	12.4	4.1	34.3	100.0
Foreign born	55.8	13.4	7.6	23.1	100.0
Mexico	60.2	14.9	11.7	13.3	100.0
Asia	63.3	9.2	5.2	22.2	100.0
Caribbean	42.3	24.2	6.9	26.6	100.0
Central America	49.5	19.5	12.1	18.9	100.0
South America	50.8	16.6	8.7	23.9	100.0
Middle East	60.1	7.5	7.1	25.4	100.0
All Other	51.6	9.2	3.7	35.5	100.0

Source: Pew Hispanic Center (2006), "Tabulations using data from the 2005 American Community Survey," October 2006, Tables 15 and 16.

access to bank financing, they cannot acquire the required permits and licenses to operate businesses, and they cannot use the courts to protect themselves against fraud, theft, and delinquent payments. Or, the lack of self-employment and, presumably, entrepreneurship may itself be a direct result of the slow assimilation of Hispanics into U.S. society.

The low rate of self-employment among Hispanics not only contributes to Hispanics' lack of income mobility, it may also be preventing the U.S. economy from gaining the full growth dividend from immigration. Recall from Chap. 9 that Joseph Schumpeter considered the entrepreneur as something of a social deviant because his or her attitude was different from the average member of society. Schumpeter pointed out that entrepreneurs were often recent immigrants because immigrants tend to be less attached to the traditions of society and, therefore, less reluctant to innovate. Furthermore, through natural selection, immigrants tend to be people who are more willing to take risks in exchange for potential future gains. Chiswick (2000) wrote that immigrants self-select in terms of personal characteristics favorable to economic growth: "The greater the out of pocket (direct) costs of migration and return migration, the greater the effect of ability on lowering the costs of migration, and the smaller are the wage differences by skill in the lower income origin than in the higher income destination." International migration, therefore, provides a natural selection process that distinguishes exceptionally adventuresome and enterprising people.

This discussion suggests that unless the U.S. finds ways to reduce the barriers to entrepreneurship that seem to apply disproportionately to Hispanic immigrants, the U.S. economy will suffer. Assimilation will be slower than necessary, which means that Hispanic immigrants will add less to U.S. output and demand. The barriers to entrepreneurship that Hispanics seem to face imply that the U.S. economy will continue to miss the full growth effect of immigration.

Finally, Lazear (2006) blames Hispanic immigrants' slow assimilation on the way the U.S. has designed its immigration policies. He argues, first of all, that U.S. immigration policy results in a very large proportion of Mexicans and Hispanics entering the country either illegally because of Latin America's proximity to the U.S. and lax U.S. border enforcement. And when Hispanics immigrate legally, it is almost always under the family reunion criterion rather than on the basis of their skills, educational attainment, or job prospects. Both unauthorized immigration and family reunion tend to promote settlement in ethnic enclaves. According to Lazear, the large numbers of Hispanic immigrants means that they live in very large enclaves that encourage immigrants to hold on to their own customs longer and assimilate more slowly than other ethnic groups that begin in small enclaves. There are Spanish language newspapers, radio stations, and television stations in nearly all cities where there are Hispanic enclaves. The larger populations in the Hispanic enclaves also result in more second and third generation Hispanics marrying other Hispanics rather than partners with other ethnic backgrounds.

12.2.3 Perhaps It Is All a Data Problem

Duncan and Trejo (2005) suggest a completely different reason why the data shows Hispanic immigrants to have assimilated so slowly. They argue that the census data used in most studies give an inaccurate impression because the children of mixed parents, e.g., when a Mexican American marries a non-Mexican American, are often not reported as being Mexican Americans. Also, the children of mixed couples most likely assimilate much faster, and such children are increasingly unlikely to classify themselves in the Census as Hispanics. In other words, the data may be tracing mostly the assimilation histories of the children of parents who assimilated less, in part because they married a spouse from the same ethnic group. The Census data are likely to miss many of the children of the parents that assimilated more quickly and found spouses in other ethnic groups. Hence, true assimilation of Mexican Americans is faster and more complete than the Census data suggest.

In a study that pre-dated many of the recent studies which find that assimilation stagnates after the second generation, Jasso and Rosenzweig (1988) used data that tracks individuals over time rather than the standard Census data to argue that assimilation of Hispanics was not any slower than previous large immigrant groups in the early twentieth century. Their time-series data for individual households indicate faster occupational mobility than the Census data suggest.[5]

12.2.4   Political Attitudes of Hispanic Immigrants

The slower assimilation of Hispanic immigrants may be, in part, the result of the strong ties to their native countries that many immigrants maintain. Such ties are often encouraged by the governments of the native countries. In fact, a number of Western Hemisphere countries have recently changed their national laws to encourage permanent immigrants to maintain ties with their native country. In the past, most countries cut off citizenship when citizens immigrate and acquire citizenship in another country, but in recent years Colombia, Ecuador, Brazil, Mexico, and the Dominican Republic, among others, have changed their laws to permit dual citizenship. Mexico even allows former citizens to reclaim Mexican citizenship after they had lost it by becoming citizens in the United States. In 2004, President Fox asked the Mexican Congress to approve letting millions of Mexican citizens living in the United States vote in the 2006 Mexican presidential election.[6] The Mexican state of Zacatecas passed a law in 2003 to let the 800,000 Zacatecans who now live in the United States run for local political office.[7] The President of the Dominican Republic in 2004, himself a former resident of New York, attributed his electoral victory to the huge number of votes by Dominicans living in New York who, like Mexicans living abroad, had gained the right to vote in their native country.[8]

A 2004 Pew Hispanic Center survey of Mexican immigrants who visited a Mexican consulate in the U.S. to apply for a *matricula consular*, an identity card issued by the Mexican government that helps unauthorized immigrants open a U.S. bank account, acquire medical services in the U.S., and provide proof of age,

---

[5]Jasso and Rosenzweig (1988).

[6]Weiner (2004).

[7]Authers (2004).

[8]Bernstein (2004).

suggests that many Mexican immigrants living in the U.S. intend to continue voting in Mexican elections.[9] Nearly 9 out of 10(87%) respondents said they would vote in the next elections if they could. Granted, the survey sample was biased; Mexican immigrants who seek a *matricula consular* are almost always unauthorized immigrants who cannot obtain U.S. identity documents. On average, unauthorized immigrants are less likely to assimilate because they face many barriers to jobs, education, and social organizations.[10]

These suggestions that today's Hispanic immigrants are less likely to assimilate than earlier U.S. immigrants should be kept in perspective, however. The fact is that newly arriving immigrants to the U.S. have always maintained close ties with their native countries. Most immigrant communities a century ago had newspapers in the native languages of immigrants, ethnic food stores and restaurants, and clubs and associations organized along national lines. When radio became a dominant medium in the early twentieth century, foreign language programs were regularly broadcast in cities with significant immigrant enclaves. There was a Hibernian Hall in most cities of the U.S. Northeast where Irish immigrants met. The Sons of Italy sponsored sports and social activities for Italian immigrants in many of the same cities. Of course, many churches and other religious organizations established in the U.S. reflected specific national origins and ethnic traditions. In any case, the high rates of return immigration discussed in Chap. 10 suggest that in the nineteenth and early twentieth centuries cultural and family ties to the homeland often trumped assimilation.

12.3   Geographic Diffusion

One common characteristic of immigration is that immigrants tend to cluster together in the destination countries, often in what become easily identifiable ethnic communities. In the United States, Hispanic immigrants have tended to also cluster in certain urban areas and certain states. What is also well known is that Hispanic immigrants from specific towns and regions of their native countries cluster together in specific towns and regions in the United States.

12.3.1   Networks and Herding

An accepted explanation for clustering is the presence of network externalities. In the case of immigration, earlier immigrants provide assistance to new immigrants, and previous immigrants can provide trusted information about the destination to

---

[9]Suro (2005).
[10]As quoted in Pascal (1998).

other immigrants. Bauer, Epstein, and Gang (2002) differentiate between network effects and what they call *herding behavior*. They define immigrant network effects as immigrants deciding "I will go to where my people are, since it will help me." Herding behavior, on the other hand, implies immigrants tell themselves: "I will go to where I have observed others go, because all these others who went before me probably have information that I do not have, even though I would have chosen independently to go elsewhere." Herding behavior effectively assumes that people have little confidence in their own information, and they feel that others' information must be better than theirs. In either case, networks or herding, immigrants from the same source countries tend to concentrate in certain communities, states, or regions. Hispanic immigrants have certainly done this, as suggested in Table 12.7.

Bauer, Epstein, and Gang examine data for Mexican immigrants to the United States to test for the relative importance of herding and network effects in determining immigrant location decisions. They label as herding the practice of natives from the same local community following fellow community members to specific locations in the U.S. Network externalities are measured by the share of Mexican immigrants in the population of a specific community in the U.S. Bauer, Epstein, and Gang find that both herding and network effects matter; one reinforces the other. The network effect is not linear, however. Network effects expand immigration to a specific community up to where Mexicans account for about 10% of the community's population, after which the strength of network externalities declines. The network effect is U-shaped, therefore. Herding effects are similarly U-shaped. In addition, network and herding effects are significantly stronger for illegal immigrants and poorly-educated immigrants.

12.3.2   Towards the South and the Midwest

There has been a noticeable diffusion of Hispanic immigrants to a more diverse set of destinations in recent years. Kochlar, Suro, and Tafoya (2005) report that the Hispanic population is growing faster in the Southern states than anywhere else in the United States. Table 12.8 presents some of these authors' data showing that the highest growth rates of Hispanic immigration were in Southern states. They describe how the economies in the South and the Midwest are changing rapidly, and they are growing rapidly as well: "Such conditions have acted as a magnet to young, male, foreign-born Latinos migrating in search of economic opportunities."

Card and Lewis (2005) analyze the spread of Mexican immigrants beyond the traditional destination cities in California and Texas to "new" destinations like Atlanta, Georgia, Denver, Colorado, Portland, Oregon, and Raleigh-Durham, North Carolina. They are surprised by how these flows to "new" destinations parallel the growth of employment without very large changes in wage rates in those destination economies. Card and Lewis conclude that they are "left with the 'puzzle' of explaining the remarkable flexibility of employment demand in different cities to local variations in supply." Is this a case of immigrants arriving and jobs then

Table 12.7 Foreign born by state and region of birth: 2005

State	Percent of all Foreign born	Percentage of region of birth						
		Mexico	Asia	Caribbean	Central America	South America	Middle East	All Other
California	27.0	38.8	34.3	2.2	31.4	9.0	30.0	15.1
New York	11.1	1.8	10.1	30.7	9.5	23.2	12.0	14.3
Texas	9.9	20.6	6.2	1.6	10.9	3.8	4.7	4.1
Florida	9.0	2.6	2.9	39.6	11.9	2.4	5.0	7.6
Illinois	4.8	6.4	4.4	0.9	1.7	2.2	4.3	6.3
New Jersey	4.6	0.8	5.3	8.0	4.3	11.2	5.6	5.9
Massachusetts	2.5	0.1	2.5	4.3	2.3	5.3	2.7	4.6
Arizona	2.4	5.3	1.0	0.3	0.9	0.6	1.1	1.8
Georgia	2.2	2.5	2.1	1.7	2.2	2.4	1.3	2.3
Washington	2.1	1.8	3.2	0.2	0.6	0.5	1.3	3.5
All Other States[a]	24.4	19.3	28.0	10.5	24.3	39.4	32	34.5
Total	100.0	100.0	100.0	100.0	100.0	100.0	100.0	100.0

[a]Calculated as the sum of the percentages of the ten states shown minus 100

Source: Pew Hispanic Center (2006), "Tabulations using data from the 2005 American Community Survey, October 2006.

Table 12.8 Hispanic population change in the U.S: 1990–2000

	Hispanics 1990	Hispanics 2000	% Change
6 Southern states	293,445	1,195,800	308
North Carolina	76,726	378,963	394
Arkansas	19,876	86,866	337
Georgia	108,922	435,227	300
Tennessee	32,741	123,838	278
South Carolina	30,551	95,076	211
Alabama	24,629	75,830	208
Traditional settlement states	11,546,271	16,481,592	43
Carolina	7,687,938	10,966,556	43
New York	2,214,026	2,867,583	30
Illinois	904,446	1,530,262	69
New Jersey	739,861	1,117,191	51

Source: Table 2 from Kochlar, Suro, and Tafoya (2005).

suddenly appearing to employ them? Or do the immigrants respond quickly to the opening of new jobs in these "new" destination cities?

12.3.3 The Dispersal of Manufacturing Jobs and Immigrant Dispersal

This dispersal of the growing number of Hispanic immigrants is not such a puzzle when it is viewed in light of the gradual shifts in manufacturing activity in the U.S. over the past half century. Hispanic immigrants have largely followed the dispersion of manufacturing activity to rural areas in the South, Midwest, and Great Plains regions. The current shift of manufacturing from the traditional manufacturing centers to rural regions of the American Midwest and Great Plains is fundamentally a continuation of the earlier trends that saw manufacturing shift from the traditional urban centers of the Northeast and North central regions of the country toward those regions in the South where wages are lower and unions are less powerful. The current growth of manufacturing in traditionally agricultural communities is also being driven by the arrival of foreign firms setting up manufacturing in the U.S. for the first time. These foreign *greenfield* investments similarly seek low labor costs, lower living costs for prospective employees, and business friendly environments.

This geographic shift in manufacturing has been well documented and studied. However, commentators and researchers have largely overlooked a very important detail about the growth of manufacturing in rural America: The revival of the rural South, Midwest, and Great Plains depends on foreign immigrants. The people moving in to take the new manufacturing jobs are often recent immigrants, and a substantial portion of them are undocumented. Rural communities in the United States enjoy a comparative advantage in infrastructure and location; the United

States' modern transportation infrastructure places most rural communities within the distribution systems serving the U.S. market for most products. The only thing lacking in these communities is a large labor force. Immigration effectively provides this missing labor force. The fact that it is manufacturing that is driving the immigration flows is compatible with the observation that the "new" immigrant destinations are not seeing a reduction in white and black populations; to the contrary, the main immigrant destinations are experiencing increases in new black and white populations as well. For example, Kochlar, Suro, and Tafoya (2005) report that even in the six Southern states, where Hispanic populations grew so rapidly, white and black populations still grew by 11 and 21%, respectively, from much higher bases over the same 1990–2000 period.

It is immigration that is the key to the growth of manufacturing in rural communities in the U.S. There is a seemingly endless "reserve army of labor" in the developing economies of the world. Their distant locations, poorly developed transportation systems, and lack of human and physical capital are all factors that have kept returns to labor very low in those countries. Failing institutions, furthermore, cause economic failures and unemployment. Modern communications and cheap transport make it increasingly possible for labor to move across borders in response to wage differences. Hence, producers prefer to operate in the U.S. where infrastructure is ample and distances to markets are short.

Our broad model of technological progress and shifting production patterns suggests that rural communities in areas like Appalachia and the Great Plains would not be able to reverse their declines without immigration. Indeed, if manufacturing continues to face increasing labor costs in the highly agglomerated urban regions of the United States, manufacturers and producers of services will increasingly look to lower cost locations. If low cost labor is not available somewhere within the U.S., the likelihood increases that manufacturing will instead move to China, India, or Brazil. In this case, the rural economies of Appalachia and the Great Plains will not enjoy their revival, and their economic decline will continue. The U.S. will have a smaller population as a result, and geographic agglomeration will likely actually increase. Overall U.S. GDP will be lower, and the Americans working in the agglomerated sectors will have lower incomes.

The U.S. press has been full of stories about the changes brought to the "new" immigrant destinations. For example, *The Wall Street Journal* described Dalton, Georgia, the home of three major carpet manufacturing plants, Shaw Industries Inc., Mohawk Industries Inc., and Beaulieu of America LLC. Job opportunities for immigrants are plentiful in Dalton. The U.S. carpet industry faces a situation similar to that of many U.S. industries faced with international competition and an increasingly scarce native work force:

> It didn't make sense to leave. Carpet mills here have made huge investment in giant tufting machines that stitch yarn into plastic backing and dye tanks that soak color into bolts of weave the length of football fields. If the mills cut labor costs by moving offshore, they'd still face the extra expense of shipping heavy carpet back to their major market. Dalton is within a 24-hour drive of about 85% of all U.S. buyers. Industry consolidation over the past two decades strengthened carpet makers' ties to the area, not only making Dalton a

one-industry town but also making Dalton a one-town industry. So, with the industry's roots entrenched, Mexico has come to Dalton.[11]

The community is changing along with the carpet industry's workforce. In 2000, one-third of the children born in Dalton's Hamilton Medical Center were from Hispanic families. There were 12,000 Hispanics in Dalton in 2000, and they have become noticeable in the community:

> The sights and sounds of rural Mexico are everywhere along Dalton's main drag, Walnut Street, where accordion-rich music from Mexico's north blares from quick-stop taco shops. Poster and fliers in Spanish tout at least 10 different agencies offering ways for recent migrants to send money home. Each morning, a refrigerator truck of an Atlanta-based food distributor, Al Maizal, darts in and out of the local strip malls, stocking more than two dozen Mexican restaurants and convenience stores. Florists, funeral homes and pharmacies all promise walk-in customers that "se habla espanol"[12]

Not everyone in Dalton is happy about the changes their community is going through. Some years ago, the local newspaper had to stop running letters to the editor about immigration because the tone had gotten too angry. "Quit employing them, quit renting to them, quit educating them," wrote one local citizen back in 1995. In 2005, over half the incoming kindergarten students were Hispanic.

12.4   Explaining Hispanic Immigration

According to Card and Lewis (2005), Mexican immigration to the U.S. was driven, on the supply side, by population growth, falling real wages, and persistently weak economic conditions in Mexico. They also point out that immigrants tend to follow prior immigrants from the same cities and regions, and they find that prior immigrants also explain the supply of Mexican immigrants to the various regions of the U.S. On the demand side, they hypothesize that immigrants are attracted by employment and wages. They find that supply side factors explain 75% of the variation in immigration, demand factors only another 10%. In fact, they find that after 1990, demand factors are not significant in explaining inflows of Mexican immigrants; only supply push and prior flows determine immigrant inflows into specific counties in the U.S. Similarly, Richter, Taylor, and Yunes-Naude (2006) find that the effects of changes in U.S. immigration policy or macroeconomic conditions on Mexican immigration to the U.S. are small compared to the network effects.

There were some special events that help to explain the surge in Hispanic immigration to the U.S. For example, Martin (2004) describes how unauthorized immigration from Mexico to the United States grew after the ratification of the North American Free Trade Agreement (NAFTA) because free trade in corn pushed

---

[11]Millman and Pinkston (2001).
[12]Millman and Pinkston (2001).

many Mexican farmers off the land. Corn production in Mexico had been protected from imports, and a domestic price twice the world price had for years served as a social safety net in rural Mexico. When NAFTA came into effect in the mid-1990s, Mexico had about 3 million corn farmers. This compared to the 75,000 corn farmers in just the state of Iowa in the United States, who produced nearly twice as much corn as Mexico at half the price. In part, the U.S. price of corn was low because of the U.S. government's direct subsidies and years of indirect subsidies through technical extension services and federally funded university research. It was not long after the establishment of free trade between the U.S. and Mexico that Mexican corn farmers abandoned their farms in great numbers. Many of these farmers migrated to the United States, most illegally. Richter, Taylor, and Yunez-Naude (2006) dispute this explanation of unauthorized Mexican immigration, however. Their statistical results do not give NAFTA a major role in driving Mexican immigration to the United States; as reported above, they find that overall macroeconomic trends in Mexico and the U.S. and immigrant network effects dominate in explaining immigrant flows.

12.4.1 The Welfare Effects on the Source Hispanic Countries

There has been little analysis of how the large outflows of Hispanic immigrants to the U.S. have affected the source economies. Clearly, the large numbers of people involved suggest that the effects of the departure of so many people must have been substantial. For example, since the civil war in the 1980s, the rise in crime, and the brutal government crackdowns on dissent in El Salvador, over 15% of that Central American country has moved to the United States. Table 12.1 showed that there are about 11 million Mexican-born immigrants in the United States; that is more than 10% of Mexico's current population.

Mishra (2006) applied immigration data for 1970 through 2000 in a standard theoretical framework, similar to the immigration model used throughout this book. She concludes that the departure of Mexican immigrants to the U.S. raised the wage of the average Mexican remaining in Mexico by about 8%. The wage effects differ greatly depending on Mexicans' levels of education, however. The wages of Mexicans with less than a high school education rose by only 5%, while the wages of high school graduates rose by about 15%. The reason for this disparity in wage effects is that a higher proportion of the relatively small group of high school graduates left the country. The great majority of Mexican immigrants have less than a high school education, but an even greater majority of all Mexicans have not graduated from high school. Mishra also calculates that the overall effect of Mexican immigration to the United States is to reduce Mexico's 2000 GDP of $580 billion by about one-half of 1%, or $3 billion. The gain for workers staying behind is 5.9% of GDP, and the loss to the owners of the fixed factors is about 6.4% of GDP. In terms of the standard labor market model of immigration for the source

country, which was illustrated in Fig. I.4 in the Introduction to Part I, p. 24, the area
e = 5.9% of GDP, and the sum of e + g = 6.4% of Mexican GDP.

12.4.2 The Demand Effects of Hispanic Immigration

The theoretical models of immigration discussed in earlier chapters suggest that
immigrants have labor and product demand effects, as well as labor supply and
complementary factor supply effects. The 41 million Hispanics in the United States
clearly constitute a very large ethnic market. Spending by Hispanic households is
estimated to exceed 8% of total household spending in the U.S. The size of this
market will continue to grow with the above average birth rates for Hispanics in the
U.S. Also, as incomes rise from first- to second-generation Hispanic immigrants,
the market grows further. And, it will grow if Hispanic immigration to the U.S.
continues growing.

It is interesting to note that marketers have suddenly recognized the importance
of the Hispanics' product demand effect on the U.S. economy. The Bank of
America Corp. has begun offering credit cards to customers without social security
numbers. Advertising revenue at Univision, the large U.S. Spanish language television network, and its smaller rival Telemundo grew by over 20% per year in the
early 2000s, about double the increase of overall television advertising revenue in
the U.S. Marketers have been especially keen to identify themselves with Mexican
holidays such as *Cinco de Mayo*. Corona beer, the Mexican brand that sells as a
premium beer in the U.S., now uses cinco de Mayo to tout its Mexican heritage to
all U.S. consumers, spending over $2 million during the first week of May alone.[13]
Sears, Roebuck & Co. has recently begun to shift advertising expenditures from
Cinco de Mayo to Mexican Independence Day on September 16 because it felt
Cinco de Mayo was becoming too much of an "American" holiday, much the way
St. Patrick's Day or Oktoberfest are enthusiastically celebrated by Americans of all
ethnic backgrounds.[14] Clearly, even though the simple labor market model of
immigration does not recognize the growth in demand after the arrival of immi-
grants, the firms that supply the U.S. market certainly do.

12.5 Future Hispanic Immigration

Mexico's Ministry of the Interior did a study on the future of Mexican immigration
to the United States. This study, prepared by the Ministry's Consejo Nacional de
Población (2001), provided alternative estimates under different assumptions about

economic growth in Mexico and the U.S. as well as different assumptions about future population growth in Mexico. The study concludes that with rapid economic growth in Mexico and moderate growth in the demand for labor in the U.S., Mexican immigration to the U.S. will remain steady at about 400,000 per year. Such annual flows of immigrants imply that another 10 million Mexican immigrants will arrive in the U.S. by the year 2030. On the other hand, slow economic growth in Mexico and robust labor demand in the U.S. would swell Mexican immigration to over half a million per year by 2030.

The study's conclusions reflect some of the empirical studies of Hispanic immigration discussed earlier in this chapter:

> The narrow range in which these situations vary indicate that other factors closely related to the migration tradition of more than 100 years and the operation of complex social networks are apparently more determinative of international emigration than the impact of economic fluctuations in the labor markets in both countries.[15]

In other words, most future immigrant flows from Mexico to the U.S. are inevitable. Simcox (2002) attributes the government study's conclusions to international politics: the alleged inevitability of more immigration could be used by Mexico to pressure the U.S. government into adapting a more comprehensive immigration policy that permits more Mexicans to enter the U.S. legally. However, the Mexican government's study does not conflict with existing evidence on immigration.

12.5.1 Will Hispanic Immigration Continue?

Not all studies predict continually increasing immigration flows from Mexico and other Latin American countries. The fact is that population growth in Latin America is slowing rapidly. This means that 20 years from now, there will be fewer young workers. As already pointed out at the start of this chapter, Hispanic immigrants to the U.S. are disproportionately young and of working age, which has to some degree mitigated the problems associated with the ageing of U.S. society. But, it appears that Hispanic countries will not have as many young people to send to the U.S. in the future. Also, the currently young Hispanic population will age too, and Hispanics will eventually reach retirement age.

Table 12.9 presents alternative estimates of the future size of the Hispanic population in the U.S. by Roberto Suro and Jeffrey Passel of the Pew Hispanic Center. The number of Hispanic immigrants is predicted to continue growing, and the growth is spread across first, second, and third generation Hispanics. These predictions suggest that Hispanics will have a strong impact on the U.S. economy and U.S. society in the future. The growing size of the Hispanic community in the U.S. will, no doubt, lead to increased interest in assimilation. Time will tell whether the Hispanic population in the U.S. will increase its rate of assimilation or whether

---

[15]Quote is a translation provided in Simcox (2002).

Table 12.9 Alternative immigration scenarios for Hispanics: 2000–2020

	Total Hispanic	1st generation	2nd generation	3rd generation
Mid-range estimate:				
2000	35,306,000	14,158,000	9,887,000	11,261,000
2010	47,696,000	18,126,000	15,404,000	14,167,000
2020	60,424,000	20,555,000	21,659,000	18,210,000
High-range Estimate:				
2000	35,306,000	14,158,000	9,887,000	11,261,000
2010	51,013,000	20,761,000	16,086,000	14,167,000
2020	67,282,000	25,090,000	23,970,000	18,221,000

Source: Table 3 from Suro and Passel (2003).

the sheer size of the Hispanic community will continue to hamper the assimilation process.

12.5.2   Temporary Immigration Programs

There have been suggestions that the U.S. should combat unauthorized immigration by instituting temporary immigration programs, such as the Bracero Program after World War II. Temporary immigration programs in Europe ended up increasing the permanent immigrant populations of many European countries, however. In order to assess whether temporary worker programs in the U.S. will end up reducing the unauthorized entry of Hispanic immigrants without adding to the further growth of the permanent Hispanic population, it is informative to look at a recent opinion survey of Hispanic immigrants by the Pew Hispanic Center described in Suro (2005).

The survey covers a large number of Mexican immigrants who visited a Mexican consulate in the U.S. in 2004 in order to apply for a *matricula consular*, the widely used identity card issued by the Mexican government. Most Mexicans applying for such cards are unauthorized immigrants unable to gain U.S. documents. Therefore, the survey clearly presents a biased sample of Mexican immigrants. Mexicans who would normally immigrate illegally would be the primary applicants for temporary work visas if they were made available.

The survey results show that by a 4 to 1 margin, respondents said they would participate in a temporary worker program that would allow Mexicans to work in the U.S. for a limited number of years and then return permanently to Mexico. Yet, 42% of the respondents replied they would stay in the U.S. "As long as I can" and another 17% said they wanted to stay "for the rest of my life." Only 27% said they intended to stay for less than 5 years. About three out of four respondents said they would participate in a program that offered the prospect of permanent legalization of unauthorized immigrants. In short, one could reasonably expect that many participants in any temporary immigration scheme would do what they could to remain in the U.S. when their temporary permit expired. Like what happened in Europe in the 1960s, many guest workers would become permanent residents and citizens.

12.6   Conclusions

This chapter has presented some of the exceptional characteristics of the recent Hispanic immigration to the United States. In 2005, there were nearly 40 million Hispanic immigrants and descendants of Hispanic immigrants living in the U.S. The assimilation experience of this large cultural group does not seem to have followed the path past immigrants to the U.S. followed, and even most third generation Hispanics in the U.S. still find themselves with income and education levels substantially below the U.S. averages. Some forecasts predict that as many as 60 million Hispanics will be living in the U.S. by 2020. It is no wonder that many Americans worry about the cultural effects of Hispanic immigration.

Few other countries in the world are experiencing such a large inflows of people from a single foreign culture. Even if we recognize, and we should, that not all Hispanics are similar, it is still the case that nearly 60% of all Hispanic immigrants and descendants are from a single country, Mexico. Sociologists have studied Hispanic immigration much more thoroughly than economists because the cultural implications are so important. However, economists also need to pay more attention to Hispanic immigration because the size of Hispanic immigration implies that assimilation is likely to be much slower than would normally be the case for smaller immigrant groups. The slower pace of assimilation has very real economic implications. Also, the expansion of Hispanic ethnic enclaves has clear demand side implications. American business has already effectively recognized this in the form of more focused marketing aimed at the Hispanic market. It may also be interesting to study whether the predominantly Hispanic immigration to the United States brings substantially different outcomes compared to the more diverse immigration into the high income countries of Europe and to Canada or the greater Asian immigration flows to Australia, for example. In any case, the study of Hispanic immigration should not belong exclusively to sociologists.

Finally, the following quote helps to keep the often-emotional discussions of Hispanic immigration in a broader perspective:

> Few of their children in the country learn English ... The signs in our streets have inscriptions in both languages ... Unless the stream of their importation could be turned they will soon so outnumber us that all the advantages we have will not be able to preserve our language, and even our government will become precarious.[16]

These words seem to represent the sentiments often displayed toward Hispanic immigration by commentators and Americans on the street. You will be interested to know that they were written nearly 250 years ago by Benjamin Franklin!

---

[16]Benjamin Franklin, quoted in Kenneth C. Davis (2007).

Franklin was referring to German immigrants who had arrived in Pennsylvania in the 1750s! Those German immigrants, or at least their descendants, were eventually fully absorbed into U.S. society, and few Americans today could imagine why anyone would make such a fuss about German immigrants. Time will tell whether the fear that pervades discussions of Hispanic immigrants will eventually be looked back on as having been just as misguided as Benjamin Franklin's assessment of the Germans in eighteenth century Pennsylvania.

References

Authers, J. (2004, 1 July). Tomato King looks to make mark for Mexican migrants. *Financial Times.*

Bauer, T., Epstein, G., & Gang, I. N. (2002). Herd effects or migration networks? The location choice of Mexican immigrants in the U.S. IZA Discussion Paper No. 551, August.

Bernstein, N. (2004, 5 December). Dominican President visits, reaching out to diaspora. *New York Times.*

Blau, F. (1980). Immigration and labor earnings in early twentieth century America. *Research in Population Economics, 2,* 21–41.

Blau, F., & Kahn, L. (2005). Gender and assimilation among Mexican Americans. In G. Borjas (Ed.), *Mexican immigration.* Chicago: University of Chicago Press.

Borjas, G. (1994). The economics of immigration. *Journal of Economic Literature, 32*(4),1667–1717.

Borjas, G. (1985). Assimilation, changes in cohort quality, and the earnings of immigrants. *Journal of Labor Economics, 3,* 463–89.

Card, D., & Lewis, E. (2005). The diffusion of Mexican immigrants during the 1990s: Explanations and impacts. NBER Working Paper No. 11552, August.

Chiswick, B. (1978). The effect of Americanization on the earnings of foreign-born men. *Journal of Political Economy, 86*(5), 897–921.

Chiswick, B. (2000). Are immigrants favorably self-selected? An economic analysis. IZA Discussion Paper No. 131, March, 2000.

Consejo Nacional de Población, Dirección de Communicación Social (2001). *Migración méxico-estados unidos 2001.* Mexico City: November.

Davis, K. C. (2007, 3 July) The founding immigrants. *New York Times.*

Duncan, B., & Trejo, S. (2006). Ethnic identification, intermarriage, and unmeasured progress by Mexican Americans. In G. Borjas, (Ed.), *Mexican immigration.* Chicago: University of Chicago Press.

Fairlie, R., & Woodruff, C. (2006). Mexican entrepreneurship: A comparison of self-employment in Mexico and the United States. In G. Borjas, (Ed.), *Mexican immigration.* Chicago: University of Chicago Press.

Huntington, S. (2004). The Hispanic challenge. *Foreign Policy* March/April.

Jasso, G., & Rosenzweig, M. (1988). How well do U.S. immigrants do? Vintage effects, emigration selectivity, and occupational mobility. *Research in Population Economics, 6,* 229–253.

Kochlar, R., Suro, R., & Tafoya, T. (2005). *The new Latino South: The context and consequences of rapid population growth.* Pew Hispanic Center Report, July 26.

Lazear, E. P. (2006). Mexican assimilation in the United States. In G. Borjas, (Ed.), *Mexican immigration.* Chicago: University of Chicago Press.

Livingston, G., & Kahn, J. (2002). An American dream unfilled: The limited mobility of Mexican Americans. *Social Science Quarterly, 83*(4), 1003–1012.

Martin, P. (2004). Mexican migration to the United States: The effect of NAFTA. Chapter 7 in D. Massey, J. E. & Taylor (Eds.), *International migration: Prospects and policies in a global market* (pp. 120–130). Oxford: Oxford University Press.

Millman, J. (2001, 1 May). U.S. marketers adopt cinco de mayo as National fiesta. *Wall Street Journal*.

Millman, J., & Pinkston, W. (2001, 30 August). Mexicans transform a town in Georgia – and an entire industry. *Wall Street Journal*.

Mishra, P. (2006). Emigration and wages in source countries: Evidence from Mexico. IMF Working Paper WP/06/86, International Monetary Fund, March.

Pascal, G. Z. (1998, 25 March). Dual citizenship is double-edged sword. *The Wall Street Journal*,

Pew Hispanic Center (2006). *Tabulations using data from the 2005 American Community Survey*. October.

Perlmann, J., & Waldinger, R. (1997). Second generation decline? Children of immigrants, past and present – a reconsideration. *International Migration Review, 31*(4), 893–922.

Richter, S., Taylor, J. E., & Yunez-Naude, A. (2006). Impacts of policy reforms on labor migration from rural Mexico to the United States. In G .Borjas, (Ed.), *Mexican immigration*. Chicago: University of Chicago Press.

Simcox, D. (2002). *Another 50 years of mass Mexican immigration*. Center for Immigration Studies, March.

Suro, R. (2002). *Counting the 'other Hispanics': How many Colombians, Dominicans, Ecuadorians, Guatemalans and Salvadorans are there in the United States?* Report by the Pew Hispanic Center, May 9.

Suro, R. (2005). *Survey of Mexican migrants, part two-attitudes about voting in Mexican elections and ties to Mexico*. Pew Hispanic Center, March 14.

Suro, R., & Passel, J. S. (2003). *The rise of the second generation: Changing patterns in Hispanic population growth*. Pew Hispanic Center Study, October.

Trejo, S. J. (1997). Why do Mexican Americans earn low wages. *Journal of Political Economy, 105*(6), 1235–1268.

Trejo, S. J. (2003). Intergenerational progress of Mexican-origin workers in the U.S. labor market. *Journal of Human Resources 38*(3), 467–489.

Weiner, T. (2004, 16 June). Fox seeks to allow Mexicans living abroad to vote in 2006. *Wall Street Journal*.

Yuengert, A. M. (1995). Testing hypotheses of immigration self-employment. *Journal of Human resources, 30*(1),194–204.

Part III
Immigration Policy: Introduction

Despite the huge and obvious income differences across countries and the natural desire for people to improve their lives, nearly all people in the world continue to live in their native countries. Even in the global economy of today, only about 200 million, or three percent, of the world's 6.5 billion people are living outside the country they were born in. The numbers suggest that we should not focus all of our attention on the question of why people immigrate; rather, we should also ask why most people do not immigrate. This section of the book examines one of the main reasons more people do not move to foreign countries: Countries generally restrict entry to foreigners.

Nearly all countries maintain formal restrictions on immigration. Some countries prohibit almost all immigration. And, most countries that do permit immigrants to enter accept them only under strict conditions and according to precise criteria. Some countries accept refugees on humanitarian grounds, and many countries accept some immigrants with specialized skills. A few countries, such as Australia, Canada, New Zealand, the United States, and the United Kingdom, accept very large numbers of immigrants as permanent residents. But even these countries are far from open to immigrants; they still go to great efforts to limit and restrict entry to foreigners.

Immigration policies usually specify the criteria under which immigrant visas can be issued or refused. Some countries tie immigrant visas to specific skills or employment opportunities. Employment visas are often of limited duration. Many immigrant destination countries limit immigrant visas to people with family or close ethnic/cultural ties to the destination country.

III.1 The Goals of Immigration Policy

Before we can analyze immigration policies, we need to ask what we expect immigration policy to accomplish. The chapters on the theory and evidence on immigration suggest that immigration has many causes and consequences. Accordingly, it is very difficult to determine the goals of immigration policy by which to ultimately judge the success or failure of such polices. According to the immigration economist George Borjas (1995):

> ...the positive theory of immigration policy...is based on the idea that, distributional issues aside, the main objective of immigration policy should be to increase the national income accruing to natives. It is far from clear that immigration policy *should* pursue this objective. The immigration statutes reflect a political consensus that incorporates the conflicting social and economic interests of various demographic, socioeconomic, and ethnic groups, as well as political and humanitarian concerns.[1]

A country has to answer some very difficult questions when it formulates its immigration policies. For example, should a country's immigration policies be designed with the objective of maximizing the welfare of natives, or should immigration policies also be concerned with the welfare of immigrants? To what degree should immigration policy take the well being of other countries into consideration? The immigration policies that we observe being applied by countries throughout the world reflect how we have effectively answered these types of questions.

This is not to say that countries explicitly debate such tough questions. Often, immigration policy seems to hinge on issues related to only a few of the many real causes and consequences of immigration. Immigration policy also reflects a society's culture. For example, immigration policies depend on whether a society's culture leads people to view human society from the classic liberal perspective of the *individual* or from the perspective of a collective *community*. If the pursuit of individual freedom is foremost, then people will be less likely to impose barriers to the free exit and entry of people into their countries. On the other hand, if people have a strong sense of community or common culture, then they are more likely to favor restrictions on the entry of foreigners.

Carens (1987) points out that the liberal view offers "little basis for drawing fundamental distinctions between citizens and aliens who seek to become citizens."[2] For example, classic liberals from the *libertarian school* like Robert Nozick (1974) would give national governments few roles beyond the protection of property and individual safety from abuse or intimidation by others.[3] On the other hand, *objectivists* like the philosopher Ayn Rand would limit government to supporting a capitalist system, similarly limiting government to protecting persons and property from theft, fraud, and intimidation.[4]

Interestingly, not every school of thought inspired by classic liberalism has concluded that government should be severely limited in its scope. Classic liberalism

---

[1]George J. Borjas (1995), "The Economic Benefits from Immigration," *Journal of Economic Perspectives*, Vol. 9(2), p. 19.

[2]Joseph Carens (1987), "Aliens and Citizens: The Case for Open Borders," *The Review of Politics*, Vol. 49(2), pp. 251–273 [quote omn p. 251].

[3]Robert Nozick (1974), *Anarchy, State and Utopia*, Oxford: Basil Blackwell.

[4]Ayn Rand (1967), *Capitalism: The Unknown Ideal*, New York: Signet Books.

also led to the *social-contractionist* philosophy of John Rawls (1971).[5] In seeking to define what makes a society "just," Rawls reasoned that a truly unbiased definition of social justice can only be arrived at from behind a "veil of ignorance" that hides one's own circumstances. That is, a just society is the one people would choose to be born in if, hypothetically, they did not know their actual social class, race, gender, sexual orientation, level of wealth, education, talent, and other personal and social characteristics. Rawls reasoned that people should be especially concerned about the conditions of the least well-off people in a society because, from behind their veil of ignorance, they know that they could end up being one of those unfortunate people. Under Rawls' definition of social justice, government has the expanded role of not only providing people personal freedom and equal opportunities in acquiring education, wealth, and social status, but it should also provide assistance for the unfortunate and the unlucky.

It is not clear that Rawls' concept of social justice leads to conclusions about immigration policy that differ substantially from the libertarian and objectivist descendants of classic liberalism. One could argue that social justice points to keeping the borders open for immigrants. People would certainly choose to have the freedom to immigrate to another country if, after emerging from behind their veil of ignorance, they found themselves living in a country with civil war, widespread poverty, or active discrimination against specific personal characteristics they might happen to be born with. However, if people's sense of nationalism is sufficiently strong, Rawls' philosophy of justice could perhaps be used to argue for a socially just national society that must be "protected" from the disruptive inflow of foreign immigrants. Indeed, we often hear groups opposed to immigration arguing that the entry of foreigners into the country changes the income distribution, lowers wages of the least fortunate, and causes some people to suffer difficult changes in life styles. Note, however, that Rawls himself never intended his veil of ignorance to stop at the border.

Finally, yet another strand of classic liberalism led to the type of utilitarian thinking that lies behind the traditional models of immigration we have presented in this book. These models suggest that the net gains from immigration are positive under most reasonable assumptions, although there are substantial shifts in welfare among distinct groups. While these models show why some people and groups might oppose open immigration, the social welfare functions that underlie these utilitarian models usually lead to the conclusion that open borders are the welfare-maximizing immigration policy. We can conclude, therefore, that most major schools of liberal thought tend to oppose widespread restrictions on immigration, but there is plenty of room for argument about specific policies and goals, especially when there is doubt about exactly how immigrants affect the welfare of natives.

Contrary to the classic liberal perspective, the *community* perspective appears more likely to justify raising barriers to immigration. This perspective accepts that a sense of community is fundamental to human behavior because humans evolved as

---

[5]John A. Rawls (1971), *A Theory of Justice*, Cambridge, MA: Harvard University Press.

members of small hunter-gatherer groups, protective of each other and fearful of outsiders. Psychology, neuroscientific studies, and experimental economics have provided ample research confirming that people care about others, but they tend to have empathy and demonstrate altruism mostly for people they identify with. Modern societies have grown to where the nation is now the basic political unit for making rules and governing human activity, and modern humans tend to view the nation as their community. Hence, people care much more about the welfare of their compatriots than they do about the welfare of foreigners. Kopczuk, Slemrod, and Yitzhaki (2002) analyze people's actual willingness to provide assistance to people inside and outside their countries, and they interpret the results as showing that observed behavior suggests Americans' value of a foreigner's welfare may be as little as 1/2000 of the value they put on the welfare of an American.[6] Whether or not classic liberals would find such attitudes "just," actual human behavior seems to indicate that people would prefer their government to restrict the movement of people across the nation's borders whenever their arrival threatens the welfare of the community, the national culture, or a significant number of fellow citizens.

In sum, immigration policy is the outcome of a complex interaction of economic forces, political systems, social structures, and basic human behavior. How culture and people's hard-wired mental thought processes shape their attitudes towards foreigners may shape a country's immigration policy more than the actual economic forces detailed earlier in this book.

III.2 Classifying Immigration Policies

In analyzing and comparing immigration policies across countries and over time, it will prove useful to classify immigration policies according to set of goals that immigration policies are intended to accomplish. Specifically, a nation's immigration policy consists of a set of laws, regulations, and bureaucratic procedures that address the following questions:

1. Is immigration to be restricted?
2. If immigration is to be restricted, how many immigrants will be allowed to enter the country?
3. If the number of foreigners seeking to immigrate exceeds the number of immigrants to be allowed into the country, what criteria will be used to ration the scarce entry permits?
4. How many resources will be devoted to enforcing the immigration restrictions?
5. What methods will be used to enforce immigration restrictions?

---

[6]Wojcech Kopczuk, Joel Slemrod, and Schlomo Yatzaki (2002), "Why World Redistribution Fails," NBER Working Paper 9186, September.

6. How are immigrants to be treated compared to citizens of the country?
7. Will all immigrants be treated the same, or will some categories of immigrants be favored over others?

Every country answers these questions differently. Some countries severely limit the number of entry visas, but they turn a blind eye to unauthorized immigrants who sneak across the border. Other countries severely punish unauthorized immigrants. In some countries immigrants enjoy virtually all the rights accorded to native citizens, but in other countries immigrants are never able to gain the full rights and privileges enjoyed by natives. In the chapters of this section of the book, our descriptions of immigration policy will be framed around these seven questions.

Chapter 13 of this Section presents the history of U.S. immigration policy, from before independence through the middle of the first decade of the twenty first century. The United States makes for a very good case study because it is the country that has accepted more immigrants than any other country over the past 200 years, and it continues to be the most popular immigrant destination today. Also interesting about U.S. immigration policy is the way it has shifted over the past 200 years. The radical shifts in U.S. immigration policy facilitate distinguishing how economic, political, and demographic forces shape the formation and application of immigration policy.

Chapter 14 describes immigration policy in Canada, and Chap. 15 covers the interesting case of Western Europe. Western European countries were the source of so many immigrants between 1500 and the late twentieth century, but now they are themselves the destination for large numbers of foreign immigrants. Not all countries have followed the same paths as have U.S. policymakers, and the variations in experiences and policies across countries and regions provide further insight into the complex economic and political processes that shape immigration policies.

The study of immigration policy actually provides us with an opportunity to apply and evaluate the models and evidence introduced earlier in this book. The policies adopted by a government tend to reflect a country's national goals and interests, the gains and losses experienced throughout the economy, and the motivations for people to immigrate, just as theory and evidence suggests. In short, the study of immigration policy provides a most interesting way to bring everything together from the previous two sections of the book.

Chapter 13
Immigration Policy in the United States

Abstract This chapter presents a brief history of U.S. immigration policy. U.S. immigration policy has varied greatly over the country's history, going from complete openness at the time of independence to a rigid ethnic quota system in the early twentieth century, and now back to a more open, albeit confusingly regulated, system at the start of the twenty first century. The chapter attempts to answer the seven questions posed in the Introduction to this section for each of the distinct immigration policy regimes.

> "Give me your tired, your poor,
> Your huddled masses yearning to breath free,
> The wretched refuse of your teeming shore.
> Send these, the homeless, tempest-tost to me:
> I lift my lamp beside the golden door."[1]

Chapter Overview

The renowned historian, Oscar Handlin, wrote that the history of the United States is fundamentally "the history of immigration."[2] Indeed, the United States has received more immigrants over the past two centuries than any other country in the world, and it continues to receive more immigrants than any other country today. That is not to say that the United States always welcomed, or today still welcomes, all immigrants. To the contrary, the wide fluctuations in immigration over the past two centuries were in large part due to shifts in U.S. immigration policy. The U.S. has moved from nearly completely unrestricted entry of foreign

---

[1] The last lines of "The New Colossus," the poem Emma Lazarus wrote for an 1883 New York auction to raise money for building the pedestal that now supports the Statue of Liberty on Liberty Island in New York harbor.

[2] Handlin (1951).

Ö.B. Bodvarsson and H. Van den Berg, *The Economics of Immigration*,
DOI: 10.1007/978-3-540-77796-0_13, © Springer-Verlag Berlin Heidelberg 2009

Table 13.1 Immigration to the United States

Decade	Number (thousands)	Rate[a]
1820–1830	152	1.3
1831–1840	599	3.9
1841–1850	1,713	8.3
1851–1860	2,598	9.4
1861–1870	2,315	6.4
1871–1880	2,812	6.2
1881–1890	5,247	9.2
1891–1900	3,688	5.4
1901–1910	8,795	10.4
1911–1920	5,736	5.7
1921–1930	4,107	3.5
1931–1940	528	0.4
1941–1950	1,035	0.7
1951–1960	2,515	1.5
1961–1970	3,322	1.7
1971–1980	4,493	2.1
1981–1990	7,256	3.0
1991–2000	9,081	3.4
2001–2006	6,168	3.5

[a]Number of immigrants per thousand residents of the United States
Source: United States Department of Commerce, Bureau of the Census, *Statistical Abstract of the United States 2003*, 117th Edition, Washington, DC, 2003.

immigrants to very tight and discriminatory restrictions and back again to a more liberal stance. Shifts in U.S. immigration policy were driven by complex relationships between economic conditions and political developments. Often, immigration policy reflected the cultural clash between native-born Americans and the "new immigrants." Whatever their causes, these immigration policy shifts clearly shaped the flow of immigrants to the U.S.

Table 13.1 shows how immigration to the United States grew throughout the nineteenth and twentieth centuries. From what today seems like a trickle, just 50,000 or so immigrants per year during the early part of the nineteenth century, immigration grew persistently and rapidly throughout that century. By the end of the nineteenth century, annual inflows of immigrants reached nearly one million persons per year. During the first decade of the twentieth century, 8.8 million immigrants arrived in the U.S. In the year 1910 annual arrivals exceeded 1 million people, or 1% of the U.S. population at that time. In that same year, about 15% of the U.S. population was foreign-born.

After 1913, World War I clearly interfered with the movement of people across oceans during the 1910s and 1940s. The Great Depression of the 1930s, when the unemployment rate surpassed 20% in the U.S., greatly reduced inflows of foreign immigrants. The decline in immigration began before the Depression, however.

In 1924, for the first time, U.S. immigration policy began to sharply restrict the entry of new immigrants.

As Table 13.1 shows, in the latter half of the twentieth century, official U.S. immigration again grew steadily. Immigration reached nearly 1 million persons per year by the year 2000 and 1.3 million per year by 2006. This latest growth in U.S. immigration matches the increases in immigration worldwide that are an integral part of the overall globalization of economic activity, but it also reflects the U.S.'s increasingly accommodating immigration policies.

U.S. immigration policy was not entirely open, however, as evidenced by the steady growth of unauthorized immigration to the U.S. during the latter half of the twentieth century. By the year 2000, there were an estimated 8.5 million unauthorized immigrants in the U.S.; by 2005, the number had grown to somewhere between 10 and 12 million. The growth of unauthorized immigration reflects the difficulties of applying immigration regulations in the face of economic incentives and the increasing ease with which people move between countries in the global economy.

U.S. immigration has also varied in terms of the source countries and the permanence of the immigrants in the U.S. Whereas most immigrants to the U.S. during the 1800s were mostly from the British isles and northern Europe, during the very early twentieth century most immigrants were from southern and eastern Europe. Then, toward the latter part of the twentieth century, most immigrants came from developing countries in Latin America and Asia.

The very early immigrants to the U.S. were mostly permanent immigrants. Toward the end of the nineteenth century, however, there was a noticeable rise in the percentage of immigrants who eventually returned to their native countries. Figure 13.1 shows that net immigration, the difference between new immigrant

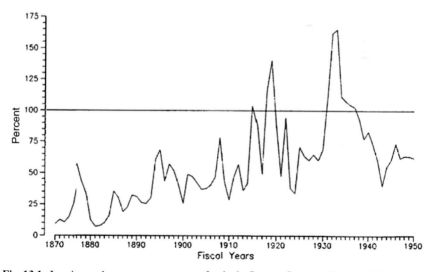

Fig. 13.1 Immigrant departures as a percent of arrivals. Source: Carter and Sutch (1997), Table 11

arrivals and immigrant departures, was not always positive. Unfortunately, data on return immigration was not collected before 1870, but the trend is obvious from the post-1879 data. As international transportation became less dangerous and much less expensive, immigrants moved in both directions more frequently. The shorter-term fluctuations in return immigration reflected economic conditions in the U.S. and abroad. Note that during several years of the Great Depression, many more people left the U.S., where unemployment was especially high. Other evidence suggests that nearly all of these departures were former immigrants returning to their native countries.

13.1 Early Immigration Policy

After the United States established its independence from Britain more than 200 years ago, its borders were effectively open to most immigrants. Immigration from Europe was, in fact, often encouraged, an understandable policy for a large country with relatively few inhabitants. The interest of the early leaders of the United States in promoting immigration is clearly revealed by the inclusion of the British Crown's restrictions on immigration to the 13 colonies as one of the justifications for *The Declaration of Independence* in 1776:

> When in the Course of human Events, it becomes necessary for one People to dissolve the Political Bands which have connected them with another... a decent Respect for the Opinions of Mankind requires that they should declare the causes which impel them to the Separation....

> ... the present King of Great Britain... has endeavored to prevent the Population of these States; for that Purpose obstructing the Laws of Naturalization of Foreigners; refusing to pass others to encourage their Migrations hither, ...

In 1787, many of the same leaders who signed the Declaration of Independence, plus a number of other prominent individuals from the various 13 United States of America, met again to draft a Constitution. The U.S. Constitution contained provisions giving the Congress the power to "establish a uniform Rule of Naturalization." The Constitution also stipulated that immigrants, once they gained citizenship, became eligible to hold all government offices except the Presidency. At the insistence of the delegates from the Southern states, the Constitution also condoned the forced immigration from Africa by banning the Federal Government from interfering with the slave trade for 20 years, until 1808.

Pro-immigration sentiment remained strong in the U.S. well into the nineteenth century. In a speech on December 2, 1783, not long after the he led the definitive defeat of the British forces in the Battle of Yorktown, George Washington told an audience of Irish immigrants:

> The bosom of America is open to receive not only the opulent and respectable stranger, but the oppressed and persecuted of all nations and religions, whom we shall welcome to participate in all of our rights and privileges, if by decency and propriety of conduct they appear to merit the enjoyment.[3]

Nearly 60 years later, President John Tyler would openly invite foreigners "to come and settle among us as members of our rapidly growing family."[4]

13.1.1 The Borders were not Entirely Open

In 1790, as permitted by the Constitution, the Congress passed its first immigration legislation. Among other things, this legislation set a period of 2 years for an immigrant to become eligible for citizenship. The 1790 act also established that immigration was open to "free white persons." In 1895, the number of years of residency required before citizenship could be applied for was increased to 5 years. Then, the *Alien and Sedition Acts* passed during the John Adams administration restricted the entry of even some "free white persons," largely those people that the Federalists thought might vote for Thomas Jefferson. In 1798, the period required before citizenship could be applied for was increased to 14 years. In 1802, during the Jefferson administration, it was changed back to 5 years, where it has remained through today. Beyond these early acts, there was no other important immigration legislation until after the Civil War.

The free importation of African slaves was no longer permitted after its Constitutional authorization ended in 1808. At the invitation of President Jefferson, Congress passed a law in that year banning the further arrival of slaves. However, there is evidence that as many as 50,000 additional African slaves may have been brought into the country illegally after 1808.

13.1.2 Assessing the Early Policies

In terms of the seven questions that immigration policy must answer, as discussed in the previous chapter, during the early 1800s the United States answered the first question in the negative, which implied it did not have to address questions 2 through 5. Questions 6 and 7 were dealt with rather simply as well in the case of "free white persons" who arrived in the United States voluntarily: immigrants were treated the same as citizens except that they did not have the right to vote or hold political office until they acquired full citizenship. Permanent immigrants, if they so desired, were usually able to acquire full citizenship after 5 years of

---

[3]Fitzpatrick (1931).
[4]Richardson (1903).

continuous residence in the U.S. Immigrants from Africa, on the other hand, were slaves and enjoyed few if any rights. It would take the Civil War and many additional laws well into the twentieth century before the descendants of African slaves would gain full and equal citizenship. It would be 200 years after the import of African slaves was banned before an African-American would be nominated by a major political party to run for President.

The 1790 immigration law establishing unrestricted immigration for "free white people" would eventually be used against Asian immigrants later in the nineteenth century. Before then, however, Asian immigrants were not refused entry and the law was interpreted as applying to everyone except Africans. In sum, most immigration was open, and most immigrants enjoyed full rights in the U.S. during the first half of the nineteenth century. Racial discrimination was a prominent and dismal characteristic of the nineteenth century U.S., however, and it was clearly reflected in immigration law and policy.

13.2   The Latter Half of the Nineteenth Century

Table 13.1 above showed that during the 1830s about 60,000 immigrants arrived in the U.S. each year. By the 1850s, the number of immigrants had increased almost 5-fold to over 250,000 per year. Relative to the U.S. population, from just 2 or 3 new immigrants per year for every thousand residents, toward the end of the 1840s and into the 1850s, each year nearly ten new immigrants arrived for every thousand residents. That is, the U.S. population was growing by about 1% per year just from immigration.

13.2.1   Religion and Immigration

During the 1850s, many of those immigrants were Irish escaping the potato famine. The Irish immigrants were often criticized because they were Catholic. There had been anti-Catholic riots in several northeastern cities of the U.S. as early as the 1830s, fueled by the fear that the growth of Catholicism would undermine traditional Protestant society of the United States. Increasing numbers of Germans were also arriving by mid-century, and the majority of them were Catholic too. This anti-Catholic sentiment was easily transformed into anti-immigrant sentiment.

An exclusive and secret society of white Protestant men called the Order of the Star-Spangled Banner arose in the 1850s to protest the threats of different cultures like Roman Catholicism. Because they would always reply, "I know nothing," when questioned about their organization, members of the Order were referred to as the *Know-Nothings*. By the mid-1850s, the Order of the Star-Spangled Banner had over a million white males as members, which amounted to about one-eighth of all eligible white male voters in the country. Remember, only men could vote in the nineteenth century, and in the Southern states, only whites could vote. The Order formed a political party, the American Party, whose candidate, the former President Millard Filmore, captured 20% of the vote in 1856. The Civil War, in which many recent immigrants fought, lowered the anti-immigrant fervor, however, and the Know-Nothings gradually faded into obscurity. Similar groups would appear again from time to time throughout American history.

13.2.2 Growing Opposition to Immigration Spurs New Legislation

After the Civil War and the Emancipation Declaration, Congress began to draft legislation to modify the 1790 Immigration Act, which still required immigrants to be "free white persons." The new legislation soon came under attack not because it enabled African Americans to be naturalized as full citizens, but because there was growing opposition to allowing Chinese immigrants into the country. In the 1860s, thousands of Chinese immigrants had come to work on the transcontinental railroad. The census showed that, by 1870, there were 63,000 Chinese in the U.S., almost all males and almost all living in California. In 1880, the number had risen to over 100,000. The anti-Chinese sentiments were strong in California, where most Chinese immigrants resided. But when, in 1870, a shoe factory in North Adams, Massachusetts, brought in 75 Chinese workers from California to replace striking workers, labor organizations were quick to exploit racial biases to depict Chinese immigrants as a threat to American workers. When organized labor targeted Chinese immigration, they effectively provided economic cover for various explicitly racist and cultural supremacist groups.

Congress passed several laws restricting Chinese immigration, but the presidents vetoed them because established trade treaties between the U.S. and China prohibited restrictions on Chinese immigration. In 1875, more general immigration laws were passed that prohibited the entry of foreigners who were "destitute," engaged in "immoral activities," or suffered from obvious health or physical problems. This law was not very explicit, and there was little money allocated for enforcement. In 1876, the Congress again passed legislation specifically banning Chinese immigration, and while President Rutherford B. Hayes' again vetoed it, he did promise to renegotiate the country's treaties with the Chinese so as to permit the restriction of Chinese immigration. In 1882, after a new trade treaty with China was negotiated, the Congress passed a bill entitled "To Execute Certain Treaty Stipulations Relating to Chinese" but popularly known as the *Chinese Exclusion Act of 1882*. This legislation banned further immigration from China for 10 years except for immediate family of Chinese already in the country. Three months later, also in 1882, a general immigration law was passed that placed a tax on immigrants in order to pay for the new immigration bureaucracy that the law also authorized and placed under the supervision of the Secretary of the Treasury. This second 1882 law is best known for establishing the criterion that immigration authorities could deny entry to "paupers or persons likely to become a public charge." Beginning in 1892, a special Commissioner General of Immigration was appointed by the President to run the immigration bureaucracy with its inspectors, examiners, translators, border guards, and administrators.

13.2.3 The Chinese Exclusion Act

The *Chinese Exclusion Act* was blatantly racist as it specifically limited Chinese immigrants. The prevailing anti-Chinese sentiment was bolstered by growing anti-immigrant sentiment during the recessionary years of the early 1890s, when unemployment was very high throughout the country. In 1892, the *Geary Act* extended the ban on Chinese immigration for another 10 years and added new restrictions on Chinese living in the U.S. For example, the Geary Act denied the right of bail to Chinese in habeas corpus proceedings, and all Chinese immigrants were required to obtain an identification document called a *certificate of residence*. Chinese American community organizations urged Chinese in the U.S. to refuse to acquire the certificates, and perhaps 90% engaged in this passive protest. A case was taken to the Supreme Court to try to overturn the Geary Act as unconstitutional. With a stunning 5–3 vote, the Supreme Court decided that the U.S. Congress had the power to monitor and deport resident aliens if "their removal is necessary or expedient for the public interest."

The Supreme Court decision effectively confirmed that unnaturalized immigrants were at the mercy of the Congress and did not enjoy the full rights accorded U.S. citizens under the Constitution. Lucy Salyer (1995) studied the legal implications of these laws and the Supreme Court decision, and she underscores their importance when she concludes that "the doctrines providing the foundation for immigration law arose out of the struggles on the West Coast among Chinese immigrants, government officials, and federal judges over the enforcement of the Chinese exclusion laws."[5] Chinese immigrants often challenged the U.S. government in court, and this led government officials to pressure Congress and the Supreme Court to rule "that the nation's gates could be effectively guarded only if they were allowed full authority and discretion over immigration policy without interference from the federal courts."[6] The support of the Supreme Court of the centralization of immigration procedures in the Presidency did not result in the wholesale loss of rights by non-naturalized residents, but it certainly supported the legitimacy of what became increasingly arbitrary processes and made the final decisions of the U.S. immigration authorities and bureaucrats uncontestable in the courts. The recent arbitrary and seemingly unconstitutional ways in which the U.S.

---

[5]Salyer (1995), p. 247.
[6]Salyer (1995, p. 248).

government has dealt with suspected terrorists and their alleged supporters in the U.S., who are generally non-naturalized foreigners are not as radical as modern commentators make them out to be; they reflect a long-running drift of U.S. law toward giving immigrants substantially less rights than native-born Americans.

13.2.4 Controlling the Border

Another important feature of the 1891 legislation was the creation of the Office of Immigration. This agency later came to be called the Immigration and Naturalization Service (INS), a name it maintained for nearly a century until a very recent reorganization of national security following the September 11, 2001 terrorist attacks. The purpose of the new agency was to enforce the immigration laws, and Congress gave it the power to deport non-citizens residing in the United States deemed by the agency to be undesirable in some defined way. The power to instantly deport non-citizens implied that this agency effectively had the power to limit the due process of law under the U.S. Constitution and the Bill or Rights for non-citizens. Immigrant processing centers were established on Ellis Island in New York and San Francisco to check to see if people met the health and moral conditions mandated by the laws.

The establishment of the immigrant processing center on Ellis Island is a landmark in U.S. immigration policy. It represents the beginning of serious control of immigrant inflows. Beginning in 1892, over 12 million immigrants would pass through Ellis Island before the present procedure of processing immigrants overseas at U.S. embassies and consulates went into effect in 1924. Despite Ellis Island's reputation, however, the screening was not terribly rigorous. First of all, not everyone was even required to pass through Ellis Island. Ships bringing immigrants would routinely dock at a pier on the Hudson or East River sides of Manhattan Island in New York, and first and second class passengers were immediately passed through customs and granted entry to the U.S., "the theory being that if a person could afford to purchase a first or second class ticket, they were unlikely to become a public charge in America."[7] Nearly all immigrants were third class and steerage (deck) passengers, however, and these passengers were ferried to Ellis Island. There they were given a quick physical exam (often lasting a mere 5 or 6 seconds) consisting of a quick check of the eyes and the skin. Then the immigrants were briefly questioned by inspectors in order to ascertain whether they were likely to become a burden on society. Immigrants were generally treated respectfully, and within a few hours nearly all were returned to Manhattan to travel on to their final destinations in the United States. Records show that fewer than 2 out of every 100 arrivals were refused entry. Of course, steamship lines were careful to screen their passengers before sailing because U.S. authorities required the shipping

---

[7]National Park Service (2001).

lines to return those passengers who were refused entry to their original ports of embarkation.

Not as well known as Ellis Island is its counterpart on the West Coast, Angel Island in San Francisco Bay. Angel Island processed several hundred thousand immigrants between 1910 and 1940. Similar to Ellis Island in New York, first class passengers were disembarked in San Francisco, and the remainder were ferried to Angel Island for processing. The processing at Angel Island took much longer than Ellis Island, however, because it was designed to prevent unauthorized Chinese immigrants from gaining entry to the U.S. The Chinese Exclusion Act banned all Asian immigrants except immediate relatives of persons already living in the U.S. Chinese immigrants were often kept in detention for a month or more before being allowed to enter the U.S. as immigration officials attempted to verify the alleged family ties to Chinese-Americans already living in the U.S. Fearing that some would-be Chinese immigrants claimed kinships that did not exist, officials subjected both the immigrants and the supposed American relatives to extensive, and often abusive, questioning. If the detainees and their alleged relatives on shore did not give identical answers to the officials' questions, that was often taken as proof the immigrants were lying about their kinship. Some Chinese and Japanese immigrants took advantage of an existing treaty between China and the U.S. that allowed businessmen to enter the country by pretending to be high-level business representatives or merchants, but that effectively required that they purchase first class passage, a cost that was beyond the financial capacity of most immigrants.

There was corruption within the administration of Angel Island. Well-connected immigrants were processed much more quickly than others. For example, thousands of Japanese "mail-order brides" were quickly admitted into the U.S. under prior arrangements between the brokers and immigration inspectors. There are many stories of personnel on Angel Island passing information between detainees and on-shore relatives about the questions being asked so that they could coordinate their answers. After the 1906 San Francisco earthquake destroyed all immigration records, all Chinese in the country, whether they entered fraudulently or legally, were effectively accepted as legal residents for lack of evidence to the contrary. Despite this evasion of the restrictions, however, Angel Island must be recognized for its role in enforcing the discriminatory and racist Chinese Exclusion Act (also, no italics here). It served to prevent many would-be Chinese and Japanese immigrants from entering the U.S.

13.2.5   Immigration Remained Mostly Open

Inflows of immigrants to the United States grew rapidly during the 1880s and again during the first decade of the twentieth century. In 1910 annual arrivals exceeded 1 million people, or 1% of the U.S. population at that time. In that same year, about 15% of the U.S. population was foreign-born. It should, perhaps, not be too surprising that political pressure for curbs on immigration gained strength in the late nineteenth century and the first decade of the twentieth century. That was also a period characterized by occasional economic panics and recessions, especially during the early 1890s. As unemployment rose during those panics and recessions, many Americans came to believe that the large number of immigrants somehow added to their economic hardship. Many politicians were only too happy to demonize the non-voting new arrivals in the hope of attracting the votes of citizens. The growth of Catholic immigrants from Ireland and Germany had already spooked many natives earlier in the nineteenth century, so it is not surprising that, given human nature, the increasingly even more diverse ethnic backgrounds of immigrants later in the nineteenth century would rekindle religious, racial, and ethnic biases and sensitivities. Opponents of immigration increasingly lamented the poor "quality" of new immigrants, which was a code word for immigrants from countries other than the traditional sources of U.S. immigration like England, Scotland, Germany, and Scandinavia.

Yet, somehow legislation to curb immigration fell short of gaining majority support in the U.S. Congress. Legislation to place strict limits on all immigration came within a few votes of passing through Congress in 1897 and again in 1898, but somehow no major restrictions on immigration would actually be imposed for another 20 years. Perhaps it was the improved economy or the lobbying by the owners of industry and commerce that pushed immigration curbs to the back burner of the legislative process. In any case, another 17 million immigrants would arrive in the U.S. before restrictive immigration legislation would finally be enacted.

Claudia Goldin (1994) documents that immigrants themselves were a decisive political force that was crucial in shaping legislation and preventing immigration restrictions from gaining enough votes for passage. Recall that in 1910 about 15% of U.S. residents were immigrants. The growing numbers of naturalized, and thus voting, immigrants in the large urban areas became a political force that kept urban politicians solidly pro-immigrant. In cities like New York and Chicago, immigrants made up as much as half the population. The corrupt political machines in the large cities looked at arriving immigrant arrivals as future voters whose loyalty could be guaranteed by an openly pro-immigrant stance. Representatives of political machines often made it a point to court new immigrants to build political loyalties.

13.2.6 Assessing the Early Policies

At the end of the nineteenth century, U.S. immigration policies explicitly answered the seven policy questions as follows:

1. Some foreigners were no longer permitted to freely immigrate to the U.S., but white Europeans continued to have almost unrestricted entry.
2. There were no numerical limits to immigration, except that Asians without immediate family ties were completely banned.
3. The rationing issue did not come up because there were no numerical limits.

4. The U.S. devoted very few resources to enforce the restrictions on immigration, although an immigration bureaucracy was created and processing centers were built.
5. Immigrants were to pass through Ellis Island or, later, Angel Island, where they were questioned and given a health exam.
6. Immigrants continued to enjoy most of the rights that native Americans enjoyed under the Constitution, although court cases determined that the U.S. Congress had the power to limit the Constitutional rights of non-naturalized residents.
7. Only Asian immigrants were explicitly identified and treated differently from the traditional European immigrants. African slaves were emancipated after the Civil War, although many formal and informal types of legal, social, and economic discrimination against African Americans continued.

In sum, except for the specific restrictions listed above, the United States remained open to most foreign immigrants at the turn of the century.

13.3   The Shift in Policy in the Early Twentieth Century

Opposition to immigration continued to fester after 1900, even though formal measures to curb immigration failed to muster a majority in the Congress. During the first decade of the twentieth century, the annual number of immigrants arriving in the United States exceeded 1% of the total U.S. population in some years. The late 1800s and early 1900s was also a period of very rapid industrialization and technological progress in the United States, and not all the accompanying changes in the way of life were to everyone's liking. The increasing numbers of foreign immigrants were a convenient group of people to blame for all kinds of problems that people did not understand.

13.3.1   The First General Restrictions of Immigration

There were bills introduced in the Congress to require literacy tests for immigrants in 1903 and 1907. Similar bills were actually passed in 1913 and 1915. These bills were vetoed by President Wilson. In 1917, Congress again passed the literacy test, and this time it easily mustered the necessary two-thirds majority in both the House and the Senate to override President Wilson's veto. It should be noted that the literacy test did not require literacy in English, only in the native language of the immigrant. For example, literacy in Yiddish, the German dialect spoken by many Jewish immigrants, was accepted as satisfying the literacy requirement under the law. A provision requiring literacy in English was considered but never included in law. The ease with which the presidential vetoes were overridden in 1917 reflected a change in the scope of anti-immigrant feeling in the country. After World War I, opposition to open immigration became even more pronounced.

13.3.2   The Post-World War I Shift in Policy

Several trends combined to shift U.S. immigration policy after the close of the war. First of all, the unsatisfactory ending to the war turned many Americans more isolationist. Equally important, the economic policy of seeking to return to the gold standard after the war led to tight monetary policy and a sharp increase in unemployment. The rise of communism in Russia may also have fueled the perception that foreign immigrants would bring alien political ideas to the U.S., and anti-Semitism may also have played a role. Mostly, though, it was the election of an isolationist Republican president in 1920 combined with a severe economic recession in the U.S. that finally enabled restrictive immigration legislation to become law. This time, the usual cries about immigrants taking Americans' jobs quickly swung the legislative debate toward serious restrictions on immigration.

In 1921, Congress passed the *Emergency Quota Act*. This Act for the first time set strict limits on immigration. The act restricted immigration from outside the Western Hemisphere to about 350,000, and it was to remain in effect for just 1 year, but in 1922 the Congress renewed it for two more years. Opponents to open immigration gained strength in both the House and Senate in 1924, and there was now momentum for a new permanent law regulating immigration, including immigration from neighboring countries Mexico and Canada. The result was the *Immigration Act of 1924*.

This act mandated that immigration from each foreign country be limited to 2% of the total number of descendants of immigrants of that national origin residing in the United States, with an overall limit of 150,000 people per year. Immediate family members and other close relatives were exempt from the overall limits, which still allowed about 300,000 immigrants to enter the U.S. each year during the remaining 1920s. Also, there was considerable argument about how to calculate national origins. It was proposed that a "scientific" study on the ethnic composition of the U.S. population be carried out, but in the meantime the latest census should serve as the guide for determining the ethnic makeup of the U.S. population. However, during the long deliberations leading up to the final bill the House of Representatives went along with its more "nativist" members and agreed to use the 1890 census, the first U.S. census to ask people about their ethnic and national origins. Using the 1890 census appealed to those people who feared that the post-1890 immigration from Southern and Eastern Europe was upsetting what they perceived as the "traditional" ethnic makeup of the United States. Critics of the bill sarcastically referred to the 1890 census as the "Anglo-Saxon census."

This use of the 1890 census lasted only for a few years, however, and in 1929 the quotas were adjusted to reflect the results of a panel of experts that had worked under the auspices of a group called the American Council of Learned Societies.

This panel somehow came to the conclusion that 43.4% of Americans traced their origins back to people who were in the country at the time of the American Revolution and, presumably, of Anglo-Saxon descent. This revision actually reduced the quotas for nearly all immigrants except those applying from the United Kingdom. Effectively, the "scientific" quotas were even more restrictive and biased.

One of the consequences of the strict quotas was the beginning of unauthorized immigration. While the flow of legal immigrants was restricted, the incentives for people to immigrate had not changed. In fact, incentives to immigrate to the United States may have gotten stronger during the 1920s. While many European economies suffered severe economic downturns, most segments of the United States economy grew fairly rapidly during the "Roaring Twenties." As immigrants began evading the new restrictions policymakers faced a serious failure of their new policies. Congress reacted in a way that has become familiar in the latter half of the twentieth century: It allocated more funds for enforcement of the immigration laws. The Bureau of Immigration was expanded, and the United States Border Patrol was established to guard the Mexican and Canadian borders against the unauthorized entry of foreigners.

In summary, the early part of the twentieth century saw a complete revision of U.S. immigration policy. By the end of the 1920s, immigration was tightly limited. U.S. immigration policies explicitly answered all seven of the questions listed above as follows:

1. Immigration was to be strictly limited.
2. There was an overall limit of 150,000 immigrants plus exceptions for, among other things, family reunions and residents of the Western Hemisphere.
3. Country quotas not to exceed 2% of that national origin already in U.S.
4. The U.S. Border Patrol was created to enforce immigration restrictions.
5. Immigrants were first required to pass through Ellis Island, Angel Island, and other border inspection stations; later, the task was passed to U.S. Consulates overseas staffed with immigration personnel.
6. Aliens' rights were further restricted by court decisions that recognized the power of the Congress to legislate how foreigners were treated.
7. Once in the country, all aliens had nearly the same rights as citizens.

13.3.3 Immigration During the Great Depression

Immigration into the United States fell drastically in the 1930s, and the quotas had little to do with the decline in immigration. The Great Depression and high unemployment reduced the economic incentives for foreigners to come to the United States. As Table 13.1 showed, in many of the Great Depression years, the number of people leaving the country exceeded the number of new arrivals. During the 1930s, unemployment exceeded 20% of the workforce, and there was no welfare system in place to provide support. U.S. streets were clearly no longer paved with gold.

The Great Depression makes it difficult to assess the effect of the *Immigration Act of 1924*. Immigration seldom exceeded even the tight quota limits for most nationalities, so the restrictions were not often tested. However, there were a number of policy issues that developed during the 1930s that reflect the difficulties in answering the seven policy questions once the decision was made to restrict immigration. For example, the so-called "likely to become a public charge" clause that appeared in a 1882 immigration law was increasingly used by many overseas consuls to restrict specific categories of immigrants. In 1930, perhaps as a reaction to the rising unemployment, President Hoover explicitly instructed consular offices to refuse an immigrant visa to anyone suspected as a likely public charge. The clause was increasingly used to bar prospective Mexican immigrants in the 1920s and 1930s.

Another problem was the high degree of discretionary power of overseas American consulates in granting immigrant visas. This discretionary power was derived from earlier court decisions upholding the executive branch's power over immigration. This power was used very inconsistently during the 1930s when it came to refugees from Nazi Germany. Some consuls granted as many visas as they could to persecuted Jews and other intellectuals, others granted very few. Incredibly, U.S. Consuls in Germany, where Jews were openly and clearly persecuted by the Nazi regime, granted only half as many immigrant visas as actually allowed under the quota system. Attempts by some legislators to pass bills allowing more refugees to enter the United States failed, and the Roosevelt administration, despite its liberal credentials, did not address the issue.

There are many stories of would-be refugees who, after failing to gain visas to enter the U.S., perished in German concentration camps. A most shameful example was the 1938 voyage of a Hamburg-Amerika Line ship with 933 mostly Jewish refugees. The refugees had been put on the quota list at U.S. consulates in Germany, but the final documents were delayed for unknown reasons. The refugees feared for their lives, so they boarded the ship bound for Havana, Cuba. They hoped to wait for their documents in the Western Hemisphere, far from Hitler's police. Cuba already had over 2,000 refugees waiting in Havana, and they refused entry to the 933 passengers. The ship then sailed for Miami, hoping to find sympathetic U.S. authorities. Instead, after docking, the ship was ordered to leave U.S. waters, and a Coast Guard cutter was assigned to follow the ship to make sure no passengers tried to swim ashore. Eventually the ship returned to Europe, where France, Belgium, the Netherlands, and Great Britain each agreed to take a fourth of the passengers. Unfortunately, a few months later, Germany invaded the first three of those countries, and many of these Jewish refugees still perished at the hands of the Nazis. Today, it is impossible to understand how the U.S. authorities could have been so callous.

13.3.4 Immigration Policy During the War

While Mexican immigration was strongly discouraged during the Great Depression, once the U.S. entered World War II, Mexican workers were actively encouraged to immigrate by new U.S. government measures. A special *Bracero Program* authorized temporary work permits for Mexicans working in agriculture and performing jobs formerly held by Americans who now joined the armed forces. The U.S. has often treated Mexican immigrants as it found convenient, changing policy as conditions changed.

One of the most shameful episodes of U.S. history is the "internment" of some 125,000 Japanese Americans after Japan attacked Pearl Harbor. U.S. law permits the government to imprison persons 14 years old or older who are citizens of countries that the U.S. is at war with. However, the Japanese Americans imprisoned during World War II were American citizens, and most were born in the U.S. They were held in 10 internment camps, most of which were in desolate areas and provided the most rudimentary living conditions. At the time, this action by the U.S. government was not sanctioned under U.S. law. A later Supreme Court decision retroactively approved the government's actions.

13.4 Post World War II Immigration Policy

Economic and political conditions were much changed after the close of World War II. The changed conditions soon began to shift immigration policy. For example, in 1945 the *War Brides Act* permitted the spouses and children of overseas U.S. citizens to immigrate to the U.S. outside the established quotas. Still, the shift in policy was slow and inconsistent.

13.4.1 Policy Immediately After the War

After World War II, the large numbers of refugees, or what were then called *displaced persons*, motivated special legislation authorizing the U.S. to accept about 400,000 immigrants outside the usual quotas. The target of this legislation were the people who had been separated from their native countries by the war and by the Soviet Union's occupation of many Eastern European countries. Also included under these special provisions were people who had been imprisoned and persecuted in the Axis countries, many of whom were still housed in various refugee camps around Europe. The 1948 *Displaced Persons Act* was a milestone in that it introduced the concept of sponsorship, under which some person or group in the U.S. assumed certain responsibilities for immigrants' welfare after their arrival. Sponsorship enabled immigration authorities to satisfy earlier immigration legislation requiring it to refuse visas to persons "likely to become public charges." There was a second bill, the *Refugee Relief Act of 1953*, authorizing another 200,000 visas for refugees outside the quota.

These small openings for more immigrants to enter the U.S. did not imply an end to the anti-immigrant and nativist sentiments that had closed the country to immigration two decades earlier, however. In fact, after World War II new legislation was proposed to reinforce the existing ethnic quota system. Many Americans were worried the large numbers of Eastern European, Jewish, and other non-traditional refugees coming to the U.S. would undermine American culture. Anti-immigrant feeling was also fueled by the Cold War paranoia about communist infiltrators in the U.S., which peaked during the McCarthy hearings in the early 1950s. The Republican-controlled House and Senate began work on a new immigration bill that both strengthened the existing system of ethnic quotas and added explicit restrictions on the immigration of suspected subversives. The *1952 Immigration and Nationality Act*, also known as the *McCarran-Walter Act*, was drafted by Senator McCarran of Nevada, the head of the Senate Judiciary Committee. McCarran had long sought to further restrict immigration, and the Act kept most quotas in place, increased border patrols, and mandated new entry restrictions for persons with un-American political philosophies. This latter provision would end up keeping noted intellectuals such as Jean Paul Sartre from ever coming to the United States to give even a single lecture. Ironically, McCarran's legislation required quite a few compromises with politicians who favored various openings to immigration, and some provisions of the act effectively began the movement toward liberalizing immigration to the U.S. The McCarran-Walter Act eliminated the anti-Asian bias in the quota system, and it reinforced the provisions of the 1924 legislation that immigrants from the Western Hemisphere and spouses and minor children of U.S. citizens did not fall under the quota system. The act also included the unlimited authorization of immigrant visas for spouses and children of Americans and authorized immigrants. This "family reunion" criterion for awarding visas caused an immediate increase in immigration during the 1950s.

13.4.2 A New Immigration Law in 1965

Some liberal Democrats already began to push for eliminating ethnic quotas in U.S. immigration policy in the early 1950s. It is also worth noting that two different government studies authorized during the Truman administration (1948–1952) had called for the elimination of the national origins system. The rise to the Presidency of John F. Kennedy in 1960 definitely changed the discourse on immigration. In 1963, Kennedy proposed that the quota system be replaced by a system based on (1) skills and national labor requirements, (2) family reunion, and (3) the first-come, first served principle. No action had yet been taken by the Congress when Kennedy was assassinated in the fall of 1963. But, after Lyndon Johnson signed the Civil Rights Act of 1964, the blatantly racist and discriminatory immigration statutes came under renewed attack. In 1965, the Johnson administration and the Democratic leadership of the Congress pushed through new legislation to replace the clearly unconstitutional discriminatory ethnic quota system.

The *Immigration and Nationality Act Amendments of 1965* abolished the national quota system in favor of a new set of criteria for the granting of permanent resident visas. The 1965 legislation prescribed that 80% of the numerical limits were to be allocated to relatives of persons already living in the United States, and the remaining were to be allocated to those with desirable skills and their family members. Immediate family, that is, spouses and children, of U.S. citizens were no longer subject to numerical limits at all.

13.4.3 The Economic Effects of the 1965 Act

Few suspected that the new immigration law would lead to sharp increases in the number of immigrants, but that is indeed what happened. Table 13.1 shows how immigration increased in the 1970s and 1980s. Also not foreseen was the change in the mix of nationalities of immigrants. Europe recovered from World War II and, by the 1960s and 1970s, reached standards of living comparable to those in the United States. Thus, the economic incentives for Europeans to immigrate to the United States were no longer as strong as they had been. Some Europeans still sought out the United States because of family ties or more subtle incentives such as a freer environment for entrepreneurs, but overall immigration from Europe declined sharply relative to immigration from Latin America and Asia. Also, the emphasis on family ties tended to favor the more recent immigrants, who were more likely to be from Latin America and Asia; most European immigrants from the nineteenth century had long since cut their ties to Europe.

It is this change in the composition of immigrants that seems to have attracted the greatest amount of attention. According to Borjas (1985, 1994), the skill levels of successive immigrant waves to the United States have declined over the post-World War II period. Blau (1980) and Chiswick (1978) showed that before the 1970s, immigrants as a group reached income parity with United States native workers within their lifetime, but Borjas presented data showing that was no longer the case toward the end of the twentieth century. He argues that current immigrants are mostly low-skilled individuals who will never become as productive as the average United States native. There is still considerable debate on Borjas' contention, and the issue will probably not be settled until more evidence on income trends become available.

Critics of Borjas' thesis reply by asking: If the low-skilled immigrants improve their own well-being, which they usually do when they come from low-income countries where wages are just a very small fraction of U.S. wages, and they cause the returns to other factors in the U.S., including human capital, to rise, why is there so much opposition to the current high rate of immigration? There are, in fact, two concerns that are not fully satisfied by looking only at the overall income gains from immigration: (1) immigration seems to be contributing to the growing wage spread between low-income and high-income workers in recent years, and (2) certain types of U.S. workers compete directly with immigrants, and whose wages have indeed been adversely impacted. This latter concern fits perfectly with the simple labor market model of immigration: Low-skilled immigrants will put downward pressure on wages in those labor markets where they compete, while increasing the returns to other factors of production, including human capital.

The increased wage differential does not necessarily represent a problem for the United States if the increasing differential serves as an incentive for low-skilled workers, or the children of low-skilled workers, to acquire the skills that are most in demand in the labor markets. But, as shown in several studies detailed in the previous chapter on Hispanic immigration, the children and grand-children of low-skilled Hispanic immigrants do not seem to be catching up to median incomes or median levels of educational attainment. Hence Borjas' fear that "the huge skill differentials observed among today's foreign-born groups become tomorrow's differences among American-born ethnic groups."[8]

13.4.4 The Growth of Unauthorized Immigration

One very prominent characteristic of recent U.S. immigration has been the increase in unauthorized immigration to the U.S. Despite permitting a substantial increase in the number of immigrant visas issued, the 1965 immigration reform has clearly not increased the supply of immigrant visas in line with the growth of demand. One major factor in the rise in unauthorized immigration was the expiration in 1964 of the *Bracero* program that had permitted the temporary entry of Mexican workers in agriculture and other manual labor jobs. The end of this program effectively cut off any possibilities for Mexicans without advanced education levels or special skills to come to the U.S. unless they had immediate family in the country. The 1,500 mile border was largely unguarded, however, and because labor market conditions had not changed, many former *braceros* continued to enter the U.S. to work illegally in the same jobs they held when the program still operated. U.S. employers were willing accomplices, as were American landlords, retailers, and many other economic interests that stood to gain from the presence of foreign workers and consumers.

13.5 Recent United States Immigration Policy

Legal and unauthorized immigration both grew substantially during the 1970s and 1980s. Additional legislation during the 1970s permitted increasing numbers of refugees from Cuba and Vietnam to enter the country. By 2000, there would be

---

[8]Borjas (1994).

about 1.5 million Vietnamese and other Southeast Asian immigrants in the U.S. The economic recession in the 1970s seemed to validate the common belief that immigrants were "taking Americans' jobs."

13.5.1 IRCA

In 1979, Congress authorized the creation of the *Select Commission on Immigration and Refugee Policy* (SCIRP), with instructions to report by 1981 on how to deal with growing legal and unauthorized immigration. The final 1981 report concluded that unauthorized immigration was a major problem. To deal with the issue, the SCIRP report recommended (1) increased border patrols, (2) forgery-proof identification cards for legal immigrants so that employers could be held responsible for hiring unauthorized workers, and (3) amnesty for unauthorized immigrants who had been in the country for a long time. In 1981, President Reagan established another task force to study immigration, and it came to the same conclusions that SCIRP did. After another 5 years of further debate, legislation finally emerged: *The Immigration Reform and Control Act of 1986* (IRCA).

IRCA generally followed the recommendations by SCIRP and Reagan's task force. The combination of amnesty, holding employers responsible for hiring unauthorized immigrants, and tougher border controls was a compromise that both sides of the issue, namely those in favor of tougher enforcement and those against harsh punishment of unauthorized immigrants, could accept. However, the legislation was fundamentally contradictory or inconsistent in that it both welcomed past unauthorized immigrants and threatened potential new unauthorized immigrants. On the one hand, IRCAs one-time amnesty for unauthorized immigrants resulted in about 2.7 million unauthorized aliens already living in the United States gaining legal residence status. Perhaps the law's apparent inconsistency was avoided when the Congress effectively failed to adequately fund the border and employer enforcement measures. Twenty years later, measures to require forgery-proof identification documents for immigrants and to enforce employer responsibility had still not been put into effect.

IRCA authorized sharply higher expenditures for the Border Patrol and, for the first time, established penalties on employers who knowingly employ unauthorized aliens. However, Hanson, Robertson, and Spilimbergo (1999) find that increased border patrols had no noticeable effect on the number of people entering the U.S. illegally. Nor did the threatened punishment of employers slow the hiring of unauthorized immigrants. Even though the new law prohibited employers from "knowingly hiring, recruiting, or referring for a fee aliens not authorized to work in the United States," punishment was not very harsh, however. The term "knowingly" guaranteed that IRCA would never have much legal strength. More fundamentally, the required checks by employers to verify their employees' legal status in the United States conflicted directly with the cherished United States legal principle of "innocent until proven guilty," and many groups worked to reduce or invalidate the measures. What these requirement for employers to verify citizenship did do was create a new industry supplying forged copies of the U.S. Social Security cards, driver's licenses, and birth certificates needed to prove legal status. Some politicians have claimed that the amnesty actually increased unauthorized immigration to the United States. Even though the amnesty was advertised as a one-time event, never to be repeated, some prospective immigrants could also have interpreted it as a signal that if enough new unauthorized aliens enter the U.S., eventually their status will again have to be legalized with yet another "one-time" amnesty. Orrenius and Zavodny (2001) present evidence that suggests flows of unauthorized immigrants after 1986 merely followed long-run trends and were, therefore, unaffected by the amnesty. Predictions that there would be further amnesties were not wrong, however. In 2000, President Clinton called for new legislation authorizing the legalization of the status of some additional unauthorized aliens living in the United States, and in 2006 the issue of amnesty for some or all of the 10–12 million unauthorized immigrants in the U.S. was a central piece of new immigration legislation. In any case, the number of unauthorized immigrants living in the U.S. continued to grow after the passage of the 1986 act.

13.5.2   After IRCA

The *Immigration Act of 1990* again altered the mix of immigrants permitted to enter the United States. This Act continued the policy of allowing unlimited numbers of entry visas for close relatives of U.S. citizens. But the act also acknowledged the arguments of those who lamented the decline in the average skill and education levels of U.S. immigrants by reducing residence visas for unskilled labor and increasing visas for "priority workers" and professionals with job offers from U.S. employers in hand. The 1990 Act also made 10,000 permanent residence visas available to foreign investors who brought more than $1 million with them for investments that create employment for at least ten U.S. residents. The *Illegal Immigration Reform and Immigrant Responsibility Act of 1996* introduced new measures to reduce the flow of unauthorized immigrants, which continued to grow despite IRCA. This new legislation set up a clearing house that employers could call to verify the status of prospective immigrant employees. This measure was deemed necessary because the proliferation of forged documents had made employer checks of standard documents almost meaningless. Funds for the Border Patrol were further increased. Finally, a perverse incentive was inadvertently also introduced into this act. By setting higher income requirements for some sponsors of legal immigrants, legal immigration became more difficult. Hence, prospective immigrants who were formerly eligible to immigrate legally to the U.S. no longer could because they now had to find a sponsor. Some simply came illegally instead.[9]

---

[9]See Espenshade, Baraka, and Huber (1997).

Other recent U.S. legislation that affects immigrants is the *Personal Responsibility and Work Opportunity Reconciliation Act*, which reformed U.S. public assistance programs in 1996. Non-citizens were barred from some types of public assistance, and eligibility for some other types of assistance was made more difficult. It was hoped that these measures would reduce the burden of immigrants on the budgets of those states receiving the greatest number of immigrants, such as California, New York, and Florida. The budgetary effect was not as great as hoped; after denying government benefits to non-citizens, there was a sharp increase in applications for U.S. citizenship by those permanent resident foreigners most interested in using government services.

When the United States economy achieved very low levels of unemployment in the late 1990s and leading high-tech industries faced severe shortages of skilled workers, pressure began to mount for increasing the number of immigrant visas for educated people. In 2000, a bipartisan bill passed through Congress authorizing an increase in the number of H-1B visas from 115,000 in 1999 to 195,000 in 2000. H-1B visas are temporary work visas for foreigners with talents and skills that are in short supply in the U.S. At the height of the "high-tech" economic boom in 2000, the inflation-conscious Federal Reserve Chairman Alan Greenspan went on record to endorse an increase in immigrant visas for labor categories in short supply.[10] Of course, by 2001, after the information technology stock market bubble had burst and the U.S. economy slowed, some of the foreign workers admitted under H-1B visas lost their jobs and there was less demand for new H-1B visas. The increase in H-1B visas was a one-time authorization by the U.S. Congress, and when the authorization for the increased allotment of annual H-1B visas ended in 2003, it was not renewed.[11]

13.5.3 Summarizing Recent U.S. Policy

In the year 2000, the end of the twentieth century, the United States answered the six questions that define immigration policy as follows:

1. Immigration was restricted by a complex set of criteria for allocating permanent residence visas and by additional programs for temporary work visas.
2. There were numerical limits for many categories of immigrants defined by family relationships, skills, education, etc. and for the special legislation such as the H-1B work visas in 2000–2002.
3. Most visas were awarded to people meeting the criteria for any given category of immigrant on a first-come, first-served basis. The market for immigrant visas essentially used a queuing (wait in line) system rather than a price system to

---

[10]Reported in the "Work Week" column of *The Wall Street Journal*, March 14, 2000.

[11]Townsend (2001) and Silverman (2001).

allocate scarce visas, and delays often amounted to years of waiting. The wait was much shorter in some categories than others, however.

4. The U.S. devoted more resources to enforce the restrictions.
5. The U.S. created additional agencies to administer and enforce the immigration laws.
6. Until foreigners gain permanent residence status, they do not enjoy the full rights accorded by the U.S. Constitution and laws.
7. Some immigrants, such as spouses of American citizens, and people with exceptional qualifications are treated more favorably after being admitted into the country.

By 2000, there were also repeated calls for reform of the immigration bureaucracy. The huge backlogs, confusing regulations, inconsistent treatment of applicants, lax enforcement of the immigration laws, widespread presence of unauthorized immigrants, and rapid expansion of the non-native population in the U.S. left few people satisfied. Discussions on how to reform immigration policy were interrupted by the terrorist attack on the World Trade Center on September 11, 2001, however.

13.6 Post 9/11 Immigration Policy

Following the September 11, 2001, terrorist attacks, U.S. laws have further reduced the rights of foreigners in the United States. *The Patriot Act* of 2001 gave the government increased powers to control, apprehend, and deport foreign citizens in the U.S. Even foreigners who have been awarded permanent residence status in the country no longer enjoyed full civil and political rights; these are only gained when, after a minimum of 5 years, foreigners gain full citizenship. And even then, the Patriot Act even allows the government to revoke citizenship if ties to terrorists are alleged. Temporary student visa applications have been subject to more extensive security checks, and student visas have effectively become more restricted.

13.6.1 Reform of the Immigration Bureaucracy and Enforcement

In 2003, the Immigration and Naturalization Service (INS) was split into two separate agencies and moved into the new Department of Homeland Security. The first is U.S. Citizenship and Immigration Services (USCIS), which now handles citizenship issues, applications for permanent residence, non-immigrant visitor and student applications, asylum, and refugees. The second agency is the Bureau of Immigration and Customs Enforcement (BICE), which consolidates all border enforcement activities. The U.S. Border Patrol, whose job has been to enforce the regulations covering the movement of people across the United States' borders, is now part of BICE.

In some ways, the new split of the old Immigration and Naturalization Service (INS) into two separate agencies makes sense. The activities the INS used to perform were, contradictory. On the one hand, the INS was charged with processing new immigrant applications and welcoming immigrants to the country, but the same agency was also charged with enforcing and investigating violations of immigration laws, which meant they were also acting to prevent people from entering the country. The question that the INS never satisfactorily answered was: Was it supposed to make it difficult for someone to immigrate, or was it supposed to facilitate the process? The separation of the INS' immigrant processing duties and border inspection duties into the separate USCIS and BICE agencies will hopefully improve their performances. USCIS employs about 18,000 people, plus the overseas consular staffs at U.S. embassies and consulates augment the USCIS staff. BICE employs 40,000 police, investigators, and administrative staff.

The growth of unauthorized immigration has been an especially difficult problem for the United States. As the differences in incomes across countries has become more obvious to more people throughout the world, as communications and transportation have improved, and as the number of relatives and fellow countrymen already in the U.S. has grown, more and more unauthorized immigrants have entered the U.S. It is estimated that 10–12 million foreigners reside in the U.S. illegally. Public sentiment toward immigration in the United States has changed in recent years. For example, 49% of respondents to a 1986 survey considered immigration to be a "bad thing" for the U.S. economy. By 1994, 61% of respondents held such a negative opinion on immigration.[12] A series of surveys throughout the 1990s showed that, when asked whether immigration should be allowed to increase, kept at current levels, or be reduced, only about 5% of respondents favored an increase.[13]

13.6.2   Employment-Based Permanent Residency

Recent immigration laws have partially reversed the emphasis on family ties for granting immigrant visas following the Immigration and Nationality Act Amendments of 1965. The 1965 Act abolished the national quota system dating back to 1924 in favor of new regulations that allocated 80% of all permanent resident visas to relatives of persons already living in the United States. The remaining 20% of immigrant visas are mostly allocated to immigrants with desirable skills and their family members; these are the so-called "employment-based," or EB-1 through

---

[12]Reported in Miller (1994).
[13]Reported in Scheve and Slaughter (2001, p. 37).

EB-5, visas. The first three categories, EB-1 through EB-3 visas, cover foreigners who have special talents, hold advanced degrees, are managers for multinational firms, are exceptionally skilled in specific types of work, or can perform work for which there are few workers available in the U.S. Specifically, these three categories of visas are:

- First Preference (EB-1 *Priority workers*): Foreigners with extraordinary ability, outstanding professors and researchers, and certain multinational executives and managers.
- Second Preference (EB-2 *Workers with advanced degrees or exceptional ability*): Foreigners who are members of the professions holding advanced degrees or their equivalent and foreigners who because of their exceptional ability in the sciences, arts, or business will substantially benefit the national economy, cultural, or educational interests or welfare of the United States.
- Third Preference (EB-3 *Professionals, skilled workers, and other workers*): Foreigners with at least 2 years of experience as skilled workers, professionals with baccalaureate degrees, and others with less than 2 years experience, such as an unskilled worker who is qualified to perform a job for which workers are not available in the United States.

A Nobel laureate from Canada, the newly assigned Toyota manager assigned to head Toyota of America, or a major-league caliber baseball shortstop from the Dominican Republic would be obvious candidates for EB-1 visas. Foreign graduate students who earn PhDs at U.S. universities often end up working in academia or as researchers in the private sector under an EB-2 visa. The EB-3 category is a catch-all that covers skilled craftsmen and tradesmen as well as specialized workers for jobs for which there are few applicants from among the resident U.S. labor force.

The other two employment-based permanent residence visas are fundamentally different from the previous three:

- Fourth Preference (EB-4 *Special workers such as those in a religious occupation or vocation*): Foreigners who, for at least 2 years before applying for admission to the United States, have been a member of a religious denomination that has a non-profit religious organization in the United States, and who will be working in a religious vocation or occupation at the request of the religious organization.
- Fifth Preference (EB-5 *Employment Creation*): This category covers foreigners who will live in the United States for the purpose of establishing a new business and who will employ U.S. workers.

Applications for these two types of visas generally do not require U.S. Department of Labor certification, but in the case of the EB-5 visa, the petition process can be quite complex. The visas listed above are those that would be most applicable to businesspeople seeking to permanently work in the United States or U.S. employers looking to hire foreign workers on a permanent basis.

13.6.3 Temporary Work Visas

The United States issues a variety of temporary residence visas. These visas permit a worker to work and the worker's family to live in the United States for a specified period of time, after which the foreigners must depart the country. In some instances, these visas can be extended or converted to permanent residence visas. These visas are easier to obtain than permanent residence visas, and it normally takes 45 days or less to complete the application process.

In this category are visas that fall under the H-1B program. The *American Competitiveness in the Twenty-First Century Act of 2000* about doubled the number of temporary H-1B work visas that can be issued. Before 2000, there was a ceiling of 65,000 H-1B visas per year. This was raised to 115,000 in 2000, and 195,000 for 2001, 2002, and 2003. Employment with universities and non-profit research organizations are exempt from the numerical limits, and thus the 2000 act actually expands the number of temporary work-related visas by even more than the explicit numbers suggest. Statistics show that in 2001 384,200 H-1B visas were issued. However, beginning in 2004 the annual ceiling was again lowered to 65,000 per year. Prospective employers have mounted strong campaigns to raise this number again, but through 2009, the ceiling had not been raised.

Another important category of temporary work visas are L1 visas for "intracompany transfers." In 2001, 328,500 L1 Visas were issued, about double the number from 5 years earlier. The large rise in L1 visas has stimulated some debate, with some suggestions that both U.S. multinational firms and foreign multinationals operating in the U.S. are abusing the category in order to bring less expensive workers from overseas. On the other hand, the large increase in foreign direct investment in the U.S. by foreign multinational firms over the past 10 years would naturally tend to increase the number of L1 visa requests as the foreign owners of U.S. businesses shuffle in employees from foreign branches. As firms become increasingly oriented to the global economy, this category of visas is destined to continue growing. In 2002, new legislation reduced the former requirement that recipients of L1 visas have been employed by the multinational company for a full year to just 6 months.

13.6.4 Immigration Reform Stalls in 2006 and 2007

With growing unauthorized immigration and the foreign-born residents reaching 12% of the total U.S. population, immigration became a serious issue that was taken up by both the U.S. Senate and the House of Representatives. In 2006, the U.S. Senate approved a comprehensive immigration bill that combined an amnesty of many unauthorized immigrants living in the country, a new program of temporary work visas, workplace enforcement of documentation, a new border fence, and sharply increased border security personnel. The House of representatives, on the other hand, passed a bill that included only increased border security and increased punishment of unauthorized immigrants already in the country. An initial version of the House bill even included a provision making all unauthorized immigrants, and any Americans who assisted unauthorized immigrants, felons. Given these very different approaches to immigration reform, no legislation was passed in 2006. Immigration policy, therefore, remained unchanged, the only possible outcome when there are widely opposing interests and no one interest group can dominate the political debate.

In 2007, with the Democratic Party having gained control of both the Senate and the House of representatives, Republican President George W. Bush and the legislative leaders attempted again to pass a comprehensive immigration bill similar to the one passed by the Senate in 2006. However, there was strong opposition to giving unauthorized immigrants amnesty within both political parties, and opponents in the Republican Party were especially aggressive in blocking the bill in the Senate. Supporters of the bill were not able to muster the needed 60% of votes to overcome a threatened Republican filibuster and move the bill to final vote on the Senate floor, so the effort died.

At the end of 2007, therefore, U.S. immigration policy was still characterized by the answers given to the 7 questions in 2000, except for those answers modified by the Patriot Act of 2001. Over 1 million new immigrants were entering the country legally each year. The basic rules remain the same as in 2000, but resident aliens enjoy even fewer Constitutional protections than they did in 2000. The Patriot Act, passed in a frenzy about terrorism in 2001, enabled the immigration authorities to exercise power even more arbitrarily and unencumbered by legal challenges than the complex, contradictory, and confusing maze of regulations and provisions of two centuries of different immigration laws already allowed. Nevertheless, unauthorized immigrants continued to arrive, employers were seldom pursued much less penalized, and as many as 12 million unauthorized immigrants had spread throughout the U.S. labor market.

13.7 Summary and Conclusions

The United States attracts more immigrants than any other country. Its large economy and high standard of living serve as strong pull factors. Also, its large immigrant population helps to attract new immigrants, both legal and unauthorized. Improved communications and transportation continue to strengthen the incentives for people to move across borders and to weaken the forces that would keep people at home. As immigration continues to grow, the debate over immigration policy promises to heat up even more in the future, and we can probably expect changes in immigration policies in the United States in the future. The difficulty, of course, is in predicting the direction of such policy shifts. Immigration policies reflect a complex set of political, social, as well as economic factors.

How the United States and its immigration policies changed over the past 200 years represents a valuable case study. The highlights of this chapter's detailed description of U.S. immigration policy over the past 200 years were:

- Throughout the 1800s, immigration was largely unrestricted.
- Immigration gradually grew throughout the nineteenth century, and it reached nearly 1 million persons per year over the period 1900–1910.
- There was increased political support for curbs on immigration in the late 1800s and early 1900s, but it took until the 1920s before legislation was passed to sharply limit immigration by means of a quota system aimed at keeping the ethnicity/nationality of the U.S. population from changing.
- The 1965 Immigration and Nationality Act Amendments, which abolished the quota system for a new set of criteria permitting effectively unlimited immigrant visas for relatives of persons already living in the United States and people with special skills, education, and talents, resulted in rapid growth of immigration. By the year 2000, close to 1 million persons were immigrating legally to the U.S. each year.
- Because the worldwide economic, social, and political integration associated with globalization has increased the incentives for people to move to other countries, the inevitable clash between these incentives and restrictive immigration policies has created a large new class of immigrants that has grown to large proportions in most high-income countries: illegal aliens.

By the turn of the millennium, the surge in immigration had not yet resulted in new laws curtailing immigration. The lack of a clear direction in immigration policy is due to the complexity of the issue in our global economy. Immigration, including unauthorized immigration, has become such an integral part of the U.S. economy that there are strong vested interests simultaneously favoring and opposing immigration.

And so the debate goes on. Nativists, business interests, social libertarians, academics, human rights advocates, economists, government officials, politicians, and many other groups have joined the discussions. While there is no indication that the debate is about to reach a consensus, more immigrants keep arriving in the United States from Latin America, Asia, the Caribbean, and elsewhere. The flow only seems to have subsided somewhat with the beginning of the recession in late 2008, but history suggests that economic slowdowns only temporarily reduce immigration, all other things equal. In the meantime, most Americans simply go about their daily lives, which are increasingly intertwined with and dependent on immigrants.

It is worth noting that potentially revolutionary changes in immigration policy festered for decades in the second half of the nineteenth century and the early twentieth century only to explode after World War I. The failure of the 2007 comprehensive immigration bill suggests opposition to immigration is festering today as well. Time will tell whether there will soon be substantial changes in the United States' current immigration policies and how those policies are enforced.

References

Blau, F. (1980). Immigration and labor earnings in early twentieth century America. *Research in Population Economics, 2*, 21–41.

Borjas, G. (1985). Assimilation, changes in cohort quality, and the earnings of immigrants. *Journal of Labor Economics, 3*, 463–489.

Borjas, G. (1994). The economics of immigration. *Journal of Economic Literature, 32*(4), 1667–1717.

Carter, S. B., & Sutch, R. (1997). Historical Perspective on the Economic Consequences of Immigration into the United States. NBER Working paper H0106.

Chiswick, B. (1978). The effect of Americanization on the earnings of foreign-born men. *Journal of Political Economy, 86*, 897–921.

Espenshade, T., Baraka, J., & Huber, J. (1997). Implications of the 1996 welfare and immigration reform acts for U.S. immigration. *Population and Development Review, 23*(4), 769–801.

Fitzpatrick, J. C. (Ed.). (1931). *The writings of George Washington* (p. 254). Washington, DC: Government Printing Office.

Goldin, C. (1994). The political economy of immigration restriction in the United States, 1890 to 1921. In C. Goldin, & G. Libecap (Eds.), *The regulated economy: An historical analysis of political economy*. Chicago: University of Chicago Press.

Handlin, O. (1951). *The uprooted*. Boston: Little, Brown.

Hanson, G., Robertson, R., & Spilimbergo, A. (1999). Does border enforcement protect U.S. workers from illegal immigration?" *Review of Economics and Statistics, 84*(1), 73–92.

Orrenius, P., & Zavodny, M. (2001). Do amnesty programs encourage illegal immigration? Evidence from IRCA. Federal Reserve Bank of Dallas Working Paper, October.

Miller, J. J. (1994, 8 March). Immigrant-bashing's latest falsehood. *The Wall Street Journal*.

National Park Service, (2001). Ellis Island history. www.nps.gov/stli/serv02.htm, March 7.

Richardson, J. D. (Ed.). (1903). *Messages and papers of the presidents*. Washington, DC: Bureau of National Literature and Art.

Salyer, L. (1995). *Laws harsh as tigers: Chinese immigrants and the shaping of modern immigration law*. Chapel Hill, NC: University of North Carolina Press.

Scheve, K., & Slaughter, M. (2001). *Globalization and the perceptions of American workers*. Washington, DC: Institute for International Economics.

Silverman, R. E. (2001). For foreign workers here on special visas, tech bust hits hard. *The Wall Street Journal*, June 21.

Townsend, K. (2001). High-tech hard times bring rude awakening for foreign workers on three-year US visas. *Financial Times*, (2001, 14 May).

Chapter 14
Immigration Policy in Canada

Abstract This chapter presents a brief history of Canadian immigration policy. Like U.S. immigration policy, Canadian immigration policy has shifted from openness at the start of the nineteenth century to a rigid ethnic quota system in the early twentieth century, and now back to a more open policy regime. The current immigration policy in Canada differs from U.S. policy in one important way: Canadian policy is more selective but admits many more immigrants on a per capita basis than does U.S. policy. The chapter attempts to answer the seven questions posed in the Introduction to this section for each of the distinct immigration policy regimes.

> *We know we start having demographic problems starting in 2010, so we'd better do something before then.*[1]

> (Canadian Minister of Immigration, Elinor Caplan)

Chapter Overview

The previous chapter showed that immigration policies played a major role in shaping the flows of immigrants to the United States. That is not to say that economic conditions did not play a major role in determining the push, pull, stay, and stay away forces highlighted in our models of immigration. The sharp decline in immigration during the 1930s was clearly the result of high unemployment during the Great Depression. Population pressure in Europe drove the exit of many people from Europe during the eighteenth and nineteenth centuries. And the potato famine drove large numbers of Irish immigrants to the U.S. in the latter half of the nineteenth century. Nevertheless, the barriers that the U.S. government erected in the 1920s to keep out immigrants also greatly reduced the number of immigrants that would otherwise have entered the United States.

---

[1]The Canadian Minister of Immigration, Quoted in 2000 in Beltrame (2000).

Ö.B. Bodvarsson and H. Van den Berg, *The Economics of Immigration*,
DOI: 10.1007/978-3-540-77796-0_14, © Springer-Verlag Berlin Heidelberg 2009

It is difficult to determine the importance of the various economic and social influences on immigration relative to explicit government immigration policies. Policy shifts and social conditions are related. For example, when jobs are scarce, people will pressure their government to reduce the labor market competition from immigrants. On the other hand, when economic growth is rapid, employers will ask their government for more open immigration policies to expand the availability of labor. Politics can take strange turns because the relationship between politics and economic policies is based on complex simultaneous relationships, omitted variables, errors in variables, truncated data sets, and many other problems familiar to social scientists who have experience in confronting economic hypotheses with real world evidence. For the researcher seeking to determine the role of policy in economic outcomes like immigration, the solution. The solution to these difficulties is to seek more evidence. That is the purpose of this chapter on immigration policy in Canada and the next chapter on immigration policy in Europe.

14.1 Overview of Immigration Policy in Canada

The history of immigration policy in Canada is, in many ways, similar to that of the United States. Canada too allowed virtually unlimited immigration during its early years of existence, then around the turn of the twentieth century it began to limit immigrant flows according to the national origin of the immigrants, and, more recently, it has based the rationing of immigrant visas on family relationships and skills. Canada has seen a change in the nationality of immigrants, just like the United States. Most immigrants arriving in Canada now are from Asia, the Caribbean, and Africa as opposed to the traditional western European source countries.

There have been some important differences between Canadian and U.S. immigration policies, however. Even today, Canada's immigration policies are noticeably different from U.S. immigration policies. Among other things, Canada's visa criteria are much more skewed toward admitting immigrants based on skills rather than the principle of family reunion that dominates U.S. policy.

14.1.1   Overview of Immigration and Population Growth in Canada

Because Canada is a much smaller country than the U.S., total numbers of immigrants have not been as large in Canada as in the U.S. But, on a per capita basis, immigration has been more important as a source of population growth in Canada. Table 14.1 shows that in the most recent decade, immigration contributed more to Canadian population growth than the difference between natural births and deaths. Table 14.1 also reveals another important difference between the U.S. and Canadian

Table 14.1 Canadian population growth and immigration

	Total Population at end of period	Population added during period	Births	Deaths	Immigration	Emigration
Decades:						
1851–1861	3,230,000	793,000	1,281,000	670,000	352,000	170,000
1861–1871	3,689,000	459,000	1,370,000	760,000	260,000	410,000
1871–1881	4,325,000	636,000	1,480,000	790,000	350,000	404,000
1881–1891	4,833,000	508,000	1,524,000	870,000	680,000	826,000
1891–1901	5,371,000	538,000	1,548,000	880,000	250,000	380,000
1901–1911	7,207,000	1,836,000	1,925,000	900,000	1,550,000	740,000
1911–1921	8,788,000	1,581,000	2,340,000	1,070,000	1,400,000	1,089,000
1921–1931	10,377,000	1,589,000	2,415,000	1,055,000	1,200,000	970,000
1931–1941	11,507,000	1,130,000	2,294,000	1,072,000	149,000	241,000
1941–1951	13,648,000	2,141,000	3,186,000	1,214,000	548,000	379,000
5-Year Periods:						
1951–1956	16,081,000	2,433,000	2,106,000	633,000	783,000	185,000
1956–1961	18,238,000	2,157,000	2,362,000	687,000	760,000	278,000
1961–1966	20,015,000	1,777,000	2,249,000	731,000	539,000	280,000
1966–1971	21,568,000	1,553,000	1,856,000	766,000	890,000	427,000
1971–1976	23,450,000	1,488,000	1,760,000	824,000	1,053,000	358,000
1976–1981	24,820,000	1,371,000	1,820,000	843,000	771,000	278,000
1981–1986	26,101,000	1,281,000	1,872,000	885,000	678,000	278,000
1986–1991	28,031,000	1,930,000	1,933,000	946,000	1,164,000	213,000
1991–1996	29,611,000	1,580,000	1,936,000	1,024,000	1,118,000	338,000
1996–2001	31,021,000	1,410,000	1,705,000	1,089,000	1,217,000	376,000

Source: Statistics Canada (2005), "Population and growth components (1851–2001 Censuses)". Downloaded 9 December, 2007 from Statistics Canada site.

experiences, namely that Canada often lost as many people to emigration as it gained from immigration. Emigration from Canada was predominantly to the United States, which suggests that many immigrants used Canada as a way station to the United States.

14.1.2   The Early Years

The first of a continuous flow of European immigrants to Canada were the French traders who followed the routes established by the French explorer Jacques Cartier in the early 1500s.[2] The first permanent settlements by the French in the "New World" did not occur until 1604, when a group of French colonizers led by Samuel de Champlain established a colony at Port Royal, off the Bay of Fundy in what is today Nova Scotia. Other French and British colonists settled in parts of what is today eastern Canada over the remainder of the seventeenth century. European immigration to either British or French territories in Canada was slow. There were many setbacks from attacks by the natives, disease, hunger, and the harsh climate. Another factor that limited immigration to Canada was the proximity of the 13 British colonies that would become the Untied States; these colonies were often more attractive to immigrants. French colonists likewise found French colonies in other parts of the world more attractive than the forested lands of Canada. In 1763, when all of the French territory in what is now Canada was ceded to the British, there were only about 65,000 European colonists in the combined territory.[3]

The end of the American Revolution brought a wave of immigrants from the United States. Many of the loyalists who openly sympathized with the British during the Revolutionary War in the U.S. elected to move to the British territory of Canada rather than return to Britain or face possible retaliation by remaining in the independent United States. After the War of 1812 between Britain and the United States, another wave of immigrants settled in Canada. These were mostly British army soldiers who had served in the war and were encouraged to stay by the colonial governors anxious to have more English-speaking British citizens to counter the influence of French-speaking residents of Quebec. New roads were opened to encourage settlement in what is today the province of Ontario. Scottish and Irish immigrants comprised an increasing share of immigration. The Irish potato famine of 1846–1849 brought hundreds of thousands of Irish to Canada, although more than half of these Irish immigrants eventually moved on to the United States. The U.S. border was open to Canadian immigrants in the 1800s.

---

[2]The Norse explorer Lief Ericson landed in what is now Newfoundland around the year 1000, but his arrival did not lead to permanent European settlements.
[3]W.A. Carrothers (1948).

14.1.3 Late Nineteenth Century Immigration

European immigration to Canada increased rapidly during the latter half of the nineteenth century, as it did in the United States and many other destination countries such as Australia, New Zealand, Argentina, Brazil, and South Africa. Political pressure developed to limit immigration, and eventually Canadian authorities began to impose restrictions on immigration. These restrictions were not always consistent, nor were they part of major legislation. For example, in 1885 the Canadian government imposed a Chinese head tax of $50 to reduce the Chinese immigration. The parallel with the United States is obvious; recall the *Chinese Exclusion Act of 1882* discussed in the previous chapter.

Chinese immigrants first arrived in Canada in 1858 from California. They were attracted to the Fraser Canyon Gold Rush in what is today the province of British Columbia. Later, they came to the Cariboo Gold Rush in the same region, and Chinese immigrants made up over half of the 20,000 population in the Cariboo town of Barkerville. The largest groups of Chinese immigrants arrived in the late 1870s and early 1880s to build the western section of the Canadian Pacific Railway. The British colony of British Columbia had agreed to join the Canadian Confederation on the condition that a transcontinental railway be built to link British Columbia to the rest of Canada. Canada's first Prime Minister, John MacDonald, wanted to meet the obligation at the lowest cost possible to the government. When objections arose to the recruitment of Chinese labor to build the railroad, he argued in Parliament: "It is simply a question of alternatives: either you must have this labour or you can't have the railway."[4] Thousands of Chinese workers were attracted first from California. The railway had to compete with the attraction of the goldfields in British Columbia, however. Many of the California Chinese tired of the drudgery of railroad construction and left for the goldfields. Additional Chinese workers were brought directly from Guangdong Province in China, but many of these underpaid and overworked workers soon also left for the goldfields. So more workers had to be contracted. By the time the Canadian Pacific Railway was completed, several tens of thousands of Chinese men were in Canada.

Once the railroad was completed, the Canadian government sought to curtail further immigration from China. The government instituted a head tax of $50 on Chinese immigrants in 1885. It is difficult to stop additional immigration between two countries once a number of immigrants have paved the way, and more Chinese immigrants continued to arrive despite the head tax. The head tax was, therefore, increased from $50 to $100 in 1900. Three years later, in 1903, the head tax on Chinese immigrants was raised to $500, equivalent to $8,000 today. Needless to say, that was quite a sum at the time. The Canadian Council for Refugees (2007) notes that between 1901 and 1918 the Canadian government collected $18 million from Chinese immigrants, while it spent $10 million to promote immigration from

---

[4]Quote from Wikipedia (2007).

Europe over the same period.[5] There clearly was a strong anti-Chinese bias in Canadian immigration policy

Other than the strong measures to reduce immigration from Asia, European immigrants continued to arrive in Canada. Canada had ample land available for immigrants. The first Canadian transcontinental railway, the Canadian Pacific, openly promoted settlement on lands bordering their rights of way in order to generate traffic. A second transcontinental railway that ran to the north of the Canadian Pacific, the Grant Trunk Pacific, did the same around the turn of the century. In 1905, two new provinces were created (Saskatchewan and Alberta) as immigrants expanded the population of the Canadian Plains region. Table 14.1 shows that during the first decade of the twentieth century, immigration exceeded 1.5 million.

14.1.4   Summary of Nineteenth Century Canadian Immigration Policy

To summarize Canada's nineteenth century immigration policies, we again refer to the set of seven questions introduced at the start of this policy section of the book.

1. Is immigration to be restricted?

In answering this question, it is important to keep in mind that Canada has maintained a close relationship with Great Britain throughout its history. Canada did not have a war for independence, which meant that well into the nineteenth century Canada's immigration policies reflected the interests of Britain as much as they reflected local Canadian interests. Overall, there was little interest in actively restricting immigration, and during most of the nineteenth century Canadian authorities instituted many explicit measures to encourage immigration. Early in the nineteenth century, there was a strong interest in shifting Canada's population balance away from French speaking Quebec towards the English speaking areas of the country.

The remaining questions were answered in ways that were surprisingly similar to those of the United States.

2. If immigration is to be restricted, how many immigrants will be allowed to enter the country?
3. If the number of foreigners seeking to immigrate exceeds the number of immigrants to be allowed into the country, what criteria will be used to ration the scarce entry permits?
4. How many resources will be devoted to enforcing immigration restrictions?
5. What methods will be used to enforce immigration restrictions?

---

[5]Dench (2007).

6. How are immigrants to be treated compared to citizens of the country?
7. Will all immigrants be treated the same, or will some categories of immigrants be favored over others?

For the nineteenth century, these last six questions were answered with a set of measures that largely encouraged immigration but nevertheless imposed subtle measures that favored some immigrants over others.

According to Kelley and Trebilcock (2000):

> The location of immigration agents and the focus of financial incentives indicated the groups of immigrants which the government preferred. Throughout these years, Britons, northern Europeans, and Americans received the most attention and the most generous offers of assistance in emigrating to Canada. And while formal barriers to entry on the basis of race did not exist until the passing of the Chinese Immigration Act in 1985, the manner in which promotional activities and incentives were distributed exhibited strong racial preferences.[6]

There were no numerical restrictions, nor were many resources devoted to enforcing the restrictions. In part, the treatment of immigrants was influenced by Canada's ambiguous status within the British Empire. British citizens remained British citizens when they immigrated to Canada, since Canada was British territory. Other immigrants could become British subjects after three years residency in Canada. Interestingly, the issue of citizenship remained somewhat confused by the fact that Canada was not entirely an independent country. Were Canadians British citizens or Canadian citizens? Only in the twentieth century would that question be clearly answered.

14.2 Canadian Immigration Policy in the Twentieth Century

At the turn of the century, and after substantial inflows of immigrants in the latter half of the nineteenth century, there was a growing sentiment to limit immigration to Canada. These sentiments reflected explicitly racist attitudes, not unlike U.S. attitudes at that same time. There was obvious support of continued immigration on the part of corporate interests in Canada, which enjoyed the benefits of the increased labor supply. Nevertheless, Canada's Chinese Immigration Act similarly revealed a latent cultural resistance to immigration that would, in the early twentieth century, bring about a major shift in Canadian immigration policy.

14.2.1 The First Half of the Twentieth Century

In 1910 Canada adopted a major piece of immigration legislation, the *1910 Immigration Act*. This law gave the government a great deal of discretionary power over who could enter Canada. The Act specifically gave the government

---

[6]Kelley and Trebilcock (2000, p. 107).

legal authority to prohibit immigrants "belonging to any race deemed unsuited to the climate or requirements of Canada." The "climate" criterion was often applied to non-white applicants.[7] In 1923 the government first issued an order limiting Chinese immigration to "agriculturalists, farm labourers, female domestic servants, and wife and children of a person legally in Canada." Then, later that year, the legislature passed the *Chinese Immigration Act*, which banned Chinese immigrants altogether. The latter law went into effect on July 1, a day known as Canada Day to most Canadians; to Chinese Canadians it became known as "Humiliation Day." This exclusion remained in effect until 1947. In 2006, Canada issued an official apology and compensation for having discriminated against Chinese immigrants.

The year 1923 saw other new restrictions on immigration. The government, under its authority to regulate the entry of immigrants, left the border open to British subjects, Americans, and citizens of "preferred countries," the latter defined as Norway, Sweden, Denmark, Finland, Luxembourg, Germany, Switzerland, Holland, Belgium, and France. But it ruled that only agriculturalists, farm laborers, female domestic servants, and sponsored family members would be admitted from "non-preferred countries," which were listed as being Austria, Hungary, Poland, Romania, Lithuania, Estonia, Latvia, Bulgaria, Yugoslavia, and Czechoslovakia. Immigrants from Southern European countries or non-European countries were not permitted at all.

The previous chapter pointed out the difficulties Jewish refugees from Nazi Germany encountered in gaining entry to the United States. Despite explicitly recognizing Germany as a "preferred country," Canada similarly blocked the entry of Jewish refugees during the 1930s. This fact makes it clear, if there ever was any doubt, that strong ethnic sentiments lay behind the designation of countries as "preferred." Canada only admitted about 5,000 Jewish refugees during the 1930s.[8] In comparison, Argentina admitted 63,000 Jewish refugees. Canada had never formulated a policy towards refugees, which meant refugees had to deal with the existing immigration bureaucracy and procedures that were largely shaped by ethnic biases and the high unemployment rate during the Great Depression.

The economic conditions during the 1930s greatly changed the way immigrants were treated. Not only were new immigrants prevented from entering the country, but there were also more deportations of immigrants previously permitted to enter the country. Specifically, between 1930 and 1935, some 28,000 immigrants were deported from Canada for becoming a "public charge."[9] In effect, the consequences of the Great Depression became grounds for deportation.

---

[7]Dench (2007).
[8]Bélanger (2006).
[9]Bélanger (2006).

14.2.2 After World War II

Canadian immigration policy began to shift after World War II. On Labor Day in 1947, Prime Minister MacKenzie King made a speech outlining his vision for post-war Canadian immigration policy:

> The policy of the government is to foster the growth of the population of Canada by the encouragement of immigration. The government will seek by legislation, regulation, and vigorous administration, to ensure the careful selection and permanent settlement of such numbers of immigrants as can advantageously be absorbed in our national economy.[10]

MacKenzie noted that "objectionable discrimination" in earlier legislation and administration of immigration should be removed, but he was clearly not abolishing all the previous discriminatory restrictions on immigration:

> ...the people of Canada do not wish, as a result of mass immigration, to make a fundamental alteration in the character of our population. Large-scale immigration from the orient would change the fundamental composition of the Canadian population."[11]

Despite the continuation of blatant discrimination against Asians, the speech did signal quite a shift in policy compared to the inter-war period. Soon, additional legislation began to fill in the details on Canada's more open immigration policy.

There were several reasons for the changes in immigration policy. First of all, World War II directly changed Canadian public opinion on human rights and tolerance of other cultures. There was also some sense of guilt about Canada's failure to accept Jewish immigrants fleeing Nazi Germany before the war. A strong anti-communist sentiment led the Canadian government to formulate, for the first time, a refugee policy, now effectively focused on persons fleeing communism in Eastern Europe. This legislation also served to increase Canada's acceptance of increasing numbers of refugees from countries that were not the traditional sources of Canadian immigrants.

Economic conditions probably played an important role in Canada's policy shift. Canadians were highly suspicious of immigrants during the high-unemployment years of the Great Depression, but during the post-World War II years the Canadian economy again began to grow and modernize. Immigrants were increasingly viewed less as threats to Canadians' well being and viewed favorably as contributors to Canadian economic growth. Immigrants were also seen as a way to increase the relative size of the national economy compared to its huge southern neighbor.

The 1946 *Canadian Citizenship Act* established Canadian citizenship for the first time. Because Canada was part of the British Commonwealth, Canadians had been British subjects. With the 1946 Act, Canada became the first Commonwealth country to establish citizenship distinct from British citizenship. New legislation began to open Canada to increasing entry of immigrants after World War II. Table 14.1

---

[10]Quoted in Dench (2007).

[11]Quoted in Dench (2007).

shows that immigration rose sharply after the war, and it has continued growing to where today most of Canada's population growth is due to immigration, not natural population growth.

14.2.3   Comparing Immigration Legislation

Towards the end of the twentieth century, the seven policy questions for Canada have very different answers than they did at the end of the nineteenth century. The answer to the first question "Is immigration to be restricted?" is clearly "yes," although how Canada restricted immigration changed continually during the twentieth century. The remaining questions are, perhaps, best addressed by contrasting the language of Canadian immigration acts from 1910, 1952, and 1976. For example, the *Immigration Act of 1910* states that the government may block the entry of:

1. Those belonging to nationalities unlikely to assimilate and who consequently prevent the building up of a united nation of people of similar customs and ideals.
2. Those who from the mode of life and occupations are likely to crowd into urban centers and bring about a state of congestion which might result in unemployment and a lowering of the standards of our national life.

The *Immigration Act of 1952* defines a number of categories of immigrants who may be excluded from entering the country:

1. Nationality, citizenship, ethnic group, occupation, class or geographical area of origin.
2. Peculiar customs, habits, modes of life, or methods of holding property.
3. Unsuitability with regard to climatic, economic, social conditions.
4. Probable inability to become readily assimilated or to assume the duties or responsibilities of citizenship.

The *1976 Immigration Act* established the following objectives of immigration policy:

1. To enrich and strengthen the cultural and social fabric of Canada, taking into account the federal and bilingual character of Canada.
2. To ensure that any person who seeks admission to Canada in either a permanent or temporary basis is subject to standards of admission that do not discriminate on grounds of race, national or ethnic origin, colour or sex.[12]

---

[12]These excerpts of past laws were provided by the Marianopolis College site on Quebec History, Documents of Canadian History, "Contrasting Canadian Immigration Regulations (1910, 1952, 1970s)," downloaded on 8 December, 2007 from http://faculty.marianopolis.edu/c.belanger/ QuebecHistory/readings/CanadianImmigrationRegulations/

Notice that Canadian immigration law in the twentieth century progressed from a strong bias against non-white immigrants from countries other than Northern Europe to an explicit ban on discriminating purely on the basis of ethnic or racial origins. The 1952 legislation was less openly discriminatory, but it still gave the government and immigration officials ample room to arbitrarily limit the entry of immigrants from specific countries or of specific ethnic backgrounds. Admittedly, the 1976 legislation still leaves some opening to discriminate against people who are judged to be less likely to assimilate quickly into Canadian society, but at least blatant racial or ethnic discrimination is banned.

14.3 Canada's Immigration Policy Today

Today, Canadian immigration law establishes three categories of immigrants: (1) family and closely related persons, (2) independent immigrants admitted on the basis of skill, capital, and labor market requirements, and (3) refugees. In the latter two categories, Canadian government officials have considerable discretion in how they award immigrant visas. Recently, to minimize the arbitrariness of their decisions for immigrants admitted on the basis of skills and labor market needs, Canadian authorities have established an objective point system to rate prospective immigrants.

14.3.1   The Canadian Point System

The Canadian points system for awarding permanent residence visas is clearly skewed toward admitting immigrants based on skills; family ties count for less. Most working-age people with advanced skills or a university degree can satisfy the visa criteria. You can go to Canada's immigration web site at www.cic.gc.ca, and in a matter of minutes you can tell whether you exceed the number of points required for a permanent immigrant visa. Points are awarded for education, English and French language skills, age, occupation, and whether you have a job offer in Canada. Essentially, if you are under 40, have a university degree or good qualifications in a profession, and are fluent in English or French, you will most likely qualify for a permanent residence visa.

A recent newspaper story describes how Amr Elimam, a highly-educated Egyptian, looked at Canada's immigration web site, counted his points, sent in his form, and some time later after providing more information and documents, received a visa in the mail.[13] Mr. Elimam now works in Toronto as a management consultant with KPMG, one of the major accounting firms. An interesting detail about Mr. Elimam is that he attended high school and college in the United States, but not having any

---

[13]Newman (1999).

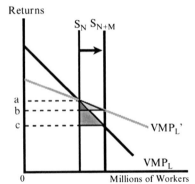

Fig. 14.1 The net gains from immigration depends on how quickly the VMP of labor falls

family ties in the U.S., Mr. Elimam did not think he would have much of a chance getting a green card in the U.S. So after graduating from college in the U.S., he sat down in front of the computer and tallied up his points. Getting the Canadian visa was "straightforward," he says.

14.3.2   Should Policy Discriminate in Favor of Highly Educated Immigrants?

Immigration policies in destination countries increasingly seem to favor immigrants with large amounts of human capital. Such policies imply that immigrants with more human capital are in some way more beneficial for the destination countries. There are several reasons why that might be the case.

Suppose the goal of immigration policy in the destination country is to maximize the welfare of the native population. Then, in the absence of demand effects, externalities, or growth effects, the policy should seek to maximize the sum of the returns to all native-owned factors of production. In terms of the standard labor market model of immigration, illustrated in Fig. 14.1, the net gain in welfare to the native population from immigration that shifts the labor supply curve from S_N to S_{N+M} is the darkened triangle if the demand for labor curve is VMP_L. This area is equal to the increase in national output minus the wages paid to the newly-employed immigrants. Alternatively, if the demand for labor curve is VMP_L', then the gain in welfare to the native population from the same quantity of new immigrants is the smaller gray triangle. The comparison of the two VMP curves shows that the more slowly the value of the marginal product of labor declines with the arrival of immigrants, the less is the net welfare gain to the destination country. Therefore, one way to determine whether immigrants with high levels of human capital are more beneficial to destination countries is to compare the slope of the VMP curve for educated labor to the slope of the VMP curve for uneducated labor. The steepness of the VMP curve ultimately depends upon the underlying production

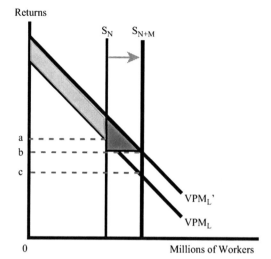

Fig. 14.2 The net gains from immigration also depend on whether externalities or demand and growth effects shift the VMP curve

function, e.g. the elasticities of substitution between capital and labor, or between native- and foreign-born labor.

The empirical evidence on the wage effects of immigration suggests that these are very small. These results could be interpreted as suggesting the demand for labor curve is very flat. Recall that studies on the wage effects of immigration have found that, although they are small, there are modest negative wage effects in the labor markets for workers with relatively little human capital. In the United States, it has been estimated that immigrants caused no reduction in the wages of educated workers, but the least educated workers, such as high school graduates, have experienced a decline in wages of over 5% because of immigration, all other things equal. According to the model above, this implies that the net welfare gains from immigration would be greatest if destination countries favor workers with little education and human capital!

The predominance of immigration policies, in Canada and elsewhere, to attract highly educated immigrants over poorly educated immigrants, provides just one more indication that the simple labor supply model of immigration is regarded as accurate. As discussed in the theory chapters of this book, a small wage effect may also mean that immigration has demand effects, growth effects, and positive externalities. That is, immigrants are likely to cause the demand curve to shift along with the labor supply curve. Note that in the case of a parallel outward shift of the VMP curve, illustrated in Fig. 14.2, the darkened net gain triangle from Fig. 14.1 still adds to the total welfare of the native population, but there are further gains. The overall purchasing power of the native population also adds the gray area between the original and new labor demand curves. The distribution of the benefits from immigration may not be as bad as in the labor supply case of Fig. 14.1, because the wage may not fall as much, or at all, when the immigrants generate positive externalities, demand effects, or growth effects. In Fig. 14.2, a parallel shift in the demand for labor means that the wage falls only slightly from a to b, not all the way to c, as in Fig. 14.1.

The empirical results from studies of the United States, a country where the majority of immigrants are poorly educated and qualified for mostly low-wage jobs, show that immigrants as a group have little effect on the wages overall while they have depressing effects on wages in the low-skill sectors of the labor market. These results suggest that low-wage immigrants generate relatively few externalities, demand effects, and/or growth effects. Indeed, high-income immigrants, all other things equal, will generate a greater demand effect in the destination economy. Highly educated immigrants are also more likely to have greater growth effects in that they are more likely to contribute to the creation of new knowledge and entrepreneurial activities. Finally, immigrants with higher education levels, and higher incomes, are less likely to cause negative externalities in the form of difficulties in adapting to their new culture, the need for government services, or burdening the native population, although these costs are often exaggerated even for poorly educated immigrants. Therefore, the Canadian policy of encouraging immigration of highly educated working-age people while refusing entry to immigrants destined for the low-wage sectors of the economy may indeed maximize net national welfare gains once the demand effects, the externalities, and the growth effects are factored in.

14.3.3   The Seven Questions in the Early Twenty First Century

At the start of the twenty first century, Canadian immigration policy remains relatively favorable to immigrants, although Canada increasingly qualifies who is eligible to enter the country.

1. Is immigration to be restricted?

There are strict restrictions on immigration to Canada. Would-be immigrants must qualify for an immigrant visa.

2. If immigration is to be restricted, how many immigrants will be allowed to enter the country?

There are no strict numerical limits on immigration. Rather, under Canada's point system, the quantity of immigrants is continually adjusted by means of increasing or decreasing the number of points required for entry.

3. If the number of foreigners seeking to immigrate exceeds the number of immigrants to be allowed into the country, what criteria will be used to ration the scarce entry permits?

Points are awarded in accordance with labor market conditions and the principle of family reunion.

4. How many resources will be devoted to enforcing the immigration restrictions?
5. What methods will be used to enforce immigration restrictions?

Canada maintains a growing immigration bureaucracy to handle immigration and citizenship matters for its high proportion of foreign-born residents. Border controls have been increased, in part at the insistence of the United States, its security-conscious southern neighbor.

6. How are immigrants to be treated compared to citizens of the country?

Canada has strict laws protecting human and civil rights, and those laws usually extend to all people residing in the country.

7. Will all immigrants be treated the same, or will some categories of immigrants be favored over others?

Canada clearly discriminates according to its point system for awarding permanent residence visas. Specifically, Canada favors immigrants with advanced educational degrees, special talents, English and/or French language proficiency, and the presence of immediate family in Canada. Canadian law explicitly bans discrimination on the basis of race, gender, sexual orientation, and national/ethnic background.

14.4 Some Final Observations

Canadian immigration has varied greatly over the years, with both economics and politics contributing to the variation. Clearly, immigration policy has tracked economic conditions fairly closely, although there have been exceptions. Most notably, today Canadian immigration policy seems to be more closely linked to Canada's long-term development than current economic conditions or even public sentiment. The fact that Canada receives, as a percentage of its population, a larger number of immigrants than do the United States and most other high-immigration countries of Europe is not to all Canadians liking. For example, the columnist Daniel Stoffman writes about the widespread concern that assimilation of immigrants seems to be slowing: "The solution is not more ESL (English as a second language) teachers. Kids don't learn English from teachers. They learn it from other kids. But they can't if the other kids don't speak English. If the flow of new immigrants were more moderate, this problem would disappear."[14] Despite such concerns, the government of Canada is pushing on with its active encouragement of immigration.

One stated reason for Canada's active promotion of immigration, in addition to the obvious support for the policy by prospective employers of immigrants, is the fear that the slowdown of the natural rate of population growth and the resulting rapid aging of the Canadian population will put severe pressure on the future

---

[14]Stoffman (2006).

provision of social services and retirement benefits. Current projections are that by 2021, Canada will have only two working Canadians for each retiree, compared to the current 6-to-1 ratio.[15] Canada now even has an Immigration Minister. In 2000 the Minister vowed to increase immigration by 50%. As quoted at the start of this chapter, she stated: "We know we start having demographic problems starting in 2010, so we'd better do something before then."[16] In recent years, the number of immigration officers has been increased in order to speed the processing time for immigrants. The province of Manitoba even sends officials overseas to recruit immigrants as a means of offsetting the departure of native Canadians for the rapidly growing urban centers in the eastern and western provinces.

Time will tell whether immigration solves the problem of Canada's ageing population, or whether it merely postpones the ageing process, as Cooper (2002), Fehr, Jockisch, and Kotlikoff (2004), and others have suggested. Even more of an open question is whether Canadians will continue to support the relatively open immigration policy that brings in such large numbers of immigrants. If history is any indication, policy may again shift if economic and social problems concern the native population.

References

Beltrame J. (2000, July 10). Canada is taking steps to boost immigration. *The Wall Street Journal.*

Bélanger, C. (2006). *L'Encyclopééde l'histoire du Québec*, Marionapolis College (downloaded from the website http://faculty.marianopolis.edu/c.belanger/QuebecHistory/readings/).

Carrothers, W. A. (1948). Immigration. In W.S. Wallace (Ed.), *The encyclopedia of Canada.* (vol. III, pp. 239–249). Toronto: University Associates of Canada.

Cooper, R. (2002). The economic impact of demographic change: A case for more immigration. In J. Sneddon Little, & R. Triest(Eds.), *Seismic shifts: The economic impact of demographic change.* Boston: Federal Reserve Bank of Boston.

Dench, J. (2007). *A hundred years of immigration to Canada, 1900–1999: A chronology focusing on refugees and discrimination.* Canadian Council for Refugees; downloaded on 9 December, 2007 from www.ccrweb.ca//history.html.

Fehr, H., Jokisch, S., & Kotlikoff, L. (2004). The role of immigration in dealing with the developed world's demographic transition. *Finanzarchiv, 60*, 296–324.

Kelley, N., & Trebilcock, M. (2000). *The making of the mosaic.* Toronto: University of Toronto Press.

Newman, B. (1999, December 9). In Canada, the point of immigration is most unsentimental. *The Wall Street Journal.*

Stoffman, D. (2006, 26 July). Too much, too soon. *Globe and Mail.*

Wikipedia (2007) *History of Chinese immigration to Canada.* downloaded 9 December, 2007.

---

[15]Beltrame (2000).

[16]Quoted in Beltrame (2000).

Chapter 15
Immigration Policy in Europe

Abstract This chapter presents a brief history of European immigration policy. Europe shifted from being a major source of immigrants for several centuries to itself becoming a major destination of immigrants after the middle of the twentieth century. European immigration policy today is an interesting compromise between mitigating the difficulties of absorbing large numbers of foreigners, expanding the free movement of people among the member states of the European Union, and respecting high standards for civil and human rights. This chapter concludes with discussions on temporary immigration programs and to what degree immigration can mitigate the problem of population ageing.

> *My mother insisted we were going to stay in Germany just long enough to earn money for a new sewing machine, to start a tailor shop back home. Now we're into the third generation, and my mother still hasn't bought her sewing machine. Of course, that's because they made comfortable lives. No one really wanted to go home.*
>
> (Eren Uesnal, A Berlin sociologist whose parents emigrated to Germany from Turkey in 1972)[1]

Chapter Overview

One of the most interesting immigration episodes is the post-World War II shift of Europe from being the largest source of immigrants to one of the major destination regions for immigrants. Table 15.1 details the size of the flow of Europeans to the main immigrant destinations of Argentina, Australia, Brazil, Canada, and the United States. As stated earlier, the United States was the single biggest recipient of immigrants from Europe during the nineteenth and early twentieth centuries. Together, these five countries received well over 50 million immigrants. Britain and Italy were the sources of about 20% of this total each. Ireland accounted for nearly

---

[1]Quoted in Nickerson and Globe Staff (2006).

Ö.B. Bodvarsson and H. Van den Berg, *The Economics of Immigration*,   395
DOI: 10.1007/978-3-540-77796-0_15, © Springer-Verlag Berlin Heidelberg 2009

Table 15.1 The great European migration: 1815–1930 (millions of persons)

To		From	
United States	37.3	Britain	11.4
Canada	4.7	Italy	9.9
Australia	3.5	Ireland	7.3
Brazil	4.3	Austria-Hungary	5.0
Argentina	6.4	Germany	4.8
		Spain	4.4
		Russia	3.1
		Portugal	1.8
		Sweden	1.2
		Norway	0.8
		Finland	0.4
		France	0.4
		Denmark	0.4
		Switzerland	0.3
		Netherlands	0.2
		Belgium	0.2

Source: Ferenczi and Wilcox (1929).

15%, and Germany and Austria-Hungary about 10% each. Interestingly, these European countries are among the largest recipients of immigrants today.

Table 15.2 shows the percentage of foreign-born living in a sample of European and traditional immigrant destination countries. Some European countries now have percentages of foreign-born populations that are approaching the foreign-born ratios in the traditional immigrant destination countries of the past. Table 15.3 provides further details.

During the post-World War II period, European countries have shifted gradually from being a source of immigrants to becoming net recipients of immigrants. Each country has followed its own pattern, however. A variety of factors, some worldwide, some continental, and some unique to each country, shaped immigrant flows. Specifically, the Northern European countries became net receivers of immigrants in the 1960s, when large numbers of Southern Europeans, notably Italians, Spaniards, and Portuguese, moved north to work in the booming economies, such as Belgium, Germany, Netherlands, and Switzerland. Thus, some European countries were net senders and others were net recipients. Table 15.4 shows how immigrant flows have varied over the past four decades in four Southern European countries.

In the 1960s, many Greeks, Italians, Portuguese, and Spaniards emigrated, mostly to Northern Europe. Beginning in the 1970s, however, Greece, Italy, and Spain began receiving immigrants from North Africa and the Middle East, among other sources. Portugal received many overseas Portuguese citizens during the early 1970s when overseas Portuguese colonies, such as Angola and Mozambique, were granted independence, but after that Portugal continued to send immigrants to the rest of Europe until well into the 1990s. By the 1990s, both Spain and Portugal began to receive immigrants from Latin America. Each of the four countries shows

Table 15.2 Percentages of Foreign-born populations: 1870–2000

	1870–1871	1890–1891	1910–1911	2000–2001
Europe:				
Germany	0.5	0.9	1.9	8.9
France	2.0	3.0	3.0	10.0
United Kingdom	0.5	0.7	0.9	4.3
Denmark	3.0	3.3	3.1	5.8
Norway	1.6	2.4	2.3	6.3
Sweden	0.3	0.5	0.9	11.3
New World:				
Australia	46.5	31.8	17.1	23.6
New Zealand	63.5	41.5	30.3	19.5
Canada	16.5	13.3	22.0	17.4
United States	14.4	14.7	14.7	11.1
Argentina	12.1	25.5	29.9	5.0
Brazil	3.9	2.5	7.3	

Source: Hatton and Williamson (">2005).

Table 15.3 Foreign-born population and labor force: 2004[1]

% of	Population	Labor force
Europe:		
Austria	13.0	15.3
Belgium	11.5	11.4
Denmark	6.3	5.9
France	10.0	11.3
Germany	13.0	12.2
Luxembourg	33.1	45.0
Ireland	11.0	10.0
Italy	2.5	5.9
Netherlands	10.6	11.1
Spain	5.3	11.2
Sweden	12.2	13.3
Switzerland	23.5	25.3
United Kingdom	9.3	9.6
Traditional immigrant destinations:		
Australia	23.6	24.9
Canada	18.0	17.8
United States	12.8	15.1

Source: OECD (2006), Chart 1.4 and Table 1.8.

a slightly different immigration pattern, but the overall trends are similar in that each of the four countries shifts from being a net source to a net destination country.

The large variations in immigrant flows invite economists and other social scientists to come up with explanations. In short, the European immigration experience

Table 15.4 Net migration 1960–1999

	Greece	Italy	Portugal	Spain
1960–69	−385,190	−918,981	−1,240,136	−887,508
1970–79	205,874	−195,084	218,895	−12,807
1980–89	208,215	−151,508	− 204,810	−920,759
1990–99	400,091	1,163,397	−2,652	274,289

EUROSTAT (1995), *Migration Statistics*; EUROSTAT (1999), *Demographic Statistics.*

offers yet another set of evidence with which to confront, and amend, our economic models of immigration.

15.1   European Migration During the Colonial Era

Early European emigration consisted largely of people moving to overseas colonies. For example, Spaniards emigrated to Spanish colonies in Latin America, Portuguese emigrated to Brazil, and British citizens emigrated to British colonies around the world. The emigration policies of the colonial powers explicitly shaped these migration patterns. Specifically, colonial powers often strongly encouraged their citizens to emigrate to their own colonies. For example, the British government subsidized emigrants to many of its colonies. One form of subsidy was the awarding of special privileges and land ownership that could, potentially, enrich colonists. Successful colonists, in turn, were expected to subsidize the immigration of family and other compatriots.[2] These colonial ventures were not always successful, as evidenced by the well-known Jamestown colony in Virginia, which failed miserably and left nearly all of the colonists dead from disease and starvation.

15.1.1   Colonial Regimes and Immigration

The special privileges that European colonial powers offered colonists varied greatly. Whereas Britain and the Netherlands sought to encourage large numbers of its citizens to move to its colonies in North America, Australia, and New Zealand by awarding smaller amounts of land to many immigrants, Spain and Portugal effectively created aristocracies in the Latin American colonies that were intentionally set up to rule over the native population or the slaves forced to migrate from Africa. Histories of Latin America, such as Lang (1979), Baer (1995), Burkholder and Johnson (1990) and Meyer and Sherman (1991), describe in detail how Spain and Portugal put in place, respectively, the encomienda and capitânia systems, which awarded large areas of

---

[2]The British policies are described in World Economic Survey 2004 (2004).

Latin America to entrepreneurial emigrants willing to invest in overseas plantations and mines. These awards of foreign territory included the implicit authorization to exploit the native populations living on the lands. The colonists were, of course, also implicitly subsidized by the military support provided by the European kingdoms. The crown's armies usually initiated the conquest of colonial territory, the crown's bureaucrats helped to establish the colonial administration of the conquered territory, and the crown's navy protected the trans-Atlantic transportation of people and goods that was critical to the eventual earnings from the colonial enterprises. Under the encomienda and capitânia systems, the colonists were required to turn over some percentage, usually between 10 and 20%, of their earnings to the crown.

As described by Cameron (1993), in some regions of Asia and Africa colonial powers such as Britain, France, and the Netherlands established control by using divide and conquer tactics to co-opt and control native political groups. These latter cases had interesting consequences that became obvious only in the twentieth century. When these colonies gained independence in the latter half of the twentieth century, these tactics of colonial conquest would result in large immigrant inflows to the colonial powers because the co-opted native elites in the colonies came to be seen by their compatriots as collaborators with the colonialists. The colonial powers felt obligated to take in these threatened elites when they granted independence to their overseas colonies.

Often, the colonizers also set strict rules forbidding the colonies to engage in economic activities that competed directly with the home countries. For example, many colonies were prohibited from setting up manufacturing firms, imports by the colonies had to come from the "mother countries," and transportation of colonial products had to be carried in ships owned by the colonial powers. Colonialism was an integral component of the economic systems of sixteenth and seventeenth century Europe that we now often refer to as mercantilism. Mercantilist economic systems were characterized by their explicit protection by the government of certain commercial interest groups. This protection was provided by monarchs who were interested in consolidating their power after the feudal epoch, which was noted for its dispersion of power among large cadres of hereditary local rulers. As part of this system, the subsidized immigrants became the political leaders in the colonies, the representatives of the colonial power's monarchy. Their offspring eventually became the leaders of the countries that remained after independence from the colonial powers. The highly skewed distributions of wealth in many Latin American countries date from this system of special privileges for immigrants and economic restrictions imposed on the colonies by the colonial powers.

In the American and Latin American colonies, the native populations were greatly reduced by the diseases brought by the colonists. In the plantation economies of Latin America and the Southern colonies of North America the new owners of the plantations and mines responded by acquiring large numbers of African slaves. In contrast, in the Northern colonies of North America, where the available land was not appropriate for growing cotton or tobacco, the economies of the eighteenth centuries were characterized by large numbers of small European immigrant farmers.

It has often been noted that the part of Brazil where most plantations were located is today much poorer than the southern part of the country that was colonized by large numbers of small farmers in the late nineteenth century. Similarly, the southern U.S. states became poorer than the northern states, where small landholdings by many European immigrants were the norm.[3] From an immigration perspective, this difference in development outcomes is compatible with the growth models discussed in Chap. 9. Large plantations operated by the people who also held political power in the colonies tended to block economic change and development. Economies with large numbers of small farmers proved to be more conducive to economic growth.

In short, European migration during the sixteenth and seventeenth centuries was far from homogeneous. However, this period did stand out for the predominance of immigrant flows consisting of (1) natives of the colonial powers to their own colonies, (2) the forced migration of slaves from Africa to colonies where labor intensive plantation and mining activities were important economic activities, and (3) increasing flows of immigrants from nearly all European countries to North America, several southern South American countries, and the British colonies Australia and New Zealand.

15.1.2 The Nineteenth Century

Even though the United States gained political autonomy from Britain after 1776, most British immigrants went there throughout the nineteenth and twentieth centuries. Policy played some role in this case, but, clearly, other factors also mattered. The colonies that received the largest numbers of European immigrants ended up with cultures that largely mirrored the cultures of the colonizing powers. These colonies adopted the colonizing country's language, religion, and other elements of culture, a trend that was further reinforced by the fact that immigrants from outside the realm of the colonial power were either banned or, because of discrimination, language, and cultural barriers, discouraged from entering the colony. Acemoglu, Johnson, and Robinson (2002), in fact, argue that the reverse relationship between pre-colonial income levels and subsequent economic growth in the European colonies can be explained by immigration. These authors hypothesize that, before 1500 and the start of European colonization in Africa, Asia, and America, tropical countries had the highest per capita incomes. A combination of dense native populations and, compared to Europe, poor health conditions limited immigration to those who came to manage plantations and mines for temporary periods of time. Mass European immigration occurred in Canada, the United States, and Australia,

---

[3]See, for example, Tanner (1995) for a description of U.S. immigration patterns.

where land was available and where health conditions were more benign. As a result, the latter countries ended up with European culture and institutions, which supported economic growth, while the former ended up with exploitative plantation economies and poor governance, which retarded economic development. Acemoglu, Johnson, and Robinson effectively argue that immigration and economic growth are positively correlated, as Chap. 9 suggested, and that the correlation is the result of European immigrants establishing growth-enhancing institutions in the European colonies.

This trend for people to migrate along colonial lines began to dissipate in the nineteenth century. First of all, the same economic forces that drove people to emigrate to the colonies of the major European colonial powers were also pushing people from countries without colonial empires to emigrate too. Towards the latter part of the nineteenth century, more and more people from Scandinavia, Switzerland, Greece, Italy, Russia, Czechoslovakia, and many other non-traditional immigrant sources emigrated to the newly independent and land-abundant countries in the Western Hemisphere, such as the United States, Brazil, and Argentina, or they went to land-abundant British colonies such as Australia, Canada, New Zealand, and South Africa. For example, it is estimated that as late as 1870, over half of all foreign-born persons in the U.S. were British, including Irish, natives, but by the early twentieth century, only a little more than 10% of the rapidly rising volume of new immigrants to the U.S. were from Great Britain and Ireland.

Note, however, that the patterns of European emigration defy simple descriptions. For example, between 1850 and 1910, the period during which the great European migration was at its peak, France had a very low emigration rate of less than two persons per thousand of mean population per decade, while Ireland's emigration rate between 1850 and 1910 averaged more than 90 persons per 1000 population per decade. The Austro-Hungarian, Italian, Portuguese, Polish and Russian rates of emigration trended upward after 1871, while the Danish, German, Irish, and Swedish rates trended downward. Hatton and Williamson (2005) point out that immigration rates among the New World destination countries varied significantly. Although the U.S. was the largest receiver of immigrants in number of persons, it did not experience the highest rate of immigration between 1850 and 1910, compared to other New World destinations. According to Hatton and Williamson's (2005) calculations, of a sample of five New World destination countries, Argentina had the highest average decadal immigration rate during this period (155 per thousand of mean population each decade), followed by Cuba (118), Canada (89), the U.S. (76), and finally Brazil (42).

15.1.3 The Emigration Life Cycle

Hatton and Williamson (2005) argue that European immigration followed a clear pattern of what they call an *emigration life cycle*. They interpret the available data as showing that between 1850 and 1910, a source country's emigration rate was not constant; rather, it first tended to accelerate from very low levels, then decelerated, and finally fell off again. Hatton and Williamson suggest that this emigration life cycle tended to coincide with a period of sustained economic growth in the European source countries when their economies were experiencing rapid technological and structural change, shifting from agrarian to industrial societies. More generally, the growth of emigration during the Industrial Revolution when most European source countries experienced accelerating economic growth and rising real wages seems to refute the standard immigration model, which links immigration to the differences in economic growth and living standards across countries. Note also that some of the poorest European countries had the lowest emigration rates during certain decades of the nineteenth century.

One suggested explanation for the weak correlation between emigration rates and home/destination wage differences is that rising emigration is a form of labor market arbitrage that directly narrowed the differences between source and destination country wages. On the other hand, wage differences may not be sufficient by themselves to explain the behavior of the emigration rate. Hatton and Williamson (2005) test the latter hypothesis with a model of how a country's emigration evolves over time. They argue that as the source country's wage rises from initially low levels, emigration evolves from being "supply constrained" to "demand constrained." Specifically, when wages are very low family resources are too low to make migration affordable, and many would-be émigrés are caught in a "poverty trap" in their home countries. When some economic growth occurs and wages rise in the home country, the poverty trap disappears and the migration decision falls primarily under the influence of relative earnings opportunities in the destination country, i.e. labor demand conditions. At this stage of the evolution of emigration, higher home wages are more closely correlated with rising levels of emigration.

Hatton and Williamson also incorporate aspects of Easterlin's (1961) hypothesis that nineteenth century European emigration was directly related to the acceleration of European population growth. Easterlin argued that industrialization in the earlier part of the nineteenth century generated spikes in the natural rate of population growth in European countries, and the resulting rise in labor supply then caused real wages to fall and, therefore, emigration to rise. Hatton and Williamson suggest another, more direct but related effect: The spike in population growth caused a spike in the number of young adults 20 years later, and these younger adults had a higher likelihood of migrating away from their local communities, all other things equal. Hatton and Williamson's demographic effect on emigration is compatible with the hypothesis, often suggested in the sociology literature, that European population growth created pressure on the stock of land and made emigration to land-abundant countries like Australia, Argentina, southern Brazil, Canada, and the United States attractive for young Europeans in the nineteenth century. In Hatton and Williamson's (2005) model, the demographic effect causes the observed correlation in the late 19th century of rising emigration rates and rising real wages.

When Hatton and Williamson test their model, they find that fundamental economic, demographic, and other social variables can explain a major part of the variations in European emigration. It should be obvious that one reason that European economic and demographic factors were the dominant influence on nineteenth century European emigration was that there were few barriers to immigration in the principal destination countries. Recall from the previous chapter and the first part of this chapter that Canada and the U.S. effectively left their borders open to European immigrants, and Australia, Argentina, Brazil, Canada, New Zealand, Uruguay, and many other land-abundant countries similarly welcomed European immigrants in the nineteenth century. The importance of open borders for the surge in immigration in the late nineteenth century is perhaps best evidenced by the precipitous fall in immigration in these destination countries when all of them imposed immigration restrictions in the twentieth century.

15.1.4   European Emigration After World War I

European emigration slowed sharply after World War I, partly because of poor economic conditions in the traditional destination countries, but also because the major immigrant destinations erected substantial barriers to immigration. These new barriers were imposed in response to domestic political pressures driven by growing unemployment and, after 1929, the Great Depression. Nevertheless, several million more Europeans still emigrated to the traditional destinations during the 1920s.

When the Great Depression hit the traditional immigrant destinations especially hard, there were actually large net flows of immigrants back to Europe. And, with the streets obviously no longer paved with gold in the traditional destinations, it could be argued that the rise in barriers to immigration were non-binding in that few people would have come anyway. The shifts in immigration policy, in part endogenously determined by destination country economic conditions, are still very important, however. When a different world emerged after World War II, and new economic and social incentives for people to migrate appeared, the immigration policies enacted between the World Wars would become more influential and binding on actual immigrant flows.

15.2   The Post-World War II Period

After World War II, large-scale European emigration resumed, but when in the late 1950s and the entire 1960s Europe not only recovered from World War II but experienced unprecedented economic growth, emigration slowed drastically. In fact, by the early 1960s, Europe became a destination for immigration. As economic conditions improved, European immigration policies changed. Also, when European countries began to grant independence to their colonies Europeans could no longer emigrate to those colonies as freely as before. More important, many former European immigrants and their descendents preferred to return, or were forced to return, to Europe as the newly independent former colonies struggled to reform their colonial social and political structures.

There were also migrations related to the disruptive effects of World War II. For example, West Germany received about 8 million ethnic Germans who were expelled from Eastern Europe in the early 1950s, and then another 2.6 million Germans immigrated from East Germany between 1950 and the erection of the Berlin wall by East Germany in 1961. Several hundred thousand Indonesians who had worked for the Dutch administration in Indonesia were more or less forced to flee to Holland after an extended conflict led to Indonesian independence from Holland in 1949. More than 1 million French residents returned from Algeria during and after that country's war of independence in the late 1950s.

The returning colonialists and post-war population adjustments were one-time events that were soon to be dwarfed by a permanent shift in immigration flows caused by the impressive economic recovery of Europe during the 1950s and 1960s. Economic recovery created an acute labor shortage in a number of European countries, most notably Germany, Holland, Belgium, and France, that began to pull in foreign immigrants. Initially, most of the immigrants to Northern European countries came from Southern European countries such as Italy, Spain, and Portugal. Soon, however, these destination countries began to attract workers from North Africa and Turkey, thus initiating the cultural diversity that now characterizes many European societies.

15.2.1   Guest Workers

During the 1950s and 1960s, most of the Northern European countries welcomed immigrants through the implementation of migrant recruitment policies. For example, Germany started a "guest worker" system, negotiating recruitment treaties with various Southern European countries, Morocco and Tunisia. The German Federal Labor Office operated 400 overseas recruiting offices abroad on behalf of German firms. Former colonial powers such as France and the UK drew on their former colonies for unskilled labor, while other countries such as Germany, Austria and the Scandinavian countries recruited workers primarily from Southern Europe, the Mediterranean countries and Turkey. In addition, when the UK, France, Netherlands, Belgium and Portugal, relinquished their colonies following the Second World War, many residents of those colonies flocked to the former mother countries. The former colonial powers typically granted rights to citizens of former colonies and many Europeans residing in the colonies returned home. Zimmerman (1995) estimates that about 5 million people migrated to the North from the Mediterranean countries during this period.

The economic recession that hit Europe after 1973 put a stop to the guest worker programs. However, many of the guest workers ended up staying in Germany,

Holland, Switzerland, and the other Northern European countries they had been working in. The immigration laws permitted workers to remain permanently after working for some number of years, and, because most of the countries allowed immigration for family reunions, immigration actually continued because family members of permanent residents were also permitted to immigrate. Also, many guest workers put down roots in the destination countries, and they used these countries' liberal policies on human and civil rights to eventually gain permanent legal status or citizenship in the destination countries.

The European experience with guest workers is now being studied by other countries seeking guest workers today. For example, the ageing of developed country populations is seen as potentially causing labor shortages in the future, which could be mitigated by temporary immigration. Recall the discussion of Canada's efforts to recruit immigrants in the previous chapter. When the first guest workers, or *gastarbeiter*, arrived in Germany from Turkey in 1961 under a special government program to provide workers for Germany's "economic miracle," no one envisioned these workers remaining in the country for more than a few years. "The idea, originally, was that the foreign workers would stay for as long as economically necessary, then go home. It didn't go like that," according to Michael Bommes, the Director of the Institute for Migration at Osnabrueck University in Germany. In 2004, immigrants made up 13% of Germany's population and over 12% of its workforce. Many of those *gastarbeiter* found ways to stay, and they brought the rest of their families. The same thing happened in the other Western European countries that sought guest workers during the 1960s. And the same thing is likely to happen in other countries where standards of living are likely to remain well above those of the countries the guest workers come from. If the destination countries also have liberal political and legal institutions that respect the welfare and interests of immigrants, then some of the temporary immigrants are likely to become permanent residents. In his introduction to the 2008 edition of the OECD's *International Immigration Outlook* (2009, p.20), Martin (2009, p. 20) warns that the "expectation of temporary stay by labour immigrants does not appear to be a foundation on which one can construct a solid immigration policy."

The Arab oil embargo of 1973 suddenly slowed economic growth in most of the Western and Northern European economies. Guest worker programs were abruptly ended, and active recruitment of immigrant workers stopped. While immigration dropped during 1974–1975, especially in France and Germany, to many people's surprise, it began to rise again starting in 1976. Zimmerman (1995) points out that not only was it difficult for governments to induce return migration, the foreign population in Europe went up because of higher fertility rates for immigrants and the arrival of those immigrants' spouses, children, parents, other relatives, and many friends who learned about life in Western Europe.

These guest worker episodes illustrate the complexity of immigration policy. Clear rules for guest workers can be overruled by other institutions and human behavior. Also, additional laws, rules, regulations, and government institutions are often enacted on top of earlier laws, rules, and regulations, thus providing immigrants and their legal advisors plenty of room to convert temporary immigrant status to permanent status.

15.2.2   The Post-Soviet Era

The fall of the Berlin Wall in 1989 and the subsequent collapse of the Soviet Union and Iron Curtain triggered internal migration on the continent, coupled with steady inflows of migrants from outside Europe. The political upheaval following the Soviet collapse triggered a large movement of persons from Eastern to Western Europe. A large early component of this movement consisted of about 400,000 ethnic German *Aussiedler*, who moved from Eastern Europe and the former Soviet Union to Germany. The Balkan wars after the collapse of Yugoslavia created large numbers of refugees who fled to other European countries. Again, the liberal legal environment and the human rights principles in most European countries have enabled these refugees to remain in their destinations.

Immigration into Germany was especially large in the 1990s, in per capita terms reaching the high levels of 1–2% per year experienced by the United States at the beginning of the twentieth century. Most of the recent immigrants to Germany have been ethnic Germans that had been living in Eastern European countries. It has remained difficult for other foreigners to immigrate to Germany, although in 2001 the government began permitting about 50,000 immigrants of non-German descent to gain permanent resident visas. Immigration for non-EU citizens has been easier in most other countries of the European Union than in Germany.

Since 1992, when the European Union became a full-fledged common market, citizens of one member country can immigrate freely to any other EU member with full labor rights. Immigration from neighboring countries is still slow, however, as many informal barriers continue to hamper the flow of people. Many immigrants continue to come from outside the EU, especially from Eastern Europe, because of the large wage differences between EU and non-EU countries. The common economic policies of the EU also imply that immigration policies vis-a-vis outside countries are common to all the EU countries. When the EU took up the issue of expansion beyond its 15 members in 2001, the potential immigrant flows from the new members, predominantly Eastern European countries, were a sticking point during the accession negotiations. The negotiations resulted in an agreement to delay the liberalization of immigration so that it would lag behind the scheduled liberalization of trade and investment. It is also interesting to note that the EU was willing to sign a free trade agreement with Turkey, the source of many immigrants in the past, but it still has not yet moved definitively toward full membership for Turkey in the EU. Full membership would imply completely unhindered immigration.

Finally, by the last decade of the twentieth century, all Western European countries were net recipients of immigrants, with immigrants from Eastern Europe supplementing increasing numbers of immigrants from Africa.

15.2.3 Recent EU Immigration Policy

The first of two agreements on freedom for people to cross borders within Europe was signed in the Luxembourg town of Schengen in 1985 by Germany, France, and the Benelux countries. This agreement led to the elimination of internal border checks. A second *Schengen Agreement* liberalizing movement across European Union borders was signed in 1990, and together these two agreements became part of the *Treaty of Amsterdam* on basic human rights in the European Union. In 1990, a consensus developed on a set of rules and judicial procedures for dealing with the growing phenomenon of unauthorized immigration. Included in a new set of regulations was a joint project to computerize information on immigrants. These procedures were implemented in 1994. In the early 1990s, Italy, Spain, Portugal, Greece, Austria, and Finland joined the so-called *Schengen Area* within which there were no border checks. There were further agreements on admission policies, and specific criteria relating to family reunion, employment, and long-term residency were adopted.

Despite the harmonization of immigration procedures among the Schengen countries, it was left to the individual destination countries to negotiate with source countries on agreements to take back unauthorized immigrants. The *Dublin Convention of 1990* also established that each country was responsible for setting its own asylum policy. Other humanitarian concerns were also left to individual countries to deal with. On a practical level, individual countries maintained quite a bit of local control over immigration for the simple reason that all of the Schengen rules and procedures had to be implemented by the individual countries. We know from the examinations of U.S. and Canadian immigration policy that there are likely to be large differences between the letter of the law and the final application of the laws. Those differences are likely to vary across the diverse members of the EU as well.

The European Union has effectively created an immigration system that is a mixture of regional and national policies. Individuals seeking entry into Europe are often able to exploit differences in national policies in order to, eventually, gain entry to all European countries under the provisions of the European Union. Wihtol de Wenden (2007) notes the potential for conflicts between countries. She also notes an interesting paradox: Political groups that in the past opposed Europeanization now demand better coordination among European countries in sharing information and the elimination of differences in national regulations that permit more foreigners to take up residence in European countries.

15.3 The Interesting Case of Ireland

Ireland is an especially interesting example of how economics and policy combine to influence immigration flows. During the nineteenth and early twentieth centuries, Ireland was the third-largest source of European immigrants to the rest of the world.

As a percentage of the population, Ireland's rate of emigration was more than double that of any other European source country. And, for most of the twentieth century, Ireland remained a source of immigrants. The United Kingdom became the largest destination of Irish immigrants. Ireland's population peaked at 8.5 million in 1845, the year the potato famine began. That is not to say there was no Irish emigration before 1845; to the contrary, about 0.7% of the Irish emigrated each year between 1820 and 1845. However, the potato famine caused emigration to soar to well over 3% of the population per year for several years running, and the combination of emigration and mass starvation caused Ireland's population to decline precipitously to 6.5 million by 1851. Even after the effects of the famine dissipated, emigration continued. It was not until the early 1900s that the rate of Irish emigration returned to its pre-famine level of less than 1% of the population per year.

Eighty percent or more of Irish emigrants went to the United States, with England and Canada, respectively, the second and third most important destinations. Protestant Irish from the Ulster region of Ireland more often emigrated to Britain or Canada, whereas the great majority of Catholic Irish emigrated to the United States. As we noted earlier in this chapter, a large proportion of Irish immigrants in Canada eventually moved on to the United States too. Also of note is that nearly all Irish immigrants to the United States remained there; Hatton and Williamson (2005) estimate that the return rate was only about 5%, a much lower rate than for most other nineteenth century immigrants to the United States.

Hatton and Williamson's (1993) statistical analysis of Irish emigration finds that more Irish emigrated when unemployment rates in destination countries were lower, when economic conditions in Ireland were below average, when the wage differentials between Ireland and destination countries were greater, and the greater was the number of Irish in the destination countries. The gradual decline in Irish emigration over the course of the nineteenth century is statistically explained by the economic recovery of Ireland and the decline in wage differentials between Ireland and the destinations countries. Looking at individual propensities to emigrate, Hatton and Williamson found that average family size had a large influence; the larger the family, the more likely someone from that family would emigrate. Hence, demographic factors were important determinants of Irish emigration. Hatton and Williamson (1993) thus conclude that: "Overall it appears that income, poverty, and demographic variables were the key determinants of county [Irish] emigration rates."[4]

Over the next 100 years, emigration consistently exceeded the natural increase in Irish population, and the population of Ireland declined from 6.5 million in the middle of the nineteenth century to 2.8 million in 1960. Even today, 3 million Irish citizens live abroad, 1.2 million of which were born in Ireland. In total, more than 10 million Irish emigrated during the 150 years following the potato famine in the middle of the nineteenth century.

---

[4]Hatton and Williamson (1993), p. 594.

There was a sudden shift in the Irish migration pattern in 1996. In that year, Ireland became a country of net immigration, one of the last Western European countries to do so. Then, immigration to Ireland accelerated enough for Ireland's 2005 population to reach its 1851 level of population. There are several causes of this sudden turnabout of immigration in Ireland. First of all, the European countries opened their borders to the free movement of people within the European Union, and Ireland instituted economic policies that caused its economy to grow faster than any other European economy. During the latter part of the 1990s and the first decade of the twenty first century, the Irish economy became one of the wealthiest members of the European Union. While Irish wages averaged less than 70% of European wages at the start of the 1980s, they reached parity with the rest of Europe in the 1990s, and they had exceeded average European wages by the early 2000s. Also, the fall of the Iron Curtain, and the accession to membership in the European Union by many of the former Eastern European Soviet "satellites," encouraged workers in those latter countries to seek to immigrate to other European countries where wages were higher.

Ruhs (2004) distinguished some other important characteristics of recent Irish immigration. First of all, since the 1980s Irish return migration has accounted for about half of total Irish immigration. That is, improved economic conditions stimulated a substantial portion of the huge overseas Irish population to come back home. Also of interest is the sharp increase in applications for asylum by immigrants from, in order of importance, Nigeria, Romania, Moldova, Zimbabwe, Ukraine, and Poland. In the most recent years, an increasing proportion of Irish immigrants come from the recent new members of the European Union.

When the European Union expanded its membership from 15 Western European countries to 25 members, it added a number of low-wage Eastern European countries that had been part of the former Soviet bloc: Poland, Lithuania, Latvia, the Czech Republic, Estonia, Slovakia, Hungary, and Slovenia. The original 15 members agreed that they would be permitted to block the entry of immigrants from the new member states for up to 7 years. Many governments were afraid a sudden opening of their borders to the lower-wage Eastern European countries would have adverse effects on their labor markets. Ireland, however, decided to grant workers from the new member states immediate access to its labor market. Ireland, along with Sweden and the U.K., was just one of three EU countries that did not opt to place restrictions on immigrants from the new accession countries. By the early 2000s, Ireland was issuing upwards of 50,000 work permits to foreigners each year.

Most recently, Ireland also provides an example of how domestic immigration policy adjusts to reflect the interests of native citizens when faced with large numbers of new immigrants. By 2008, Ireland had begun monitoring immigrants' usage of public services such as health, education, and unemployment assistance in order to determine to what extent immigrants come to Ireland to work and how many immigrants come for government benefits. Also, in 2004, the Irish government put up for referendum a measure that ends the automatic granting of permanent residence status to foreign-born parents of Irish-born children. This measure, which won a very large majority vote, was aimed at ending the practice where foreign asylum seekers would have children in Ireland while awaiting a decision on their status and thus gain permanent residency even though their cases for asylum were eventually judged to be unfounded. In 2005, the government also decided to begin moving towards a skill-based immigration policy for immigrants from the new members of the EU and from countries outside the EU. These shifts in policy were overshadowed by the severe economic contraction in 2008, however. The effects of economic recession quickly reduced immigration much faster than Ireland's gradual shift in policy ever could.

15.4   Recent Immigration Policy in Spain

Immigration policy in Europe may be influenced by recent changes in immigration policy in Spain, which is one of the European Union member countries that have recently received large numbers of unauthorized immigrants. Like many European countries, Spain has a high unemployment rate, but there are plenty of low-paying jobs that native workers do not want to fill. Spain is home to many illegal immigrants from North and Central Africa and Latin America, perhaps over 1 million in total. The Strait of Gibraltar, which separates Spain from Africa, is only 15 kms across at its narrowest point. Latin Americans are attracted to Spain because they share a common language. At the start of 2005, Spain changed its immigration policies in an attempt to deal with the large illegal immigrant population. The policy shift may also reflect the terrorist attacks in Madrid in 2004, which heightened the fear that more terrorists could be hiding among the many illegal immigrants from North Africa and the Middle East living in Spain.

Spain's new immigration policies are in some ways similar to recent policy reforms in the United States. For example, more funds will be devoted to guarding the border. For one thing, electronic barriers are being built along Spanish coastlines. Spain has also begun to sign bilateral agreements that permit the prompt repatriation of unauthorized immigrants caught in Spanish territory. On the other hand, the new reforms recognize that many unauthorized immigrants have been in Spain for some time and are employed in jobs crucial to the economy. The strategy is to draw the illegal immigrants out into the open and to have them employed legally. An amnesty was therefore established in 2004, and workers with a six-month labor contract issued by a legal employer were to be given permanent residence papers. After the amnesty ended in May of 2005, fines for unauthorized workers and their employers rose sharply to as much as 160,000 per illegal employee. Legalizing the status of unauthorized foreign workers enables the government to keep better track of foreigners, and it meant that social insurance contributions would be paid by employers and income taxes were more likely to be collected. The Spanish reforms also include a measure to attract highly skilled immigrants. Skilled workers will be permitted to live in Spain for a limited amount of time while they look for work, and their temporary visa is converted to a permanent residence visa when they show they have been permanently employed in their skill.

15.6   Can Immigration Solve the Demographic Burden?

One of the common themes among pundits in the news media is that Western European countries need immigration in order to offset the economic consequences of the rapid ageing of the native-born population. The sharp decline in birth rates in post-World War II Western Europe is destined to sharply raise the percentage of retired Europeans relative to working Europeans. Immigration can change the evolving course of Europe's demographic profile because, on average, immigrants tend to be younger and of working age. Immigration is seen by some as the solution to the rising burden of an ageing population. After analyzing the incentives to move and the increasing ease with which people can travel from one country to another, Cooper (2002) writes:

> . . . the prospective decline of natural population growth likely to be observed in the coming decades suggests a prediction: Immigration into all rich countries will occur on a much greater scale than is currently envisioned in official population projections, illegally if not legally; on balance such immigration will be more welcome than it seems to be at present. Indeed, it will even be encouraged.

Are Cooper's predictions about immigration and immigration policy accurate? The youthfulness of immigrants is an unmistakable fact. There are several reasons for the relative youthfulness of immigrants. In part, the lowering of transportation costs has increased the flows of temporary immigrants, who are especially likely to be young and of working age. That is, more and more immigrants move to other countries just to work, and more and more countries attempt to attract immigrants who only want to come and work for some temporary period. We have noted how such policies have often failed to prevent immigrants remaining in the destination countries, but even in these cases, the population of the destination countries remain relatively young because the immigrants that switch from temporary to permanent status tend to call for their equally youthful spouses and even more youthful children to come to join them in their new homes. The fact that more immigrants are children does not weaken immigration's effect on the worker-retiree ratio, however, since those children will also help to support retirees later in their lives.

Another reason for the youthfulness of immigrants to Western European countries is that population growth has been much faster in the developing countries from which immigrants come. That is, the overall populations from which the immigrants self-select contain, on average, a very high percentage of young people. In China, for example, about one quarter of the population is under the age of 15, and only 7% of the population is over 65. In India, the population between the ages of 15 and 59 will within 20 years account for three-fourths of the total population, which implies a very high worker–retiree ratio. Over the next two decades these countries have to provide employment for rapidly increasing working age populations, and they are thus in a position to provide labor to high-income countries in the rest of the world where marginal returns to labor are higher. Maximizing the incomes of their populations is important for these countries, of course, because in the latter half of the century, these countries will also go through the same demographic transition that today's high-income countries are experiencing.

Many writers have, probably correctly, observed that it is difficult to imagine Europe, Japan, and other developed countries willingly opening their borders to the very large immigrant inflows necessary to prevent a decline in their workers-per-retiree ratios. According to the United Nations' *2004 World Economic and Social Survey*, for immigration to eliminate the rising economic burden of ageing populations in Western Europe, North America, and Japan, "incoming migration would have to expand at virtually impossible rates to offset declining support ratios, that is, workers per retiree."[5] According to one estimate, the European Union countries as a group will have to accept between 50 and 75 million immigrants from outside the region over the next 50 years if the future burden on working people is to remain manageable.[6] Such levels of immigration equal about 20% of Europe's total population. According to the United Nations report, Japan's very low birth and death rates imply that it would have to receive 600,000 immigrants per year for the next half century just to keep its total working age population from shrinking. But, if that many foreign immigrants arrive in Japan, then by 2050 one-third of the Japanese population will be either foreign-born or a child of an immigrant.

Weil (2002) has observed that the immigrant arrivals required to keep the support ratios constant calculated by the United Nations imply annual immigrant inflows for Europe and Japan that are less than 0.5% of their total populations. Such a rate of immigration is just half of what annual per capita immigrant inflows to the United States were in the first decade of the twentieth century. Of course, those high rates did foment political opposition to immigration that ultimately resulted in a sharp policy shift toward tight curbs on immigration in the United States in the early 1920s. The *Financial Times* economic policy pundit Martin Wolf writes: "Immigration could solve the west's ageing population problem but the numbers required would be unacceptable. Free migration is economically logical but politically impossible."[7]

Predicting how immigration flows affect how a country's ability to handle the demographic transition is not easy. There are a number of offsetting factors to consider. First of all, while immigrants increase the size of the labor force, they have a variety of influences on income in the country, as the models of immigration have made clear. Secondly, most immigrants increase their human capital after they arrive in the country, which will increase their productivity and marginal effect on national income. Thirdly, immigrants, like natives, are eligible for a variety of government transfers, and how those transfer programs evolve over time influences the calculations. Finally, immigrants themselves eventually age and require pension payments and other assistance. After looking at many of these potential changes, Fehr, Jokisch, and Kotlikoff (2004, p. 322) reach the sobering conclusion that even

---

[5]Quoted in Williams (2004).

[6]Crawford (2001).

[7]Wolf (2001).

a large expansion of immigration, "whether across all skill groups or among particular skill groups, will do remarkably little to alter the major capital shortage, tax hikes, and reductions in real wages that can be expected along the demographic transition."

Regardless of how immigration policies shift in the future, the global economy will continue to provide incentives for people to immigrate. In fact, the demographic transitions will radically change countries' demographic profiles, and that will change the marginal returns to labor and other factors across countries, increasing the incentives for people to move. But cultural factors and political expediency will also play a role in shaping immigration policy. It remains to be seen whether the rich country governments will respond to the demographic transition by liberalizing immigration as Cooper predicts.

15.7 Conclusions

Immigration policies in Canada and Europe provide contrasts to the immigration policies that evolved in the United States over the past 200 years. Interestingly, there seem to be more similarities than differences. The U.S., Canada, and Europe all experienced continual changes in immigration policies as economic, social, and political conditions changed. Certainly economic conditions, and unemployment specifically, played important roles in shaping immigration policy. In short, a country's immigration policy, like all government policy, is endogenous to its economic and social systems. On the other hand, the fields of political science, sociology, and psychology, no doubt, have much to tell us about the various lags between economic events and changes in immigration policy. An especially troubling aspect of immigration policy is the huge gap between policymakers' stated intentions and actual outcomes. Did policymakers really believe that the 1986 IRCA law in the U.S. would end unauthorized immigration or that Europe's guest worker programs would attract only immigrants content to just work for a brief period and then go back to their poor native countries?

The huge gap between the stated intent and the actual results of immigration policies reflects either a lack of understanding of immigration on the part of policymakers or the intentional misleading by policymakers of electorates who lack an understanding of the causes and consequences of immigration. Either way, economists have much work to do.

References

Acemoglu, D., Johnson, S., & Robinson, R. (2002). Reversal of fortune: Geography and institutions in the making of the modern world income distribution. *Quarterly Journal of Economics*, *107*(4), 1231–1294.

Baer, W. (1995). *The Brazilian economy: Growth and development* (4th ed.). Westport, Connecticut: Praeger.

Burkholder, M., & Johnson, L. (1990). *Colonial Latin America*. Oxford: Oxford University Press.

Cameron, R. (1993). *A concise economic history of the world*. Oxford: Oxford University Press.

Cooper, R. (2002). The economic impact of demographic change: A case for more immigration. In J. Sneddon Little, & R. Triest (Eds.), *Seismic shifts: The economic impact of demographic change*. Boston: Federal Reserve Bank of Boston.

Crawford, L. (2001, 27 June). Migrant workers obeying the cold laws of Economics. *Financial Times*, Special section on Europe Reinvented.

Dustmann, C., & Glitz, A. (2005). *Immigration, jobs and wages: Theory, evidence and opinion*. Report to Centre for Research and Analysis of Migration (CREAM), London, UK (www.econ.ucl.ac.uk/cream).

Easterlin, R. A. (1961). Influences on European overseas emigration before World War I. *Economic Development and Cultural Change, 9*, 331–351.

Ferenczi, L., & Wilcox, W. F. (1929). *International migrations* (vol. 1). New York: National Bureau of Economic Research.

Fehr, H., Jokisch, S., & Kotlikoff, L. (2004). The role of immigration in dealing with the developed world's demographic transition. *Finanzarchiv, 60*, 296–324.

Hatton, T., & Williamson, J. (2005). *Global migration and the world economy*. Cambridge, MA: MIT.

Hatton, T., & Williamson, J. (1993). After the famine: Emigration from Ireland, 1850–1913. *Journal of Economic History, 53*(3), 575–600.

Hornbeck Tanner, H. (1995). *The settling of North America*. New York: MacMilllan.

Lang, J. (1979). *Portuguese Brazil: The King's plantation*. New York: Academic Press.

Martin, J. (2009). Temporary labour migration: An illusory promise? Editorial. International migration outlook SOPEMI 2008. Paris: OECD.

Meyer, M., & Sherman, W. (1991). *The course of Mexican history*. Oxford: Oxford University Press.

Nickerson, C., & Staff, G. (2006, 19 April). A lesson in immigration: Guest worker experiments Transformed Europe. *Boston Globe*.

OECD, (2006). *International migration outlook*. Paris: OECD.

Ruhs, M. (2004). Ireland: A crash course in immigration policy. Working paper, Centre of Migration, Policy and Society, Oxford University, October 2004.

Weil, D. (2002). Comment on "Demographic shocks: The view from history" by Massimo Livi-Bacci. In J. Sneddon Little, & R. Triest (Eds.), *Seismic shifts: The economic impact of demographic change*. Boston: Federal Reserve Bank of Boston.

Wihtol de Wenden, C. (2007). The frontiers of mobility. In A. Pécoud, & P. de Guchteneire, (Eds.), *Migration without borders: Essay on the free movement of people*. Geneva: UNESCO.

Williams, F. (2004, 30 November). Migrants cannot fix pension crisis. *Financial Times*.

Wolf, M. (2001, 28 November). Fighting for economic equality. *Financial Times*.

World Economic Survey 2004 (2004). Chapter 1, Migration during 1820–1920, the first global century. Paris: OECD.

Zimmerman, K. (1995). European migration: Push and pull. In *Proceedings of the World Bank Annual Conference on Development Economics 1994* (pp. 313–341). New York, NY: The International Bank for Reconstruction and Development/The World Bank.

Chapter 16
Conclusions and Final Observations

Abstract This book's survey of what economists have written about immigration concludes that neither the theoretical models nor their supporting evidence provide accurate information on which to base efficient immigration policies. To develop more accurate models and more accurately test those models, economists must take a broader, holistic view of immigration. Immigration is a complex and dynamic process that cannot be captured in a partial equilibrium static model. Even with a better understanding of the economics of immigration, however, it is not clear that policymakers will embrace more efficient internationally-coordinated immigration policies.

> *We wanted workers, we got people.*
>
> (Max Frisch, noted Swiss writer)[1]

Chapter Overview

In the introductory first chapter of this book, we warned that this book's survey of the economics of immigration would show that much work remains to be done before we can achieve a full understanding of the economic and social causes and consequences of people's rapidly increasing international mobility. We also noted that the subject of immigration is a most fascinating phenomenon to study. We hope that, indeed, this book has revealed both the challenges and the excitement of the subject of immigration.

It is fair to say that the field of economics has not paid nearly enough attention to the phenomenon of immigration. This is somewhat puzzling given that the subject of "globalization" permeates many fields, including economics, business, sociology, political science, and anthropology. In the research, writing, and teaching of international economics, only two of the three categories of international economic

---

[1]Quoted in Nickerson, *Globe* Staff (2006).

Ö.B. Bodvarsson and H. Van den Berg, *The Economics of Immigration*,
DOI: 10.1007/978-3-540-77796-0_16, © Springer-Verlag Berlin Heidelberg 2009

activity are prominently covered: international trade and investment. The contrast between economists' often esoteric and narrow analysis of immigration issues on the one hand and the political and social reactions to rapidly growing immigration flows on the other is nothing short of stunning.

While economists debated over the past two decades whether the immigration surplus is some infinitesimal positive or negative fraction of national GDP, the proportion of the world's population living outside their native countries doubled. In most high-income countries, non-natives now make up more than ten percent of the population and workforce, and in Canada and Switzerland these percentages approach one quarter of the population. More troublesome, millions of people went to live in other countries illegally, lacking formal rights and protections. The unauthorized population today exceeds 10 million people in the United States and at least half that many in Europe. Economists seem to have been largely oblivious to the political frictions caused by the presence of these cadres of clandestine foreigners implicitly invited by employers and government officials, but increasingly feared by native residents of the destination countries. Economists have continued to argue about the size of welfare triangles in misleading static labor market models even as the U.S. government began making mass arrests and criminal prosecutions that destroy human lives and violate the U.S.' most hallowed principles of human rights.

In early 2008, for example, 270 Guatemalan immigrants in the state of Iowa were arrested in a raid on a local meatpacking plant, subjected to an assembly-line legal procedure in temporary courts set up at a local fairground, and kept from contacting their families or legal counsel. Despite protests by the American Immigration Lawyers Association, the workers faced the judges without the usual counseling, and each worker ended up pleading guilty to poorly understood charges and accepting sentences of 5 months in Federal prison to be followed by deportation, or what the U.S. government now simply calls "removal." Such events beg the question we wish to address here in the concluding chapter: What can economics add to the difficult and often-emotional discourse on immigration? Our answer is: A lot! If the movement of people across borders is going to be used to justify violations of countries' basic principles of civil rights, we had better have an accurate idea about what is really at stake.

16.1 Immigration: A Fundamental Economic Phenomenon

In order to understand immigration, economists first need to recognize its dynamic and evolutionary nature. The immigration we study today is just the latest manifestation of a fundamental human trait, which is to walk, sail, and ride across the surface of the earth. Ever since the human race evolved in Africa some 200,000 years ago, humans have spread to all corners of the globe in search of better living conditions. This global spread of humanity is what distinguishes humans from most other living species.

Humans have the incredible ability to live in nearly all climates, at nearly all altitudes, and within just about every natural environment found on earth. Most other living species are restricted to specific areas on earth, unable to survive outside limited climate zones and natural landscapes. Humans have somehow evolved the mental and physical capabilities that permit them to survive and, judging by their growing numbers, thrive almost anywhere. As discussed and detailed by Seabright (2004) in his fascinating account of the development of human society, humans have evolved the mental capacity for abstract thought. Humans are able to conceptually analyze their situation and redesign their rules of behavior to alter the collective outcomes of their economic and social activities. Humans have also developed the means to accumulate knowledge outside the evolutionary biological confines of the human body, including language, writing, and art. Such disembodied knowledge can be expanded much more quickly than the biological process of evolution can increase a living organism's capacity to deal with its changing environments. These capabilities enabled humans to adapt to nearly every natural environment across the globe. Hence, migration became a distinguishing trait of humans.

Migration did not end with the complete occupation of all parts of the world, however. Humans' capacity for abstract thought also enabled them to survive after they reached the capacity of the earth's available resources for current levels of human technology. Humans were able to change their social environment and raise their production technologies much faster than the process of evolution could ever have done. Some 10,000 years ago, humans adjusted from living in small hunter-gatherer societies to permanent settlements based on agriculture. Much more recently, the Industrial Revolution accelerated the shift towards large urban societies, a transformation of human society that has accelerated recently with the recent expansion of the service sectors of human economies. Today, humans are tightly packed into a global economy that links all parts of the world through a complex economic and social system in which everyone is fully dependent on strangers throughout the world. Immigration has now become a prominent economic and social phenomenon within an extremely complex global society.

Unfortunately, the much slower process of human evolution has not enabled basic human emotions and instincts to keep up with the complexity of human society. The human capacity for abstract thought has not always been able to design the assorted rules, regulations, governing structures, and cultures that induce people to behave in ways that sustain today's complex human society. In the case of immigration, we humans continue to fear foreigners, to ignore our long-run common interests, and to deny our dependence on strangers for our daily existence.

Economists in particular have not exploited our capacity for abstract thinking to gain a better understanding of the economic and social complexity we have created for ourselves. So far, economists have permitted special interests and human emotions to drive the political debate on immigration and shape economic policy. Economists would do well to memorize Max Frisch's quote above and repeat it to themselves every time they think about immigration. Immigration is not exclusively a labor issue. Rather, it is a phenomenon within the evolving larger human economic and social environments.[2] In short, we can no longer ignore the complexity within which economic phenomena occur.

16.2   We Must Think Outside our Little Boxes

Chapters 2 through 7 presented the theory and empirics of the standard labor market approach to the economics of immigration. To their credit, labor economists analyzed immigration when other fields of economics paid it no attention. If any field should have analyzed the economic causes and effects of immigration it should have been international economics. However, international economists have concentrated their attention on international trade and finance, and they dealt with the international movement of labor in only the most tangential way. One only has to pick up an international economics textbook to see that, at most, one or two pages are devoted to immigration. The field of regional economics has analyzed migration more, but its focus has been exclusively on internal migration. Even in the economic development literature the analysis has been focused on internal migration. The unfortunate lack of communication between regional and international economics has prevented research in regional economics in internal migration from being applied to international migration. The bias towards viewing immigrants exclusively as workers and describing the effects of immigration almost entirely in terms of changes in labor market outcomes is the result of centering the economics of immigration in the field of labor economics.

The labor market approach has added much useful information to the immigration debate. The evidence examined in Chap. 5 suggests that immigration has very little effect on destination country labor markets. Immigration tends to be complementary to most categories of labor, and even in the cases where immigrants are substitutes for domestic labor the wage effect is negative but small. The owners of business and capital are also complementary to immigrant labor and are, therefore, positioned to gain from immigration. These gains by capital and other factors also appear to be small, although we have little confidence in such a conclusion because the labor market focus has not paid nearly as much attention to the gains or losses to factors of production beyond labor. The fact that business often lobbies hard for expanding immigration suggests that the gains may be substantial. However, the evidence from estimating the short run wage effects of immigration, covered in Chap. 6, suggests that it is the immigrants themselves who reap most of the gains from moving across borders to work and live.

Chapter 7 looked at the empirical evidence on the distributional effects of immigration more broadly. It was noted in that chapter that immigration triggers

---

[2]It can be argued, in fact, that the past and current migrations that have built the global economy now give humans the capacity to change their natural environment in potentially disastrous ways. The natural environment should probably also be incorporated into the study of immigration, both as a cause and a consequence of immigration.

a whole set of reactions throughout the economy beyond the labor supply shift that the labor market model hypothesizes. For example, native labor is likely to migrate away from those regions where immigrants arrive, or it may migrate to other industries and professions. In each of these cases, the net labor supply curve shifts by less than the immigrant inflow. Also, other complementary factors, such as capital and other types of labor, are likely to move toward those regions and industries where immigrants add to the labor force. Most important, perhaps, is the finding by a small number of studies that the arrival of immigrants increases *both* the demand and supply curves of labor. Immigrants are consumers as well as workers, after all. Finally, immigrants can generate a variety of externalities, some positive and some negative. Immigrants demand a share of "the commons" in destination countries, for example, and the resulting rise in congestion is costly to natives. More directly, studies have shown that, contrary to popular myth, immigrants generally do not use as many public services per capita as natives in most countries. On the positive side, immigrants add to the size of an economy and, therefore, may generate economies of scale effects.

Chapter 8 looked at the effects of immigration on the source country. Again, the economic effects are not clearly positive or negative. Even the brain drain, which is one of the few popular topics related to immigration in the development economics literature, is not necessarily a bad outcome for developing countries once remittances and return migration are factored in. Chap. 10 examined the economic effects of temporary immigration. As important as this form of international migration is, there are few models and even less evidence of its impact.

Chapter 9 surveys literature that pushes the economics of immigration into completely new territory. It is the static nature of the economic analysis covered in Chaps. 2–7 that is potentially most damaging to the conclusions about the gains and losses from immigration. The fact is that immigration is part of an evolving process of economic development. Ever since humans abandoned the lifestyle of a hunter-gatherer society, in which they interacted with relatively small numbers of other people, human societies have become more "global" in that individuals expanded the number of strangers they transacted and dealt with. Also, the rise of permanent settlements that accompanied the development of agriculture also meant that the movement of people across the earth clashed with more permanent boundaries between societies and cultures. To make a long story short, today's immigration flows across national borders is just the latest installment of a long history of gradual globalization of human society. The pace of globalization has accelerated sharply over the past two centuries, and international migration has grown along with all other forms of globalization, such as international trade, international investment, and international business organizations. In such a dynamic economic and social environment, it is not possible for a static or partial equilibrium model to accurately explain the causes and consequences of immigration.

Growth is a compound process, and, like the race between the hare and the tortoise, the "power of compounding" will sooner or later see the long-run growth effects of immigration overwhelm even a large one-time change in the economy. Therefore, if immigration changes an economy's growth rate, such an effect is much more important than a short-run change in welfare estimated using a static labor market model of immigration. In general, if immigration increases the overall growth of the destination economy, as some evidence suggests is indeed the case, then all workers and owners of other factors are likely to gain, regardless of the short-run adjustments. The problem is that economists have developed few dynamic models of immigration beyond the ad hoc approach, such as we described in Chap. 9, of inserting immigration into the standard Solow and "Schumpeterian" endogenous growth models. Economists have also generated very little statistical evidence linking immigration to economic growth. As a result, there are few off-the-shelf analytical procedures to answer questions about immigration's long-run growth impacts and welfare implications. When it comes to the relationship between immigration and economic growth, empirical work has not yet really begun.

16.3   An Appeal to Holism

The complexity of the process of globalization and the specific roles of immigration within that process mean we need to expand our analysis beyond the familiar economic relationships studied by traditional mainstream economics. To accurately discern the causes, effects, and long-run consequences of immigration, we need to formally recognize the interdependence of all social, and natural, phenomena. These concerns suggest that the economics of immigration should embrace a perspective known as *holism*. The perspective of holism takes the analyst across disciplinary boundaries to many other fields of the natural and social sciences, and it views economic phenomena as part of an on-going dynamic process. Most important, it views any single phenomenon within a broader system rather than in isolation.

16.3.1   Defining Holism

The term holism is derived from the Greek word holos, meaning entire, total, whole. The term was first used by Jan Christiaan Smuts, who in his 1926 book entitled *Holism and Evolution* used the term to describe new dynamic theories in the physical sciences, such as Charles Darwin's theory of evolution, Henri Becquerel's theory of radioactivity, and Albert Einstein's theory of relativity. These new theories described the world as evolving dynamic systems, in which the parts are related to all other parts in complex ways that condition how each observed part actually functions. Essentially, holism recognizes that the component parts of the whole cannot be understood in isolation and their functions cannot be predicted without knowing the environment in which they exist.

Holism has been described as the diametric opposite to scientific reductionism. Scientific reductionism refers to the approach to understanding the whole by learning about its parts. Clearly, there is some relationship between the whole and its component parts, and in this sense there appears to be no inherent conflict between scientific reductionism and holism. However, to understand a complex process or system, one obviously must understand not only the parts, but also how the parts interact. Focusing only on the parts is not scientific when there are good reasons to suspect that the interactions between the parts help to determine the outcomes of the overall system.

Holism has been pursued in many fields other than economics. In sociology, Emile Durkheim argued against the notion that society was nothing more than a collection of individuals. He showed that a community can take on many different forms depending on how the individuals who make up the society organize themselves and behave within that organization. In medicine, the holistic approach to healing recognizes that the emotional, mental, and physical elements of each person work together. Most psychologists recognize that a person's relationship to society shapes behavior. The International Electrical Engineering Association recently published guidelines suggesting engineers should take a holistic approach to their work in order to avoid incompatibilities between specific projects and the societies in where the projects are carried out. And, of course, holism is fundamental to the field of ecology. Economists, therefore, are in good company when they embrace holism, which Kenneth Boulding (1956, p. 197) appropriately described half a century ago as the approach that links "the specific that has no meaning and the general that has no content."

16.3.2   The Economics of Immigration Must Embrace Holism

There is no better indication of the dual need to understand the parts and the way the parts interact and function as a whole than when we analyze immigration. Immigration is clearly a holistic phenomenon that is related in complex ways to the social and natural environments humans live in. People migrate for many reasons, and their decisions and actions are shaped by factors such as expected income differences, family conditions, immigration policies in the source and destination countries, public and private institutions in the source and destination countries, and the adjustments in the source and destination countries in response to immigration flows. The models and statistical evidence presented in this book also suggest that immigration both causes wages to change and is itself a function of wages at home and abroad.

Furthermore, immigration both affects and is affected by economic growth, or the lack of it. Immigration changes the demographics of countries, just as demographic differences can influence immigration flows. The chapters on immigration policy showed that immigration influences, and is influenced by, shifts in immigration policies. In fact, gradual changes in immigration flows can trigger sudden sharp reversals in immigration policy, suggesting that the relationship between immigration policy and actual immigration flows is not linear, as so many economic models assume. Nonlinearities are a common feature of complex systems.

In short, immigration can only be understood as a holistic social and economic phenomenon that is, on the one hand, a part of human society and the earth's natural environment but, on the other hand, interacts with those social and natural environments in complex ways. Hopefully, the chapters on unauthorized immigration, Hispanic immigration, return immigration, and immigration policy have provided some insight into the "holistic" nature of immigration and its broad causes and consequences. Clearly, attempts to analyze immigration using models that isolate just one aspect of the immigration process, as the labor market models of immigration effectively do, are doomed to failure. Similarly, empirical models based on partial and static models cannot accurately distinguish the causes or consequences of immigration.

The jump from the labor market model of immigration, in which all other things remain the same in response to a shift in the labor supply curve, to true holism, in which immigration interacts dynamically with all other human activities in earth's natural environment, is a major challenge for economists to meet. Even at the Santa Fe Institute, the think tank where holism and the study of complex systems has been actively pursued, the holistic methods for analyzing human society are still quite experimental. We do not wish to infer that a more holistic perspective is something that makes the life of economists easier. The technical difficulty of incorporating holism into economic research such as insufficient mathematics, does not disqualify it from still providing guidance for practical analysis. The shortcomings of much of the analysis of immigration is not the result of a conscious decision by economists to avoid holism because it was too difficult to bring more complexity into their analysis. The problem has been that economists used familiar methods when they began to analyze immigration, and those methods ignored the complexity of human social and economic activity. By not looking outside the box, economists missed out on many easy opportunities to improve and expand their analysis.

16.3.3   The Holistic Approach to the Study of Immigration: An Example

Why would economists blindly continue to devote years of effort to the study of partial equilibrium relationships that are not only often refuted by the data, but are wrong from a holistic perspective? More specifically, how is it possible that economists ignored the need to adjust their models of immigration's wage effects for internal migration, capital investment, product demand effects, and endogenous policy adjustments? Even a superficially holistic perspective would have warned them about these, and many other effects. At the very minimum, economists would have run regressions that controlled for some of these factors.

All economists would agree that sound empirical analysis begins with well-conceived, thorough and realistic theoretical analysis. Much of the literature on the economics of immigration is devoid of high quality theoretical analysis that captures the "big picture" and also incorporates the many complex relationships associated with immigration. Most empirical analyses are based on the elementary textbook style single-period partial equilibrium model of a labor market, where natives and immigrants are perfect substitutes, there are no secondary adjustments to immigration, and no policy or growth considerations. A holistic approach to modeling immigration would, most likely, point to a general equilibrium, dynamic model where natives and immigrants are imperfect substitutes, which explains both immediate and longer-run adjustments to immigration, which endogenizes immigration policy, which captures growth responses to immigration, and which links international trade with international labor mobility. An especially important requirement of this "unifed" theory is that it accounts for bi-directional causality between variables and that it links the different markets that cause, as well as are affected by, immigration. A more holistic view provided by such a unified theory would provide researchers with the guidance they need for deriving an empirical specification that ensures robust hypothesis testing. Furthermore, success in testing the model requires complete and intricate data, which at present are unavailable for many countries. No one claims that a holistic approach will be easy!

To elaborate further on the value of a holistic approach, consider the following simple regression model that relates immigration to the wage differential. For example, suppose we use data on immigration flows between two countries for a sample of 20 countries to estimate the coefficient a_1 in the regression equation

$$\text{Imm} = a_0 + a_1(w_1/w_2) + \varepsilon \tag{16.1}$$

where Imm is the emigration rate from countries 1 to 2, w_1 (w_2) is the wage in country 1(2), and ε is an error term. Applying Ordinary Least Squares would provide an inaccurate indication of how immigration is related to the wage differential; the estimated value of a_1 would be subject to omitted variable bias because other determinants of immigration are not "controlled" for in the equation.

A solution to omitted variable bias is to add more variables to the regression model, say by applying data on 20 countries using the following model

$$\text{Imm} = a_0 + a_1(w_1/w_2) + \mathbf{b}\mathbf{X} = \varepsilon \tag{16.2}$$

in which b is a vector of coefficients and X is a matrix of data for 20 countries on a set of other variables hypothesized to affect immigration.

In the case of immigration, such an equation will still be biased, however. As has been found in many studies, immigration both influences, and is influenced by, a great variety of factors. That is, estimates using (16.2) are subject to simultaneity bias. Fortunately, there are two ways to deal with simultaneity bias: (1) replace the variables that are bi-directionally related or correlated with other variables within the model with instrumental variables that, somehow, are correlated with the endogenous variables but are not related to any other variables in the model, or (2) use a simultaneous-equations model that explicitly recognizes the various interrelationships between the variables in the model. Convenient computer programs to estimate simultaneous-equations models are readily available. Unfortunately, estimation procedures limit the number of variables in the model to some number less than the number of observations (the degrees of freedom problem), while data for many countries tend to be annual or even just decennial. Furthermore, good instrumental variables are hard to find.

An even more serious challenge for statistical analysis of evolving social phenomena such as immigration is the need for dynamic analysis to test for relationships over time. For example, we have noted in various places in this book that current immigration is related to past immigration. In general, immigration is part of the continually evolving process of human social change, and there are many lagged influences and lagged effects to be considered. Obviously, the use of time-series data that trace immigration over various periods of time can be used to estimate the coefficients in dynamic regression models, but consistent observations of variables over the years are also hard to come by. And, the degrees of freedom problem still remains; only a few time-series variables can be entered into the model to mitigate omitted variable bias when there are just a few observations for different years or decades.

Finally, it is not at all clear that the relationship between immigration and the many hypothesized social, environmental, political, and other relevant variables are linear in nature. Social systems are complex and, most likely, non-linear. Regressions to test economic relationships are often estimated with the variables in logarithmic form, but that only linearizes variables subject to constant growth rates over time. Complex and potentially explosive or implosive systems require much more complex and presently unknown functional forms.

One way to deal with some of these problems in applying the principle of holism to statistical analysis is to do many different statistical studies for different countries using many different data sets, empirical specifications, and statistical tests. Then, after many of these independent estimations have been completed, a "meta-study" of all of the results can be carried out to determine whether the results across these many studies constitute a robust conclusion. This was, for example, the purpose of the meta-analytic study of Longhi, Nijkamp, and Poot (2005) on the wage effects of exogenous immigration. Robustness is achieved when the results across all the different studies consistently lead to a similar conclusion. The idea behind robustness is that, even though any individual statistical study suffers from a variety of data problems and sources of estimation bias, if enough different studies using different data sets, control variables, empirical specifications, and statistical methods come to the same conclusion, then perhaps we can begin to feel confident about the result.

The economics of immigration is not yet close to claiming even a modest degree of robustness for the statistical results we have reported in this book. There simply have not been enough studies, and researchers have not exhibited sufficient respect for the holistic nature of immigration by venturing beyond the most simple regression models and the convenient applications for which data was easily available. Much work remains to be done. New data must be collected, especially for unauthorized immigration, two-way migration, migration between developing countries, and for return immigration. More sophisticated theoretical and empirical models must be specified, and, given the dynamic and complex nature of immigration, panel data must be used. Hopefully, economists will embrace the principle of holism and abandon narrow empirical studies that insert exclusively cross-section or time-series data into single-equation regression models that effectively ignore the true nature of human migration.

16.4 Developing International Institutions for an International Phenomenon

The models and empirical evidence examined throughout this book suggest that, overall, immigration increases world income. If, despite our concerns discussed in the previous section, these conclusions are indeed correct, then a strong case can be made for reducing the restrictions that countries have placed on immigration. Of course, the partial equilibrium static models of immigration, as well as most of the evidence generated by these models, suggest that there are likely to be both gainers and losers when people move between countries. Therefore, there will always be some resistance to the liberalization of international migration. Immigration seems to be similar to international trade, which also generates gains and losses that sum to a substantial net gain for the world as a whole and, as a consequence, is always subject to lively political debate. We conclude, therefore, by asking whether the world should seek to establish some kind of international organization, like the World Trade Organization (WTO) for trade, to facilitate multilateral negotiations on an international agreement that would bring the world closer to the global optimum? Do we need a World Migration Organization?

16.4.1 The Global Commission on International Migration

The United Nations established a Global Commission on International Migration in 2003. However, this international commission has not yet moved much beyond a study group. There has been little interest among member nations for a major round of negotiations to liberalize international migration, as the World Trade Organization and its predecessor, the General Agreement of Trade and Tariffs (GATT), have organized for international trade over the past 50 years. Hatton (2006) argues that such an agreement would be very difficult because, in fact, international migration is not the same as international trade.

Hatton describes trade as determined, in the long run, by comparative advantage, but international migration is determined by absolute advantage. Specifically, it is well known that total factor productivity, or more generally the level of technology, varies greatly across countries. In high-income countries all factors of production are much more productive than they are in low-income countries. Such technology differences do not stand in the way for balanced trade based on comparative advantage. However, there will not be balanced migration in both directions; people will largely move from the low-wage, low-income countries to the high-wage, high-income countries. Hatton (2006, p. 24) therefore concludes that "it will be hard, if not impossible, to reach the sorts of global agreements for migration as have been negotiated for trade." Jagdish Bhagwati, the well-known trade economist does not agree with Hatton; Bhagwati has repeatedly called for creating a World Migration Organization to begin negotiations for some degree of international coordination of immigration policies across countries. He claims that immigration needs to expand, but the current confusing array of national immigration policies and the growth of unauthorized immigration call out for a more coordinated approach to managing and safeguarding the flows of humans across borders.

16.4.2   What is the Optimal Flow of Immigrants?

Benhabib and Jovanovic (2007) perform an interesting exercise in which they calculate the optimal immigration flows under different international welfare functions. They find that, depending on how the world welfare function weighs the incomes of people in poor countries relative to the incomes of people in rich countries, very different patterns of immigration are required to maximize world welfare. For example, they find that in a case of an egalitarian welfare function that weighs everyone's welfare equally across the world's population, world welfare would be maximized by having 3.2 billion low-skilled people emigrate from third world to OECD countries. In another case that weighs the welfare of natives of high-skill OECD countries much higher than the welfare of natives in third world countries, the optimal immigration policy may be to prohibit all immigration or to restrict immigration to high-skilled workers (a brain drain). Benhabib and Jovanovic hypothesize many other cases by varying the weights in the welfare function, making diverse assumptions about the distribution of skills across countries, and assuming different migration costs and immigration externalities. Their exercises make an interesting point, however, which is that an international agreement on immigration may be difficult to achieve given countries' diverse populations and the need for political leaders to serve the interests of their citizens.

Still, it may be possible to reach some agreement on how to deal with the brain drain, human trafficking, unauthorized immigration, temporary immigration, and immigrant remittances. With regard to these issues, there are mutual gains and losses across countries, and cooperation among countries can clearly reduce the losses and increase the gains for all. The European Union, which now consists of 26 countries at substantially different levels of development and per capita income, has in fact negotiated a very detailed agreement on migration among the EU member countries. Granted, migration among EU countries does not provide nearly as great an economic gain as would migration between the poorest and richest nations of the world. On the other hand, as Corner (2008) and McClintock (2008) argue, a move toward global governance and the unequal sharing of costs and benefits that characterizes issues such as international migration necessarily involves the loss of national sovereignty.

16.4.3   Small Steps Towards Global Governance

McClintock (2008) suggests that the difficult expansion of international cooperation is more likely to succeed if it starts with regional groups of countries such as the European Union. Sovereignty will only be ceded gradually as specific issues arise, and even then only when there are good relations among the countries involved. The set of issues and the number of countries with good relations can grow over time, much as the scope and membership of the EU has grown over the past 50 years. But, McClintock explicitly argues that the United Nations is currently not designed to deal with real sovereignty issues. Regional groups such as the EU are better positioned. Their regional structure of governance, which includes a real transfer of sovereignty from nations to a multinational institution, can then gradually expand to include a greater share of the world's nations.

Freeman (2007) takes a less global approach to bringing world migration flows closer to their optimum. In light of the evidence showing that the greater portion of the economic gains from international migration accrue to immigrants while all the other interest groups in the source and destination countries are left to fight over the remainder of the economic gains and losses, Freeman suggests that immigrants be taxed or charged a high fee for permitting them to migrate to another country. He specifically suggests that countries with long waiting lists for immigrant visas, such as the United States, Western Europe, or Canada, should auction a limited number of visas or, better yet, charge a high fee – perhaps as much as $50,000 – for each permanent residence visa. Chap. 13 on U.S. immigration policy mentioned that the U.S. has already raised fees for processing immigrant visas, but these higher fees were only raised to cover the high costs incurred by the U.S. government for processing the heavy load of visa applications. Freeman is proposing much higher fees to raise money to directly compensate those who are negatively impacted by the arrival of immigrants or to fund education and job subsidies that mitigate the negative effects of immigrants. Given the holistic nature of immigration, it is difficult to see how Freeman's ideas could be applied accurately and fairly. Opening the door to fees could en up legitimizing the high barriers to the movement of people between countries that xenophobes demand.

Clearly, much more abstract thought needs to be applied to the issue of international migration before we can determine the best mix of national and international policies to deal with the fundamental human desire to migrate. Seabright (2004) convincingly argues that we, and that includes economists, can do this very well.

16.5   Final Comment

And now we conclude our survey of the economics of immigration. We may have left you with more questions than answers, but that is to be expected given the small number of questions economists have tried to answer. In fact, we hope that we have made you aware of many new questions that did not occur to you before. The economics of immigration is, first and foremost, the study of human beings. More important, it is the study of human beings in what is most likely one of the most active and vulnerable times of their lives. Moving between countries and cultures is not an easy decision for most people to take. On top of the inherent difficulties of leaving home and moving to another country, governments and people on both sides of the world's borders continue to make international migration quite difficult for immigrants. We were reminded of these difficulties once again as we completed this book just as the United States held its 2008 elections. In many states and communities around the country, immigration in general and immigrants in particular were sometimes praised but mostly demonized. The tone of the debate often turned ugly and even cruel, as opportunistic politicians repeatedly exploited the basic human mistrust of foreigners to promote their own political ambitions. Note that such political opportunism occurred routinely in a country that has received more immigrants than any other country in the world.

It is our hope that this book, by spreading the knowledge economists have accumulated and motivating more economists and other social scientists to actively add to our knowledge, can help to broaden and humanize the public debate on immigration. As Max Frisch reminds us, immigrants are people, just like all of us.

References

Benhabib, B., & Jovanovic, B. (2007). Optimal migration: A world persepctive. NBER Working Paper 12871, January.

Boulding, K. (1956), General systems theory, the skeleton of science. *Management Science* **2–3,** 197–208.

Corner, M. (2008). Towards a global sharing of sovereignty. European Essay No. 44, The Federal Trust for Education & Research, Brussels, August.

Freeman (2007). People flows in globalization. NBER Working Paper 12315.

Hatton, T. (2006). Should we have a WTO for international migration? The Julian Simon Lecture, IZA Bonn, May 20.

Longhi, S., Nijkamp, P. & Poot, J. (2005). A Meta-analytic assessment of the effect of immigration on wages. *Journal of Economic Surveys,* 19, 451–477.

McClintock, J. (2008). *The uniting of nations: An essay on global governance.* Brussels: Peter Long Press.

Seabright, P. (2004). *The company of strangers: A natural history of economic life.* Princeton, NJ: Princeton University Press.

Printed in the United States
150944LV00001B/88/P